The Collected Courses of the Academy of
Series Editors: Professor Gráinne de Búrca,
Professor Bruno de Witte, and
Professor Francesco Francioni,
European University Institute,
Florence
Assistant Editor: Barbara Ciomei, *European University*
Institute, Florence

VOLUME XV/1
Human Rights Obligations of Non-State Actors

The Collected Courses of the Academy of European Law
Edited by Professor Gráinne de Búrca,
Professor Bruno de Witte, and Professor Francesco Francioni
Assistant Editor: Barbara Ciomei

This series brings together the Collected Courses of the
Academy of European Law in Florence. The Academy's mission is to
produce scholarly analyses which are at the cutting edge of the two
fields in which it works: European Union law and human rights law.
A 'general course' is given each year in each field, by a
distinguished scholar and/or practitioner, who either examines the
field as a whole through a particular thematic, conceptual, or
philosophical lens, or who looks at a particular theme in the context
of the overall body of law in the field. The Academy also publishes
each year a volume of collected essays with a specific theme in each
of the two fields.

Human Rights Obligations of Non-State Actors

ANDREW CLAPHAM

Academy of European Law
European University Institute

OXFORD
UNIVERSITY PRESS

OXFORD
UNIVERSITY PRESS

Great Clarendon Street, Oxford OX2 6DP

Oxford University Press is a department of the University of Oxford.
It furthers the University's objective of excellence in research, scholarship,
and education by publishing worldwide in

Oxford New York

Auckland Cape Town Dar es Salaam Hong Kong Karachi
Kuala Lumpur Madrid Melbourne Mexico City Nairobi
New Delhi Shanghai Taipei Toronto

With offices in

Argentina Austria Brazil Chile Czech Republic France Greece
Guatemala Hungary Italy Japan Poland Portugal Singapore
South Korea Switzerland Thailand Turkey Ukraine Vietnam

Oxford is a registered trade mark of Oxford University Press
in the UK and in certain other countries

Published in the United States
by Oxford University Press Inc., New York

© A. Clapham 2006

The moral rights of the author have been asserted
Database right Oxford University Press (maker)

Crown copyright material is reproduced under Class Licence
Number C01P0000148 with the permission of OPSI
and the Queen's Printer for Scotland

First published 2006

All rights reserved. No part of this publication may be reproduced,
stored in a retrieval system, or transmitted, in any form or by any means,
without the prior permission in writing of Oxford University Press,
or as expressly permitted by law, or under terms agreed with the appropriate
reprographics rights organization. Enquiries concerning reproduction
outside the scope of the above should be sent to the Rights Department,
Oxford University Press, at the address above

You must not circulate this book in any other binding or cover
and you must impose the same condition on any acquirer

British Library Cataloguing in Publication Data
Data available

Library of Congress Cataloging in Publication Data
Clapham, Andrew.
Human rights obligations of non-state actors / Andrew Clapham.
p. cm.
Includes index.
ISBN-13: 978–0–19–829815–1 (hardback : alk. paper)
ISBN-13: 978–0–19–928846–5 (pbk. : alk. paper)
1. Human rights. 2. Social responsibility of business. 3. Non-
governmental organizations. I. Title.
JC571.C597 2006
323—dc22
2005031871

Typeset by Newgen Imaging Systems (P) Ltd., Chennai, India
Printed in Great Britain
on acid-free paper by
Biddles Ltd., King's Lynn

ISBN 0–19–829815–3 (hbk) 978–0–19–829815–1 (hbk)
ISBN 0–19–928846–1 (pbk) 978–0–19–928846–5 (pbk)

3 5 7 9 10 8 6 4 2

Acknowledgements

Several years ago Ian Brownlie kindly asked me to prepare a second edition of my book, *Human Rights in the Private Sphere*; when I began work it transpired that there was no electronic version of the book. Oxford University Press were ready to retype the relevant chapters, but I came to realize (helped by Philip Alston) that the absence of computer files might be a blessing in disguise, it seemed I had better write a new book. The project took a new turn when I was asked by Gráinne de Búrca and Bruno de Witte to give the General Course on Human Rights for the Academy of European Law at the European University Institute in Florence. This book is the result of the lectures given in Florence in 2004 and has benefited from the challenging and stimulating discussion provoked by the Academy's participants. I should like to thank all those involved with the Academy for making the experience so pleasurable. Thank you Bruno, Philip, and Gráinne for having me, thanks also to Francesco Francioni and Wojciech Sadurski for their warm hospitality, and a special thank you to Anny Bremner and Barbara Ciomei for the royal treatment I received during my stay and in the preparation of this publication. Oxford University Press has provided encouragement and wonderful editorial assistance throughout the publication process. I should like to thank John Louth, Gwen Booth, Rowena Lennon, Rebecca Smith, and Alison Floyd for their hard work and patience.

I have been lucky to be able to work on this project with talented students from the Graduate Institute of International Studies. At an early stage Silvia Danailov helped me to research and define the context for a study of non-state actor obligations under international law, her continuing interest in the topic is helping to shape thinking about the recruitment of child soldiers and to find new ways of holding armed groups accountable. Later on, Michelle Healy worked on the manuscript, skilfully adjusting the prose, and improving the argumentation. In the final stage Claire Mahon cast an expert eye over the whole manuscript. Thank you Silvia, Michelle, and Claire for all your input.

I should also like to thank those friends and colleagues who have invited me to try out the ideas developed in this book on various audiences, and then encouraged me to continue to look for new ways of thinking about the problem. Thank you Ben Emmerson, Walter Kälin, Jonathan Cooper, Mary Robinson, Bill Schabas, and Susan Marks for giving me the opportunity to air some of these ideas. Lastly, special thanks to my wife Mona Rishmawi, whose unfailing support ensured that the book was written, and whose human rights insights have certainly improved the final product.

A.B.C.

Graduate Institute of International Studies,
Geneva

Contents

Table of Cases

EUROPEAN COURT OF HUMAN RIGHTS

INTER-AMERICAN COMMISSION ON HUMAN RIGHTS

INTER-AMERICAN COURT OF HUMAN RIGHTS

INTERNATIONAL CENTRE FOR SETTLEMENT OF INVESTMENT DISPUTES

INTERNATIONAL COURT OF JUSTICE

INTERNATIONAL CRIMINAL TRIBUNAL FOR RWANDA

INTERNATIONAL CRIMINAL TRIBUNAL FOR THE FORMER YUGOSLAVIA

INTERNATIONAL MILITARY TRIBUNAL AT NUREMBERG

SPECIAL COURT FOR SIERRA LEONE

UNITED NATIONS ADMINISTRATIVE TRIBUNAL

ADMINISTRATIVE TRIBUNAL OF THE ILO

UNITED NATIONS COMMITTEE AGAINST TORTURE

UNITED NATIONS COMMITTEE ON THE ELIMINATION OF RACIAL DISCRIMINATION

UNITED NATIONS HUMAN RIGHTS COMMITTEE

NATIONAL COURTS

Canada

France

Table of Treaties, Legislation, and other Relevant Instruments

NATIONAL LEGISLATION

Table of Abbreviations

General

ACHPR	African Charter on Human Peoples' Rights
ACHR	American Convention on Human Rights
ACP	African, Caribbean and Pacific Group of States
ATCA	Alien Tort Claims Act (US) (see also ATS below)
ATS	Alien Tort Statute (US)
BIAC	Business and Industry Advisory Committee (OECD)
CAT	Convention Against Torture and Other Cruel, Inhuman or Degrading Treatment or Punishment
CEDAW	Convention on the Elimination of All Forms of Discrimination against Women
CERD	Convention on the Elimination of All Forms of Racial Discrimination
CIME	Committee on International Investment and Multinational Enterprises (also known as the Investment Committee)
CSR	corporate social responsibility
DSU	Dispute Settlement Understanding (WTO)
ECGD	Export Credit Guarantees Department (UK)
ECHR	European Convention on Human Rights
ECJ	European Court of Justice
ECOMOG	ECOWAS Cease-fire Monitoring Group
ECOSOC	UN Economic and Social Council
ECOWAS	Economic Community of West African States
EPZs	export processing zones
FTZs	free trade zones
GA	General Assembly of the United Nations
GATT	General Agreement on Tariffs and Trade
IACHR	Inter-American Commission on Human Rights
ICC	International Chamber of Commerce
ICCPR	International Covenant on Civil and Political Rights
ICESCR	International Covenant on Economic, Social and Cultural Rights
ICFTU	International Confederation of Free Trade Unions
ICHRP	International Council on Human Rights Policy

ICRC	International Committee of the Red Cross
ICSID	International Centre for the Settlement of Investment Disputes
ICTY	International Criminal Tribunal for the former Yugoslavia
IFIs	international financial institutions
ILC	International Law Commission
ILO	International Labour Organization
IMF	International Monetary Fund
IMT	International Military Tribunal (at Nuremberg)
IOE	International Organisation of Employers
IPPR	Institute for Public Policy Research
KFOR	NATO Kosovo Force
MEA	multilateral environmental agreement
MNCs	multinational corporations
MNEs	multinational enterprises
MSF	*Médecins sans frontières*
NAFTA	North American Free Trade Agreement
NATO	North Atlantic Treaty Organization
NCPs	national contact points
NGOs	non-governmental organizations
OAS	Organization of American States
OAU	Organization of African Unity
OECD	Organization for Economic Co-operation and Development
OHCHR	Office of the High Commissioner for Human Rights (UN)
OSCE	Organization for Security and Co-operation in Europe
PCC	Press Complaints Commission (UK)
PSF	private security firm
RAID	Rights and Accountability in Development
TEC	Treaty Establishing the European Community
TNCs	transnational corporations
TRIPS	Agreement on Trade-Related Aspects of Intellectual Property Rights
TUAC	Trade Union Advisory Committee (OECD)
UNESCO	United Nations Educational, Scientific and Cultural Organization
UNMIK	United Nations Interim Administration Mission in Kosovo
UNPF	United Nations Peace Forces
UNTS	United Nations Treaty Series

| VCLT | Vienna Convention on the Law of Treaties |
| WTO | World Trade Organization |

Journals

AJIL	*American Journal of International Law*
AJPIL	*Austrian Journal of Public and International Law*
ALJ	*Alternative Law Journal*
AYBIL	*Australian Year Book of International Law*
Berkeley JIL	*Berkeley Journal of International Law*
BJIS	*British Journal of International Studies*
Brooklyn JIL	*Brooklyn Journal of International Law*
Col JTL	*Columbia Journal of Transnational Law*
EHRLR	*European Human Rights Law Review*
EJIL	*European Journal of International Law*
Ford ILJ	*Fordham International Law Journal*
Harv CR-CLLR	*Harvard Civil Rights-Civil Liberties Law Review*
Harv HRJ	*Harvard Human Rights Journal*
HICLR	*Hastings International and Comparative Law Review*
HLR	*Harvard Law Review*
HRLJ	*Human Rights Law Journal*
HRQ	*Human Rights Quarterly*
ICLQ	*International and Comparative Law Quarterly*
IJRL	*International Journal of Refugee Law*
ILM	*International Legal Materials*
IRRC	*International Review of the Red Cross*
JIEL	*Journal of International Economic Law*
LQR	*Law Quarterly Review*
Mich LR	*Michigan Law Review*
MJIL	*Michigan Journal of International Law*
MLR	*Modern Law Review*
NILR	*Netherlands International Law Review*
NJIL	*Nordic Journal of International Law*
NQHR	*Netherlands Quarterly of Human Rights*
RCADI	*Recueil des Cours de l'Académie de Droit International de la Haye*
SAJHR	*South African Journal on Human Rights*

UCLA JIL & FA	*University of California Los Angeles Journal of International Law and Foreign Affairs*
UPLR	*University of Pennsylvania Law Review*
URLR	*University of Richmond Law Review*
Van JTL	*Vanderbilt Journal of Transnational Law*
Virg JIL	*Virginia Journal of International Law*
Yale HRDLJ	*Yale Human Rights and Development Law Journal*
YLJ	*Yale Law Journal*

Introduction

This book examines the legal protection of human rights in situations where the threats to the enjoyment of human rights come from non-state actors rather than directly from state agents. Such an application of human rights law to the private sphere has implications for the ways in which we conceive human rights generally. In turn it also affects the ways in which we imagine and promote human freedom, human security, and human development.

The premise of this book is that through the analysis of recent human rights cases we can elaborate ideas in order to develop an understanding of the importance of human rights accountability for corporations, international organizations, multilateral development banks, multinational peace-keeping operations, and even for individuals and their associations.

Rethinking human rights obligations in this way will inevitably affect the implementation of a wide range of programmes and legal protection. In particular, it forces us to reconfigure traditional approaches to violence against women, working conditions, and unfair discrimination of all kinds. This paradigm shift, away from what has usually been an exclusively state-centric approach to human rights protection, also means that our appreciation of the traditional importance of the boundary between public and private may need adjusting if we are going to develop a coherent theory of human rights protection capable of practical application to protect the victims of indignities everywhere. We need not only to develop a framework for non-state actors, but also to re-examine the effect of the distinction we make between state and non-state activity—between public and private—between governmental and non-governmental. To highlight this distinction is to admit that: 'Today, the heart of political debate is about choosing among competing conceptions of what should be treated as public and what should not.'[1] We cannot pretend that the public/private distinction is a pre-ordained static border. It is closer to a battleground, with ideological forces wishing to shift the frontline in order to consolidate their own gains.

In order to 'privatize' human rights in this way, we will have to consider many of the pitfalls of such an approach. For many, the sanctity of a private sphere, protected from invasion by the state or the law, is an ideal which goes to the heart of the way we want to live with each other. This study will, among other things, seek to show that one can retain respect for privacy through law without excluding abuses committed in the private sphere from the world of human rights.

[1] P. Cerney, 'Globalization, governance and complexity', in A. Prakash and J. Hart (eds) *Globalization and Governance* (London: Routledge, 1999) 188–212, at 199.

The basic premise of my book *Human Rights in the Private Sphere* (1993) was that we need to think about human rights law in new ways in order to meet the challenges posed by private actors to the enjoyment of human rights. Two approaches were suggested. First, it was suggested that international human rights law demands that states protect individuals from private acts which threaten their rights; and that where a state has failed to take preventive or punitive action with regard to this abuse, then that state could be found in violation of its international obligations. The second approach suggested that the difference between private and public acts may be a difficult, even dangerous, distinction to draw, and that, in some circumstances, human rights obligations may give rise to directly enforceable duties on the private actors themselves. This may not be the case for all rights in all circumstances. But in some jurisdictions such direct enforceability is already legally possible in order to prevent the dangerous public/private distinction being used to shield private power from human rights scrutiny.

The present study takes a fresh look at the scope of human rights law today. The *problèmatique* of the human rights obligations of non-state actors has been at the heart of discussions within human rights organizations over the last twenty years. The issue has proven difficult for all concerned. It was often felt that by investigating and reporting on abuses committed by armed opposition groups, the human rights movement would play into the hands of those governments which wanted the international debate to shift to the human rights violations committed by rebels or terrorists. Such a shift in focus might remove the spotlight from governments and unwittingly 'legitimize' crackdowns on their opposition that might involve further violations of human rights.

This apparent conundrum has been partly resolved at one level due to the greater use of the international humanitarian law of armed conflict in human rights monitoring and reporting. This international law applies in part to armed opposition groups in times of armed conflict and allows for a degree of specificity and certainty with regard to the behaviour expected of all parties to an armed conflict. Furthermore, the adoption in 1998 of the Rome Statute for an International Criminal Court has clarified the international obligations that attach to individuals, from both the government side and from the non-state actor side, in different types of armed conflict. In addition to clarifying who can be tried for such international war crimes, the Rome Statute includes genocide and other crimes against humanity that can be committed outside the context of any armed conflict. Again, these definitions have dissipated much of the confusion and doctrinal debate which surrounded the issue of international human rights obligations of non-state actors in conflict and non-conflict situations. The Statute is clear that crimes against humanity can be committed not only by state actors but also by non-state actors where the individual attacks on the civilian population are pursuant to, or in furtherance of, an organizational policy to commit such attack. With regard to war crimes and crimes against humanity, there are international yardsticks against which to judge criminal acts by certain non-state actors. But, as we shall see, this development has not resolved the debate.

In this introduction I should like to highlight four forces, or phenomena, which I consider are important for understanding the relevance of the question of the obligations of non-state actors. These forces recur as background elements to the situations discussed throughout the book.

First, the *globalization* of the world economy has highlighted the power of large corporations and their limited accountability in law for human rights abuses. The emerging framework for ensuring greater responsibility in this sphere is international human rights law.

The second phenomenon is *privatization*. The privatization of sectors such as health, education, prisons, water, communications, security forces, and military training has forced us to think again about the applicability of human rights law in the private sector. When *Human Rights in the Private Sphere* was published, few observers imagined that privatization meant much more that insisting that the state retain some supervision over traditional functions of the state. The debate is set to move into a new phase as claims are brought directly against the private contractors that operate prisons, detention centres, and hospitals, alleging violations of international standards.

Third, the increase in internal armed conflict situations involving the *fragmentation* of states has led to greater demands on non-state rebel groups. Such demands may go beyond the accepted core minimum of international humanitarian law. The debate over 'fundamental standards of humanity' has evolved at the United Nations into an attempt to consider what sorts of human rights demands one might make on an armed group. The demands go beyond the law of international individual criminal responsibility and the developing body of international criminal law. Human rights reporting in the United Nations' Charter-based bodies already includes reports on human rights violations by all sides to a conflict, and the state/non-state actor boundary again seems less and less relevant. In this context we should also consider the assumption of state-like tasks carried out by the United Nations in situations such as those of Kosovo and East Timor. This has led to new developments as to the applicability of human rights law to the United Nations and other international organizations in the context of protection work in fragmented states.

Fourth, the developments surrounding the international human rights of women have led to a complete reappraisal of the way in which the public/private divide has been constructed to delimit human rights law. Some treaties now specifically require the state to take action to protect women in the 'private sphere' or to guarantee women's rights in public and private life.[2] International obligations and commitments have been redesigned to ensure that they cover daily harm to women and not only a narrow range of concerns of men. The *feminization* of

---

[2] See Inter-American Convention on the Prevention, Punishment and Eradication of Violence Against Women (1994), Art. 1. See also the Protocol to the African Charter on Human and Peoples' Rights on the Rights of Women in Africa (2003) which covers violence whether committed in 'private or public' as well as covering rights in the 'private sector'.

human rights has shifted the emphasis to issues of violence against women, certain unfair labour practices, sexual exploitation, trafficking, and traditional practices. Let us look now at each of these phenomena in a little more detail.

GLOBALIZATION

Familiar aspects of globalization include: the sense that breaking news on one side of the world is simultaneously broadcast to the rest of the world through global communications giants like CNN, the BBC, and Reuters; the sense that decision-making is conducted away from national parliaments and under the influence of powerful states; the realization that large multinationals may not only control more resources than the smallest states, but that corporate global influence can overwhelm local cultures and initiatives; and lastly, a realization that national policies are sometimes dictated with deference to certain economic models which aim almost exclusively to provide the conditions for 'free markets' and foreign direct investment, with little regard for the immediate effect of these policies on the marginalized or the poor.

Governments and individuals have for a long time been subject to a sense that their future is governed by forces outside their territory. For centuries there have been networks of economic and cultural interaction that have never corresponded to the political space of states. Governments have always been constrained, and have had to cope with extensive extra-territorial networks of cultural, economic, and military power. What is new about the contemporary processes, described as global-ization, however, is the speed at which changes in these processes are taking place.

What is interesting in the context of a book about non-state actors is the stress which commentators place on an appreciation that the state's traditional capabili-ties are being undermined by globalization. Caroline Thomas suggests: 'Globalization is privileging the private over the public sphere and over the com-mons. It is eroding the authority of states differentially to set the social, economic and political agenda within their respective political space. It erodes the capacity of states in different degrees to secure the livelihoods of their respective citizens by narrowing the parameters of legitimate state activity.'[3] There is a assumption among some commentators that states are no longer in a position to function as the main actors on the international stage and that their room for manoeuvre has been diminished.

We are often reminded of the increased power of associations of states (such as the European Union or NAFTA), global corporations, and global non-governmental organizations.[4] Particular concern is focused on the role of international financial

---

[3] C. Thomas, 'International Financial Institutions and social and economic rights: an exploration' in T. Evans (ed) *Human Rights Fifty Years On: A reappraisal* (Manchester: Manchester University Press, 1998) 161–185, at 163.

[4] I. Ramonet, 'La mutation du monde' *Le Monde Diplomatique*, October 1997.

institutions such as the World Bank and the IMF which, despite their insistence on the rule of law and good governance, are seen to act outside any global good governance regime for the protection of the rights of those affected by their policies. It is clear that there has been a profound transformation of the world economy over recent decades through the progressive elimination of barriers to trade and investment and the international mobility of capital. In turn, the state's role is seen as changing due to the growing importance and pressures of global forces outside the state's control, and social justice is seen as increasingly threatened.[5]

According to the UN Committee on Economic, Social and Cultural Rights, the actual developments associated with globalization are not themselves 'necessarily incompatible with the principles of the Covenant [on Economic, Social and Cultural Rights of 1966] or with the obligations of governments thereunder'. Nevertheless, they go on to warn that:

> Taken together, however, and if not complemented by appropriate additional policies, globalization risks downgrading the central place accorded to human rights by the United Nations Charter in general and the International Bill of Rights in particular. This is especially the case in relation to economic, social and cultural rights. Thus, for example, respect for the right to work and the right to just and favorable working conditions of work is threatened where there is an excessive emphasis upon competitiveness to the detriment of respect for the labour rights contained in the Covenant. The right to form and join trade unions may be threatened by restrictions upon freedom of association, restrictions claimed to be 'necessary' in a global economy, or by the effective exclusion of possibilities for collective bargaining, or by the closing off of the right to strike for various occupational and other groups. The right of everyone to social security might not be ensured by arrangements which rely entirely upon private contributions and private schemes.[6]

It is not simply the development of the global market, deregulation, or privatization which is threatening the enjoyment of human rights, but rather, it is the ways in which governments are responding to these developments. Instead of abandoning the state as a focus for human rights activism, we may need to refocus on the existing obligations of the state. Whether globalization is really leading to the demise of the nation state is still an open question. It may be argued that, in at least some contexts, the globalization of certain decision-making processes is actually leading to a greater role for the state, and for international law, and

---

[5] Theo van Boven put it as follows: 'In this process, the interdependent and joint powers of national and international economic and financial actors, in particular transnational corporations and financial institutions, are gaining a great deal of strength and influence at the expense of the state, thus weakening the state's role as the protector of social rights and social welfare. Due to the process of globalization, the imperatives of social justice aimed at promoting and protecting the rights of the weak and the marginalized are increasingly being jeopardized. The gap between the rich and the poor is becoming more pronounced, in both the North and the South.' 'A Universal Declaration of Human Responsibilities?' in B. Van der Heijden and B. Tahzib-Lie (eds) *Reflections on the Universal Declaration on Human Rights* (The Hague: Martinus Nijhoff, 1998) 73–79, at 76.

[6] Statement by the Committee on Economic, Social and Cultural Rights, 11 May 1998.

international decision-making processes. Indeed, globalization may in fact be stimulating new forms of accountability for non-state actors and a new global polity which increasingly finds a place for international law. Many do not share this proposition—indeed some would argue that international law is part of the problem rather than part of the solution.

First, there is a counter-assumption that because international law is almost exclusively about inter-state relations it is useless to expect this legal order to be of much use in regulating the behaviour of non-state actors.[7] Second, for many commentators, globalization has to be understood as operating through new networks operating transnationally and outside the state.[8] Rather than an accumulation of power through superpower hegemony or a federation of nation states, globalization is seen as a social phenomenon driven by non-state actors outside the control of individual states; the protection of human dignity required civil society mobilization around the language of human rights rather than relying on states and their institutions. Third, the very process of globalization could be seen as the antithesis of human rights accountability. As Philip Alston explains:

> Globalization (at least as an ideal type) is premised upon flexibility, adaptability, poly-centrality, informality, and speedy, tailored and innovative responses to rapidly changing circumstances. In less positive terms it conjures up adjectives such as opportunistic, ad hoc, uncontrollable, unprincipled, and undemocratic (in the sense that many of its targets have no choice but to conform to its imperatives). The human rights regime (especially the non-ideal type portrayed by its critics) is very different. In positive terms it might be characterized as being solid, principled, not easily manipulated, committed to procedural integrity, and careful not to reach beyond its authorized grasp. In more pejorative terms it might be considered to be stolid, excessively gradualist, cautious, rigid, resistant to innovation, and legalistic. In essence then, globalization has a variety of characteristics that are largely alien to the regime of human rights accountability, and the latter is not at all well constructed in order to enable it to adapt, let alone transform itself, in response to new challenges.[9]

For Anne-Marie Slaughter, the bankers, lawyers, business people, public-interest activists, and criminals look to transnational government networks as the foci of decision-making processes. The state is not disappearing, it is disaggregating into its separate, functionally distinct parts. These parts—courts, regulatory agencies, executives, and even legislatures—are networking with their counterparts abroad,

---

[7] E.g. Thomas (1998: 182) 'International law is a legal code operating between states. This applies equally to the international law of human rights. Yet the institutions of globalization which are intimately involved in eroding social and economic rights, such as multinational banks and transnational corporations, can operate largely outside of national regulation, and outside of international law pertaining to rights.'

[8] A. Brysk, *Human Rights and Private Wrongs: Constructing Global Civil Society* (New York and London: Routledge, 2000).

[9] P. Alston, 'Downsizing the State in Human Rights Discourse' in N. Dorden and P. Gifford (eds) *Democracy and the Rule of Law* (Washington, DC: Congressional Quarterly Press, 2001) 357–368, at 359 (footnote omitted).

creating a dense web of relations that constitutes a new transgovernmental order. Today's international problems—terrorism, organized crime, environmental degradation, money laundering, bank failure, and securities fraud—created and sustain these relations.[10]

This implies a move away from arenas of relative transparency into back-rooms; the bypassing of the national political arenas. However, as Alston remarks, there are multiple strata of decision-makers, including a variety of public, private, and 'transgovernmental' fora with many interactions between them. 'While ease of travel and communications have enhanced and facilitated their functioning, it is far from clear that the result has involved such a fundamental shift in the locus of power that one can conclude that the state is "disaggregating". '[11]

The planned 'burial' of the state as the central player in the international context is still premature. From a human rights perspective, this issue is not so much about increasing complexity in decision-making at the international level, but rather, what can be done to adapt our thinking and procedures to ensure the best protection of human rights. Clearly, the traditional understanding of the human rights dynamic—as protecting individuals from an overarching state—is inadequate.

There is also what could be called a 'bottom-up' globalization (as opposed to a 'top-down' globalization, implied principally by the globalization of trading systems). These bottom-up demands relate to general objectives such as 'better living standards', the 'good life', and universal respect for all human rights. A growing mobilization against the perceived dangers posed by global economic forces and actors has created a network of civil society groups which are trying to act with regard to new challenges. And indeed, accompanying the development of global actors and forces, there is a global spread of ideas, which include debates over the advantages of respecting human rights and fundamental freedoms as well as different democratic forms of governance. An important consequence of this interdependence of civil responses to 'top-down' globalization is that the global peoples' networks, by their common action, are claiming rights that need to be protected from non-state actors in the sphere of economics and finance.

If one regards globalization in terms of the top-down effects of more open markets for transnational actors, as well as the opportunities created by a bottom-up network of global demands, one could start to exploit the dynamics to ensure better respect for human rights.[12] To demonize globalization or the World Trade Organization, *per se*, is to let those with international responsibilities off the hook.

---

[10] A.-M. Slaughter, 'The Real New World Order', 76 *Foreign Affairs* (1997) 183, at 184.

[11] P. Alston, 'The Myopia of the Handmaidens: International Lawyers and Globalization' 8 *EJIL* (1997) 435–448, at 441.

[12] Cf N. Aziz, 'The Human Rights Debate in an Era of Globalization' in P. Van Ness (ed) *Debating Human Rights* (London: Routledge, 1999) 32–55.

Thinking about globalization means considering the new ways in which states are acting at the international level. It would be short-sighted indeed to consider that states are somehow less important as attention switches to the global trading system, the international financial institutions (IFIs), and regional organizations. States themselves are creating these new regimes and those states remain more than ever responsible for the evolving international law in this field.[13] Part of the challenge is to find ways to hold governments accountable for these new diffuse activities, activities which tend to take place in fora which, while not opaque, are less than transparent. Analysing globalization highlights change and developments in various sectors—but human rights abuses are committed by legal entities, not by an abstract phenomenon named globalization.

PRIVATIZATION

The phenomenon of privatization should force us to think about the implications of the shrinking nature of state functions at the national level. As Alston notes: 'insufficient attention has been given to the implications for international law of the changing internal role of the state, as opposed to the implications of the changing international context for the state's external relations'.[14]

The end of the Cold War and the collapse of the Soviet Union have paved the way for a yen for privatization in many former communist countries. At the same time, global trade liberalization, an ideological predilection for privatization in a number of Western countries, and the convergence criteria demanded for entry into European Monetary Union, have ensured a shift in many fields from the public to the private sector. In addition, international financial institutions and other lenders have increasingly imposed conditions on debtors that include accelerated privatization of state concerns. Often the transition to a market economy, or the rush to privatize, is at the expense of established economic and social state-provided benefits. Little attention has been paid to considering how to ensure that such transitions do not lead to violations of the international human rights obligations which the state has undertaken in the economic and social rights sphere. Furthermore, the privatization of functions such as law enforcement, health care, education, telecommunications, and broadcasting has meant in some cases the evaporation of controls which were placed on these sectors to ensure respect for civil and political rights. Similarly, it is even more difficult to apply the benchmarks and procedures for 'achieving progressively the rights recognized' in the International Covenant on Economic, Social and Cultural Rights. At the international level, the problem is exacerbated by the fact that most procedures for ensuring the protection of human rights and accountability for

---

[13] Cf S. V. Scott, 'International Lawyers: Handmaidens, Chefs, or Birth Attendants: A Response to Philip Alston' 9 *EJIL* (1998) 750–756.   [14] Alston (1997: 446).

violations are designed to bring states, and only states, to account. These international procedures are ill-equipped to tackle violations committed in these 'new private spheres'.

However, one must admit that the move to privatize is tied to the move to deregulate global markets. To start to impose new restrictions (albeit for the protection of fundamental human rights) runs counter to the *Zeitgeist* for less law and more market 'freedom'. The ideology of privatization has captured the imagination of certain sectors of public opinion and of decision-makers in governments and in opposition. The controversial approach taken by Robert Nozick in his 1974 book *Anarchy, State and Utopia* no longer seems to attract the sort of dismissive attitude he himself expected. The opening page of his book contains the following passage:

> Our main conclusions about the state are that a minimal state, limited to the narrow functions of protection against force, theft, fraud, enforcement of contracts, and so on, is justified; that any more extensive state will violate persons' rights not to be forced to do certain things, and is unjustified; and that the minimal state is inspiring as well as right. Two noteworthy implications are that the state may not use its coercive apparatus for the purpose of getting some citizens to aid others, or in order to prohibit activities to people for their own good or protection.
>
> Despite the fact that it is only the coercive routes towards these goals that are excluded, while voluntary ones remain, many persons will reject our conclusions instantly, knowing that they don't *want* to believe anything so apparently callous towards the needs and suffering of others. I know that reaction; it was mine when I first began to consider such views.[15]

Alston has highlighted the fact that:

> ... the means which are always assumed to be an indispensable part of the globalization process, have in fact acquired the status of values in and of themselves. Those means/values include, for example: privatization of as many functions as possible; deregulation, particularly of private power, at both national and international levels; reliance upon the free market as the most efficient and appropriate value-allocating mechanism; minimal government except in relation to law and order functions narrowly defined; and minimal international regulation except in relation to the 'new' international agenda items.[16]

According to Alston, the supreme value of respect for the free market has been introduced

> ... as an element which is capable of trumping other values. Thus, even some human rights norms are increasingly subject to an assessment of their market friendliness in order to determine what, if any, weight will be accorded to them... In at least some respects, the burden of proof has been shifted—in order to be validated, a purported human right must justify its contribution to a broader, market-based 'vision' of the good society.[17]

[15] R. Nozick, *Anarchy, State and Utopia* (Oxford: Basil Blackwell, 1974) at ix.
[16] Alston (1997: 442).   [17] Ibid.

   The World Bank's 1997 report, *The State in a Changing World*, showed that over the last century the size and scope of government have expanded enormously, and even at the end of the century, state spending constituted almost half of total income in the established industrial countries, and around a quarter in developing countries.[18] However, following the collapse of the Soviet Union, 'government failure, including the failure of publicly owned firms, seemed everywhere glaringly evident. Governments began to adopt policies designed to reduce the scope of the state's intervention in the economy'.[19] The report goes on to conclude that this 'overzealous rejection of government' has led in some cases to outright collapse of the state and that: 'State-dominated development has failed, but so will stateless development. Development without an effective state is impossible.'[20] But the report takes the opportunity to reaffirm the advantages of liberalization and privatization. 'With economic liberalization, many areas of regulation have been recognized as counterproductive, and wisely abandoned. Yet in some areas the traditional rationales for regulation remain, and market liberalization and privatization have brought new regulatory issues to the fore. The challenge . . . is not to abandon regulation altogether. Instead it is to find regulatory approaches in each country that match both its needs and its capabilities.'[21]

   At the national level, the privatized body may or may not be covered by the protections offered by the national Bill of Rights or Constitution. This will depend on the wording of the national Bill and the interpretation of the Bill by the national judges. The national legal orders of various countries are examined in Chapter 10. As discussed in Chapter 6, dealing with the responsibility of corporations, the international law of state responsibility covers privatized entities that exercise elements of governmental authority. But traditional concepts of what could be considered such elements of governmental authority are changing. The Supreme Court of the United States has decided that the tradition that prison services were run by public authorities was a short-lived tradition, as in the eighteenth century, prisons were run by corporations, and the trend is now towards the privatization of detention facilities. In this particular case (which is discussed in Chapter 10) the Supreme Court ruled that a prison guard in a private prison could not therefore rely on the public nature of his function to claim immunity from suit.[22] Such a finding demonstrates the difficulty of distinguishing 'traditional' governmental activity from something which is 'obviously' private.

   Furthermore, developments in the United States point towards new models of private law enforcement and policy development: around 30 million Americans have now bought private housing in 'common interest developments'; in effect leading to a privatization of local government and police functions in certain areas.[23] In his book, *Privatopia*, Evan McKenzie describes the rise of residential

---

[18] World Bank, *World Development Report 1997: The State in a Changing World* (New York: Oxford University Press, 1997) at 2.   [19] Ibid, at 23.
[20] Ibid, at 25.   [21] Ibid, at 65.   [22] *Richardson et al v McKnight* 521 US 399 (1977).
[23] E. McKenzie, *Privatopia* (Newhaven: Yale University Press, 1994).

private government. A few examples suffice to give a flavour of the direction in which some parts of the United States may be heading:

> Some community associations have banned political signs, prohibited distribution of newspapers, and forbidden political gatherings in the common areas...In Fairbanks Ranch, an affluent CID [common-interest development] that lies behind six locked gates, there are forty-five private streets patrolled by private security officers who enforce a private speed limit. First-time speeders get a warning; the second offense brings a hearing and a reprimand; a third offense means a five-hundred dollar fine, and the car and driver are banned from the private streets for a month.[24]

A traditional international lawyer's response to such developments might be to say that because the state has privatized these activities, it remains responsible for how they are conducted and for the way in which they are privatized. Certainly, the International Law Commission (ILC) or the European Court of Human Rights might approach the problem from this perspective. But the problem is really much wider than holding the state accountable for the privatization of its state-like activities. First, as already suggested, it is now no longer clear what are the traditional functions of the state. The ILC's articles on state responsibility attribute to the state conduct of a non-state entity 'empowered by the law of that State to exercise elements of the governmental authority'.[25] But the scope of what should be considered governmental is itself a deeply contested concept. Any insistence on a pre-ordained public/private divide can lead to dangerous distinctions between the public and private spheres which simply reinforce the unequal status of women in society, and further shield powerful non-state actors from scrutiny under international law.[26]

Second, new powerful elements often operate without specific empowering internal law. New entities or powerful associations spring up to exercise power without any sort of delegated authority or state regulation. In the context of residential private government in America, McKenzie asserts that: 'the move toward privatization was a matter of inaction. It was de facto privatization; it was done over decades, without a public discussion of whether it should take place; it happened not by government action, but by inaction, as private developers gradually transferred local government functions to private corporations'.[27]

---

[24] Ibid, at 15–16.

[25] International Law Commission's articles on responsibility of states for internationally wrongful acts, *Report of the ILC, 53rd Session*, adopted 10 August 2001, UN Doc. A/56/10, Art. 5. Discussed further in Ch 6, at 6.7.1 below. The UN General Assembly took note of the articles, 'commended them to the attention of Governments', and annexed the articles to its Resolution 56/83, 12 December 2001. See further J. Crawford, *The International Law Commission's Articles on State Responsibility: Introduction, Text and Commentaries* (Cambridge: Cambridge University Press, 2002a); and J. Crawford and S. Olleson, 'The Nature and Forms of International Responsibility' in M. Evans (ed) *International Law* (Oxford: Oxford University Press, 2003) 445–472.

[26] Discussed by Christine Chinkin with regard to the specific discussions concerning the draft articles on state responsibility developed by International Law Commission. 'A Critique of the Public/Private Dimension' 10 *EJIL* (1999) 387–395.   [27] McKenzie (1994: 180).

Throughout this book we shall encounter examples of privatization (with regard to water services, prisons, peace-keeping, shopping areas, and so on) which will suggest that human rights law should continue to apply even after such functions have moved to the private sector. Talking about privatization highlights the possible dangers for human rights protection of simple transfers of certain state activity to the private sphere. It does not mean that privatization *as such* is a violation of human rights or that the purpose of privatization necessarily violates human rights obligations. The issue is twofold. First, the non-state actor in control of the 'private' activity now has human rights claims that the old state actor could not make. Claims by commercial companies for respect of property rights have proven successful in situations where the previous public owners would have had no such claim. Second, through privatization, governments may decrease the level of human rights accountability for the sector concerned. Although it is possible to build in new layers of accountability as functions pass from the public to the private sphere, the point of privatization is usually to introduce flexibility rather than extra accountability.[28]

FRAGMENTATION

International humanitarian law has adapted in the last few decades to encompass the behaviour of armed opposition groups and national liberation armies, but the framework for ensuring compliance (appeals by the International Committee of the Red Cross, prosecution before the International Criminal Tribunals, condemnations by the states parties, training programmes in military academies, and so on) is not yet well suited to really ensuring that armed groups have an incentive to comply with principles of humanitarian law. From the perspective of the legal framework applicable, it is well known that states are still often unwilling to admit the applicability of the Geneva Conventions or Protocol II for fear of recognizing that 'terrorists' are engaged in an internationally recognized armed struggle which might encourage claims taking them outside the realm of the normal criminal law. The following is a brief outline of some of the problems encountered by the International Committee of the Red Cross (ICRC) in seeking to promote respect for international humanitarian law. The legal aspects of this issue are dealt with in more detail in Chapter 7.

---

[28] Alston (2001: 362) observes that the objectives of privatization and deregulation 'include the promotion of greater enterprise efficiency, the development of a more service-oriented mentality, the elimination of loss-making assets that drain the capacity of the state to fulfil its core functions, the achievement of the degree of flexibility—in the markets for labour, capital and production—that is conducive to efficiency, and the provision of the incentive needed to unleash the spirit of enterprise that can energize a free market. It is not necessary to contest the validity of any one of these objectives in order to observe that many of the measures taken in the name of these objectives have the capacity to reduce very significantly the element of accountability that is central to the human rights regime'.

The ICRC has detailed the essential characteristics of what they call 'anarchic' conflicts: 'The disintegration of the organs of central government, which is no longer able to exercise its rights or perform its duties in relation to the territory and the population; the presence of many armed factions; divided control of the national territory; the breakdown of the chain of command within the various factions and their militias.'[29] The problems for the promotion of international humanitarian law are clear: 'The extreme individualization of the factions has made contacts and negotiations very uncertain. Every soldier—adult or child—virtually becomes a spokesperson, or in any case someone with whom to negotiate.'[30] Furthermore the 'concept of a "war ethic" becomes a delusion', it becomes necessary to reach the population at large rather than members of a military hierarchy, and the loose structure of the factions 'makes it more and more difficult, if not impossible, to distinguish between combatants and civilians'.[31] These contemporary aspects of armed conflict and internal violence threaten to undermine the whole humanitarian logic.

Michael Ignatieff, after a trip to Afghanistan, was dismayed to see that humanitarian notions seem suddenly quaint when confronted with today's realities:

> The Red Cross acknowledges that a warrior's honor is a slender hope, but it may be all there is to separate war from savagery. And a corollary hope is that men can be trained to fight with honor. Armies train people to kill, but they also teach restraint and discipline; they channel aggression into ritual. War is redeemed only by moral rules, and, as Holleufer says, 'the Red Cross is the guardian of the rules'. The problem, he concedes, is that more and more warriors no longer play by the rules. Modern technology has steadily increased the distance, both moral and geographic, between the warrior and his prey. What sense of honor can possibly link the technician who targets the Tomahawk cruise missile and the civilians of Baghdad a thousand miles away? At the other end of the scale, the global market in small arms is breaking up the modern state's monopoly on the means of violence. The disintegrating states of the world are literally flooded with junk weapons, old Kalashnikovs for the most part, which can be bought in the marketplace for the cost of a loaf of bread. With weapons this cheap, violence becomes impossible for the state to contain. The history of war has been about the state's confiscating violence from society and vesting it in a specialized warrior caste. But if the state loses control of war, as it has in so many of the world's red zones of insurgency and rebellion—if war becomes the preserve of private armies, gangsters, and paramilitaries—then the distinction between battle and barbarism may disappear.[32]

In such situations where the state is collapsing, or has already collapsed, it is almost perverse to insist that human rights norms and procedures only be invoked through the prism of the state and the government authorities. Of course the lack of government will make it harder in practice to carry out human rights

---

[29] ICRC, *Preparatory document for the first periodical meeting on international humanitarian law: Armed conflicts linked to the disintegration of State structures* (Geneva) 19–23 January 1998, at 4.

[30] Ibid, at 5.   [31] Ibid, at 6.

[32] M. Ignatieff, *The Warrior's Honor: Ethnic War and the Modern Conscience* (New York: Metropolitan Books, 1998) at 157.

promotion, and a formal legal approach might suggest that there may even be no state to fulfil the human rights obligations and hence no human rights under international law,[33] but an alternative approach would insist that local human rights programmes can be launched even in a situation as 'collapsed' as that of Somalia.[34] We need not abandon human rights thinking in the absence of a government ready to carry out all the traditional functions of statehood.

There are situations where the non-state actors themselves have agreed to respect or follow certain international human rights and humanitarian norms, and Chapter 7 examines some initiatives designed to get armed opposition groups to sign up to certain 'commitments'. But these voluntary initiatives do not lead to the conclusion that in the absence of such agreement, the non-state actor is not bound to abide by basic human rights law or humanitarian law. Human rights and humanitarian law is not now something one can opt in or out of. The sorts of rights at issue in this context are usually binding customary international law and not really dependent on unilateral declarations and signatures.

Several projects are currently under way to clarify the exact scope of these customary rules. Three may be mentioned here. First, for some time scholars such as Theodor Meron have drawn attention to the legal problems associated with the protection of human rights in times of armed conflict and proposed a new Declaration to fill a number of gaps.[35] The Turku Declaration on Minimum Humanitarian Standards was adopted by a group of experts in 1990 and slightly modified in 1994.[36] Now the topic has been re-titled as concerning the 'fundamental standards of humanity' and remains on the agenda in the inter-governmental system at the United Nations.[37] Second, the International Committee of the Red Cross has conducted its own study of customary international humanitarian law. This study includes a set of principles concerning human rights applicable in times of armed conflict.[38] Third, the June 1998 Rome Conference on Establishment of an International Criminal Court set out a series of crimes that

---

[33] R. Koskenmäki, 'Legal Implications Resulting from State Failure in Light of the Case of Somalia' 73 *NJIL* (2004) 1–36.

[34] M. Rishmawi, 'Situation of human rights in Somalia', UN Doc. E/CN.4/1998/96, 16 January 1998.

[35] T. Meron, 'On the Inadequate Reach of Humanitarian and Human Rights Law and the Need for a New Instrument' 77 *AJIL* (1983) 589; T. Meron, *Human Rights in Internal Strife: Their International Protection* (Cambridge: Grotius, 1987).

[36] A. Eide, T. Meron, and A. Rosas, 'Combating Lawlessness in Gray Zone Conflicts Through Minimum Humanitarian Standards' 89 *AJIL* (1995) 215.

[37] UN Doc. E/CN.4/1998/87/Add. 1, 12 January 1998. See J.-D. Vigny and C. Thompson, 'Fundamental Standards of Humanity: What Future?' (2002) 20 *NQHR* 185–199.

[38] J.-M. Henckaerts and L. Doswald-Beck, *Customary International Humanitarian Law—Volume 1: Rules* (Cambridge: Cambridge University Press, 2005) esp. Ch 32. The study mysteriously asserts that the 'majority view' is that international human rights law (in contrast to international humanitarian law) only binds governments and not armed opposition groups (at 299). For those who do not accept this apparent limitation on human rights law, the set of customary rules will provide a useful normative framework for holding non-state actors accountable in times of armed conflict for violations of international human rights law.

are not only justiciable at the international level but also, for those states that have incorporated the crimes from the Rome Statute in their national legal orders, triable before national courts. The Statute has confirmed that there are obligations under international law for individuals (whether acting on behalf of a state or as non-state actors). Because the Rome Statute specifically extends to internal armed conflicts, and even covers conflict between non-state groups, it is clear that specific war crimes can be committed by individual non-state actors under Article 8(2)(c) and (e) and, according to a report of the Secretary-General written after the adoption of the Rome Statute, 'the prohibition of these acts has been widely recognized as customary international law'.[39]

FEMINIZATION

More than the other forces of globalization, privatization, and fragmentation, the feminization dimension permeates all the above dynamics. The connections have been made by many commentators. As Anthony Giddens put it:

> It is wrong to think about globalisation as just concerning the big systems, like the world financial order. Globalisation isn't only about what is 'out there', remote and far away from the individual. It is an in-here phenomenon too, influencing intimate and personal aspects our lives. The debate about family values, for example, which is going on in many countries might seem far removed from globalising influences. It isn't. Traditional family systems are becoming transformed, or are under strain, in many parts of the world, particularly as women stake claim to greater equality. There has never been a society, so far as we know from the historical record, in which women have been even approximately equal to men. This is a truly global revelation in everyday life, whose consequences are being felt around the world in spheres from work to politics.[40]

The series of global conferences held in the first half of the 1990s activated an impressive network of women's groups that has succeeded in making women's rights a global issue. The United Nations itself highlighted the resultant redefinition of human rights:

> Notwithstanding efforts at the non-discriminatory application of human rights to all without distinction, it has been increasingly recognized that the vision of human rights and the mechanisms that exist to concretize this vision, although supposedly available to women and men on an equal basis, have profited women less than men. As a result, significant efforts have been applied to redefine the meaning of human rights to encompass the specific experiences of women at all stages of their lives.[41]

---

[39] Report of the Secretary-General submitted pursuant to Commission Res. 1998/29, 18 December 1998, UN Doc. E/CN.4/1999/92, at para. 12.

[40] A. Giddens, *Runaway World* (London: Profile Books, 1999) at 12.

[41] Report of the Secretary-General, UN Doc. E/CN.4/1998/22–E/CN.6/1998/11, at 4.

In looking at what is meant by feminization, it may help to consider it from various perspectives. First, the 'feminization' of poverty is now becoming more serious in most of the countries of the world. A human rights agenda that attaches importance to violations of human rights in the private sphere has to start to address the fundamental inequality it finds here. More women than men are found in the poorest sections of the population and, at the same time, greater demands are made on women in a 'flexible' and deregulated labour market while they are paid less. While poverty is affecting households as a whole, because of the gender division of labour and responsibilities, women bear a disproportionate burden, the situation being even worse for women in rural areas. As the gender-related development index and the gender empowerment measure have shown, the achievements of states with regard to human development—i.e. whether people lead long and healthy lives, are educated and knowledgeable, and enjoy a decent standard of living—have to be re-evaluated when inequality in achievement between women and men is taken into account.[42]

Second, when one considers the question of discrimination within the national economic and social spheres, it is evident that pressures to adapt to global competitiveness and the new economic models of minimal public spending have meant that states have sought to avoid protective labour standards and have cut back on education and health care facilities paid for out of the public purse. Free trade zones (FTZs) continue to be developed by host countries as areas with little or no social regulation or respect for the right to form trade unions or other associations. In fact, states often advertise abroad the fact that no unions are allowed in such areas and redefine the area so that it exists in a sort of legal limbo where constitutional and other rights do not apply. The idea is to achieve a comparative advantage by driving down wages and attracting transnational corporations that are offered tax breaks and reduced customs duties. According to one study: 'The workforce is mostly composed of unmarried women between the ages of seventeen and twenty-three. In Mexican FTZs, these women account for about 50 per cent of the workforce. They are the preferred workers, as their wages tend to be lower (often less than $1 per day), and they are considered better suited to repetitive tasks that require nimble fingers.'[43]

When one considers the issue of the cut-backs in public spending on health, education, and basic social services, this has meant in turn that families have had to make choices about which children they can afford to educate or insure for privatized health care. There is here a sort of 'double privatization'. The dynamic of privatizing state functions has led to a new set of private actors (families) as violators of human rights due to the choices they may be forced to take. As with all

---

[42] *Human Development Report 1997* (Oxford: Oxford University Press, 1997) at 41, 149–151, 152–154.

[43] A. Goldsmith, 'Seeds of Exploitation: Free Trade Zones in the Global Economy' in J. Mander and E. Goldsmith (eds) *The Case against the Global Economy: and for a turn toward the local* (San Francisco, Cal: Sierra Club Books, 1996) 267–284, at 268.

the other examples touched on, this represents a new challenge for human rights lawyers as they grapple with new forms of accountability and human rights education.

Third, the issue of violence against women in the home is clearly part of international human rights law and the state has legal obligations to prevent, prosecute, punish, and protect in this domestic/private sphere. But the questions facing human rights organizations no longer concern the need to fix a legal duty on the state, but rather the failure of the state to take rights in this sphere seriously. 'A police chief in Rio de Janeiro told Americas Watch that to her knowledge, of more than 2,000 battery and sexual assault cases registered at the station in 1990, not a single one had ended in punishment of the accused.'[44] Should policing become even more orientated to ensuring a minimal state of law and order, rather than a state function with multiple responsibilities within society, it seems likely that the home may remain assimilated with the sphere of competitive commerce— a zone which is better left unregulated and unpoliced. The familiar mantra that there must be 'no interference in domestic affairs' often seems to have been absorbed at the national level as some sort of excuse for inaction. To generate a greater state of obligation to deal with violence in the private sphere seems to go against the grain. But that is precisely what women's human rights groups are suggesting, and this is precisely what the current state of international human rights law demands. It suffices here to quote from the UN General Assembly Declaration on Violence against Women, adopted by consensus on 20 December 1993:

> Article 4.   States should condemn violence against women and should not invoke any custom, tradition or religious consideration to avoid their obligations with respect to its elimination. States should pursue by all appropriate means and without delay a policy of eliminating violence against women and, to this end, should: . . . (c) Exercise due diligence to prevent, investigate and, in accordance with national legislation, punish acts of violence against women, whether those acts are perpetrated by the State or by private persons; . . .[45]

As the human rights movement has become increasingly feminized, gender-based considerations are becoming integrated in the domestic and international human rights agenda. The 1995 Beijing Declaration and Platform of Action called for this incorporation of a gender perspective as 'mainstreaming'.[46] The Beijing Platform for Action further outlined what is expected in this field:

> 224.   Violence against women both violates and impairs or nullifies the enjoyment by women of human rights and fundamental freedoms. Taking into account the

---

[44] Human Rights Watch, *Criminal Injustice Violence against Women in Brazil* (1991) at 5.

[45] GA Res. 48/104.

[46] 'The Beijing Declaration and Platform for Action: Fourth World Conference on Women, Beijing, China', 4–15 September 1995, UN Doc. DPI/1766/Wom, see e.g. (at para. 229): 'In addressing the enjoyment of human rights, Governments and other actors should promote an active and visible policy of mainstreaming a gender perspective in all policies and programmes so that, before decisions are taken, an analysis is made of the effects on women and men, respectively.'

Declaration on the Elimination of Violence against Women and the work of Special Rapporteurs, gender-based violence, such as battering and other domestic violence, sexual abuse, sexual slavery and exploitation, and international trafficking in women and children, forced prostitution and sexual harassment, as well as violence against women, resulting from cultural prejudice, racism and racial discrimination, xenophobia, pornography, ethnic cleansing, armed conflict, foreign occupation, religious and anti-religious extremism and terrorism are incompatible with the dignity and the worth of the human person and must be combated and eliminated. Any harmful aspect of certain traditional, customary or modern practices that violates the rights of women should be prohibited and eliminated. Governments should take urgent action to combat and eliminate all forms of violence against women in private and public life, whether perpetrated or tolerated by the State or private persons.

Fourth, women's human rights advocates have highlighted the ways in which women have been targeted for rape and sexual abuse in recent armed conflicts and have made a series of suggestions for tackling the issue. One could cite the success in getting the issue of rape in times of internal and international armed conflict to be treated as an international crime. In the cases of the former Yugoslavia and Rwanda this has resulted in trials before the International Tribunals in The Hague and Arusha and the affirmation that the prohibition of rape and sexual assault in armed conflict and the individual criminal responsibility for the commission of these crimes have acquired the status of customary international law. The Rwanda Tribunal has suggested definitions of rape and classified some rape as torture.[47] A Trial Chamber of the Tribunal for the former Yugoslavia referred to this categorization of rape as torture under international human rights law.[48] Crucially in the present context, the International Tribunal for the former Yugoslavia has confirmed that the customary international crime of torture can be committed by a non-state actor with no nexus to a state.[49] In the Tribunal's assessment, the definition in Article 1 of the Convention Against Torture, which demands that the actual act be committed by or with the acquiescence of a public official, does not 'wholly [reflect] customary international law regarding the meaning of the crime of torture generally'.[50] In particular, 'the public official requirement is not a requirement under customary international law in relation to the criminal responsibility of an individual for torture outside the framework of the Torture Convention'.[51]

In situations of armed conflict, not only are societies fragmented, but people are set against each other in a cycle of violence where civilians, and women and children in particular, are often the primary targets. The fact that most refugees are women is fairly well known but new issues of claims for refugee status because of sexual oppression are taxing national and international lawyers around the

[47] *Prosecutor v Akayesu* Case ICTR–96–4–T, judgment of 2 September 1998.
[48] See *Prosecutor v Furundžija* Case IT–95–17/1–T, judgment of 10 December 1998.
[49] *Prosecutor v Kunarac, Kovač and Vuković* Case IT–96–23 and IT–96–23/1–A, judgment of 12 June 2002, para. 147.   [50] Ibid, para. 147.
[51] Ibid, para. 148.

world. A fifth dimension of the feminization dynamic relates to women and girl-children who claim asylum due to fear of a general level of violence against women, yet are still unlikely to receive refugee status. Refugee law requires a degree of individual persecution. Women who flee internal armed conflict for fear of being raped may not meet the requirements of refugee law in some countries; women fleeing domestic or communal violence may not be seen as subject to individual persecution. The legal developments concerning this issue are discussed in more detail in Chapter 8. In some cases, national decision-makers have moved away from exclusively examining state-sponsored persecution and have developed tests based on the idea that protection has to be offered where the state of origin is unwilling or unable to offer protection from the non-state violence.

This introduction simply serves to explain some of the reasons as to *why* human rights law is developing to fix human rights obligations on non-state actors. With these background factors in mind, let us turn to a brief explanation of the structure of this book which is focused on explaining *how* and *where* these legal changes are taking place. Chapter 1 examines some of the broader objections to such an extension of human rights law into the world of non-state actors. These are grouped around five sets of objections: the trivialization argument, the legal impossibility argument, the foreign policy tactical argument, the legitimization of violence argument, and the rights as a barrier to social justice argument. I respond to these objections and suggest new ways of looking at human rights violations. These involve the removal of the filter which only allows international lawyers to see the world through the rules of state responsibility and courts with limited international jurisdiction. I suggest that we allow ourselves a wider field of vision which permits us to look at a wide range of actors and a multiplicity of jurisdictions and accountability mechanisms.

In Chapter 2 it is suggested that the concept of international personality may be a help or a hindrance in determining the scope of existing responsibilities. Everything depends on one's approach to the doctrines of personality and subjectivity. Of course, this is a problematic area, as personality is often seen as the capacity to exercise rights and undertake responsibilities. The use of personality to determine rights and responsibility is therefore circular. But one can go beyond the tired question of the international capacity of the United Nations, to look at entities which enjoy a degree of international capacity, and see to what extent human rights and humanitarian law obligations now fix on these entities. Such an approach reinforces the challenge to traditional assumptions about international law only binding states and what are the proper 'subjects' of international law. Starting with the United Nations and the European Community, it is fairly easy to show that customary international law is considered binding on non-state actors such as these. Customary international law will also bind other non-state actors in fields such as the prohibition on slavery or genocide. This is not startling with regard to individuals, but it will be suggested that the obligation attaches to legal persons, such as corporations, as well. Several international treaties now address non-state actors as juridical persons. Even though states usually remain the sole parties to the treaties, the criminalization of corruption, transfer of toxic waste, mercenarism, and certain crimes under humanitarian law may create international crimes or delicts so that entities are subject to the jurisdiction of state parties. We have here the development of key rules which are precise enough to bind non-state actors. Even if all of these treaties do not yet reflect obligations under customary international law for non-state actors, such treaties have focused the attention of those who direct corporate non-state actors on the possibilities of obligations stemming from international law.

Chapter 3 provides a general overview of the different categories of international human rights law that will be encountered in the course of the book. Consideration is given to the meaning of terms such as *jus cogens* and *erga omnes*, and the elaboration, status, and interaction of customary international law and treaty law is considered against the background of the burgeoning number of non-binding Declarations adopted at the inter-governmental level. The purpose of the Chapter is to highlight the proposition that a doctrinaire approach to the sources of international law, which separates treaties and customary international law from non-binding instruments such as resolutions of the General Assembly, blinds us to the hybrid varieties of international human rights law which have merged to meet new challenges to the enjoyment of human rights.

The next four chapters examine the ways in which human rights compliance has arisen for different types of non-state actors. We look at inter-governmental organizations such as the United Nations and the World Bank (Chapter 4) and the World Trade Organization and the European Union (Chapter 5). The different functions of these organizations raise very different human rights concerns. The Chapters focus on the interlocking legal orders to discover which human rights obligations might be binding on these non-state actors.

Chapter 6 considers the various regimes which have been implemented to address the human rights obligations of corporations. Starting with the Guidelines adopted by the Organization for Economic Cooperation and Development, the International Labour Organization, and the UN Global Compact, we highlight the existing procedures established to examine human rights abuses committed by corporations. The case-law of the US courts with regard to cases brought against corporations for violations of international human rights law under the Alien Tort Claims Act is considered; particularly the case-law dealing with the notion of accountability for corporate complicity in human rights violations.

Chapter 7 is dedicated to certain non-state actors in times of armed conflict and addresses the obligations of belligerents, national liberation movements (NLMs), and insurgents as entities with international obligations. This Chapter also considers some of the dilemmas facing humanitarian non-governmental organizations and the putative regime emerging to cover their actions.

The legal argument developed throughout this book is that customary international law, international treaties, and certain non-binding international instruments already create human rights responsibilities for non-state actors. This is a radical departure from the traditional approach to customary international law. But today, customary international law is already considered to be binding on some non-state actors by those same non-state actors themselves (as we shall see, for example, with regard to the European Community). Even though international obligations cannot presently be enforced through the majority of international courts (the main exception being the International Criminal Tribunals which may have jurisdiction over individuals accused of genocide, crimes against humanity, and war crimes), these international obligations are being invoked before national courts. Furthermore, it is possible to argue that they do begin to form a legal framework (albeit in the absence of a standing international jurisdiction) which operates to delimit the behaviour of actors such as corporations and international organizations.

Chapter 8 covers refugee law as well as international human rights treaty law as monitored by the UN treaty bodies. We will tackle the issue of protection from expulsion to a country where the threat emanates from non-state actors as opposed to the state itself.

Chapter 9 looks in detail at some of the cases which have arisen under the regional human rights treaties. The judgments regarding states' obligations under the treaties to prevent, control, and punish private abuses of human rights often contain explanations as to the scope of the duty of the private actors themselves to respect the human rights in the treaty. If the state fails to prevent individuals from ill-treating others, this sometimes implies that the individuals and other non-state actors have an obligation to respect human rights. The international ruling will have to address the extent of the obligation on the private actor in order to see if the state has prohibited the behaviour by the relevant non-state actor, and in addition, whether the state has taken effective measures to ensure protection from such violations, by these non-state actors. Where the issue involves the right to a remedy for human rights violations, the international decision may imply that the state has to provide a remedy for abuses of international human rights committed by private bodies. While the international bodies in this context do not usually need to define the exact limits of non-state obligations, the decisions are of particular relevance for determining not only the scope of positive obligations on the state party, but also the likely scope of the non-state actor obligation. In some states, rights in the human rights treaties already take effect between private parties at the national level. In such situations, such pronouncements by international bodies can have a critical effect in determining the scope of non-state human rights obligations at the national level.

Chapter 10 examines the situation in various national law jurisdictions. This Chapter illustrates how the lack of international jurisdiction over non-state actors has not prevented national courts from developing human rights obligations for non-state actors. Sometimes these obligations are international law obligations simply enforced at the national level (such as in the US Alien Tort Claims Act). In several situations, national courts will enforce constitutional (or human) rights against non-state actors where there is deemed to be an appropriate link to a governmental function or to the state. National courts may also simply incorporate human rights values and obligations into their reasoning to determine the outcome of a case, even where both parties to the case are disconnected from the state and recognized by the court as purely 'private' entities. The national case law highlights how the values of dignity and democracy are at the heart of judicial reasoning in human rights cases, and yet a simple appeal to these values rarely resolves the competing claims before the court.

Chapter 11 examines the paradoxes which arise when we seek to resolve cases through appeals to the need to protect dignity and democracy.

In essence, I am suggesting that the human rights obligations of non-state actors can be considered under three broad headings: first, the international obligations on non-state actors themselves; the suggestion that non-state actors have such obligations is an important step in the development of a coherent concept of complicity under international law. Non-state actors, such as corporations or multilateral development banks, are typically accused of facilitating violations of human rights law by governments. They emerge as accomplices with international obligations and are accused of *complicity*. Second, the international obligations on states to protect everyone from human rights abuses committed by non-state actors; these obligations include duties to create remedies at the national level and to ensure that individuals and organizations can claim their human rights against the relevant non-state actor. These obligations have been explicated in a number of General Comments and judgments from human rights treaty monitoring bodies and courts. The obligation on the state is often to ensure that individuals are protected through national law from infringements on their human rights by non-state actors. There are then two sets of obligations that have to be respected: first, the obligation of the state to ensure protection through national law; and second, the obligation of the non-state actor itself. Sometimes these obligations can both be generated from the international norm in question and the obligation in international law will automatically take effect in the national legal order; at other times the national law may offer insufficient protection and the state will be obliged to change the law in order to ensure human rights protection from non-state actors. These multiple obligations, which apply to a multiplicity of actors, create a situation of *complexity*. Third, are the obligations on non-state actors which take effect in national jurisdictions depending on the constitutional and other arrangements in national law. In some cases, these obligations may go beyond what is demanded by international law, and in other cases, such national arrangements may fail to meet the obligations imposed on the state through its international obligations. The dialectic between the international and national law of human rights gives rise to complementary legal orders. The human rights obligations we observe will depend on the jurisdictional filter we are looking through. The obligations apply simultaneously but we can only focus on one legal order at a time. I hope to demonstrate that it may make more sense to see these variegated obligations, not in hierarchical terms, but rather through the concept of *complementarity*.

1

Old Objections and New Approaches

This book is concerned with those occasions when non-state actors act in ways which threaten the enjoyment of human rights. We will focus on international organizations, transnational corporations, and armed opposition groups. As the human rights debate has expanded to address these actors, the response has been far from uniform. At the legal level, much depends on one's approach to international law. Reflecting this we can identify multiple responses by lawyers to ensuring the accountability of non-state actors for human rights abuses. Let us condense these to three broad approaches.

The first approach would insist on the importance of states as the main actors in the international system and the only bearer of human rights obligations under international law. Such an approach focuses on state responsibility and demands that human rights problems concerning non-state actors are simply dealt with as questions of the relevant government's obligation to ensure respect for human rights. Human rights law is said to be adequate, in that it already demands that governments protect everyone from those who might undermine those rights. The whole human rights system has been based on the responsibility of states and this is said to be the best medium through which to tackle the growing concern over threats emanating from non-state actors. It is said that attempting to extend legal duties under human rights law to non-state actors bestows on such actors an unfortunate legitimacy, which will undermine the authority of the state and dilute the responsibilities of states with respect to their human rights obligations. According to this first approach, to change course now would allow the whole human rights project to unravel. The state is, at least in many cases, already accountable for failing to enforce its own laws against abusive non-state actors. In addition, there are several ways in which popular participation can influence outcomes in government policy and improve legislation to constrain abuses by non-state actors. Better to put our faith in the current state-centred system than in a new, unknown, and necessarily diffuse accountability arrangement which would inadvertently give non-state actors greater 'status'.

The second approach suggests that governments are increasingly irrelevant and powerless and that attention should focus on other actors such as transnational corporations and international institutions such as the International Monetary Fund and the World Bank. According to this approach, we should face up to the fact that, in a globalized economy, the trading which accompanies economic exploitation or civil wars is no longer in the hands of governments (even if they were minded to seriously tackle these issues). New ways of understanding transnational justice and global law are needed to respond to globalization. For Gunther Teubner: 'Today's globalization is not a gradual emergence of a world society under the leadership of interstate politics, but is a highly contradictory and highly fragmented process in which politics has lost its leading role.'[1] In this vein, global law is not bound by the territories of nation states but 'rather, by "invisible colleges", "invisible markets and branches", "invisible professional communities", "invisible social networks" that transcend territorial boundaries but nevertheless press for the emergence of genuinely legal forms'.[2] Teubner's response is a proposed legal pluralism 'defined no longer as a set of conflicting social norms but as a multiplicity of diverse communicative processes in a given social field that observe social action under the binary code of legal/illegal'.[3] The emphasis is on a plurality of legal discourses rather than a hierarchy of legal orders. This approach may also combine with a vision of human rights as pre-existing moral claims, derived from moral philosophy rather than positive law.[4] In particular, when one encounters attempts to make human rights legitimate and effective at a popular level, the foundations and justifications for human rights obligations may build on religion and inductive appreciations of the importance of human dignity.[5] As Andrea Bianchi suggests, it may be that transnational civil society networks and non-governmental organizations 'create our understanding of human rights' even where this operates 'independently of the existence of binding obligations under international law'.[6]

Such an approach may come close to explaining the normative forces at work in various sectors, but is difficult for international human rights lawyers to embrace fully, as many work from the assumption that human rights norms have some sort of special status which is legitimized through the accepted law-making process of national and international law. In some circumstances, it has even been agreed that human rights laws should have a higher status than other norms and should be given priority over other goals. Many human rights lawyers would be loathe to abandon the special status accorded to human rights as law (traditionally understood) and move to law as a *multiplicity of communicative processes*, or accept

---

[1] G. Teubner, ' "Global Bukowina": Legal Pluralism in the World Society' in G. Teubner (ed) *Global Law Without a State* (Aldershot: Dartmouth, 1997) 3–28, at 5.   [2] Ibid, at 8.
[3] Ibid, at 14.
[4] C. Jones, *Global Justice: Defending Cosmopolitanism* (Oxford: Oxford University Press, 1999). See also A. Brysk, *Human Rights and Private Wrongs: Constructing Global Civil Society* (New York and London: Routledge, 2000).
[5] See A. A. An-Na'im, 'The Synergy and Interdependence of Human Rights, Religion, and Secularism' in J. Runzo, N. M. Martin, and A. Sharma (eds) *Human Rights and Responsibilities* (Oxford: Oneworld Publications, 2003) 27–49.
[6] A. Bianchi, 'Globalization of Human Rights: The Role of Non-state Actors' in G. Teubner (ed) *Global Law Without a State* (Aldershot: Dartmouth, 1997) 179–212, at 201.

arguments about *world law*, *multi-level governance*, or the identification of accountable non-state actors through the use of criteria such as *autonomy* or *representativeness*.[7]

Asserting the importance of non-state actors cannot easily be equated with an assertion that international law must therefore (obviously) impose duties on them. Most international lawyers still adhere to a vision of international law as the product that emerges from an established law-making process, starkly described by Anthony Clark Arend as follows:

> ... states are still the main actors in the international system and the primary creators of international law. Even though nonstate actors exist, and, in some cases, these nonstate actors have entered into international agreements, these actors do not enter the process of creating general international law in an unmediated fashion. In other words, the interactions of nonstate actors with each other and with states do not produce customary international law. Only state interactions can produce custom.[8]

Having presented the traditional understanding of international law formation, Arend goes on to imagine a possible future system, inspired by the medieval international society evoked by Hedley Bull in *The Anarchical Society*. In such a future system, he suggests, the rules for the formation of customary international law would change.

> If, however, the state were to lose its monopoly in a neomedieval system, the most basic general principle about the nature of international law—the notion that *states* create international law through their consent—would now have to be expanded. If this were to be the case, the international law-creating process would be fundamentally changed ... [T]he process of creating customary international law could become much more complex. There could, in fact, be multiple levels of customary international law. At one level, there could be some rules of customary international law that were binding on all types of international actors. In those cases, instead of authoritative state practice alone producing customary legal rules, the mutual interactions of a variety of international actors—states, substate actors, 'peoples,' and international organizations—would constitute general customary international law. If a scholar or other observer wished to determine the existence of a rule of international law of this nature, he or she could not examine merely state practice, but would need to examine the practice of this entire panoply of actors.[9]

This approach suggests a future legal order where the rules for who has the authority to develop the rules have developed to include non-state actors as rule-makers. Arend points to the disintegration of states and the ensuing emergence on the scene of non-state actors such as the Bosnian Serbs, the rise of authorities such as the European Community, organized private violence committed by criminal

[7] For a thought-provoking essay on these possibilities, see C. Harding 'Statist assumptions, normative individualism and new forms of personality: evolving a philosophy of international law for the twenty-first century' 1 *Non-State Actors and International Law* (2001) 107–125, esp. 112, 121.

[8] A. C. Arend, *Legal Rules and International Society* (New York: Oxford University Press, 1999) at 176.   [9] Ibid, at 176–177.

gangs and terrorists, and asks whether the state system will be replaced 'by a fundamentally different paradigm for. international relations'.[10] His prediction is that in a new system: 'General international law will come about through the many interactions of the multiple international actors . . . It does not seem unreasonable to expect the emergence of such a system in the early part of the twenty-first century.'[11]

I should like to suggest a third approach. My approach retains as a starting point the principles and rules of public international law with its origins in the law-making power of the nation-state. But I want to go beyond the traditional, narrow, state-focused approach and argue that some of the obligations found in public international law, and traditionally only applied to states, also apply to non-state actors. I recognize the importance of non-state actors and their influence without suggesting that they have achieved the role of law-maker. We should indeed examine their activity and their interaction with states and others to determine the duties and rights that states have fixed them with. Such an examination elevates them to subjects of interest without any automatic legitimizing effect. Such an examination will reveal the concern of states to address the behaviour of non-state actors that threatens international human rights.

My main argument is that the existing general rules of international human rights law, created and acknowledged by states, now fix on non-state actors so that they may be held accountable for violations of this law. Of course this radical rethink could be dismissed by proponents of the first approach as simply incorrect. But I am going to challenge the assumptions they have built into their approach. This may betray an adherence to a legal method which accepts that values are omnipresent as we seek to determine the applicability of rules. In this sense, I would follow the approach of Rosalyn Higgins when she writes: 'Reference to "the correct legal view" or "rules" can never avoid the element of choice (though it can seek to disguise it), nor can it provide guidance to the preferable decision. In making this choice one must inevitably have consideration for the humanitarian, moral, and social purpose of the law.'[12] I would submit that one can accept that international law is mostly generated by accepted processes between nation states,[13] but still reject the prevalent assumptions that: first, the bearers of international obligations are limited to presumed, so-called, 'subjects' of

---

[10] A. C. Arend, *Legal Rules and International Society* at 179.   [11] Ibid, at 185.

[12] R. Higgins, *Problems and Process: International Law and How We Use It* (Oxford: Clarendon Press, 1994) at 5.

[13] In considering the international legal order, Christian Tomuschat points to the policy school which 'deals with law, but totally refrains from referring to the norms as they appear in "normal" text books'. International Law: Ensuring the Survival of Mankind on the Eve of a New Century: *General Course on Public International Law* 281 RCADI (The Hague: Nijhoff, 2001) at 54. The subsequent construction of a 'contextual norm for the case at hand according to a cannon of preferential criteria unilaterally proposed by the authors' is said to give rise to 'absolute freedom to revise the existing law at any time according to a balancing of the pros and cons that can be identified in a given case, without having to go through the normal processes available for reviewing and reforming deficiencies in the law that have emerged in the course of its application'. Our approach will be to apply law which would be recognizable to the readers of 'normal' textbooks, the values identified to contextualize

international law;[14] and second, that public international law is inoperative outside established enforcement regimes such as international tribunals. I would also argue that public international law can apply in the networks and sectors that focus on duties for non-state actors. And, I would suggest we can construct such a framework without the existing law of state responsibility crumbling and without inappropriately legitimizing the relevant non-state actors.

1.1　THE EXPANDING SCOPE OF INTERNATIONAL LAW

International law has for some time served to tackle individual criminal responsibility for certain acts committed by individuals: slavery, war crimes, genocide, crimes against humanity, disappearances, and torture. International law can attach to certain non-state actors at all times and irrespective of their links to the state. Article I of the Convention on the Prevention and Punishment of the Crime of Genocide confirms that 'genocide, whether committed in time of peace or in time of war, is a crime under international law'. Article IV reminds us that persons committing acts of genocide shall be punished 'whether they are constitutionally responsible rulers, public officials or private individuals'. The key obligations under this treaty have clearly become customary obligations for all states, even regarding crimes committed outside their territory.[15] Furthermore, genocide 'is a crime under international law for which individuals shall be punished'.[16] This means in effect that there are international obligations for every individual. In fact, although at one stage it was said that the broader category of crimes against humanity had to be pursued in furtherance of a *state* policy, this restriction is no longer applied. In the words of the Trial Chamber of the International Criminal Tribunal for the former Yugoslavia 'although a policy must exist to commit these acts, it need not be the policy of a State'.[17] The Chamber relied on the work of the International Law Commission of the United Nations as well as practice from the courts of the United States in reaching this conclusion:

> Importantly, the commentary to the draft articles of the Draft Code [of Crimes Against the Peace and Security of Mankind], prepared by the International Law Commission in

interpretation will be self-consciously chosen but there will be an attempt to derive the legitimacy of such value choices from the reasoning of recognized institutional authorities within the legal order. The legitimacy of the process for the evolution of the legal order may not be recognized by some as part of the 'normal' process for law reform—but our understanding of what is normal in the present context may be changing.

[14] The issue of subjectivity under international law is dealt with in Ch 2.

[15] See the International Court of Justice *Case concerning application of the Convention on the Prevention and Punishment of the Crime of Genocide (Bosnia-Herzegovina v Yugoslavia)* (Preliminary Objections), (1996) ICJ Reports para. 31.

[16] Report of the Secretary-General Pursuant to Paragraph 2 of Security Council Resolution 808 (1993) S/25704, 3 May 1993, para. 45.

[17] *Prosecutor v Tadić* Case IT–94–1–AR72 and Case IT–94–1–T, Judgment of 7 May 1997, para. 655.

1991, which were transmitted to Governments for their comments and observations, acknowledges that non-state actors are also possible perpetrators of crimes against humanity. It states that:

> [i]t is important to point out that the draft article does not confine possible perpetrators of the crimes [crimes against humanity] to public officials or representatives alone... the article does not rule out the possibility that private individuals with de facto power or organized in criminal gangs or groups might also commit the kind of systematic or mass violations of human rights covered by the article; in that case, their acts would come under the draft Code.[18]

Similarly, the United States Court of Appeals for the Second Circuit recently recognized that 'non-state actors' could be liable for committing genocide, the most egregious form of crimes against humanity, as well as war crimes.[19]

In other words, for some behaviour, customary international law has fixed obligations on the individual, even in the absence of a state nexus, and the violation of these international obligations will be punishable at the national and international level.

Does international law confine its reach to states and individuals? No, there are well-known categories of entities besides states and individuals that are capable of bearing rights and obligations under general international law. Inter-governmental organizations such as the United Nations have the requisite international personality to claim rights and fulfil their duties on the international plane.[20] A further category comprises certain parties to internal armed conflicts sometimes described as 'civil wars'.[21] A vexed question is the status of corporations or legal persons in general. We shall discuss this in detail in Chapter 2; for present purposes let us simply refer to the discussions during the Rome Conference for an International Criminal Court. The draft Statute for the International Criminal Court before the delegates at the start of the Rome Conference in 1998 actually included a paragraph in brackets, which ensured the possibility of trying 'legal persons, with the exception of States, when the crimes were committed on behalf of such legal persons or by their agents or representatives'.[22] This paragraph did

---

[18] At this point, footnote 167 in the original reads: '*I.L.C. 1991 Report*, 266.'

[19] At this point, footnote 168 in the original reads: '*Kadic v. Karadžić*, 70 F.3d 232 (2nd Cir. 1995), cert. denied, 64 U.S.L.W. 3832 (18 Jun. 1996).'

[20] We discuss this in further detail in Ch 2, at 2.2. For a general overview see P. Sands and P. Klein, *Bowett's Law of International Institutions* (London: Sweet and Maxwell, 2001) Ch 15, 'Legal Personality'.

[21] We discuss this further in Ch 7. Note the recent elaboration of this issue by the International Law Institute, Resolution adopted 25 August 1999 in Berlin: 'The Application of International Humanitarian Law and Fundamental Human Rights, in Armed Conflicts in which Non-State Entities are Parties.' See also W. Kälin, *Guiding Principles on Internal Displacement: Annotations* (Washington, DC: Studies in Transnational Legal Policy No. 32, American Society of International Law, 2000) at 9. 'Humanitarian law applicable in situations of noninternational armed conflicts (common Article 3 Geneva Conventions and Protocol II) binds not only state actors but all parties to the conflict.'

[22] Art. 23(5), UN Doc. A/CONF.183/2/Add.1, 14 April 1998. The background and fate of this proposal is discussed in Ch 6 and in greater detail in A. Clapham, 'The Question of Jurisdiction Under International Criminal Law Over Legal Persons: Lessons from the Rome Conference on an International Criminal Court' in M. Kamminga and S. Zia-Zarifi (eds) *Liability of Multinational Corporations Under International Law* (The Hague: Kluwer, 2000) 139–195.

not survive, due in part to the fact that, according to the Co-ordinator of the working group on general principles, 'Time was running out'.[23] However, there is no reason to believe that certain international law obligations cannot attach to non-state actors in the form of legal persons. At no point during the drafting of the Rome Statute was it claimed by any delegation that the 'legal persons' referred to in the draft could not demonstrate the requisite legal capacity to be the bearers of international obligations.

The point is that international law is already concerned with the duties of individuals both in their public and private capacities. International law has already extended this concern to inter-governmental organizations, and there is no evidence that the international legal order cannot accommodate duties for other kinds of actor. Although there are only rare instances where a corporation could be the respondent in a dispute before an international tribunal (such as a case before the Seabed Disputes Chamber of the Law of the Sea Tribunal),[24] a non-state actor such as a corporation can still be the bearer of international duties outside the context of international courts and tribunals. Lack of international jurisdiction to try a corporation does not mean that the corporation is under no international legal obligations. Nor does it mean that we are somehow precluded from speaking about corporations breaking international law.

In fact, states can be bound in international law to ensure that the corporations respect duties defined in international treaties. The Bamako Convention on the Ban of the Import into Africa and the Control of Transboundary Wastes within Africa goes further than most treaties and explicitly demands national legislation 'for imposing criminal penalties on all persons who have planned, committed, or assisted in such illegal imports. Such penalties shall be sufficiently high to both punish and deter such conduct'.[25] The Convention defines 'person' as meaning 'any natural or legal person'.

In thinking about the obligations which arise with regard to conduct prohibited under international law, it is crucial to understand that the same act, say an act of genocide, can violate multiple obligations. The single action can constitute a violation of the international obligations of the person committing the act— constituting an international crime under customary international law; and should the person's acts be attributable to a state, then that state may have violated the state's international treaty obligations to other states parties as well as its obligations under customary international law. There may even be additional

---

[23] See P. Saland 'International Criminal Law Principles' in R. Lee (ed) *The International Criminal Court: The Making of the Rome Statute—Issues, Negotiations, Results* (The Hague: Kluwer, 1999) 189–215, at 199.

[24] See Arts 187 and 291(2) of the UN Convention on the Law of the Sea (1982).

[25] Reproduced in 30 *ILM* (1991) 773. See especially Arts 1(16) (definition); 4(1) 'Such import shall be deemed illegal and a criminal act'; and 9(2) (Obligation on States parties to introduce criminal penalties on all persons guilty of illegal imports).

breaches of non-binding guidelines or codes of conduct applicable to a corporate or non-governmental actor.[26]

Apart from multiple violations, there could be multiple fora in which to hold the various actors accountable—the national courts (for criminal and civil liability of the natural and legal persons), an international criminal court (for individual criminal responsibility), and the relevant international human rights treaty monitoring bodies and courts (to hold the state accountable for violations of its treaty obligations). There may even be arrangements made under non-binding schemes for investigations by the designated authority.[27]

There is little controversy over a multiplication of obligations concerning a crime such as genocide. However, a more general extension of human rights obligations towards non-state actors has met with a series of objections. Those who have built up the state-centred approach seem sometimes to suggest that an extension of human rights scrutiny to non-state actors will chip away at the foundations of the human rights monument, thereby accelerating the chances of its eventual disintegration and ruin. But I would suggest that the strength of the human rights system has always been its ability to adapt to new demands and new needs. There are now demands for protection from the effects of big business and non-state actors. The human rights machinery and norms are pliant enough to be reoriented to cope with these new demands. In response to those concerned about the strain such a reorientation would place on the system, we might consider the following passage by Christine Chinkin:

> There is apprehension that to transform the vision of human rights to include acts by private individuals would disturb and undermine the entire edifice of human rights. Women in turn argue that the system has excluded harms most frequently inflicted upon them and that the vision has never held out the same promise of fulfilment of human dignity to them as to men. If human rights law is so fragile that it can not withstand such reconceptualization, then it is barely worth preserving.[28]

But suggesting that we should 'privatize' our thinking about human rights, or that non-state actors and private individuals have duties under human rights law that can be judicially enforced, has been met, not only with apprehension, but also with several argued objections. These can be grouped under five headings.

---

[26] An example of such a non-binding obligation is the OECD Guidelines for Multinational Enterprises discussed in Ch 6 below.

[27] E.g. the OECD procedures for bringing complaints before the National Contact Points (NCPs) have referred to allegations of 'violations' or 'breaches' of the OECD Guidelines; see, e.g. the statement by the UK NCP concerning De Beers (undated 2004); the French NCP was seized by various trade unions with regard to forced labour in Myanmar and the subsequent recommendation suggests practical steps to be taken by the multinationals; see statement of 28 March 2002.

[28] C. Chinkin, 'International law and human rights', in T. Evans (ed) *Human Rights Fifty Years On: A reappraisal* (Manchester: Manchester University Press, 1998) 105–129, at 115.

1.2   THE TRIVIALIZATION ARGUMENT

First, there are those who object that applying human rights obligations to private actors trivializes human rights and ignores their historical pedigree. They argue that the thing that makes human rights important is the fact that they relate only to serious abuses of state power, and this is what distinguishes human rights from ordinary crime or breaches of the law. In response to a ruling of the Constitutional Court of Malta that the prohibition on inhuman and degrading treatment applied, not only to state actors, but also to private actors, a serious letter appeared in the Maltese *Sunday Times*. The letter to the editor complained that this sort of extension of human rights law into the private sphere undermines the human rights project. The author of the letter welcomed the first part of the judgment whereby the Court:

> . . . recognized the *principle* that only the state is actionable for the violation of human rights. Human rights are what the state owes to the individual, and it is only the state that can infringe them. A *private* violation of human rights by a private individual is, on principle, constitutional heresy. It would have been amazing had the Court held otherwise. Our supreme tribunal has finally recognized what for the rest of the world has been elementary doctrine since the beginning of codified human rights.
>
> The Constitutional Court then went on to observe that the makers of Constitutions may, and sometimes do allow some specific exceptions to this principle. Of course, if the Constitution so wills, some specific human rights may be made actionable against individuals. Here too one finds nothing to dispute. What I must respectfully, but very forcefully, disagree with is how the Court is to identify those specific human rights provisions which are actionable not only against the state, but against private individuals as well.
>
> The Constitutional Court seems to have laid down the test that when the wording of the human rights provision is generic, and is not limited to protection against state action, then that particular human right is actionable against private individuals too.
>
> This, I submit, is totally untenable. If the wording of the constitutional provisions does not expressly, or by necessary implication, make individuals actionable, then it is the general rule that must apply, viz, that only the state is actionable for breaches of human rights. Obviously, it is always the exception to the rule that must be specifically spelt out, not the other way around.[29]

We are told there is a 'general rule' that only the state is actionable for breaches of human rights. If we look for evidence of the general rule the results are inconclusive. International human rights are usually traced to the Universal Declaration of Human Rights of 1948. Early drafts mentioned the duties of the individual at the beginning of the Declaration, stating that 'Man is essentially social and has fundamental duties to his fellow men. The rights of each are therefore limited by the rights of others'.[30] The Declaration starts with a recognition of the inherent

[29] Maltese *Sunday Times*, 22 October 1989.
[30] Draft Art. 3 presented by Cassin, as cited by J. Morsink, *The Universal Declaration of Human Rights: Origins, Drafting, and Intent* (Philadelphia: University of Pennsylvania Press, 1999) at 243. For the full drafting history of the duties under the final Declaration see 239–252.

dignity and inalienable rights of everyone. It proclaims rights for everyone and defines them with no reference to the state or any other duty-holder. Everyone has the rights to life, no one shall be held in slavery, no one shall be subjected to torture or to cruel, inhuman, or degrading treatment or punishment, 'no one shall be subjected to arbitrary interference with his privacy, family, home or correspondence, nor to attacks upon his honour and reputation'.[31] Whilst one paragraph mentions the family's entitlement to 'protection from society and the State',[32] there is only one concrete individual entitlement expressed as an entitlement *vis-à-vis* the state (with regard to social security).[33] The last two Articles in the Declaration proclaim that 'Everyone has duties to the community' and that the Declaration does not imply that any 'State, group or person' has a right to engage in activity aimed at the destruction of the rights in the Declaration.[34]

So only some rights are specifically concerned with the relationship between the individual and the state. In general, rights are simply proclaimed as belonging to individuals. Individuals and groups are precluded from relying on their right to infringe or destroy the rights of others. The rule appears to be that most human rights are not defined with regard to a specific duty-holder. If other rights are exclusively applicable only against the state, these should be spelt out expressly.

The author of the letter to the Maltese *Sunday Times* concludes that the Court's generic test invited 'judicial bedlam' (chaos). For him:

> The decision can only bring a regrettable involution of human rights and a trivialization of the formidable concept of protection against abusive state action. The teenager whose love letters are opened by her mother now has an action for human rights redress just like the political dissenter whose correspondence is spied on by the political police. The wife who is beaten up by her husband henceforth has an action for fundamental rights redress on an equal footing with the political detainee who is beaten up by his interrogators! Which with all due respect, pulls inside out the very concept of human rights.[35]

In response, one might argue that to confine examination of human rights violations to violence by the state in this way excludes certain important categories of violence from serious discussion and attention. From this perspective, domestic violence and violence against prisoners both deserve attention and remedies. One

---

[31] See Arts 3, 4, 5, and 12.   [32] See Art. 16(3).

[33] Art. 22 reads: 'Everyone, as a member of society, has the right to social security and is entitled to realization, through national effort and international co-operation and in accordance with the organization and resources of each State, of the economic, social and cultural rights indispensable for his dignity and the free development of his personality.'

[34] See Arts 29 and 30. Art. 29: '1. Everyone has duties to the community in which alone the free and full development of his personality is possible. 2. In the exercise of his rights and freedoms, everyone shall be subject only to such limitations as are determined by law solely for the purpose of securing due recognition and respect for the rights and freedoms of others and of meeting the just requirements of morality, public order and the general welfare in a democratic society. 3. These rights and freedoms may in no case be exercised contrary to the purposes and principles of the United Nations'. Art. 30: 'Nothing in this Declaration may be interpreted as implying for any State, group or person any right to engage in any activity or to perform any act aimed at the destruction of any of the rights and freedoms set forth herein.'   [35] Maltese *Sunday Times*, 22 October 1989.

victim should not be prejudiced by the 'private' nature of the violence. As will be discussed, international law (as a regime that focused on inter-state relations) has inevitably skewed the rules and procedures one way, towards an examination of state action. In addition, the focus has been on prohibitions on states rather than demands for action. As Catherine MacKinnon put it: 'The role of international law has been largely, in Isaiah Berlin's sense, negative. It could be more, but it fosters human rights less through mandating governmental interference than through enforcing governmental abstinence. In other words, if your human rights are going to be violated, pray it is by someone who looks like a government, and that he already acted, and acted wrong.'[36]

At this point one might suggest that, rather than trivializing human rights, it is possible to apply human rights obligations to non-state actors in a way which shifts human rights discourse from the realms of rhetoric and ideology into the sphere of daily reality and social progress. Two counter-arguments present themselves in response to the trivialization argument. First, the trivialization argument is based on an assumption that human rights, as a rule, are only actionable against the state, and that exceptions to this rule have been explicitly spelt out. In fact, a case can be made that, as a rule, human rights are to be respected by all persons, groups, and states, and that exceptional additional duties for the state have been explicitly articulated. The second counter-argument tackles the very premise of trivialization, i.e. that political prisoners are a legitimate subject of concern and violence against women in the home is not. What can be considered trivial depends on who you are and what are your interests.

1.3   THE LEGAL IMPOSSIBILITY ARGUMENT

A second line of resistance is presented as a legal argument that private non-state actors simply cannot incur responsibilities under international law. Partisans of this thesis point to a lack of evidence that international law accepts such a general development. They argue that treaties are negotiated and entered into by states and that these treaties cannot bind those who are not a party to them. In addition, other forms of international law, such as customary international law, result from the behaviour of states and their willingness to accept new rules as binding on them. These rules should be seen as binding only those explicitly addressed by states. Adherents to the legal impossibility argument would admit that some non-state entities, such as inter-governmental organizations, can incur duties under international law through entering into treaties or through the application of customary international law. So, for example, the United Nations and the European Community can violate international law binding on them. The fact

---

[36] C. MacKinnon, 'Crimes of War Crimes of Peace' in S. Shute and S. Hurley (eds) *On Human Rights: the Amnesty Lectures* (New York: Basic Books, 1993) 83–110, at 92.

that they cannot be parties to a case before the International Court of Justice does not mean that they do not have rights and obligations under international law; disputes have to be settled in a different forum.[37] Even where an international regime allows for individual complaints against the state, one should not assume that these procedural possibilities (rights) determine the reach of the substantive rights under the treaty.[38]

Those who insist on an approach based on the traditional scope of international law would also admit that international law creates international crimes for individuals in fields such as piracy, genocide, crimes against humanity, and war crimes. But these are explained away as explicit exceptions for individuals. For some lawyers, such as Liesbeth Zegveld, the answer lies in the assertion that 'human rights law purports to govern the relations between the government representing the state and the governed', so that any suggested extension to armed opposition groups would be unintended and inadequate.[39] Furthermore, Zegveld suggests that, with regard to international criminal law, criminal responsibility for the group would be unnecessary due to the existence of both civil responsibility for the group and criminal responsibility for the individual members.[40] Room is left for 'application of human rights law to armed opposition groups that act as de facto governments or groups with a stable presence in part of the state territory. In those cases, the basic features of human rights law, namely the relationship between government and governed, is present'.[41] However, this concession should be of limited impact as, according to Zegveld: 'Armed opposition groups rarely function as de facto governments.'[42]

In response, it is possible to point to situations where armed groups that cannot be compared to governments, such as the rebel groups in Sierra Leone, have been

---

[37] E.g. the treaty obligations of the European Community under the UN Convention on the Law of the Sea (1982) can be litigated before the Law of the Sea Tribunal or under some appropriate arbitration arrangement.

[38] See R. Higgins, 'Conceptual thinking about the individual in international law' 4 *BJIS* (1978) 1–19, esp. at 4; and *Problems and Process: International Law and How We Use It* (Oxford: Clarendon Press, 1994) at 48–55. Note also the suggestion by Martin Scheinin that, with regard to a new World Human Rights Court, non-state actors such as international organizations and corporations could make unilateral declarations accepting the jurisdiction of a new court. M. Scheinin 'Towards a World Human Rights Court?' Conference at the Graduate Institute of International Studies, Geneva, 18 December 2002 (unpublished mimeograph on file with the author).

[39] L. Zegveld, *Accountability of Armed Opposition Groups in International Law* (Cambridge: Cambridge University Press, 2002) at 54–55.   [40] Ibid, at 58.

[41] Ibid, at 54. Note also the approach adopted by the Truth Commission in El Salvador: 'It is true that, in theory, international human rights law is applicable only to Governments, while in some armed conflicts international humanitarian law is binding on both sides: in other words, binding on both insurgents and Government forces. However, it must be recognized that when insurgents assume government powers in territories under their control, they too can be required to observe certain human rights obligations that are binding on the State under international law. This would make them responsible for breaches of those obligations.' 'From Madness to Hope: the 12-year war in El Salvador: Report of the Commission on the Truth for El Salvador', UN Doc. S/25500, 1 April 1993, at 20.   [42] Ibid, at 152.

investigated for committing human rights abuses. The Truth and Reconciliation Commission of Sierra Leone had a mandate which read as follows:

> 6. (1)   The object for which the Commission is established is to create an impartial historical record of violations and abuses of human rights and international humanitarian law related to the armed conflict in Sierra Leone, from the beginning of the Conflict in 1991 to the signing of the Lomé Peace Agreement; to address impunity, to respond to the needs of the victims, to promote healing and reconciliation and to prevent a repetition of the violations and abuses suffered.[43]

The Commission's Report contains detailed examinations of activity by multiple actors, including not only the insurgents, rebels, and international peace-keepers, but also the private security firm, Executive Outcomes. It 'found the RUF [Revolutionary United Front] to have been responsible for the largest number of human rights violations in the conflict'[44] and uses the expression 'human rights violations' with regard to all actors.

The earlier report of the Guatemalan Historical Clarification Commission similarly referred to human rights violations by the insurgents. The legal analysis is perhaps more developed as it refers to 'general principles common to international human rights law', thus suggesting that the insurgents could not be burdened with all the human rights obligations of the state:

> 127.   The armed insurgent groups that participated in the internal armed confrontation had an obligation to respect the minimum standards of international humanitarian law that apply to armed conflicts, as well as the general principles common to international human rights law. Their high command had the obligation to instruct subordinates to respect these norms and principles.
>
> 128.   Acts of violence attributable to the guerrillas represent 3% of the violations registered by the CEH. This contrasts with 93% committed by agents of the State, especially the Army. This quantitative difference provides new evidence of the magnitude of the State's repressive response. However, in the opinion of the CEH, this disparity does not lessen the gravity of the unjustifiable offences committed by the guerrillas against human rights.[45]

---

[43] Supplement to the Sierra Leone Gazette, vol. CXXXI, No. 9, dated 10 February 2000.

[44] Para 15 of the 'Overview' accessible at http://www.nuigalway.ie/human_rights/publications. html. See also vol. Two, Ch Two, paras 106 and 107, where the Commission found that the RUF was 'the primary violator of human rights in the conflict' and responsible for 60.5% of the violations (24,353 out of 40,242 violations). See further paras 115–172. The RUF were not the only non-state actor dealt with in the report. ECOMOG (the Ecowas Cease-Fire Monitoring Group and Executive Outcomes (the Military Security Company) are both considered. With regards to ECOMOG, the Report points (at para. 396) to 'human rights violations' including summary executions of civilians. With regard to Executive Outcomes, the Report states (at para. 402) that the Commission recorded no 'allegation of any human rights violation against the mercenaries'.

[45] *Guatemala Memory of Silence*, Executive Summary Conclusions and Recommendations, UN Doc. A/53/928 Annex, 27 April 1999. For the relevant part of the full Spanish report see paras 1699–1700 in vol. II at pp 312–313. Christian Tomuschat, Chair of the Commission and has highlighted the way in which the Commission determined that outside times of armed conflict the insurgents were bound by these common principles. See C. Tomuschat, *Human Rights: Between Idealism and Realism* (Oxford: Oxford University Press, 2003) at 261 and cited in Ch 7 below.

Today one can point to the international preoccupation with terrorism and suggest that it has opened the door even further to an approach which simply admits that insurgents, guerrillas, or terrorists do indeed violate human rights in the course of some of their attacks. A background paper for an expert meeting on 'Human Rights, the United Nations and the Struggle Against Terrorism' explained the issue in the following way:

> The proposition that terrorism violates human rights should not be controversial. Yet classical interpretations of human rights hold that only states can violate human rights. Only states are bound by human rights treaties, not individuals, non-state actors or others. Fortunately, human rights thinking and even jurisprudence has evolved and now certain non-state actors like rebel groups and multi-national corporations can be held responsible for rights violations. Certainly organizations like al Qaeda would fall into this category…[46]

The point here is that preoccupations with terrorism have led to a number of assertions, not only by commentators and non-governmental organizations but also by key UN organs, that terrorists violate human rights. Already in 1994, the UN General Assembly's Declaration on Measures to Eliminate Terrorism contains a preambular paragraph which expresses concern that terrorists resort to violence 'violating basic human rights'.[47] Two years later in 1996, following the hostage-taking at the Japanese Embassy in Peru, the President of the Security Council responded with the following statement: 'The Security Council has always firmly condemned terrorist acts, whatever the circumstances, in the most unequivocal terms. Such acts constitute a violation of the basic principles of international law and of human rights.'[48] More recently the UN Secretary-General transmitted a report to the General Assembly and Security Council which simply asserted: 'it must be understood clearly that terrorism itself is a violation of human rights. Terrorist acts that take life violate the right to life set forth in article 6 of the International Covenant on Civil and Political Rights'.[49] We might mention the voted 2003 Resolution of the UN Commission of Human Rights which expressed the Commission's concern at 'the gross violations of human rights perpetrated by terrorist groups' and condemned terrorist acts and 'the violations of the right to life, liberty and security'.[50] Lastly, we can note that the United Nations may condemn terrorist attacks as attacks on rights such as the right to life.[51]

[46] William O'Neill, unpublished paper on file with the author.
[47] Annexed to Res. 49/60 of 9 December 1994, the full paragraph reads: 'Concerned at the growing and dangerous links between terrorist groups and drug traffickers and their paramilitary gangs, which have resorted to all types of violence, thus endangering the constitutional order of States and violating basic human rights.'
[48] Statement at press conference by Ambassador Fulci, 19 December 1996.
[49] Report of the Policy Working Group on the United Nations and Terrorism established by the Secretary-General UN Doc. A/57/273–S/2002/875, 6 August 2002, at para. 26.
[50] Human rights and terrorism, Res. 2003/37, adopted by a recorded vote of 30 votes to 12, with 11 abstentions.
[51] See, e.g. 'The acting High Commissioner condemns this attack on the right to life in the strongest possible terms.' *Acting Rights Chief Condemns Kandahar Bombings*, UN Press Release, 7 January 2004.

The explicit focus by the UN Human Rights Commission on violations of human rights by terrorist groups has met with opposition from some governments that fear such a focus could distract from the Commission's task of holding governments accountable. Whether or not this is a reasonable policy to adopt with regard to the work of the Commission, it does not really determine whether non-state actors have human rights obligations.

The UK Foreign and Commonwealth Office's 2004 position with regard to the obligations of non-state actors focused on the direct obligations of states as parties to international instruments to protect and promote human rights for all individuals within its jurisdiction. But the position also reiterated the state's duty to protect people from non-state actors that threaten human rights, and recognized the possibility of human rights obligations applying to non-state actors:

> States must not themselves violate those rights or, through inaction or negligence, allow non-state actors to prevent people from enjoying those rights. Non-state actors are not parties to international human rights instruments and not bound directly by them. However, whether and how to make human rights obligations binding on e.g. insurgent groups, multinational corporations is likely to be one of the main debates in the human rights field in the years to come.[52]

The position of various other governments can be gleaned from statements submitted to the UN Special Rapporteur on terrorism and human rights which, on the whole, avoid the theoretical issue.[53] We might simply extract here a few submissions. The Argentinian Government stated:

> The Government noted that it does not accept the argument that the acts of international terrorism constitute a human rights violation, since, by definition, only States are capable of violating human rights. To consider acts of terrorism as violating human rights often conceals the intention to justify the use of anti-terrorist methods and practices by States agencies which themselves ignore human rights standards.[54]

This approach defines non-state actors as outside the category of duty-holders under the international law framework without further explanation. Some may say it is *obvious* that human rights are defined as rights exclusively applicable against the state, but no international definition states this in these terms. In fact, as we saw above, the Universal Declaration was carefully drafted to avoid suggesting that the

---

[52] *Human Rights Guidelines*, Human Rights Policy Department (Foreign and Commonwealth Office), June 2004, at 8. The UK has also suggested that: 'Any ongoing process should not seek to place companies in the same position as States with regard to obligations in international human rights law. To avoid confusion of their legal status, texts relating to the responsibilities of business with regard to human rights should not use legally-binding treaty language.' Reply to the request by the Office of the High Commissioner for Human Rights (OHCHR) for input from states regarding the report concerning 'Responsibilities of transnational corporations and related business enterprises with regard to human rights', at para. 3; see Decision of the Commission 2004/116. See also http://www.ohchr.org/english/issues/globalization/business/contribution.htm.

[53] UN Doc. E/CN.4/Sub.2/2003/WP.1/Add.2, 8 August 2003, Sub-Commission on the Promotion and Protection of Human Rights, Additional progress report prepared by Ms Kalliopi K. Koufa, Addendum, Summary of comments received.　　　　　　[54] Ibid, para. 2.

state has specific duties, the rights are written in the form 'everyone has the right to . . .'. The focus is on the inherent possession of the right, and references to duties can be found to society, the state, groups, and individuals.

Moreover the Argentine position is bolstered, not by reference to legal arguments but rather by invoking a policy argument suggesting that pointing to human rights obligations for terrorists allows states to use the fight against terrorism as an excuse to violate human rights themselves. This policy argument is further examined in the next section. Nevertheless, the position of the Argentinian Government is ambivalent. The submission later concludes:

> The Government noted that it espouses the concept that human rights violations can only be committed by the State or State agents, which was at the heart of the international codification of human rights. In recent years, however, the theoretical basis of this concept has been reappraised so as to extend it to non-State actors, in much the same way as humanitarian law was extended to non-governmental armed groups.[55]

The submission seems ambivalent; on the one hand it is said that human rights violations can only be committed by the state, on the other hand the theoretical basis of this notion has been *reappraised* so that human rights violations can be committed by non-state actors. The submission of Cuba is much less ambiguous:

> In its view, terrorism is an unacceptable practice and a violation of the most basic human rights, whoever the victims or the terrorists might be. The Government did not share the view that only States are capable of committing human rights violations. Individuals and groups of individuals have not only rights but also duties and human responsibilities.[56]

The Indian Government put the issue as follows:

> The Government also noted that it is inevitable that in tackling terrorism, some of the measures may impact on the unfettered exercise of human rights. The challenge is to get the necessary balance between the imperative of dealing with terrorism and safeguarding human rights. It has to be recognized that [the] terrorist is a violator of human rights. In finding the requisite balance, States are currently engaged in adopting new measures with built in safeguards to ensure that they are not abused or misused.[57]

Kuwait noted that it 'participates in all international efforts to combat international terrorism and affirmed that terrorism, at whatever form or manifestation and by whomever committed, is a grave crime against humanity and a violation of human rights'.[58] Turkey stated that it held 'the firm belief that the terrorists violate the most sacred human right, the right to life'.[59]

Some lawyers might still argue that such official statements by governments are not enough to create international human rights obligations for terrorists; but taken together, the statements suggest that in various contexts some governments already consider that at least one type of non-state actor—terrorists—has international

---

[55] See n 53 above, para. 4.　　　[56] Ibid, para. 10.　　　[57] Ibid, para. 19.
[58] Ibid, para. 22　　　[59] Ibid, para. 28.

human rights obligations.[60] Just as the Second World War ushered in a shift in legal thinking, so that it was thereafter assumed that individuals could commit international war crimes and crimes against humanity, so the terrorist attacks at the beginning of the twenty-first century are ushering in an era when states acting in the United Nations are willing to attach human rights obligations to non-state actors in general and to terrorists in particular.

Whatever semantic or definitional position governments may take, there are numerous examples in everyday media reports of armed groups being described as abusers of human rights. For example, on the eve of the release of the International Monitoring Commission report in 2004, an Irish newspaper reported that the document 'examines continuing human rights abuses by both loyalist and republican paramilitaries'.[61] There are many other examples of injustices of all sorts being characterized as human rights abuses. Of course, *claiming* a human rights abuse does not generate a human rights duty in law; but the term 'human rights' has generated meanings and significance beyond the realm of international legal obligations owed by states. It is commonplace that government ministers from all over the world refer to rights carrying with them corresponding responsibilities.[62] Some governments may wish to restrict the meaning or understanding of the term 'human rights', but excluding any obligations for non-state actors through appeals to the 'definition', 'essence', or 'original sense' of the term 'human rights' are unconvincing.

1.4   THE POLICY TACTICAL ARGUMENT

A third set of objections emerges from what could be called 'tactical' considerations. These objections centre on the fact that some governments may choose to

---

[60] Although Zegveld (2002: 45) considers that references to human rights violations by armed groups in the context of the UN Human Rights Commission and peace agreements such as the San José agreement in San Salvador are of little evidentiary weight in determining the extension of human rights obligations to armed opposition groups; she also rejects the argument 'that the characterization of acts committed by armed opposition groups as human rights violations might legitimize human rights violations by the state', citing the rules which ban reprisals in armed conflict.

[61] Alan Murray, 'Report on NI paramilitaries "won't miss" ' *Sunday Independent*, 11 April 2004, at 4. The Irish Independent Monitoring Commission Act 2003 states in Art. 4: 'In relation to the remaining threat from paramilitary groups, the Commission shall: (a) monitor any continuing activity by paramilitary groups including: i. attacks on the security forces, murders, sectarian attacks, involvement in riots, and other criminal offences; ii. training, targeting, intelligence gathering, acquisition or development of arms or weapons and other preparations for terrorist campaigns; iii. punishment beatings and attacks and exiling; (b) assess: i. whether the leaderships of such organisations are directing such incidents or seeking to prevent them; and ii. trends in security incidents.'

[62] See, e.g. letter from Keith Vaz MP, Minister for Europe, with regard to the EU Charter of Fundamental Rights stating that the Charter might 'Underline the fact that all rights carry with them a matching responsibility, on individuals as well as governments, to respect the rights of others'. Letter to Lord Tordoff, Chairman of the European Communities Committee, House of Lords, 8 December 1999 (on file with the author).

concentrate on individual duties in order to highlight the actions of rebels, or what they may prefer to label as 'terrorists'. This shift in focus then opens the way for the implicit, or even explicit, suggestion that governmental measures that respond to these actions are actually designed to protect human rights. In this way, human rights law may be cynically captured and abused to justify further oppression. The fear is that, by allowing the language of human rights to be applied to the actions of insurgents, we are seduced away from the international responsibility of governments to secure human rights for everyone within their jurisdiction. Absolute distrust of governments is difficult to maintain in a climate where there is a genuine fear of terrorism and terrorist networks. Some of the security measures being taken in the name of the 'war on terrorism' may be disproportionate and unnecessary; but others are indeed appropriate in order to protect the human rights of others.

There is a longstanding concern that an extension of human rights into the realm of duties for non-state actors would allow governments to deflect criticism by pointing to violations committed by armed opposition groups. In an influential article, Nigel Rodley outlined a legal framework which would exclude applying the term human rights violations to anybody except states, death squads acting in collusion with the government, and armed opposition groups exercising effective power over a significant segment of the population and conducting sustained, organized armed hostilities.[63] His main argument was as follows: 'A government, particularly one facing activities of an armed opposition group that commits acts which, if committed by a government, would be called human rights violations, will wish to discredit that group and call its activities human rights violations.'[64] According to Rodley, it will be especially inclined to do this if its own agents are committing violations 'with the aim of dissipating the discredit'.[65] In turn, the government may discredit those non-governmental organizations (NGOs) that bring attention to the government's violations and identify those involved in reporting human rights violations as collaborators with the opposition, or as terrorists themselves. For Rodley, to use the language of human rights violations is not only wrong legally speaking, but amounts to taking a policy approach he suggests it is not even in the interests of governments and NGOs. It is not in the interests of governments as they may in fact 'dignify' the armed opposition 'as having government-like attributes'.[66] And he states that, in any event, such use of the language of human rights to denounce the violence of such groups may simply encourage governmental counter-insurgency policies which are not in the long-term

---

[63] 'Can Armed Opposition Groups Violate Human Rights' in K. E. Mahoney and P. Mahoney (eds) *Human Rights in the Twenty-first Century* (Dordrecht: Martinus Nijhoff, 1993) 297–318. The reference to 'effective power' is taken from the Resolution by which the General Assembly adopted the Declaration on the Protection of All Persons from Being Subjected to Torture and Other Cruel, Inhuman and Degrading Treatment, UN GA Res. 3452(XXX), 9 December 1975.
[64] Ibid, at 314.   [65] Ibid, at 315.   [66] Ibid, at 315.

interests of the state. Turning to look at the issue from an NGO perspective, Rodley's policy arguments are more radical:

> The 170-odd governments of the world owe their positions to various factors, ranging from popular legitimation by pluralist, constitutional institutions to the threat or use of naked terror. Adherents of all the political doctrines, except perhaps absolute pacifism, would encompass the legitimacy of internal resort to armed force to displace governments at the latter end of the range. Yet they would not agree on which those governments are, nor could they do so without abandoning the principle of impartiality towards all governments. So a politically viable conception of human rights must avoid ruling out resort to armed opposition. And, until an armed opposition group has succeeded in becoming an entity exercising effective power as defined in the previous section, there are few traditional manifestations of armed resistance that could not also be described as human rights violations, were they to be undertaken by governments.[67]

This politico-tactical objection is echoed by others looking at the issue in terms of NGO reporting.[68]

In response, however, I suggest that by blinkering our outlook so as to focus on governments and exclude armed opposition groups, we also blind ourselves to the opportunities presented by including corporations, mercenaries, international organizations, criminal organizations, and terrorists within the category of those capable of committing human rights violations. The policy argument deserves a policy-orientated response. It is necessary to weigh up the risks of further governmental violations due to the governments succeeding in 'dissipating the discredit', as against a human rights strategy that would encompass a much broader range of actors, including not only terrorists but also other powerful non-state entities.

Terrorist attacks may violate international law when they amount to war crimes, genocide, crimes against humanity, or the international crime of terrorism.[69] Where such acts deny people their human rights, it seems doctrinaire to insist that terrorists cannot violate human rights. To avoid the conclusion that terrorists can be said to violate human rights is to risk being seen to apologize for terrorist violence in violation of international law. On balance, the risk to the human rights movement of losing the backing of those that support armed struggle no longer seems as pressing as it once perhaps seemed. Moreover, the inevitability of taking

---

[67] Ibid, at 317.
[68] E.g. Ravi Nair warns against 'taking an overall moral position on violence and getting confined within the liberal framework of the State, which suggests that the State has the sole and legitimate right to recourse to force. It is often argued that the increased recourse to violence by political opposition groups is a reflection of the generalized closure of legitimate, democratic space for dissent, that it is State terrorism and lawlessness that begets political terrorism and violence'. 'Confronting the Violence Committed by Armed Opposition Groups' 1 *Yale HRDLJ* (1998) 1–15, at 13. Nair agues for a cautious approach and (at 14) urges NGOs 'to be careful that their critique of abuses perpetrated by *certain* armed opposition groups not be taken to mean a condemnation of *all* such violence'.
[69] For the argument that terrorism is already a crime under international law, see A. Cassese 'Terrorism as an International Crime' in A. Bianchi (ed) *Enforcing International Norms against Terrorism* (Oxford: Hart Publishing, 2004) 213–235; and see further Ch 3, at 3.4 below.

civilian casualties no longer seems central or even acceptable to many of those who might support armed opposition today.

A further corollary and striking dimension to the exclusion of non-state actors from human rights obligations is the fact that, by allowing private violence to be relegated to a blindspot, the human rights movement would be unable to accommodate the main concerns of those fighting to protect women's rights in the context of violence against women. If the concern is consistency and maintaining a broad support base, then the political arguments favour a wider, rather than a narrower, definition of those who can be accused of human rights violations. Once one accepts that governments are not the sole centres of power capable of violating human rights, it may indeed be logical that the pressure will inevitably be partly eased on governments as we come to cover the full range of threats to the enjoyment of human rights. But in fact, it is perhaps more likely that governments will come under new pressures to introduce human rights protection in spheres which had not previously been given such attention.

A second tactical issue relates to the extension of human rights norms to cover the activity of corporations. From one perspective it is self-evident that the power and influence of some corporations rival those of some governments; moreover, the corporate responsibility movement has extended corporations' 'horizon of interest beyond the traditional areas of markets and the workplace, to include the community (both proximate and distant) and the natural environment'.[70] Does this mean that governments should encourage a normative extension—or should we consider such activity as voluntary initiatives based on enlightened self-interest and as outside the scope of human rights law?

As with the extension of human rights scrutiny to terrorists, diplomats at the UN Human Rights Commission fear that a focus on corporations will allow some governments to shift attention from their own behaviour.[71] The United States' position has been articulated as follows: 'attempts to craft norms of this nature dangerously shift the focus of accountability for human rights violations away from States and toward private actors, thus creating the perception that States have less of a responsibility to end human rights abuses for which they are responsible'.[72]

---

[70] M. McIntosh, M. R. Thomas, D. Leipziger and G. Coleman, *Living Corporate Citizenship: Strategic routes to socially responsible business* (London: Prentice Hall, 2003) at 47.

[71] In the words of one observer, Koen De Feyter, there is a 'perception that the raising of the responsibility of transnational corporations at human rights fora is a ploy by developing countries to escape monitoring of their domestic human rights record'. K. De Feyter, 'Corporate Governance and Human Rights', Institut international des droits de l'homme, *Commerce mondial et protection des droits de l'homme: les droits de l'homme à l'épreuve de la globalisation des échanges economiques* (Brussels: Bruylant, 2001) 71–110, at 106.

[72] Response from the US Government to the request by OHCHR for input from states regarding the report concerning 'Responsibilities of transnational corporation and related business enterprises with regard to human rights', Decision of the Commission 2004/116, at p 3, see: http://www.ohchr.org/english/issues/globalization/business/contributions.htm.

The detailed foreign policy arguments are sometimes surprising and contradictory. On the one hand, governments have been prepared to participate in the elaboration of international texts that direct corporations to respect human rights and labour standards. On the other hand, governments, such as the US Administration, have been at pains to prevent any legal accountability for human rights violations where this involves companies acting abroad. In one well-known case, the Department of State suggested that, should the US Court allow a case regarding human rights abuses allegedly committed in Indonesia by the US corporation EXXON to proceed, this would undermine the 'war on terrorism', as the Indonesian Government might thereafter be disinclined to cooperate with the United States.[73] The US Justice Department filed an *amicus curiae* brief in a similar case before the US federal courts concerning the oil company Unocal, relating to human rights abuses in Myanmar; arguing in similar terms that such extraterritorial suits could undermine the Government's 'war on terrorism' as officials from allied governments in that fight could find themselves subjected to claims in the US courts.[74]

In response, one is struck by the fact that such consequentialist reasoning sits uneasily with policies dedicated to spreading respect for human rights, the rule of law and transparency. The US courts have not yet addressed such foreign policy arguments based on the need to ensure cooperation in the 'war on terrorism'. US courts have, however, reasserted that corporations do have obligations under international human rights law. In the preliminary stages of a case against Talisman Energy Inc, concerning abuses in Sudan, expert briefs were produced by the oil company which argued that international law had no regime under which to hold companies liable. In response, Judge Schwartz concluded: 'substantial international and United States precedent indicates that corporations may also be held liable under international law, at least for gross human rights violations. Extensive Second Circuit precedent further indicates that actions under the ATCA [Alien Tort Claims Act] against corporate defendants for such substantial violations of international law, including *jus cogens* violations, are the norm rather than the exception'.[75]

Two years later, the company again sought dismissal of the case, this time on the grounds that new case-law cast doubt on the existence of corporate aider and

---

[73] The State Department argued that the case should not proceed as anti-terrorist efforts in Indonesia might be 'imperiled in numerous ways if Indonesia and its officials curtailed cooperation in response to perceived disrespect for its sovereign interests'. 'State Dept. opposes suit against Exxon over Indonesian venture' *International Herald Tribune*, 8 August 2002, at 4. See also 'Human rights and terror' *International Herald Tribune*, 14 August 2002, at 4, and K. Roth 'U.S. hypocrisy in Indonesia', ibid.

[74] United States Court of Appeals for The Ninth Circuit, *John Doe I, et al v Unocal Corp, et al.* Brief for the United States of America, as *amicus curiae*, 8 May 2003, esp. at 3.

[75] *The Presbyterian Church of Sudan et al v Talisman Energy Inc, Republic of the Sudan* Civil Action 01 CV 9882 (AGS), US District Court for the Southern District of New York, Order of 19 March 2003, at p 47.

abettor liability in international law.[76] District Court Judge Cote was careful to canvass the ways in which customary international law is formed and concluded that international law did indeed bind corporations. Judge Cote paid particular attention to the fact that no state had ever objected to US courts exercising jurisdiction over corporations on the grounds that these corporations have been accused of having violated international law:

> . . . in this action, the Government of Canada ('Canada') has transmitted a letter via the U.S. Department of State to this Court expressing political concerns about the foreign policy implications of exerting extraterritorial jurisdiction over a Canadian corporation based on events occurring in Sudan. Pointedly, Canada has not objected to the notion that customary international law provides for corporate liability for violations of jus cogens norms. Indeed, Talisman has not cited a single case where any government objected to the exercise of jurisdiction over one of its national corporations based on the principle that it is not a violation of international law for corporations to commit or aid in the commission of genocide or other similar atrocities. If this issue was a genuine source of disagreement in the international community, it would be expected that the assertion of such a rule as customary would provoke objections from States whose interests were implicated by the assertion of the rule in those cases against their nationals.[77]

1.5   THE LEGITIMIZATION OF VIOLENCE ARGUMENT

A fourth objection has arisen out of the debate as to whether non-governmental organizations (NGOs) should condemn armed groups for violent acts. Let us first consider the application of humanitarian law, as this is seen as the 'obvious' starting point for a situation involving serious armed violence. Some activists (especially those that promote non-violence) have argued that when NGOs address armed opposition groups as entities with obligations under international law, this may seem to legitimize the use of violence by both sides.

Rachel Brett explains the reticence of human rights groups to adopt or adapt a humanitarian law framework to report on incidents in internal armed conflict:

> In Northern Ireland, for example, to oppose the killing of 'civilians' (those not taking active part in the conflict) by the IRA on the basis of common Article 3 could be seen as legitimizing IRA killings of members of the British armed forces. Moreover, if application of Article 3 implies that this is an armed conflict, could it not also legitimize the alleged 'shoot to kill' policy of the government, since international humanitarian law permits members of the armed forces to kill members of the opposing armed forces? For human rights NGOs, the possibility of legitimizing killings is an issue even though there

---

[76] *The Presbyterian Church of Sudan et al v Talisman Energy Inc* [2005] WL 1385326 (SDNY) Opinion and Order of 13 June 2005.
[77] Ibid, at para. 4.

is definitely an armed conflict. But the question becomes thornier if, as in the example of Northern Ireland, there is not in fact an armed conflict, or where the situation is in doubt. In such circumstances, human rights NGOs are invoking the *principles* of common Article 3 in their dealings with the non-State entities involved in the situation, rather than the provision itself. This avoids the problem of having to hold the government to this same standard and it ensures that certain conduct, such as deliberately killing innocent bystanders, is condemned.[78]

A strict application of humanitarian law generates dilemmas for such organizations. Part of the problem is that the thresholds for the application of the law of internal armed conflict can be quite high, and there are situations where armed non-state actors are involved in violent incidents even where that threshold has not been reached, thus reliance on international humanitarian law leaves one unable to comment in obviously violent situations. Decisions concerning condemnation could become exercises in determining whether the conflict had reached the intensity necessary to trigger the application of international humanitarian law. If one relies on international humanitarian law to guide one in this field then certain sporadic violent acts would have to go uncondemned as they would fall outside the humanitarian law framework. The accountability exercise would get caught in subjective argumentation about whether the threshold has been reached.[79] In addition, it is well known that governments actually involved in an internal armed conflict situation often deny the applicability of humanitarian law, and although UN bodies may from time to time make a determination, this is done in a selective and tardy way; a fundamental problem remains the denial of the applicability of humanitarian law by the states concerned.[80]

Turning to international human rights law, even when the threshold for an armed conflict is reached, human rights law continues to apply to governments. NGOs taking a traditional legal approach to such situations, whereby human rights law only applies to states, thus risk creating an imbalance. In this way Brett argues:

> Human rights NGOs could, therefore, find themselves invoking both human rights law and international humanitarian law vis-à-vis the government while referring only to international humanitarian law vis-à-vis [the] armed opposition group. Does it matter whether the government is held to higher or different standards than the opposition? Furthermore, Protocol II only applies if the State concerned is a party to it. Should the non-adherence of a government prevent human rights NGOs from insisting that its provisions be complied with by non-State-entities to whom those provisions would otherwise apply?[81]

---

[78] R. Brett, 'Non-governmental human rights organizations and international humanitarian law' 324 *IRRC* (1998) 531–536, at 535.

[79] For an example of a report condemning non-state violence outside the context of an armed conflict, see Human Rights Watch, *No Exit: Human Rights Abuses Inside the MKO Camps* (May 2005).

[80] See Zegveld (2002: 12–13) for further discussion.   [81] Brett (1998: 534).

In response, one might suggest that the problems stem not from the application of the international humanitarian law framework, but rather, from the selective application of human rights law. Looked at another way, the problems outlined by Brett can be easily dispatched. It is not that international humanitarian law really permits or 'legitimizes' lethal force against hostile forces engaged in attacks in an *internal* armed conflict? International humanitarian law simply does not prohibit this. In an internal armed conflict, international humanitarian law does not grant any sort of immunity to anyone using lethal force against the enemy—it simply fails to outlaw it.[82] Lethal force in such a situation falls to be governed by human rights law, national law, and the international standards on the use of force and firearms. In the context of the internal armed conflict in Chechnya, the UN Human Rights Committee recently stated that the Committee acknowledges:

> ...that abuse of and violations against civilians also involve non-State actors, but reiterates that this does not relieve the State party of its obligations under the Covenant. In this regard, the Committee is concerned about the provision in the Federal Law 'On Combating Terrorism' which exempts law enforcement and military personnel from liability for harm caused during counter-terrorist operations.[83]

Looking at the other side, killings of members of the armed forces and civilians by the rebel fighters will remain individual crimes under national law and no combatant immunity will apply.[84] And where these acts involve intentionally targeting civilians such acts could be international crimes where the fighting develops into the sort of armed conflict covered by international humanitarian law.[85] In situations of armed conflict, the deliberate killing of civilians will remain a crime and will be contrary to the principles of humanitarian law and represent international war crimes where the civilians are targeted as such. Holding rebel forces to these norms of behaviour, to the rules of armed conflict, need not imply that they have the right to kill the government's armed forces—nor does it permit the claim that the government has the right to shoot to kill in counter-insurgency or counter-terrorism operations.

---

[82] On the other hand, in a conventional international armed conflict, one cannot ordinarily try lawful combatants from one state for simply engaging in combat with combatants from armed forces of the other state.

[83] Concluding Observations of the Human Rights Committee, Russian Federation, 6 November 2003, CCPR/CO/79/RUS, at para. 13.

[84] Unless the relevant government recognizes the insurgents as belligerents, see A. Cassese, *International Law* (Oxford: Oxford University Press, 2nd edn, 2005) at 126, or unless Protocol I Additional to the Geneva Conventions of 1949 applies and the people are fighting in the exercise of their right to self-determination as defined in Art. 1(4) and are represented by an authority which has taken the requisite steps under Art. 96(3).

[85] See the Rome Statute for the International Criminal Court, Art. 8(2)(e)(i). For the threshold for armed conflict see Common Art. 3 to the Geneva Conventions 1949 and Protocol II Additional to those Conventions. The test in customary international law can be found in the *Tadić* appeal judgment of the ICTY, Case IT–94–1, AR72, Judgment of 2 October 1995, para. 70: 'an armed conflict exists whenever there is a resort to armed force between States or protracted armed violence between governmental authorities and organized armed groups or between such groups within a State'.

Internal armed conflicts in places such as Rwanda, Colombia, and Chechnya have led human rights groups to re-examine the utility of the humanitarian law framework contained in Common Article 3 to the Geneva Conventions of 1949 and Protocol II.[86] With regard to situations such as Colombia, the UN Commission on Human Rights calls directly on the rebel groups to comply with international humanitarian law and to respect the right of the population to exercise their human rights.[87] For some time there has been an attempt to tackle this issue by admitting that non-state actors have to obey human rights norms but distinguishing them from state actors by labelling them human rights *abusers* rather than *violators*. According to David Weissbrodt: 'When non-State actors do not comply with human rights norms, they should be criticized for "abusing" the rights of individuals rather than committing "violations".'[88] But the reasons for such a distinction are, seemingly, tactical and political rather than imbued with legal meaning. According to Weissbrodt: 'The term "human rights violation" should be limited to misconduct by governments, so as to avoid giving greater recognition and undue status to non-State entities.'[89] This approach has been the dominant approach of groups such as Amnesty International and has also been adopted by the United Nations in its training materials: 'While most human rights are perceived as individual rights vis-à-vis the Government, human rights norms may also apply to non-State actors (such as *armed opposition groups*, corporations, international financial institutions and individuals who perpetrate domestic violence) who commit human rights abuses.'[90]

Amnesty International explains its position as follows:

> As a matter of customary law (law which is binding on all states, whether or not they are bound by treaty law), basic human rights norms (directed for the most part at states) might apply to armed groups where they exercise de facto control over territory and take on responsibilities analogous to a government. Indeed, in a number of situations armed groups have expressly indicated their commitment to human rights principles.[91]

---

[86] Carrillo-Suárez, 'Hors de logique: contemporary issues in international humanitarian law as applied to internal armed conflict' 15 *American University International Law Review* (1999) 1–149.

[87] Note the Commission on Human Rights' Chairperson's Statement in 2003: '25. The Commission firmly condemns all acts of violence and breaches of international humanitarian law committed by paramilitary groups, particularly against the civilian population. It also strongly condemns the growing practice of extrajudicial, summary and arbitrary executions. 26. The Commission strongly condemns all breaches of international humanitarian law committed by other illegal armed groups, especially FARC, in particular through attacks on the civilian population. It urges all illegal armed groups to comply with international humanitarian law and to respect the legitimate exercise by the population of their human rights.' OHCHR/STM/CHR/03/2 Situation of human rights in Colombia.

[88] D. Weissbrodt, 'Non-State Entities and Human Rights within the Context of the Nation-State in the 21st Century' in M. Castermans, F. van Hoof, and J. Smith (eds) *The Role of the Nation-State in the 21st Century* (Dordrecht: Kluwer, 1998) 175–195, at 194.   [89] Weissbrodt (1998: 195).

[90] Office of the High Commissioner for Human Rights, *Professional Training Series No. 7, Training Manual on Human Rights Monitoring* (New York and Geneva: United Nations, 2001) at para. 26.

[91] Amnesty International, *It's in our hands: Stop violence against women*. AI Index ACT 77/001/2004, at 56. The report explains: 'There are many different—and passionate—views on whether and when it is legitimate to use violence to achieve change or to confront state power.

In practice, so far, most armed opposition groups have been addressed through the prism of the principles in Common Article 3 to the Geneva Conventions of 1949, and as groups in control of territory with attendant human rights responsibilities. But the issue does arise of how to deal with interferences with, what Ravi Nair calls, 'intermediate, gray situations of political violence. The gray situation can be distinguished from situations of "normal" crime or war'.[92] Moreover human rights groups have been confronted with dilemmas over how to report on abuses of rights committed by criminal organizations taking on a political role as well as political organizations engaging in criminal activity.[93]

It is suggested that is clearly no longer feasible for human rights groups to avoid reporting the killings by rebels on the ground that they are mandated simply to apply a strict framework of international humanitarian law and human rights law as traditionally understood. The moral and political context is too fraught to rely on such a formulaic approach. Imagine the head of a human rights organization having to explain to a government why the organization condemns the army's violence in the search for terrorists—yet never says a word about organized rebel attacks on civilian targets. One could say one is strictly applying a humanitarian law framework and the bombings have not reached the required threshold—but this is unlikely to convince any government that there is no bias involved.[94] Writing from his experience in India, Ravi Nair points out:

> By not criticizing armed opposition groups, human rights organizations also threaten their legitimacy as unbiased observers. The repeated and vociferous criticism of the government on the human rights front, when seen in conjunction with the apparent silence of some human rights groups regarding the abuses committed by armed opposition groups, meets with a hostile reception. The activities of the human rights groups can be construed as partisan and unfair, if not fundamentally misdirected, leading to an increasing loss of credibility and further marginalization, even within the victim groups.[95]

Human rights organizations have met this challenge in two ways. First, an organization such as Amnesty International has, through its publications and the media, simply 'opposed' torture, hostage taking, and unlawful killings by non-governmental groups

Amnesty International takes no position on this issue—we do insist, however, that groups which resort to force respect minimum standards of international humanitarian law, justice and humanity. Armed groups, no less than governments, must never target civilians, take hostages, or practise torture or cruel treatment, and they must ensure respect for basic human rights and freedoms in territory they control.'

[92] Nair (1998: 11). Nair gives the examples of Jammu and Kashmir, Assam, other parts of North East India, and areas in Andhra Pradesh.   [93] Nair (1998: 5).

[94] Similarly, with regard to bodies such as the Inter-American Commission on Human Rights, it has been pointed out that: 'If a human rights body does not also direct its attention to the actions of a nonstate actor in terms of compliance with international humanitarian law, it may leave the perception of not being evenhanded. The body may even come to be seen as a tool for restricting the activities of one party to a conflict.' K. Watkin, 'Controlling the Use of Force: A Role for Human Rights Norms in Contemporary Armed Conflict' 98 *AJIL* (2004) 1–34, at 30.   [95] Nair (1998: 10).

that use armed force for political reasons.[96] Similarly, Human Rights Watch has published reports detailing the human rights abuses by, for example, the Mojahedin Khalq Organization, an armed Iranian opposition group operating out of a camp in Iraq. In its reports it details policies of compulsory divorce, prolonged incommunicado detention, coerced confessions, beatings, and torture that in two cases were said to have led to death.[97] The significance of these reports is that the organizations neither see a need to establish the application of the laws of armed conflict, nor to assimilate the armed opposition group to a *de facto* government. The armed opposition group is simply treated as having human rights obligations.

It is further suggested that the use of some of the rules from international humanitarian law does not necessarily legitimize violence on either side of an internal armed conflict.[98] International humanitarian law simply adds a more detailed set of prohibitions for both parties to the internal armed conflict. In an internal armed conflict, applying the applicable international humanitarian law does not entitle the rebels to privileges such as combatant and prisoner of war status.[99] This means that governments can try rebels for treason or taking up arms. Such trials would not be allowed if the conflict were an international armed conflict or an internationally recognized war of national liberation.[100] The use of international humanitarian law to judge the conduct of all sides in an internal armed conflict does not lead to a new legitimacy for the fighters, or to impunity for those who have used violence. In formal terms, the international humanitarian law instruments explicitly state that the application of the norms to a party 'shall not affect the legal status of the Parties to the conflict',[101] and in general terms, the provisions do not legitimize any violence; they only set down further international prohibitions to complement applicable law.

With regard to impunity, it is clear that the winning side may try the fighters it has captured as they enjoy no combatant immunity in a strictly internal armed conflict. However, Protocol II, while not demanding the release of those captured

---

[96] See *Amnesty International Handbook*, AI Index ORG 20/001/2002, at 33. More detail is given with regards to a wider range of abuses addressed in AI reports in Ch 7 below.

[97] Human Rights Watch, *No Exit: Human Rights Abuses Inside the MKO Camps* (May 2005).

[98] Should the conflict between the armed group and the state or states be considered part of an armed conflict between states (whereby the armed group was actually working as part of the armed forces of a state), such a categorization would in effect mean that one accepts that the rules of international armed conflict apply and this would indeed legitimize attacks by the military on military objectives of the adversary. The consequent combatant immunity would mean that captured combatants would enjoy prisoner of war status and would have to be released at the end of the conflict. See further Ch 7, 7.1 below.

[99] The parties remain free to accord such a status, and Common Art. 3 specifies that the provisions are not only a minimum but that the parties should endeavour to apply as much as possible of the Geneva Conventions of 1949. See H. McCoubrey, *International Humanitarian Law* (Aldershot: Ashgate, 2nd edn, 1998) at 264.

[100] For a discussion of when international law recognizes the legitimacy of an NLM and the applicable international humanitarian law, see H. A. Wilson, *International Law and the Use of Force by National Liberation Movements* (Oxford: Oxford University Press, 1988) and G. Abi-Saab, 'Wars of National Liberation in the Geneva Conventions and Protocols' (1979) 165 *Recueil des cours* IV, at 353–445.　　[101] Common Art. 3 to the Geneva Conventions and Art. 4 of Protocol I.

(as would be the situation in an international armed conflict), does include a provision on amnesty. Article 6(5) reads: 'At the end of hostilities, the authorities in power shall endeavour to grant the broadest possible amnesty to persons who have participated in the armed conflict, or those deprived of their liberty for reasons related to the armed conflict, whether they are interned or detained.' This provision requires some explanation. According to McCoubrey:

> ... the Protocol in no way denies the right of the lawful authority to try those who have set up armed opposition to it—an activity which almost any state would tend to categorize as criminal, if not treasonable. The great question is what, in a context of non-international armed conflicts, is a lawful authority. In practice, this tends to be whatever authority has emerged victorious in the territory, or part thereof, in question. The reference of Protocol II is to criminal proceedings, and whilst offences such as treason clearly have a 'political' element in their motivation, it may be suggested that this should not extend to merely having sympathised with a losing and/or subversive party. The call for amnesty goes further, and suggests that merely *fighting* on an adverse side should not lead to punishment in such circumstances, although this may not include higher command functions and other more specific offences such as terrorism and war crimes *stricto sensu*.[102]

In any event, the application of the laws of war contained in Protocol II, designed to better protect human rights, can not really be seen to endorse violence or legitimize the use of force against the state or any other group. The provision on amnesty relates to the larger problem of ensuring national reconciliation after an internal armed conflict.

The fourth objection, which we have labelled 'the legitimization of violence argument', seeks to fix governments with the highest standards and avoid legitimizing violence on either side. It argues that human rights organizations should steer clear of reporting on violations/abuses committed by rebels or terrorists in times of armed conflict. In reality this argument turns on a view of humanitarian law as a legal regime that seems to authorize lethal force by both sides in internal armed conflict. It is suggested that humanitarian law does no such thing. It simply supplements and interprets existing human rights rules.[103] Fixing human rights and humanitarian obligations on non-state actors in an internal armed conflict, or even human rights obligations in the context of internal disturbances which do not rise to this level, in no way legitimizes violence; nor does it change the rules about who is or is not a legitimate target, or who should be granted prisoner of war status or amnesty.

The legitimization of violence argument rests on two pillars. Both can be demolished. First, it is wrong to presume that the application of international obligations to armed opposition groups, as such, entitles them to use any sort of violence. It simply further limits them with regard to their legal obligations. Second, to suggest that the application of international duties to an armed group

---

[102] McCoubrey (1998: 275).   [103] See Ch 4, at 4.1.3 below.

increases its legitimacy in the eyes of observers has no basis in law and would be hard to demonstrate empirically. There may be a problem of perception, but this argument, like the others, depends more on policy preferences of the objector rather than any inherent legal or practical impossibility with regard to the application of international law to the behaviour of non-state actors.

1.6   THE RIGHTS AS BARRIERS TO SOCIAL JUSTICE ARGUMENTS

The last type of objection builds on the critique of rights which has questioned the utility of human rights as tools for social justice. Philip Alston summarizes this critique as follows: 'it has often been said that the international human rights system makes an important contribution to the legitimacy of states, both by enabling them to claim the moral high ground and by giving them the opportunity to take on obligations which, in effect, legitimize a more activist or interventionist role for the government within society'.[104] For those who critique the human rights movement from such a perspective, there is a fear that one 'legitimizes' actors by giving them human rights obligations and implies powers which may themselves erode, rather than enhance, human freedom and autonomy. Such a critique is hard to dismiss out of hand, but the idea that labelling someone a human rights violator dignifies them with legitimacy only holds true if one has already assumed that only legitimate actors, such as states, have human rights obligations. Ever since the Nuremberg Tribunal held individuals accountable for war crimes and crimes against humanity,[105] it has been clear that having international law obligations does not imply respectability, legitimacy, or decency. If this point holds with regard to the law of crimes against humanity, it can also hold for the law of human rights violations.

We can also see that, to deny the applicability of human rights law to powerful non-state actors, is to deny the empowerment which accompanies human rights claims. As Chris Jochnick explains, referring to a failed approach by his human rights organization, one can not expect to get very far by telling communities in Ecuador threatened by the activities of an oil company that 'private companies are technically immune to human rights claims, that they do not sign covenants guaranteeing human rights, and that only the state is responsible for ensuring these rights'.[106] In

---

[104] P. Alston, 'Downsizing the State in Human Rights Discourse' in N. Dorden and P. Gifford (eds) *Democracy and the Rule of Law* (Washington, DC: Congressional Quarterly Press, 2001) 357–368, at 359.

[105] *Trial of Major War Criminals (Goering et al)*, International Military Tribunal (Nuremberg) Judgment and Sentence, 30 September and 1 October 1946 (London: HMSO) Cmd. 6964. This judgment is discussed in Chs 6 and 12 below.

[106] C. Jochnick 'Confronting the Impunity of Non-State Actors: New Fields for the Promotion of Human Rights' 21 *HRQ* (1999) 56–79, at 58.

fact, holding the public/private line in this way risks actually undermining the opportunities for progressive change by shielding the nature of private activity that threatens human well-being. As he explains: 'the intended approach risked the uncomfortable prospect of doing more harm than good. Insisting solely on governmental obligations would obscure the true nature of the violation, reinforce Texaco's impunity, and most importantly, detract from the communities' long-overdue sense of injustice and resolve'.[107] To apply the traditional state/non-state distinction risks obfuscating the real violators; to insist on the exclusive applicability of human rights law to governments generates a dangerous sense of impunity for those who are undermining people's rights.

At another level the critique has been put forward that rights have historically been used to protect a private sphere from public interference. This has in many cases resulted in the protection of private power from attempts to ensure social justice. According to this argument, it is unrealistic to expect the law, and the judges, to turn rights on their head and use them against the same private interests they have historically protected. My approach, which looks to judicial enforcement of human rights in the private sphere, has been specifically criticized in a considered and constructive way by Gavin Anderson. He suggests that such a 'jurisdictional approach' is 'self-limiting, and thus fails to take into account ways in which human rights discourse itself contributes to the protection of private power'.[108] For Anderson 'the history of rights is not one of neutrality, but of partiality: in juridical form, human rights have been largely synonymous with the protection of private activities from public power'.[109] This may be true from a constitutional law perspective that is concerned about the role of a Supreme Court in building a theory of constitutional rights in the national polity.[110] In some constitutional arrangements, decisions by judges over the scope of constitutional rights may override the will of the people, as expressed through legislation, and commentators have been wary of new applications of constitutional (supreme) rights as law. Scholars such as Tushnet and Fudge, writing about the judiciary in the United States and Canada respectively, voice considerable scepticism over the faith placed in judges as the ultimate arbiters of conflicting policies and

---

[107] C. Jochnick *HRQ*, at 58.

[108] G. W. Anderson 'Rights and the Art of Boundary Maintenance' 60 *MLR* (1997) 120–132, at 121. (Book review article on *Human Rights in the Private Sphere* (1993)). See also in this context L. M. Seidman, 'Public Principle and Private Choice: The Uneasy Case for a Boundary Maintenance Theory of Constitutional Law' 96 *YLJ* (1987) 1006–1059.   [109] Anderson (1997: 122).

[110] Anderson also refers to the problems associated with a rights theory that fails to tackle the 'reality of constitutional adjudication which prohibits governmental interference with private power' (1997: 129). Anderson also refers to the discussion by B. A. Ackerman, 'Beyond *Carolene Products*' 98 *Harv LR* (1985) 713–746. Ackerman's concerns rest in part on the fact that the promise of *Carolene Products* is deceptive as: 'The victims of sexual discrimination or poverty, rather than racial or religious minorities, will increasingly constitute the groups with the greatest claim upon *Carolene's* concern with the fairness of pluralist process' (at 718).

freedoms.[111] Reviewing the record of the courts in the United States and Canada, they argue that courts should not be the only forum for enforcing fundamental human rights. And in the words of Fudge: 'Ultimately, the question of whether an entrenched bill of rights enforced by the ordinary common law courts enhances respect for fundamental rights and democracy is an empirical question.'[112]

Although much of this book will focus on the decisions of courts, this does not imply that human rights claims are confined to litigation and fora where remedies exist. The focus on courts in this book is, in part, to illustrate that human rights arguments are already used to hold non-state actors accountable for actions in the private sphere. By honing the arguments used in litigation, I aim to develop a more coherent approach to the human rights obligations of non-state actors, even in the absence of applicable tribunals entitled to hand down binding decisions. We might also suggest that the dangers of entrenching subjective values through judicial activism are of a different order when applied outside the context of a constitutional court with the ultimate legal say over the validity of national legislation. We shall mainly focus on the scope of international human rights as applied on the international plane rather than the scope of constitutionally protected rights in national law. The two sets of rights are not congruent in their scope or enforcement.

In the end, Anderson's objection to extending rights into the private sphere rejoins the first type of argument, labelled the 'trivialization thesis' in section 1.2 above; namely, that our suggested approach ignores the historical pedigree of rights. Anderson's approach emphasizes that: 'Rights have not been about the limitation of power, with the nature of that power just happening to be public in most cases— their whole purpose and analytical framework has had public power as their specific object. Thus their enforcement against private actors is not a simple matter of extending existing practice and beliefs but, as it seeks to reverse the focus of protection of private power, would in fact entail standing them on their heads.'[113]

Both arguments consider that the application of human rights obligations to non-state actors distorts our understanding of human rights. Such an application is said to pull 'inside out the very concept of human rights'.[114] Alternatively, we are accused of 'standing them on their heads'. Of course most people's historical understanding of rights is that rights are embodied in a contract between government and the individual, and that rights protect individuals and private groups from state interference in a number of specified domains. In this conception, rights operate as a sort of buffer between the state and the private sector. Moreover,

---

[111] M. Tushnet, 'Scepticism about Judicial Review: A Perspective from the United States' in T. Campbell, K. D. Ewing, and A. Tomkins (eds) *Sceptical Essays on Human Rights* (Oxford: Oxford University Press, 2001) 359–374; J. Fudge, 'The Canadian Charter of Rights: Recognition, Redistribution, and the Imperialism of the Courts', also in Campbell *et al* (2001: 335–358).

[112] Ibid, at 357.   [113] Anderson (1997: 123).

[114] Letter to the Maltese *Sunday Times*, see 1.2 above.

the private sector has relied on human rights to protect the boundaries of its private sphere. But these physical analogies have limitations; they can no longer explain how human rights are observed in action today as limitations on private power.

I suggest that, at the beginning of the twenty-first century, we need a paradigm shift in our understanding of the power and utility of human rights. If human rights once offered a shield from state oppression in the vertical relationship between the individual and the state, they now also represent a sword in the hands of victims of private human rights abuses. Perhaps we do have to pull human rights inside out and acknowledge that they can be used against other human rights holders. Perhaps we have to turn human rights on their heads and realize that while they have protected private power, they also contain the seeds for action against private power—in the same jurisdictions that have historically curtailed public power when such power has threatened private autonomy.

1.7   NEW WAYS OF LOOKING AT HUMAN RIGHTS

The metaphors that suggest physical deformation of our traditional understanding of human rights entrench a traditional approach to civil rights, which prevents us imagining a different set of qualities for human rights. Why not imagine a system where human rights obligations attach both to states and to non-state actors? Is such an attachment really as contradictory and impossible as the various arguments outlined above suggest? In the world of physics there were conundrums that confronted scientists for a great part of the last century. Assumptions were challenged and a new vocabulary emerged.

In classical physics it was assumed that light had to be described either in terms of particles, or as waves, even though scientists seemed to discern both properties in different experiments. The elusive search for the true nature of light (particles or waves) is partially resolved by the notion of *complementarity*.[115] In 1927, Niels Bohr formulated a new way of looking at the dilemma. He considered that, although wave and particle behaviour seem to mutually exclude each other, we need to understand both qualities for a proper appreciation of the object's properties. Most importantly, he pointed out that whether or not the object behaves as a wave or a particle depends on the experiment you use for looking at it. This has been explained as follows: 'To decide if it's a wave, [physicists] diffract it through slits and see whether they get interference fringes. To decide whether it's a particle, they bounce it off things and see if it holds together. They ask wavy questions to decide whether it's a wave, particley questions to decide whether it's a particle.'[116]

---

[115] We return to this concept, along with those of complexity and complicity in Ch 12 below, in the guise of a conclusion.

[116] J. Cohen and I. Stewart, *The Collapse of Chaos: Discovering Simplicity in a Complex World* (Harmondsworth: Penguin, 1994) at 276.

Just as light was understood to have different qualities depending on the apparatus used to experiment on it, we cannot describe with certainty the nature of the object under investigation as either one thing or the other. The uncertainty of the state of an atomic system is much more complicated than suggested here; but the principle of complementarity helps us to see that conflicting views of the quality of something may not necessarily be contradictory. Different views may have to be seen as complementary in order to get a better understanding of the object under scrutiny.

Does this reductive excursus into nuclear physics help? Perhaps, it may be that human rights can indeed be used by private power and against private power at the same time. This may seem counterintuitive, or naïve, but it is possible. Perhaps human rights do indeed have this double quality and it is not necessarily misguided to propose greater attention to the possibility of human rights having the necessary qualities to act as a check on private power. At least we should perhaps admit that our appreciation of human rights has been skewed by the jurisdictional filters that have been employed in our experiments to examine them.

Anderson asks us to explain *why* courts have consistently exercised their options against public power as opposed to private power. He points to the case-law of the European Court of Human Rights to back his argument that courts administering the key human rights instruments 'have been in the business of limiting, public, not private power'.[117] This is true, but I suggest here that this is not due to some essential nature of human rights, but simply because human rights lawyers are over-focusing on a handful of jurisdictions. In setting up a particular apparatus to examine human rights we are precluding the chance to observe human rights in action under other experimental conditions. If we set up our monitors in Strasbourg at the European Court of Human Rights, we shall find evidence of human rights being enforced against the state rather than against private power.[118] *Why* is this so? Because, under the jurisdictional treaty establishing the Court, only states can be defendants before the Court. If we examine rights in certain constitutions, we will find human rights as mainly opposable against the government. Again, this is so because the constitutional document limits, or appears to limit, such cases to abuse of public power. But if we look elsewhere, we may find evidence of human rights obligations being opposable to private power. In other words, the results of our investigation depend on where we set up our experiment and the filter we are looking through. With a multiplicity of jurisdictions for human rights claims, we have to accept that human rights obligations may attach to non-state actors in some jurisdictions and not in others. These different jurisdictional appreciations of the nature of human rights need not be contradictory. They can be considered complementary.

---

[117] Anderson (1997: 123).

[118] R. Lawson, 'Out of Control, State Responsibility and Human Rights: Will the ILC's Definition of the "Act of State" Meet the Challenges of the 21st Century?' in M. Castermans, F. Van Hoof, and J. Smith (eds) *The Role of the Nation-State in the 21st Century* (The Hague: Kluwer, 1998) 91–116.

In sum, all of the arguments outlined above boil down to two claims: first, that an application of human rights obligations to non-state actors trivializes, dilutes, and distracts from the great concept of human rights. Second, that such an application bestows inappropriate power and legitimacy on such actors. The counter-argument is that we can legitimately reverse the presumption that human rights are inevitably a contract between individuals and the state; we can presume that human rights are entitlements enjoyed by everyone to be respected by everyone. Once we accept that human rights obligations can apply in this way, the idea of legitimizing non-state actors by subjecting them to human rights duties becomes illogical.

The message is that international human rights obligations can fall on states, individuals, and non-state actors. Different jurisdictions may or may not be able to enforce these obligations, but the obligations exist just the same. With more and more national jurisdictions applying international human rights law as the law of the land, we look set to see an increasing acknowledgement of the relevance of human rights norms for judging the conduct of private actors. We may be witnessing a shift in emphasis. In the words of the distinguished British academic lawyer, the late Professor Sir William Wade:

> It is true that the original purpose of the human rights Convention was to prevent the emergence of dictatorial and oppressive governments such as that of Nazi Germany. But in the intervening half century a new culture of human rights has developed in the Western world, and the citizen can legitimately expect that his human rights will be respected by his neighbours as well as his government.[119]

---

[119] H. W. R. Wade, 'Horizons of Horizontality' 116 *LQR* (2000) 217–224, at 224. See also H. R. W. Wade, 'Paradoxes in Human Rights Act', letter to *The Times*, 1 September 2000. See also, from a comparative law perspective, the comment by B. Markesinis and S. Enchelmaier, 'Nowadays, therefore, the new paradigm of a human right violation may be that of an "individual" (to be understood here as referring to any natural or legal person which is not acting with public authority) encroaching upon the freedom of another individual' in their chapter, 'The Applicability of Human Rights as between Individuals under German Constitutional Law' in B. S. Markesinis (ed) *Protecting Privacy: The Clifford Chance Lectures Volume Four* (Oxford: Oxford University Press, 1999) 191–243, at 192. Cf B. Markesinis, 'Privacy, Freedom of Expression, and the Horizontal Effect of the Human Rights Bill: Lessons from Germany' 115 *LQR* (1999) 45–88; A. Lester and D. Pannick, 'The Impact of the Human Rights Act on Private Law: The Knight's Move' 116 *LQR* (2000) 380–385; J. Beatson and S. Grosz 'Horizontality: a Footnote' 116 *LQR* (2000) 385–386; M. Hunt, 'The Horizontal Effect of the Human Rights Act', *Public Law* (1998) 423–443. The issue of private discrimination was already of concern to Hersch Lauterpacht in his early work, *International Law and Human Rights* (London: Stevens and Sons, 1950) at 340–343, where he highlighted the duties of a state to refrain from lending the 'arm of the law' to enforce discrimination by private individuals, such as inn-keepers, performing a public function. He went on, however, to pose (at 343) an 'urgent question whether in modern conditions, the duty of the State ought not to go beyond that and whether there ought not to be a right of protection against organized oppression from whatever source it may originate'.

2

Thinking Responsibly about the Subject of Subjects

2.1 SUBJECTS AS PRISONERS OF DOCTRINE

The traditional treatment of the question of the subjects of international law is confusing and incomplete. Although few authors, or even states, hold out that states are the sole subjects of international law, the question of international legal personality has remained entangled with the misleading concept of 'subjects' of international law and the attendant question of attributions of statehood under international law. It seems assumed that increasing the categories of international legal persons recognized under international law will lead to an expansion of the possible authors of international law.[1] This, of course, is seen to threaten the viable development of a decentralized, state-centred international legal order.

Most doctrine would include as subjects of international law entities on their way to becoming states, and actors with state-like qualities, such as: *de facto* regimes, insurgents recognized as belligerents, national liberation movements (NLMs) representing peoples struggling for self-determination, the Holy See, and even the Order of Malta.[2] Furthermore, as the principal subjects of international law (states) discover that they need to include further subjects of international law, they can demonstrate this through the recognition of, not only entities such as NLMs, but also of inter-state organizations such as the United Nations. However, even these bodies are not detached from the states themselves, as the doctrine suggests that they are created by them to fulfil objectives which cannot be fulfilled by states acting individually.[3]

[1] See H. Lauterpacht, 'General Laws of the Law of Peace' in E. Lauterpacht (ed) *Collected Papers, Volume 1* (Cambridge: Cambridge University Press, 1970) at 280: 'Much of the opposition to the predominant doctrine with regard to the subjects of international law is undoubtedly due to such reasons as the reaction against the recognition of sovereign States as the only authors of international law, or to the desire to vindicate the rights of man in the international sphere.'

[2] See G. Abi-Saab, *Cours Général de Droit International Public*, Vol. 207 *RCADI* (The Hague: Nijhoff, 1996) at 81, and P. Cahier, *Changements et Continuité du Droit International*, Vol. 195 *RCADI* (Dordrecht: Nijhoff, 1992) at 92. See also J. A. Frowein, 'De Facto Régime' in R. Bernhardt (ed) *Encyclopedia of Public International Law*, Vol. 1 (Amsterdam: Elsevier, 1992) 966–968 'State practice shows that entities which in fact govern a specific territory will be treated as partial subjects of international law. They will be held responsible, treaties may be concluded with them' (at 966).

[3] Abi-Saab, ibid, at 82.

The concept of a *subject* of international law is today often deemed unhelpful; and scholars increasingly avoid speculation on which non-state actors can be described as subjects.[4] It is suggested that much of the contemporary doctrine on this topic simply reflects whether the commentators see any policy advantage to extending the traditional notion of subjects of international law.[5] Even those commentators who take a functional approach to the necessity of addressing non-state actors have, however, failed to conclude whether formal status should be extended to non-state actors. For example, Ruth Wedgwood exhorts us to be functional:

> The test for the 'privatization' of the international legal order must be a functional one. In the case of non-governmental organizations, their role has been seen as beneficial and creative, subject to suitable cautions. In the case of non-state political entities, the international community has treated them from necessity where the nation state did not have full control of its own domain, but it remains to be seen whether these political imperatives may require a more formal status outside the state orientation of the Westphalian system.[6]

But Wedgwood then chooses to reject the utility of the subject of subjects: 'in general, it is not clear that analytic purity about the nature of a "subject" of international law will serve much point in describing the real evolution of the international system'.[7] Similarly, Daniel Thürer suggests a constitutional approach which would provide 'a way of escaping from the rigidly defined circle of traditional subjects of international law. Thereby we can avoid the intensely debated but largely sterile question as to whether or not NGOs or transnational enterprises have emerged as new subjects within the international legal order'.[8]

These views, pronounced at a conference entitled, *Non-State Actors as New Subjects of International Law*, are mirrored in countless symposia and suggest that international lawyers realize that the role of non-state actors is too important to be

---

[4] See, e.g. Société Française pour le Droit International, *Colloque du Mans: Le sujet en droit international* (Paris: Pedone, 2005).

[5] For an introduction to the debate as to whether non-state actors should fit in a theory of international relations, see A. Weenink, 'The Relevance of Being Important or the Importance of Being Relevant? State and Non-State Actors in International Relations Theory' in B. Arts, M. Noortmann, and B. Reinalda (eds) *Non-State Actors in International Relations* (Aldershot: Ashgate, 2001) 59–76.

[6] 'Legal Personality and the Role of Non-Governmental Organizations and Non-State Political Entities in the United Nations System' in R. Hofmann (ed) *Non-State Actors as New Subjects of International Law: International Law—From the Traditional State Order Towards the Law of the Global Community* (Berlin: Duncker & Humblot, 1999) 21–36, at 36.

[7] Remarks in Hofmann (1999: 93).

[8] D. Thürer, 'The Emergence of Non-Governmental Organizations and Transnational Enterprises in International Law and the Changing Role of the State' in Hofmann (1999) 37–58, at 53. See also T. Franck 'Individuals and Groups of Individuals as Subjects of International Law' in Hofmann (1999) at 97–113. Franck avoids the issue of legal subjectivity altogether and concludes with a *moral* priority for the individual as a rights claimant with regard to groups and states. We can find similar equivocation with regard to minorities: Stephen Hobe suggests minorities may be becoming limited subjects of international law, 'a position they arguably do not yet possess'. 'Individuals and Groups as Global Actors: The Denationalization of International Transactions' in Hofmann (1999) 115–133, at 128.

ignored, yet feel constrained by the 'rules' on subjectivity to develop a framework to explain the rights and duties of non-state actors under international law. To take one further example, Cees Flinterman, in his concluding remarks at a conference entitled, *The Legitimacy of the United Nations: Towards an Enhanced Legal Status of Non-State Actors*, limited himself to stating that 'most Non-State Actors, both political and humanitarian, have at present no legal status or at best a limited legal status under international law'.[9]

Let us step back and consider whether the rules for determining whether an entity has become a 'subject' with 'status' under international law are coherent or helpful. We can see straight away that the rules of the game are self-consciously subjective. The 1920 edition of a well-known treatise on international law introduces the topic in this way:

> The conception of International Persons is derived from the conception of the Law of Nations. As this law is the body of rules which the civilised States consider legally binding in their intercourse, every State which belongs to the civilised States, and is, therefore, a member of the Family of Nations, is an International Person. And since now the Family of Nations has become an organised community under the name of the League of Nations with distinctive international rights and duties of its own, the League of Nations is an International Person *sui generis* besides the several States. But apart from the League of Nations, sovereign States exclusively are International Persons—*i.e.* subjects of International Law.[10]

Everything turns on the conception that one has of the Law of Nations. The same treatise was equally dogmatic about the meaning of the Law of Nations: 'The Law of Nations is a law for the intercourse of States with one another, not a law for individuals. As, however, there cannot be a sovereign authority above the several sovereign States, the law of nations is a law *between*, not above, the several States, and is therefore, since Bentham, also called "International Law".'[11]

Of course, later editions of the treatise have been amended to take into consideration the role of the United Nations and of individuals. But such amendments beg the question: why do we stop here? If individuals are to be deemed subjects of international law with international legal personality, why not non-governmental organizations? And if we add non-governmental organizations, why not transnational corporations? Such doubts are creeping into the practice and doctrine of international lawyers.

Let us consider how the International Law Commission (ILC) came to delimit its work on its draft articles on the responsibility of international organizations. In his first report, the Special Rapporteur, Giorgio Gaja, recalls the familiar line that

---

[9] *SIM Special No. 19*, Utrecht, SIM Studie- en Informatiecentrum Mensenrechten (Netherlands Institute of Human Rights) (1997) at 187.
[10] L. Oppenheim, *International Law: A Treatise*, R. F. Roxburgh (ed) (London: Longmans, 3rd edn, 1920) at 125.   [11] Ibid, at 2 (footnote omitted).

international rights and duties depend on the entity being considered a subject of international law.[12]

> When considering a definition of international organizations that is functional to the purposes of draft articles on responsibility of international organizations, one has to start from the premise that responsibility under international law may arise only for a subject of international law. Norms of international law cannot impose on an entity 'primary' obligations or 'secondary' obligations in case of a breach of one of the 'primary' obligations unless that entity has legal personality under international law. Conversely, an entity has to be regarded as a subject of international law even if only a single obligation is imposed on it under international law. Thus, should an obligation exist for an international organization under international law, the question of that organization's responsibility may arise. Logically, a study on responsibility of international organizations should consider all the organizations that are subjects of international law.

But Gaja later addresses the issue, raised by a number of governments, as to whether non-governmental organizations (NGOs) should be included in the scope of the ILC's work. Here the doctrine concerning the current category of subjects seems to exclude NGOs, but Gaja, having recalled the International Court of Justice's conclusions regarding the United Nations and its specialized agencies, exposes the indeterminate nature of the concept (or conception) of subjects of international law. Gaja recognizes that the recent approach of the International Court of Justice opens the door to accepting that NGOs could be subjects of international law.

> The Court's assertion of the legal personality of international organizations needs to be viewed in the context of its more recent approach to the question of legal personality in international law. The Court stated in the *LaGrand* case that individuals are also subjects of international law.[13] This approach may lead the Court to assert the legal personality even of non-governmental organizations. It would be difficult to understand why individuals may acquire rights and obligations under international law while the same could not occur with any international organization, provided that it is an entity which is distinct from its members.[14]

Scholars are increasingly rejecting the whole notion of subjects, and exposing the fact that there seem to be no agreed rules for determining who can be classed a subject. According to Rosalyn Higgins: 'We have all been held captive by a

---

[12] 'First report on responsibility of international organizations', UN Doc. A/CN.4/532, 26 March 2003, para.15.

[13] Footnote 47 in the original reads: '*I.C.J. Reports 2001*, para. 77. The Court referred to the Vienna Convention on Consular Relations of 24 April 1963 and concluded that "article 36, paragraph 1, creates individual rights".'

[14] First report (see n 12 above) at para. 17. See also the Report of the ILC Working Group 'The responsibility of international organizations: scope and orientation of the study': 'The topic would be considerably widened if the study were to comprise also organizations that States establish under municipal laws, for example under the law of a particular State, and non-governmental organizations. Thus, it may seem preferable to leave questions of responsibility relating to this type of organization aside, at least provisionally.' UN Doc. A/CN.4/L.622, 6 June 2002, at para. 11.

doctrine that stipulates that all international law is to be divided into "subjects"—that is, those elements bearing, without the need for municipal intervention, rights and responsibilities; and "objects"—that is, the rest.'[15] Higgins seems to suggest that the whole edifice is built on the myth that we have a rule for determining when something should be classed as a subject, and that the whole enterprise is constructed by doctrine and can therefore be dismantled by doctrine. She concludes: 'the positivist definition assumed that some specific rule is required "permitting" the individual to be a "subject" of international law. Finally, the whole notion of "subjects" and "objects" has no credible reality, and, in my view, no functional purpose. We have erected an intellectual prison of our own choosing and then declared it to be an unalterable constraint'.[16]

Jan Klabbers playfully asks us to think who invented the notion of subjects and the overbearing tradition to which the young legal scholar is expected to conform:

> To be a subject of international law is to be given an academic label: a subject of international law is a legitimate subject of international research and reflection. Any attempt by an international lawyer to study, for example, the workings of the city of Amsterdam, or of the Finnish Icehockey Association, or the Roman Catholic church, can be challenged in terms of subjectivity: as these are not generally regarded as subjects of international law, the international law scholar may have to address claims that he or she could have spent his or her time better.[17]

2.2   THE *REPARATIONS FOR INJURIES* OPINION, THE UNITED NATIONS, AND UN AGENCIES

A first port of call for anyone seeking to understand the doctrine surrounding the notion of international legal 'subjectivity' is the crucial step taken by the International Court of Justice in the *Reparations for injuries* opinion. The Court was concerned with the question whether the United Nations, as an organization, had the capacity to bring an international claim against a state where an agent of the United Nations suffered injuries in circumstances involving the responsibility of that state. The background to the request for the advisory opinion was the killing of the UN Chief negotiator for Palestine, Count Bernadotte. An important aspect of the opinion is that it specifically dealt with the objective personality of the United Nations *vis-à-vis* a non-member state (the reparations were being sought against Israel, not at that time a member of the United Nations).

The Court came to the conclusion that 'the Organization is an international person'.[18] The Court explained that this meant that: 'it is a subject of international law

---

[15] R. Higgins, *Problems and Process: International Law and How We Use It* (Oxford: Clarendon Press, Oxford University Press, 1994) at 49.   [16] Ibid.

[17] J. Klabbers, *An Introduction to International Institutional Law* (Cambridge: Cambridge University Press, 2002) at 43.

[18] *Reparations for injuries suffered in the service of the United Nations*, ICJ Reports (1949) 174, at 179.

and capable of possessing international rights and duties, and that it has the capacity to maintain its rights by bringing international claims'.[19]

The reasoning is quite open-ended and certainly allows for a changing conception of what is an international person. The Court stated:

> The subjects of law in any legal system are not necessarily identical in their nature or in the extent of their rights, and their nature depends on the needs of the community. Throughout its history, the development of international law has been influenced by the requirements of international life, and the progressive increase in the collective activities of States has already given rise to instances of action upon the international plane by certain entities which are not States. This development culminated in the establishment in June 1945 of an international organization whose purposes and principles are specified in the Charter of the United Nations. But to achieve these ends the attribution of international personality is indispensable.[20]

As Ian Brownlie points out, the definition of a subject of international law as 'an entity capable of possessing international rights and duties and having capacity to maintain its rights by bringing international claims' is circular.[21] International law recognizes the capacity to act at the international level of an entity that is already capable of acting at the international level. Furthermore, the needs of the community and the requirements of international life will throw up new subjects and new capabilities according to those needs; where those needs require the capacity to act, there will be recognition of that personality. In the words of the International Court of Justice:

> In the opinion of the Court, the Organization was intended to exercise and enjoy, and is in fact exercising and enjoying, functions and rights which can only be explained on the basis of the possession of a large measure of international personality and the capacity to operate on an international plane.[22]

International personality and capacity to act on the international plane are presented as necessary conditions for the exercise of these functions and rights. But the Court also said that when it spoke of 'international personality', it meant the capacity to have rights and exercise them! To break out of this circle, let us reconsider the traditional contexts where the issue of international legal personality has arisen.

Brownlie suggests three contexts: 'capacity to make claims in respect of breaches of international law; capacity to make treaties and agreements valid on the international plane; and the enjoyment of privileges and immunities from national jurisdictions'.[23] Because states have these capacities, they have been used to determine international personality for other entities. Such capacities in a non-state actor may even be seen by some as evidence of international personality.

---

[19] *Reparations for injuries* (n 18 above) at 179.   [20] Ibid, at 179.
[21] I. Brownlie, *Principles of Public International Law* (Oxford: Oxford University Press, 6th edn, 2003) at 57.   [22] *Reparation for injuries* (n 18 above) at 179.
[23] Brownlie (2003: 57).

However, if we look at other areas of international law aside from treaty-making powers, claims for reparation under general international law, and immunity before national courts, we may find that international personality is necessary *not because the capacity to bring a claim exists, but in order to ensure that the intention of states to confer rights and duties is effective.* A re-reading of the last-cited passage from the Court's statement in the *Reparations for injuries* opinion allows us to separate two different concepts which have usually been confusingly intertwined. First, the Court points to a large measure of international personality, and second, it refers to the capacity to *operate* on an international plane. Recall that the question of capacity to actually bring an *international claim* was at the heart of the original request for an advisory opinion. The Court seems to be saying that the Organization has international personality; and also, in this context, it has the capacity to bring an international claim similar to a claim for diplomatic protection under the rules of inter-state responsibility. Simultaneously with its finding that the United Nations possesses a large measure of personality, the Court is assuming that the states intended the UN Organization to be *effective*, and thus the right to make a claim is implied.

While the capacity to make claims has generated considerable theoretical interest, less attention has been paid to the general question of the *capacity to fulfil obligations*, and indeed, what those obligations might be.[24] We shall see in the chapters dealing with the United Nations and the European Union that there is a recognition that these entities accept that they are bound by customary international humanitarian law and customary international human rights law. But the issue in broader terms has rarely been addressed. In 1980, the International Court of Justice recalled its earlier opinion regarding reparations to the United Nations, and in a separate advisory opinion stated:

> ... there is nothing in the character of international organizations to justify their being considered as some form of 'super-State'. ... International organizations are subjects of international law and, as such, are bound by any obligations incumbent upon them under general rules of international law, under their constitutions or under agreements to which they are parties.[25]

---

[24] Peter Bekker focuses on the immunities of international organizations and how disputes with third parties may be resolved but does not tackle the non-contractual obligations that could arise under general international law. *The Legal Position of Intergovernmental Organizations: A Functional Necessity Analysis of Their Legal Status and Immunities* (Dordrecht: Nijhoff, 1994); Klabbers (2002: 310) refers to the treaty obligations of organizations, breaches of customary international law, failure to live up to unilateral promises made by the organization, and possible violations of general principles of law. Focus usually turns to the indirect or secondary responsibility of the member states rather than the concurrent and parallel responsibility of the organization itself. Klabbers (2002: 311). The work of the ILC on the responsibility of international organizations, while it will not look at the content of those obligations, will inevitably lead to greater attention to the substantive obligations of international organizations under general rules of international law.

[25] *Interpretation of the Agreement of 25 March 1951 Between the WHO and Egypt*, ICJ Reports (1980) 73, at 89–90.

In this case the Court found that there were obligations on the World Health Organization (WHO) to give a reasonable period of notice to Egypt for the termination of the existing arrangement. Additionally, the WHO and Egypt were to consult together in good faith regarding a transfer of the regional office of the organization.[26] This opinion was given in the context of host state agreements; what might be the wider scope of such 'general rules of international law'? Amerasinghe suggests: 'Generally, organizations have been found at fault in connection with damage resulting from conduct of their servants or agents or persons or groups under their control, such as armed forces.'[27] (We will deal with the UN response to claims against it relating to peace-keeping in Chapter 4.) Amerasinghe goes on to consider what might be the positive obligations of an organization such as the United Nations. 'There is no reason why, where necessary, analogies should not be borrowed from the principles of imputability applied in the customary law of State responsibility, particularly, for injuries to aliens.'[28] It remains to be seen how exactly such analogies will be drawn.[29]

The work of the International Law Commission's Special Rapporteur with regard to diplomatic protection, John Dugard, suggests that the traditional substantive standards on injuries to aliens have been overtaken by the customary international law of human rights.[30] The proposed draft article is clear that

---

[26] *Interpretation of the Agreement of 25 March 1951 Between the WHO and Egypt*, at 95–96.

[27] C. F. Amerasinghe, *Principles of the Institutional Law of International Organizations* (Cambridge: Cambridge University Press, 1996) at 241. See also the International Court of Justice' Advisory Opinion on *Difference relating to immunity from legal process of a special rapporteur of the Commission on Human Rights*, 29 April 1999, at para. 66.

[28] Amerasinghe (1996: 241). For the substantive obligations of states towards aliens under international law and the influence of human rights law with regard to the right to life, liberty, and security of the person, the right not to be subjected to cruel inhuman or degrading treatment or punishment, the right to be free from arbitrary arrest, detention and expulsion, and the right to property, see R. B. Lillich, 'Duties of States Regarding the Civil Rights of Aliens', vol. 161 *Collected Courses of the Hague Academy of International Law* (Alphen aan den Rijn: Sijthoff and Noordhoff, 1980) 329–442.

[29] E.g. the work of Giorgio Gaja, the Special Rapporteur on responsibility of international organizations of the International Law Commission, deals with the secondary rules of attribution by analogy but is unlikely to deal with the substantive obligations which surround the protection of aliens under customary international law. UN Doc. A/CN.4/532, 26 March 2003. For the other reports see UN Docs A/CN.4/541, 2 April 2004 and A/CN.4/553, 13 May 2005. For the draft Articles adopted by the Commission on first reading see A/CN.4/L.632, 4 June 2003, A/CN.4/L.648, 27 May 2004, and A/CN.4/L.666/Rev.1, 1 June 2005. Note draft Art. 2: 'For the purpose of the present draft articles, the term "international organization" refers to an organization established by a treaty or other instrument governed by international law and possessing its own international legal personality. International organizations may include as members, in addition to States, other entities.'

[30] See 'First report on diplomatic protection', UN Doc. A/CN.4/506, 7 March 2000: 'Contemporary international human rights law accords to nationals and aliens the same protection, which far exceeds the international minimum standard of treatment for aliens set by Western Powers in an earlier era' (at para. 32). For an overview of some of the traditional categories of 'nonwealth' claims see Yates, who splits such claims into 'nonwar' and 'war' claims. Nonwar claims are further divided into personal injury and death, denial of justice, failure to protect, and expulsion. War claims are divided into internment, forced military service, maltreatment of prisoners of war, other personal injury and death claims, and miscellaneous claims resulting in *ex gratia* payments. G. T. Yates, 'State Responsibility for Nonwealth Injuries to Aliens in the Postwar Era' in R. B. Lillich (ed) *International Law of State Responsibility for Injuries to Aliens* (Charlottesville, Virg: University Press of Virginia, 1983) 213–279.

diplomatic protection lies for any injury to an alien arising from an internationally wrongful act by the state concerned.[31] Dugard was aware that an analogy can be drawn in this context with internationally wrongful acts committed by international organizations but suggested that the matter would be better dealt with in the context of responsibility of international organizations. He nevertheless drafted a savings clause which read: 'These articles are without prejudice to the right of a State to exercise diplomatic protection against an international organization.'[32]

Pierre Klein, in a scholarly and careful study of the responsibility of international organizations, points to several categories of obligations.[33] He notes that the International Law Commission confirmed in 1986 that international organizations are bound by norms of *jus cogens*. This confirmation came in the context of the commentary to the Vienna Convention on the Law of Treaties between States and International Organizations or Between International Organizations (1986).[34]

---

[31] 'First report on diplomatic protection', UN Doc. A/CN.4/506, at para. 73, and see draft Art. 1: 'Diplomatic protection consists of resort to diplomatic action or other means of peaceful settlement by a State adopting in its own right the cause of its national in respect of an injury to that national arising from an internationally wrongful act of another State.' UN Doc. A/CN.4/L.647, 24 May 2004. See also the discussion of various approaches by Dugard at paras 17ff of his first report. He is careful to avoid suggesting any primary rules of conduct for states and has dropped the expression 'denial of justice' from the ILC's earlier meaning given to diplomatic protection in 1997 (where it was said to cover situations where a state's natural or legal persons had 'suffered injury and/or a denial of justice in another State'), explained at para. 40. Dugard refers to the suggestion made in the past that the equal treatment standard and the international minimum standard have been replaced by an international human rights standard, which accords nationals and aliens alike a standard incorporating 'the core provisions' of the Universal Declaration of Human Rights (at para. 17). Dugard also notes the relevance of the guarantee of access to consular officials as mentioned in the General Assembly's Declaration on the Human Rights of Individuals Who are not Nationals of the Country in which They Live, GA Res. 40/144 of 13 December 1985 (at para. 28). He separates out the rights that aliens have as human beings from their absence of remedies under international law (at para. 28).

[32] 'Fifth report on diplomatic protection', UN Doc. A/CN.4/538, 4 March 2004, draft Art. 24, discussed at paras 19–20. This article was not retained by the Drafting Committee; see UN Doc. A/CN.4/L.647, 24 May 2004.

[33] P. Klein, *La responsibilité des organisations internationals: dans les ordres juridiques internes et en droit des gens* (Brussels: Bruylant, 1998) at 312–375. Klein lists eight types of obligation: those resulting directly from treaties entered into by the organization, those resulting from obligations contracted by the member states, obligations resulting from the acts of other international organizations, those under customary international law, those which flow from general principles of law, those which result from unilateral acts of institutions, those which result from the decisions of international judicial decisions, and those obligations which result from the succession of one international organization to the obligations of another. For our purposes, the key categories are those of customary international law and of general principles of law. With regard to general principles, principles of national law (such as the duty to give a fair hearing and the duty to pay reparations for a breach of the law) are obviously relevant and are applied by the international administrative tribunals of international organizations. See further Ch 3, at 3.7.

[34] See *Yearbook of the ILC* (1982) vol. II, Part 2, at 56: 'It is apparent from the draft articles that peremptory norms of international law apply to international organizations as well as to States, and this is not surprising. International organizations are created by treaties concluded between States, which are subject to the Vienna Convention by virtue of Article 5 thereof; despite a personality which is in some respects different from that of the States Parties to such treaties, they are nonetheless the creation of those States. And it can hardly be maintained that States can avoid compliance with peremptory norms by creating an organization.'

That treaty states that treaties entered into between states and international organizations that violate peremptory rules of international law (*jus cogens*) are null and void. The scope of *jus cogens* norms is discussed in Chapter 3.

An interim conclusion could be that international organizations have a duty to protect the customary international human rights of everyone[35] in their control to the extent that their functions allow them to fulfil such a duty.[36] Such responsibility includes not only the duty to respect human rights (the negative obligations) but also the duty to protect human rights (the positive obligations). Amerasinghe makes this point at the end of his review of the responsibility of organizations under international law: 'Responsibility of course, could be ascribed to the international organization, as in the case of State responsibility, if there had been some element of negligence on the part of the international organization in allowing the offense to occur.'[37]

The International Court of Justice was careful to state that the possession of international personality did not imply that the organization had the same rights and duties as those of a state. The variegated approach to the rights and responsibilities of particular international persons considered in the *Reparations* opinion was critical to the denial by the International Court of Justice of the right of the WHO to request an advisory opinion on whether the use of nuclear weapons by a state in war, or other armed conflict, would be a breach of its obligation under international law, including the WHO constitution. The Court's opinion included the following passage:

> The Court need hardly point out that international organizations are subjects of international law which do not, unlike States, possess a general competence. International organizations are governed by the 'principle of speciality', that is to say, they are invested by the States which create them with powers, the limits of which are a function of the common interests whose promotion those States entrust to them.[38]

We have an international legal order that admits that states are not the only subjects of international law. It is obvious that non-state entities do not enjoy all the competences, privileges, and rights that states enjoy under international law, just as it is also clear that states do not have all the rights that individuals have under international law. A state could not claim to have been subjected to torture under the law of human rights; a state could not claim that she had been denied the right to marry. We need to admit that international rights and duties depend

---

[35] Amerasinghe (1996: 247) makes the point that with regard to international organizations 'it is irrelevant that the victim is or is not a national of the territorial State'.

[36] See also the *Effect of Awards of Compensation Made by the United Nations Administrative Tribunal* ICJ Reports (1954) 47, at 57, where the ICJ determined that the power to create an Administrative Tribunal derived from the need 'to do justice as between the Organization and the staff members [which] was essential to ensure the highest standards of efficiency, competence and integrity'.   [37] Amerasinghe (1996: 247).

[38] *Legality of the Use by a State of Nuclear Weapons in Armed Conflict (Request of the World Health Organization)* (1996) at para. 25.

on the capacity of the entity to enjoy those rights and bear those obligations; such rights and obligations do not depend on the mysteries of subjectivity.

2.3   CERTAIN NON-UNIVERSAL INTER-GOVERNMENTAL ORGANIZATIONS

It is interesting to note that, one year before the Court's *Reparations* opinion was handed down, states had completed their work at the United Nations Conference on Trade and Development, held in Havana, Cuba, from 21 November 1947 to 24 March 1948, and drafted a Charter to establish an International Trade Organization (ITO). Although the organization was never established, the states had at that time included an express provision entitled 'International Legal Status of the Organization'. Article 89 read: 'The Organization shall have such legal personality and shall enjoy such legal capacity as may be necessary for the exercise of its functions.'[39] Another Article set out the legal status in the territory of the members, and follows the wording of Articles 104 and 105(1) of the UN Charter. By highlighting the 'International Legal Status' of the organization in the ITO Charter, the membership seemed to imagine international legal personality which went beyond the separate legal status that an organization might have *vis-à-vis* its members or enjoy in the national legal order of its members. The capacity to exercise its functions was a further quality bestowed on the organization. It would appear that there are two different qualities for any entity: explicit legal personality (international or national), and necessary legal capacity for the fulfilment of functions accorded to the entity. The Marrakesh Agreement of 1994 which established the World Trade Organization separates these two aspects with a comma. Article VIII entitled 'Status of the WTO' starts as follows: '1. The WTO shall have legal personality, and shall be accorded by each of its Members such legal capacity as may be necessary for the exercise of its functions.' The Rome Statute of the International Criminal Court of 1998 elegantly further divides the qualities: international legal personality, necessary legal capacity, and powers and functions within different states:

Article 4 Legal status and powers of the Court.

1. The Court shall have international legal personality. It shall also have such legal capacity as may be necessary for the exercise of its functions and the fulfilment of its purposes.
2. The Court may exercise its functions and powers, as provided in this Statute, on the territory of any State party and, by special agreement, on the territory of any other State.

[39] Art. 89, Final Act and Related Documents, Interim Commission for the International Trade Organization, Lake Success, New York, April 1948.

Other treaties for non-universal organizations create similar separations between the assertion of legal personality and the legal capacities to be accorded to the entity in the national legal orders of the member states.[40] One recent treaty, however, the Treaty Establishing a Constitution for Europe, simply states: 'The Union shall have legal personality.'[41]

We might then conclude that, whereas a special case was made for the United Nations in 1949 due to its universal mission, any more general rule concerning the rights and duties of international organizations is difficult to draw. Even where treaties explicitly confer international legal personality, it is hard to understand what this really means in terms of substantive rights and obligations on the international plane. There is clarity only in relation to the status in the national law of the member states, and this takes effect according to the domestic legal systems of the member states.

2.4   ACQUIRING RIGHTS AND DUTIES THROUGH CAPACITY RATHER THAN SUBJECTIVITY

Personality is a central concept in domestic legal systems which allows judges to know whether an entity exists for the purposes of the national legal system. Each system may have its own particularities ('Rights have been ascribed to white elephants in Siam and cats in Egypt').[42] By contrast, international law has *doctrinal filters* for determining personality/subjectivity. The list of subjects of international

---

[40] Art. 281 of the Treaty Establishing the European Community reads: 'The Community shall have legal personality.' Art. 282 reads: 'In each of the Member States, the Community shall enjoy the most extensive legal capacity accorded to legal persons under their laws; it may, in particular, acquire or dispose of movable property and may be a party to legal proceedings. To this end, the Community shall be represented by the Commission.' With regard to the question of the EU's legal personality, see J. Klabbers, 'Presumptive Personality: The European Union in International Law' in M. Koskenniemi (ed) *International Law Aspects of the of the European Union* (The Hague: Kluwer, 1998) 231–253; see also E. Cannizzaro (ed) *The European Union as an Actor in International Relations* (The Hague: Kluwer, 2002) particularly the contribution by C. Tomuschat, 'The International Responsibility of the European Union', at 177–191, esp. at 183, where it is asserted that the EU is subject to the rules that govern international organizations and 'Because of the proximity of the EU to States proper, one might even think of applying to it the traditional rules governing state conduct'. In his *General Course on Public International Law*, Tomuschat addressed the particularities of the EU, as opposed to the European Community, and argued that the EU must be liable for violations of international law: 'the European Union lacks the autonomy which characterizes an international organization proper. It partakes more of the nature of an international conference. And yet, in cases where it acts under its name of European Union at the international level, for instance by issuing declarations on a given situation, it could not escape international responsibility if it committed a wrong by such an act. Member States may withhold rights of active participation in international life, but they cannot thereby shield their creation from becoming liable towards other subjects of international law on account of its activities'. *International Law: Ensuring the Survival of Mankind on the Eve of a New Century*, vol. 281 *RCADI* (The Hague: Martinus Nijhoff, 2001) at 131–132.

[41] Art. I–7, EU Doc. CIG 87/2/04, Rev. 2, 29 October 2004.

[42] O. H. Phillips, *A First Book of English Law* (London: Sweet & Maxwell, 2nd edn, 1953) at 252.

law is determined by the text-book writers and not by any authoritative decision-making body. Even if bodies such as the International Court of Justice and the International Tribunal for the former Yugoslavia have pronounced on the topics of subject and personality, this can only represent an *ad hoc* declaration of the situation rather than a constitutive act creating personality. As Klabbers concludes: 'After all is said and done, personality in international law, like "subjectivity", is but a descriptive notion: useful to describe a state of affairs, but normatively empty, as neither rights nor obligations flow automatically from a grant of personality.'[43]

Let us abandon for the moment the concepts of subjectivity and personality and instead consider the status of non-state actors in the following contexts: first, does the entity have the requisite legal capacity directly to acquire rights and obligations under international law? And, second, in what circumstances do these actors have the capacity to be party to a claim (either as a claimant or as a defendant) at the international level?

For Daniel O'Connell:

> Capacity implies personality, but always it is capacity *to do those particular acts*. Therefore 'personality' as a term is only shorthand for the proposition that an entity is endowed by international law with legal capacity. But entity A may have capacity to perform acts X and Y, but not act Z, entity B to perform acts Y and Z but not act X, and entity C to perform all three. 'Personality' is not, therefore, a synonym for capacity to perform acts X, Y and Z; it is an index, not of *capacity per se*, but of specific and different capacities.[44]

O'Connell asked us to admit that there are entities that do not enjoy all the capacities that states do under international law. From here he separated capacity from personality:

> So a State may have the capacity to do acts X, Y and Z, the United Nations to do acts Y and Z, the International Labour Organisation to do act X, and the human being to do acts X and Y. All four entities have capacities. To deny that all three have personality is to argue that only entities with all capacities are persons, an argument that removes all meaning from the term 'personality.' This was the error of generations of international lawyers who asserted that 'States only are the subjects of international law.'[45]

O'Connell's framing of the issue allows us to imagine a matrix with various non-state actors on the vertical axis and different international capacities on the horizontal axis. It is only a short jump from here to imagining that such non-state actors may have, not only the capacity to enjoy rights and obligations, but also the capacity to be held accountable for failure to fulfil those obligations to which they have been subjected. How to determine whether particular non-state actors have been subjected to international obligations is a difficult question.

---

[43] Klabbers (2002: 57).
[44] D. P. O'Connell, *International Law*, vol. 1 (London: Stevens and Sons, 2nd edn, 1970) at 81–82. [45] Ibid, at 82.

For Sir Hersch Lauterpacht, the opinion of the Permanent Court of International Justice with regard to the *Jurisdiction of Danzig Courts* meant that: 'The acquisition of treaty rights directly by individuals was made a function of the intention of the parties. The view that they can acquire rights only through the instrumentality of municipal law of States was rejected.'[46] The key passage from the opinion is as follows:

> It may be readily admitted that, according to a well established principle of international law, the *Beamtenabkommen*, being an international agreement, cannot as such, create direct rights and obligations for private individuals. But it cannot be disputed that the very object of an international agreement, according to the intention of the contracting Parties, may be the adoption by the parties of some definite rules creating individual rights and obligations and enforceable by the national courts.[47]

Lauterpacht developed a line of thinking which is convincing and far-reaching:

> It may also be noted, for the sake of completeness, that individuals are the real subjects of international duties not only when they act on behalf of the State. They are the subjects of international duties in all cases in which international law regulates directly the conduct of individuals as such. This applies, for instance, with regard to piracy. Individuals engaged in piracy break a rule of international law prohibiting piracy. They would not, but for the rule of international law, be subject to the jurisdiction of any foreign State into whose hands they fall. The position is analogous in cases in which in numerous anti-slavery and similar treaties the injunction is addressed directly to individuals or in which the contracting parties grant one another the right to punish offenders who are nationals of the other party.[48]

After explaining that individual members of the armed forces of a belligerent are directly subjects of the international laws of war, and that there will be no defence of superior orders where the crime is obvious and a generally recognized rule of international law, Lauterpacht goes on to outline the possibility of an evolving set of international duties for individuals as well as the philosophical logic of extending international duties beyond states:

> ...these examples show that there is nothing in the existing international law which makes it impossible for individuals to be directly subjects of international duties imposed on them as such. The question is one of technique and procedure which at present tends to impose upon the State as such the direct responsibility for the fulfilment of the object of the treaty. Secondly, reasons have been given why even in those cases in which States are formally made subjects of international duties, the actual centre of legal

---

[46] *The Development of International Law by the International Court* (London: Stevens, 1958; republished Cambridge: Grotius, 1982) at 175.

[47] *Pecuniary Claims of Danzig Railway Officials who have passed into the Polish Service, against the Polish Railways Administration. Advisory Opinion No. 15*, 3 March 1928, Series B, at pp 17–18.

[48] H. Lauterpacht, 'General Rules of the Law of Peace' in E. Lauterpacht (ed) *Collected Papers*, vol. 1 (Cambridge: Cambridge University Press, 1970) at 284. See also O'Connell (1970: 111–112) who separates the rights in national law from the question of whether customary international law creates rights in individuals.

and moral responsibility is in the individual and not in the metaphysical personality of the State. Decisive reasons of progress of international law and morality seem to favour that construction.[49]

Drawing on this approach, Theodor Meron has pointed to direct obligations created by humanitarian and human rights treaties.[50] He gives examples of such direct obligations for individuals: Article 5 of Geneva Convention IV and Articles 5(1) and 20 of the International Covenant on Civil and Political Rights. He separates these from the individual criminal responsibility which arises from grave breaches of the Geneva Conventions.[51] Meron accepts that 'the imposition of direct rights and responsibilities on individuals, or on organizations, of course'[52] will raise the important question of the political and legal status of such organizations, and he highlights the refusal of states to apply Common Article 3 out of fears for their sovereignty.

The problem is not really a conceptual one. The issue is one of emphasis. As we saw in Chapter 1, there is a perception, among those opposed to this new emphasis on responsibilities, that governments are seeking to reorientate the human rights message so as to shift the focus away from their own responsibilities. In 2005, however, the Commission on Human Rights adopted the Basic Principles and Guidelines on the Right to a Remedy and Reparation for Victims of Gross Violations of International Human Rights Law and Serious Violations of International Humanitarian Law.[53] It is of interest that they include the following injunction: 'In cases where a person, a legal person, or other entity is found liable for reparation to a victim, such party should provide reparation to the victim or compensate the State if the State has already provided reparation to the victim.'[54] The liability of non-state actors is clearly admitted. Part of the explanation may lie in the conjunction of human rights and humanitarian law in the same normative text. Humanitarian law now knows no conceptual barrier to imposing duties on non-state actors;[55] the design of a set of principles focused on victims and their right to reparation would make little sense if it insisted on a doctrinal division between violations committed by non-state actors in times of armed conflict and violations committed during peace-time.

---

[49] Ibid, at 285.

[50] *Human Rights in Internal Strife: Their International Protection* (Cambridge: Grotius, 1987) at 33–40.

[51] See the grave breach provisions Arts 50, 51, 130, and 147 of the four Geneva Conventions respectively. One might also recall the criminal responsibility that stems from individual violations of Common Art. 3 to the four Conventions and the grave breach provision of Protocol I (Arts 85, 11(4)). [52] Ibid, at 36.

[53] See UN Doc. E/CN.4/RES/2005/35, adopted 19 April 2005.

[54] Ibid, Annex at para. 15.

[55] The detailed rules are discussed in Ch 7 below. For a clear statement that the non-state party to an armed conflict is bound by the international humanitarian law obligations found in Common Art. 3 to the Geneva Conventions of 1949 as well as Protocol II, see C. Greenwood, 'The Law of War (International Humanitarian Law)' in M. Evans (ed) *International Law* (Oxford: Oxford University Press, 2003) 789–823, at 816.

2.5 RIGHTS WITHOUT REMEDIES—DUTIES WITHOUT JURISDICTIONS

Of course not all treaties that mention individuals can be said to be intended to impose rights and obligations directly. But some treaties do have this effect, so that the individual can be said to acquire these rights without the intervention of municipal legislation.[56] This potential acquisition of rights on the international plane need not be made dependent on the existence of an international remedy. Although the international procedural rights granted to individuals and corporations can be said to highlight their 'status as actors on the international stage',[57] this status is not dependent on an institutionalized remedy. It is suggested that it is possible to enjoy a right without a remedy.[58] This already happens, for example, under human rights treaties where the state has failed to allow for the international tribunal to have jurisdiction over claims coming from individuals under its jurisdiction. The right exists during this period even if there is no procedural remedy at the international level. Once the procedural international remedy is granted by the state, the right becomes more effective, but the remedy does not generate the right. As Higgins points out, international lawyers are 'all too familiar with the realities of power, we have long had a vested interest in rejecting the Austinian and Kelsenian precept of the dependence of international law on the existence of effective sanction. I realize of course, that effective remedy and sanction are not wholly coterminous, and I simply make the point that we are not unaccustomed to separating our definition of a right from our appraisal of a remedy'.[59]

A recent example of a human rights treaty attempting to create duties for individuals and groups is the Optional Protocol to the Convention on the Rights of the Child on the involvement of children in armed conflicts. The issue arose as to whether the treaty should place obligations on armed opposition groups that recruit children who then participate in armed conflict. Interestingly, the conceptual confusion about the possibility of imposing duties through a human rights

---

[56] R. Jennings and A. Watts (eds) *Oppenheim's International Law*, vol. i (London: Longman, 9th edn, 1996) at 847.

[57] E. Lauterpacht 'International Law and Private Foreign Investment' (1998) available at http://www.law.indiana.edu/glsj/vol4/no2/laupgp.html, 12 pages, at p 9. He continues 'For decades the procedural incapacity of non-State entities was proclaimed as an article of faith. Today that incapacity is scarcely recognizable.'

[58] See further H. Lauterpacht (1970: 286–287) 'It is important not to exaggerate the importance of what is, in the last resort, a procedural rule. The faculty to enforce rights is not identical with the quality of a subject of law or of a beneficiary of its provisions. A person may be in possession of a plenitude of rights without at the same time being able to enforce them in his own name. This is a matter of procedural capacity. Infants and lunatics have rights; they are subjects of law. This is so although their procedural capacity is reduced to a minimum. Secondly, the rule preventing individuals from enforcing their rights before international tribunals is a piece of international machinery adopted for convenience. It is not a fundamental principle.'   [59] Higgins (1994: 53).

treaty split the drafters. For some governments, it was preferable to include a prohibition on the recruitment of children under 18 by non-governmental armed groups.[60] For others, this should be mentioned but could not be a legal obligation created by treaty. The state would simply have the treaty obligation to take all appropriate measures to prevent recruitment of persons under the age of 18 years by non-governmental armed groups involved in hostilities. The final version of the Protocol states in Article 4 that:

1. Armed groups that are distinct from the armed forces of a State, should not, under any circumstances, recruit or use in hostilities persons under the age of 18 years.
2. States Parties shall take all feasible measures to prevent such recruitment and use, including the adoption of legal measures necessary to prohibit and criminalize such practices.
3. The application of the present article under this Protocol shall not affect the legal status of any party to an armed conflict.

Some states wishing to see a stronger legal obligation preferred the word 'shall' instead of 'should'; and UN practice suggests that the use of *shall* in a treaty creates a 'harder' sense of obligation than the use of *should*, which arguably belongs to the category 'soft law'.[61] Using an interpretation that stresses ordinary meaning, the word 'should' normally denotes an obligation when addressed to a third person (here the opposition groups were not part of the treaty-making process). The difference between 'you should leave' and 'you shall leave' seems more semantic than substantive at this point. Moreover, the assertion that children should not be recruited or used *'under any circumstances'* makes it clear that the drafters intended to create an obligation that allowed for no derogation; it is suggested here that such language points to the strongest kind of international legal obligation, rather than a 'soft' non-binding exhortation.[62]

---

[60] See the position of Switzerland reported in the Report of the Working Group UN Doc. E/CN.4/1998/102, 23 March 1998, para. 41 and Colombia at para. 57, where the delegate suggests seeing human rights and humanitarian law as one universe in which the prime subject is the human person. The obligations which emanated from the draft, 'should not only be assumed by States but should also be extended to all parties involved in an armed conflict'. See also the report of the Working Group: '37. While some speakers argued that non-State parties could not be bound by an inter-State treaty and that it was therefore a matter to be dealt with through domestic law, another view was that the optional protocol should address non-State actors directly and provide for criminalization of their actions in cases where they were in violation of the protocol.' E/CN.4/2000/74, 27 March 2000. See also Brett (1998: 534).

[61] P. C. Szasz, 'General Law Making Processes' in O. Schachter and C. C. Joyner (eds) *United Nations Legal Order*, vol. 1 (Cambridge: Cambridge University Press, 1995) 35–108, at 46.

[62] According to Ulrika Sundberg, Minister at the Permanent Mission of Sweden to the UN in Geneva, the rules in the Protocol 'also apply to armed groups, distinct from armed forces'. She pointed to the lengthy debates during the drafting and characterized those as debates about whether the non-state actors could be bound by human rights law as opposed to international humanitarian law. The issue seems to be finessed by simply stating that the 'rules apply to armed groups'. Paper entitled 'The Role of the United Nations Commission on Human Rights in Armed Conflict Situations' presented to the XXXVIIIth Round Table on Current Problems of International Humanitarian Law, International Institute of Humanitarian Law, San Remo 2–4 September 2004. (The paper carries the usual disclaimer that it is written in a personal capacity.)

2.6　THE INTERNATIONAL COMMITTEE OF THE RED CROSS

A functional international personality similar to that of the United Nations has been claimed by the International Committee of the Red Cross,[63] and was recognized by the International Criminal Tribunal for the former Yugoslavia in a decision concerning the testimony of an ICRC witness.[64] Although the question of international personality was not contested by the prosecution, the evidence of the recognition of the international personality of the ICRC was presented as stemming from various factors: the recognition of the work of the ICRC in various treaties,[65] the ability of the ICRC to conclude treaties, and the capacity of the ICRC to enter into diplomatic relations through agreements which suggest that states treat ICRC delegations in the same way they would treat a diplomatic envoy from a state.[66] The third suggested criterion is the capacity to bring a claim at the international level under general international law.[67] Applying these criteria, Christian Dominicé concluded in 1984, that the ICRC has the capacity to fulfil these functions and that states recognize that the ICRC has these three essential capacities.[68]

2.7　THE LEGAL SUBJECTIVITY OF TRANSNATIONAL CORPORATIONS

There has been strong resistance to including entities such as transnational corporations in a discussion about the subjects of international law, and, until recently, it was hardly ever suggested that corporations have international legal personality.[69] Some legal scholars leave the question

[63] See the information document prepared by the ICRC for the Preparatory Commission for the Establishment of an International Criminal Court, 'The ICRC's Confidentiality Rule and the International Criminal Court', July 1999, at paras 19–35.

[64] *Prosecutor v Simic*, decision of 27 July 1999, at para. 35

[65] Geneva Convention relative to the Treatment of Prisoners of War 1929, and the four Geneva Conventions of 1949, and the First Protocol of 1977 to the 1949 Conventions.

[66] See C. Dominicé, 'La personalité juridique internationale du CICR' in C. Swinarski (ed) *Studies and essays on international humanitarian law and Red Cross principles in honour of Jean Pictet* (The Hague: Martinus Nijhoff, 1984) 663–673, at 669.　　[67] Ibid, at 670–671.

[68] Ibid, at 672. See also P. Reuter 'La personalité juridique internationale du Comité international de la Croix-Rouge' in C. Swinarski (ed) *Studies and essays on international humanitarian law and Red Cross principles in honour of Jean Pictet* (The Hague: Martinus Nijhoff, 1984) 783–791, who emphasizes the possibility of the ICRC concluding agreements which take effect according to the rules of public international law ('C'est bien pourquoi la possibilité de conclure des accords soumis à des régles du droit international public est la pierre de touche d'une personalité juridique internationale') (at 791).

[69] For an exception, see D. A. Ijalaye, *The Extension of Corporate Personality in International Law* (New York: Oceana, 1978) esp. 221–246. He reviews the increasing references to international law in the contracts concluded between corporations and states, evaluates the doctrinal response (of

open,[70] while others suggest that 'in principle' corporations do not have international personality.[71] Pierre-Marie Dupuy suggests that corporations enjoy a temporary and limited status on the international level, to the extent that they are given the right to defend rights accorded under special contracts in international arbitral bodies.[72] David Kinley and Junko Tadaki, having reviewed the rights and obligations of transnational corporations (TNCs) under international treaties, suggest that 'it is possible to invest in TNCs sufficient international legal personality to bear obligations, as much as to exercise rights'.[73] In 1983, Fatouros wrote 'it is possible for the international legal process to acknowledge that TNEs [transnational enterprises] are significant actors in the world economy and thus to recognize that they have a degree of legal capacity in international law'.[74] He concluded his review: 'there is still considerable room for the exercise of legal ingenuity and originality in shaping new structures, informing new relationships, and to some extent, avoiding formalistic legal problems in the pursuit of the goals of a new, and more just, international legal and economic order'.[75]

It is possible to move beyond the self-imposed formalistic legal problem of subjectivity and concentrate on capacity. Moreover, even without an international

---

Friedmann, Schwarzenberger, Fatouros, Abi-Sabb, Mann, and McNair) and makes the following appeal: 'Since the participation of private corporations at the level of international law would now seem to be a *fait accompli*, international lawyers should stop being negative in their approach to this obvious fact. They must realize that as a result of these new arrivals in the international scene, the commercial law of nations, more than ever before, now constitutes a formidable challenger to international and comparative lawyers alike. It is only by their co-operation and positive contribution, (rather than by their cowardice, pessimism and conservatism, evident in their out-moded dogmas or concepts) that this new branch of law can be developed into an acceptable part of extension of public international law' (at 245). See also M. T. Kamminga, 'Holding Multinational Corporations Accountable for Human Rights Abuses: A Challenge for the EC' in P. Alston, M. Bustelo, and J. Heenan (eds) *The EU and Human Rights* (Oxford: Oxford University Press, 1999) 553–569.

[70] M. Shaw, *International Law* (Cambridge: Cambridge University Press, 5th edn, 2003) at 255. Theodor Meron reviews some of the scholarship but eschews the terminology of subjects and personality in favour of considering participants and the scope of participation in the system of international law, *International Law in the Age of Human Rights—General Course on Public International Law*, vol. 301 *RCADI* (Leiden: Martinus Nijhoff, 2004) at 336–340 and 369–372. See also A. A. Fatouros, who, writing in 1987, compares a 'number of writers' who have 'suggested that current developments and arrangements point to the possible emergence of transnational enterprises as relatively independent legal entities, possessing a degree of legal capacity' with 'a solid majority of scholars and . . . the apparent totality of governments' that reject this view 'at least as far as any explicit recognition of their international status is concerned'. 'National Legal Persons in International Law' in R. Bernhardt (ed) *Encyclopedia of Public International Law*, vol. 1 (Amsterdam: Elsevier, 1997) 495–501, at 500.

[71] I. Brownlie, *Principles of Public International Law* (Oxford: Oxford University Press, 6th edn, 2003) at 65.

[72] P.-M. Dupuy, *L'unité de l'ordre juridique international: Cours général de droit international public*, vol. 297 *RCADI* (Leiden: Martinus Nijhoff, 2002) at 105 (with specific reference to *Texaco v Libya* 53 ILR [1977] 389) and at 117 as a provisional conclusion.

[73] D. Kinley and J. Tadaki, 'From Talk to Walk: the Emergence of Human Rights Responsibilities for Corporations at International Law' 44 *VJIL* (2004) 931–1022, at 947.

[74] A. A. Fatouros, 'Transnational Enterprise in the Law of State Responsibility' in R. B. Lillich (ed) *International Law of State Responsibility for Injuries to Aliens* (Charlottesville, Virg: University Press of Virginia, 1983) 361–403, at 389.　　　　　　　　　　[75] Ibid, at 390–391.

jurisdiction, the acts of corporations can be regarded as international crimes (recall the discussion at the Rome Conference in 1998 discussed at the beginning of Chapter 1) and it therefore makes complete sense to talk about limited international personality. Resistance to the recognition of international legal personality for corporations owes much to two fears. First is a fear that foreign corporations would somehow be able more easily to interfere in the political and economic affairs of states if they were acknowledged to possess a degree of international legal personality. Second is a fear that these foreign corporations would be able to trigger excessive diplomatic protection for national companies of the host state where the foreign nationals are controlling shareholders in those national companies.

Georges Abi-Saab has suggested that proponents of international legal personality for companies display theoretical incoherence by suggesting that 'internationalizing' contracts between governments and alien companies allows one to conclude that the company has achieved international personality.[76] For him, the additional argument that 'transnational law' has elevated the status of multinationals is unconvincing due to the absence of a separate transnational legal order which is more than 'an amalgam of rules' from which the judge makes 'an eclectic choice'. For Peter Malanczuk, the problem is that: 'A unilateral elevation by the host state of the foreign company to the international level is not possible because it would also interfere with the rights of the home state of the company.'[77] This interference would occur 'whether this State is determined on the basis of the seat theory, the control theory or any other theory relevant to the difficult problem of identification of the nationality of multinational companies'.[78] Malanczuk sees such an attempted elevation as an attempt to create a subject of international law having *erga omnes* effect.[79] His conclusion is clear but does not actually depart from our suggestion that we look at capacity and discreet obligations:

> Multinational companies are still formally not 'subjects of international law' in any meaningful sense of the term, although there is limited recognition of their legal personality in certain dispute settlement mechanisms. As such, their existence is barely recognized by general international law (in contrast to a few . . . special soft law instruments aiming at the regulation of their activities).[80]

Similarly, Antonio Cassese has suggested that 'States have not upgraded these entities [private companies] to international subjects proper'. Writing in 1986, he stated:

> Socialist countries are politically opposed to them and the majority of developing countries are suspicious of their power; both groups will never allow them to play an

---

[76] See G. Abi-Saab, 'The International Law of Multinational Corporations: A Critique of American Legal Doctrines' *Annales d'études internationales* (1971) 97–122.

[77] *Akehurst's Modern Introduction to International Law* (London: Routledge, 7th edn, 1997) at 102.

[78] P. Malanczuk, 'Multinational Enterprises and Treaty-making—A Contribution to the Discussion on Non-State Actors and the "Subjects of International Law"' in V. Gowlland-Debbas (ed) *Multilateral Treaty-Making: The Current Status of Challenges to and Reforms Needed in the International Legislative Process* (The Hague: Martinus Nijhoff, 2000) 45–72, at 62.

[79] Ibid, at 62.   [80] Malanczuk (2000: 71).

autonomous role in international affairs. Even Western countries are reluctant to grant them international standing; they prefer to keep them under their control—of course, to the extent that this is possible. It follows that multinational corporations possess no international rights and duties: they are only subjects of municipal and 'transnational law'.[81]

Wolfgang Friedmann suggested that any such extension of subjectivity is subversive and as untenable as eliminating the public/private division in national law. But he contrasted the suggestion that corporations should have a legal status equivalent to international organizations with the 'entirely different proposition' that private corporations 'acquire a limited *ad hoc* subjectivity to the extent that their transactions are controlled by the norms of public rather than private international law'.[82]

These concerns lose much of their sting when one reorientates the issue and simply asserts that corporations have limited international legal personality rather than pretending that multinationals are proper/primary subjects of international law with the 'status' that implies. As long as we admit that individuals have rights and duties under customary international human rights law and international humanitarian law, we have to admit that legal persons may also possess the international legal personality necessary to enjoy some of these rights, and conversely to be prosecuted or held accountable for violations of the relevant international duties.[83]

By definition, a corporation has legal personality under the national law of the state of its incorporation or establishment. Various theories have been put forward to explain how and why corporations achieve this status. These theories often emerge in the context of seeking a justification in political morality to ensure constitutional rights and privileges for corporations in national jurisdiction.[84] Some have emphasized the idea that the corporation owes its origin to individuals and so takes on some of the rights and duties of those individuals. Others focus on the centrality of the corporation in the market as an actor with contractual relations. This approach starts from the premise that all jurisdictions have a form

---

[81] *International Law in a Divided World* (1986) at 103. In his later book, *International Law* (Oxford: Oxford University Press, 2nd edn, 2005), Cassese avoids any discussion of the status of corporations in international law. In his conclusion to the chapter 'Other international legal subjects', corporations are perhaps conspicuous by their absence: 'To differentiate the position of individuals from that of States, it can be maintained that while States have international legal personality proper, individuals possess a *limited* locus standi *in international law*. Furthermore, unlike States, individuals possess a limited array of rights and obligations, that is, a *limited legal capacity* (to some extent they can therefore be equated with other non-State international subjects: insurgents, international organizations, and national liberation movements)' (at 150).

[82] W. Friedmann, *The Changing Structure of International Law* (London: Stevens and Sons, 1964) at 223.

[83] Civil actions brought against companies in the US for violations of international law represent torts in federal common law and under the Alien Claims Tort Act. The cases are discussed in more detail in Ch 6, at 6.8 and Ch 10, at 10.1.1 below.

[84] R. A. Shiner, *Freedom of Commercial Expression* (Oxford: Oxford University Press, 2003) at 178–191 outlines and criticizes the following theories: the legal fiction theory, the moral agency theory based on internal decision-making, the partnership theory, and the contract theory.

of corporate law. 'The first and most important contribution of corporate law, as of other forms of organizational law, is to permit a firm to serve [as a nexus of contracts for suppliers and consumers] by providing for the creation of a legal person—a contracting party distinct from the various individuals who own or manage the firm, or are suppliers or customers of the firm.'[85] Both approaches can be criticized for failing to appreciate the impact of the corporation beyond corporate law and the corporation's contractual relations. My approach appeals to the effectiveness principle. If international law is to be effective in protecting human rights, everyone should be prohibited from assisting governments in violating those principles, or indeed prohibited from violating such principles themselves.

References to the subjects of international law are obviously misleading. Conflating the question of subjectivity with the concepts of international legal personality and international capacity has prevented a clear appreciation of the fact that non-state actors can bear international rights and obligations (even where they have no state-like characteristics or pretensions). Trying to squeeze international actors into the state-like entities box is, at best, like trying to force a round peg into a square hole, and at worst, means overlooking powerful actors on the international stage.[86] While the ICRC can claim to fulfil some of the criteria for international personality, by highlighting the quasi-diplomatic nature of some of its activities and the similarity with other international organizations recognized in international law, such as the United Nations, other organizations with very different characteristics have succeeded in making claims directly against states in the past (consider the arbitration between Greenpeace and France over the *Rainbow Warrior*, where France was responding to an allegation of an international delict rather than a breach of contract). When we leave the arena of treaty making, diplomatic relations, and immunity before the courts we see a panoply of possible legal rights and obligations which can be applied to non-state actors without suggesting that they have state-like qualities or privileges. In fact, if we turn to treaty law, a raft of non-state actors have acquired rights and may enjoy the legal capacity to bring a claim before an international instance under various treaties, including the European Convention on Human Rights.[87]

---

[85] H. Hansmann and R. Kraakman, 'What is Corporate Law?' in R. Kraakman, P. Davies, H. Hansmann, G. Hertig, K. Hopt, H. Kanda, and E. Rock (eds) *The Anatomy of Corporate Law: A Comparative and Functional Approach* (Oxford: Oxford University Press, 2004) 1–19, at 7.

[86] Some commentators see the formalism of the subjects debate as a deliberate way of rendering transnational corporations invisible. See Claire A. Cutler, 'Critical Reflections on the Westphalian assumptions of international law and organization: a crisis of legitimacy' 27 *Review of International Studies* (2001) 133–150, at 147.

[87] See Art. 34: 'The Court may receive applications from any person, non-governmental organization or group of individuals claiming to be the victim of a violation by one of the High Contracting Parties of the rights...' According to Jacobs and White: 'The term "person" [*personne physique* in the French text] includes only natural persons but an application may be brought by any corporate or unincorporated body. Thus applications have been brought by companies, trade unions, churches, political parties, and numerous other types of body. Article 25 [now Article 34] should be understood as excluding from the right of petition only governmental bodies, whose rights are protected, if only

2.8   INTERNATIONAL CAPACITY DERIVED FROM THE RIGHTS OF NON-STATE ACTORS TO COMPLAIN TO INTERNATIONAL INSTANCES UNDER TREATY LAW

Interestingly, in some circumstances it may only be the company and not its individual or corporate shareholders who can complain to the European Court of Human Rights. The Court recognizes, in some cases, the *legal person* as the *only appropriate victim* who can make the application and has stated that shareholders are not entitled to apply to the Court under the Convention.[88] In an authoritative article, Krüger and Nørgaard explain that the jurisprudence of the European Commission determined that in the Convention's Article regarding victims as extending to legal persons: 'legal persons come under the concept of "non-governmental organizations" '.[89] The Court's case-law has included numerous cases brought by corporations acting as NGOs in this way. One of the seminal judgments of the European Court of Human Rights was *Sunday Times v United Kingdom*, the first applicant being Times Newspapers Ltd.[90] The term 'non-governmental organizations'

against infringement by other States, under Article 24 [now Article 33]. A corporate body has some but not all of the rights of individuals: thus it has the right to fair trial under Article 6, to protection of its correspondence under Article 8, and is expressly granted property rights under Article 1 of the First Protocol, but it does not have the right to education under Article 2.' (Footnotes omitted). *The European Convention on Human Rights* (Oxford: Clarendon Press, 2nd edn, 1996) at 349. According to Gomien, Harris, and Zwaak 'Local authorities and other autonomous or semi-autonomous governmental bodies' do not come within the non-governmental organizations category in Art. 34 ECHR. *Law and Practice of the European Convention on Human Rights and the European Social Charter* (Strasbourg: Council of Europe, 1996) at 43. See further Ch 9 at 9.1.10. The full sentence in Art. 34 in French reads: 'La Cour peut être saisie d'une requête par toute personne physique, toute organisation non gouvernementale ou tout groupe de particuliers qui se prétend victime d'une violation par l'une des Hautes Parties contractantes des droits reconnus dans la Convention ou ses Protocoles.' The Convention on the Settlement of Investment Disputes between States and Nationals of Other States (1965) is clear that natural and juridical persons may under certain circumstances consent in writing to a dispute being submitted to the Centre established under the Treaty. E. Lauterpacht (1998) has highlighted the important theoretical point that since the creation of the Additional Facility, which allows for the settlement of disputes even where the state of nationality of the investor is not a party to the treaty, it is clear that the ICSID system is not dependent on a treaty relationship between the host state and the state of nationality of the investor.

[88] *Case of Agrotexim and ors v Greece*, judgment of 24 October 1995: 'the Court considers that the piercing of the "corporate veil" or the disregarding of a company's legal personality will be justified only in exceptional circumstances, in particular where it is clearly established that it is impossible for the company to apply to the Convention institutions through the organs set up under its articles of incorporation or—in the event of liquidation—through its liquidators.' (at para. 66). Judge Walsh dissented: 'It appears to me to be anomalous that the defence of human rights in the field of property, or otherwise, should yield to the commercially sacred impenetrability of the "corporate veil" ' (at para. 3 of the dissenting opinion).

[89] H. C. Krüger and C. A. Nørgaard, 'The Right of Application', in R. St J. Macdonald, F. Matscher, and H. Petzold (eds) *The European System for the Protection of Human Rights* (Dordrecht: Nijhoff, 1993) 657–675, at 666.   [90] Judgment of 29 March 1979.

has been interpreted to allow applications from bodies that have no legal personality under national law. Partnerships, associations, or even unregistered associations that have been denied the right to constitute themselves as associations have been able to bring applications under the European Convention. The jurisprudence has produced a curious public/private distinction. 'The "non-governmental" character of the organizations concerned means that they must not be public corporations participating in the exercise of State power.'[91] Yet religious organizations that are recognized as public law corporations can lodge applications, and it apparently flows from this that the action of a church incorporated as a public law corporation is not attributable to the state for the purposes of an application concerning an alleged violation by the church. The 'publicness' of the public law corporation is not enough to bar it from bringing an application,[92] and it is not enough to imply direct state responsibility under the Convention. Where allegations are brought against the behaviour of a church, the European Convention institutions will search to see if the state has fulfilled its positive obligations in the field, rather than imputing the action to the state.

2.9   FINAL REMARKS ON THE INTERNATIONAL LAW OBLIGATIONS OF NON-STATE ACTORS

We have argued that various non-state entities today have enough international legal personality to enjoy directly rights and obligations under general international law as well as under treaties. The burden would now seem to be on those who claim that states are the sole bearers of human rights obligations under international law to explain away the obvious emergence onto the international scene of a variety of actors with sufficient international personality to be the bearers of rights and duties under international law. If *The Sunday Times* has sufficient personality and the capacity to enjoy rights under the European Convention on Human Rights, it might surely have enough personality and capacity to be subject to duties under international human rights law. Similarly, if non-governmental organizations can claim their internationally protected rights in multiple international fora, they might also have the capacity to be the bearers of appropriate international obligations.[93]

I agree with Klabbers in his suggestion that 'the existence of certain rights, privileges, powers or immunities may lead to the conclusion that the entity concerned

---

[91] Krüger and Nørgaard (1993: 666).

[92] *The Holy Monasteries v Greece*, judgment of 9 December 1994, European Court of Human Rights.

[93] See K. Nowrot, 'Legal Consequences of Globalization: The Status of Non-Governemental Organizations Under International Law' 6 *Global Legal Studies Journal* (1999) 579–645, who concludes after a lengthy survey of the international arrangements for NGOs that these can 'be regarded as partial subjects of international law, with the consequence that they are also bound by the norms of the international legal order applicable to them' (at 635).

may be classified as an international legal person'.⁹⁴ I suggest that we concentrate on the rights and obligations of entities rather than their personality. A starting point may be the International Court of Justice's assertion that international organizations are subject to 'general rules of international law'.⁹⁵ As Tomuschat points out, it makes little sense to look for evidence of custom in this context.

> Generally, customary international law has evolved through practice in dealings between States. Consequently, it could be argued that international organizations, being autonomous subjects of international law, cannot be bound by such rules in whose formation they did not participate. The rationale behind this argument is far from convincing, however. Substantively, international organizations may be characterized as common agencies operated by States for the fulfilment of certain common tasks. Now, if States acting individually have been subjected to certain rules thought to be indispensable for maintaining orderly relations within the international community, there is no justification for exempting international organizations from the scope *ratione personae* of such rules.⁹⁶

Tomuschat notes that the European Community is bound by 'general rules of customary international law',⁹⁷ that NATO is 'bound to respect the humanitarian rules applicable in armed conflict',⁹⁸ and that military units under the command of the United Nations are subject to the 'general rules of humanitarian law governing international armed conflict'.⁹⁹ Dismissing arguments that Security Council operations could be described as police actions for the re-establishment of international peace and security, he concludes: 'Even those engaged in "just" military action are therefore bound to abide by the minimum requirements of humanity.'¹⁰⁰

I am simply suggesting that these rules, applicable to international organizations, include the customary international law of human rights. Just as the rules of humanitarian law have not been specifically extended to international organizations, so the customary international law of human rights has remained state-focused. Many agree that, even if states can limit the powers of the organization they create, they 'cannot thereby shield their creation from becoming liable towards other subjects of international law on account of its activities'.¹⁰¹

---

⁹⁴ Klabbers (1998: 253).
⁹⁵ *Interpretation of the Agreement of 25 March 1951 Between the WHO and Egypt* (1980) ICJ Reports 73, at 89–90 (quoted in 2.2 above).   ⁹⁶ Tomuschat (2001: 34–35).
⁹⁷ Ibid, at 137.   ⁹⁸ Ibid, at 137.   ⁹⁹ Ibid, at 137.   ¹⁰⁰ Ibid, at 137.
¹⁰¹ Ibid, at 129–130.

3

Characteristics of International Human Rights Law

This chapter invites the reader to take a fresh look at the way human rights are classified. Rather than seeing human rights as belonging to 'generations', I suggest a new typology which concentrates on the legal characteristics of the right rather than its historical or philosophical foundations. This categorization allows us to see what obligations might formally bind a non-state actor. I suggest that it makes sense to look at six overlapping types of human rights law and to allow for the evolution of certain hybrids which combine these types and their characteristics. I shall consider human rights under the following headings: customary/general international law, *jus cogens*, treaty law, international crimes, *erga omnes*, and inter-governmental standards.

3.1 CUSTOMARY INTERNATIONAL LAW

Although today less attention is given to the customary international law of human rights, due to the increasing ratification of the human rights treaties, it is suggested that renewed attention to the dynamics of customary international law is relevant for a number of reasons: first, not all states are parties to the relevant international treaties. Second, reservations to treaties may preclude international jurisdiction under treaty law. Third, customary international law is relevant to limit treaty derogations in situations of armed conflict, states of emergency, and other internal disturbances.[1] Fourth, some human rights treaties may contain specific clauses which entitle the control body to have regard to customary international law.[2] Fifth, customary international law may take effect as the law of the

---

[1] Human rights treaties allow for certain derogations in situations of emergency but refer to other international obligations outside the treaty itself and demand that no state party may derogate from its treaty obligations in a way that violates its other international obligations. See, e.g. Art. 4 of the International Covenant on Civil and Political Rights 1966 and Human Rights Committee, General Comment 29 (states of emergency), 24 July 2001.

[2] See, e.g. Art. 61 of the African Charter of Human and Peoples' Rights 1981: 'The Commission shall also take into consideration, as subsidiary measures to determine the principles of law, other general or special international conventions, laying down rules expressly recognized by member states

land at the level of domestic law. (This means that, in contrast to treaty law, the national legal order may demand no specific implementing legislation and the rights and obligations may be enforceable in the national courts.) Sixth, customary international law may be more relevant than treaty law in terms of ensuring liability and accountability at the national level for non-state actors.[3]

Rules of customary law emerge when two essential criteria are met: first there must be some unambiguous and consistent practice by a state in a particular field (state practice), and second, the state must have followed that practice out of a sense of legal obligation (*opinio juris*).[4] In the field of human rights law, customary rules have evolved primarily from those norms that are considered to be universal in character and that are proclaimed in various international instruments. For example, several of the principles proclaimed in the Universal Declaration of Human Rights have acquired the status of customary international law, and are therefore legally binding. Although an ongoing debate exists over the extent to which each of the provisions of the Declaration have achieved customary law status, the rules prohibiting arbitrary killing, slavery, torture, detention, and systematic racial discrimination—such as apartheid—are now recognized as rules of customary international law binding on all states. Other rights, including the right to self-determination, the right to basic sustenance, freedom of opinion, equality rights, and the right to fair trial have entered the realm of customary international law, but the scope of the protection offered by the right and the permissible restrictions mean that a more detailed examination is required in order to determine the parameters of the customary obligations. A recent detailed study of the customary law nature of the rights in the Universal Declaration highlights the fact that, even if social and economic rights often receive less attention, certain economic and social rights in the Declaration 'enjoy sufficiently widespread support as to be at least potential candidates for rights recognized under customary international law: the right to free choice of employment; the right to form and join trade unions; and the right to free primary education, subject to a state's available resources'.[5]

of the Organization of African Unity, African practices consistent with international norms on human and people's rights, customs generally accepted as law, general principles of law recognized by African states as well as legal precedents and doctrine.'

³ For a discussion of the application of customary international law to corporations in the US domestic courts, see the Ch 6, at 6.7 and Ch 10, at 10.1.1 below.

⁴ Described in the Statute of the International Court of Justice as 'international custom, as evidence of a general practice accepted as law', Art. 38(1)(b).

⁵ H. Hannum, 'The Status of the Universal Declaration of Human Rights in National and International Law' 25 *Georgia Journal of International and Comparative Law* (1995/6) 287–397, at 349 (footnotes omitted). Philip Alston has suggested that with regard to economic, social, and cultural rights, it is possible to consider the adoption of the Millennium Declaration and the Millennium Development Goals (MDGs) as significant and that 'it can plausibly be claimed that at least some of the MDGs reflect norms of customary international law . . . it can be observed that the case would be most easily made in relation to the first six of the Goals. And parts at least of the seventh would also be strong candidates'. P. Alston, *A Human Rights Perspective on the Millennium*

As will be discussed in the following chapters, it is customary international law (what is sometimes referred to as general international law, as opposed to treaty law) that is often employed to hold non-state actors accountable under international law. Some international organizations are considered to have the necessary capacities to enjoy international rights and bear international obligations under general international law. The adjective 'general' is employed here because it is misleading to suggest that international organizations have generated these rights and obligations through 'custom'. It is not the sustained practice and sense of obligation that have generated the rights and duties of international organizations. The obligations arise because the international legal order considers these rights and obligations as generally applicable and binding on every entity that has the capacity to bear them. This process started with the 1946 Nuremberg Trial of the Major War Criminals (where individuals were held to have duties under international criminal law), was developed by the International Court of Justice through advisory opinions declaring the United Nations and its agencies as entities with international rights and obligations under general international law, and now finds its application in the litigation brought against corporations in the United States for violations of the 'law of nations'.

3.2   *JUS COGENS* OR PEREMPTORY NORMS OF INTERNATIONAL LAW

While, on the one hand, customary international law rules usually take time to evolve due the requirement that there is evidence of states acting out of a sense of legal obligation, on the other hand, *jus cogens* rules on human rights need to be simply accepted by the international community of states as a whole. Courts have been willing to accept, for example, that the prohibition on torture is a rule of *jus cogens* without a painstaking search for evidence of states acting out of a sense of legal obligation. The International Tribunal for the former Yugoslavia has not only asserted the prohibition of torture as a rule of *jus cogens*,[6] but also referred to the demands of humanity and the dictates of the public conscience, notions reflected in the judgments of the International Court of Justice and the Martens Clause,[7] to

---

Development Goals: Paper prepared as a contribution to the work of the Millennium Project Task Force on Poverty and Economic Development (2004) at para. 42, on file with the author. The customary law status of certain economic, social, and cultural rights is considered in greater detail in Ch 4, at 4.2.2 below.

   [6] *Prosecutor v Furundžija* Case IT–95–17/1–T, judgment of 10 December 1998, at paras 153ff.

   [7] This clause is found in slightly different forms in the 1899 Hague Convention Concerning the Laws or Customs of War on Land, the 1907 Hague Convention IV, and Art. 1(2) of Protocol I of 1977. This last version reads: 'In cases not covered by this Protocol or by other international agreements, civilians and combatants remain under the protection and authority of the principles of international law derived from established custom, from the principles of humanity and from the dictates of public conscience.' Note also the impossibility of avoiding these rules through denunciation of the Geneva Convention of 1949. Arts 63, 62, 142, and 158, of the four Geneva Conventions

suggest that these imperatives drive the necessary mental element (*opinio juris*) which heralds 'the emergence of a general rule or principle of humanitarian law'.[8] In the *Kupreskić* judgment, the Tribunal suggested that 'Due to the pressure exerted by the requirements of humanity and the dictates of public conscience, a customary rule of international law has emerged' (on the prohibition of reprisals against civilians in combat zones).[9] In short, our changing notions of what is considered humane can generate new binding rules in the field of international human rights and humanitarian law without recourse to the mysteries of evaluating state practice and *opinio juris*. But why single out some norms as *jus cogens* norms? And what norms are considered to fall within this variety of human rights law?

Chapter III of the International Law Commission's (ILC's) Articles on state responsibility is entitled 'Serious breaches of obligations under peremptory norms of general international law'. The Commentary states: 'Those peremptory norms that are clearly accepted and recognized include the prohibitions of aggression, genocide, slavery, racial discrimination, crimes against humanity and torture, and the right to self-determination'.[10] Other examples included in Commentary are 'the slave trade...and apartheid...the prohibition against torture as defined in article 1 of the Convention against Torture and Other Cruel, Inhuman or Degrading Treatment or Punishment...the basic rules of international humanitarian law applicable in armed conflict'.[11] This list is carefully described as exemplary rather than definitive. For completeness one should note that the UN Human Rights Committee has referred to the following as acts which would violate *jus cogens* norms: arbitrary deprivations of life, torture and inhuman and degrading treatment, taking hostages, imposing collective punishments, arbitrary deprivations of liberty, or deviating from fundamental principles of fair trial, including the presumption of innocence.[12]

---

respectively, state that denunciation shall 'in no way impair the obligations which the Parties to the conflict shall remain bound to fulfil by virtue of the principles of the law of nations, as they result from the usages established among civilized peoples, from the laws of humanity and the dictates of the public conscience'. See A. Cassese, 'The Martens Clause: Half a Loaf or Simply Pie in the Sky?' 11 *EJIL* (2000) 193–202; and V. Chetail, 'The contribution of the International Court of Justice to international humanitarian law' 85 (850) *IRRC* (2003) 235–269.

[8] *Prosecutor v Kupreskić* Case IT–95–16, judgment of 14 January 2000, at para. 527. 'This is however an area where *opinio iuris sive necessitatis* may play a much greater role than *usus*, as a result of the aforementioned Martens Clause. In the light of the way States and courts have implemented it, this Clause clearly shows that principles of international humanitarian law may emerge through a customary process under the pressure of the demands of humanity or the dictates of public conscience, even where State practice is scant or inconsistent. The other element, in the form of *opinio necessitatis*, crystallising as a result of the imperatives of humanity or public conscience, may turn out to be the decisive element heralding the emergence of a general rule or principle of humanitarian law.'

[9] Ibid, at para. 531.

[10] Commentary to Art. 26, para. 5. Report of the ILC, GAOR, Supp. No 10 (A/56/10) p 208.

[11] Commentary to Art. 40, paras 3–5, ibid, at pp 283–284.

[12] See General Comment 29, Art. 4: Derogations during a state of emergency, at para. 11, adopted 24 July 2001, UN Doc. HRI/GEN/1/Rev.6, 12 May 2003.

To fall within this Chapter of the ILC's Articles (special obligations) the violations of the peremptory norms have to involve 'a gross or systematic failure by the responsible State to fulfil the obligation' (Article 40(2)). According to the Commentary: 'To be regarded as systematic, a violation would have to be carried out in an organized and deliberate way. In contrast, the term "gross" refers to the intensity of the violation or its effects; it denotes violations of a flagrant nature, amounting to a direct and outright assault on the values protected by the rule.'[13] The consequences of such a serious breach are set out in Article 41. States have to cooperate to bring the serious breach to an end and no state shall recognize as lawful such a breach nor render aid or assistance in maintaining that situation. This regime for serious breaches has obvious implications for holding all states accountable for allowing serious human rights violations to be perpetrated by any other state.

The ILC has also included a reference to *jus cogens* with regard to circumstances precluding wrongfulness and the lawfulness of counter-measures. Counter-measures may not affect *jus cogens* obligations (Article 50(1)(d)). In the words of the Commentary, 'for example, a genocide cannot justify a counter-genocide'.[14] With regard to a conflict with a pre-existing treaty obligation which is not by its terms contrary to *jus cogens*, the ILC seems to suggest that a state will be justified in refusing to comply with a treaty obligation where its observance is incompatible with a *jus cogens* prohibition.[15] Antonio Cassese has highlighted the approach of the Swiss Tribunal Fédéral which prioritized the *jus cogens* norm concerning the prohibition of torture over a binding obligation contained in a bilateral extradition treaty.[16] Nevertheless, this is not an area replete with state practice. The ILC's Commentary deals with the conflict of norms question in fairly terse terms: 'Where there is an apparent conflict between primary obligations, one of which arises for a State directly under a peremptory norm of general international law, it is evident that such an obligation must prevail. The processes of interpretation and application should resolve such questions without any need to resort to the secondary rules of State responsibility.'[17]

In addition to these consequences, under the rules of state responsibility (and one can expect that similar rules will be codified or developed with regard to the responsibility of international organizations)[18] a number of further consequences arise when human rights abuses fall into the category of *jus cogens*. First, under the

---

[13] Ibid, para. 8 at p 285.

[14] Commentary to Art. 26, at para. 4. Report of the ILC, GAOR, Supp. No. 10 (A/56/10) at p 208. We should add that Art. 50 also excludes counter-measures that affect 'obligations for the protection of fundamental human rights' and 'obligations of a humanitarian character prohibiting reprisals'.   [15] Commentary to Art. 26, at para. 2, ibid, at p 207, citing Fitzmaurice.

[16] *International Law*, (Oxford: Oxford University Press 2nd edn, 2005) at 210–211.

[17] Commentary to Art. 26 at para. 4. Report of the ILC, GAOR, Supp. No. 10 (A/56/10) at p 207.

[18] See the reports of the Special Rapporteur of the ILC on responsibility of international organizations, Giorgio Gaja, UN Docs A/CN.4/532, 26 March 2003; A/CN.4/541, 2 April 2004; and A/CN.4/553, 13 May 2005.

law of treaties developed through the two Vienna Conventions, a treaty may be held to be invalid if it conflicts with a norm of *jus cogens*.[19] This should apply not only for inter-state treaties but also for treaties entered into by international organizations.[20] This is, of course, further evidence that international organizations have obligations to respect certain human rights norms. But the implications for treaty law probably go beyond the drastic scenario of a treaty being held to be void as conflicting with *jus cogens*. Cassese has suggested that a court 'will simply *disregard* or declare *null and void* a single treaty provision that is contrary to *jus cogens*, if the remaining provisions of the treaty are not tainted with the same invalidity'.[21] He also suggests that 'a court may be led to *construe* a treaty provision possessing a dubious scope in a sense consistent with a peremptory norm on the matter, rather than in any other sense.'[22]

Second, violations of *jus cogens* have been invoked outside the law of treaties, with regard to the accountability of state and non-state actors, particularly individuals. It is the non-state actor's violation of international law that is at issue; the responsibility of any state for the acts of that individual is not determinative of the individual responsibility under international law. In fact, even where the individual has no state function (or is operating as a non-state actor) the *jus cogens* norms may apply, with consequences not only for the individual (in this case individual criminal responsibility discussed below), but also for other actors. The International Criminal Tribunal for the former Yugoslavia, in the *Furundžija* case, explained some special consequences that arise in the context of a violation of the *jus cogens* norm of torture: first, the higher rank of the principle at issue means that it cannot be derogated from by states through treaties or customary international law;[23] second, the principle serves to internationally de-legitimize any legislative, administrative, or judicial act authorizing torture;[24] third, 'the victim could bring a civil suit for damage in a foreign court, which would therefore be asked *inter alia* to disregard the legal value of the national authorising act';[25] fourth, 'at the individual level, that is, that of criminal liability, it would seem that one of the consequences of the *jus cogens* character bestowed by the international community upon the prohibition of torture is that every State is entitled to investigate, prosecute and punish or extradite individuals accused of torture, who are present in a territory under its jurisdiction'.[26] Lastly, the Tribunal mentions that 'other consequences include the fact that torture may not be covered by a statute of

---

[19] See Vienna Convention on the Law of Treaties (1969) Arts 53, 64, 65, and 66(a) (this last provision establishes the jurisdiction of the ICJ with regard to disputes concerning *jus cogens* in this context). See also Vienna Convention on the Law of Treaties Between States and International Organizations or Between International Organizations (1986) (not yet in force) Arts 53, 64, 65, and 66 (the provisions regarding the ICJ provide for an advisory opinion where one or more parties to the dispute is an international organization).   [20] See the Vienna Convention of 1986 (n 19 above).

[21] Cassese (2005: 206).   [22] Ibid.

[23] IT–95–17/1–T, Judgment of 10 December 1998, at para. 153.   [24] Ibid, at para. 155.

[25] Ibid, at para. 155.   [26] Ibid, at para. 156.

limitations, and must not be excluded from extradition under any political offence exemption'.[27]

As we shall see, the notion of *jus cogens* has also been commented on in national courts, not only with regard to issues of immunity and criminal jurisdiction over individuals, as highlighted in the *Furundžija* case, but also with regard to the obligations of corporations under violations of the customary/general international law, or as the US Alien Tort Claims Act terms it, the 'law of nations'.[28]

3.3   HUMAN RIGHTS TREATIES

Human rights treaties codify and develop international human rights and obligations. A human rights treaty can give rise to a number of legal effects.

First, it creates a set of multilateral obligations between the parties to the treaty. For the moment, human rights treaties are confined to states parties, but the European Union may yet become a party to the European Convention on Human Rights, and Protocol 14 to that treaty has already been adopted by the states of the Council of Europe in order to make this possible.[29] It therefore makes sense to talk about the *parties* to a human rights treaty rather than use the expression *states parties*, which suggests that states are the exclusive members of every human rights treaty regime.

Any party to a human rights treaty can complain about a violation by another party. The complaining party would not have to show that it was a direct victim or that it had an interest in the alleged violation. In some cases, such as the Conventions on the Elimination of All Forms of Racial Discrimination (CERD) and on the Elimination of All Forms of Discrimination against Women (CEDAW), as well as the International Convention on the Protection of the Rights of All Migrant Workers and Members of their Families, the treaty includes a provision for the eventual settlement of unresolved disputes by the International Court of Justice.[30] The International Covenant on Civil and Political Rights (ICCPR) and the Convention Against Torture and Other Cruel, Inhuman or Degrading Treatment or Punishment (CAT) provide for an optional procedure of state complaints to the relevant Committee, which can result in an *ad hoc* Conciliation Commission.[31] The Covenant explicitly states that states parties may use other procedures for the settlement of disputes in accordance with the

---

[27] Ibid, at para. 157, footnotes omitted.

[28] See, e.g. *The Presbyterian Church of Sudan et al v Talisman Energy Inc, Republic of the Sudan*, Civil Action 01 CV 9882 (AGS), US District Court for the Southern District of New York, order of 19 March 2003, esp. p 47, discussed in Ch 10, at 10.1.1 below.

[29] See Protocol 14 to the European Convention on Human Rights (ECHR) (2004) Art. 17. Note also Art. I–9(2) of the Treaty Establishing a Constitution for Europe (2004) discussed in Ch 5, at 5.2.2.2 below.   [30] CERD, Art. 22; CEDAW, Art. 29; Migrant Workers Convention, Art. 92.

[31] ICCPR Arts 41–44; CAT, Arts 21–23.

agreements in force between them.[32] This could include recourse to the International Court of Justice.[33]

Some treaties at the regional level currently provide for inter-state cases to be determined before the relevant regional body or court.[34] For present purposes we simply highlight the point that human rights treaties create multilateral regimes in which any member can insist on compliance by any other member, even in the absence of actual damage to the complaining treaty party.[35]

Second, the human rights treaties also create rights for individuals and groups. In some cases, these rights can be directly vindicated at the international level through complaints to international courts; this is the case at the regional level under the European Convention on Human Rights. The African Court of Human and Peoples' Rights has jurisdiction over such complaints under certain conditions.[36] The Inter-American Commission hears complaints from persons under the American Convention on Human Rights and the Inter-American Court of Human Rights can hear these cases where the Commission submits them to the Court. These and other treaties often allow for complaints to be brought before international monitoring bodies[37] which, even if they cannot issue a binding decision as such, adopt 'views' and decisions that given a degree of publicity can have some impact on the relevant governments. Two treaties provide for the treaty bodies to receive information which could lead to a confidential inquiry.[38]

Third, human rights treaties may create reporting obligations for the states parties. These reports are sent to the United Nations, or to the relevant international body at the regional level, they are examined by the treaty body concerned, and a

[32] ICCPR, Art. 44.

[33] R. Higgins, 'The International Court of Justice and Human Rights' in K. Wellens (ed) *International Law: Theory and Practice* (The Hague: Martinus Nijhoff, 1998) 691–705, at 694.

[34] See, e.g. European Convention on Human Rights (ECHR), Art. 33. Note that Art. 55 precludes recourse to other forms of dispute settlement for disputes concerning the interpretation or application of the Convention; American Convention on Human Rights (ACHR), Arts 45, 61–62; African Charter on Human and Peoples' Rights (ACHPR), Arts 47–49 and Protocol to the African Charter on Human and Peoples' Rights on the Establishment of an African Court on Human and Peoples' Rights, Art. 5. Regulations on the Human Rights Commission of the Commonwealth of Independent States, Section II. Cf the Arab Charter of Human Rights (revised version 2004) (not yet in force).

[35] See on this point the draft Articles on State Responsibility, UN Doc. A/CN.4.600, 21 August 2000, Arts 43(b)(ii) and 49(1)(a) which define injured states and other states that are entitled to invoke the responsibility of another state.

[36] See Arts 5(3) and 34(6) of the Protocol (n 34 above).

[37] See, e.g. CERD, Art. 14; First Optional Protocol to the ICCPR; CAT, Art. 22; Optional Protocol to CEDAW, Art. 2; Convention on the Rights of Migrant Workers, Art. 76; ACHR, Art. 44, and Art. 19(6) of the Additional Protocol to the ACHR in the Area of Economic, Social and Cultural Rights; 'Protocol of San Salvador' regarding trade union rights and the right to education, as defined by Arts 8 and 13 of the Protocol; ACHPR, Art. 55; Additional Protocol to the European Social Charter Providing for a System of Collective Complaints, Arts 1–2.

[38] See CAT, Art. 20 and the Optional Protocol to CEDAW, Arts 8–10. Each ensures that the respective Committee publishes a summary of its activities, therefore some details of the inquiry will enter the public domain.

dialogue starts between the treaty body and the relevant government.[39] This process is currently under strain.[40] The human rights treaties have attracted a large number of ratifications, and the treaty bodies have too many reports to consider with too few resources. Governments are obliged to report every few years under seven possible treaties at the universal level and in many cases others at the regional level.

Fourth, treaty rights may give rise to rights which are effective at the national level. Of course, in many situations states will pass implementing legislation in order to give the rights effect in the domestic legal order. But it has also been suggested that it is possible that human rights treaties create rights that are clear and precise enough for individuals to rely on at the national level.[41] Many states accept that some human rights contained in human rights treaties are clear and precise enough to be considered self-executing, and so take effect in national law. Some states, such as the United States, have been careful to state that their ratification of a certain human rights treaty, such as the racial discrimination Convention (CERD), does not mean that the rights contained should be considered self-executing in US law.[42] A treaty therefore can create rights for individuals which may or may not be enforceable at the national or international level.

Fifth, a treaty can oblige or permit states to exercise criminal jurisdiction over international crimes such as torture or disappearances. It can even require states to submit cases of international crimes to their prosecutorial authorities where there is no jurisdictional link between the crime and the state with custody of the accused. So, for example, the United Kingdom was obliged under the Torture Convention (CAT) to submit the case of Pinochet to its prosecutorial authorities in the event of non-extradition to Spain or any other requesting state.[43] In another

---

[39] See CERD, Art. 9; International Covenant on Economic, Social and Cultural Rights (ICE-SCR), Arts 16–18 (includes reports by specialized agencies of the UN); International Covenant on Civil and Political Rights (ICCPR), Art. 41; CEDAW, Art. 18; CAT, Art. 19; Convention on the Rights of the Child, Art. 44; Convention on the Rights of Migrant Workers, Art. 73; ECHR, Art. 52; European Social Charter 1961, Art. 21; Revised European Social Charter, Part IV, Art. C; ACHR, Arts 42 and 43; ACHPR, Art. 62; African Charter on the Rights and Welfare of the Child, Art. XLIII.

[40] See J. Crawford and P. Alston (eds) *The Future of UN Human Rights Treaty Monitoring* (Cambridge: Cambridge University Press, 2000) 175–198.

[41] Recall the discussion, in Ch 2, at 2.4 above, of the advisory opinion of the Permanent Court of International Justice, *Pecuniary Claims of Danzig Railway Officials who have passed into the Polish Service, against the Polish Railways Administration*. Advisory Opinion No. 15, 3 March 1928, Series B, esp. at pp 17–18.

[42] On ratification, the US made the following declaration: 'II. The Senate's advice and consent is subject to the following declaration: "That the United States declares that the provisions of the Convention are not self-executing." '

[43] The concluding observations of the Committee against Torture addressed this point on 17 November 1998, UN Doc. CAT/C/UK. E. Recommendations: '(f) The Committee finally recommends that in the case of Senator Pinochet of Chile, the matter be referred to the office of the public prosecutor, with a view to examining the feasibility of and if appropriate initiating criminal proceedings in England, in the event that the decision is made not to extradite him. This would satisfy the State party's obligations under articles 4 to 7 of the Convention and article 27 of the Vienna Convention on the Law of Treaties of 1969.'

more recent case, the United Kingdom prosecuted an Afghan 'warlord', Faryadi Zardad, for torture and hostage-taking committed in Afghanistan against Afghanis. The subsequent conviction represents an unusual exercise of national jurisdiction to successfully prosecute human rights crimes which have no nationality or territorial connection with the human rights violation.[44]

Sixth, the treaty can, as in the case of Pinochet, be considered to have removed immunity from foreign jurisdiction that might be invoked under customary international law or even under prior treaty law.[45] Finally, as we saw above in the section on *erga omnes partes* obligations, the treaty can form the basis of obligations owed to a group of states 'for the protection of a collective interest' and thus ground claims for violations of state responsibility by other states parties.[46]

3.4   INTERNATIONAL CRIMES

Some of the obligations described above can give rise to *individual* international criminal responsibility. This creates, in a way, another type of international human rights law. The criminalization of certain international human rights violations has a number of effects. First, the accused can be arrested outside the jurisdiction where the crime took place, and even tried abroad. Second, the accused may lose immunities which might otherwise be applicable. Third, the accused may be unable to claim refugee status or asylum. Fourth, statutes of limitations may not be applicable in some cases, and fifth, the crime may be automatically included in extradition treaties.

Some of these international crimes will fall into the category of crimes of universal jurisdiction. In this situation, even in the absence of an applicable international treaty, governments will be able to try individuals who committed an offence outside the jurisdiction even where there is no link to the commission of the offence through the nationality of the perpetrator or the victims. Moreover, once conduct can be categorized as an international crime, this may have the effect of ensuring that there is civil jurisdiction for a state's courts over the conduct, even when the events took place outside the territory of that state and none of the parties is normally resident in that state.[47]

---

[44] Discussed in Ch 8, at 8.7 below. 'Afghan warlord guilty of torture', 18 July 2005, http://news.bbc.co.uk/2/hi/uk_news/4693239.stm.

[45] *R v Bow Street Metropolitan Stipendiary Magistrate and Others, ex p Pinochet Ugarte (No. 3)* [1999] 2 W.L.R. 827.

[46] See Articles of the International Law Commission, Art. 48(1)(b) discussed below at 3.5.

[47] See the draft Convention on Jurisdiction and Foreign Judgments in Civil and Commercial Matters; Art. 18 in its present form covers conduct which constitutes (1) 'genocide, a crime against humanity or a war crime' or (2) 'a serious crime under international law, provided that this State has exercised its criminal jurisdiction over that crime in accordance with an international treaty to which it is a Party and that claim is for civil compensatory damages for death or serious bodily injuries arising from that crime'. Summary of the Outcome of the Discussion in Commission II of the First Part of the Diplomatic Conference 6–20 June 2001, Interim Text. See generally on civil actions for

Some crimes are crimes of universal jurisdiction with an obligation to prosecute or extradite. Such crimes include grave breaches of the Geneva Conventions and their Additional Protocol I of 1977. Another category of crimes may simply be acts which states parties are obliged to criminalize at the national level, but which have not yet risen to the category of crimes under general international law, as there is no general prohibition on such conduct: see, for example, activity related to an organized criminal group in the context of the UN Convention Against Transnational Organized Crime (2000) and its three protocols on trafficking in persons, the smuggling of migrants, and the illicit manufacturing of and trafficking in firearms.[48] Where tribunals exist to try individuals for international crimes, human rights crimes, such as the recruitment of child soldiers, can pass from being treaty crimes to crimes under general international law in a relatively short period of time. In fact, in such situations, it may be more accurate to see the adoption of treaties including human rights crimes as a reflection of the fact that the crime has already become a crime under general international law, with binding effects for the individual under international law.[49]

Even in the absence of an international jurisdiction, authors such as Cassese have suggested that terrorist crimes are now likely to be accepted more rapidly as international crimes. He argues that terrorism is already an individual crime under customary international law. The conditions for such a criminalization at the international level are, according to Cassese, as follows: first, the acts must constitute a criminal offence under most legal systems (assault, murder, kidnapping, hostage-taking, extortion, bombing, torture, arson, etc.); second, the act is aimed at the spreading of terror by violent means against a state or the public (or a section thereof); and third, the act is politically, religiously, or otherwise ideologically motivated (i.e. not done for private ends).[50]

---

human rights crimes such as torture, C. Scott (ed) *Torture as Tort: Comparative Perspectives on the Development of Transnational Human Rights Litigation* (Oxford: Hart Publishing, 2001).

[48] For a discussion of some of the human rights obligations arising in this context, see T. Obokata, 'Smuggling of Human Beings from a Human Rights Perspective: Obligations of Non-State and State Actors under International Human Rights Law' 17 *IJRL* (2005) 394–415.

[49] See further *Prosecutor v Sam Hinga Norman* Case SCSL–2004–14–AR72(E), Decision on preliminary Motion Based on Lack of Jurisdiction (Child Recruitment), Decision of 31 May 2004.

[50] A. Cassese, 'Terrorism as an International Crime' in A. Bianchi (ed) *Enforcing International Law Norms Against Terrorism* (Oxford: Hart Publishing, 2003) 213–225 at 219; see also A. Cassese, *International Criminal Law* (Oxford: Oxford University Press, 2003) at 124. International treaties contain various crimes; see further: Convention on Offences and Certain other Acts Committed on Board Aircraft (1963); Convention for the Suppression of Unlawful Seizure of Aircraft (1970); Convention for the Suppression of Unlawful Acts against the Safety of Civil Aviation (1971); Convention on the Prevention and Punishment of Crimes against Internationally Protected Persons, including Diplomatic Agents (1973); International Convention against the Taking of Hostages (1979); Convention on the Physical Protection of Nuclear Material (1980); Protocol for the Suppression of Unlawful Acts of Violence at Airports Serving International Civil Aviation, supplementary to the Convention for the Suppression of Unlawful Acts against the Safety of Civil Aviation (1988); Convention for the Suppression of Unlawful Acts against the Safety of Maritime Navigation

3.5   *ERGA OMNES* OBLIGATIONS

The International Court of Justice asserted in the *Barcelona Traction* case that certain basic human rights give rise to international obligations owed by states to all other states which the Court characterized as *erga omnes* obligations.[51] Literally translated, the expression *erga omnes* means 'towards everyone'. The *erga omnes* concept explains which human rights violations are capable of giving rise to a separate right for a state to complain about the violating state's breach of its obligations concerning these basic rights. The *Barcelona Traction* case was concerned with whether one state had the right to complain about breaches of international law by another state. As such, it reveals little about the *erga omnes* obligations of actors other than states.[52]

More recently, the ILC has adopted the *erga omnes* notion as developed by the Court and confirmed, in the context of their articles on state responsibility, that every state can complain about a violation of international law where another state has breached an obligation 'owed to the international community as a whole'.[53] The ILC Articles are clear that a state *other* than an *injured* state is entitled to *invoke the responsibility* of another state if the obligation breached falls into either of two categories: first, where the obligation is owed to the international community as a whole (Article 48(1)(b)); or, second, if the obligation breached is owed to a group of states, including that state, and is established for the protection of the collective interest of the group (Article 48(1)(a)).

(1988); Protocol for the Suppression of Unlawful Acts against the Safety of Fixed Platforms located on the Continental Shelf (1988); International Convention for the Suppression of Terrorist Bombings (1997); International Convention for the Suppression of the Financing of Terrorism (1999). At the regional level, see OAS Convention to Prevent and Punish Acts of Terrorism Taking the Form of Crimes against Persons and Related Extortion that are of International Significance (1971); European Convention on the Suppression of Terrorism (1977), and Protocol amending the European Convention on the Suppression of Terrorism (2003, not yet in force); States of the South Asian Association for Regional Cooperation Regional Convention on Suppression of Terrorism (1987); and Inter-American Convention Against Terrorism (2002).

[51] (1970) ICJ Reports 4 at para. 33: 'In particular, an essential distinction should be drawn between the obligations of a State towards the international community as a whole, and those arising vis-à-vis another State in the field of diplomatic protection. By their very nature the former are the concern of all States. In view of the importance of the rights involved, all States can be held to have a legal interest in their protection; they are obligations *erga omnes*.' See further at para. 34: 'Such obligations derive, for example, in contemporary international law, from the outlawing of acts of aggression, and of genocide, as also from the principles and rules concerning basic rights of the human person, including protection from slavery and racial discrimination. Some of the corresponding rights of protection have entered into the body of general international law (*Reservations to the Convention on the Prevention and Punishment of the Crime of Genocide, Advisory Opinion (1951) ICJ Reports* at 23); others are conferred by international instruments of a universal or quasi-universal character.'

[52] For this see the Advisory Opinion of the Inter-American Court of Human Rights OC–18/03 of 17 September 2003, *Juridical Condition and Rights of the Undocumented Migrants*, esp. para. 110, discussed in Ch 9, at 9.2.3. below.

[53] Art. 48 of the Articles adopted by the ILC on 31 May 2001, annexed to UN GA Res. 56/53, 12 December 2001.

The ILC Special Rapporteur, James Crawford, was clear that human rights obligations are either obligations in the first category (*erga omnes*) or the second category (*erga omnes partes*) 'depending on their universality and significance', and that 'Human rights treaties are plainly (even if not always explicitly) designed to protect a general common interest'.[54] The Articles suggest that the complaining state is entitled to ask for the violations to stop (cessation and assurances and guarantees of non-repetition) and can seek reparations in the interests of the injured state or of the *beneficiaries* of the obligation breached (Article 48(2)).[55] In other words, international law entitles a state to obtain reparation for the victims of human rights violations, where the violations relate to obligations owed to the international community as a whole (and for present purposes one may assume that these obligations are the *jus cogens* obligations discussed above),[56] or from a multilateral treaty to which both states are party.

The fact that states rarely, if ever, actually use a legal forum, such as the International Court of Justice, to enforce human rights law where they have no direct interest,[57] should not blind us to the relevance of this wider recognition of

[54] See Third Report, UN Doc. A/CN.4/507, at para. 92. The relevant Article is now Art. 48 'Invocation of responsibility by a State other than an injured state'. Note also para. 89, where Crawford points out the difference between human rights obligations and other obligations under international law: 'What does seem to be special about human rights obligations (as compared with these other fields) is that they are specifically formulated in terms of the rights of individuals, whereas, for example, international environmental instruments speak of the obligations of States.'

[55] The right to take counter-measures (reprisals) seems to be limited by the Articles to an injured state (Arts 49 and 54) even if general international law may evolve to accept certain sanctions in this area. See Commentary to Art. 54, esp. paras 6 and 7. Report of the ILC, GAOR, Supp. No. 10 (A/56/10) at 355.

[56] According to the third report of the Special Rapporteur, James Crawford, the scope of these obligations can be divined from the Court's judgment. 'From the Court's reference to the international community as a whole, and from the character of the examples it gave, one can infer that the core cases of obligations *erga omnes* are those non-derogable obligations of a general character which arise directly under general international law or under generally accepted multilateral treaties (e.g. in the field of human rights). They are thus virtually coextensive with peremptory obligations (arising under norms of *jus cogens*). For if a particular obligation can be set aside or displaced as between two States, it is hard to see how that obligation is owed to the international community as a whole.' UN Doc. A/CN.4/507, at para. 96. See 3.2 above for the the scope of the *jus cogens* obligations.

[57] As explained by Christian Tomuschat (a former member of the ILC): 'But for an individual third State to claim reparation to the benefit of the victims is something almost unknown in international practice. In venturing so far ahead a State not directly affected would certainly not feel at ease. Taking a stand to defend the rights and interests of the citizens of a third country is already a noble gesture which inevitably has its political costs. But no government can really feel motivated to go into the fine work of bringing redress to an afflicted foreign population. Here, the limits of what altruism can achieve are obviously reached. The situation is totally different if a State has been hurt in the person of its citizens. Then its general duty to protect the rights and interests of its national community is activated. Diplomatic protection in the international sense has its strong incentives in the accountability of any democratic government towards its electorate as well as in the interest to shield national assets from any harmful interference by other States. To espouse the cause of foreign citizens in a foreign country, however, is always a discretionary decision which even a strong State is normally extremely reluctant to take. In other words, the system for the reparation of human rights violations as conceived by the ILC is hardly workable.' C. Tomuschat, 'Individual Reparation Claims in Instances of Grave Human Rights Violations: The Position under General International Law' in A. Randelzhofer and C. Tomuschat (eds) *State Responsibility and the Individual: Reparation in Instances of Grave Violations of Human Rights* (The Hague: Martinus Nijhoff, 1999) 1–25, at 5–6.

the scope of state responsibility. Already, the European Community links cooperation and the conclusion of other agreements to respect for human rights from its partners. The way in which a state or international organization treats those under its jurisdiction or control can trigger legitimate legal responses from other states or international organizations even where they have no nationals affected. Of course, the response cannot amount to a reprisal involving violations of fundamental human rights or humanitarian obligations prohibiting any form of reprisals against protected persons.[58] But there is an expectation that human rights violations can lead to sanctions, cancellation of contracts, and other proportionate reprisals which can be justified in law. Even in the context of action short of reprisals, such as public condemnation, international law has evolved to a point where it is admitted that human rights violations are matters of 'legitimate concern' which may be discussed without this discussion being construed as interference in internal affairs.

The United Nations Organization may legally employ any and all measures appropriate under the UN Charter to deal with human rights violations.[59] These measures may include: the discussion of the situation by the UN Secretary-General; discussion by the Security Council; and debates in other UN organs and bodies such as the General Assembly,[60] the Economic and Social Council, or the Commission on Human Rights.[61] Discussions may occur in the form of an open debate, or in the context of a procedure designed to deal with communications confidentially. Sometimes a commission of inquiry or a Special Rapporteur may be appointed to investigate a situation.

At the end of the second World Conference on Human Rights, held in Vienna in 1993, more than 170 states agreed to the adoption of the Vienna Declaration and Programme of Action, which includes the following paragraph:

> The promotion and protection of all human rights and fundamental freedoms must be considered as a priority objective of the United Nations in accordance with its purposes and principles, in particular the purpose of international cooperation. In the framework of these purposes and principles, the promotion and protection of all human rights is a legitimate concern of the international community.[62]

---

[58] See Art. 50 of the Articles (n 53 above).

[59] UN Charter, Arts 1(3), 14, 55(c), and 56. See also: The Competence of a Special Rapporteur. Views of the Special Rapporteur on the Situation of Human Rights in Chile, 1980 UN Doc. A/34/583, at paras 1–13. Extract reprinted in B. G. Ramcharan (ed) *The Principle of Legality in International Human Rights Institutions* (The Hague: Martinus Nijhoff, 1997) at para. 9.

[60] See, e.g. UN GA Res. 721(VIII), 8 December 1953.

[61] See the Economic and Social Council Resolution authorizing the Commission on Human Rights and the Sub-Commission on Prevention of Discrimination and Protection of Minorities to examine information relevant to gross violations of human rights and fundamental freedoms, E/RES/1235(XLII), 6 June 1967.

[62] Vienna Declaration, World Conference on Human Rights, 14–25 June 1993, UN Doc. A/CONF.157/24, Part 1, para. 4.

While a state which is the focus of a discussion on human rights may raise various objections to such a dialogue taking place, in the post-Vienna world, it is no longer legitimate for a state to argue that discussions related to its human rights record are not permitted under international law.

3.6   UNIVERSAL STANDARDS

A further and final type of human rights law includes universal standards, which may not necessarily be legally binding as such, but which have been developed and accepted at the international level and which make up the main corpus of human rights law. Of course, where these standards create clear rules, they may become rules of customary international law. Whether or not they evolve in this way is probably not as important as is often assumed. Few governments today denounce as 'not-binding' the human rights standards which are applied to them. Whether such standards are legally binding or not at the international level may in many cases simply turn out to be 'academic'.

Declarations adopted by governmental representatives in bodies such as the General Assembly, or at a UN inter-governmental Crime Congress, are certainly worth more than the paper they are printed on. In the words of a memorandum by the UN Office of Legal Affairs to the UN Commission on Human Rights: 'it may be said that in United Nations practice, a "declaration" is a solemn instrument resorted to only in very rare cases relating to matters of major and lasting importance where maximum compliance is expected'.[63]

The use of UN declarations, as well as documents containing principles, standards, minimum rules, and other non-binding instruments, is essential to the world of human rights law and provides the detail which gives meaning to the abstract binding obligations such as the right to life, or women's rights to equality with men. Again we can list some of the reasons why we consider these texts require special attention. First, these standards are used every day to train officials and ensure a rights-based approach in sectors such as policing, justice, development, violence against women, and the rights of minorities. Second, the instruments may contain ideas which are used to develop best practices and take the authorities beyond what has been agreed to at the level of binding treaty law. For example, with respect to human rights defenders the Declaration spells out a number of detailed guarantees.[64] Third, these instruments often point the way for new binding treaties and monitoring procedures. Fourth, in some cases principles have been formulated in a flexible way, so they guide not only the behaviour of states

---

[63] 'Use of the terms "Declarations" and "Recommendation" ' UN Doc. E/CN.4/L.610, 2 April 1962.

[64] See GA Res. A/RES/53/144, Declaration on the Right and Responsibility of Individuals, Groups and Organs of Society to Promote and Protect Universally Recognized Human Rights and Fundamental Freedoms, 9 December 1998.

and state agents but they are also addressed to international agencies and even to parties engaged in an armed conflict. Declarations and principles often give guidance which is universally applicable for all relevant actors, including non-state actors.[65]

3.7   RECATEGORIZATION OF HUMAN RIGHTS VIOLATIONS AND HYBRID TYPES OF OBLIGATION

What has not yet been explored is the full scope of these international human rights obligations, or the ways in which one type of international human rights law can evolve into another type, or how there may be hybrid situations resulting from complex interaction among types of international human rights obligations.

For an example of such an evolution, consider the following situations: as a treaty attracts near universal ratification, it is often said that the principles contained therein can be assumed to have achieved customary international law status. Some resolutions adopted by near consensus at the international level will similarly contain concrete principles and rules which reflect the state of customary international law, and their constant invocation in international relations, together with arrangements for follow-up, may permit the conclusion that values, principles, and rules contained in these texts are transposed into concerns reflecting customary international law applicable to all.

The General Assembly's law-making activity has gone beyond the production of human rights treaties. Although the Assembly has drafted and adopted a number of Declarations as preludes to international treaties, in many cases the General Assembly's Resolutions contain Declarations which are of considerable legal significance in their own right. Scholarly debate still continues as to the legal status of certain Declarations contained in General Assembly Resolutions.[66] In

---

[65] Particularly interesting examples in this regard are the Guiding Principles on Internal Displacement, which even though they have not been adopted in the form of a General Assembly Declaration, have been developed in a way that reflects existing principles of human rights and humanitarian law. They have also been supported by the Inter-Agency Standing Committee which deals with humanitarian assistance, and they provide a framework for these humanitarian agencies, as well as guidance for governments. The Principles are included in UN Doc. E/CN.4/1998/53/Add.2, 11 February 1998. See further W. Kälin, *Guiding Principles on Internal Displacement: Annotations* (Washington, DC: ASIL and the Brookings Institution, 2000).

[66] See G. Abi-Saab, 'Diplomatie multilatérale et développement du droit international: le rôle des résolutions de l'Assemblée générale' in V.-Y. Ghebali and D. Kappeler (eds) *Multiple Aspects of International Relations: études à la mémoire du professeur Jean Siotis* (Brussels: Bruylant, 1995) 83–99; B. Sloan, *United Nations General Assembly Resolutions in Our Changing World* (New York: Transnational, 1991), O. Schachter, *International Law in Theory and Practice* (Dordrecht: Martinus Nijhoff, 1991) 84–94, A. Cassese, *International Law in a Divided World* (Oxford: Oxford University Press, 1986) 174–175, 192–195, A. Cassese and J. H. H. Weiler (eds) *Change and Stability in International Law-Making* (Berlin: Walter de Gruyter, 1988) 33–62, R. Higgins, *The Development of International Law through the Political Organs of the United Nations* (Oxford: Oxford University Press, 1963).

some cases, the content of the Declaration and its manner of adoption have led to the conclusion that certain Declarations can provide evidence of the crystallization of norms of customary international law. In fact, the International Court of Justice has used some of these Declarations as a sort of *short cut* to determining the applicable law in its opinions and judgments.[67] A number of resolutions include the word 'declaration' in the title or 'declare' a number of principles. Because the dynamic of the adoption of human rights Declarations suggests that they arise out of the breach of the rights concerned, it seems fair to distinguish them from General Assembly Resolutions, which have a programmatic or even codificatory function.[68] This latter type of resolution may be framed as a recommendation or simply endorse standards elaborated elsewhere. Recommendatory resolutions rarely create controversial new duties—but rather recommend that states base their practices on certain existing principles.

The General Assembly Resolutions listed in the following footnote are all of importance in understanding the scope of international human rights law.[69] This

---

[67] E.g. the *Advisory Opinion on Western Sahara* (1975) ICJ Reports 12, relied heavily on GA Res. 1514(XV), 1541(XV), and 2625(XXV) to determine the content of the right to self-determination, see paras 55–59; in the *Case Concerning Military and Paramilitary Activities in and against Nicaragua* (1986) ICJ Reports 14, the Court construed the consent to the text of resolutions such as GA Res. 2625(XXV) as an acceptance of the rules declared in the resolution (para. 188), and determined that the 'resolution demonstrates that the States represented in the General Assembly regard the exception to the prohibition on the use of force constituted by the right of individual or collective self-defence as already a matter of customary international law' (para. 193). The Court also relied on GA Res. 3314(XXIX), which annexed the Definition of Aggression, and found that the description of an armed attack as including the sending of armed bands which carry out acts of armed force against another state 'may be taken to reflect customary international law' (para. 195).

[68] See O. Schachter: 'Declarations that affirm the prohibitions against aggression, genocide, torture or systematic racial discrimination would not be deprived of their legal value because they are not uniformly observed. On the other hand, declarations asserting or affirming legal rules of a less peremptory character would not prevail over evidence that such rules were not generally observed by affected states.' 'The UN Legal Order: An Overview' in O. Schachter and C. C. Joyner (eds) *United Nations Legal Order* (Cambridge: Cambridge University Press, 1995) 1–31, at 5.

[69] Resolutions affirming the principles of international law relating to war crimes and crimes against humanity (1946) GA Res. 95(I) and (1947) Res. 170(II); Declaration of the Rights of the Child (1959) GA Res. 1386(XIV); Declaration on the Granting of Independence to Colonial Countries and Peoples (1960) GA Res. 1514(XV); Resolution on Permanent Sovereignty over Natural Resources (1962) GA Res. 1803(XVII); Declaration on the Elimination of All Forms of Racial Discrimination (1963) GA Res. 1904 (XVIII); Declaration on the Promotion among Youth of the Idea of Peace, Mutual Respect and Understanding Between Peoples (1965) GA Res. 2037(XX); Declaration on the Elimination of Discrimination against Women (1967) GA Res. 2263(XXII); Declaration on Social Progress and Development (1969) GA Res. 2542(XXIV); Declaration on Principles of International Law Concerning Friendly Relations and Cooperation of States in Accordance with the Charter of the United Nations (1970) GA Res. 2625(XXV); Basic Principles for the Protection of Civilian Populations in Armed Conflicts (1970) GA Res. 2675(XXV); Declaration on the Rights of Mentally Retarded Persons (1971) GA Res. 2856(XXVI); Principles of International Co-operation in the Detection, Arrest, Extradition and Punishment of Persons Guilty of War Crimes and Crimes against Humanity (1973) GA Res. 3074(XXVIII); Declaration on the Protection of Women and Children in Emergency and Armed Conflict (1974) GA Res. 3318(XXIX); Declaration on the Use of Scientific and Technical Progress in the Interests of Peace and for the Benefit of Mankind (1974) GA Res. 3384(XXX); Declaration on the Protection of All Persons from being Subjected to Torture and Other Cruel, Inhuman or Degrading Treatment or Punishment

book refers throughout to the key General Assembly Declarations in order to inform the reader of the full scope of the human rights obligations which have been agreed by states at the international level. As discussed above, Declarations may be adopted in circumstances where states expect 'maximum compliance'. I have sought to go beyond the arguments over the normativity of these resolutions and advocate allowing their content to flesh out skeletal human rights and duties contained in the basic rules.

Perhaps the clearest example of a declaration that has been recognized as reflecting general international law is the 'Friendly Relations' Declaration of 1970. It is worth pausing to consider the qualities of this Declaration that have allowed it to achieve this status. First, it is often remarked that the Declaration was adopted after a decade of negotiations and without objections. Second, it represents an interpretation of the Charter—a legally binding treaty for all members of the United Nations. Third, the content suggests legally binding principles. The fact that the International Court of Justice has had occasion to pronounce on the legal status of the norms enumerated in the Resolution means that this is one of the few resolutions acknowledged as representing international law. However, most of the other Resolutions of the General Assembly mentioned in the previous footnote can also be said to add flesh to the bare bones of binding international law. Moreover, they were nearly all adopted by consensus[70] and very often after a long drafting process.

(1975) GA Res. 3452(XXX); Declaration on the Rights of Disabled Persons (1975) GA Res. 3447; Code of Conduct for Law Enforcement Officials (1979) GA Res. 34/169; Declaration on the Elimination of All Forms of Intolerance and of Discrimination Based on Religion or Belief (1981) GA Res. 36/55; Principles of Medical Ethics Relevant to the Role of Health Personnel Particularly Physicians, in the Protection of Prisoners and Detainees against Torture and Other Cruel, Inhuman or Degrading Treatment or Punishment (1982) GA Res. 37/194; Declaration on the Right of Peoples to Peace (1984) GA Res. 39/11; United Nations Standard Minimum Rules for the Administration of Juvenile Justice ('The Beijing Rules') (1985) GA Res. 40/33; Declaration of Basic Principles of Justice for Victims of Crime and the Abuse of Power (1985) GA Res. 40/34; Declaration on the Human Rights of Individuals Who are not Nationals of the Country in Which They Live (1985) GA Res. 40/144; Declaration on Social and Legal Principles Relating to the Protection and Welfare of Children, with Special Reference to Foster Placement and Adoption Nationally and Internationally (1986) GA Res. 41/85; Declaration on the Right to Development (1986) GA Res. 41/128; Body of Principles for the Protection of All Form of Detention or Imprisonment (1988) GA Res. 43/173; Basic Principles for the Treatment of Prisoners (1990) GA Res. 45/111; United Nations Rules for the Protection of Juveniles Deprived of their Liberty (1990) GA Res. 45/113; United Nations Standard Minimum Rules for Non-custodial Measures ('The Tokyo Rules') (1990) GA Res. 45/110; Principles for the Protection of Persons with Mental Illness and the Improvement of Mental Health Care (1991) GA Res. 46/119; Declaration on the Rights of Persons Belonging to National or Ethnic, Religious and Linguistic Minorities (1992) GA Res. 47/135; Declaration on the Protection of All Persons from Enforced Disappearances (1992) GA Res. 47/133; Declaration on the Elimination of Violence against Women (1993) GA Res. 48/104; Declaration on the Right and Responsibility of Individuals, Groups and Organs of Society to Promote and Protect Universally Recognized Human Rights and Fundamental Freedoms (1998) GA Res. 53/144.

[70] Note the US voted against the Declaration on the Right to Development. However, more recently it joined the consensus in Vienna for the adoption of the Declaration and Programme of Action and did not dissent during the adoption by consensus of the resolution at the 50th Session of the GA on the Right to Development, which in its first preambular paragraph reaffirmed the Declaration on the Right to Development. GA Res. 50/184, adopted 22 December 1995.

In the decision on jurisdiction by the Appeals Chamber of the International Criminal Tribunal for the former Yugoslavia in the *Tadić* case, the Chamber quoted extensively from two General Assembly Resolutions containing basic humanitarian principles in order to justify its conclusion that it had jurisdiction over 'breaches of the laws and customs of war' in an internal armed conflict. The Resolutions were building blocks in the argument that the relevant crimes could be considered to be international crimes for which individuals can be held responsible. The Chamber referred to General Assembly Resolution 2444 of 1968 and Resolution 2675 of 1970.[71] The latter Resolution affirmed a number of 'basic principles for the protection of civilian populations in armed conflicts'.[72] The Chamber took note of the fact that one of the sponsors of the Resolution, Norway, had explained that in this Resolution 'the term "armed conflicts" was meant to cover armed conflicts of all kinds—an important point, since the provisions of the Geneva Conventions and the Hague Regulations did not extend to all conflicts'.[73] The Chamber explains the twofold nature of the role of these Resolutions: 'they were declaratory of the principles of customary international law regarding the protection of civilian populations and property in armed conflicts of any kind and, at the same time, were intended to promote the adoption of treaties on the matter, designed to specify and elaborate upon such principles'.[74]

Both of the Resolutions used by the Chamber were adopted with no negative votes. General Assembly Resolutions adopted over the objections of the states most affected by their legal status provide weaker evidence of the *opinio juris* necessary for the formation of customary international law, and it is more difficult to argue that they contain general principles of international law. In the 1996 *Advisory Opinion of the International Court of Justice on the Legality of the Threat or Use of Nuclear Weapons*, the International Court of Justice noted that the relevant

---

[71] Res. 2444 relative to the respect for human rights in armed conflict affirmed Res. XXVIII of the XXth International Conference of the Red Cross held in Vienna, 1965. The resolution laid down, *inter alia*, the following principles: 'a) That the right of the parties to a conflict to adopt means of injuring the enemy is not unlimited; b) That it is prohibited to launch attacks against the civilian populations as such; c) That distinction must be made at all times between persons taking part in the hostilities and members of the civilian population to the effect that the latter be spared as much as possible.' This resolution, together with five resolutions adopted by the GA in 1970, were part of the basis for the draft protocols drawn up by the ICRC which eventually became the two 1977 Protocols additional to the Geneva Conventions of 1949. The five Resolutions are 2673, 2674, 2675, 2676, and 2677.

[72] These included: '1. Fundamental human rights, as accepted in international law and laid down in international instruments, continue to apply in situations of armed conflict. 2. In the conduct of military operations during armed conflicts, a distinction must be made at all times between persons actively taking part in the hostilities and civilian populations. 3. In the conduct of military operations, every effort should be made to spare civilian populations from the ravages of war, and all necessary precautions should be taken to avoid injury, loss or damage to civilian populations.'

[73] Quoted at para. 111 of the decision of 2 October 1995, the Chamber cites the reference for the quote as (UN GAOR, 3rd Comm, 25th Sess, 1785th Mtg., at 281, UN Doc. A/C.3/SR.1785 (1970). The Chamber's decision also refers to a statement by the Cuban delegate UN GAOR, 25th Sess, 1922nd Mtg., at 3 UN Doc. A/PV.1922 (1970). [74] Advisory Opinion, 8 July 1996, para. 112.

General Assembly Resolutions were adopted with a 'substantial number of negative votes and abstentions' and 'fell short of establishing *opinio juris*'.[75]

The Court, however, noted that General Assembly Resolutions, even if they are not binding, may sometimes have normative value. They can, in certain circumstances, provide evidence important for establishing the existence of a norm or the emergence of *opinio juris*. To establish whether this is true of a given General Assembly Resolution, it is necessary to look at its content and the conditions of its adoption; it is also necessary to see whether an *opinio juris* exists as to its normative character. Or a series of resolutions may show the gradual evolution of the *opinio juris* required for the establishment of the rule.[76]

Rather than attempting to determine whether declarations of principles by the General Assembly are legally binding as 'black letter law', it seems more pertinent to accept their increasing influence at both the international and the national level. Together with the Universal Declaration of Human Rights, these declarations are legitimately used to hold up the standards of achievement that the member states of the United Nations have set. This means that the texts are used as instruments for reform by national and international NGOs seeking changes in the laws and institutions of the countries around the world. But these standards are more than mere exhortations and, as already stated, they are nearly all expressed as *principles*.[77] Sometimes dismissed as 'soft law', these declarations clearly harden when conceived of as explanatory to treaty law or as principles which persuade decision-makers when faced with ambiguity.[78]

Resolutions may also encapsulate or express the opinion of states with regard to the interpretation of existing international law. In human rights declarations, this could be by the fleshing out of international law obligations (either under treaty law or general international law) or by categorization of certain acts as human rights violations of one type or another. An example of the first situation is the Declaration on the Elimination of Violence against Women,[79] which was adopted

---

[75] At para. 71.   [76] At para. 70.

[77] On general principles, see B. Simma and P. Alston, 'The Sources of Human Rights Law: custom, jus cogens, and general principles' 12 *AYBIL* (1992) 82–108. It has been suggested in the context of a study of law-making at the UN that: 'the general principles of law are those not easily or frequently legislated. Nevertheless, it is not to be excluded that certain principles emphasized repeatedly by the international community through organs such as the General Assembly, for example the prohibition of torture, may through such repetition and sponsorship come to be generally accepted (at least in principle) by all states and thus become part of international law even before customary law has developed in the same sense'. P. Szasz, 'General Law-Making Processes' in Schachter and Joyner (1995) 35–108, at 44.

[78] On the use of General Assembly Resolutions containing human rights declarations by the International Court of Justice, see F. Francioni, 'International "soft law: a contemporary assessment' in V. Lowe and M. Fitzmaurice (eds) *Fifty Years of the International Court of Justice: Essays in Honour of Sir Robert Jennings* (Cambridge: Grotius/Cambridge University Press, 1996) 167–178, esp. at 170–174.

[79] GA Res. 48/104, adopted 20 December 1993. The Resolution '*Solemnly proclaims*' a Declaration the content of which is such that it contains definitions and imperatives. Art. 4 contains a number of exhortations and suggestions but it also includes clear wording which suggests that states are entering into an obligation which 'fleshes out' or is parasitic on existing legal obligations. 'States

by the General Assembly by consensus. It is an expression of states' interpretation of their obligations under the Convention on the Elimination of All Forms of Discrimination against Women, as well as their international law obligations under the Charter and general international law. An example of the second type of resolution is the Declaration on the Protection of All Persons from Enforced Disappearance, adopted by consensus by the General Assembly.[80] The wording is clearly intended to confirm that certain acts violate legal obligations contained in specific rules of international law:

> 2. Any act of enforced disappearance places the persons subjected thereto outside the protection of the law and inflicts severe suffering on them and their families. It constitutes a violation of the rules of international law guaranteeing, *inter alia*, the right to recognition as a person before the law, the right to liberty and security of the person and the rights not to be subjected to torture and other cruel, inhuman or degrading treatment or punishment. It also violates or constitutes a grave threat to life.

More subtly, the Declaration also nudges the systematic practice of enforced disappearances into the category of 'crimes against humanity'.[81] As noted in the

should condemn violence against women and should not invoke any custom, tradition or religious consideration to avoid their obligations with respect to its elimination.' The Declaration was heavily influenced by the General Recommendation No. 19 (11th Session, 1992) adopted by the Committee on the Elimination of Discrimination Against Women. The importance of the General Assembly Declaration is that states themselves have adopted the text and therefore it is conclusive proof of the minimal scope of the obligations under the treaty. States cannot contest the text adopted by the General Assembly in the same way that they might argue about the obligations contained in a recommendation of the expert treaty body. In addition, the obligations in the Declaration are of course binding on states which are not yet parties to the Convention of the Elimination of All Forms of Discrimination against Women (CEDAW). Cf the Inter-American Convention on the Prevention and Eradication of Violence against Women. This should be seen as a demonstration of the legal nature of some of the obligations contained in the UN Declaration, rather than evidence of the necessity of drafting a convention before the obligations have any legal effect. A further role for the General Assembly Declaration has been to give a normative framework to various Special Rapporteurs, including the Special Rapporteur on traditional practices affecting the health of women and children, and the Special Rapporteur on violence against women. These Special Rapporteurs, appointed by the Sub-Commission and Commission on Human Rights respectively, do not confine their activities and reports to states parties to CEDAW, and so the Declaration provides an important catalogue of the obligations the states have freely entered into in this field. See UN Doc. E/CN.4/Sub.2/1995/6 for the preliminary report on traditional practices and UN Doc. E/CN.4/1996/53 for a relevant report of the Special Rapporteur on violence against women.

80   GA Res. 47/133, adopted 18 December 1992.

81   The fourth preambular paragraph reads: '*Considering* that enforced disappearance undermines the deepest values of any society committed to respect for the rule of law, human rights and fundamental freedoms, and that the systematic practice of such acts is of the nature of a crime against humanity.' See also Arts 4, 14, and 15, which cover the criminalization of enforced disappearances. For a preliminary draft of an 'international convention on the prevention and punishment of enforced disappearances' see UN Doc. E/CN.4/Sub.2/1996/WG.1/CRP.2, 7 August 1996. Art. 2 of the draft reads: 'The systematic or widespread practice of forced disappearance constitutes a crime against humanity.' Compare the Inter-American Convention on the Forced Disappearance of Persons, 9 June 1994, in force since 29 March 1996, which states in its sixth preambular paragraph: '*Reaffirming* that the systematic practice of the forced disappearance of persons constitutes a crime against humanity.'

discussion on violation of *jus cogens*, categorizing a human rights violations as more than a simple violation of international law can have a number of legal consequences. Categorizing a human rights violation as a crime against humanity (in addition to the consequences resulting from a violation of a norm of *jus cogens*) entails the following consequences: the crime may be excluded from statutes of limitations which forbid prosecution after a certain period of time,[82] the perpetrators can be denied refugee status[83] or asylum,[84] there will be added obligations on states to cooperate, and in some jurisdictions the crime may come within a state's national criminal jurisdiction whereas without the label 'crime against humanity' it might not. Moreover, crimes against humanity have been specifically held to generate obligations for non-state actors which may give rise to civil or criminal liability. In *Kadic v Karadžić*, the US Court of Appeals for the Second Circuit concluded that 'subject matter jurisdiction exists, that Karadžić may be found liable for genocide, war crimes, and crimes against humanity in his private capacity'.[85]

Let us briefly look at what we called 'hybrid' types of human rights obligation. First, several key human rights treaties include the rule that one cannot be prosecuted for a crime which was not a crime at the time it was committed. This rule includes in the definition of triable criminal offences under international law, or in the European Convention on Human Rights, any act or omission which was 'criminal according to the general principles of law recognised by civilised nations'.[86] Evolving rules of international criminal law will change the scope of the protection under these human rights treaties. Similarly, derogations under human rights treaties may not involve measures that are inconsistent with a state's other obligations under international law. These will include customary international obligations. Where states find themselves in a state of emergency or armed conflict, the court or body that supervises compliance with the treaty will consider these other obligations and may have to decide whether there has been a violation of the other obligation in order to see if there has been a violation of the human

---

[82] See the Convention on the Non-Applicability of Statutory Limitations to War Crimes and Crimes Against Humanity (1968) in force since 11 November 1970, *Compilation* 678–681; see also GA Res. 3074(XXVIII), 3 December 1974, Principles of international cooperation in the detection, arrest, extradition and punishment of persons guilty of war crimes and crimes against humanity.

[83] Art. 1F(a) of the Convention Relating to the Status of Refugees (1951) states that: 'The provisions of this Convention shall not apply to any person with respect to whom there are serious reasons for considering that: he has committed . . . a crime against humanity, as defined in the international instruments drawn up to make provision in respect of such crimes.'

[84] GA Res. 2312(XXII), 14 December 1967 contains the Declaration on Territorial Asylum which, in Art. 1(2), states that: 'The right to seek and enjoy asylum may not be invoked by any person with respect to whom there are serious reasons for considering that he has committed a crime against peace, a war crime or a crime against humanity, as defined in international instruments drawn up to make provision in respect of such crimes.'   [85] 13 October 1995, 34 *ILM* (1995) 1592, at 1597.

[86] Art. 7(2), see also the International Covenant on Civil and Political Rights, Art. 15(1); Universal Declaration of Human Rights, Art. 11(2); American Convention on Human Rights, Art. 9; and African Charter on Human and Peoples' Rights, Art. 7(2).

rights convention at issue. The African and American regional treaties go even further and graft on obligations under Declarations so that respect for the treaty may involve hybrid rights created from a combination of treaty rights and declaration rights.[87] The African Charter on Human and Peoples' Rights (1981) includes the following: 'Article 18(3): The State shall ensure the elimination of every discrimination against women and also ensure the protection of the rights of the women and the child as stipulated in international declarations and conventions.'

International human rights law is therefore a complicated branch of international law. Although historically seen as neatly divided between different generations of civil and political rights on the one hand, and economic, social, and cultural rights on the other, it may be time to conceive of human rights law as a complex set of international legal obligations. The obligations are contained in a variety of types of international law; and human rights obligations can evolve so that simple declarations of principle can become strict rules or even the basis for an international crime. However one conceives human rights law, it is surely not static. Human rights law is driven, not by the steady accretion of precedents and practice, but rather by outrage and solidarity.

[87] See, e.g. the complaints concerning the incidents at La Tablada in Argentina: *Report 55/97, case 11,137 v Argentina* approved by the Inter-American Commission on Human Rights, 30 October 1997. The American Convention includes a number of references to other treaties and obligations and the Commission may even control the extent to which remedies are provided in national law for violations of these obligations where they have been incorporated into national law. See Arts 25, 27, and 29 for the complex interaction of Declarations, treaties, customary obligations, and national law.

4

The United Nations

Let us turn to consider some human rights problems associated with a number of inter-governmental organizations. This chapter concentrates on the United Nations and in the next chapter we address the World Trade Organization and the European Union. Before looking at each organization in its context, I would like to make some general observations based on arguments developed in previous chapters.

First, international organizations with the capacity to bear rights and obligations at the international level may have human rights obligations under international law. Such obligations are not restricted to those obligations which are explicitly accepted by the international organization.[1]

Second, I suggest it is uncontroversial that all states have human rights obligations under customary international law and, in addition, have obligations under the human rights treaties they have ratified. It has been held that states cannot simply divest themselves of such human rights obligations when they empower an international organization to take decisions or act on their behalf.[2] In sum, international organizations are capable of violating international obligations with regard to human rights; and, where these organizations remain unaccountable for such violations, states retain their own international obligations to ensure respect for human rights. The acts and omissions of international organizations may then give rise to both international human rights violations by the organization and, in some circumstances, also for the relevant states. This is so where the 'international organization aids or assists, or directs or controls, a State in the commission of a

---

[1] C. Tomuschat, *International Law: Ensuring the Survival of Mankind on the Eve of a New Century: General Course on Public International Law*, vol. 281 *RCADI* (The Hague: Martinus Nijhoff, 2001) at 34–35, quoted in Ch 2, at 2.9 above.

[2] This point is developed in Ch 5 below, with regard to the European Community and the supervision of its member states' obligations under the European Convention on Human Rights by the European Court of Human Rights. The key sentence from the Grand Chamber of the Court reads: '67. The Court is of the opinion that where States establish international organisations in order to pursue or strengthen their cooperation in certain fields of activities, and where they attribute to these organisations certain competences and accord them immunities, there may be implications as to the protection of fundamental rights. It would be incompatible with the purpose and object of the Convention, however, if the Contracting States were thereby absolved from their responsibility under the Convention in relation to the field of activity covered by such attribution. It should be recalled that the Convention is intended to guarantee not theoretical or illusory rights, but rights that are practical and effective.' *Waite and Kennedy v. Germany*, Judgment of 18 February 1999, at para. 67. See also C. Tomuschat (n 1 above).

wrongful act'.[3] The International Law Commission (ILC) has approved, on a first reading, a draft Article on the responsibility of international organizations which states that the organization will be responsible where it 'aids or assists a State or another international organization in the commission of an internationally wrongful act by the State or the latter organization is internationally responsible for doing so if: (a) That organization does so with knowledge of the circumstances of the internationally wrongful act; and (b) The act would be internationally wrongful if committed by that organization'.[4] In other words, the international organization may be *complicit* in the violations of international law where the organization has the same obligations as the principal perpetrator.

4.1   THE UNITED NATIONS ORGANIZATION

The United Nations has multiple tasks and myriad bodies carrying out a variety of functions around the world. Rather than trying to develop an abstract framework of human rights duties, I shall concentrate on some areas where human rights accusations have been levelled at the United Nations and the organization has responded with an attempt to set out human rights obligations. By examining these situations in detail it may later be possible to unearth some general principles. Such principles might apply not only to the United Nations but also to all inter-governmental organizations carrying out similar functions.[5]

4.1.1   Obligations on the UN and Other Entities Engaged in Armed Conflict, Multilateral Peace-Keeping, and Peace-Enforcement Operations

Ever since the first peace-keeping operations, the International Committee of the Red Cross has reminded the United Nations and the troop contributing states of

---

[3] G. Gaja, 'Second report on responsibility of international organizations', UN Doc. A/CN.4/541, 2 April 2004, at para. 9, and on joint a several responsibility, see generally paras 5–13.

[4] Draft Article 12, UN Doc. A/CN.4/L.666/Rev.1, 1 June 2005, adopted by the ILC on first reading on 5 June 2005. For the rule with regard to state complicity, see Ch 6, at 6.9 below.

[5] Regional peace-keeping and peace-enforcement has been criticized in various reports. With regard to NATO, see Amnesty International, ' "Collateral Damage" or Unlawful Killings? Violations of the Laws of War by NATO during Operation Allied Force', AI Index EUR 70/025/2000; with regard to ECOMOG in Sierra Leone and Liberia, see, e.g. Letter from Amnesty International to the Special Representative of the Secretary-General for Liberia, 14 August 2003, AI Index: AFR 34/018/2003: 'Amnesty International, for example, documented human rights violations and other criminal acts by forces of the Economic Community of West African States (ECOWAS) deployed in both Liberia and Sierra Leone. ECOWAS Cease-fire Monitoring Group (ECOMOG) forces in Liberia and Sierra Leone were responsible for indiscriminate aerial bombardments resulting in civilian casualties, extrajudicial executions of captured or suspected rebel combatants, torture, ill-treatment and illegal detention of both combatants and civilians, harassment of civilians and widespread looting. None were known to have ever been brought to justice.'

their obligations under international humanitarian law.[6] The international obligations of inter-governmental organizations engaged in multilateral peace-keeping have been studied and debated in numerous conferences and fora.[7] Most of this discussion has turned on the applicability of international humanitarian law. More recently, however, the issue has been addressed in a wider perspective by the Institut de Droit International, which, in 1999, adopted a Resolution that clearly stated: 'All parties to armed conflicts in which non-State entities are parties, irrespective of their legal status, as well as the United Nations, and competent regional and other international organizations have the obligation to respect international humanitarian law as well as fundamental human rights.'[8] The commentary to the Resolution states that there was an unsuccessful attempt to define 'fundamental human rights' as those which are non-derogable under human rights treaties. This was rejected 'in a fairly categorical way'. The commentary states: 'One must therefore assume that the expression "[fundamental] human rights" refers back to general international law, and even to the law of human rights, in which context one can find definitions of the concept.'[9] The debate itself reveals that the category of non-derogable rights was considered too narrow to be used to describe the human rights obligations applicable in times of armed conflict.[10] This expert declaration confirms that both human rights law and international humanitarian law can apply to the United Nations in times of armed conflict, but the detailed application of this principle is more complex.

Concern about the behaviour of UN personnel hit the headlines in 1993 with reports of abuses by UN forces in Somalia.[11] While primary responsibility for prosecution and military discipline was said to lie with the authorities of the troop

[6] A. Ryniker, 'Quelques commentaires à propos de la Circulaire du Secrétaire général des Nations Unies du 6 août 1999' 836 *Revue internationale de la Croix-Rouge* (1999) 795–805.

[7] See, e.g. L. Condorelli, A.-M. La Rosa, and S. Scherrer (eds) *Les Nations unies et le droit international humanitaire: Actes du colloque international 19,20, 21 octobre 1995* (Paris: Pedone, 1996).

[8] 'The Application of International Humanitarian Law and Fundamental Human Rights, in Armed Conflicts in which Non-State Entities are Parties', Resolution adopted at the Berlin Session, 25 August 1999, Art. II. See also the Resolution of 13 August 1975, 'Conditions of Application of Rules, other that Humanitarian Rules, of Armed Conflict to Hostilities in which United Nations Forces may be engaged.'

[9] Institute of International Law, *'L'application du droit international humanitaire et des droits fondamentaux de l'homme dans les conflits armés auxquels prennent part des entités non étatiques: résolution de Berlin du 25 août 1999—The application of international humanitarian law and fundamental human rights in armed conflicts in which non-state entities are parties: Berlin resolution of 25 August 1999 (commentaire de Robert Kolb) Collection 'résolutions' n° 1*' (Paris: Pedone, 2003) at 25 (square brackets in the original).

[10] See Bernhardt in 68-II *Yearbook of the Institute of International Law* (1999) at 304; and, according to Tomuschat, 'the most important rights to protect during armed conflict were the rights to life, liberty, and freedom of the person, which were not necessarily non-derogable' (ibid, at 305); Meron 'signalled his agreement with the suggestion to drop the word "imperative" and to make reference to fundamental human rights as opposed to non-derogable rights. He pointed out that different human rights conventions contained varying lists of non-derogable rights' (ibid, at 305).

[11] On these and other incidents, see African Rights, *Somalia: Human Rights Abuses by United Nations Forces* (1993).

contributing countries, the United Nations had to react, not only by condemning the actions of the individuals, but also by seeking to take preventive action for the future. As the trials of two Belgian paratroopers opened, Kofi Annan, as Secretary-General, stated: 'While soldiers are under the control of their own superior officer, I wish to assure that every possible effort will be made on the part of the United Nations to ensure that such incidents do not recur.'[12] Moreover, the personal injury claims made against the United Nations in the context of the Somalia operation triggered further reflection on the public international law obligations which apply.[13]

In response to the Somalia incidents, the Canadian Airborne Regiment was disbanded and the Canadian Commission of Inquiry published a 2,000-page report entitled *Dishonored Legacy: The Lessons of the Somalia Affair* (1997). From the UN perspective, the situation is complicated by the fact that some of the abuses committed by Belgian, Canadian, and Italian troops may have been committed during the period when they were part of a multinational coalition (Unified Task Force, UNITAF) rather than under the UN operation (UNISOM II),[14] and the fact that some national authorities saw the operations not as war (for the purposes of national law) but, rather, as 'a police operation aiming at restoring public order'.[15] Furthermore, even during the UNISOM II phase, some national contingents remained outside the command and control of the United Nations.[16] The UN Independent Expert on Somalia, Mona Rishmawi, detailed the allegations and the follow-up by the three Governments in her 1998 report to the UN Commission on Human Rights. The key issue for her was the future credibility of action in the name of human rights. Rishmawi recommended:

> ... that allegations of abuses committed by the international troops which were present in Somalia from 1992 be fully investigated. The perpetrators of wrongful acts that amount to grave breaches of the Geneva Conventions, and other serious violations of humanitarian law, must be brought to justice. This is essential not only for the credibility of the international human rights and humanitarian action in Somalia, but also because Somalis must not be taught the wrong lessons about the respect of human rights and humanitarian law.[17]

The Canadian Report avoids a legalistic approach to the applicable standards, but highlights the failure to issue clear rules of engagement that are specific enough to

---

[12] Reuters and Associated Press, 'Growing reports of UN Somalia atrocities anger Annan', *The Globe and Mail*, 24 June 1997, A15.

[13] UN Doc. A/C.5/49/65, 24 April 1995, 'Report of the Secretary-General', at para. 20.

[14] See R. M. Young and M. Molina, 'IHL and Peace Operations: Sharing Canada's lessons learned from Somalia' 1 *YBIHL* (1998) 362–370, at 366; K. Boustany, 'Brocklebank: A Questionable Decision of the Court Martial Appeal Court of Canada' 1 *YBIHL* (1998) 371–374; and N. Lupi, 'Report by the Enquiry Commission on the Behaviour of Italian Peace-keeping Troops in Somalia' 1 *YBIHL* (1998) 375–379.   [15] Lupi (1998: 379).

[16] See C. Greenwood, 'International Humanitarian Law and United Nations Military Operations' 1 *YBIHL* (1998) 3–34, at 13.

[17] 'Situation of human rights in Somalia', UN Doc. E/CN.4/1998/96, 16 January 1998, Conclusions and Recommendations.

indicate when lethal force can be used. The report criticizes the lack of adequate training regarding this issue and states that scenario-based, fact-driven training 'could have reinforced the requirement for necessity, proportionality and restraint in the use of force'.[18]

At one level, the United Nations has responded to the challenge posed by the concern over the abuses in Somalia and elsewhere with a number of training manuals and cards for civilian police and military observers which include references to human rights.[19] These include: the 'Ten Rules—Code of Personal Conduct for Blue Helmets', rule number 5 of which obligates blue helmets to 'Respect and regard the human rights of all'.[20] Furthermore, there are Bulletins issued by the Secretary-General on the observance of international humanitarian law by UN forces, and on special measures for protection from sexual exploitation and sexual abuse.[21] This last Bulletin responded to concerns that UN personnel have been implicated in trafficking in women, demanding sexual favours in refugee camps, violence against civilians, and organizing prostitution.[22] This human rights issue

[18] Report of the Commission of Inquiry into the Deployment of Canadian Forces to Somalia, *Dishonored Legacy: The Lessons of the Somalia Affair*, vol. 2 (Ottawa, Minister of Public Works and Government Services) at 661.

[19] UN, *United Nations Civilian Police Handbook* (Turin: International Training Centre of the ILO, 1995) includes as an annex the UN handbook on criminal justice standards for peace-keeping police. The foreword states (at D5): 'The international standards and norms summarized in this handbook incorporate basic principles of criminal justice, human rights and humanitarian law, for the use of the civilian police components of United Nations peace-keeping operations. One of their main responsibilities is to monitor law enforcement activities of local officials, so that they carry out their tasks with full respect for universally-accepted human rights and criminal justice standards. In view of these important functions, it is expected that United Nations personnel would set an example, in strictly adhering to the spirit and the letter of the principles contained therein and in overviewing their applications.' The Universal Declaration of Human Rights is also annexed. The UN *Military Observers Handbook* (1995) also includes as an annex the Universal Declaration, which should be seen in the light of the card issued to peacekeepers which pledges compliance with the applicable portions of the Declaration.

[20] Issued by the UN Department of Peacekeeping Unit Operations Training Unit along with another card headed 'We are United Nations Peacekeepers' which states in its second paragraph: 'We will comply with the Guidelines on International Humanitarian Law for Forces Undertaking United Nations Peacekeeping Operations and the applicable portions of the Universal Declaration of Human Rights as the fundamental basis of our standards.'

[21] Secretary-General's Bulletin 'Observance by United Nations forces of international humanitarian law', UN Doc. ST/SGB/1999/13, 6 August 1999, in force from 12 August 1999. 'Special measures for protection from sexual exploitation and sexual abuse', UN Doc. ST/SGB/2003/13, 9 October 2003, which states at para. 3.1: 'Sexual exploitation and sexual abuse violate universally recognized international legal norms and standards and have always been unacceptable behaviour and prohibited conduct for United Nations staff.'

[22] Two reports on trafficking of women in Bosnia were particularly notable at the time; see the testimony in the US Congress 'The UN and the Sex Slave Trade in Bosnia: Isolated Case or Larger Problem in the UN System?' Sub-Committee on International Operations and Human Rights, 24 April 2002. See also B. Limanowska, *Trafficking in Human Beings in Southeastern Europe: Current Situation and Responses to Trafficking in Human Beings in Albania, Bosnia and Herzegovina, Bulgaria, Croatia, The Federal Republic of Yugoslavia, The Former Yugoslav Republic of Macedonia, Moldova, Romania* (2002) UNICEF, OHCHR, OSCE/ODIHR, esp. at 96, where there are references to

has dominated discussions concerning the acts of UN peace-keepers. In this context, the UN High Commissioner for Human Rights has issued guidelines which contain specific injunctions not only for states but also for inter-governmental organizations and non-governmental organizations. The UN High Commissioner's *Recommended Principles and Guidelines on Human Rights and Human Trafficking* contain a specific Guideline addressed to those working for non-state actors, such as inter-governmental or non-governmental organizations. Guideline 10 entitled, '*Obligations of peacekeepers, civilian police and humanitarian and diplomatic personnel*', reads:

> The direct or indirect involvement of peacekeeping, peace-building, civilian policing, humanitarian and diplomatic personnel in trafficking raises special concerns. States, intergovernmental and non-governmental organizations are responsible for the actions of those working under their authority and are therefore under an obligation to take effective measures to prevent their nationals and employees from engaging in trafficking and related exploitation. They are also required to investigate thoroughly all allegations of trafficking and related exploitation and to provide for and apply appropriate sanctions to personnel found to have been involved in trafficking.[23]

Unfortunately, further reports of sexual exploitation and rape have surfaced since the adoption of these texts.[24] The human rights obligations with regard to protection of individuals from abuse in this context should, in theory, make immediate disciplinary action easier. But even if individual disciplinary measures remain primarily an issue for the state of nationality, the international human rights obligations on the United Nations itself operate in a parallel and complementary way. To understand fully the legal framework, one needs to step back and consider

UNMIK international police officers suspected of trafficking and being repatriated. And see 166 for the recommendation concerning the establishment of mechanisms for implementing anti-trafficking regulations for all international personnel. See also UNHCR/Save the Children UK, note for implementing and operational partners, 'Sexual Violence and Exploitation: the experience of refugee children in Liberia, Guinea and Sierra Leone', February 2002.

[23] Report of the United Nations High Commissioner for Human Rights to the Economic and Social Council, UN Doc. E/2002/68/Add.1, 20 May 2002. The Guidelines use the following definition of trafficking: 'the recruitment, transportation, transfer, harbouring or receipt of persons, by means of the threat or use of force or other forms of coercion, of abduction, of fraud, of deception, of the abuse of power or of a position of vulnerability or of the giving or receiving of payments or benefits to achieve the consent of a person having control over another person, for the purpose of exploitation. Exploitation shall include, at a minimum, the exploitation of the prostitution of others or other forms of sexual exploitation, forced labour or services, slavery or practices similar to slavery, servitude or the removal of organs'. Source: Protocol to Prevent, Suppress and Punish Trafficking in Persons, Especially Women and Children, supplementing the United Nations Convention against Transnational Organized Crime (2000) (Art. 3(a)).

[24] UN Secretary-General, Kofi Annan, issued a press release on 19 November 2004 which read, in part: 'I am afraid there is clear evidence that acts of gross misconduct have taken place. This is a shameful thing for the United Nations to have to say, and I am absolutely outraged by it.' UN Doc. SG/SM/9605, AFR/1069, PKO/115; see also 'U.N. Probes Congo Sex-Abuse Allegations', Associated Press, 23 November 2004.

how the United Nations has historically dealt with claims against it for 'unnecessary damage' in the context of peace-keeping missions.

4.1.2 Claims against UN Peace Operations

It is clear that the United Nations accepts that it has international obligations and that it incurs responsibility for acts that violate those obligations. The United Nations sees the rules on state responsibility as applicable to it by analogy.[25] In addition, Section 29 of the Convention on the Privileges and Immunities of the United Nations (1946) obligates the United Nations to provide a means of settling contractual disputes or 'other disputes of a private law character'.[26] It is this provision which has been at the heart of the framework for complaints against the United Nations. In the context of this study, it is perhaps ironic that in order to fall within the rule, human rights victims have to show that their injuries are connected to obligations which are of a 'private law character'.[27]

In the context of a UN deployment of personnel to a country, the settlement of disputes would be governed by the status of forces agreement. The model treaty for the United Nations to apply with host states (status of forces/mission agreements) provides for a 'standing claims commission' to settle such disputes of a private law character. No such standing claims commission has ever been established,[28] and it has been argued that, in the light of the fact that the United Nations may be engaged in situations such as Somalia, where it is not clear who would represent the state on such a commission,[29] there will, in any event, remain a need for alternative methods for resolving such claims. So far, *local claims review boards* have dealt with claims against UN peace-keeping operations. These boards are UN bodies, and in the words of the Secretary-General's report: 'the Organization, rightly or wrongly, may be perceived as acting as a judge in its own case. Based on the principle that justice should not only be done but also be seen to be done, a procedure that involves a neutral third party should be retained in

---

[25] 'The international responsibility of the United Nations for the activities of United Nations forces is an attribute of its international legal personality and its capacity to bear international rights and obligations. It is also a reflection of the principle of State responsibility—widely accepted to be applicable to international organizations—that damage caused in breach of an international obligation and which is attributable to the State (or to the Organization), entails the international responsibility of the State (or of the Organization) and its liability in compensation.' 'Report of the Secretary-General', UN Doc. A/51/389, 20 September 1996, at para. 3.

[26] 'Section 29   The United Nations shall make provisions for appropriate modes of settlement of: (a) Disputes arising out of contracts or other disputes of a private law character to which the United Nations is a party; (b) Disputes involving any official of the United Nations who by reason of his official position enjoys immunity, if immunity has not been waived by the Secretary-General.'

[27] For a full discussion of the immunities of international organizations and the procedures for dealing with contractual obligations of such organizations, as well as other claims of a private law nature, see P. H. F. Bekker, *The Legal Position of Intergovernmental Organizations: A Functional Necessity Analysis of Their Legal Status and Immunities* (Dordrecht: Martinus Nijhoff, 1994).

[28] See 'Report of the Secretary-General' UN Doc. A/51/903, 21 May 1997, at paras 7–8.

[29] UN Doc. A/C.5/49/65, 24 April 1995, 'Report of the Secretary-General', at para. 17.

the text of the status-of-forces agreement as an option for potential claimants'.[30]
The failure of the United Nations to establish clear and efficient procedures
for the operation of these boards has been criticized by its own Office of Internal
Oversight, which highlighted the fact that at the end of the UN Peace Forces
(UNPF) operation in the former Yugoslavia (1992–1996), there were pending
claims worth US $32 million.[31] In the context of the liquidation of that opera-
tion, the Secretary-General prepared a report that looked more generally at third-
party claims. Although some claims would not normally be labelled human
rights claims, the report stated that, in the context of peace-keeping, the claims
against the United Nations relate mostly to: 'non-consensual use and occupancy
of premises, personal injury and property loss or damage arising from the ordinary operation of the force, and such injury and damage as result from combat
operations'.[32] A follow-up report set out proposed limitations to third-party
claims against the United Nations regarding its peace-keeping operations, and the
General Assembly subsequently decided the legal limitations that apply to
such claims.[33] The limitations on claims against the United Nations have been
circumscribed by a General Assembly Resolution.[34] In brief, the limitations on
third-party claims for personal injury, illness, or death resulting from UN peace-
keeping operations are as follows: only economic loss will be compensated—no
compensation for pain and suffering, etc., the maximum payment for the injury,
illness, or death of any individual is $50,000 (although an exception can be
made); for property loss and damage the rates for non-consensual use of premises
are fixed according to the pre-mission rental value; and no liability is engaged in
relation to claims connected to activities of members of peace-keeping operations
arising from 'operational necessity'.[35] In the context of a death or personal injury
claim representing a human rights complaint, the concept of operational necessity

---

[30] UN Doc. A/51/903, 21 May 1997, 'Report of the Secretary-General', at para. 10.
[31] UN Doc. A/53/394, 23 September 1999, 'Note by the Secretary-General', paras 63–64.
[32] UN Doc. A/51/389, 20 September 1996, 'Report of the Secretary-General', at para. 3.
[33] Daphna Shraga, Senior Legal Officer, Office of the Legal Counsel, Office of Legal Affairs, UN,
writing in an unofficial capacity, has explained the way in which the Resolution has binding legal
effects: 'A General Assembly resolution on the limited liability of the United Nations, while recommendatory for member states, is mandatory for the Organization and binds the Secretary-General to
compensate claimants within the temporal and financial limitations prescribed; when incorporated
by reference in a status of forces agreement, it also constitutes the legal basis for the parties' consent to
abide by the limitations. If, as is expected, UN claims review boards continue to settle private-law
claims between the Organization and third-party claimants, the incorporation of the financial and
temporal limitations in their terms of reference will constitute the applicable law by which third-
party claims will be decided.' 'UN Peacekeeping Operations: Applicability of International
Humanitarian Law and Responsibility for Operations-Related Damage' 94 *AJIL* (2000) 406–412, at
411–412.   [34] UN Doc. A/RES/52/247, adopted 26 June 1998.
[35] See UN Doc. A/51/389, 20 September 1996 'Report of the Secretary-General', at paras 13ff
and fn 5: 'The concept of "operational necessity" as used herein has been developed in the practice of
United Nations operations. It is distinguishable from the concept of "military necessity", which is
limited to combat operations and is governed by the laws of war. Both concepts are, however, concep-
tually similar in that they serve as an exemption from liability, or a legitimization of an act that would
otherwise be considered unlawful.'

could be understood as similar to a limitation clause in human rights law. Nevertheless, simply claiming operational necessity does not mean that there has been a legitimate limitation on an international human right. The legitimacy of any interference has to be determined according to international human rights law. Some human rights allow for no limitations. For example, there can never be such a limitation, necessity, or justification regarding torture.[36]

It is worth recalling the early recognition by the United Nations of its international obligations, when it negotiated a settlement regarding unlawful acts and omissions by the military operation in Egypt (UNEF) and in the Congo (ONUC).[37] The United Nations articulated a policy to compensate individuals who had suffered damage for which it is legally liable. The arrangement was made by the Secretary-General, acting as chief administrative officer, settling claims brought by private individuals against the United Nations.[38] Compensation was also paid directly to the International Committee of the Red Cross for the death of their principal representative and two staff in a shooting incident in Elizabethville in 1961. In this case, there was no conclusion on the facts as to whether the United Nations had acted unlawfully.[39]

The terms of the 1965 treaty between the United Nations and Belgium relating to the settlement of 581 claims filed by Belgian nationals read as follows:

> The United Nations has agreed that the claims of Belgian nationals who may have suffered damage as a result of harmful acts committed by ONUC personnel, and not arising from military necessity, should be dealt with in an equitable manner.
>
> It has stated that it would not evade responsibility where it was established that United Nations agents had in fact caused damage to innocent parties...
>
> [T]he Secretary-General shall, without prejudice to the privileges and immunities of the United Nations, pay the Belgian Government the sum of one million five hundred thousand United States dollars in outright and final settlement of all claims arising [for damage to persons and property arising from the operations of the UN force in the Congo].[40]

The US $1.5 million compensation was set off against unpaid assessments to the ONUC operation. It is of interest that, in the opinion of the United Nations, its

---

[36] Note Art. 3 of the Article 3 UN General Assembly's Declaration on the Protection of All Persons from Being Subjected to Torture and Other Cruel, Inhuman or Degrading Treatment or Punishment (1975) GA Res. 3452: 'No State may permit or tolerate torture or other cruel, inhuman or degrading treatment or punishment. Exceptional circumstances such as a state of war or a threat of war, internal political instability or any other public emergency may not be invoked as a justification of torture or other cruel, inhuman or degrading treatment or punishment.' See also *Chahal v UK*, Judgment of the European Court of Human Rights, 25 October 1996, and see in this regard M. K. Addo and N. Grief, 'Does Article 3 of the European Convention on Human Rights Enshrine Absolute Rights' 9 *EJIL* (1998) 510–524.

[37] See the discussion and references in C. F. Amerasinghe, *Principles of the Institutional Law of International Organizations* (Cambridge: Cambridge University Press, 1996) 239–247.

[38] See the letters from the Secretary-General to the Acting Permanent Representative of the USSR, of 6 August 1965, discussed and cited in R. Simmonds, *Legal Problems Arising from the United Nations Military Operations in the Congo* (The Hague: Martinus Nijhoff, 1968) at 239–241.

[39] Ibid, at 190–191.

[40] UNTS 7780, United Nations and Belgium, in force 17 May 1965.

liability stems from three multiple sources: 'generally recognized legal principles', the Convention of Privileges and Immunities, reinforced by the 'principles set forth in the international conventions concerning the protection of life and property of civilian population during hostilities', and 'considerations of equity and humanity which the United Nations cannot ignore'.[41]

4.1.3   The Principles and Spirit of General Conventions Applicable to the Conduct of Military Personnel

Steps were taken at this time to include a reference to the laws of war and the Geneva Conventions in agreements between the United Nations and troop contributing countries.[42] The Regulations for the Cyprus operation contained in its final provision the terse injunction: 'The Force shall observe the principles and spirit of the general international Conventions applicable to the conduct of military personnel.'[43] This was elaborated on in agreements with troop contributing countries. One such agreement with Canada in 1966 (which was copied in later agreements) stated: 'The international Conventions referred to in this Regulation include, *inter alia*, the Geneva (Red Cross) Conventions of 12 August 1949 to which your Government is a party and the UNESCO Convention on the Protection of Cultural property in the event of armed conflict, signed at the Hague on 14 May 1954.'[44] At the time, commentators concluded that these provisions 'really constitute a recognition of the applicability of the general (or customary) international law of war rather than of those detailed provisions of the relevant conventions which do not as yet constitute customary international law.'[45]

Regulations for the early UN operations in Egypt, the Congo, and Cyprus therefore included a general clause demanding respect for the principles and spirit of general international conventions applicable to the conduct of military personnel. Since 1992, the Secretary-General has also included in status of forces agreements with host states a clause relating to the applicable international law. For example, the agreement with the Rwandan Government stated:

> The United Nations shall ensure that UNAMIR shall conduct its operations in Rwanda with full respect for the principles and spirit of the general conventions applicable to the conduct of military personnel. These international conventions include the four Geneva Conventions of 12 August 1949 and their Additional Protocols of 8 June 1977

[41] Letter from the Secretary-General to the Acting Permanent Representative of the USSR, UN Doc. S/6597, 6 August 1965, at 1.

[42] See the details in D. Shraga, 'The United Nations as an actor bound by international humanitarian law' in L. Condorelli, A.-M. La Rosa, and S. Scherrer (eds) *Les Nations unies et le droit international humanitaire: Actes du colloque international 19, 20, 21 octobre 1995* (Paris: Pedone, 1996) 317–338, at 325–326.   [43] UN Doc. ST/SGB/UNFICYP/1, 25 April 1964, Reg. 40.

[44] Exchange of Letters Constituting an Agreement, 21 February 1996, deemed to take effect from 13 March 1964, UNTS 8107, at para. 11 of the annexed letter of the Secretary-General. See also the discussion by Simmonds (1968: 192).   [45] Simmonds (1968: 192).

and the UNESCO Convention of 14 May 1954 on the Protection of Cultural Property in the Event of Armed Conflict.... UNAMIR and the Government shall therefore ensure that members of their respective military personnel are fully acquainted with the principles and spirit of the above-mentioned international instruments.[46]

Similar obligations have been included in subsequent peace-keeping operations and are also included in the model agreement between the United Nations and the troop contributing states.[47] Whatever the exact nature of the applicability of these Conventions, it is important to note that the customary international law obligations exist in parallel to the obligations included in the treaties. Indeed, the United Nations is considered as already bound by such customary international law. In a contribution to a symposium on 'Humanitarian Action and Peace-Keeping Operations', Daphna Shraga and Ralph Zacklin, from the UN Legal Office, stated: 'The Geneva Conventions which have by now been widely accepted as part of customary international law are binding upon all States, and, therefore, also upon the United Nations, irrespective of any formal accession.'[48] Note, however, that we should be clear that UN officials such as Ralph Zacklin were also careful to state that the United Nations is: 'not a State and does not possess the juridical and administrative powers necessary to independently discharge many of the obligations provided for under international humanitarian law'.[49]

What exactly can be expected of the United Nations in such contexts? The clarification of what the United Nations should be expected to do and what is meant by the 'principles and spirit' of such conventions has now been achieved through expert work conducted under the auspices of the International Committee of the Red Cross. This in turn led to the Secretary-General's Bulletin, 'Observance by United Nations forces of international humanitarian law'.[50] That this is the fulfilment of a legal obligation (rather than an internal directive) is evidenced by the Secretary-General's explanation that, by promulgating and disseminating Directives for UN Peace-keeping Forces regarding respect for international humanitarian law, 'the United Nations will be complying with its *obligation* under common article 1 of the Geneva Conventions to respect and to ensure respect for the principles of international humanitarian law'.[51]

---

[46] Quoted by D. Shraga and R. Zacklin, 'The Applicability of International Humanitarian Law to United Nations Peace-keeping Operations: Conceptual, Legal and Practical Issues' in U. Palawankar (ed) *Symposium on Humanitarian Action and Peace-Keeping Operations* (Geneva: ICRC, 1994) 39–48, at 45.   [47] UN Doc. A/46/185, Annex, para. 28.

[48] Shraga and Zacklin, 'The Applicability of International Humanitarian Law to United Nations Peace-keeping Operations: Conceptual, Legal and Practical Issues', *Symposium on Humanitarian Action and Peace-keeping Operations*, 22–24 June 1994 (Geneva: ICRC, 1994) 39–48, at 47. The authors include the usual disclaimer that the views in the paper 'do not necessarily reflect the views of the Office of Legal Affairs or of the United Nations'.

[49] R. Zacklin, 'General Report' in L. Condorelli, A.-M. La Rosa, and S. Scherrer (eds) *Les Nations unies et le droit international humanitaire: Actes du colloque international 19, 20, 21 octobre 1995* (Paris: Pedone, 1996) 39–53, at 51.   [50] 6 August 1999, ST/SGB/1999/13.

[51] Report on the work of the Organization (August 1996) UN Doc. A/51/1, para. 117 (emphasis added).

The scope of the Bulletin is quite narrow: first, it covers only UN forces conducting operations under UN command and control; and second, it applies only to UN forces 'when in situations of armed conflict they are actively engaged therein as combatants, to the extent and for the duration of their engagement'.[52] In addition to the 'fundamental rules and principles of international humanitarian law' outlined in the Bulletin, there is a reference to the obligations traditionally included in status of forces agreements. Section 3 states: 'the United Nations undertakes to ensure that the force shall conduct its operations with full respect for the principles and rules of the general conventions applicable to the conduct of military personnel'. Because the Bulletin is limited to combat situations, it was not considered necessary to refer explicitly to human rights obligations.

The problem remains, however, that most complaints relate to situations outside actual combat situations; complaints relate to the more usual scenario where the UN forces are acting as police or in assuring humanitarian assistance. What other obligations beyond the laws of armed conflict apply to UN forces and the United Nations as such? The list of conventions mentioned in the status of forces agreements is not stated to be exhaustive. Should human rights obligations also be considered obligations derived from 'general conventions applicable to the conduct of military personnel'? When this phrase appeared in the agreement with Canada (cited above), no UN human rights treaties were in force, and so it is not surprising that they were not mentioned. The scope of the 'general conventions', considered in the context of status of forces agreements and agreements with troop contributing countries, should today arguably include human rights conventions. A treaty such as the Convention on the Rights of the Child (1989) has over 190 states parties, and military personnel and war situations are not excluded from its scope. In fact, some obligations in the Convention specifically deal with the rights of the child during armed conflict, and one of the Protocols is explicitly addressed to obligations relating to the involvement of children in armed conflict.[53] Other conventions, such as the conventions on discrimination against women (CEDAW) and racial discrimination (CERD) are clearly relevant, as are the International Covenant on Civil and Political Rights (ICCPR), and the International Covenant on Economic, Social and Cultural Rights (ICESCR). The Convention against Torture and Other Cruel, Inhuman, or Degrading Treatment or Punishment (CAT) is equally pertinent, although torture and inhuman or degrading treatment is in any case prohibited in customary international law.

At this point one might question whether human rights treaties are relevant at all to the situation where states parties send their troops abroad as part of a multilateral force. The UN Human Rights Committee, in a 2004 General Comment

---

[52] UN Doc. ST/SGB/1999/13, Section 1.1.
[53] See Art. 38 of the Convention on the Rights of the Child, in force since 2 September 1990, and see also the Optional Protocol to the Convention on the Rights of the Child on the involvement of children in armed conflict (2000).

on the general legal obligations imposed on states parties to the Covenant on Civil and Political Rights, has specifically addressed this issue:

> States Parties are required by article 2, paragraph 1, to respect and to ensure the Covenant rights to all persons who may be within their territory and to all persons subject to their jurisdiction. This means that a State party must respect and ensure the rights laid down in the Covenant to anyone within the power or effective control of that State Party, even if not situated within the territory of the State Party. As indicated in General Comment 15 adopted at the twenty-seventh session (1986), the enjoyment of Covenant rights is not limited to citizens of States Parties but must also be available to all individuals, regardless of nationality or statelessness, such as asylum seekers, refugees, migrant workers and other persons, who may find themselves in the territory or subject to the jurisdiction of the State Party. This principle also applies to those within the power or effective control of the forces of a State Party acting outside its territory, regardless of the circumstances in which such power or effective control was obtained, such as forces constituting a national contingent of a State Party assigned to an international peace-keeping or peace-enforcement operation.[54]

The applicable conventions should definitely include the Covenant on Civil and Political Rights. The International Court of Justice's Advisory Opinion on the Legal Consequences of the Construction of a Wall in the Occupied Palestinian Territory, has more recently confirmed that this treaty, and other human treaties such as the Covenant on Economic, Social and Cultural Rights and the Convention on the Rights of the Child, do indeed apply where a state exercises jurisdiction outside its own territory.[55]

A second question should also be addressed. It has been argued that in times of armed conflict, only the rules of international armed conflict apply and that human rights rules are somehow displaced. This argument has been rejected by the International Court of Justice, and the Human Rights Committee has offered further clarification. The 1996 Advisory Opinion of the International Court of Justice on the *Legality of the Threat or Use of Nuclear Weapons* was clear that human rights norms can continue to apply alongside international humanitarian law.[56]

> It was suggested that the Covenant was directed to the protection of human rights in peacetime, but that questions relating to unlawful loss of life in hostilities were governed by the law applicable in armed conflict. The Court observes that the protection of the International Covenant on Civil and Political Rights does not cease in times of war, except by operation of Article 4 of the Covenant whereby certain provisions may be derogated from in a time of national emergency. Respect for the right to life is not, however such a provision. In principle, the right not arbitrarily to be deprived of one's life applies also in hostilities.[57]

---

[54] General Comment No. 31 (on Art. 2 of the Covenant: The Nature of the General Legal Obligation Imposed on States Parties to the Covenant) adopted 21 April 2004, UN Doc. CCPR/C/74/CRP.4/Rev.6, para. 10.   [55] 9 July 2004, at paras 111–113.
[56] *Legality of the Threat or Use of Nuclear Weapons*, Advisory Opinion of 8 July 1996, (1996) ICJ Reports 66.   [57] Ibid, at paras 24–25.

The Court explained how recourse to international humanitarian law may in some circumstances be necessary to explain the content of a human rights obligation in the context of an armed conflict.

> The test of what is an arbitrary deprivation of life, however, then falls to be determined by the applicable *lex specialis*, namely the law applicable in armed conflict which is designed to regulate the conduct of hostilities. Thus whether a particular loss of life, through the use of a certain weapon in warfare, is to be considered an arbitrary deprivation of life contrary to Article 6 of the Covenant, can only be decided by reference to the law applicable in armed conflict and not deduced from the terms of the Covenant itself.[58]

This issue has since been addressed by the UN Human Rights Committee in the following way:

> As implied in General Comment 29, the Covenant applies also in situations of armed conflict to which the rules of international humanitarian law are applicable. While, in respect of certain Covenant rights, more specific rules of international humanitarian law may be specially relevant for the purposes of the interpretation of Covenant rights, both spheres of law are complementary, not mutually exclusive.[59]

Again the flexible notion of *complementarity* can be deployed to apply two frameworks of legal analysis simultaneously. There is no longer any question of being forced to choose either a human rights filter or a humanitarian law filter. In its more recent Advisory Opinion on the *Construction of a Wall in the Occupied Palestinian Territory*, the Court explained the interrelationship between these two branches of international law in general terms, going beyond the question of the right to life in the context of the specific regime governing the use of prohibited weapons.

> 106.   More generally, the Court considers that the protection offered by human rights conventions does not cease in case of armed conflict, save through the effect of provisions for derogation of the kind to be found in Article 4 of the International Covenant on Civil and Political Rights. As regards the relationship between international humanitarian law and human rights law, there are thus three possible situations: some rights may be exclusively matters of international humanitarian law; others may be exclusively matters of human rights law; yet others may be matters of both these branches of international law. In order to answer the question put to it, the Court will have to take into consideration both these branches of international law, namely human rights law and, as *lex specialis*, international humanitarian law.

As discussed in Chapter 3, human rights law cannot be gleaned by a restrictive application of human rights conventions, human rights law emerges through the practice of evolving universal standards adopted in international fora. It is these standards which put flesh on the bones of the generally formulated principles

---

[58] *Legality of the Threat or Use of Nuclear Weapons* (n 21 above) at para. 25.
[59] General Comment 31 (n 54 above) at para. 11, footnote omitted.

found in the treaties. I suggest that the obligations to respect the principles of conventions applicable to military personnel must include respect for the standards which explicate these principles.

Evidence that UN personnel are also bound by such international human rights standards can be found in the adoption by the UN General Assembly in 1995 of the text of the Convention on the Safety of United Nations and Associated Personnel.[60] The Convention opens its savings clauses in the following way: 'Nothing in this Convention shall affect: (a) the applicability of international humanitarian law and *universally recognized standards of human rights as contained in international instruments* in relation to the protection of United Nations operations and United Nations and associated personnel or *the responsibility of such personnel to respect such law and standards.*'[61]

The scope of such universally recognized standards of human rights should cover, not only customary international law, but also the standards contained in UN instruments such as the UN Code of Conduct for Law Enforcement Officials[62] and the UN Basic Principles on the Use of Force and Firearms.[63] At the time of the drafting of the Convention on the Safety of United Nations and Associated Personnel, Amnesty International had been highlighting the need to ensure an explicit recognition of incorporation of such standards into UN peace-keeping work. The Amnesty International report, *Peacekeeping and Human Rights* argued:

> ... the UN must ensure that troops under its command carrying out law enforcement functions, such as arrest, detention, search and seizure, crowd dispersal or ensuring public order, are trained in and abide by international human rights and criminal justice standards. Such standards should include, among others, the Code of Conduct for Law Enforcement Officials and the Basic Principles on the Use of Force and Firearms by Law Enforcement Officials ... If troops are to carry out these policing functions they must abide by and be trained in international standards of policing, rather than the practices of war.[64]

In addition to the Code of Conduct and the Basic Principles, there is the UN Body of Principles for the Protection of All Persons under Any Form of Detention or Imprisonment which provides the detail necessary to understanding terms such as 'cruel, inhuman or degrading treatment'. Principle 6 reads:

> No person under any form of detention or imprisonment shall be subjected to torture or to cruel, inhuman or degrading treatment or punishment.* No circumstance whatever

---

[60] For an overview, see M.-C. Bourloyannis-Vrailas, 'The Convention on the Safety of United Nations and Associated Personnel' 44 *ICLQ* (1995) 560–590. Note that the Norwegian proposal to allow non-state actors in control of territory to adhere to the Convention was rejected as giving too much recognition to such groups (at 588).

[61] See GA Res. 49/59, adopted 9 December 1994, Art. 20(a) (emphasis added).

[62] Adopted by the General Assembly in Res. 34/169, 17 December 1979.

[63] Adopted in September 1990 by the Eighth UN Congress on the Prevention of Crime and the Treatment of Offenders, Havana, Cuba.

[64] Amnesty International, *Human Rights and Peacekeeping* (1994) AI Index IOR 40–001/1994, Section 2.2 at 21.

may be invoked as a justification for torture or other cruel, inhuman or degrading treatment or punishment.

> * The term 'cruel, inhuman or degrading treatment or punishment' should be interpreted so as to extend the widest possible protection against abuses, whether physical or mental, including the holding of a detained or imprisoned person in conditions which deprive him, temporarily or permanently, of the use of any of his natural senses, such as sight or hearing, or of his awareness of place and the passing of time.[65]

In sum, the United Nations is responsible for any violations of international humanitarian law and international human rights law committed by its forces or agents.[66] The scope of the international human rights obligations on the United Nations covers at least the customary international law rights identified by the Human Rights Committee,[67] and must be considered to extend, through the use of the phrase 'general conventions applicable to the conduct of military personnel', to applicable rights in widely ratified human rights treaties. For a human rights policy to be meaningful in this context, the principles enumerated in these treaties have to be understood by reference to detailed human rights standards covering the use of force and detention.

The next section looks more closely at some further legal arguments which have arisen regarding application of international human rights law to the United Nations outside the context of UN peace-keeping.

4.1.4   UN Human Rights Obligations and the Issue of Discrimination in Employment

Frédéric Mégret and Florian Hoffmann suggest that: 'One can think of three main ways that the United Nations can possibly be bound by international

---

[65] Approved by the UN General Assembly, A/RES/43/173, 9 December 1988, footnote * in the original.

[66] Note the draft Article on the responsibility of international organizations adopted on first reading by the ILC: 'Article 4   General rule on attribution of conduct to an international organization   1. The conduct of an organ or agent of an international organization in the performance of functions of that organ or agent shall be considered as an act of that organization under international law whatever position the organ or agent holds in respect of the organization.   2. For the purposes of paragraph 1, the term "agent" includes officials and other persons or entities through whom the organization acts.   3. Rules of the organization shall apply to the determination of the functions of its organs and agents.   4. For the purpose of the present draft article, "rules of the organization" means, in particular: the constituent instruments; decisions, resolutions and other acts taken by the organization in accordance with those instruments; and established practice of the organization.' UN Doc. A/CN.4/L.648, 27 May 2004.

[67] Discussed in Ch 3 above, the key part of the General Comment reads: 'a State may not reserve the right to engage in slavery, to torture, to subject persons to cruel, inhuman or degrading treatment or punishment, to arbitrarily deprive persons of their lives, to arbitrarily arrest and detain persons, to deny freedom of thought, conscience and religion, to presume a person guilty unless he proves his innocence, to execute pregnant women or children, to permit the advocacy of national, racial or religious hatred, to deny to persons of marriageable age the right to marry, or to deny to minorities the right to enjoy their own culture, profess their own religion, or use their own language. And while reservations to particular clauses of article 14 may be acceptable, a general reservation to the right to a fair trial would not be.' General Comment No. 24, (Issues relating to reservations made upon ratification or accession to the Covenant or the Optional Protocols thereto, or in relation to declarations under article 41 of the Covenant) 4 November 1994, para. 8.

human rights standards.'[68] First, they posit an 'external' conception, whereby the United Nations is bound by the customary international law of human rights as a subject of international law, and, moreover, as human rights treaties are often drafted with the intention of creating universal law, the United Nations is bound by the general principles of law reflected in these treaties. Second, an 'internal' conception argues that the United Nations is bound by human rights standards due to its own obligation to promote human rights under its Charter. Third, Mégret and Hoffmann point to what they term a 'hybrid' conception whereby the United Nations cannot be allowed to escape the obligations of its members.

The United Nations has taken on board a number of human rights obligations in the context of peace-keeping, without necessarily articulating any theoretical justification for such steps. It seems that a mixture of the routes for binding the United Nations identified by Mégret and Hoffman play in the background. There are, in fact, few legal fora in which human rights can be claimed as a matter of right against the United Nations. The UN Tribunals with competence over employment matters have been unsympathetic to certain discrimination-based claims.[69] In the rare cases where human rights obligations have been raised as a matter of law, they have not yet been determinative. This is partly explained by the fact that the issue has most obviously arisen in the controversial context of 'same-sex marriage'. These cases are worth examining.

In a case against UNESCO, the Appeals Board suggested a human rights approach but this was rejected by the Director-General; the rejection was, in turn, upheld by the relevant UN Tribunal (the ILO Administrative Tribunal).[70] The dissent of Mr Justice Hugessen explains the recommendations of the Appeals Board:

> By a majority the Board recommended that UNESCO:
>
> '... recognize the national law of the staff members to determine his/her marital status including those of homosexuals. Equally, the Organization should recognize the French law which recognizes homosexual partnership as ... marriage-like.'
>
> (4) Alternatively, in the event that the Director-General had difficulty accepting the above-mentioned position, the Board recommended that he make an exception to the Staff Rules, pursuant to Rule 112.2 in order to:
>
> '... protect the human rights of homosexuals, prevent discrimination on the ground of sexual orientation and fulfill the object of the rules to protect a domestic partner by granting the necessary family allowances and manifest the culture of tolerance of the Organization.'

---

[68] F. Mégret and F. Hoffmann, 'The UN as Human Rights Violator? Some Reflections on the United Nations Changing Human Rights Responsibilities' 25 *HRQ* (2003) 314–342, at 317.

[69] Amerasinghe (1996: 348) discussing *Mullan* UNAT Judgment No. 162 [1972], JUNAT Nos 114–166, 387 (sex discrimination).

[70] *Mr R. A.-O. against the United Nations Educational, Scientific and Cultural Organization (UNESCO)*, Administrative Tribunal of the International Labour Organization, 94th Session, Judgment No. 2193, 5 February 2003.

(5) Finally, the Board recommended that the Director-General:

'. . . specifically amend the rules to leave no room for doubt and to define the word "spouse" or domestic partner appropriately and remove any kind of discrimination against homosexual partners assuming that every kind of mutual loving and caring assistance, transforms the two domestic partners into spouses.'

(6) On 28 June 2001 the Director-General decided not to endorse the Board's recommendations and upheld his decision not to recognise the complainant's partner as a dependant within the meaning of the Staff Rules.

As explained above, the ILO Tribunal dismissed the appeal by the complainant. In dissent, Judge Hugessen (endorsed on this point by Judge Rondón de Sansó) considered that general principles of law, as well as international conventions on human rights, meant that the appeal should have been allowed and the discriminatory rules declared ineffective against the complainant.[71] The separate UN Administrative Tribunal has also refused to read 'spouse' to include same-sex partners.[72]

The Tribunal notes the evolution of the pledges being made by couples and, especially, the changing nature of the parties involved. Other bodies, from the International Civil Service Commission to the Committee on Human Rights, the World Bank and many others outside the United Nations system, are considering and ruling positively on the implications of this social change that is affecting part of the world. These efforts are in keeping with the principles of the Charter. However, as stated, law and custom still interpret a spouse as a partner in a legal marriage, whatever the nature of that marriage.

UN Secretary-General Kofi Annan later issued a Bulletin stating that: 'a legally recognized domestic partnership agreement under the law of the state of nationality of the staff member would count as a marriage for the purposes of the UN Staff Rules'. Whether or not this resulted from an appreciation of human rights obligations is hard to say, but the logic remains one of respect for the law of nationality rather than respect for international human rights obligations.[73]

---

[71] 'For all the above reasons, the Tribunal should conclude that Rules 103.7 and 103.9 are unenforceable vis-à-vis the complainant because they are contrary to fundamental principles of law. The provisions improperly discriminate between staff members for the purpose of entitlement to family allowances and benefits on the ground of sexual orientation. Discrimination on such a ground is contrary to the Charter of the United Nations, general principles of equality of treatment and respect for the human dignity of employees, principles which govern the international civil service, as well as international instruments on human rights. Since the provisions had no effect vis-à-vis the complainant, there was no authority to withhold the benefits. Consequently, the impugned decision, being based on these provisions, cannot stand' (at para. 40 of his dissent).

[72] Judgment No. 1063 of July 26, 2002, Case No. 1169: *Berghuys v The United Nations Joint Staff Pension Board* UN Doc. AT/DEC/1063, 26 July 2002, see para. VIII.

[73] A legally recognized domestic partnership contracted by a staff member under the law of the country of his or her nationality will also qualify that staff member to receive the entitlements provided for eligible family members. The Organization will request the Permanent Mission to the United Nations of the country of nationality of the staff member to confirm the existence and validity of the domestic partnership contracted by the staff member under the law of that country.

In the absence of a clear legal logic articulated by the United Nations, we might suggest a fourth, perhaps rather prosaic, approach. The United Nations is bound to respect human rights because it has unilaterally declared that it expects its personnel to act in accordance with the Universal Declaration of Human Rights and acts as if it were itself bound. The Secretary-General's Bulletin concerning international humanitarian law in conflict situations clears up part of the puzzle by concretizing what is meant by the 'spirit and principles' of international humanitarian law. But the abundance of official training manuals and courses on the duty of UN personnel to protect and respect human rights makes it quite clear that the UN itself sees that it, and its personnel, must respect international human rights.[74] We could call this the 'axiomatic' approach.[75] How can the United Nations call for respect for human rights without acknowledging that it must itself respect the same principles? In fact, much of the impetus behind the United Nations' training of its own field personnel for human rights has been to ensure that the understanding of the human rights standards as exemplified by the UN civilian police and military personnel is passed on to the personnel of the host countries.[76]

The important issue remains that, for some, human rights law remains of ambiguous applicability. The obstacles probably do not relate to the lack of a theoretical basis as such (given that there are multiple bases). Opposition endures due, first, to an abiding sense that soldiers should be focused on the laws of war rather than human rights standards (in some contexts it has even been suggested that human rights training will make soldiers 'too soft' for fighting). Second, there is a sense that human rights norms are less universally accepted than the laws of war. Some of this opposition is currently waning; in part this must be due to the publicity generated around the sexual abuse scandals which have plagued the United Nations in the 1990s. It is hard to argue that the United Nations is not obligated not to abuse children or to refrain from sexual violence against women. Because such human rights abuses may take place outside the context of armed conflict, it is clear that the laws of war are not the exclusive legal framework. Human rights law and the employment bulletins of the Secretary-General provide a clear set of obligations. The challenge remains the development and implementation of an effective strategy for prevention, and, in cases of abuse, appropriate disciplinary action and reparations.

Secretary-General's Bulletin, 'Family status for purposes of United Nations entitlements', UN Doc. ST/SGB/2004/4, 20 January 2004.

[74] See the Code of Conduct for Peacekeepers and the Handbooks for Military Observers and Civilian Police, published in 1995, referred to n 19 above.

[75] A. Clapham and M. Henry, 'Peace-keeping and Human Rights in Africa and Europe' in A. Henkin (ed) *Honoring Human Rights* (The Hague: Kluwer, 2000) 119–150.

[76] See, e.g. UN, *United Nations Civilian Police Handbook* (Turin: International Training Centre of the ILO, 1995) excerpted in n 19 above.

4.1.5   UNMIK in Kosovo and the Issue of UN Administration of Territory

Perhaps the clearest example of the application of international human rights law to the United Nations has been in the context of Kosovo.[77] Security Council Resolution 1422 stated that one of the main responsibilities of the international civil administration included 'Protecting and promoting human rights'.[78] The Secretary-General's report on the UN Interim Administration Mission in Kosovo (UNMIK) is explicit that this mandate carries with it human rights obligations for the Mission and its staff: 'In exercising their functions, all persons undertaking public duties or holding public office in Kosovo will be required to observe internally recognized human rights standards, and shall not discriminate against any person on any grounds, such as sex, race, colour, language, religion, political or other opinion, national, ethnic or social origin, association with a national community, property, birth or other status.'[79] Crucially, the Secretary-General went on to outline an accountability mechanism: the Ombudsperson Institution. The reports stated that this institution would receive complaints concerning any abuse 'of authority by the Interim Civil Administration and any emerging local institutions and any non-state actors claiming or exercising authority'.[80]

A second human rights accountability mechanism was set up in the form of the Temporary Media Commissioner and Media Appeals Board. The relevant framework refers to human rights: 'The Board shall determine its own rules of procedure, which rules shall guarantee fair and impartial proceedings in accordance with internationally recognized human rights standards.'[81]

Decisions of these institutions have relied on international human rights law, as well as judgments of the European Court of Human Rights. In fact, the Ombudsperson's mandate is to protect the rights of all persons (natural and legal)

---

[77] For a detailed report, together with proposals for greater human rights accountability for UNMIK and KFOR, see the European Commission for Democracy through Law (Venice Commission) *Opinion on Human Rights in Kosovo: Possible Establishment of Review Mechanisms,* Adopted by the Venice Commission at its 60th Plenary Session (Venice, 8–9 October 2004) Opinion No. 280/2004, CDL–AD (2004)033, Strasbourg, 11 October 2004. Available from http://www.venice.coe.int/docs/2004/CDL-AD(2004)033-e.pdf. Note the UN Committee on Economic, Social and Cultural Rights and the Human Rights Committee have requested reports regarding UNMIK's activities and respect for human rights under the relevant treaties. At the time of writing, it looked as though UNMIK would report to these human rights bodies.

[78] S/RES/1244 (1999), 10 June 1999, at para. 10(j).

[79] 'Report of the Secretary-General on the United Nations Interim Administration Mission in Kosovo', UN Doc. S/1999/779, 12 July 1999, at para. 38, and see UNMIK Regulation No. 1999/1, 25 July 1999, at Section 2: Observance of internationally recognized standards. Note also the Constitutional Framework for Provisional Self-Government, Art. 10.1: 'Natural and legal persons in Kosovo shall have the right, without threat of reprisal, to make complaints to an independent Office concerning human rights violations or actions constituting abuse of authority by any public authority in Kosovo.'   [80] Ibid, at para. 89.

[81] UNMIK Regulation No. 2000/36, 17 June 2000, on the licensing and regulation of the broadcast media in Kosovo, at Section 4.6.

under the European Convention on Human Rights and its Protocols and under the International Covenant on Civil and Political Rights.[82] The Media Appeals Board has also read international human rights law into the requirements for procedural fairness. In the words of the Board:

> Drawing by analogy upon Article 6(1) of the European Convention on Human Rights, the Board is of the view that in deciding the grant of a benefit, such as a broadcasting licence, every applicant is entitled to a fair hearing before an independent and impartial tribunal. This requires that applicants should be informed of the procedure and of the information which they are expected to provide, that they should have an opportunity to present their case, and they should be able to correct any errors, misunderstandings or inconsistencies in the evidence.[83]

The Ombudsperson Institution has used the Convention, and its case-law, to determine not only rules of procedural fairness, but to determine violations of human rights by UNMIK officials, even where the United Nations has admitted the abuse and disciplined the officer. The Ombudsman has taken UNMIK to task for not providing the victim with a remedy within the meaning of human rights law. In a 2002 decision, the Ombudsperson concluded that there had 'been a violation of the right of the applicant to be free from ill-treatment guaranteed under Article 3 of the European Convention on Human Rights', and went on to examine whether the right to an effective remedy has been violated. The Ombudsperson found a violation of Article 13 of the Convention.

> 19.   The Ombudsperson recalls the case-law of the European Court of Human Rights holding that an investigation into allegations of ill-treatment must be capable of leading to the identification and punishment of those responsible for the breach of Article 3. The Court stressed the importance of these two elements in the Assenov and others v. Bulgaria judgment of 28 October 1998, in which it stated:

> > If this were not the case, the general legal prohibition of torture and inhuman and degrading treatment and punishment, despite its fundamental importance, ... would be ineffective in practice and it would be possible in some cases for agents of the State to abuse the rights of those within their control with virtual impunity.

> 20.   The Ombudsperson observes that the investigation into the alleged ill-treatment of the applicant was not only capable of leading to the identification of the individual responsible, but in fact did so. The Ombudsperson also observes that the UNMIK Police Commissioner has stated that the UNMIK Police had taken 'the necessary steps

---

[82] UNMIK Regulation No. 2000/38, on the Establishment of the Ombudsperson Institution in Kosovo, at Section 1.1: 'The Ombudsperson shall promote and protect the rights and freedoms of individuals and legal entities and ensure that all persons in Kosovo are able to exercise effectively the human rights and fundamental freedoms safeguarded by international human rights standards, in particular the European Convention on Human Rights and its Protocols and the International Covenant on Civil and Political Rights.'

[83] *Nexhmedin and Radio Mitrovica v Temporary media Commission, OSCE Respondent*, 14 February 2001, at para. 35, and note the Rules of Procedure 001/2000 and 002/2000, which were drawn up taking into account the standards in Art. 14 ICCPR, Art. 6 ECHR and the case-law of the European Court of Human Rights.

to discipline' the responsible Officer. However, the Ombudsperson emphasizes that the taking of disciplinary action against a police officer transgressing the bounds of correct police conduct, including even the ill-treatment of a detainee, constitutes a necessary but not sufficient element of an effective remedy for the individual suffering the harm. The Ombudsperson stresses, in this regard, that the taking of an undefined 'steps to discipline' a police officer found to have ill-treated a detainee does not adequately address the seriousness of the violation. In such circumstances, criminal prosecution is called for.

21.   The Ombudsperson further observes that Article 13 requires that the individual whose rights have been violated must be provided with effective access to any criminal investigative proceedings against the agent who has ill-treated him. Furthermore, the individual must also be able to pursue proceedings with a view to obtaining compensation where appropriate (see above-cited Assenov and others v. Bulgaria judgment). In this regard, the Ombudsperson reiterates his serious and ongoing concern about the wide scope and continuing applicability of UNMIK Regulation 2000/47 granting immunity to UNMIK and its personnel in Kosovo (cf. Special Report No. 1). This immunity places insurmountable obstacles before any resident of Kosovo wishing to enjoy an effective remedy for the violation of his or her rights by a member of UNMIK. In addition to the concerns raised therein, the Ombudsperson observes that for the United Nations itself to maintain a dual policy of anonymity of its international police officers and a refusal even to identify the country from which a police officer abusing rights comes, creates a fertile environment for 'virtual impunity' to flourish.[84]

Such developments are pertinent, as they enforce and apply human rights as such and not simply as guiding principles.[85] Moreover, the United Nations went

---

[84] Registration No. 361/01, Shefqet Maliqi, against The United Nations Mission in Kosovo (UNMIK), 13 March 2002. Note the immunities are contained in: UNNMIK/REG/2000/47, 18 August 2000, on the status, privileges and immunities of KFOR and UNMIK and their personnel in Kosovo. Note the immunity of two UNMIK CIVPOLS was lifted by the UN Secretary-General in connection with the killing of two other CIVPOLS and the wounding of a number of others. 19 April 2004 UNMIK News.

[85] Reg. 2000/59 amending 1999/1: '1.1 The law applicable in Kosovo shall be: (a) The regulations promulgated by the Special Representative of the Secretary-General and subsidiary instruments issued thereunder; and (b) The law in force in Kosovo on 22 March 1989. In case of a conflict, the regulations and subsidiary instruments issued thereunder shall take precedence.   1.2 If a court of competent jurisdiction or a body or person required to implement a provision of the law, determines that a subject matter or situation is not covered by the laws set out in section 1.1 of the present regulation but is covered by another law in force in Kosovo after 22 March 1989 which is not discriminatory and which complies with section 1.3 of the present regulation, the court, body or person shall, as an exception, apply that law.   1.3 In exercising their functions, all persons undertaking public duties or holding public office in Kosovo shall observe internationally recognized human rights standards, as reflected in particular in: The Universal Declaration on Human Rights of 10 December 1948; The European Convention for the Protection of Human Rights and Fundamental Freedoms of 4 November 1950 and the Protocols thereto; The International Covenant on Civil and Political Rights of 16 December 1966 and the Protocols thereto; The International Covenant on Economic, Social and Cultural Rights of 16 December 1966; The Convention on the Elimination of All Forms of Racial Discrimination of 21 December 1965; The Convention on Elimination of All Forms of Discrimination against Women of 17 December 1979; The Convention Against Torture and Other Cruel, Inhumane or Degrading Treatment or Punishment of 17 December 1984; and The International Convention on the Rights of the Child of 20 December 1989.   1.4 No person

beyond the human rights treaty law that was binding on the Federal Republic of Yugoslavia at the time.[86] These accountability mechanisms are part of a unilateral commitment to use human rights law as part of the parameters for governance by the United Nations and the Organization for Security and Co-operation in Europe (OSCE). They also illustrate the fact that the United Nations is prepared to be subject to obligations *beyond* some universally accepted common lowest denominator and include standards and rules from treaties which are not binding on the relevant national government. Ralph Wilde, in a carefully researched and thoughtful series of publications, has demonstrated that what he terms the 'International Territorial Administration' in Kosovo, or East Timor, is not as exceptional as is often claimed. Wilde's work suggests that we should see the acts of the international actors in a bifurcated way: the acts of the UN personnel are the acts of national governments because they are acting as the agents of national governments, but they are also the acts of the international organizations and they are bound by the law that binds the international organizations as such. The international norms applicable to the state, 'and the norms applicable to international organizations, are not just both in play—they are both in play with respect to the same acts'.[87] Wilde is not necessarily suggesting that the non-state actor and the state actor have exactly the same obligations; only that the non-state actor may in addition, as an agent of the state, have to fulfil human rights obligations usually considered as applicable to states. In such situations of proxy government, the non-state actor has human rights obligations that extend beyond those fundamental obligations that apply to the non-state actor as an actor bound by general customary international law.

> Whatever the scope of the international human rights obligations applicable to the international organization, the full range of State obligations are also applicable when the governmental role is performed. Officials need to be aware of this latter set of obligations and ensure that their behaviour is in conformity with them. If they do not, their acts will give rise to violations of international law, in this case violations committed by the State or non-State-sub-State unit in whose name they act.[88]

---

undertaking public duties or holding public office in Kosovo shall discriminate against any person on any ground such as sex, race, colour, language, religion, political or other opinion, natural, ethnic or social origin, association with a national community, property, birth or other status. In criminal proceedings, the defendant shall have the benefit of the most favourable provision in the criminal laws which were in force in Kosovo between 22 March 1989 and the date of the present regulation.'

[86] The Federal Republic of Yugoslavia became a party to the European Convention on Human Rights in March 2004. See also UNTAET/REG/1991/1, 27 November 1999, for East Timor, which included the same clause as the UNMIK Regulation with the exception of the reference to the European Convention and its Protocols.

[87] R. Wilde, 'The Complex Role of the Legal Adviser when International Organizations Administer Territory', *Proceedings of the 95th Annual Meeting of the American Society of International Law* (2001) 251–258, at 256; R. Wilde, 'From Danzig to East Timor and Beyond: The Role of International Territorial Administration' 95 *AJIL* (2001) 583–606.

[88] R. Wilde, 'The Accountability of International Organizations and the Concepts of Functional Duality' in W. P. Heere (ed) *From Government to Governance: The Growing Impact of Non-State Actors on the International and European Legal System* (The Hague: TMC Asser Press, 2004) 164–170, at 170.

Again the *complementarity* concept perhaps helps us to see that such acts can be two things at the same time—one single action giving rise to parallel responsibilities. Wilde also asks us to consider expanding our conception of UN administration to other situations, such as development camps run by the UN High Commissioner for Refugees, and to start to reflect on why, and how, such camps should be subject to human rights law, in particular with regard to governance rights to participation in decision-making and the inclusion of women in that process.[89]

In short, it has become clear that the United Nations and other international organizations, when administering territory, under whatever legal authority, are going to rely on a wide range of human rights instruments and, where there are accountability mechanisms, the rules can be applied as binding obligations. Even where the United Nations as UNMIK is held accountable by non-governmental organizations, with regard to issues such as trafficking, the rules of international human rights law are being applied in ways which substitute UNMIK for the authorities, with attendant international human rights obligations to protect people from violence and traffickers.[90]

4.1.6   Action by the UN Security Council

A further question concerns the human rights impact of the activities of the Security Council. Where the Security Council acts to impose sanctions,[91] to set up subsidiary organs, such as the international criminal tribunals for the former Yugoslavia and Rwanda,[92] or to demand measures in the context of counter-terrorism,[93] there has been considerable attention given to the need to ensure that the resulting action is in conformity with human rights law.

Michael Reisman and Douglas Stevick have argued that international law suggests that the framework for deciding the legitimacy of military action in time of war be applied to any determination of the legality of UN sanctions. They suggest

---

[89] R. Wilde, '*Quis Custodiet Ipsos Custodes?*'; Why and How UNHCR Governance of Development Refugee Camps Should be Subject to International Human Rights Law' 1 *Yale HRDLJ* (1998) 107–128.

[90] See Amnesty International, *Kosovo (Serbia and Montenegro): 'So does that mean I have rights?' Protecting the human rights of women and girls trafficked for forced prostitution in Kosovo* (2004) AI Index EUR 70/010/2004.

[91] This discussion draws on A. Clapham, 'Sanctions and Economic, Social and Cultural Rights' in V. Gowlland-Debbas (ed) *United Nations Sanctions and International Law* (The Hague: Kluwer, 2001) 131–141.

[92] For a study of the role of human rights law in this context, see S. Zappalà, *Human Rights in International Criminal Proceedings* (Oxford: Oxford University Press, 2003).

[93] Although there has been speculation as to whether, as a result of Art. 103 of the UN Charter, Security Council demands on states override obligations under international human rights law, this clash of norms scenario is not a real legal problem. Security Council Resolution 1456 of 20 January 2003 includes the following key paragraph: '6. States must ensure that any measures taken to combat terrorism comply with all their obligations under international law, and should adopt such measures in accordance with international law, in particular international human rights, refugee, and humanitarian law.'

the following five principles to guide the Security Council when imposing mandatory economic sanctions: that highly coercive sanctions be based on lawful contingencies (an approval by the Security Council); that the sanctions be necessary and proportionate; that they reasonably maximize the distinction between combatants and non-combatants; that they be periodically assessed; and that relief be provided to injured third parties.[94] The problem is that such tests seem even more subjective than the tests applied in the laws of war. The necessity of sanctions depends on one's view of the importance of the goal which sanctions are supposed to produce. Some human rights can never be balanced against foreign policy goals.

The UN Economic Social and Cultural Rights Committee, in its General Comment on the Right for Food, stated:

> States parties should refrain at all times from food embargoes or similar measures which endanger conditions for food production and access for food in other countries. Food should never be used as an instrument of political and economic pressure. In this regard, the Committee recalls its position, stated in its General Comment No. 8, on the relationship between economic sanctions and respect for economic, social and cultural rights.[95]

In its separate General Comment on Sanctions, the Committee had stated that:

> In considering sanctions, it is essential to distinguish between the basic objective of applying political and economic pressure upon the governing elite of the country to persuade them to conform to international law, and the collateral infliction of suffering upon the most vulnerable groups within the targeted country. For that reason, the sanctions regimes established by the Security Council now include humanitarian exemptions designed to permit the flow of essential goods and services destined for humanitarian purposes. It is commonly assumed that these exemptions ensure basic respect for economic, social and cultural rights within the targeted country.[96]

The Comment referred to the inclusion of humanitarian exemptions designed to permit the flow of essential goods and services for humanitarian purposes, but goes on to explain how these exemptions are very limited in scope: 'They do not address, for example, the question of access to primary education, nor do they provide for repairs to infrastructures which are essential to provide clean water, adequate health care, etc.'.[97] The Comment pointed out that insufficient attention is paid to the impact of sanctions on vulnerable groups and called for the injection of a human rights dimension into deliberations on the issue of sanctions.

---

[94] 'The Applicability of International Law Standards to United Nations Economic Sanctions Programmes' 9 *EJIL* (1998) 86–141.

[95] General Comment 12 (1999) 'The right to adequate food (art. 11)', 12 May 1999, at para. 37, UN Doc. HRI/GEN/1/Rev.6, 12 May 2003.

[96] General Comment 8 (1997) 'The relationship between economic sanctions and respect for economic, social and cultural rights', 12 December 1997, at para. 4, UN Doc. HRI/GEN/1/Rev.6, 12 May 2003.   [97] Ibid, at para. 5.

It is outside the scope of this book to consider in depth the separate responsibility of member states of the Security Council for the results of the Council's actions and sanctions. I have simply suggested that the United Nations will itself be responsible for violations of customary international law. The doctrine on this topic has revolved around the dissolution of international organizations and the question of whether the member states should be liable for the debts of the organization. The lack of convincing international legal authority in this area has led some scholars to fall back on policy considerations. In a thorough examination of the question, the Institute of International Law canvassed all possible perspectives. The rapporteur, Rosalyn Higgins (now Judge Higgins at the International Court of Justice), came to the following preliminary conclusion: 'By reference to the accepted sources of international law, there is no norm which stipulates that member states bear a legal liability to third parties for the non-fulfilment by international organizations of their obligations to third parties.'[98] Turning to questions of policy, she weighed, on the one hand, the 'efficient and independent functioning of international organizations, and on the other, the protection of third parties from undue exposure to loss and damage'.[99] She was concerned that 'if members know they are potentially liable for contractual damages or tortious harm caused by the acts of an international organization, they will necessarily intervene in virtually all decision-making by international organizations'.[100] Higgins suggested that third parties can be protected though insurance and *ad hoc* guarantees from members.

The policy implications of the human rights impact of sanctions are rather different. It is not a question of a member state interfering in the decision-making process of the organization, but of certain member states creating the policy of the organization with binding effect for all the member states; this policy and its implementation then has possible consequences for inhabitants in every state in the world. The question is not really about quantifiable contractual or tortious harm, but rather about possible violations of fundamental human rights. The majority of members of the Institute shared the views of the Rapporteur that: 'there was no rule of international law providing for the liability of states members for the defaults of international organizations', and that: 'Any liability could only be determined by reference to the particular provisions governing the operation of specific international organizations.' Nevertheless, a minority stressed that there was no rule saying that there was no liability. For some, the question is the function of the organization. Where the functions are governmental, rather than commercial, states retain a financial responsibility. Although the final resolution states that 'there is no general rule of international law whereby States members are, due solely to their membership, liable concurrently or subsidiarily, for the

---

[98] 'The legal consequences for member states of the non-fulfilment by international organizations of their obligations toward third parties, Preliminary Exposé and Draft Questionnaire' *Annuaire de l'Institut de droit international* (1995) 287.   [99] Ibid, at 288.
[100] Ibid, at 288.

obligations of an international organization of which they are members', the minority view was accommodated through the inclusion of an exception. The exception, which was accepted by the majority, reads: 'In particular circumstances, members of an international organization may be liable for its obligations in accordance with a relevant general principle of international law, such as acquiescence or the abuse of rights.'

The debate at the Institute took place against the controversy over the obligations of member states of the Tin Council for its debts.[101] It is therefore perhaps inappropriate to draw from their debate general conclusions about the obligations of member states for the acts of international organizations. I suggest that, in the context of the United Nations and the Security Council, some continuing separate responsibility for member states continues, and that this is particularly the case with regard to human rights obligations.[102] Furthermore, in a case brought against the British Government concerning British troops in the UN Cyprus mission, the two lower courts in the United Kingdom held that responsibility for the non-payment for occupation of a hotel lay with the United Nations alone, and that the Government was not liable. The House of Lords, however, overturned this finding and found, as a preliminary matter, that the courts had jurisdiction and the Government could be liable to pay compensation for the occupation by British troops arising from the UN operation of a British-owned hotel in Cyprus.[103] The case is sometimes referred to in the doctrine to illustrate the possibility of *concurrent* responsibility of the United Nations and the contributing states. According to Amerasinghe: 'What this case illustrates is that in such instances there may be concurrent responsibility because of dual control,

---

[101] *Maclaine Watson & Co Ltd v Department of Trade and Industry and related appeals; Maclaine Watson and Co Ltd v International Tin Council* [1989] 3 All ER 523; for discussion see Bekker (1994: 211–237), on the liability of member states more generally, see Amerasinghe (1996: 249–289).

[102] In a discussion of the Security Council and the rule of law, Brownlie concludes: 'Even if the political organs have a wide margin of appreciation in determining that they have competence by virtue of Chapter VI or Chapter VII, and further, in making dispositions to maintain or restore international peace and security, it does not follow that the selection of the modalities of implementation is unconstrained by legality. Indeed when the rights of individuals are involved, the application of human rights standards is a legal necessity. Human rights now form part of the concept of international public order and the International Court, in dictum supported by 12 judges, has asserted that the obligations of States deriving from the "basic rights of the human person" are obligations *erga omnes*. [*Barcelona Traction* case (Second Phase), ICJ Reports 3, at 32.] This discipline is no less applicable when Member States are discharging their responsibilities as members of the Security Council.' I. Brownlie, 'The Decisions of Political Organs of the United Nations and the Rule of Law' in R. St. J. Macdonald (ed) *Essays in Honour of Wang Tieya* (Dordrecht: Martinas Nijhoff, 1993) 91–102, at 102.

[103] *Attorney-General v Nissan* [1969] 1 All ER 629. Note the House of Lords considered that the Security Council had recommended that all costs pertaining to the UN force should be determined by an agreement between the troop contributing countries and Cyprus, *per* Lord Morris at 646, and that the UN would use voluntary contributions to settle claims that remain unsettled by the Governments providing contingents (Reg. 16, 25 April 1964), as explained by Lord Pearce (at 647–648). To be clear, the case was not really dealing with responsibility for an internationally unlawful act arising under international law, but rather a contract, quasi contract, implied contract, or claim for unjust enrichment (Lord Reid at 639). The issue focused in part on who had primary financial responsibility (see Lord Morris at 648).

so to speak. It may mean that the UN does not have exclusive responsibility, but this does not mean that the organization cannot be held responsible.'[104]

Before leaving this topic, it is worth highlighting the approach of the Economic Social and Cultural Rights Committee when it has addressed states parties to its Covenant as members of International Financial Institutions. In 2000, the Committee's concluding observations regarding Belgium's report stated that:

> The Committee encourages the Government of Belgium, as a member of international organizations, in particular the International Monetary Fund and the World Bank, to do all it can to ensure that the policies and the decisions of those organizations are in conformity with the obligations of States parties to the Covenant, in particular the obligations contained in article 2.1 concerning international assistance and cooperation.[105]

Furthermore, various General Comments by the Committee address the International Financial Institutions themselves. For example, with regard to the right to food, the Committee stated:

> The international financial institutions, notably the International Monetary Fund (IMF) and the World Bank, should pay greater attention to the protection of the right to food in their lending policies and credit agreements and in international measures to deal with the debt crisis. Care should be taken, in line with the Committee's general comment No. 2, paragraph 9, in any structural adjustment programme to ensure that the right to food is protected.[106]

The next section looks more generally at the obligations of the World Bank and the IMF.

4.1.7   Summary of Legal Issues Related to the Human Rights Obligations of the United Nations

• The United Nations currently settles claims against its peace-keeping operations through local claims review boards based on its general liability under law according to the limits fixed by the General Assembly Resolution 52/247. One of these limits, the operational necessity limitation, should be assimilated to the proportionality inquiry which is a part of determinations under human rights or humanitarian law. An arbitrary deprivation of the right to life would be subject to such a necessity test (with a humanitarian law framework being used in an actual armed conflict situation and a human rights framework being used in a non-armed conflict situation). On the other hand, there can be no necessary limitation on the right not to be tortured or subjected to inhuman and degrading treatment.

---

[104] C. F. Amerasinghe, *Principles of the Institutional Law of International Organizations* (Cambridge: Cambridge University Press, 1996).
[105] UN Doc. E/C.12/1/Add.54, 1 December 2000, at para. 31.
[106] General Comment 12 (n 95 above) at para. 41.

- The United Nations' own training manuals and Code of Conduct now include, not only the Universal Declaration of Human Rights, but also detailed explanations of the scope of instruments such as the Basic Principles on the Use of Force and Firearms.[107] The United Nations' own willingness to accept such obligations suggests that it is bound by such human rights law. Further bases for obligations in human rights law can be found in the explicit references to the *spirit and principles* of general conventions, and the *universally recognized standards of human rights as contained in international instruments.*

- The UN Security Council, through its binding decisions on member states, requires states to act; but all such action has to take place in conformity with international human rights law. The Security Council explicitly stated this in Resolution 1456 in the context of counter-terrorism.

4.2   THE OBLIGATIONS OF THE UNITED NATIONS' INTERNATIONAL FINANCIAL INSTITUTIONS

Institutions such as the World Bank and the International Monetary Fund (IMF) have been accused of being 'secretive, unaccountable and ineffective',[108] however, they are also said to be moving to becoming 'more transparent, more accountable and more participatory'.[109] The transparency and accountability of such financial institutions under 'general principles of good global governance' are issues beyond the focus of this book.[110] We will concentrate on the accountability of such institutions under *international human rights law.*[111]

Two opposing views are sometimes seen as irreconcilable in the context of discussion over human rights and the international financial institutions. On the one hand, some argue that it is legitimate and important for international financial institutions, such as the World Bank,[112] to compel borrowers to adhere to conditions

---

[107] See *United Nations Civilian Police Handbook 1995* (n 19 above) Annex D.

[108] N. Woods, 'Making the IMF and World Bank more accountable' 77 *International Affairs* (2001) 83–100, at 83.   [109] Ibid.

[110] See R. Foqué, 'Global Governance and the Rule of Law: Human Rights and General Principles of Good Global Governance' in K. Wellens (ed) *International Law: Theory and Practice* (The Hague: Martinus Nijhoff, 1998) 25–44, who argues for a legal framework based on general principles to cover the 'multitude of actors in the *global public realm.* Not only nation-states or large globalising international concerns, but also and increasingly, even more actors such as the World Bank and the International Monetary Fund by their actions and decisions directly determine the position of individuals, groups and societies. The Legal protection of these individuals, groups and societies is often directly or indirectly at stake, as well as the respect for their (basic) rights.' Foqué (at 33) seeks a legal theoretical framework to 'establish the public realm guaranteed by the rule of law, as a safehaven for freedom, participation and plurality, without having to fall back on universality claims of pre-political and pre-natural law and on an idealistic view of man'.

[111] For details of the early debates see generally: Lawyers Committee for Human Rights, *The World Bank: Governance and Human Rights* (1993).

[112] The World Bank Group encompasses the International Bank for Reconstruction and Development (IBRD), the International Development Association (IDA), the International Finance

involving human rights in addition to the existing conditions concerning policies on the environment, military spending, anti-corruption and information disclosure. In this vein, the considerable financial resources, technical assets, and global presence of international financial institutions puts them in a position to assist in encouraging and creating the necessary conditions for the respect of international human rights standards. On the other hand, it has been argued that human rights considerations are inappropriate in this context because human rights are not included in the Articles of Agreement of institutions such as the World Bank.[113] Therefore to introduce human rights as relevant factors in this context would, it is said, violate the injunction not to interfere in the political affairs of the member states.

This summary of the poles of opinion fails to reflect the complexity of the situation or reveal the different layers of legal obligation. It is quite clear that the objectives of an institution such as the World Bank include, in a general way, the realization of human rights.[114] However, the aims of these institutions are rarely expressed in human rights terms, or organized with serious attention being paid to the actual rights concerned. This is in part because the use of the vocabulary of human rights is seen to politicize the debate,[115] and in part, because of the focus on economic considerations.

But the Bank has not excluded civil and political rights, such as freedom of expression and participatory democracy, from consideration. Explaining the

Corporation (IFC), the Multilateral Investment Guarantee Agency (MIGA), and the International Centre for Settlement of Investment Disputes (ICSID). Many of the points developed in this chapter will be of general relevance to all members of the group, however the IBRD and IDA are the only members that are subject to the Inspectional Panel procedure; MIGA and the IFC have a separate mechanism, the Compliance Adviser Ombudsman, who as an Ombudsman may respond to 'complaints by those who are affected, or likely to be affected, by the social or environmental impacts of projects'. Operational Guidelines of the CAO 'Introduction'. See generally http://www.cao-ombudsman.org. The present Chapter focuses on the IBRD and uses 'Bank' mainly to refer to that organization.

[113] I. F. I. Shihata, 'The World Bank and Human Rights: An Analysis of the Legal Issues and the Record of Achievements' 17 *Denver Journal of International Law and Policy* (1988) 39.

[114] The Bank see its role as follows: 'The Bank contributes directly to the fulfillment of many rights articulated in the Universal Declaration. Through its support of primary education, health care and nutrition, sanitation, housing, and the environment, the Bank has helped hundreds of millions of people attain crucial economic and social rights. In other areas, the Bank's contributions are necessarily less direct, but perhaps equally significant. By helping to fight corruption, improve transparency and accountability in governance, strengthen judicial systems, and modernize financial sectors, the Bank contributes to building environments in which people are better able to pursue a broader range of human rights.' World Bank, *Development and Human Rights: The Role of the World Bank* (Washington, DC: World Bank, 1998a) at 3.

[115] James D. Wolfensohn, President of the World Bank, has put it as follows: 'to some of our shareholders the very mention of the word human rights is inflammatory language. And, it's getting into areas of politics, and it's getting into areas that they're very concerned about. We decide to just go around it and we talk the language of economics and social development'. Remarks at a Dialogue on Human Rights and Development Organized by the Ethical Globalization Initiative and New York University Law School, New York City, 1 March 2004.

legitimacy of attention to such rights, Ibrahim Shihata, a Senior Vice-President and General Counsel of the World Bank, conceded that:

> It should be noted that in extreme cases, where the violations of political human rights in a country are pervasive, there will inevitably be economic repercussions to these political events which the Bank may have no choice but to take into account as relevant economic considerations in its decisions. Also, the Bank is bound to pay due regard to the binding decisions of the Security Council taken under Articles 41 and 42 of the UN Charter (to maintain peace and security).

Shihata suggested that the Bank could best respond to a 'despotic government' by 'improving the elements of governance that the Bank takes into account at present (i.e. the rule of law, accountability and transparency, in particular through support of legal, judicial and civil service reform)'.[116] Shihata's real fear, when faced with the issue of the Bank paying attention to human rights, was that the Bank might get dragged into questions of conditionality and 'plain intervention in the domestic affairs of a country' and that 'further politicization of the Bank's work, even for a moral purpose, could undermine its ability to play the roles for which it was created and for which no other institution is nearly so well qualified'.[117]

Conditionality in general is increasingly seen as inappropriate and difficult to manage.[118] In the context of the IMF, where various conditionalities relating to concepts such as governance became prevalent, there is continuing suspicion of further conditions creeping into IMF country work. In 2001, the International Monetary and Financial Committee endorsed the principle that: 'Fund conditionality should focus on those measures, including structural, that are critical to a program's macroeconomic objectives. While this principle needs to be interpreted carefully on a case-by-case basis, the Committee notes that it shifts the presumption of coverage from one of comprehensiveness to one of parsimony.'[119]

Human rights issues remain (especially for those working for the international financial institutions) mired in ideology and selectivity; human rights are not seen as simple international legal entitlements. Shihata expressed this as follows: 'Drawing the Bank into a direct and explicit political role for which it has neither the mandate nor the competence would not only raise major legal and policy

---

[116] I. F. I. Shihata, 'The World Bank and Human Rights', *Österreichische Außenpolitische Dokumentation*, Special Issue 'The universal protection of human rights: Translating international commitments into national action', 40th International Seminar for Diplomats, Helbrunn Castle, Salzburg, Austria, 28 July–1 August 1997 (1997b) 191–205, at 198.   [117] Ibid, at 199.

[118] For criticism of the way conditionality is managed within the institutions, see D. Kapur and R. Webb, *Governance-Related Conditionalities of the International Financial Institutions* (New York and Geneva: United Nations, UNCTAD, Centre for International Development Harvard University, 2000).

[119] Press Release No. 01/20, 29 April 2001, Communiqué of the International Monetary and Financial Committee of the Board of Governors of the International Monetary Fund. See generally 'Conditionality in Fund-Supported Programs Overview' Prepared by the Policy Development and Review Department, 20 February 2001, at http://www.imf.org/external/np/pdr/cond/2001/eng/overview/index.htm.

issues; it would also threaten its existing practice of promoting a large number of human rights while avoiding the use of this term in its work as part of its continuous attempts to insulate its operations from the partisan politics of its members.'[120] A similar position has been taken by the IMF:

> ... the Fund does not have a mandate to promote human rights. It is not bound by the various declarations and conventions. Human rights are not mentioned in the Articles of Agreement; nor were human rights issues raised in the process of amending the articles four times. Moreover, the autonomy of the Fund in the UN system was established in its agreement with the UN signed in 1947.
>
> But let me assure you this is all too narrow—the question might be, what is the Fund effectively doing to promote human rights? And I would confidently claim that the Fund is indeed promoting human rights through a variety of channels. The emphasis by the Fund on poverty reduction, higher spending on education and health, the preparation of PRSPs [Poverty Reduction Strategy Papers] in a broad participatory process with active involvement of civil society, the enhancement of governance through all possible channels (improvements in information availability to facilitate accountability and dialogue, the strengthening of the rule of law, the promotion of transparency in government policies), and the push for a reduced role of the state in economic activity are all critical areas for the empowerment of the civil society and preconditions for the attainment of human rights in their broad sense.[121]

Before embarking on a closer legal analysis of the relevant obligations, we should mention that, in practice, the Bank and the IMF have responded in quite public ways to major human rights incidents, such as the events in East Timor following the referendum in September 1999.[122] Not only are there important precedents of international financial institutions reacting to human crises by imposing relevant conditions on finance, but there is also, today, a greater awareness that decision-making is not actually based on pure economic policy considerations. It is not only that governments seek informally to influence the decisions taken by the Bank with regard to the human rights situation in recipient countries, but that the United States actually imposes a duty on its Executive to do so. The United States has legislation which calls on the government to 'advance the cause of human rights' in 'connection with its voice and vote' in the international financial institutions. This includes 'seeking to channel assistance toward countries other

---

[120] I. F. I. Shihata, 'Democracy and Development' 46 *ICLQ* (1997c) 635–643, at 642.

[121] G. B. Taplin, 'Speaking Points: Globalization and its Impact on the Full Enjoyment of Human Rights, Speech to Sub-Commission on the Promotion and Protection of Human Rights', 8 August 2001.

[122] See 'World Bank Statement on East Timor', News Release No. 99/035/EAP, 7 September 1999: 'We join with the International Monetary Fund (IMF) and our other partners in supporting a rapid response to the deteriorating security situation, in order that initiatives for economic recovery and poverty reduction may proceed in both Indonesia and East Timor.' See also 'The Situation in Indonesia and the IMF' by an IMF spokesman, William Murray, on 16 September 1999 stating that the IMF had decided not to send any missions to Indonesia for the time being and that discussions concerning the eventual disbursement of the next installment of the IMF's financing package scheduled for mid-September 'will take place once the right conditions exist.'

than those whose governments engage in...a pattern of gross violations of internationally recognized human rights'.[123] In the determination of such violations, the government is to give consideration to how the country under consideration is cooperating with human rights or humanitarian investigations by organizations' including the International Committee of the Red Cross, Amnesty International, and the International Commission of Jurists. The US Executive Directors are authorized and instructed to oppose 'any loan, any extension of financial assistance, or any technical assistance', to countries committing such violations unless 'such assistance is directed specifically to programs which serve the basic human needs of the people of such country'. By opposing suggested projects, the United States, and other G7 governments, can effectively block proposals, even if this is done pre-emptively by simply letting it be known that projects will not be approved. According to research by David Gillies, the Executive Directors [EDs] from the G7 countries 'bluntly informed Barber Conable, the President of the World Bank that there would be no lending to China [in the aftermath of the events in Tiananmen Square in 1989] and that if staff presented any new loans for consideration by the Board, the G7 EDs would vote against them'.[124]

The selectivity with which the United States acted in the past has drawn criticism from human rights groups,[125] and added to the general suspicion of human rights as a relevant topic in World Bank and IMF circles. Observers have highlighted the fact that international financial institutions are clearly sometimes used by governments to pursue foreign policy by other means. The attitude of the IMF and the World Bank towards Indonesia in September 1999 was reported as contributing to pressure to ensure the Indonesian acceptance of the multinational peace-keeping force for East Timor (Interfet).[126] In this case, there was probably broad-based support for such leverage, but the suspicion that human

---

[123] 22 USC §262d (1994): 'The United States Government, in connection with its voice and vote in the International Bank for Reconstruction and Development, the International Development Association, the International Finance Corporation, the Inter-American Development Bank, the African Development Fund, the Asian Development Bank, and the African Development Bank, the European Bank for Reconstruction and Development, and the International Monetary Fund, shall advance the cause of human rights, including by seeking to channel assistance toward countries other than those whose governments engage in—(1) a pattern of gross violations of internationally recognized human rights, such as torture or cruel, inhumane, or degrading treatment or punishment, prolonged detention without charges, or other flagrant denial to life, liberty, and the security of the person.'

[124] D. Gillies, 'Human Rights, Governance, and Democracy: The World Bank's Problem Frontiers' 11 *NQHR* (1993) 3–24.

[125] Lawyers Committee for Human Rights (1993: 31).

[126] 'Sick patients, warring doctors' *The Economist*, 18 September 1999, 93–94, at 93. Security Council Res. 1264 (1999) of 15 September 1999 stated that the Security Council, acting under Ch VII of the UN Charter, authorized 'the establishment of a multinational force under a unified command structure, pursuant to the request of the Government of Indonesia conveyed to the Secretary-General on 12 September 1999, with the following tasks: to restore peace and security in East Timor, to protect and support UNAMET in carrying out its tasks and, within force capabilities, to facilitate humanitarian assistance operations, and authorizes the States participating in the multinational force to take all necessary measures to fulfil this mandate'.

rights arguments will be used to impose the foreign policy agenda of powerful countries drives resistance by developing countries to integrating human rights into the work of the World Bank. There is a worry, from within and outside the World Bank, that the Bank could become an enforcement arm for those governments wishing to impose their own vision of human rights on other governments.

The following discussion reorientates the issue to focus on the fact that these organizations themselves have responsibilities, and such organizations should ensure that their own actions do not contribute to human rights violations. We will start with the role of human rights law in the legal regime which governs the Bank and the IMF; second, we shall consider the role of the Bank's own mechanisms for ensuring that the Bank operates in accordance with its own rules; and third, we shall consider place of international human rights law in the work of the International Centre for the Settlement of Investment Disputes (ICSID).

4.2.1   The Legal Arguments over Human Rights at the World Bank and the IMF

The normal starting point is to consider the functions, powers, and competences of the International Financial Institutions (IFIs). This leads to the conclusions, touched on above, that not only are most IFIs, such as the World Bank, not explicitly empowered by states under their constitutive instruments to tackle human rights issues, but the Bank is, in fact, specifically prohibited from interference in the political affairs of states and from conditioning loans on political or other non-economic considerations (under Article IV, Section 10 and Article III, Section 5(b) of the World Bank's Articles of Agreement).[127] The Bank's own interpretation of this prohibition, and its reliance on the prohibition in order to reject consideration of human rights issues, is well-known and will be briefly considered below. There are, of course, exceptions to the rule, for example, where the Security Council has acted to impose an embargo against a country.[128] This political affairs

---

[127] Art. IV, s 10, entitled 'Political Activity Prohibited', reads: 'The Bank and its officers shall not interfere in the political affairs of any member; nor shall they be influenced in their decisions by the political character of the member or members concerned. Only economic considerations shall be relevant to their decisions, and these considerations shall be weighed impartially in order to achieve the purposes stated in Article I.' Art. III, s 5(b) reads: '(b) The Bank shall make arrangements to ensure that the proceeds of any loan are used only for the purposes for which the loan was granted, with due attention to considerations of economy and efficiency and without regard to political or other non-economic influences or considerations.' See I. F. I. Shihata, *The World Bank in a Changing World: Selected Essays* (Dordrecht: Martinus Nijhoff, 1991) at 67–79 for an interpretation of the meaning of 'political' in this context.

[128] See Arts 41, 42, 48, and 103 of the UN Charter and Art. VI(1) of the Agreement between the United Nations and the International Bank for Reconstruction and Development (1947). The Bank's Board of Governors agreed to extend such regard for UN Resolutions to General Assembly Resolutions adopted under the 'Uniting for Peace Formula' GA Res. 377(V), but not for other types of General Assembly Resolutions.

prohibition, although not specifically included in the IMF's Articles, is said to apply in a comparable way to the activities of the IMF.[129]

The political affairs prohibition can no longer be interpreted as precluding consideration of human rights obligations under international law, because human rights law has become a matter of legitimate international concern. No state can claim that those who raise human rights issues are engaging in illegitimate interference in their domestic jurisdiction.[130] This issue has been addressed here because it is always raised as a preliminary obstacle to addressing the separate question, which is at the heart of this study, i.e.: What are the human rights obligations of non-state actors such as the World Bank and the IMF?

The rationale for the inclusion of a political affairs clause in the Articles of the Bank is attributed to Harry White from the United States and Lord Keynes from the United Kingdom. According to Shihata, they meant 'to emphasize the impartiality of the institution, when it came to political ideologies and interests, and to heighten instead its non-political character and universality'.[131] There are also suggestions in the scholarship that the ideological divide between capitalism and communism meant that there were concerns on all sides that the new institutions not be used as instruments to promote the influence of one bloc over the other.[132] To turn this attempt to constrain the potential for ideological partiality by the Bank into an assertion that it is illegitimate for the IMF or the Bank to consider the human rights implications of its own actions is to turn the prohibition inside

---

[129] The analogous situation in the IMF is dealt with by J. Gold, *Interpretation: The IMF and International Law* (Dordrecht: Kluwer, 1996) at 435 and 503. Note the IMF's Articles of Agreement, Art. IV, s 3: 'Surveillance over exchange arrangements, (a) The Fund shall oversee the international monetary system in order to ensure its effective operation, and shall oversee the compliance of each member with its obligations under Section 1 of this Article. (b) In order to fulfill its functions under (a) above, the Fund shall exercise firm surveillance over the exchange rate policies of members, and shall adopt specific principles for the guidance of all members with respect to those policies. Each member shall provide the Fund with the information necessary for such surveillance, and, when requested by the Fund, shall consult with it on the member's exchange rate policies. The principles adopted by the Fund shall be consistent with cooperative arrangements by which members maintain the value of their currencies in relation to the value of the currency or currencies of other members, as well as with other exchange arrangements of a member's choice consistent with the purposes of the Fund and Section 1 of this Article. These principles shall respect the domestic social and political policies of members, and in applying these principles the Fund shall pay due regard to the circumstances of members.'

[130] Thomas Buergenthal has written: 'today a state no longer can claim validly that the international community (of states, international organizations or NGOs) is intervening in its domestic jurisdiction in contravention of international law when it takes human rights considerations into account in shaping its policies or relations with that state or in publically criticizing it.' 'The World Bank and Human Rights' in E. Brown Weiss, A. Rigo Sureda, and L. Boisson de Chazournes (eds) *The World Bank, International Financial Institutions and the Development of International Law* (Washington, DC: American Society of International Law, Studies in Transnational Legal Policy, No. 31, 1999) 95–101, at 96. See also T. Buergenthal, 'The Normative and Institutional Evolution of International Human Rights' (1998) 19 *HRQ* 703–723, at 723.   [131] Shihata (1991: 71).

[132] See M. Darrow, *Between Light and Shade: The World Bank, the International Monetary Fund, and International Human Rights Law* (Oxford: Hart Publishing, 2003a) at 168–169, and the references therein.

out. The prohibition was, in a sense, designed to protect a human right, the right to self-determination: the right to choose one's political and economic system. Such a prohibition can hardly serve to create a general impunity from human rights accountability for the international organization.

Today, the appropriate approach should be to examine the political prohibition provision in the light of contemporary conditions and the coherence of the international legal order.[133] The political affairs prohibition cannot be read as excluding concern that governments comply with their international human rights obligations. And, in any event, the prohibition on interference in the polit-ical affairs of a state cannot be read to mean that the Bank and IMF have no human rights obligations of their own. I suggest that the IFIs have obligations with regard to general international law, including the main principles in the Universal Declaration of Human Rights as customary international law. Moreover, the IFIs are already perceived by some commentators as 'violators' of economic, social, and cultural rights,[134] and have been called on by UN bodies to avoid participation in projects which lead to violations of human rights, for exam-ple projects involving 'large scale evictions or displacement of persons without the provision of all appropriate protection and compensation'.[135]

[133] Cf Working Paper submitted by J. Oloka-Onyango and D. Udagama to the UN Sub-Commission on the Promotion and Protection of Human Rights on 'Human rights as the primary objective of international trade, investment and finance policy and practice' UN Doc. E/CN.4/Sub.2/1999/11, 17 June 1999, at para. 34: 'The principle problem with the "honouring the charter: or privileging the Articles" approach to the issue is that it subordinates the international human rights instruments to the charters of the agencies in question when, as a matter of law, the reverse should be the case. Human rights obligations emanate from the Charter of the United Nations and the Universal Declaration, and have come to represent a standard that in over 50 years of existence signifies a holistic approach to the human condition.'

[134] S. Leckie, 'Another Step Towards Indivisibility: Identifying the Key Features of Violation of Economic, Social and Cultural Rights' 20 *HRQ* (1998) 81–124 at 112: 'These institutions [the World Bank and IMF], as UN entities and subjects of international law, are bound by the United Nations' normative framework. Despite this, however, the policies of the international financial insti-tutions (IFIs) have resulted in substantial violations of economic, social and cultural rights within a range of developing nations, particularly the poorest countries with the least economic or political leverage.' Leckie cites General Comment No. 2 of the UN Committee on Economic Social and Cultural Rights, see below.

[135] The Committee on Economic Social and Cultural Rights, General Comment 2, 'International technical assistance measures (Art. 22)' 2 February 1990, reads, at para. 6: 'United Nations agencies involved in the promotion of economic, social and cultural rights should do their utmost to ensure that their activities are fully consistent with the enjoyment of civil and political rights. In negative terms this means that the international agencies should scrupulously avoid involvement in projects which, for example, involve the use of forced labour in contravention of international standards, or promote or reinforce discrimination against individuals or groups con-trary to the provisions of the Covenant, or involve large-scale evictions or displacement of persons without the provision of all appropriate protection and compensation. In positive terms, it means that, wherever possible, the agencies should act as advocates of projects and approaches which con-tribute not only to economic growth or other broadly defined objectives, but also to enhanced enjoy-ment of the full range of human rights.' Reproduced in UN Doc. HRI/GEN/1/Rev.6, 12 May 2003, at 12. See also Art. 22 of the ICESCR.

The discussion so far has focused on the question of why IFIs refuse to act as enforcers of human rights obligations, I now address more fully whether the IFIs actually have their own obligations with regard to human rights.

Two treatments of this question have looked in great detail at, and employed sophisticated legal reasoning to determine, the scope of the human rights obligations of IFIs. Sigrun Skogly, in her book *The Human Rights Obligations of the World Bank and the International Monetary Fund*,[136] concentrated on the role of these IFIs as inter-governmental organizations with international personality, as specialized agencies of the United Nations in the UN system, as entities referred to as specialized agencies in the two UN Covenants, and as objects of UN Charter obligations, as well as on the content of the Relationship Treaties between the specialized agencies and the United Nations itself. Skogly's analysis leads her to find that the IFIs have human rights obligations which flow from the UN Charter and subsequent human rights treaties. The scope of these obligations will be looked later in this Chapter.

Mac Darrow, in his book *Between Light and Shade: The World Bank, the International Monetary Fund, and International Human Rights Law*,[137] looks at the 'institutional effectiveness' of these IFIs and uses this principle of interpretation as a basis for an examination of the meaning of the 'political prohibition' and the scope of the powers of these IFI to deal with human rights. Darrow applies the international rules of treaty interpretation, including consideration of the subsequent practice of the IFIs, the rules of international law applicable between the member states, and the *travaux préparatoires*, to consider the interpretation of the political activity prohibition in the Articles of Agreement. He concludes that the prohibition is: 'A prohibition on interference in partisan politics and of discrimination against a State because of the political character of its government, without prejudice to fundamental human rights obligations.'[138]

Both these analyses do much to reorientate the debate over the human rights obligations of the World Bank and the IMF. They ought to do much to convince the legal analysts who have addressed this problem that the Articles of Agreement and the Charter of the United Nations cannot be read as prohibiting attention by the Bank and the IMF to the human rights implications of their activities.

4.2.2   The 2001 Opinion of the IMF General Counsel

One of the recent developments analysed by Darrow is a detailed legal brief by the General Counsel of the IMF, François Gianviti.[139] Although the brief emphasizes

---

[136] (London: Cavendish, 2001).   [137] (Oxford: Hart Publishing, 2003a).

[138] Ibid, at 192. This conclusion follows and updates the 1966 opinion of the UN Legal Counsel in the debate over the specialized agencies' obligations to respond to the General Assembly's Resolutions calling for the agencies to deny cooperation and assistance to South Africa and Portugal due to the respective apartheid and colonial policies of those governments.

[139] F. Gianviti, 'Economic, Social and Cultural Rights and the International Monetary Fund', 30 May 2001. Paper presented to a meeting organized by the UN Committee on Economic Social and Cultural Rights, on file with the author.

the Fund's own legal structure and mandated purposes, it touched on more general issues of possible human rights obligations of the Fund. The reasoning deserves our attention here for a number of reasons. First, the General Counsel articulated clearly the position that the human rights implications of the IMF's policies may indeed be relevant from the point of view of the macroeconomic effects and wisdom of any proposed course of action by the IMF:

> Another basis for Fund involvement is its assessment, as a condition for its assistance, that the member's program is viable and likely to be implemented. This means that, if a program is so strict that it is likely to generate strong popular opposition, it may not be implemented, and the Fund should not support it. It also means that, if egregious or systematic violations of human rights lead foreign governments or creditors to suspend their financial assistance or other forms of external financing, the program may not be implemented, and the Fund should not support it. Clearly this does not establish a direct link with the objectives of the Covenant [on Economic, Social, and Cultural Rights]. However, to the extent that major violations of economic and social human rights would trigger civil unrest or a lack of foreign financing, there would be at least an indirect link. Whether or not a program may create such problems is a matter of judgment for the Managing Director when transmitting the member's request to the Executive Board and for the Executive Board when deciding on the request.[140]

This clearly begs the questions: which procedures and expertise will the Fund employ to determine 'popular opposition'? And which sorts of human rights violation would trigger suspension of assistance by third parties?

Second, the brief rejected the direct applicability of the Covenant on Economic, Social, and Cultural Rights to the Fund on the following grounds: the Fund is not a party to the Covenant, the Covenant only imposes obligations on states, and lastly, the Covenant itself contains a savings clause that protects the constitutions of the UN specialized agencies.[141] The IMF's reasoning, which responds to those who have claimed that the IMF is bound by human rights law, is instructive. Gianviti drew the conclusion that any obligation not to violate these human rights implies that the Fund's constitution be interpreted 'in a manner consistent with the objective of promoting the rights in the Covenant, or deemed to be amended if this was necessary to achieve these objectives'.[142] He then declares that the consequences of such a result 'could be far reaching':

> For example, would the Fund be required to finance health and education projects while its mission is only to provide balance of payments assistance? Would the Fund have to

---

[140] Gianviti (2001) at para. 51.

[141] Ibid, at para. 12. Art. 24 ICESCR reads: 'Nothing in the present Covenant shall be interpreted as impairing the provisions of the Charter of the United Nations and of the constitutions of the specialized agencies which define the respective responsibilities of the various organs of the United Nations and of the specialized agencies in regard to the matters dealt with in the present Covenant.' See Darrow (2003a: 133–138) for a critical discussion of some of these and other arguments put forward by Gianviti.   [142] Gianviti (2001) at para. 14.

disregard the principle of uniform treatment, which still governs its general resources (i.e., resources not generated by capital gains on gold sales), to provide special assistance to developing countries? Would the United Nations Committee on Economic, Social and Cultural Rights exercise jurisdiction over the Fund's activities and the decisions of its organs? Once the principle is admitted that the Covenant takes precedence over the Articles, the whole institutional and legal structure within which the Fund operates can be questioned.[143]

This doomsday scenario presumes a number of leaps in argumentation that are not necessary to uphold the simple proposition that the IMF is bound by human rights law. The case for human rights obligations for the IMF does not presume an overriding obligation to promote human rights in disregard of the constitution of the IMF.[144] Nor does respect for human rights inevitably lead to a new role for the UN Committee that supervises the states' reports under the Covenant; recognizing existing customary international law obligations could not lead to an assumption of 'jurisdiction' over entities that are not formally bound by the treaty. Neither of these consequences flows from the assertion that the IMF is bound by human rights law. Some such consequences could possibly flow following accession by the IMF to the Covenant, but this is not possible under the terms of the Covenant and is unlikely to become a serious possibility in the future.

Third, the General Counsel considers the obligations of the IMF as a subject of international law with attendant legal obligations. Here it seems to be admitted that the IMF would be bound by norms which are part of general international law, to the extent that the activities of the organization overlap with the content of the norms.[145] But Gianviti concludes that: 'it is not generally accepted that the Covenant (or the norms contained in it) form part of general or customary international law'.[146] Unfortunately, this reasoning seems to be based mostly on an appreciation of *obiter dicta* in a judgment of the International Court of Justice. None of the judgments or opinions of that Court have resulted in a definitive list of customary international law human rights. Lists such as that found in the Court's judgment in the *Barcelona Traction* case were never expressed as closed, and in fact, were offered only as examples of the sorts of rights that carried general obligations owed to the international community as a whole (*erga omnes* obligations).[147] Moreover, the judgment is now over 35 years old, and came at a time when the two International Covenants on human rights had not even entered into force.[148] In more recent cases, the Court has referred to the principles in the Universal Declaration and affirmed that the right to self-determination is a

---

[143] Ibid, at para. 14.

[144] The developed arrangements setting out the human rights obligations of the EU do not imply any power to act outside the existing constitutional framework; see Ch 5 below.

[145] Ibid, at paras 18–19 and accompanying footnotes.   [146] Ibid, at para. 19.

[147] See Ch 3, at 3.1 above.

[148] The Court referred to 'the principles and rules concerning the basic rights of the human person' as giving rise to *erga omnes* obligations under international law in the *Barcelona Traction Light and Power Company* case (1970) at paras 33–34.

customary international law right which also gives rise to *erga omnes* obligations.[149] The right of self-determination is in fact a norm which is included in both Covenants.[150] Whether or not other norms contained in the Covenant can be described as general international law obligations is an issue which will give rise to differences of opinion. But it seems to be accepted by the IMF General Counsel that customary international law rights are binding on non-state actors such as the IMF. Suffice it to say that my reading of the contemporary scope of customary international law of human rights is wider than that presented by the General Counsel. Recall the discussion in Chapter 3 and the conclusion by Hurst Hannum that, even if social and economic rights often receive less attention, certain economic and social rights in the Declaration 'enjoy sufficiently wide-spread support as to be at least potential candidates for rights recognized under customary international law: the right to free choice of employment; the right to form and join trade unions; and the right to free primary education, subject to a state's available resources'.[151] Other scholars have also suggested that economic, social, and cultural rights are part of the general international law that is binding outside the treaty regimes. Christian Tomuschat has written that, following the adoption of the Declaration, the subsequent wide-scale acceptance of the two Covenants constitutes: 'a framework which might even be said to have become binding on non-signatory states, in any event as far as their substantive content is concerned'.[152] David Weissbrodt has simply applied the Universal Declaration to non-state actors.[153] And Thomas Buergenthal, just before he became a Judge of the International Court of Justice, wrote: 'The two Covenants and the Universal Declaration—which over time can be said to have acquired normative status

---

[149] See the *United States Diplomatic and Consular Staff in Tehran (United States v Iran)* case (1980) ICJ Reports 3, at para. 91, which held that 'wrongfully to deprive human beings of their freedom and to subject them to physical constraint in conditions of hardship is itself manifestly incompatible with the principles of the Charter of the United Nations, as well as with the fundamental principles enunciated in the Universal Declaration of Human Rights'. In the *East Timor (Portugal v Australia)* case ICJ Reports (1995) 90, at para. 29, the Court affirmed the *erga omnes* character of the rights to self-determination: 'In the Court's view, Portugal's assertion that the right of peoples to self-determination, as it evolved from the Charter and from United Nations practice, has an *erga omnes* character is irreproachable . . . [I]t is one of the essential principles of contemporary international law.' See also Ch 3, at 3.1 above.

[150] See Common Art. 1(1) to the two Covenants: 'All peoples have the right of self-determination. By virtue of that right they freely determine their political status and freely pursue their economic, social and cultural development.'

[151] H. Hannum, 'The Status of the Universal Declaration of Human Rights in National and International Law' 25 *Georgia Journal of International and Comparative Law* (1995/6) 287–397, at 349 (footnotes omitted).

[152] C. Tomuschat, *Human Rights: Between Idealism and Realism* (Oxford: Oxford University Press, 2003) at 4.

[153] Weissbrodt was not in fact examining customary law, but simply the normative force of the Declaration: 'although it is not its principal thrust, it appears that non-State entities have human rights duties under the Universal Declaration'. D. Weissbrodt, 'Non-State Entities and Human Rights within the Context of the Nation-State in the 21st Century' in M. Castermans, F. van Hoof, and J. Smith (eds) *The Role of the Nation-State in the 21st Century* (Dordrecht: Kluwer, 1998) 175–195, at 180.

either as customary international law or as an authoritative interpretation of the Charter—constitute what has become known as the International Bill of Rights.'[154] This last description of the normative effect of the Covenants and the Declaration was written in the context of an examination of the ways in which the World Bank has actually eschewed human rights law over the years. Buergenthal boldly stated 'Human rights issues no longer can be characterized as exclusively political',[155] and goes on to give a pertinent example of how human rights law should be properly considered by the Bank:

> . . . when the Bank embarks on projects supporting judicial reform, it has every right to, and should not be afraid to resort to the Covenant on Civil and Political Rights in fixing desirable due process of law or fair trial standards. We have a vast body of law on these and related subjects under international human rights treaties, and yet few individuals working on this subject in international development institutions are aware of them or dare to rely on them in establishing compliance and policy standards.[156]

Finally, as regards the customary international law status of economic, social, and cultural rights, Philip Alston has suggested that the adoption of the Millennium Development Goals (MDGs) must be taken to have legal significance:

> When large numbers of heads of state or government congregate together, along with foreign ministers and other dignitaries, and solemnly declare their abiding commitment to meet a set of MDGs—as they did in the context of the 2000 Millennium Declaration, and again at both the Johannesburg World Summit on Sustainable Development and the Monterrey Consensus, each in 2002—there would seem to be good reason to assume that they meant what they said and that they had thereby under-taken a form of obligation which should have some legal consequences.[157]

Alston argues that a case can be made that the six first Goals 'reflect norms of customary international law' and that parts of the seventh Goal would be 'strong candidates' for such status.[158] Because the goals are agreed to by all governments and are goals for the whole UN system, it seems appropriate to consider that they can provide a normative framework for the international financial institutions.[159]

---

[154] T. Buergenthal 'The World Bank and Human Rights' in E. Brown Weiss, A. Rigo Sureda, and L. Boisson de Chazournes (eds) *The World Bank, International Financial Institutions and the Development of International Law* (Washington, DC: American Society of International Law, Studies in Transnational Legal Policy, No. 31, 1999) 95–101, at 96.   [155] Ibid, at 95.

[156] Ibid, at 97.

[157] P. Alston, *A Human Rights Perspective on the Millennium Development Goals: Paper prepared as a contribution to the work of the Millennium Project Task Force on Poverty and Economic Development* (2004) at para. 35 (on file with the author).

[158] Ibid, at para. 42.

[159] The goals are as follows: '1. Eradicate extreme poverty and hunger. 2. Achieve universal primary education 3. Promote gender equality and empower women. 4. Reduce child mortality. 5. Improve maternal health. 6. Combat HIV/AIDS, malaria and other diseases 7. Ensure environmental sustainability. 8. Develop a global partnership for development.' For details of the actual targets and statistics charting progress see Report of the Secretary-General 'Implementation of the United Nations Millennium Declaration', UN Doc. A/59/282, 27 August 2004.

4.2.3   The Content of the Human Rights Obligations of the International Financial Institutions

In answer to the question: what are the human rights obligations of the international financial institutions, I would highlight three approaches. First, as UN specialized agencies, the IMF and the Bank must be involved in what the UN Secretary-General has called a core mission of the United Nations: the protection of human rights. From early on in his term, Secretary-General Kofi Annan articulated the importance of this constructive approach to human rights:

> There is a new realization that ensuring good governance—including securing Human Rights and the rule of law, assisting with elections and aiding development policies constitute in themselves preventive action. The weakness of these rights and structures are not only the roots of poverty. They are also the causes of conflict and the impediments to post-conflict reconstruction.[160]

A second approach concerns a more legalistic argument. Legal scholars such as Skogly have developed a thesis that ties the Bank and the IMF into human rights obligations through their position in the UN system, the agreements they have entered into with the United Nations itself, Articles of the International Covenant on Economic, Social and Cultural Rights (1966), and the fact that the governments on the boards of the international financial institutions have their own international human rights obligations. The scope of the obligations has then been circumscribed by Skogly to comprise a duty to simply *respect* human rights or not to make the situation worse.[161] She sees only limited obligations for the institutions to *protect* human rights (for example through a careful choice of sub-contractors) and no obligation to *fulfil* human rights obligations.[162]

---

[160] Address to the Danish Foreign Policy Society, 1 September 1997.

[161] Skogly (2001: 193): 'It has been argued that obligations pertaining to human rights law may be divided into three levels: to respect, to protect and to fulfil, where the respect level is connoted with a negative or neutral obligation not to make the human rights situation worse. It is argued that the two institutions are under an obligation to respect human rights in their operations, but not to protect or to fulfil, which implies a much more active human rights approach than it can be legally argued that the two obligations are under an obligation to do. To protect human rights implies that the obligation holder should make sure that third parties do not violate human rights. Only under limited circumstances could this be relevant for the institutions. For example, in their use of subcontractors, they may be under an obligation to ensure that these contractors do not violate human rights through their operations, but the institutions are not under a legal obligation to ensure that Member States, for instance, do not violate human rights. The obligation to fulfil human rights also lies beyond the legal obligations of the two institutions, as this would imply an active provision of measures to ensure that the human rights standards improved.'

[162] The UN's approach to the three dimensions of human rights obligations is explained in detail in Ch 8, at 8.3 below, with regard to, for example, the right to health. See General Comment 14 of the UN Committee on Economic, Social and Cultural Rights, 'The right to the highest attainable standard of health (art. 12)', 11 August 2000, esp. paras 33–37. Reproduced in UN Doc. HRI/GEN/1/Rev.7, 12 May 2004.

A third way of tackling the issue is through the prism of 'due diligence'.[163] Some scholars, such as Pierre Klein, start from the point that inter-governmental organizations are bound to respect general international law, and argue by analogy from the law of state responsibility. Klein asserts that an obligation of *vigilance* (or due diligence) fixes on inter-governmental organizations with regard to activities under their control which can affect the rights of other subjects of international law.[164]

In conclusion I suggest that the customary international law of human rights is certain enough in the relevant sectors to affirm that the international financial institutions are bound by customary international law. I would go beyond Skogly and suggest that, if the entity has sufficient legal capacity to be the bearer of international obligations, the relevant obligations include multiple aspects of the appropriate customary international law of human rights. The international financial institutions can therefore be said to have obligations, not only to respect human rights, but also to protect and even fulfil human rights in appropriate circumstances. Skogly's reasoning is based in part on the idea that such an extension is not 'feasible' and that the organizations have not been 'set up to handle' such an 'active human rights policy operation'.[165] A more activist approach would admit that international financial institutions do not normally fulfil the functions of states and so that the whole gamut of human rights obligations will not be transposable. Of course, international financial institutions will not have the same human rights obligations as states, for example, they are not obliged as such to 'fulfil' the right to basic primary education in the same way that a state has such an obligation. But they may indeed have obligations not to act in a way that prevents a borrowing state from fulfilling its obligations to provide such education. I prefer not to erect a barrier between the obligation to respect and the obligation to protect. This seems to be asking for trouble rather than responding to a clear dividing line in the law applicable to international financial institutions.[166] The customary law obligation will go beyond a simple injunction to *respect* the prohibition on racial discrimination in their activities, or to refrain from acting in a way that immediately denies people the right to life, or which involves facilitating forced labour. The customary obligation will be to avoid directly violating any human right and to avoid complicity in someone else's violation of human rights obligations.[167] Having

---

[163] For an extensive review of the practice concerning this term in the law of state responsibility see R. Pisillo Mazzeschi, *'Due diligence' e resonsibilità internazionale degli stati* (Milan: Giuffrè, 1989).

[164] 'Parmi les obligations que le "droit international général" impose aux organisations intergouvernmentales, l'on retrouve en effet l'obligation de vigilance que le droit international coutumier fait traditionnellement peser sur les Etats . . . On peut, à l'heure actuelle, affirmer que l'obligation de vigilance impose de manière général à son titulaire de veiller à ce que des activités qui se déroulent sous son contrôle ne portent pas atteinte aux droits d'un autre sujet de droit international.' P. Klein 'Les institutions financières internationales et les droits de la personne', *Revue belge de droit international* (1999) 97–114, at 112.   [165] Skogly (2001: 151).

[166] But cf Skogly (2001: 151, 193).

[167] Darrow (2003a) has detailed the ways in which the policy of the World Bank builds in respect for the environmental obligations of the recipient states under international law. The same process

suggested that all international financial institutions are bound as a matter of general international law to respect, protect, and fulfil human rights principles under general international law, let us turn to some of the internal guidelines and policy directives of the World Bank and examine how they contribute to greater understanding of the human rights obligations of this particular institution.

4.2.4   The World Bank's Operational Standards and the Inspection Panel

The World Bank's Inspection Panel represents a relevant mechanism for examining the behaviour of a non-state actor and considering compliance with international standards. The Panel has been the subject of different analyses and we need not examine the procedures in detail here.[168] It is sufficient to note that the Panel may deal with requests for inspection presented to it by 'an affected party in the territory of the borrower'.[169] This has been clarified to mean that the request for inspection must be presented by 'any two or more individuals with common interests or concerns'.[170] The procedure demands that 'The affected party must demonstrate that its rights or interests have been or are likely to be directly affected by an action or omission of the Bank as a result of a failure of the Bank to follow its operational policies and procedures with respect to the design, appraisal and/or implementation of a project financed by the Bank'.[171] The question in the present context is the extent to which these policies and procedures require respect for human rights.

The detailed explanation by Laurence Boisson de Chazournes has helped to clarify the different types of operational standards and policy directives that

could be applied in the human rights field. Gianviti (2001) addresses the issue of indirect obligations on the IMF through a supposed duty to ensure that the recipient country respects its international obligations under the Covenant. But he invokes the IMF mandate again and states (at para. 34): 'it must be emphasized that the Fund has no general mandate to ensure that its members abide by their international obligations. The extent to which the Fund may consider the international undertakings of its members is defined by the Fund's own purposes'. However, while the Fund indeed has no mandate to ensure compliance with all the international obligations of its members; where it does have an international obligation under general international law, it should not be complicit in a member's violation of that same obligation. (Cf Art. 16 of the ILC draft articles on state responsibility discussed in Ch 6, at 6.9 below, and see the ILC's draft articles on the responsibility of international organizations, draft Art. 12, UN Doc. A/CN.4/L.666/Rev.1, 1 June 2005, adopted by the ILC on first reading on 5 June 2005, and reproduced in the text accompanying n 4 above.)

168 L. Boisson de Chazournes, 'Le Panel d'Inspection de la Banque mondiale: à propos de la complexification de l'espace public international', *Revue Générale de Droit International Public* (2001) 145–162; J. T. Möller, 'The Independent Inspection Panel of the World Bank—Comparison with other Inspection Complaints Procedures' in G. Alfredsson and R. Ring (eds) *The Inspection Panel of the World Bank* (The Hague: Kluwer, 2001) 219–248.

169 Res. IBRD 93–10 and with regard to the IDA Res. IDA 93–6, reproduced in 34 *ILM* (1995) 503.   170 Clarification of 17 October 1996.

171 Res. IBRD 93–10, para. 12.

govern the Bank's activities.[172] The spectrum of varying degrees of obligation only makes sense against the history of the changing procedures within the Bank. Although there is no specific directive dedicated exclusively to human rights issues, several guidance measures are pertinent,[173] and one directive explicitly mentions human rights. Operational Directive (OD) 4.20 states:

> The Bank's broad objective towards indigenous people, as for all the people in its member countries, is to ensure that the development process fosters full respect for their dignity, human rights, and cultural uniqueness. More specifically, the objective at the center of this directive is to ensure that indigenous peoples do not suffer adverse effects during the development process, particularly from Bank-financed projects, and that they receive culturally compatible social and economic benefits.[174]

This directive rather suggests that respect for everyone's human rights is already a Bank policy. The particular importance of such directives is that they are central to the work of the Inspection Panel. Although the Inspection Panel has been slow to employ human rights as part of its analytical framework, there are signs that this may be changing.

4.2.5   The World Bank Inspection Panel and the Chad Pipeline Report

The Inspection Panel Report on the Chad Pipeline is perhaps the most revealing with regard to the Bank's evolving human rights policy.[175]

> 212.   As for human rights, Management states in its Response to the Panel that 'The Bank is concerned about violations of human rights in Chad as elsewhere while respecting the Bank's Articles of Agreement which require the Bank to focus on economic considerations and not on political or other non-economic influences as the basis for its decisions. In evaluating the economic aspects of any project, human rights issues may be relevant to the Bank's work if they may have a significant direct economic effect on the project. Having carefully considered all aspects of this issue, Management's conclusion is that the Project can achieve its developmental objectives.' In other words, according to the Management Response, if human rights issues have 'significant direct economic effects' on a Bank financed project, they become a matter of concern to the Bank. Otherwise they don't. In this case, Management feels that the project 'can achieve its development objectives,' so human rights issues are of no *direct* concern . . .

---

[172] L. Boisson de Chazournes, 'Policy Guidance and Compliance: The World Bank Operational Standards' in D. Shelton (ed) *Commitment and Compliance: The Role of Non-Binding Norms in the International legal System* (Oxford: Oxford University Press, 2000) 281–303.

[173] E.g. see BP 4.01 and OP 4.01 environmental assessments, OP 4.11 para. 2.A (regarding culture), OMS 2.4 (indigenous), 4.04 (natural habitats), and OP 4.36 (forests).

[174] OD 4.20, September 1991, at para. 6.

[175] Chad-Cameroon Petroleum and Pipeline Project (Loan No. 4558–CD); Petroleum Sector Management Capacity Building Project (Credit No. 3373–CD); and Management of the Petroleum Economy (Credit No. 3316–CD). Emphasis is in the original. Footnotes omitted.

214.   The Panel appreciates the fact that the frequently imprecise concepts of 'governance' and 'human rights' acquire special significance in the context of the Bank's mandate and operations. Nonetheless, the Panel takes issue with Management's narrow view, and draws attention in this connection to the United Nations Universal Declaration of Human Rights adopted in December 1948, three years after the Bank's Articles of Agreement cited above entered into effect. On the fiftieth anniversary of this Declaration, the Bank wrote; '*The World Bank believes that creating the conditions for the attainment of human rights is a central and irreducible goal of development. By placing the dignity of every human being—especially the poorest—at the very foundation of its approach to development, the Bank helps people in every part of the world build lives of purpose and hope. And while the Bank has always taken measures to ensure that human rights are fully respected in connection with the projects it supports, it has been less forthcoming about articulating its role in promoting human rights within the countries in which it operates.*'

215.   It is not within the Panel's mandate to assess the status of governance and human rights in Chad in general or in isolation, and the Panel acknowledges that there are several institutions (including UN bodies) specifically in charge of this subject. *However, the Panel felt obliged to examine whether the issues of proper governance or human rights violations in Chad were such as to impede the implementation of the Project in a manner compatible with the Bank's policies.* Determination of Management's compliance with these specific policy requirements can be found in the relevant sections of this Report.

The relevant sections of the report refer to the specific commitments regarding consultation and resettlement, but do not further elaborate on the human rights dimension. One can surmise, however, that the human rights situation was taken into account by the Board when assessing obstacles to implementing the Bank's policies. It is not so much the general situation of human rights in a country which seems to be relevant for the Panel, but the fact that the Bank made a claim that it takes measures to ensure its policies fully respect human rights. In fact, the same 1998 document referred to by the Panel also claims that:

The Bank contributes directly to the fulfillment of many rights articulated in the Universal Declaration. Through its support of primary education, health care and nutrition, sanitation, housing, and the environment, the Bank has helped hundreds of millions of people attain crucial economic and social rights.[176]

The report of the Inspection Panel continued with an explanation as to why the 'human rights as economic considerations' approach was no longer satisfactory:

The Panel differentiates the approach of Management which is to accept the legitimacy of human rights considerations only so far as they affect economic development. Nevertheless the Panel confine themselves to examining the conformity of the Bank's behaviour with regards to its own policies, the human rights dimension goes to inform the issue of the Bank's conformity with its own policies. Human rights are not considered as a policy as such. This is not surprising given the Panel's actual mandate, but the report demonstrates how far the Management are being asked to move away from an

[176] World Bank, *Development and Human Rights: The Role of the World Bank* (Washington, DC: World Bank, 1998a) at 3.

approach which only incorporates human rights considerations when they threaten development.

In effect, if the Bank is to claim that human rights considerations form part of its methodology and that it is working to fulfil human rights entitlements, then there are growing expectations that this will be done through enhanced articulation of the ways in which the Bank is contributing to respect and fulfilment of these human rights. This can only be done by including a closer examination of the actual scope of these rights, rather than simply invoking them as factors that are taken into consideration. To achieve this convincingly would require carefully organized human rights impact assessments, to be carried out before, during, and after World Bank projects.

There is now evidence that human rights issues are being taken up as matters of concern for the Bank even outside their relevance to the existing Guidelines and the Bank's duties to avoid undermining human rights through its activities. The same Panel reported that the Bank's President intervened with regard to an arrested individual: 'The Panel also takes note of the fact that on more than one occasion when political repression in Chad seemed severe, the Bank's President personally intervened to help free local opposition leaders, including the representative of the Requesters, Mr. Yorongar, who was reported as being subjected to torture.'[177] This intervention illustrates the demise of the argument that the Bank's mandate strictly prevents it from developing a human rights policy. One might hope that the emerging policy will be based on the full range of international human rights obligations and not selectively limited to certain rights.

4.2.6 International Investment Protection through ICSID at the World Bank

States have established a mechanism to settle disputes between corporations and their host states: the International Centre for the Settlement of Investment Disputes (ICSID, based at the World Bank in Washington). The awards of an Arbitral Tribunal established in this context are binding and enforceable in the jurisdiction of any of the contracting parties to the Washington Convention on the Settlement of Investment Disputes Between States and Nationals of Other States (1965). The question has arisen as to how far these decisions take into account the multiple obligations on states. Not only are states bound by their obligations under the ICSID Convention, the bilateral and other investment agreements to which they are a party, but they are bound by the international law of human rights, environmental protection, and even international criminal law. While it is possible, in some circumstances, for an Arbitral Tribunal established under the ICSID Convention to take into account applicable rules of international

---

[177] At para. 213.

law,[178] there is concern that, so far, there is little consideration of environmental or human rights obligations in such contexts.

Philippe Sands has highlighted the failure of the Arbitral Tribunal in *Compania del Desarrollo de Santa Elena SA v Republic of Costa Rica* to consider the obligations on Costa Rica under international environmental law in the context of valuing an expropriated environmental resource, in this case an area of rainforest rich in biological diversity.[179] The award includes the following paragraphs:

64.   This leaves the Tribunal in a position in which it must rest on the second sentence of Article 42(1) ('In the absence of such agreement...') and thus apply the law of Costa Rica and such rules of international law as may be applicable. No difficulty arises in this connection. The Tribunal is satisfied that the rules and principles of Costa Rican law which it must take into account, relating to the appraisal and valuation of expropriated property, are generally consistent with the accepted principles of public international law on the same subject. To the extent that there may be any inconsistency between the two bodies of law, the rules of public international law must prevail. Were this not so in relation to takings of property, the protection of international law would be denied to the foreign investor and the purpose of the ICSID Convention would, in this respect, be frustrated.

...

71.   In approaching the question of compensation for the Santa Elena Property, the Tribunal has borne in mind the following considerations:—International law permits the Government of Costa Rica to expropriate foreign-owned property within its territory for a public purpose and against the prompt payment of adequate and effective compensation. This is not in dispute between the parties.—While an expropriation or taking for environmental reasons may be classified as a taking for a public purpose, and thus may be legitimate, the fact that the Property was taken for this reason does not affect either the nature or the measure of the compensation to be paid for the taking. That is, the purpose of protecting the environment for which the Property was taken does not alter the legal character of the taking for which adequate compensation must be paid. [Footnote 32. For this reason, the Tribunal does not analyse the detailed evidence submitted regarding what Respondent refers to as its international legal obligation to preserve the unique ecological site that is the Santa Elena Property.] The international source of the obligation to protect the environment makes no difference.

72.   Expropriatory environmental measures—no matter how laudable and beneficial to society as a whole—are, in this respect, similar to any other expropriatory measures that a state may take in order to implement its policies: where property is expropriated,

---

[178] Art. 42 of the ICSID Convention reads in part: '(1) The Tribunal shall decide a dispute in accordance with such rules of law as may be agreed by the parties. In the absence of such agreement, the Tribunal shall apply the law of the Contracting State party to the dispute (including its rules on the conflict of laws) and such rules of international law as may be applicable.'

[179] P. Sands, 'Vers une transformation du droit international? Institutionnaliser le doute' in P.-M. Dupuy and C. Leben (eds) *Cours et travaux* (Paris, Université Panthéon-Assas (Paris II)/Institut des hautes études internationales de Paris: Pedone, 2000b) 180–268.

even for environmental purposes, whether domestic or international, the state's obligation to pay compensation remains.[180]

Nevertheless, despite the obvious risk that environmental or human rights obligations could be used by governments to avoid their obligations under investment agreements, there ought to be room for the argument that, in investment and trade disputes, not only do states have parallel (or even higher obligations) under human rights law,[181] but that the complainant multinational also has obligations under international law, and that failure to respect these obligations could be taken into consideration when seeking a determination based on international law. For some lawyers, such an approach may be reminiscent of the 'clean hands' doctrine, but I am suggesting that we go past notions of equity and fairness, and admit that multinationals may have obligations under international law. It seems fairly clear that in an extreme case of an expropriation resulting in crimes against humanity, the expropriation would be unlawful.[182] Surely then, confiscation in response to crimes against humanity by non-state actors could actually be lawful. In other words, it must make sense in the context of such dispute settlement to take into consideration other international obligations on the parties.[183] To go further with this line of thinking involves moving beyond the obligations of states and international organizations to a consideration of the obligations of the corporations themselves. This is the subject of Chapter 6.

4.2.7   Summary Conclusion Regarding the World Bank and the IMF

- The mandate argument has been transformed into a justification for taking human rights into consideration only as far as they affect the economic performance of a country and its ability to comply with international financial institution (IFI) requirements. Such an approach, however, opens up the possibility of a connected argument that all human rights issues can potentially affect the economy. In some circumstances it will be evident that compliance with human rights obligations may even hinder economic development as defined by the IFI in question. In such a situation the Bank

---

[180] *Compañía Del Desarrollo de Santa Elena, SA v Republic of Costa Rica*, Judgment of 17 February 2000, 39 *ILM* (2000) 1317.

[181] See, e.g. M. Sorenarajah: 'The argument can credibly be made that there are some values in international environmental law and human rights law that are so fundamental that the propositions of investment treaties which are designed to protect large multinational corporations should give way to them.' *The International Law on Foreign Investment* (Cambridge: Cambridge University Press, 2nd edn, 2004) at 265.

[182] See A. H. Qureshi, *International Economic Law* (London: Sweet & Maxwell, 1999) at 374.

[183] See P. Sands, 'Treaty, Custom and the Cross-fertilization of International Law' 1 *Yale HRDLJ* (1998) 3; and 'Arbitrating environmental disputes', Unpublished draft remarks on the occasion of the annual ICSID-ICC-AAA Colloquium, 10 November 2000, Washington, DC. For a discussion of the possibility of corporations relying on breaches of WTO treaties in the context of investment disputes, see G. Verhoosel, 'The Use of Investor-State Arbitration under Bilateral Investment Treaties to Seek Relief for Breaches of WTO Law', 6 *JIEL* (2003) 493–506.

sometimes suggests that its Articles of Agreement force it to choose economic development over respect for human rights, but the Bank's own 1998 report claims that the Bank has always taken measures to ensure that human rights are fully respected in the projects it supports. Furthermore, Operational Directive (OD) 4.20 states that the Bank's 'broad objective' for all the people in its member countries is to ensure that the development process fosters full respect for human rights. The World Bank's Inspection Panel seems prepared to consider the human rights situation as part of the context for policy implementation and scrutiny.

• The argument that IFIs should respect human rights as they are international actors capable of bearing such international responsibilities is gathering some adherents. In political terms, opposition will remain to linking human rights and the work of IFIs, and the IFIs will continue to assert that there are other international organizations that deal with such issues. But one cannot be allowed to violate international human rights norms simply because there are sister bodies charged with human rights monitoring and enforcement. The general international law obligations of IFIs include the human rights norms binding in general international law. There has been a reluctance in some quarters to see such norms as encompassing economic, social, and cultural rights. In general terms, however, recent scholarship describes key economic social and cultural rights as making up the binding obligations considered part of general international law (described as the International Bill of Rights). Indeed, the World Bank (if not the IMF) has highlighted the change in attitude to economic, social, and cultural rights: 'With the final document of the 1993 Vienna World Conference on Human Rights, the international community has moved toward accepting the equality and indivisibility of all human rights. Governments must continue to work to advance all human rights for all people.'[184]

• There is a distinction emerging between the human rights situation in the borrowing country and the human rights obligations of the Bank as such. This is helpful. With regard to the first, the reticence of the Bank will continue for the political reasons outlined above (fear of conditionality, political selectivity, etc.). As for the Bank itself, there is the beginning of a recognition that human rights are important values for the international system to work to protect, and, that human rights impacts and factors may have to be to be specifically incorporated into evaluations of loans and projects. Unfortunately, the expressed reluctance to encroach on the so-called 'political' problem of human rights hampers a transparent and explicit policy.

• This fear of conditionality can best be addressed by recognizing that the human rights obligations of IFIs do themselves demand conditionality—human rights

---

[184] World Bank (1998a: 3).

obligations demand institutional reflection on the human rights impacts of the institution's projects. It is the contribution of the IFIs to human rights abuses rather than their reaction to human rights violations that is the contemporary concern.[185]

---

[185] Cf the conclusions of a report concerning IFIs and international humanitarian law: 'A role for IFIs in the implementation and enforcement of international humanitarian law does not mean that they must always withdraw or reduce financing; rather, it requires that IFIs consider the impact of international humanitarian law violations as a factor in making policy and decisions.' K. L. Blank, *The Role of International Financial Institutions in International Humanitarian Law: Report from the International Humanitarian Law Working Group* (Washington, DC: United States Institute of Peace, 2002) at 6.

5

The World Trade Organization and the European Union

This chapter deals with two non-universal organizations: the World Trade Organization and the European Union. It is convenient to treat these non-state actors together as they both have international legal orders which illustrate how human rights obligations may be discerned, both against the organizations themselves, and within the particular legal orders that they have developed. In addition, both entities address economic actors, and an understanding of their legal regimes is relevant to our consideration of the obligations of corporations in Chapter 6.

5.1   THE WORLD TRADE ORGANIZATION

It is now quite common to find the World Trade Organization (WTO) depicted as the centre of world power, used by 'powerful multinationals' to control the lives of 'ordinary people'.[1] One journalist began his article: 'Behind the imposing entrance of a grand 1920s building on the shores of Lake Geneva lies what is probably the most powerful organization on Earth.'[2] The article, complete with pictures of banana growers in the West Indies, beef from cattle fed on hormones, and an endangered turtle, included summaries of the WTO panel decisions that are described as: 'attacks on the poor, on health and on the environment'. Such distrust is not confined to journalists. Anyone living in Geneva or in the vicinity of a WTO summit will be familiar with the graffiti and slogans such as 'WTO kills: kill the WTO' and 'OMCide'.[3] The WTO has become a lightning rod for complaints about global injustices, often articulated as human rights violations. According to the detailed account by Miloon Kothari, the People's Global Action (comprising social movements and peoples' organizations), that met in Geneva in 1998 around the WTO Ministerial Summit, elaborated a

> . . . peoples manifesto against global 'corporate rule' which argues that '[t]he WTO, the IMF, the World Bank, and other institutions that promote globalisation and liberalisation

[1] G. Lean, 'The hidden tentacles of the world's most secret body' *The Independent on Sunday*, 18 July 1999, at 13.   [2] Ibid.
[3] OMC is the French acronym for WTO.

want us to believe in the beneficial effects of global competition. Their agreements and policies constitute direct violations of basic human rights (including civil, political, economic, social, labour and cultural rights) which are codified in international law and many national constitutions, and ingrained in people's understandings of human dignity'.[4]

There is certainly a perception among some that the WTO represents a serious threat to the enjoyment of human rights, and various human rights activists are shifting their attention to this body. Peter Leuprecht, former Deputy Secretary-General of the Council of Europe, poses the question thus: 'In today's world, pan-economic ideology and its practical application are among the most serious threats to the cause of human rights. As far as the WTO is concerned, the question is whether it will be positively affected by the "mainstreaming" of human rights or whether it will be one of the playgrounds of pan-economic ideology and thus contribute to the undermining of human rights, particularly their social and cultural dimension.'[5] The issues of concern to human rights lawyers have expanded beyond general concern regarding the absence of references to environmental and labour standards in the decision-making of the WTO, beyond the disputes related to endangered turtles, cigarette advertising, and banana growers, to cover a wider range of topics: access to HIV drugs, the patenting of indigenous peoples' traditional knowledge, genetically modified crops, and threats to health from the importation of asbestos. With decisions on all of these issues seemingly more and more in the hands of the WTO, human rights activists fear that the human rights dimension will be lost, and that human rights law in general risks being marginalized, or down-graded, as emphasis shifts to compliance with trade laws rather than respect for human rights obligations.

We are all familiar with the canard that WTO really stands for 'World Take Over',[6] and it is hard to forget that demonstrations against the WTO, the World Bank, and the IMF have been some of the most violent and vociferous in recent times. But is it really right to focus on organizations such as the WTO in this way? States are still formally the actors that make the rules that are being interpreted and applied. Should we not simply look at the obligations of the governments that negotiate and decide issues of global trade law? Does it make sense in the present context to categorize the WTO as a non-state actor and consider its human rights obligations?

I suggest it does make sense because, not only is the WTO becoming symbolic of the drive towards prioritizing free trade, but the WTO mechanisms are clearly

---

[4] M. Kothari, 'Globalisation, Social Action and Human Rights' in M. Mehra (ed) *Human Rights and Economic Globalisation: Directions for the WTO* (Uppsala: Global Publications Foundation, International NGO Committee on Human Rights in Trade and Investment, International Coalition for Development Action, 1999) 37–60, at 45.

[5] P. Leuprecht, 'The World Trade Organisation—Another Playground of Pan-Economic Ideology?' in Mehra (1999) 15–22, at 15.

[6] 'The hidden tentacles of the world's most secret body' (n 1 above).

going to be asked to consider the impact of human rights law as they enforce the new international trade regime. So far, the impact of multilateral environmental agreements has been finessed by the WTO Appellate Body.[7] But the issues will inevitably have to be addressed. Even if the WTO is 'a member-driven, consensus-based organization',[8] it still exists as such, and its decisions can be said to emanate from the organization rather than the simple collective will of the members. It therefore makes sense to consider its actions and the WTO's own responsibility under international law.

The human rights concerns that arise cover issues such as access to drugs, the implications of agricultural negotiations for culture, the right to food, and the human rights impact of opening up national markets to foreign services in areas such as health and education.[9] Some of these issues have been examined in a number of detailed reports of the UN High Commissioner for Human Rights and are not elaborated on here.[10] In the present Chapter the goal is to develop a general theory of how to ensure that the WTO does not operate in clinical isolation from human rights law.

The WTO, as such, has sufficient international personality to be bound by the international customary law of human rights. At a certain point, it is the WTO itself that acts, for example, though entering into a treaty with the World Bank or advising a government through training programmes. Looked at in this way, considering the human rights aspects of the WTO's action no longer becomes a question of the WTO enforcing human rights, or of allowing human rights to be used for protectionist purposes, but one of WTO responsibility for the human rights impact of its actions. Human rights are obligations for the non-state actor bound under international law—not a policy question, or an agenda put forward by various blocs. Thinking about the WTO as an actor with human rights obligations may be the first step to ensuring that the WTO, its panels, the

---

[7] E.g. it remains uncertain how a WTO panel will deal with the international obligations of states under a treaty such as the Cartagena Protocol on Biosafety to the Convention on Biological Diversity (2000); see L. Boisson de Chazournes and M. M. Mbengue, 'Le rôle des organes de règlement des différends de l'OMC dans le développement du droit: à propos des OGM' in J. Bourrinet and S. Maljean-Dubois (eds) *Le commerce international des organisms génétiquement modifiés* (Paris: la documentation Française, 2002) 177–212.   [8] WTO, *Understanding the WTO* (2003) at 101.

[9] See OHCHR, 'Human Rights and Trade', paper presented to the 5th WTO Ministerial Conference, Cancún, Mexico, 10–14 September 2003. http://www.unhchr.ch/html/menu2/trade/index.htm (What's New? Accessed 13 July 2005); and see further S. Marks and A. Clapham, *International Human Rights Lexicon* (Oxford: Oxford University Press, 2005) at 44 (culture), 144–147 (education), 175–177 (food), 187–188, 190–191 (globalization), 203–4 (health), and 217 (housing).

[10] 'Human rights, trade and investment', report of the High Commissioner for Human Rights (E/CN.4/Sub.2/2003/9); 'Liberalization of trade in services and human rights', report of the High Commissioner for Human Rights (E/CN.4/Sub.2/2002/9); 'Globalization and its impact on the full enjoyment of human rights', report of the High Commissioner for Human Rights (E/CN.4/2002/54) (considers the WTO's Agreement on Agriculture); 'The impact of the TRIPS Agreement on the Enjoyment of all Human Rights', report of the High Commissioner for Human Rights (E/CN.4/Sub.2/2001/13).

Appellate Body, its organs, and its members take human rights obligations more seriously in all their activities.

The WTO, as an international organization with international personality, is bound by general international law. This assertion concerning international obligations of the WTO, and its human rights obligations in particular, need not be laboriously constructed from the theory of international organizations; suffice to say that in 2001, the WTO Secretariat simply acknowledged that the WTO is bound by the customary international law of human rights. The Summary Records of the UN Sub-Commission on the Promotion and Protection of Human Rights contain the following summary of an intervention by Gabrielle Marceau from the Legal Affairs Division of the WTO, who is reported as saying:

> The WTO secretariat, as a distinct legal personality, and the WTO member States, were bound by international law, and were consequently under an obligation to respect human rights instruments. Furthermore, the WTO Agreements specifically mentioned that members should interpret all the provisions of those Agreements in the light of any relevant rules of international law. The mandate of WTO dispute settlement panels was limited to deciding whether or not a violation of the WTO Agreements had occurred. They were unable to change the rules agreed upon by the member States.[11]

A later intervention by Marceau clarified that the WTO was bound by customary international law.[12] This approach is significant as it highlights three key points. First, the WTO, as such, is obliged to respect the customary international law of human rights. Second, the WTO is not mandated to enforce human rights law but only WTO law. And third, the WTO cannot override or change the international human rights obligations of states. These are separate points but are often confused in order to justify exclusion of human rights matters from the WTO processes. So, to be clear, with regard to each point: to insist that the WTO should not act in a way that violates human rights is not to give the WTO a human rights mandate through the back door—but simply to demand that it comply with existing obligations. The jurisdiction of the dispute settlement mechanism is with regard to trade treaties, not human rights treaties, but this does not mean that human rights treaties have no role to play in applying the trade treaties; no one can claim that the international rules agreed to in the WTO context override binding

---

[11] UN Doc. E/CN.4/Sub.2/2001/SR.12, at para. 24, Summary Record of the 12th meeting on 8 August 2001.

[12] See UN Doc. E/CN.4/Sub.2/2001/SR.13, at para. 40: 'Mme Marceau (Organisation mondiale du commerce) dit que son organisation est disposée à poursuivre sa collaboration avec la Sous-Commission. Elle précise que les pays membres de l'OMC, et donc l'Organisation elle-même, sont liés par le droit international coutumier. L'OMC ne fait qu'édicter des règles. Il appartient ensuite aux États membres de mettre leur politique en conformité avec ces règles.' (English translation unavailable at the time of writing.) See also the later article published by Marceau in her private capacity, and accompanied by the usual disclaimer: 'The WTO has its own international legal personality. As such the WTO is bound by international law insofar as its functional international personality permits it to be so bound.') G. Marceau, 'WTO Dispute Settlement and Human Rights' 13 *EJIL* (2002) 753–814, at 802.

international rules on human rights, in fact considering that some human rights obligations are *jus cogens* obligations, it may be that certain human rights obligations override apparent obligations under trade law.[13]

Of course, in practice, problems arise because the legal mechanisms for enforcing trade rules are more enthusiastically embraced than those for enforcing human rights rules. And because the enforcement of trade rules, whether by governments in response to new WTO agreements, or as a result of the dispute settlement mechanism, can impact on the enjoyment of human rights, the WTO is seen as undermining the enjoyment of human rights. Highlighting the WTO's own human rights obligations under international law may be an approach which could reinforce any tendency by the panels and the Appellate Body to interpret WTO agreements in a way that does not require states to violate their own human rights obligations.

The different ways in which the WTO may be confronted with obligations to respect human rights can be considered in three separate contexts. First is the way that the WTO panels that adjudicate trade disputes should deal with applicable human rights law, for example, when human rights law is used as a justification for regulating a certain product. Second, is the way that WTO law and its enforcement mechanisms are said to restrict measures, such as sanctions that are imposed as a response to human rights violations. Third, is consideration of the implications of the fact that human rights law binds both the states participating in the negotiations at the WTO and the WTO itself. We now turn to these issues.

5.1.1 Decisions by the Panels and Appellate Body

The following discussion begins with a cursory discussion of the mechanics of the dispute settlement procedure at the WTO, although it does not purport to deal with the intricacies of the system.[14] A WTO panel's interpretation of a rule contained in a WTO covered agreement could hypothetically lead to a denial of human rights through the losing government's application of the ruling. To take a simplified example: importation of a product that has been prohibited by one state on the ground that it is dangerous to health is prevented at the frontier of that state; the panel rules that the product is essentially the same as a national product and that the ban represents discrimination in favour of a national product. The panel's report is adopted by the Dispute Settlement Body of the WTO. The banning state is faced with the choice between allowing the product to be imported or ruinous trade sanctions. Assume also that the banning country is attempting to phase out its own harmful product and find alternative

---

[13] The scope of those human rights obligations that constitute *jus cogens* is dealt with in Ch 3 above.

[14] For an introduction to the topic, see E.-U. Petersmann, *The GATT/WTO Dispute Settlement System: International Law, International Organizations and Dispute Settlement* (London: Kluwer, 2002).

employment for the workers currently employed in that industry. Allowing the importation of the product will arguably undermine the efforts of the government to protect the right to health.

Such a straightforward clash is admittedly unlikely, as the disputes tend to throw up more complex scenarios. But let us look at the options for the panel under international law. Clearly, a WTO panel only has jurisdiction over a dispute concerning a relevant WTO agreement. A WTO panel cannot simply determine whether a certain measure or situation violates the international law of human rights; such a ruling would be outside its competence and *ultra vires*. But, in deciding on the *meaning* of the WTO treaty in question, a panel will apply the international law rules of treaty interpretation. Considerable effort has been expended in the doctrine to demonstrate how the rules of treaty interpretation can lead to an increasing relevance of international environmental and human rights law.[15]

5.1.1.1   Protecting Human Rights from the WTO through the Law of Treaty Interpretation

WTO scholars have pointed both to Article 3.2 of the WTO Dispute Settlement Understanding (DSU), which demands that existing provisions of WTO agreements are clarified 'in accordance with customary rules of interpretation of public international law', and to certain Articles of the Vienna Convention on the Law of Treaties (1969) (VCLT), which are said to codify those customary rules. In the first dispute to come before the Appellate Body that Body famously stated, after having considered Article 31(1) of the VCLT and Article 3.2 of the DSU,[16] that the direction contained in Article 3.2 which states that the dispute settlement system of the WTO is to clarify existing provisions of WTO covered agreements 'in accordance with customary rules of interpretation of public international law' is a direction to the Appellate Body which 'reflects a measure of recognition that the *General Agreement* is not to be read in clinical isolation from public international law.'[17]

---

[15] P. Sands, 'Treaty, Custom and the Cross-fertilization of International Law' 1 *Yale HRDLJ* (1998) 3; M. Garcia-Rubio, *On the Application of Customary Rules of State Responsibility by the WTO Dispute Settlement Organs* (Geneva: Graduate Institute of International Studies, Studies and Working Papers, 2001); G. Marceau, 'WTO Dispute Settlement and Human Rights' 13 *EJIL* (2002) 753–814; R. Howse and M. Mutua, *Protecting Human Rights in a Global Economy: Challenges for the World Trade Organization* (Montreal: International Centre for Human Rights and Democracy, 2000); J. Pauwelyn, *Conflict of Norms in Public International Law: How WTO Law Relates to other Rules of International Law* (Cambridge: Cambridge University Press, 2003) esp. 251–274.

[16] Art. 31(1) reads: 'A treaty shall be interpreted in good faith and in accordance with the ordinary meaning to be given to the terms of the treaty in their context and in the light of its object and purpose.' Art. 3.2 reads: 'The dispute settlement system of the WTO is a central element in providing security and predictability to the multilateral trading system. The members recognize that it serves to preserve the rights and obligations of members under the covered agreements, and to clarify the existing provisions of those agreements in accordance with customary rules of interpretation of public international law. Recommendations and rulings of the DSB cannot add to or diminish the rights and obligations provided in the covered agreements.'

[17] Appellate Body Report on *United States—Standards for Reformulated and Conventional Gasoline* AB–1996–1, WT/DS2/AB/R, adopted 29 April 1996, at p 17, (96–1597).

To return to our hypothetical example, where an exporting government seeks to rely on WTO-based trading rules to the detriment of the health of people in another state, the state that has prohibited the importation of the goods of the exporting state may rely, *inter alia*, on the justifications in Article XX of the General Agreement on Tariffs and Trade (GATT). This Article is entitled 'General Exceptions' and states in part that, subject to the requirement that the measures taken by a state do not constitute arbitrary or unjustified discrimination, or a disguised restriction on international trade, the GATT shall not be construed to prevent the enforcement by any contracting party of measures necessary to protect health. Returning to the relevant rules of interpretation: the terms of this Article may have to be interpreted in the light of the human rights law or other relevant rules of international law binding on the parties.[18] More concretely, WTO panels, when interpreting the meaning of a WTO provision, have to respect the rule reflected in Article 31(3)(c) of the VCLT which demands that: 'There shall be taken into account, together with the context: (c) any relevant rules of international law applicable in the relations between the parties.' The result is that the meaning of terms such as 'unjustifiable', 'arbitrary', and 'health' may be elucidated in the context of the human rights rules binding on the parties.

A tricky question which has arisen in the doctrine is whether the reference in the VCLT to the 'parties', should be considered as a reference to the *parties to the dispute*, or to *all to the parties to the treaty under interpretation*. According to Mariano Garcia-Rubio: 'It seems also reasonable to assume that the obligations "applicable in the relations between the parties" refers to the parties to the dispute rather than to the parties to the WTO Agreement. It is difficult to imagine a situation in which Article 31(3)(c) of the VCLT would be applicable if identical membership were required under both the WTO Agreement and the non-WTO treaty used to interpret the WTO obligation. In addition, it would create logical difficulties for considering customary obligations as a basis for interpretation. This would lead to a greater isolation of WTO law, rather than to a coherent integration of WTO law with general international law.'[19] In the same vein,

---

[18] Consider the rulings in the *Asbestos* dispute between Canada and the European Communities. The panel considered that France's policy of prohibiting asbestos-based products fell within the range of policies designed to protect human life or health under Art. XX(b) of GATT 1997, *European Communities—measures affecting asbestos-containing products*, Report of the Panel, 18 September 2000, WT/DS135/R, Doc. 00–3353; on appeal the Appellate Body considered that France could ban the product on the ground that the public health risks associated with the product meant that this product was not a 'like product' with similar products that did not contain asbestos for the purposes of a claim with regard to discrimination under Art. III.4 of the GATT, Report of the Appellate Body, 12 March 2001, AB–2000–11, WT/DS135/AB/R, Doc. 01–1157. The Doha Ministerial Declaration of 14 November 2001 stated (at para. 6): 'We recognize that under WTO rules no country should be prevented from taking measures for the protection of human, animal or plant life, or of the environment at the levels it considers appropriate, subject to the requirement that they are not applied in a manner which would constitute a means of arbitrary or unjustifiable discrimination between countries where the same conditions prevail, or a disguised restriction on international trade, and are otherwise in accordance with the provisions of the WTO Agreements.'

[19] Garcia-Rubio (2001: 76) footnotes omitted.

Gabrielle Marceau rejects an interpretation which demands that 'parties' in Article 31(3)(c) of the VCLT means all WTO members. She explains why, in her view, such an interpretation would be problematic:

> It would reduce the number of outside treaties and legal principles that could be used to interpret WTO obligations under Article 31(3)(c), and this leads only to inconsistencies and incoherence between systems of law. Few international agreements, if any, will have identical memberships, although some may include all WTO members or even a wider membership than the WTO. But to require that such a non-WTO treaty have at least the WTO Membership would also create illogical situations. As WTO Membership grows, fewer international agreements will match its membership. This is especially so since the WTO admits non-sovereign members: it would make it impossible for the WTO to have an identical membership to any treaty. This would lead to the paradoxical result that the WTO would, at least in theory, become more isolated from other international systems of law as its membership grows.[20]

Let us consider some of these arguments specifically with regard to human rights rules. First, no human rights treaties currently include all WTO members. As Marceau points out, the WTO membership includes non-state entities such as Hong Kong and the European Community. It is impossible for such entities to become parties to human rights treaties such as the Convention on the Rights of the Child, as this treaty is only open to states. Other treaties contain similar restrictions, and there may be further institutional complications restricting accession for entities such as the European Community to human rights treaties.[21] As the European Community is a party to a large proportion of the disputes brought under the WTO dispute settlement system, this issue cannot be sidestepped. In sum, in the context of human rights it is almost impossible to imagine a human rights treaty that will be binding on *all* WTO members. Should all the human rights treaty obligations operating between the parties to a WTO dispute be taken into account to interpret the WTO treaty provision at issue? Would this not lead to different interpretations of WTO agreements depending on the human rights treaty constellation between the parties to the dispute? Does this approach not itself lead to fragmentation and inconsistencies, rather than coherence for the WTO treaty system?

One could respond that a panel decision only binds the parties to the dispute,[22] so it is appropriate that the answer is tailored to the rules binding those parties. But even if this is strictly speaking the case, it is obvious that the decisions of panels of the Appellate Body form the 'case-law' of the WTO and set the parameters

---

[20] Marceau (2002:771).

[21] On the problems concerning European Community accession to the European Convention on Human Rights, see 5.2.2.2 below.

[22] Note the statement by the Appellate Body in *Japan—Alcoholic Beverages*, 4 October 1996, AB–1996–2, Doc. 96–3951, at Part E, that adopted panel reports 'are not binding, except with respect to resolving the particular dispute between the parties to that dispute'. Cited by Pauwelyn (2003: 28).

for the way in which WTO members expect each other to behave.[23] A further complication arises from the fact that the European Community is not yet a party to any human rights treaty. Clearly, even an interpretation which relies on human rights treaties in operation between the parties to the dispute will not take us very far in the numerous disputes involving the European Community.

Pauwelyn limits the non-WTO norms that should be taken into account by panels in their interpretations of the WTO covered agreements to those where all WTO members are bound, or, where a norm (such as a multilateral environmental agreement (MEA)) is not legally binding on all WTO members, he suggests it could still influence the meaning of the WTO norm 'if it can be shown that the MEA norm is an expression of the "common intentions" or "understanding" of all WTO members'.[24] In the context of human rights obligations, it seems sensible to simply start from the fact that all WTO members are bound by the customary international law of human rights. It is these general rules of international law that should be taken into account in interpreting WTO agreements. It is unlikely that one would need to revert to a particular human rights treaty to discern the meaning of the words at issue in the WTO treaty.[25] There is a tendency in this area to conflate questions of interpretation with the application of competing norms. In some cases one could assume that the parties to the WTO dispute could not have intended the WTO agreement to supplant customary rules concerning the international law of human rights. In this way, interpretation means not only taking into account human rights law, but may involve something which properly considers the human rights obligations of the parties. The International Court of Justice (ICJ) came close to such a manoeuvre regarding the obligation not to use force under public international law in the *Case Concerning Oil Platforms* in 2003:[26]

> Moreover, under the general rules of treaty interpretation, as reflected in the 1969 Vienna Convention on the Law of Treaties, interpretation must take into account 'any relevant rules of international law applicable in the relations between the parties' (Article 31, paragraph 3 (c)). The Court cannot accept that Article XX, paragraph 1 (d), of the 1955 Treaty was intended to operate wholly independently of the relevant rules of international law on the use of force, so as to be capable of being successfully invoked, even in the limited context of a claim for breach of the Treaty, in relation to an unlawful use of force. The application of the relevant rules of international law relating to this

---

[23] See *Japan—Alcoholic Beverages*, ibid, discussed by Pauwelyn (2003: 51–52).
[24] Pauwelyn (2003: 263).
[25] Marceau (2002: 786, footnote 105) lists a number of instruments related to health and suggests they could 'serve as useful instruments—whether in and of themselves binding or not—when interpreting WTO provisions dealing with health matters'. While the instruments would certainly be useful, the obligation on the panel to take into account relevant rules of international law suggests so far that they would have to take into account binding treaty and customary law. The non-binding instruments may provide the evidence as to what the customary law is in this context. See Ch 3 above.
[26] *Islamic Republic of Iran v United States of America*, Judgment of 6 November 2003, at paras 41–42.

question thus forms an integral part of the task of interpretation entrusted to the Court by Article XXI, paragraph 2, of the 1955 Treaty.

The Court is therefore satisfied that its jurisdiction under Article XXI, paragraph 2, of the 1955 Treaty to decide any question of interpretation or application of (inter alia) Article XX, paragraph 1 (d), of that Treaty extends, where appropriate, to the determination whether action alleged to be justified under that paragraph was or was not an unlawful use of force, by reference to international law applicable to this question, that is to say, the provisions of the Charter of the United Nations and customary international law. The Court would however emphasize that its jurisdiction remains limited to that conferred on it by Article XXI, paragraph 2, of the 1955 Treaty. The Court is always conscious that it has jurisdiction only so far as conferred by the consent of the parties.

Similarly, the WTO panels and the Appellate Body will be conscious of their limited jurisdiction. They may be able, or even obligated, to take human rights law into account in interpreting the covered agreements, but such an approach can only go so far. So, for example, in interpreting Article XX(b) exceptions to the non-discrimination obligations that the measures are 'necessary to protect human, animal or plant life or health', it will be appropriate to take into account the fact that states have obligations under human rights law to protect the right to health. The meaning of 'health' in such circumstances, as it relates to the state's human rights obligations, will be relevant for understanding the scope of 'health' in the WTO covered agreement, in this case the GATT. Of course the panel will not be determining a violation of the right to health under human rights law; but protecting health is a defence to an alleged violation or impairment of enjoyment of GATT treaty rights by states, and the scope of the concurrent right to health is surely relevant. The ICJ's use of the law on the use of force to determine the scope of the exception to the Amity Treaty at issue in the *Case Concerning Oil Platforms* (2003), provoked the following warning from Judge Higgins, who delivered a separate opinion:[27]

> It is a commonplace that treaties are to be interpreted by reference to the rules enunciated in Article 31 of the Vienna Convention on the Law of Treaties, which Article is widely regarded as reflecting general international law. Article 31, paragraph 3 *(c)*, on which the Court places emphasis, states that, in interpreting a treaty, 'There shall be taken into account, together with the context, . . . any relevant rules of international law applicable in the relations between the parties.'
>
> The Court reads this provision as incorporating the totality of the substantive international law (which in paragraph 42 of the Judgment is defined as comprising Charter law) on the use of force. But this is to ignore that Article 31, paragraph 3, requires 'the context' to be taken into account: and 'the context' is clearly that of an economic and commercial treaty. What is envisaged by Article 31, paragraph 3 *(c)*, is that a provision that requires interpretation in Article XX, paragraph 1 *(d)*, will be illuminated by recalling what type of a treaty this is and any other 'relevant rules' governing Iran-United States relations. It is not a provision that on the face of it envisages incorporating the

---

[27] See separate opinion of Judge Higgins, ibid, at paras 45–46.

entire substance of international law on a topic not mentioned in the clause—at least not without more explanation than the Court provides.

Similar complaints would arise should there be an attempt to incorporate human rights law into the WTO dispute settlement process. But the dynamic is rather different. Protecting human rights, unlike invoking the right to self-defence, does not involve a separate possible violation of a rule of general international law (the ban on the use of force). To invoke human rights as a defence to a GATT complaint does not open the door to a finding of a violation of a separate (*jus cogens*) norm as a claim to self-defence does. If a claim of self-defence fails as a defence to a bilateral treaty obligation, it probably means that the claimant has violated the rules on the use of force. If a claim regarding the need to protect human rights fails, it simply means that the GATT treaty as such has been violated. The WTO panel is not being asked implicitly to come to a conclusion with regard to compliance with a non-WTO rule. The rejection of the human rights claim simply leads to the conclusion that the defending state overestimated the extent of its human rights obligations according to the panel. There is a separate danger that embarking on this route entails surrendering to WTO panels the task of determining the scope of human rights obligations.[28] On balance, however, this is a risk worth taking when the alternative is that the WTO simply takes its decisions in ignorance of, and isolation from, the international human rights obligations that are supposed to ensure individuals a meaningful life to be lived with dignity.

Pauwelyn has rightly cautioned against assuming that conflicts of norms can be spirited away by a simple interpretive device. 'Interpretation of the terms in question may resolve apparent conflicts; it cannot resolve genuine conflicts.'[29] He suggests a series of rules for resolving such conflicts and highlights the fact that environmental and human rights agreements involve 'integral type' agreements giving rise to third-party benefits. By contrast, WTO treaties are of a reciprocal nature so that 'in most cases of conflict between, for example, human rights and environmental conventions (generally setting out obligations of an "integral type"), on the one hand, and WTO obligations (of the "reciprocal" type), on the other hand, WTO provisions will have to give way'.[30] He is not suggesting that the WTO panel would then come to a finding with regard to the human rights treaty; simply that the panel would be unable to conclude the WTO treaty dispute before them due to the limited jurisdiction of the panel. Nevertheless, for him, the applicable law includes all law which is binding on the parties.

Until we are faced with an actual controversy before a panel, where trade law and human rights law seem irreconcilably at odds, much of this debate will remain rather theoretical. What I have sought to show is that, without distorting the rules

---

[28] See Carlos Lopes Hurtado, 'The WTO Legal System and International Human Rights' (Geneva: Graduate Institute of International Studies, PhD thesis, 2005).
[29] Pauwelyn (2003: 272).   [30] Ibid, at 491.

of treaty interpretation, it is clear that WTO law does not operate in isolation from human rights law, and that there will be situations where the rules of treaty interpretation demand that relevant human rights law 'shall be taken into account'.[31]

5.1.1.2   Trade Sanctions to Protect Human Rights Precluded by WTO Rules

The issue of a 'social clause' whereby the WTO could be used to enforce core labour standards has been extensively discussed and is now more or less moribund in the context of the WTO.[32] As a WTO brochure puts it: 'Many officials in developing countries believe the campaign to bring labour issues into the WTO is actually a bid by industrial nations to undermine the comparative advantage of lower wage trading partners.'[33] But, even if the WTO has so far excluded human rights enforcement relating to conditions of work, the question arises whether human rights enforcement measures taken outside the WTO might be found not to be WTO compliant and a violation or impairment of a WTO agreement. In other words, does the WTO system actually undermine or threaten human rights by outlawing trade sanctions designed to ensure compliance with human rights?

This issue has indeed arisen in the context of unilateral sanctions imposed on Myanmar by the state of Massachusetts in the United States. The sanctions were a reaction to the human rights record of Myanmar. Although the sanctions were eventually abandoned, due to a finding by the Supreme Court that such action was unconstitutional, the prospect of the United States being eventually brought before a WTO panel loomed large. The situation was complex as it was the European Community that was threatening the United States before the WTO as the sanctions affected the European Union's companies and economic interests.[34] Let us consider the case in more detail.

---

[31] Art. 31(3)(c) of the Vienna Convention on the Law of Treaties (1969); for an interpretation of 'taken into account' in this context, see Sands (1998) at para. 39, who states that 'Ordinary usage suggests that the formulation [take account] is stronger than "take into consideration" but weaker than "apply".' (For the discussion in French see P. Sands, 'Vers une transformation du droit international? Institutionnaliser le doute' in P.-M. Dupuy and C. Leben (eds) *Cours et travaux* (Paris, Université Panthéon-Assas, Paris II/Institut des hautes études internationales de Paris: Pedone, 2000b) 180–268, at 230. See also analogous arguments made for 'applying' or 'interpreting' WTO law in the context of investment arbitrations: G. Verhoosel, 'The Use of Investor-State Arbitration under Bilateral Investment Treaties to Seek Relief for Breaches of WTO Law' 6 *JIEL* (2003) 493–506.

[32] V. Leary, 'The WTO and the Social Clause: Post Singapore' 1 *EJIL* (1997) 118–122.

[33] *Understanding the WTO* (2003) at 74.

[34] In formal terms it is the European Community which is a member of the WTO and entitled to engage the Dispute Settlement Mechanism of the WTO. An attempt is made in this Chapter to refer to the European Community rather than the EU when it is the Community that is acting in its legal capacity as an entity with international legal personality with the capacity to enter into treaties. The foreign policy of the EU goes beyond what the European Community can achieve in the WTO legal processes. Hence there are alternate references to the EU and the Community in the following passages. For a general overview of the role of the EU, see P. Alston, M. Bustelo, and J. Heenan (eds) *The EU and Human Rights* (Oxford: Oxford University Press, 1999).

In 1996, Massachusetts adopted 'An Act Regulating State Contracts with Companies Doing Business with or in Burma (Myanmar)'. On 19 June 2000, the Act was held invalid by the Supreme Court of the United States under the Supremacy Clause of the US Constitution, as it frustrated federal statutory object-ives. Interestingly, part of the reasoning of the Supreme Court stems from the fact that the European Community opposed this law and had started proceedings against the United States at the WTO. The Supreme Court's judgment quotes the State Department:

> While the [Massachusetts sanctions on Burma] were adopted in pursuit of a noble goal, the restoration of democracy in Burma, these measures also risk shifting the focus of the debate with our European Allies away from the best way to bring pressure against the State Law and Restoration Council (SLORC) to a potential WTO dispute over its consistency with our international obligations. Let me be clear we are working with Massachusetts in the WTO dispute settlement process. But we must be honest in saying that the threatened WTO case risks diverting United States' and Europe's attention from focusing where it should be—on Burma.[35]

The EU brief in the Massachusetts District Court made it clear that its opposition to the Burma law 'does not reflect indifference to the situation in Burma or sup-port for its present leadership'.[36] The brief set out a list of actions taken by the European Union (EU) to respond to the human rights situation in Myanmar (withdrawal of Generalized System of Preferences (GSP),[37] expulsion of military personnel, arms embargo, ban on entry visas for senior members of the SLORC and their families, etc.) The EU brief explained that: 'The Massachusetts Burma Law constitutes a direct interference with the ability of the EU to cooperate and carry out foreign policy with the United States.' The EU objected that Massachusetts sought 'to force the EU and its member States to impose sanctions on Burma and EU companies to abandon activities in Burma'. The EU suggested that in some circumstances such measures would be an option for the EU; but the brief continued: 'The EU and its Member States had specifically chosen not to ban such activities in favor of other policy measures toward Burma. The Massachusetts Burma law is thus aimed at influencing the foreign policy choices of the EU and its Member States, and at sanctioning the activities of EU compan-ies which are not only taking place in a third country but which are also lawful under EU and Member States laws.'

---

[35] *Crosby v National Foreign Trade Council* (99–474), 530 US 363 (2000), 181 F 3d 38 affirmed, 19 June 2000, at 20, Eizenstat testimony, App 115, the Court stated that the US continued to advance this position in its *amicus curiae* brief, at footnote 22.

[36] *National Foreign Trade Council v Charles Baker and Philmore Anderson III*, Civil Action No. 98–CV–10757 JLT, at 2.

[37] See further A. Clapham and J. Bourke Martignoni, 'Are we there yet? EU Policy on Trade and Labour Rights' in V. A. Leary and D. Warner (eds) *Social Issues, Globalization and International Institutions: Labour Rights and the EU, ILO, OECD and WTO* (Leiden: Martinus Nijhoff, forthcoming 2005).

The European Community's application to the WTO concerned the Government Procurement Agreement,[38] but there was no panel ruling as the Community's WTO complaint was abandoned once the Supreme Court had struck down the Massachusetts law. Against this background, there is some uncertainty over whether the WTO regime allows for states to impose trade sanctions on WTO members in order to enforce or encourage respect for human rights. For some, this could mean that the WTO system is restricting the possibilities for human rights enforcement. Is it desirable to build an argument that the WTO has human rights obligations and that these include ensuring that states can enforce human rights through trade sanctions?

Sanctions are often seen as a blunt and ineffective instrument. The fact that the WTO may preclude states from imposing sanctions outside the framework of the Security Council can hardly be seen today as a violation of any human rights obligations that the WTO may have. In fact, WTO agreements such as the GATT include a specific exception (Article XXI) which states that the GATT cannot be construed to prevent governments from 'taking any action in pursuance of its obligations under the United Nations Charter for the maintenance of international peace and security'. Because the Security Council has been prepared to consider human rights violations as giving rise to threats to international peace and security in situations such as Kosovo, it is quite possible that sanctions could be imposed by the Security Council in order to attempt to halt human rights violations. The expanded meaning of a threat to 'international peace and security' was first articulated by the Council at the 1992 Summit:

> . . . the absence of war and of armed conflicts between States does not alone guarantee international peace and security. Other non-military menaces to peace and security can be found in the instability which exists in economic, social, humanitarian and environmental areas. It is incumbent upon all Members of the United Nations Organization, acting within the appropriate organs, to attach the highest priority to the solution of these problems.[39]

In sum, the question of human rights and the role of the WTO is not really about states giving up the possibility of imposing trade sanctions in order to enforce human rights. Both the United States and the EU seem to have decided that engagement is preferable as a strategy and that trade sanctions may be counterproductive. Schemes such as the Generalized System of Preferences, which were conditional on human rights performance with regard to certain labour standards, seem of decreasing relevance, although their demise may in fact have been hastened by the WTO rules which circumscribed such schemes.[40] In short, the

---

[38] Request for consultations by the European Communities, WT/DS88/1, GPA/D2/1, 26 June 1997.

[39] 'Statement by the President of the Security Council on Behalf of the Council', Security Council Summit Meeting, UN Doc. S/23500, 31 January 1992.

[40] See WT/DS 246 EC—Conditions for the Granting of Tariff Preferences to Developing Countries, 1 December 2003, and WT/DS 242.

human rights complaint concerning the WTO relates not so much to the diminishing possibilities for sanctions but rather to the human rights impact of negotiations on trade, agriculture, intellectual property, services, and the power which is given to powerful actors to enforce the resultant rules through the WTO's dispute mechanism.[41]

5.1.1.3   The Threat to Human Rights and Human Rights Enforcement from WTO Agreements

Perhaps the most obvious threat to human rights has come from the inability of people to achieve access to expensive medicine, particularly in the context of HIV and AIDS. Governments such as the Government of South Africa, that introduced measures to achieve such access, were accused by the United States and the EU of violation of the WTO protected intellectual property agreement (TRIPS). These governments were thus threatened with a panel procedure, and the prospect of trade sanctions to bring them back into line in order to ensure that the patents of the pharmaceutical companies were respected. Other governments, fearful of WTO-sanctioned counter-measures, will have reflected on the consequences of introducing their own measures. Public debate raged on this topic, and as a consequence of the public outrage that commercial rights were being prioritized over human rights, pharmaceutical companies eventually abandoned their intellectual property claims before the South African courts. For some commentators, the issue now is how to prevent threats of litigation by powerful WTO members that act on behalf of commercial interests. The 'rule-based' WTO may need to start to look at how to prevent its procedures from being used to intimidate weaker members, who may in fact be operating within the rules and simply applying the exceptions laid down in agreements such a TRIPS.[42]

As regards the protection of intellectual property rights under the TRIPS agreement, and the threat to the right to health where people are denied access to certain drugs, the debate has shifted to implementation of the Doha Ministerial Declaration on the TRIPS Agreement and Public Health, adopted in 2001, which states: 'We agree that the TRIPS Agreement does not and should not prevent members from taking measures to protect public heath. Accordingly, while reiterating our commitment to the TRIPS Agreement, we affirm that the Agreement can and should be interpreted and implemented in a manner supportive of WTO Members' right to protect public health and, in particular, to promote access to medicines for all.'[43] This agreement, which introduces the idea of balancing social

---

[41] See generally Mehra (1999); and Fédération Internationale des Ligues des Droits de l'Homme, *The World Trade Organisation and Human Rights: Position paper*, No. 285/2 (November 1999).

[42] F. M. Abbott, 'The Rule of Law and the Protection of Asymmetric Risks in TRIPS' *Bridges* (2003) No. 7, 22–24.

[43] Para. 4, WT/MIN (01)/DEC/2, adopted 14 November 2001. For a discussion of the links between this agreement and human rights, see the Report of the UN High Commissioner for Human Rights, 'The Impact of the Agreement on Trade-Related Aspects of Intellectual Property Rights on Human Rights' UN Doc. E/CN.4/Sub.2/2001/13, 27 June 2001.

goals such as health against rights to trade claimed under the WTO treaties, illuminates the glaring tension between intellectual property rights and the obligation (right) of governments to protect the right to health.

This Declaration alters the expectations of developed countries as regards panels faced with a government insisting on its right to protect health. In turn, it has encouraged developing countries to grant compulsory licences for the domestic production of drugs and to take advantage of the possibility of cheaper medicines through parallel imports. The procedures for implementation of the Declaration are complex and continue to evolve.[44] Further controversy focuses on the impact of the WTO intellectual property regime on indigenous peoples and their traditional knowledge and agricultural methods.[45] The negotiations on these topics are too fluid for detailed analysis here. What is apparent, however, is a reticence on the part of governments to incorporate, or reference, human rights norms and principles. This is unfortunate, as human rights norms could provide, not only a reference point which ought to be acceptable to all sides, but also, agreed obligations under international law which have to be taken into account in any future dispute.

Similar tensions exist in the context of negotiations and disputes over trade in services with regard to rights to education or water, as private foreign corporations assume responsibility for the provision of services in these sectors. Furthermore, negotiations over agriculture threaten rights to subsistence and employment as tariff reductions force farmers out of business, with no viable alternative crops.[46] Of course, reminding the WTO and its member states of the human rights obligations and implications inherent in their work is unlikely to have much immediate impact. At one level, many officials and negotiators simply assume that trade liberalization will inevitably improve human rights in the long run. A much more complicated phase will involve developing ways to determine what are the exact human rights implications of any negotiation or adjudicated decision at the WTO. This will be a complicated exercise in prediction, and prognoses will be contested, but it is important to note that environmental impact assessments are now commonplace in various fields. Such environmental impact assessments could be tools for protectionism, but the relevant decision-makers still consider that environmental damage may be irreversible, and that the risks need to be discussed. Human rights damage can likewise be irreversible. There are some signs that human rights norms are very gradually being introduced as factors to be taken into account in new negotiations.

[44] See WT/L/540, 2 September 2003, Implementation of paragraph 6 of the Doha Declaration on the TRIPS Agreement and Public Health, 30 August 2003.

[45] For an overview see M. Khor, *Intellectual Property, Biodiversity and Sustainable Development* (Penang: Third World Network, 2002).

[46] These overlaps are discussed in the paper prepared by the UN Office of the High Commissioner for Human Rights entitled 'Human Rights and Trade', prepared for the WTO 2003 Summit in Cancún, Mexico and available at http://www.unhchr.ch/html/menu2/trade/index.htm (*What's New?* Accessed 13 July 2005).

Marceau has described the introduction by Mauritius of a number of human rights instruments into the discussion in the Committee on Agriculture. In her account, the Government argued that 'negotiations and WTO policy reform ought to be undertaken in a way that is consistent with other multilateral commitments'.[47] This represents perhaps a turning point, as until recently human rights were considered automatically inimical to the developing country agenda. Human rights were either seen as excuses for protectionism, or as part of a justification for trade sanctions.

5.1.2   Summary Conclusions Regarding the WTO

- The role of international human rights law in the deliberations of the panels and Appellate Body remains to be clarified by those bodies. There is plenty of room to legitimately take human rights obligations into account under the international law governing interpretation of treaties.

- WTO rules have prevented governments from taking action, such as special measures with regard to essential medicine, which are necessary to protect human rights. There are fears that further developments will deny groups such as farmers and indigenous peoples their human rights, as WTO agreements are interpreted to favour those capable of registering patents concerning traditional knowledge and farming techniques, including the use of seeds. Introducing human rights as ongoing obligations for the negotiating and implementing governments may shift the argument from one about 'concessions' to one about rights and existing entitlements.

- Reiterating that the WTO, as an inter-governmental non-state actor, is bound by international human rights law may help to reorientate the debate away from the misleading suggestion that introducing the human rights dimension is part of a demand for the WTO to enforce human rights. Focusing on the WTO as the bearer of international human rights obligations may help to highlight the issue of the human rights impact of the WTO, its rules, and the decisions of its dispute settlement mechanism.

5.2   THE EUROPEAN COMMUNITY AND THE EUROPEAN UNION[48]

The evolution of the European Community's human rights policy is an often-told story and open to multiple interpretations. Andrew Williams, in what he calls

---

[47] Marceau (2002: 788, footnote 113).
[48] The expression European Community is preferred in this section when we are dealing with the Community as a legal entity with specific legal rights and obligations on the international plane.

'an excavation of the plurality of the Community's institutional narratives on human rights' has highlighted the effects of the European Community's 'bificurated' approach.[49]

> Internally, the Community has adopted an assumption that human rights conditions within its borders do not require attention on the whole. Although open to some degree of institutional review, at no time has it turned its eyes with any force upon its Member States... By contrast, the Community has presented itself externally as a practising guardian of human rights, a beacon of virtue. It has attempted to impose standards and values and interpretations on the tacit understanding that, unlike its own constituents, 'others' require constant scrutiny and the presence of potential sanction to ensure human rights are respected.[50]

This critique is based, not only on the Community's policies, but also results in part from the legal framework which does indeed limit the extent to which the Community can control the human rights performance of its member states.

The Community has a welter of complex possibilities to pursue its human rights policies.[51] Such policies might lead one to assume that the Community is, not only a promoter of human rights in the rest of the world, but also imbued with human rights as part of its constitutional order. The Community is often referred to as a pillar of a European Union, which in turn according to its treaty, is 'founded on the principles of liberty, democracy, respect for human rights and fundamental freedoms, and the rule of law, principles which are common to the Member States'.[52] However, the reticence of the member states to grant the Community full powers and competences over human rights means that the situation is complex. As with the United Nations and its creations,[53] one might assume that the starting point should be that an organization such as the Community must be bound by the same human rights obligations to which it appeals with regard to its own identity and in its external relations.

5.2.1   The European Community as a Party to Treaties with Human Rights Clauses

A convenient starting point is to consider certain international agreements through which the Community has entered into treaty relations with non-Community

---

However, the European Union, even in the absence of the entry into force of the Constitution, may also have legal obligations under international law. This section refers to the EU where the relevant documents such as the Charter and draft Constitution use this term for the emerging new order.

[49] A. Williams, *EU Human Rights Policies: A Study in Irony* (Oxford: Oxford University Press, 2004) at 193.   [50] Ibid, at 200–201.

[51] For a study of these policies, see Alston *et al* (1999).

[52] Treaty of European Union, Art. 6 [2002] OJ C325/11, 24 December 2002.

[53] With regard to the UN High Commissioner for Refugees, Ralph Wilde asserts: 'On the face of its mandate, it would be inconceivable that UNHCR, as a creature set up by international law to

states. These treaties include explicit terms that make respect for human rights an essential element of the agreement. While these agreements are clearly designed to allow the European Community to suspend the agreement in response to human rights violations in the third country, the effect of these agreements is that the European Community accepts its human rights obligations as obligations arising in international law. In the words of Barbara Brandtner and Allan Rosas: 'In this respect, the Communities' activities are based on the presumption that the Universal Declaration expresses general principles which have become binding on all subjects of international law, including the Community itself.'[54]

Looking at the wording of particular treaties binding the European Community, it is clear that this presumption can translate into a binding treaty obligation which can be enforced through the rules which govern treaty relations. The Cotonou Agreement between the African, Caribbean and Pacific States (ACP) and the European Community and its member states stipulates in Article 9(2) that: 'Respect for human rights, democratic principles and the rule of law, which underpin the ACP–EU Partnership, shall underpin the domestic and international policies of the Parties and constitute the essential elements of this Agreement.'[55]

The Agreement provides that, in the event of an alleged violation of the human rights contained in Article 9, recourse will be had to the consultation mechanism established in Article 96, and in cases of special urgency[56] this could mean counter-measures under international law.[57] Under this treaty, the Community and the ACP states are bound to respect international human rights law; and there is a particular mechanism which can be triggered by each party for ensuring that respect. The obligations, strictly speaking, stem from the content of the treaty, but they build on the presumption that the Community is already bound to respect these rights under customary international law. The parties to the agreement are bound by the same human rights clause. The content of this obligation assumes a common understanding of what is meant by human rights: the customary (general) international law of human rights.

---

promote international human rights law, was not bound by international human rights law itself.' '*Quis Custodiet Ipsos Custodes?*; Why and How UNHCR Governance of Development Refugee Camps Should be Subject to International Human Rights Law' 1 *Yale HRDLJ* (1998) 107–128, at 116.

[54] B. Brandtner and A. Rosas, 'Human Rights and the External Relations of the European Community: An analysis of doctrine and practice' 9 *EJIL* (1998) 469–490, at 489.

[55] Cotonou Agreement, 23 June 2000, available at: http://europa.eu.int/comm/development/body/cotonou/index_en.htm.

[56] Art. 96(2)(b) states: '"cases of special urgency" shall refer to exceptional cases of particularly serious and flagrant violation of one of the essential elements referred to in paragraph 2 of Article 9, that require an immediate reaction.'

[57] Art. 96(2)(c): 'The "appropriate measures" referred to in this Article are measures taken in accordance with international law, and proportional to the violation. In the selection of these measures, priority must be given to those which least disrupt the application of this agreement. It is understood that suspension would be a measure of last resort.'

In truth, this aspect of the Community's human rights obligations is unlikely to be of much practical significance. It does nevertheless reinforce the overall case for the assertion that non-state actors have human rights obligations under international law. It may also make it easier to build a human rights policy with regard to the Community's humanitarian and development programmes.

5.2.2   Obligations on the Community in the Community Legal Order

Turning to the actual legal order of the Community, the focus has been on European human rights. The Treaty on European Union states that the European Union shall respect fundamental rights as guaranteed by the European Convention and the constitutional traditions common to the member states.[58] This formula derives from the case-law of the European Court of Justice (ECJ) and has been the subject of considerable commentary with regards to its application by the ECJ and the threat posed by possible divergent member state interpretation of such a ground for judicial review.[59] The new 'Treaty establishing a Constitution for Europe' reorganizes the human rights dimension of the new proposed European Union in its Article I-9, entitled 'Fundamental rights':

1. The Union shall recognise the rights, freedoms and principles set out in the Charter of Fundamental Rights which constitutes Part II.
2. The Union shall accede to the European Convention for the Protection of Human Rights and Fundamental Freedoms. Such accession shall not affect the Union's competences as defined in the Constitution.
3. Fundamental rights, as guaranteed by the European Convention for the Protection of Human Rights and Fundamental Freedoms and as they result from the constitutional traditions common to the Member States, shall constitute general principles of the Union's law.[60]

Whether or not this Constitution enters into force, the three paragraphs usefully set out three aspects of the human rights obligations of non-state actors in the present context.

---

[58] Art. 6(2): 'The Union shall respect fundamental rights, as guaranteed by the European Convention for the Protection of Human Rights and Fundamental Freedoms signed in Rome on 4 November 1950 and as they result from the constitutional traditions common to the Member States, as general principles of Community law.'

[59] See, in particular, the insightful approach of Joseph Weiler to the inherent problem of respecting constitutional traditions in the application of Community law. J. H. H. Weiler, *The Constitution of Europe: 'Do the new clothes have an emperor?' and other essays on European integration* (Cambridge: Cambridge University Press, 1999) at 102–129.

[60] Art. I-9, Treaty establishing a Constitution for Europe, 29 October 2004, CIG 87/2/04, Rev. 2.

5.2.2.1   *The European Union Charter of Human Rights and Fundamental Freedoms*

Member states determined in 1999 that 'the fundamental rights applicable at Union level should be consolidated in a Charter and thereby made more evident'.[61] The aim of this Charter has always been to highlight applicable rights rather than generate new obligations. The Charter was solemnly promulgated by the European Parliament, the Commission, and the Council in Nice in December 2000.[62] It was later incorporated in an amended form into the treaty establishing the Constitution for Europe.[63]

The European Community (through its institutions) is already accountable for violations of human rights obligations (as they constitute principles of Community law) before the European Court of Justice (ECJ). Complaints can be brought against the Commission of the Community by the member states or by natural and legal persons where those persons are directly affected.[64] Even where the Court has accepted that the European Community is bound by customary international law, this has really been in the context of a discussion as to whether individual rights derived from Community agreements with third states have been overridden by properly adopted secondary legislation. The *Racke* case[65] established that the Court considers that the Community is bound by customary international law, and that a violation of customary international law could be relevant to a determination that a piece of Community secondary legislation was invalid and inapplicable to an individual or legal person. But the circumstances of that case have left some doubt as to whether customary international law rights would be directly protected by the Court.[66]

In analysing the Charter, it is important to highlight the fact that there are a number of important limitations. These are known in this context as 'horizontal clauses'. The provisions of the Charter are only addressed to the institutions and bodies of the Union within the framework of the powers conferred on them by the Treaties, as well as to the member states exclusively within the framework of implementing Community law.[67]

---

[61] European Council, Presidency Conclusions, Cologne European Council, 3–4 June 1999, §44 and Annex IV.   [62] [2002] OJ C364/1, 18 December 2000.

[63] The final version is Part II of the treaty, CIG 87/2/04, Rev. 2, 29 October 2004. For some interesting aspects of the negotiating history, see G. de Búrca, 'Beyond the Charter: How Enlargement has Enlarged the Human Rights Policy of the EU' 27 *Ford ILJ* (2004) 679–714.

[64] Art. 230, Treaty establishing the European Community (TEC).

[65] *A. Racke GmbH & Co v Hauptzollamt Mainz* Case C–162/96, 16 June 1998 [1998] ECR I–3655.

[66] K. Lenaerts and E. De Smijter, 'The European Union as an Actor under International Law' 19 *Yearbook of European Law* (2000) 95–138, at 126: 'A rule of customary international law can thus always be invoked by an individual in the framework of a claim based on another rule of Community law. On the other hand, the question whether an individual may claim rights which derive directly from a rule of customary international remains open for the time being.'

[67] Art. 51(1): 'The provisions of this Charter are addressed to the institutions and bodies of the Union with due regard for the principle of subsidiarity and to the Member States only when they are implementing Union law. They shall therefore respect the rights, observe the principles and promote

How might the Community, or Community law, actually violate human rights in ways where there would not be the normal recourse to human rights law against the state? It is in the implementation of Community law, and in the application of derogations to primary Community law, that the ECJ has developed a layer of human rights protection from Community law itself. The ECJ gradually incorporated the protection of fundamental rights as a general principle of Community law. This came about against a background of discontent in the Constitutional Courts of Italy and Germany, which had suggested that they might one day have to review Community provisions for compatibility with basic human rights.[68] The ECJ, having rejected arguments based on human rights principles found in national law in an early case,[69] later explained that:[70]

> ...the Court is bound to draw inspiration from constitutional traditions common to the Member States, and it cannot therefore uphold measures which are incompatible with fundamental rights recognized and protected by the constitutions of those States. Similarly, international treaties for the protection of human rights on which the Member States have collaborated or of which they are signatories, can supply guidelines which should be followed within the framework of Community law.

In the *Hauer* case, in 1979, the Court found itself dealing with a concrete application of this principle with regard to the right to property;[71] the Court stated that this right is guaranteed in the Community legal order. The Court referred to Article 1 of the First Protocol to the European Convention on Human Rights and to 'ideas common to the Constitutions of the Member States'.[72]

Ten years later, in the *Wachauf* case, the Court developed its reasoning as follows:[73]

> The Court has consistently held, in particular in its judgment of 13 December 1979 in Case 44/79 *Hauer v Land Rheinland Pfalz* (1979) ECR 3727, that fundamental rights form an integral part of the general principles of the law, the observance of which is ensured by the Court. In safeguarding those rights, the Court has to look to the constitutional traditions common to the Member States, so that measures which are incompatible with the fundamental rights recognized by the constitutions of those States may not find acceptance in the Community. International treaties concerning the protection of human rights on which the Member States have collaborated or to which

---

the application thereof in accordance with their respective powers.' The Constitution adds the phrase 'and respecting the limits of the powers of the Union as conferred on it in the other Parts of the Constitution' (Art. II-111).

[68] *Frontini* Case (No. 183), Corte Costituzionale, 27 December 1973 [1974] 2 CMLR 386 and the *German Handelsgesellschaft* case, Bundesverfassungsgericht, 29 May 1974 [1974] 2 CMLR 551. See also the *Solange II* decision of 22 October 1986, *Re Wünsche Handelsgesellschaft* [1987] 3 CMLR 225.   [69] *Stork* case, Case 1/58 [1959] ECR 17.
[70] *J. Nold v Commission* Case 4/73 [1974] ECR 491, at 507.
[71] *Hauer v Land Rheinland-Pfalz* Case 44/79 [1979] ECR 3727.
[72] For speculation on why the Court referred to 'ideas', see Weiler (1999: 114).
[73] *Hubert Wachauf v FRG* Case 5/88 [1989] ECR 2609, paras 17–19.

they have acceded can also supply guidelines to which regard should be had in the context of Community law.

The fundamental rights recognised by the Court are not absolute, however, but must be considered in relation to their social function. Consequently, restrictions may be imposed on the exercise of those rights, in particular in the context of the common organization of a market, provided that those restrictions in fact correspond to the objectives of general interest pursued by the Community, and do not constitute, with regard to the aim pursued, a disproportionate and intolerable interference, impairing the very substance of these rights.

Having regard to those criteria, it must be observed that Community rules which, upon the expiry of the lease, had the effect of depriving the lessee, without compensation, of the fruits of his labour and of his investments in the tenanted holding would be incompatible with the requirements of the protection of fundamental rights in the Community legal order. Since those requirements are also binding on the Member States when they implement Community rules, the Member States must, as far as possible, apply those rules in accordance with those requirements.

The obligation under Community law is that, when member states *implement* Community law, they must, as far as possible *apply* those rules in accordance with human rights law. This means that a national court has to take human rights into account in the application of Community law to the case before it. The question which arises, in the light of the recognition of the Charter of Fundamental Rights, is the extent to which a national court, following entry into force of the new Constitution, will have to apply the rights contained in the Charter in the implementation of Union law (as it would then be called) over and above human rights as understood in Community law. The statement of reasons which accompanied the Charter in 2000, explained that the provision follows from the case-law of the ECJ, which requires member states to ensure that the result of the implementation of Community legislation is not incompatible with human rights.[74]

A second type of case added to this jurisprudence. This type of case suggests that fundamental rights, and the Convention in particular, have to be considered by national courts, not only when implementing and interpreting Community provisions in the application of the law, but also when weighing the proportionality and legitimacy of derogations from Community freedoms. In the *ERT* case, the Court stated that the permissible restrictions under Article 56 of the old Treaty of

---

[74] 'As regards the Member States, it follows unambiguously from the case law of the Court of Justice that the requirement to respect fundamental rights defined in a Union context is only binding on the Member States when they act in the context of Community law (judgment of 13 July 1989, Case 5/88 *Wachauf* [1989] ECR 2609; judgment of 18 June 1991, *ERT* [1991] ECR I–2925). The Court of Justice recently confirmed this case law in the following terms: "In addition, it should be remembered that the requirements flowing from the protection of fundamental rights in the Community legal order are also binding on Member States when they implement Community rules…" (judgment of 13 April 2000, Case C–292/97, paragraph 37 of the grounds, not yet published). Of course this principle, as enshrined in this Charter, applies to the central authorities as well as to regional or local bodies, and to public organisations, when they are implementing Union law.' CHARTE 4473/00, CONVENT 49, 11 October 2000, at 46.

the European Economic Community (EEC) (public policy, public security, or public health) had to be looked at in the light of the general principle of freedom of expression; Community law could not be used in ways which would impinge on human rights.[75]

There are then essentially two types of national implementation of Community law that are subject to review for compatibility with human rights under Community law. First, is the application of Community or secondary legislation through the national legal order (*Wachauf*). And second, is a national attempt to apply a Community right derived from the primary treaty in a way that could impinge on human rights (*ERT*). Until recently these safeguards, derived from ECJ case-law, seemed attractive to those building the theoretical case that the Community had a constitution that protected human rights. Critical voices pointed to the fact that, in practice, few human rights claimants had succeeded in invoking this doctrine in a way that had led to the ECJ choosing human rights over the alternative demands of Community economic freedoms or the 'objectives of general interest pursued by the Community'.[76] This is in part due to the sorts of human rights claims made against Community law: that it impermissibly interfered with the enjoyment of possessions. There were few cases which pitted individual human rights (outside the context of property rights) against economic actors protected by Community law. There is now some evidence from one case that the ECJ is prepared to restrict Community economic freedoms in order to ensure the protection of human rights. This case bears some examination due to the fact that the human rights claim was in effect argued against a non-state actor.

A road haulage company was operating its trucks on a route through Austria. The inhabitants of that particular mountainous region objected to the trucks crossing this part of Austria and they organized a demonstration (with the authorization of the Austrian authorities) which effectively brought the lorries to a halt on the Brenner motorway. The haulage company brought an action against

---

[75] *Elliniki Radiophonia Tiléorani-Anonimi Etairia v Dimotiki Etairia Pliroforissis* C–260/89, judgment of 18 June 1991 [1991] ECR I–2925, para. 41: 'it has no power to examine the compatibility with the European Convention on Human Rights of national rules which do not fall within the scope of Community law. On the other hand, where such rules do fall within the scope of Community law, and reference is made to the Court for a preliminary ruling, it must provide all the criteria of interpretation needed by the national court to determine whether those rules are compatible with the fundamental rights the observance of which the Court ensures and which derive in particular from the European Convention on Human Rights.' And at para. 43: 'In particular, where a Member State relies on the combined provisions of Articles 56 and 66 in order to justify rules which are likely to obstruct the exercise of the freedom to provide services, such justification, provided for by Community law, must be interpreted in the light of the general principles of law and in particular of fundamental rights. Thus the national rules in question can fall under the exceptions provided for by the combined provisions of Articles 56 and 66 only if they are compatible with the fundamental rights the observance of which is ensured by the Court.' Para. 44 states: 'It follows that in such a case it is for the national court, and if necessary, the Court of Justice to appraise the application of those provisions having regard to all the rules of Community law, including freedom of expression, as embodied in Article 10 of the European Convention on Human Rights, as a general principle of law the observance of which is ensured by the Court.'   [76] *Wauchauf* (n 73 above) para. 18.

Austria in the Austrian courts, claiming damages for the time their lorries had
been delayed. On referral to the ECJ, the Court concluded that Community
law had to be applied in a way that gave priority to the human rights of the
protesters.[77] The Court was clear that the Community itself has human rights
obligations: 'Thus, since both the Community and its Member States are required
to respect fundamental rights, the protection of those rights is a legitimate interest
which, in principle, justifies a restriction of the obligations imposed by
Community law, even under a fundamental freedom guaranteed by the Treaty
such as the free movement of goods.'[78] The upshot of the ECJ's ruling is that, not
only was it confirmed that the European Community as such has to respect
human rights, but that as a consequence of this, other non-state actors, in this case
haulage companies, can exercise their economic freedoms under Community law
only to the extent that such exercise does not disproportionately interfere with the
enjoyment of international human rights.[79]

5.2.2.2 The European Community before the European Court of Human Rights

Of course, if the complaint relates solely to rights granted through the European
Community legal order, the story would stop there. The European Court of
Justice of the Community promises to ensure that Community law is applied in
conformity with human rights. But should that Court fail to uphold a claim based
on international human rights, can one complain internationally about a failure
by the European Community *as such* to uphold one's international human rights?
As suggested in Chapter 1, much depends on the jurisdictional filter we use. The
following section contains a brief consideration of the situation before the
European Court of Human Rights.

At the time of writing, the Community was not a party to the European
Convention on Human Rights, however, the proposed Constitution includes a
commitment to accede to the European Convention on Human Rights.[80] Should

---

[77] *Eugen Schmidberger, Internationale Transporte und Planzüge v Austria* Case C–112/00,
Judgment of the European Court of Justice, 12 June 2003 [2003] ECR I–5659.

[78] Ibid, at para. 74.

[79] At para. 76 the judgment refers to the fact that Austria was seeking to uphold international
human rights: 'In the present case, the national authorities relied on the need to respect fundamental
rights guaranteed by both the ECHR [European Convention on Human Rights] and the
Constitution of the Member State concerned in deciding to allow a restriction to be imposed on one
of the fundamental freedoms enshrined in the Treaty.'

[80] See Art. I-9(2), at 5.2.2 above. The question whether the European Union, as opposed to the
European Community, has international legal personality is a complicated one that will not be dealt
with here. I shall simply refer to the European Community as the entity that is most likely to be
explicitly entitled to ratify the ECHR. (See, e.g. Art. 33 of the Convention on Human Rights and
Biomedicine (1997) which is open for the signature of the 'European Community'.) For an excellent
discussion on the international legal personality of the European Union, see J. Klabbers 'Presumptive
Personality: The European Union in International Law' in M. Koskenniemi (ed) *International Law
Aspects of the European Union* (The Hague: Kluwer, 1998) 231–253.

such an accession take place, it is clear that the Community (or under a new Constitution, the Union) would be accountable before the European Court of Human Rights. Until such accession, the issue of the human rights obligations of the Community before the European Court of Human Rights will remain rather convoluted.

Protocol 14 to the Convention now provides that the European Union may become a party to the Convention.[81] Until such an accession comes into effect, the situation remains that there is no option of complaining directly against the European Community to the European Court of Human Rights in Strasbourg. For example, one cannot complain that a decision of the European Court of Justice in Luxembourg has violated human rights, rights which are supposed to be protected for all people in Europe under the European Convention on Human Rights. Nevertheless, the Strasbourg-based European Court of Human Rights has been faced with some interesting complaints concerning the Community brought against the Community's member states but concerning the Community.

In *Matthews v United Kingdom*[82] the European Court of Human Rights found the United Kingdom to be in violation of the Convention, even though the law (which denied voting rights in Gibraltar for elections to the European Parliament) resulted from a treaty entered into by the Community's member states, rather than a piece of national legislation. The Court reiterated that it could not hold the Community as such accountable for the denial of voting rights to a Community institution:

> The Court observes that acts of the EC as such cannot be challenged before the Court because the EC is not a Contracting Party. The Convention does not exclude the transfer of competences to international organisations provided that Convention rights continue to be 'secured'. Member States' responsibility therefore continues even after such a transfer.[83]

The Court went on to explain how acceding to a treaty is an act that can give rise to a finding of a violation of human rights where the treaty organization has legislative powers and people are denied the right to participate in the election of that legislature.

> It is uncontested that legislation emanating from the legislative process of the European Community affects the population of Gibraltar in the same way as legislation which enters the domestic legal order exclusively via the House of Assembly.[84]

The Court found that the European Parliament was a legislature for the applicant in Gibraltar within the meaning of Article 3 of Protocol 1 of the European Convention on Human Rights.[85] And the Court found that the applicant's right to vote under that provision had been denied. Looked at another way, the legislative branch of the Community represents transferred powers from the

---

[81] Art. 17 inserts a new paragraph into Art. 59 of the Convention: 'The European Union may accede to this Convention.'   [82] Judgment of 18 February 1999.

[83] Ibid, at para. 32.   [84] Ibid, at para. 34.

[85] Art. 3 of Protocol 1 reads: 'The High Contracting Parties undertake to hold free elections at reasonable intervals by secret ballot, under conditions which will ensure the free expression of the opinion of the people in the choice of the legislature.'

member states, and these powers have to be exercised in accordance with the human rights provisions on the election of legislatures under the Convention. Anyone within the jurisdiction of a member state will be able to complain if this transfer of power to the Community denies that person the right to free elections with regard to a legislature passing legislation that affects that complainant.[86]

A second application concerned a complaint about a fine imposed by the Commission of the Community on a German shipping company, Senator Lines.[87] The application was subsequently withdrawn from the Court's list and will not be heard before the Court due to the resolution of the issue before the Community Court, but a few points are worth highlighting.

The complaint arises out of a Decision by the EC Commission finding an infringement of Articles 85 and 86 of the Treaty of the Economic Community (TEC) (now Articles 81 and 82 TEC) and a resultant fine for Senator Lines of €13,750,000.[88] In the words of the application: 'The Applicant is thus found guilty of an abuse of a "collective dominant position" despite the fact that it has only itself a 3.2% market share of the relevant market as defined by the Commission (i.e. the trade within the scope of TACA [Trans Atlantic Conference Agreement]). This fine represents 11.53% of the world wide annual turnover of the Applicant in the transatlantic trade in the last year of the alleged infringement.'[89]

The legality of the decision and the appropriateness of the fine by the EC Commission were challenged in the European Communities' Court of First Instance on the grounds, *inter alia*, that there had been a denial of the right to a fair hearing. Article 6 of the ECHR was raised in that context.[90]

---

[86] See further, P. Leach, *Taking a Case to the European Court of Human Rights* (London: Blackstone Press, 2001) at 187–188.

[87] The full text of the application is reproduced in 21 *HRLJ* (2000) 112–128. Other relevant applications that have addressed the question of the responsibility of member states for the actions of international organizations are *M. & Co v FRG*, App. 13258/87, 64 DR 138–146 (European Commission of Human Rights) and *Waite and Kennedy v Germany* Judgment 18 February 1999 (European Court of Human Rights).

[88] Decision 1999/243/EC of 16 September 1998 [1999] OJ L95/1–112.

[89] See the application (n 87 above) at 113.

[90] Art. 6 reads: '(1) In the determination of his civil rights and obligations or of any criminal charge against him, everyone is entitled to a fair and public hearing within a reasonable time by an independent and impartial tribunal established by law. Judgment shall be pronounced publicly but the press and public may be excluded from all or part of the trial in the interests of morals, public order or national security in a democratic society, where the interests of juveniles or the protection of the private life of the parties so require, or to the extent strictly necessary in the opinion of the court in special circumstances where publicity would prejudice the interests of justice. (2) Everyone charged with a criminal offence shall be presumed innocent until proved guilty according to law. (3) Everyone charged with a criminal offence has the following minimum rights: (a) to be informed promptly, in a language which he understands and in detail, of the nature and cause of the accusation against him; (b) to have adequate time and facilities for the preparation of his defence; (c) to defend himself in person or through legal assistance of his own choosing or, if he has not sufficient means to pay for legal assistance, to be given it free when the interests of justice so require; (d) to examine or have examined witnesses against him and to obtain the attendance and examination of witnesses on his behalf under the same conditions as witnesses against him; (e) to have the free assistance of an interpreter if he cannot understand or speak the language used in court.

The application by Senator Lines to the European Court of Human Rights clearly raised questions of the compatibility of European Community law and procedures with the European Convention on Human Rights. But the application was brought against the fifteen member states of the European Union. The Union itself was represented through written observations prepared by the EC Commission at the preliminary stage.

With regard to responsibility, the Commission supported the position of the member states that first, they have no control over the acts of the Commission and the ECJ, and, second, that the Community has a separate legal personality. The Commission then tackled the crucial issue in the following way:

> While it may be true as a matter of principle that signatories to the Convention may not evade their obligations by transferring powers to independent international organisations, it does not follow that they can be held liable for the actions of those organisations in individual cases. In order to comply with their obligations under the Convention it is sufficient that they ensure the institution of an equivalent level of protection of fundamental rights within the organisation in question.[91]

The observations then go on to explain how the Community protects fundamental rights within its own legal order. For the Commission, the key issue with regard to responsibility is that the Court should not 'equate the organisation with the collectivity of its members' as this is 'to ignore the very purpose of establishing international organizations capable of forming their own will distinct from that of individual members or the group as a whole'.[92] The Commission was careful to state that it was not claiming that the human rights obligations of the member states are satisfied 'once and for all where, having set up an international organisation such as the Community, they endow it with an appropriate internal mechanism of human rights protection'. It stated that there may be a need for vigilance on the part of member states, but that the human rights obligation under Article 1 of the European Convention on Human Rights [93] would only be triggered 'if there were clear indications that, beyond the individual case at hand, acts of the organisation *in general* did not live up to that organisation's own human rights standards and that the internal safeguard mechanism no longer afforded equivalent protection'.[94] The request to the European Court of Human Rights by the Commission is quite far reaching:

> In light of the serious and exceptional implications of such a situation, the Commission submits that this Court should continue to hold inadmissible all applications against individual Community acts unless the applicant is able, going beyond the particular

---

[91] 'Written Observations' of the Commission of the European Communities, 1 March 2001, JURM (2000) 4030, at para. 25. I am grateful to the Legal Service of the Commission for sending me their intervention.   [92] Ibid, para. 36.

[93] Art. 1 states: 'The High Contracting Parties shall secure to everyone within their jurisdiction the rights and freedoms defined in Section I of this Convention.'

[94] 'Written Observations' (n 91 above) at para. 41.

case or subject matter in issue, to show that in general the Community fails effectively to protect human rights as general principles of Community law.[95]

In the circumstances, this sounds reasonable, but the problem is that the approach of human rights law is to focus on the harm to individual victims, and not the general adequacy of the system. The Court would not take seriously a claim by a state party to the Convention that the Court should look, not at the individual facts, but rather, at the general adequacy of that state's legal system (which of course always includes the provisions and institutions for the protection for human rights).

A clue as to the way in which the Strasbourg Court would deal with a complaint about a denial of a fair hearing before the ECJ can be gleaned from the case of *Pellegrini v Italy*.[96] It that case, the Strasbourg Court held that Italy had violated the Convention, by entering into an agreement with the Vatican that it would enforce the judgments of the ecclesiastical courts, without first checking that the procedure in those courts satisfied the requirements of fair trial under the Convention.[97] One can conclude that where states parties to the European Convention on Human Rights claim they are simply enforcing the decisions of the European Union/Community (or any other state or non-state actor that is not a party to the Convention), then the Strasbourg Court will scrutinize whether the agreement to enforce such decisions carefully considered whether the party's procedures were human rights compliant. The net effect should be that such non-state actors would be forced to assume the human rights obligations of the states parties to the Convention.

5.2.2.3 *Community Law as the Source of Human Rights Obligations on Non-State Actors*

Provisions in Community law can give rise to direct obligations on non-state actors, including individuals and private corporations. For example, the principles of non-discrimination on grounds of nationality and equal pay for equal work (Articles 12 and 141 in the Treaty Establishing the European Community (TEC))

---

[95] Ibid, at para. 41.

[96] Judgment of the European Court of Human Rights, 20 July 2001. I am grateful to Judge Costa, of the European Court of Human Rights, for highlighting the analogy in his speech 'L'article 1er de la Convention européenne des droits de l'homme et la responsabilité des Etats', Journée d'études sur la Cour européenne des droits de l'homme, Institut universitaire de hautes études internationales, Geneva, 11 March 2005. Unpublished mimeograph on file with the author.

[97] See esp. para. 40: 'The Court notes at the outset that the applicant's marriage was annulled by a decision of the Vatican courts which was declared enforceable by the Italian courts. The Vatican has not ratified the Convention and, furthermore, the application was lodged against Italy. The Court's task therefore consists not in examining whether the proceedings before the ecclesiastical courts complied with Article 6 of the Convention, but whether the Italian courts, before authorising enforcement of the decision annulling the marriage, duly satisfied themselves that the relevant proceedings fulfilled the guarantees of Article 6. A review of that kind is required where a decision in respect of which enforcement is requested emanates from the courts of a country which does not apply the Convention.'

give rise to such obligations. This is sometimes known as 'horizontal direct effect'.[98] Important secondary Community legislation may also be aimed at private discrimination just as much as state discrimination. The Directives on sex discrimination,[99] racial discrimination,[100] and discrimination on the basis of religion or belief, sexual orientation, age, and disability[101] are all presented in terms of protecting human rights—and all are to apply to discrimination and harassment by private employers.

In a landmark case in 1963, the ECJ referred to the direct obligations that arise in Community law in the following way: 'Independently of the legislation of Members States, Community law therefore not only *imposes obligations on individuals* but is also intended to confer upon them rights which become part of their legal heritage.'[102] These rights and obligations are constantly evolving with the evolution of the Community, and in the same case the Court went on to state: 'These rights arise not only where they are expressly granted by the Treaty, but also by reason of *obligations which the Treaty imposes in a clearly defined way upon individuals* as well as upon the Member States and upon the institutions of the Community.'[103]

Let us turn to consider a few cases where direct obligations arose for individuals, corporations, and associations under the Community Treaty (EEC, now TEC). In *Walrave and Koch v Association Union Cycliste Internationale*[104] the EEC Treaty's prohibition of discrimination based on nationality was held by the ECJ to extend to the rules of an international cycling organization. The rule in question provided that, for a world championship race, the pacemaker (motorcyclist) must be the same nationality as the stayer (cyclist). The Court highlighted the argument that the Treaty only covered the public sphere, obligating only state actors. 'It has been alleged that the prohibitions in these Articles refer only to restrictions which have their origin in acts of an authority and not to those resulting from legal acts of persons or associations who do not come under public law.'[105] The ruling then directly addressed the particular circumstances of the case: 'Prohibition on such discrimination does not only apply to the action of public authorities but extends

---

[98] See L. Betten and N. Grief, *EU Law and Human Rights* (London: Longman, 1998) at 81.

[99] Directive 2002/73/EC of 23 September 2002, amending Council Directive 76/207/EEC on the implementation of the principle of equal treatment for men and women as regards access to employment, vocational training and promotion, and working conditions, [2002] OJ L269/15, in force 5 October 2002. Member states had until 5 October 2005 to bring in the necessary laws and such laws will cover the private sector.

[100] EU Directive 2000/43/EC, [2000] OJ L180/22, in force 19 July 2000. States had until 19 July 2003 to bring into force the necessary measures, which have to cover the private sector.

[101] EC Council Directive 2000/78/EC, adopted 27 November 2000, [2000] OJ L303/16. The Directive entered into force on 2 December 2000. With regard to religion/belief and sexual orientation discrimination, states had until 2 December 2003 to implement the Directive; for age and disability legislation, states may take an extra three years to 2 December 2006.

[102] *Van Gend en Loos v Netherlandse Administratie der Belastingen* Case 26/62 [1963] ECR 1, at 12 (emphasis added).   [103] Ibid, at 12 (emphasis added).

[104] Case 36/74 [1974] ECR 1405.   [105] Ibid, at para. 15.

likewise to the rules of any other nature aimed at regulating in a collective manner gainful employment and the provision of services.'[106]

Less than two years later, the Court gave its ruling in the *Defrenne* case.[107] The case raised similar questions to those raised in the *Walrave* case, but this time the issue was equal pay for men and women for equal work. The Court was asked to draw the conclusion that Article 119 of the EEC Treaty (now Article 141 TEC) could not create individual rights enforceable before national tribunals. Furthermore, because the Article specifically refers to 'Member States'[108] it was argued that this demonstrated that the 'authors of the Treaty' did not intend this Article to create rights and obligations between employers and employees. The Court determined that this right to equal pay has to be protected 'in particular in the case of those forms of discrimination which have their origin in legislative provisions or collective labour agreements, as well as where men and women receive unequal pay for equal work which is carried out in the same establishment or service, *whether private or public*'.[109]

More recently, the ECJ delivered a judgment concerning discrimination based on nationality. In this case, a bank required that knowledge of Italian would be proven only on the production of a certificate which could only be obtained in one particular province in the state. This was said to put other nationalities at a disadvantage and constitute prohibited discrimination under the treaty.[110] A key passage, for our purposes, makes it clear that the prohibition in Article 48, concerning free movement for persons, applies to non-state actors including private banks. According to the Court, under this provision, 'freedom of movement for workers within the Community entails the abolition of any discrimination based on nationality between workers of the Member States as regards employment, remuneration and other conditions of work and employment'.[111] The Court is explicit that the treaty prohibition is not only binding on the member states of the European Union, but also binds private actors. 'It should be noted at the outset that the principle of non-discrimination set out in Article 48 is drafted in general terms and is not specifically addressed to the Member States.'[112] The Court highlights the fact that the erection of a public/private divide would simply generate a further set of discriminations; this time, between those subject to state and non-state actor discrimination. 'Since working conditions in the different Member States are governed sometimes by provisions laid down by law or regulation and sometimes by agreements and other acts concluded or adopted by private persons, limiting application of the prohibition of discrimination based on nationality

---

[106] Ibid, at para. 17.   [107] Case 43/75 [1976] ECR 455.

[108] Art. 119 started: 'Each Member State shall during the first stage ensure and subsequently maintain the application of the principle that men and women should receive equal pay for equal work.'   [109] *Defrenne* (n 107 above) at 482 (emphasis added).

[110] *Angonese v Cassa di Risparmio di Bolzano SpA* Case C–281/98 [2000] ECR I–4139, at paras 37–42.   [111] Ibid, at para. 29.

[112] Ibid, at para. 30.

to acts of a public authority risks creating inequality in its application'.[113] The judgment is unambiguous about the outcome: 'Consequently, the prohibition of discrimination on grounds of nationality laid down in Article 48 of the Treaty must be regarded as applying to private persons as well.'[114] The thrust of the Court's approach is to extend anti-discrimination protection under the TEC to the private sphere, whether the discrimination is on grounds of sex or nationality. Non-state actors are subject to direct obligations under Community law. In this way, sporting associations and employers have been precluded from operating discriminatory policies. Most recently, the English High Court has held that Article 43 TEC on freedom of establishment has direct horizontal effect and could be directly enforced against a trade union.[115]

Although such non-discrimination provisions in the TEC may be enforced against private individuals as part of Community law,[116] the Court has ruled that rights contained in directives which are enforceable against emanations of the state are not as such to be directly enforceable against private bodies.[117] This is the consequence of the judgment in *Marshall v Southampton and SW Hampshire Area Health Authority*,[118] where the equal treatment directive was held only to bind 'organs of the State' when relied on at the national level. Complainants have to wait until the directive is transformed into national law, but as is evident with regards to the directives on issues such as discrimination, this national application can apply to the private sector as well. There may be the possibility of complaining under Community law against the state for failure to properly transpose the directive into national law.[119] Lastly, Community law may demand that national law be

---

[113] Ibid, at para. 33.

[114] *Angonese v Cassa di Risparmio di Bolzano SpA* (n 110 above) at para 36.

[115] *Viking Line Abp v International Transport Workers' Federation and Finnish Seamen's Union* [2005] EWHC 1222 (Comm) at paras 109–115.

[116] Cf B. de Witte, 'The Past and Future Role of the European Court of Justice in the Protection of Human Rights' in P. Alston *et al* (1999) 859–897 who presents the *Walrave* and *Defrenne* cases as exceptional and assumes (at 874): 'that Community fundamental rights do not directly bind private parties'. See also, S. Van Den Bogaert, 'Horizontality: The Court Attacks?' in C. Barnard and J. Scott (eds) *The Law of the Single European Market* (Oxford: Hart Publishing, 2002) 123–152.

[117] See also T. Leivo, 'Against Whom May the Direct Effect of EC Directives be Relied Upon?' 'VI *The Finnish Yearbook of International Law* (1995) 565–574, who makes the point (at 574) that the ECJ's approach may 'lead to a distortion of competition. This is the result of the fact that undertakings controlled by a member State have to comply with non-implemented directives while private undertakings functioning on the same market do not have this obligation'; see also S. Prechal, *Directives in European Community Law: A Study of Directives and Their Enforcement in National Courts* (Oxford: Clarendon Press, 1995) at 295–305.

[118] Case 152/84 [1986] ECR 723; briefly, Mrs Marshall had been employed by the authority as a senior dietician, and she was dismissed as the age of 62, whereas had she been a man she would have been entitled to continue working until at least 65. She could not rely on the Sex Discrimination Act 1975, as s. 6(4) provided that sex discrimination by employers is not prohibited in relation to death or retirement. She relied on Art. 5 of Directive 76/207, as the date for implementation of the directive had expired and the terms of the Article were clear, precise, and unconditional.

[119] See the discussion in S. Drake, 'Twenty years after *Von Colson*: the impact of "indirect effect" on the protection of the individual's Community rights' 30 *European Law Review* (2005) 329–348, at

read to take into account the purpose of the directive where this is 'possible' without contradicting the national legislation; this rule applies even in civil cases brought against non-state actors.[120]

5.2.3   Summary Conclusions Regarding the European Community and the European Union

- The European Community is said by the ECJ to be bound by the general rules of international law in its treaty relations. These treaty relations include commitments to respect human rights in the context of the treaties with ACP and other states. The assumption is that the Community considers the Universal Declaration of Human Rights as reflecting the principles of international law binding on the Community and states with which it concludes such treaties. There is no reason to believe that the EU is not similarly bound by the same international human rights obligations.[121]

- The Community and the Union are obliged under Community/Union law to respect international human rights law. It is likely that the Charter of Fundamental Rights of the Union will play a role in shaping the way these obligations are interpreted.

- The prospect of the EU acceding to the European Convention on Human Rights reminds one how obvious it has become that non-state actors have the capacity to bear international human rights obligations, and that they may be held accountable for any violations at the international level. In the absence of accession, the European Court of Human Rights in Strasbourg will continue to receive cases against EU member states and assess the adequacy of the arrangements made by the Community to ensure respect for the human rights contained in the Convention through its own procedures.

- Member states are obliged to apply human rights law when implementing Community law. This may mean that non-state actors are precluded from enforcing their economic freedoms under Community law when these disproportionately affect the enjoyment of human rights.

343–345. For completeness it should be stated that *regulations* (which may be very similar in form to directives) may be directly effective against both state and private bodies and *decisions* are similarly enforceable against both state and private bodies (where the decision has been addressed to that body).

[120] See *Von Colson and Kamann* Case 14/83 [1984] ECR 1891, and *Webb v EMO Air Cargo (UK) Ltd* Case C–32/93 [1994] ECR I–3567. For an explanation of this complicated area of EU law, see Drake (2005).

[121] Note the Treaty establishing a Constitution for Europe, signed (but not ratified at the time of writing) by the 25 member states, provides in Art. I-7: 'The Union shall have legal personality.' See further Klabbers (1998); C. Tomuschat, 'The International Responsibility of the European Union' in E. Cannizzaro (ed) *The European Union as an Actor in International Relations* (The Hague: Kluwer, 2002) 177–191.

- The Community legal order has been interpreted by the Courts as generating direct obligations on private individuals, associations, corporations, and trade unions. These obligations are of direct effect in the international and national legal orders. As obligations of non-discrimination, they could be said to be human rights obligations binding on non-state actors.

6

Corporations and Human Rights

6.1 CORPORATE RESPONSIBILITY AND CORPORATE ACCOUNTABILITY

Activists concerned with the harmful activities of corporations have drawn a distinction between corporate responsibility and corporate accountability. According to CorpWatch: 'Corporate responsibility refers to any attempt to get corporations to behave responsibly on a voluntary basis, out of either ethical or bottom-line considerations.'[1] This approach is said to be 'favoured in the earth Summit processes, the UN Global Compact and the International Chamber of Commerce'.[2] Corporate accountability (or compliance) 'refers to requiring corporations to behave according to social norms or face consequences'. The corporate preference for voluntary initiatives, as opposed to binding legal commitments, is coming under scrutiny by the same groups that throughout the 1990s encouraged such voluntary initiatives (often known as corporate social responsibility (CSR) policies). *The Economist* highlighted this apparent change of direction as a 'switch': 'CSR was conjured up in the first place because government action was deemed inadequate: orthodox politics was a sham, so pressure had to be put directly on firms by organised protest. Ten years on, instead of declaring victory, as well they might, disenchanted NGOs like Christian Aid are coming to regard CSR as the greater sham, and are calling on governments to resume their duties.'[3] Christian Aid itself stated that it 'is advocating giving "teeth" to the ethical commitments of companies by moving beyond corporate social responsibility, which does not and cannot go far enough, to corporate social accountability, to ensure that companies have a legal obligation to uphold international standards'.[4]

---

[1] Joshua Karliner and Kenny Bruno, 'Responsibility vs. accountability' *International Herald Tribune*, 1 July 2002, at 14.   [2] Ibid.

[3] 'Two-faced capitalism' *International Herald Tribune*, 24 January 2004, 57–58, at 58; see also A. Frean 'Corporate aid or plain hypocrisy?' *The Times*, 2 February 2004, at 27.

[4] Christian Aid, *Behind the mask: The real face of corporate social responsibility* (2004) at 56. See also International Council on Human Rights Policy, *Beyond Voluntarism: Human rights and the developing international legal obligations of companies* (Versoix: ICHRP, 2002), and M. Monshipouri, C. E. Welsh, and E. T. Kennedy, who conclude: 'Whether the answer lies in restructuring international organizations, linking their strengths, enhancing private actions and media exposure, or creating a single intermediary institution, or regional or global governance, the case for MNC's self-policing is utterly unpersuasive.' 'Multinational Corporations and the Ethics of Global Responsibility: Problems and Possibilities' 25 *HRQ* (2003) 965–989, at 989.

This chapter seeks to explore the legal framework which forms the backdrop to the underlying tension between corporate social responsibility and corporate accountability. It highlights the emergence of some new ways of holding corporations accountable to their human rights obligations. In other words, it looks at how some obligations are being given 'teeth'.[5] I shall not examine the complementarity which is said to exist between the so-called responsibility and accountability approaches.[6] Advocates of each approach will continue to emphasize different aspects of what is sometimes known as 'the business case for human rights'.[7] Proponents of the 'voluntary' or 'regulatory' approaches will each in turn point to the efficacy of developing regimes according to their own preferences. It is clear that, as a rule, large businesses currently favour voluntary codes of conduct, guidelines, and sectoral initiatives. In this they are supported by their home governments individually and in the context of statements issued by the G8 and the European Union.[8] Non-governmental organizations are increasingly suggesting that there is a need for a greater emphasis on law and accountability mechanisms. Trade unions, for their part, have been sceptical of the idea of CSR initiatives and the attendant industry that has grown up around CSR. According to Dwight Justice: 'Governments were using CSR as a substitute for their own failure to address the social consequences of globalization. Trade unionists often found themselves the only ones in the room to notice that business was using CSR not to

---

[5] The demand for corporate social responsibility frameworks with 'teeth' is a recurring metaphor in reports which evaluate existing arrangements, see e.g. I. Smillie, *Motherhood, Apple Pie and False Teeth* (Ottawa: Partnership Africa Canada, Occasional Paper No. 10, The Diamonds and Human Security Project, 2003); Christian Aid, *Behind the mask: The real face of corporate social responsibility* (2004) at 3 and 56 (quoted in n 4 above). See also M. Sornarajah, *The International Law on Foreign Investment* (Cambridge: Cambridge University Press, 2nd edn, 2004) at 178, who concludes that the law is set on moving from the 'smokescreen' of soft law prescriptions to law 'with sufficient teeth'.

[6] See the RSA World Leaders Lecture by Mary Robinson 'Beyond Good Intentions: Corporate Citizenship for a New Century', London, 7 May 2002. See also the approach of the Ethical Trading Initiative, which is premised on the idea that 'internationally-agreed standards (complementary to national and international regulations and frameworks) contribute to the well-being (the lives and rights of families)'. M. Blowfield, 'ETI: a multi-stakeholder approach', in R. Jenkins, R. Pearson, and G. Seyfang (eds) *Corporate Responsibility & Labour Rights: Codes of Conduct in the Global Economy* (London: Earthscan, 2002) 184–195 at 186.

[7] Amnesty International and The Prince of Wales Business Leaders Forum, *Human rights: is it any of your business?* (2000); Amnesty International, *Business and Human Rights in a time of change* (2000); International Alert, Council on Economic Priorities, and The Prince of Wales Business Leaders Forum, *The Business of Peace: The private sector as a partner in conflict prevention and resolution* (2000); OHCHR, *Business and Human Rights: A Progress Report* (Geneva: OHCHR, 2000) also available at http://www.unhchr.ch/business.htm; Financial Times Management, *Visions of Ethical Business* (London: Financial Times Professional, 1998).

[8] See the Evian Summit, June 2003, Fostering Growth and Promoting a Responsible Market Economy—A G8 Declaration, at para 2. EU Council Res. of 6 February 2003 on corporate social responsibility, EU Doc. 2003/C 39/02. For an examination of the way in which the meaning of corporate social responsibility has been shaped and contested by corporations, see R. Shamir, 'Between Self-Regulation and the Alien Tort Claims Act: On the Contested Concept of Corporate Social Responsibility' 38 *Law & Society Review* (2004) 635–663.

go beyond, but to go around regulation and trade unions.'[9] The big fear in the union movement is that CSR initiatives become a substitute for respecting legal obligations and collective bargaining with trade unions. Moreover the arrival of new players in the field of labour relations was treated with suspicion: 'CSR moved from a concept to become an industry as consultants and enterprises emerged, offering CSR services to business. Among these services were social auditing and reporting as well as "risk assessment" services. The trade union concern with this industry is that it is assisting business in redefining the expectations of society instead of responding to them.'[10]

Both sides of this debate present an overarching case for taking human rights seriously. The advantages to companies adopting a human rights policy are usually listed as: protection of reputation with regard to consumers; reduction of risk of disruption through strikes, protests, and boycotts; enhancement of attractiveness for future and current employees; and lastly, in some cases, because it is the 'right thing to do'. On the one hand, these ideas are still relatively new (and seen by some as a passing fashion). Many corporate decision-makers see no need to adjust their policies when this might radically affect short-term profits; it is sometimes argued that human rights programmes would be a breach of the duty to maximize profit. On the other hand, it is possible to highlight two recent developments that are forcing particular attention to the human rights implications of corporate activity: first, the decision by some governments to link export credit guarantees for companies to potential human rights impacts of the relevant project;[11] and second, the complex ways in which human rights compliance is increasingly factored into investment decisions regarding shares and bonds, in particular by funds that advertise an ethical investment dimension.[12] In the United Kingdom, for example, pension funds must by law disclose the extent to which any social, environmental, or ethical considerations are taken in to account in the selection

---

[9] D. W. Justice, 'The international trade union movement and the new codes of conduct', in Jenkins, Pearson, and Seyfang (2002) (n 6 above) 90–100, at 99.

[10] Ibid, at 99. For a critique of the audits carries out by Price Waterhouse Coopers, see D. O'Rourke, 'Monitoring the monitors: a critique of corporate third-party labour monitoring' in Jenkins, Pearson, and Seyfang (2002) (n 6 above) 196–208.

[11] See, e.g. the arrangements in the Netherlands and in the UK. The UK Export Credit Guarantees Department (ECGD), *Mission and Status Review* 1999–2000 (London, HMSO, 2000) Cm 4790, stated at para. 1.26: 'However, ECGD's assessment processes should be further developed, to include screening for human rights, and ECGD should ensure it has the necessary skills and capacity in-house to handle sensitive cases, as well as access to independent external expertise.' The Business Principles which were later adopted, state with regard to objectives: 'ECGD will, when considering support, look not only at the payment risks but also at the underlying quality of the project, including its environmental, social and human rights impacts.' Available at http://www.ecgd.gov.uk/ecgdbusprinciples.pdf. See also in the US, 12 USC §635(b)(1)(B), discussed by Ralph Steinhardt, 'Corporate Responsibility and the International Law of Human Rights: The New *Lex Mercatoria*' in P. Alston (ed) *Non-State Actors and Human Rights* (Oxford: Oxford University of Press, 2005) 177–226.

[12] R. Sullivan, R. Lake, and J. Kirsty Thomas, 'Why Should Investors Care *about* Human Rights', 2(1) *New Academy Review* (2003) 37–40.

and retention of investments.[13] Neither development adds to the drive for accountability through law, but it is suggested that together they provide the context for the increasing sensitization of corporations to human rights criticism and the potential impact of their future projects. Of course, the increasing emphasis on human rights with regard to ethical investment may explain in part the resistance in the corporate sector to new initiatives which would increase accountability under law. Lawsuits, settlements, and verdicts in human rights trials would do nothing to enhance ethical reputation.

A recent survey of Europe's largest 100 companies concluded that almost 90 per cent now include 'some form of ethical statement within their annual reports'; the survey nevertheless concluded that: 'While the quality of communication on environmental issues is generally convincing, when it comes to human rights, it is less effective. This could be for a number of reasons: a failure to understand the relevance of human rights, a fear of investigating this relevance, a suspicion about the introduction of human rights into the workplace or because of the complexity of reporting on these issues.'[14] Human rights policies for companies remain in their infancy, and governmental scrutiny of such policies remains embryonic, but there are developments regarding the international framework. This Chapter is confined to an explanation of some of the existing international regimes which cover the human rights obligations of corporations, the possibilities for monitoring these obligations, and even accusations that corporations have committed, or have been complicit in, international crimes.

The reaction of many lawyers to the vexing question of corporate criminal accountability is that it is hard to condemn a company when it is, first, so difficult to see into its thoughts, and second, so difficult to restrain its bulk. In a famous law review article, John Coffee quoted an eighteenth-century Lord Chancellor of England who asked: 'Did you ever expect a corporation to have a conscience, when it has no soul to be damned and no body to be kicked?'[15] Coffee then went on to outline detailed steps that could be taken in the United States to use existing possibilities within the legal system to deter corporate misbehaviour. I will take a similar approach. Instead of focusing on the supposed absence of subjectivity for corporations in international law,[16] or highlighting the lack of obvious

---

[13] See the Occupational Pension Schemes (Investment, and Assignment, Forfeiture, Bankruptcy etc.) Amendment Regulations 1999, SI 1999/1849, s. 2(4)(b), which effectively demands that trustees must state their policy in their statement of investment principles to cover '(a) the extent (if at all) to which social, environmental or ethical considerations are taken into account in the selection, retention and realisation of investments; and (b) their policy (if any) in relation to the exercise of the rights (including voting rights) attaching to investments.'

[14] M. Grenier, 'Communicating Human Rights: a summary of recent trends in European annual reports' 2(1) *New Academy Review* (2003) 76–89, at 88. See also the earlier report by Hoop Associates, *All mouth and no trousers* 2002, available at http://www.allmouthnotrousers.com.

[15] '"No Soul to Damn: No Body to Kick": an unscandalized inquiry into the problem of corporate punishment' 79 *Mich LR* (1981) 386–459.

[16] The difference between subjects of international law and bodies capable of bearing international duties is considered in Ch 2 above. For a view which restricts rights and duties under

international remedies for human rights abuses committed by corporations, I shall explore the existing international framework and highlight the existing normative obligations and procedural possibilities with regard to international human rights norms.[17]

6.2   TRANSNATIONALS, MULTINATIONALS, AND NATIONAL CORPORATIONS

Much of the commentary on the topic of corporations and human rights confusingly concentrates on the concept of the *transnational* corporation. This is due in part to the history of the topic at the United Nations in the 1980s and the concern with protection for and against foreign corporations operating in the developing world.[18] The term 'transnational corporation' emphasizes the fact that there is usually a single legal corporation operating in more than one country, with a headquarters and a legal status incorporated in the national law of the home state. According to Rigaux: 'The concept of *transnationality* comes into its own when it is applied to an autonomous corporate system and, in this sense, the transnational corporation is *one* single corporation even if it is composed of corporations with separate identities under the corporation law of the States in which they operate.'[19]

international law to subjects of international law, see I. Seidl-Hohenveldern, *Corporations in and under International Law* (Cambridge: Grotius, 1987) at 70–74. Cf M. Noortmann, 'Non-State Actors in International Law' in B. Arts, M. Noortmann, and B. Reinalda (eds) *Non-State Actors in International Relations* (Aldershot: Ashgate, 2001) 59–76, at 71: 'Corporate rights and duties have been increasingly internationalised. TNCs can make legal claims and be held responsible on the basis of international legal instruments, and as such they may be qualified as new subjects.'

[17] A discussion of claims against corporations for negligence under national law, or for violations of health and safety rules is outside the scope of this book. In many cases, the claims may not be presented as human rights claims but rather as a violation of a duty of care in tort. Important developments regarding the possibility to bring such cases in the UK led to a £21m settlement by Cape plc following a ruling by the House of Lords concerning harm done to workers, including children, from asbestos mining in South Africa (*Lubbe et al v Cape* [2000] 1 WLR 1545 (HL)); see R. Meeran 'Cape pays the price as justice prevails' *The Times (Law Supplement)*, 15 January 2002, at 5. See also C. Scott, 'Multinational Enterprises and Emergent Jurisprudence on Violations of Economic, Social and Cultural Rights' in A. Eide, C. Krause, and A. Rosas (eds) *Economic, Social and Cultural Rights: A Textbook* (Dordrecht: Nijhoff, 2nd edn, 2001) 563–595, who highlights the fact that interests that are protected from negligent harm can be formulated in the same way as interests protected by economic social and cultural rights, and so basic tort categories can be seen as remedies for human rights violations without the need to develop specific 'human rights' causes of action (at 587–595).

[18] See P. T. Muchlinski, *Multinational Enterprises and the Law* (Oxford: Blackwell, 1999) at 12. The last proposed version of the UN Code of conduct on Transnational Corporations is UN Doc. E/1990/94 of 12 June 1990; negotiations were suspended in July 1992 (Muchlinski 1999: 594). The various definitions and the UN's use of the expression transnational corporation (TNC) is discussed at 593. For an introduction to the international debate and attempts of the UN Centre on Transnational Corporations to introduce recommendations concerning TNCs in the context of the UN Conference on Environment and Development, see J. Richter, *Holding Corporations Accountable: Corporate Conduct, International Codes, and Citizen Action* (London: Zed Books, 2001) at 8.

[19] F. Rigaux, 'Transnational Corporations' in M. Bedjaoui (ed) *International Law: Achievements and Prospects* (Dordrecht: Martinus Nijhoff, 1991) 121–132, at 124.

Legal systems do actually determine the 'nationality' of companies for various purposes. These rules are evolving as companies take on more and more elements of transnationality: the headquarters may be in one state, the legal incorporation in another state, the shareholders mostly from a third state, and the operations in a fourth state. If the workers are from a fifth state and those affected by the operations from yet another set of states, it becomes clear that highlighting transnationality is, in a way, essential to capture the phenomenon under discussion.

The international texts use the terms 'transnational corporation', 'multinational enterprise', and 'business enterprise' in various contexts,[20] and this Chapter will use all of these terms as I discuss the various sets of standards. As legal systems become more comfortable with 'piercing the corporate veil', to reveal the true nature of the control by the parent over its offspring,[21] it may be that *multinationality* also usefully expresses the characteristics of these non-state actors for the purposes of legal accountability. The nationality of incorporation may no longer be the sole determinant for deciding issues of jurisdiction. In this sense, the corporation may be both operating transnationally and the bearer of multinationality.[22]

---

[20] The Draft United Nations Code of Conduct on Transnational Corporations started by stating that 'This Code is universally applicable to enterprises, irrespective of their country of origin and their ownership, including private, public or mixed, comprising entities in two or more countries, regardless of the legal form and fields of activity of these entities, which operate under a system of decision-making, permitting coherent policies and a common strategy through one or more decision-making centres, in which the entities are so linked, by ownership or otherwise, that one or more of them may be able to exercise a significant influence over the activities of others, and, in particular, to share knowledge, resources and responsibilities with the others.' UN Doc. E/1990/94, 12 June 1990. The attached letter from the Chair of the special session of the Commission on Transnational Corporations to the president of ECOSOC stated: 'Although it was not possible to agree on a final draft code of conduct, it is important to note that the vast majority of its provisions have already been accepted.' For a discussion of the differences between the Western, Socialist, and third world blocs of states over the definition, see C. Thuan, 'Sociétés transnationales et droits de l'homme' in C. Thuan (ed) *Multinationales et droits de l'homme* (Paris: PUF, 1984) 43–96, at 90. For a further set of definitions of multinational enterprises, control, parent company, subsidiary, and branch, see the resolution of the Institute of International Law on 'Obligations of Multinational Enterprises and their Member Companies' 1 September 1995, 66 *Annuaire de l'Institut de Droit International*, Part II, at 463. The OECD Guidelines for Multinational Enterprises, the ILO Tripartite Declaration of Principles concerning Multinational Enterprises and Social Policy, and the UN Sub-Commission's text are all discussed below.

[21] For developments on judicial unveiling and dismissals of claims of *forum non-conveniens* made by companies in the UK (in the context of complaints against transnationals accused of negligence concerning the health of workers in hazardous conditions), see R. Meeran, 'The Unveiling of Transnational Corporations' in M. K. Addo (ed) *Human Rights Standards and the Responsibility of Transnational Corporations* (The Hague: Kluwer, 1999) 161–170; H. Ward, *Governing Multinationals: the Role of Foreign Direct Liability* (London: Royal Institute of International Affairs, Briefing Paper New Series No. 18, 2001); P. Muchlinski, 'Corporations in International Litigation: Problems of Jurisdiction and the United Kingdom Asbestos Cases' 50 *ICLQ* (2001b) 1–25.

[22] Note Art. 25 of the Convention on the Settlement of Investment Disputes Between States and Nationals of Other States (1965). I have briefly discussed the application of this nationality rule for corporations in A. Clapham, 'The Question of Jurisdiction under International Criminal Law Over Legal Persons: Lessons from the Rome Conference on an International Criminal Court' in M. Kamminga and S. Zia-Zarifa (eds) *Liability of Multinational Corporations under International Law* (The Hague: Kluwer, 2000) 139–195, at 187–188.

So the adjective 'transnational' or 'multinational' can be employed to emphasize different characteristics of certain corporations. It does not really change the nature of the corporation as a legal entity. One might ask why purely national corporations seem to be excluded from the titles of the regimes seeking to ensure compliance with international standards by multinational corporations (MNCs), transnational corporations (TNCs), and multinational enterprises (MNEs). It is suggested here that, while larger companies may have greater responsibilities with regard to human rights obligations,[23] there is no reason to exclude purely national companies from the realm of such obligations. Although some texts, such as the OECD Guidelines, are specifically addressed to 'multinational' enterprises, the Guidelines stress that the same expectations are relevant to both multinational and domestic enterprises.[24]

6.3   THE OECD GUIDELINES FOR MULTINATIONAL ENTERPRISES

James Salzman introduces his examination of the OECD Guidelines for Multinational Enterprises by highlighting the revelations in the early 1970s of 'wide-scale unethical and illegal activities by multinational companies'.[25] He mentions two of the best known incidents: the involvement of ITT and other US companies in the 1973 Chilean coup and the bribes paid by Lockheed to Japanese officials to obtain military contracts. The Ministerial Declaration adopted by the OECD in 1976 was actually focused on the promotion of international investment. The Guidelines for Multinational Enterprises were simply an add-on to the inter-governmental Declaration on International Investment and Multinational Enterprises. This context helps to explain some of the scepticism aroused by the Guidelines. The OECD was seen by some as simply reacting to the possible threat of normative activity with regard to multinationals by the UN General Assembly. This OECD non-binding initiative could be seen as a way of stalling a potentially more obligatory framework at the UN level. At the time, the Guidelines were considered

---

[23] See International Council on Human Rights Policy (2002: 141) for a suggested framework for judging the scope of a company's responsibilities which takes into account the connections to the victims and the links to government: 'a company has the highest degree of responsibility if both connections are strong: if it has proximity to the victims as well as a close political and economic relationship with the authority violating their rights'.

[24] 'The Guidelines are not aimed at introducing differences of treatment between multinational and domestic enterprises; they reflect good practice for all. Accordingly, multinational and domestic enterprises are subject to the same expectations in respect of their conduct wherever the Guidelines are relevant to both.' OECD, *The OECD Guidelines for Multinational Enterprises: Text, Guidelines, Commentary*, DAFFE/IME/WPG(2000)15 Final, Concepts and Principles I.4.

[25] J. Salzman, 'Labour Rights, Globalization and Institutions: The Role and Influence of the Organization for Economic Cooperation and Development' 21 *Mich JIL* (2000) 769–848, at 788.

completely voluntary, and today the revised Guidelines still state in their first operative paragraph:

> The Guidelines are recommendations jointly addressed by governments to multinational enterprises. They provide principles and standards of good practice consistent with applicable laws. Observance of the Guidelines by enterprises is voluntary and not legally enforceable.[26]

Furthermore, the follow-up procedures for hearing complaints and 'clarifying' the guidelines were met with disappointment from trade unions, who invested some effort in bringing complaints, only to see little change at the national level, even in those cases where the dispute moved from the level of the National Contact Point (NCP) to the Committee on International Investment and Multinational Enterprises (CIME) (these procedures are explained below).[27] To be clear, there is still no procedure for legally enforcing any sort of finding against a multinational enterprise; but, the complaint mechanisms are beginning to attract more attention.

The OECD Guidelines have been revised several times. The 2000 annual Ministerial meeting had as its theme 'Shaping Globalization'. According to the OECD Secretary-General: 'The integration of national economies into one global economy is accelerating and intensifying, driven by new technologies and new opportunities. These new opportunities are not only to reap profit, but also to stimulate development and improved social conditions around the world.'[28] As with international instruments on corruption,[29] the Guidelines seem, in part, to respond to a concern from the corporate sector that a corporation should not be disadvantaged when it plays by the new rules. The OECD Secretary-General explicitly recognizes this dimension of the Guidelines: 'They provide a government-backed standard of good corporate conduct that will help level the playing field between competitors in the international market place.'[30]

> Governments avoided any exclusive definition of multinational enterprises: A precise definition of multinational enterprises is not required for the purposes of the Guidelines. These usually comprise companies or other entities established in more than one country and so linked that they may co-ordinate their operations in various ways. While one or more of these entities may be able to exercise a significant influence over the activities of others, their degree of autonomy within the enterprise may vary widely from one multinational enterprise to another. Ownership may be private, state

---

[26] *The OECD Guidelines for Multinational Enterprises: Text, Guidelines, Commentary,* DAFFE/IME/WPG(2000)15 Final (OECD: Paris, 2001), Concepts and Principles I.1.

[27] Salzman (2000: 790).

[28] *OECD Guidelines for Multinational Enterprises: Review 2000,* DAFFE/IME/WPG(2000)9, at 3.

[29] *The Economist* special report on bribery reports that the US Department of Justice estimated allegations of bribery by foreign firms of $200bn in 1994–2001. The claim has been consistently made by American companies that they are disadvantaged in the global market-place due to the domestic legislation outlawing bribery covering American citizens and companies abroad. 'The short arm of the law' *The Economist,* 2 March 2002, 67–70, at 67.

[30] *OECD Guidelines for Multinational Enterprises: Review 2000,* DAFFE/IME/WPG(2000)9, at 3.

or mixed. The Guidelines are addressed to all the entities within the multinational enterprise (parent companies and/or local entities). According to the actual distribution of responsibilities among them, the different entities are expected to co-operate and to assist one another to facilitate observance of the Guidelines.[31]

The reach of the Guidelines could even extend beyond the entities within the multinational enterprise.[32] In the Chapter on General Policies, enterprises are to 'take fully into account established policies in the countries in which they operate, and consider the views of other stakeholders. In this regard enterprises should: Encourage, where practicable, business partners, including suppliers and sub-contractors, to apply principles of corporate conduct compatible with the Guidelines.'[33] The reach of the Guidelines, then, extends right down the chain to the smallest sub-contractors, with the emphasis on the multinational to encourage others with which it is in contact to respect the Guidelines.

The Guidelines have been adopted by the thirty OECD states,[34] and accepted by eight non-member states: Argentina, Brazil, Chile, Estonia, Israel, Latvia, Lithuania, and Slovenia. The follow-up procedures apply to all participating states. The Guidelines are monitored through flexible complaints mechanisms, which are not necessarily to be compared to litigation or other traditional forms of legal complaint. The Guidelines are addressed to multinational enterprises operating in, or from, the thirty-eight adhering states and are to apply to business operations not only in the OECD states (as had been previously presumed) but also world-wide.

> I. 2.   Since the operations of multinational enterprises extend throughout the world, international co-operation in this field should extend to all countries. Governments adhering to the Guidelines encourage the enterprises operating on their territories to observe the Guidelines wherever they operate, while taking into account the particular circumstances of each host country.

This globalization of the Guidelines represents an important development considering the reach of multinationals from OECD countries. For some time, the Guidelines were discounted as they were seen as limited to the OECD area and thus incapable of tackling breaches by companies outside the OECD area.[35] With the explicit extension of coverage of activity to non-OECD countries, one might expect increased use of the Guidelines and the complaints mechanism.

A complaint filed shortly after the adoption of the new Guidelines illustrates the potential of the globalized scope of the Guildelines. In a letter dated 18 February 2002, the International Textile, Garment and Leather Workers'

---

[31] OECD (2001) Concepts and Principles I.3.   [32] Salzman (2000: 794).

[33] OECD (2001) General Policies II.10.

[34] Australia, Austria, Belgium, Canada, Czech Republic, Denmark, Finland, France, Germany, Greece, Hungary, Iceland, Ireland, Italy, Japan, Korea, Luxembourg, Mexico, the Netherlands, New Zealand, Norway, Poland, Portugal, Slovak Republic, Spain, Sweden, Switzerland, Turkey, the UK, and the US.   [35] Salzman (2000: 793).

Federation complained to the Vice-Minister of Commerce, Industry and Energy of South Korea (the National Contact Point under the Guidelines) concerning 'serious breaches' of the Guidelines (Chapter IV on employment and industrial relations) by Korean companies in Guatemala.[36] The plants produce garments for export to the United States, the main customer being a US company. The letter summarizes the complaints:

The companies' actions since July 2001 have included:

promoting 'solidarista' associations, under management control, as an alternative to a trade union;

offering workers bribes to resign from the union;

instilling fear in non-union workers in order to incite them to violence, to the point where the trade unionists lives may be at risk if they go to work;

failing to take disciplinary measures against workers guilty of violence;

securing letters of resignation from union supporters under duress;

allegedly engaging in criminal activity;

allegedly threatening workers and their families in their homes and neighbourhoods;

encouraging non-union workers to paint anti-union banners, during working hours and with materials supplied by the company;

unilaterally changing the working conditions of union supporters;

threatening union leaders with blacklisting;

interfering in internal union affairs by demanding a list of union members in order to prove that the union no longer meets the minimum number of members.

It is difficult to imagine a more globalized human rights complaint. A European-based Federation complains to the Korean Government about the treatment of Guatemalan workers by a Korean company operating in Guatemala.

The Guidelines set standards to be respected, in addition to relevant national law, for OECD multinationals operating at home and abroad. The Commentary states: 'The *Guidelines* are not a substitute for nor should they be considered to override local law and regulation. They represent supplementary principles and standards of behaviour of a non-legal character, particularly concerning the international operations of these enterprises.'[37] The logic remains one of ensuring a level playing field for OECD companies when operating in countries where there will be opportunities to avoid these basic guarantees. Governments have attempted to allay fears that they could be either legislating in an extraterritorial way, or seeking to put developing countries at a disadvantage. The Guidelines state that: 'Governments adhering to the Guidelines should not use them for protectionist purposes nor use them in a way that calls into question the comparative advantage of any country where multinational enterprises invest.'[38]

The revised Guidelines have added a human rights obligation in the context of general policies. They state that enterprises should: 'Respect the human rights of

---

[36] Posted on the Federation's website, 28 February 2002, http://www.itglwf.org.
[37] OECD (2001: 12).   [38] OECD (2001) Concepts and Principles I.6.

those affected by their activities consistent with the host government's obligations and commitments.'[39] One might see this guideline as exporting values, but this would be wrong. The commentary explains that enterprises are to act consistently with the host states' existing international human rights obligations. The relevant passage reads:

> ...while promoting and upholding human rights is primarily the responsibility of governments, where corporate conduct and human rights intersect enterprises do play a role, and thus MNEs are encouraged to respect human rights, not only in their dealings with employees, but also with respect to others affected by their activities, in a manner that is consistent with host governments' international obligations and commitments. The Universal Declaration of Human Rights and other human rights obligations of the government concerned are of particular relevance in this regard.[40]

General Policy II.5. states that enterprises should: 'Refrain from seeking or accepting exemptions not contemplated in the statutory or regulatory framework related to environmental, health, safety, labour, taxation, financial incentives, or other issues.' This provision is directly aimed at multinationals in the contemporary context. It is a reaction to attempts by some governments to offer 'union-free zones' or the fiction of extraterritoriality for the purposes of health and safety regulations. The Commentary retains the idea that there may be instances where exemptions from laws may be legitimate. But I would suggest here that exemptions from health, safety, or labour laws should be treated with suspicion. Furthermore, human rights protection is clearly threatened where there is no recourse to remedies under national law; the Guidelines are supposed to discourage multinationals from accepting such inducements.

The problem is that even if MNEs desist from accepting such exemptions, *de facto* exemptions may result from the authorities turning a blind eye. Export Processing Zones (EPZs), and *maquilas* (places where clothes are assembled) with tax incentives, have proven particularly controversial and a number of human rights reports have noted abuses of human rights in these and similar zones.[41] Naomi Klein's book, *No Logo*, dedicates several pages to descriptions of her visits to EPZs and *maquilas*. Her testimony points to harsh conditions, constituting degrading treatment, that represent systematic violations of the law. Such situations are usually driven by a policy which attempts to build up the idea of 'exemptions' designed to attract foreign investment in the short term. Klein portrays her experience as follows:

> The rationale goes something like this: *of course* companies must pay taxes and strictly abide by national laws, but just in this one case, on this one specific piece of land, for just

---

[39] OECD (2001) General Policies II.2.   [40] Ibid.

[41] Human Rights Watch, *From the Household to the Factory: Sex Discrimination in the Guatemalan Labor Force* (2002a) esp. Ch IV on the *maquilas* pointing out that: 'The vast majority of maquilas in Guatemala are freestanding factories, not located inside any of the nation's free trade zones.' Amnesty International (2002) refers to incidents involving a so-called 'corporate mafia state' in Guatemala. See generally the ILO report, *Labour and social issues relating to export processing zones* (1998). For further information see http://www.maquilasolidarity.org/.

a little while, an exception will be made—for the cause of future prosperity. The EPZs, therefore, exist within kind of a legal and economic set of brackets, apart from the rest of their countries—the Cavite zone, for example, is under the sole jurisdiction of the Philippines' federal Department of Trade and Industry; the local police and municipal government have no right even to cross the threshold. The layers of blockades serve a dual purpose: to keep the hordes away from the costly goods being manufactured inside the zone, but also, and perhaps more important, to shield the country from what is going on inside the zone . . . Never mind that the boundaries of these only-temporary, not-really-happening, denationalized spaces keep expanding to engulf more and more of their actual nations. Twenty-seven million people worldwide are now living and working in brackets, and the brackets, instead of being slowly removed, just keep getting wider.[42]

If one studies the reports of the human rights abuses in such zones, the problems seem to stem, not so much from the exceptions under national law, but rather from the sense of impunity among the local managers and bosses, as well as from governmental determination not to do anything which the government considers might frighten foreign investors.

Klein explains how the lack of protection in the Cavite Export Processing Zone in the Philippines stems from political decisions rather than legal exemptions:

The Philippine government . . . says that the zones are subject to the same labor standards as the rest of Philippine society: workers must be paid the minimum wage, receive social security benefits, have some measure of job security, be dismissed only with just cause and be paid extra for overtime, and they have the right to form independent trade unions. But in reality, the government views working conditions in the export factories as a matter of foreign trade policy, not a labor-rights issue. And since the government attracted foreign investors with promises of a cheap and docile workforce, it intends to deliver. For this reason, labor department officials turn a blind eye to violations in the zone or even facilitate them.[43]

Foreign investors may be increasingly exposed in such situations and persuaded into encouraging respect for fundamental rights rather than seeking to profit from such abuses. In the complaint regarding garment workers in Guatemala (referred to earlier) it is made clear that the US company, Liz Claibourne Inc, which buys 60 per cent of the output from the plants, had actually written stating that it would continue to use the plants only if the management respected the right to join a union. There are plenty of reasons to be sceptical about the prospects of companies refusing to accept exemptions from the law on ethical grounds, but some consumer focus is shifting to those companies that profit from human rights abuses, either in their own factories, or in the factories of their subsidiaries or suppliers. Where one is dealing with recognizable consumer brands it is the multinational enterprises themselves rather than governments that are most sensitive to the type of reporting and complaints highlighted here. Even though

---

[42] N. Klein, *No Logo* (London: Flamingo, 2001) at 207–208.   [43] Ibid, at 210–211.

the governments that have established these zones are mostly outside the OECD area, as explained above, the OECD companies are vulnerable to complaints wherever they operate.

In general terms, the OECD Guidelines cover, in addition to a broad category of human rights, the fields of: employment; industrial relations; protection of the environment; and the question of bribery. The Guidelines include specific obligations on enterprises: to respect the right of their employees to be represented by trade unions; to engage in constructive negotiations with worker representatives with a view to reaching agreement on employment conditions; to contribute to the effective abolition of child labour; to contribute to the elimination of all forms of forced or compulsory labour;[44] and not to discriminate against their employees.[45] Most legal commentators pass over the Guidelines with the attitude that lawyers can ignore them due to their status as non-legally binding. But, as mentioned above, a corporation's record with regard to the Guidelines may be pertinent for investment decisions, either in the form of governments' export credit guarantees, or from ethical schemes for private investors. Moreover, Peter Muchlinski has suggested that the Guidelines are likely to play a role with regard to the way that national courts treat *forum non conveniens* and related issues.

> Although the OECD Guidelines are non-binding, they do represent a consensus on what constitutes good corporate behaviour in an increasingly global economy. Furthermore, they are clear that home countries of MNEs have a moral duty to ensure that the standards contained in the Guidelines are maintained world-wide. Given that the United Kingdom adhered to the OECD Guidelines as a member of that organisation, in future the English courts may have to pay heed to their contents when determining issues of public interest in litigation involving MNEs.[46]

6.3.1 The OECD Guidelines' Implementation Procedures

The OECD complaints procedure does not represent a judicial or even quasi-judicial finding but rather a series of procedures for requesting consultations, good offices, conciliation, or mediation as well as 'clarifications' of the Guidelines.

---

[44] The formulation relating to the contribution to the abolition of child labour, rather than an injunction not to use child labour, is, according to S. Tully, due to suggestions by the employers' advisory body (BIAC) that many corporations lacked direct business involvement with child labour and that the Guidelines should avoid duplication of ILO efforts. He suggests that this formulation also finds a later reflection in the General Policy that corporate respect for human rights is to be consistent with a host state's commitments. This makes particular sense with regard to child labour where the international obligation can vary according to the exact form of the adherence to the relevant ILO Conventions such as the ILO Convention Concerning Minimum Age for Admission to Employment 138 (1973), which states that the minimum age should not be less than the age for completing compulsory schooling and in no event less than age 15—for countries whose economic and educational facilities are insufficiently developed, the age can be set initially at 14. S. Tully, 'The 2000 Review of the OECD Guidelines for Multinational Enterprises' 50 *ICLQ* (2001) 394–404, at 398–399.   [45] OECD (2001) Employment and Industrial Relations IV.1.
[46] Muchlinski (2001b: 24).

The following is only a thumbnail sketch of the procedures, and in any event, it is too early to review conclusively the efficacy of the new revised procedures.[47]

The Council decision of June 2000 replaces the previous arrangements and installs new Implementation Procedures. National Contact Points (NCPs) are to be set up by the adhering countries for handling inquiries as well as promotional activities. They are also supposed to be for 'discussions with the parties concerned on all matters covered by the guidelines so that they can contribute to the solution of problems which may arise in this connection'.[48] These facilities are addressed not only to governments, but also to the business community, employee organizations, and 'other interested parties'. The Procedural Guidance adopted by the Council clearly states that the term 'other interested parties' 'includes non-governmental organizations'.[49] Groups such as Oxfam have been focusing on the procedure and interest has broadened to other non-governmental organizations (NGOs) which have set up a monitoring body entitled OECD Watch, whose task is to facilitate NGO activities around the OECD Guidelines.

One can find examples of NCP's intervening with multinational enterprises in ways which have led to concrete human rights protection. In one case reported by Patricia Feeney, a member of the OECD Watch steering committee, following the intervention of the OECD NCP, the 'The threat of forcible eviction of squatters on mine land by the army was withdrawn and negotiations, which had broken down between the company and local community leaders, re-started. The company has begun to upgrade its staff dealing with social issues.'[50] Nevertheless, NGO assessment of the system overall is rather critical.[51] There have been attempts by NCPs to hinder NGO access by creating procedural hurdles, such as insisting that NGOs have a power of attorney before they can raise a case, or requiring that cases should be filed by NGOs based in the country where the problem occurred.[52] The OECD's own website promises: 'Any person or organization may approach a National Contact Point to enquire about a matter related to the guidelines.'[53] NGOs have also expressed frustration regarding issues of transparency. Confidentiality is understandably maintained during the performance of good offices by the NCP, and the NCP may also arrange conciliation or mediation with the agreement of the parties. However, the Procedural Guidance

---

[47] For a review of the early practice see R. Blanpain, *The OECD Guidelines for Multinationals and Labour Relations 1967–1979: experience and review* (Deventer: Kluwer, 1979).

[48] Decision of the OECD Council on the OECD Guidelines for Multinational Enterprises, June 2000, para. I.1.   [49] Procedural Guidance, para. I.A.

[50] P. Feeney, 'The Relevance of the OECD Guidelines for Multinational Enterprises to the Mining Sector and the Promotion of Sustainable Development' 10 *The Centre for Energy, Petroleum and Mineral Law and Policy Journal* (2002) 13, available at http://www.dundee.ac.uk/cepmlp/journal/html/vol10/article10-6.html.

[51] See Rights and Accountability in Development (RAID), 'Review of the UK National Contact Point for the OECD Guidelines 2004' available from RAID, Oxford.

[52] Feeney (2002) at 12.

[53] OECD, *OECD Guidelines for Multinational Enterprises: Frequently asked questions* (2000b) available at http://www.oecd.org/daf/investment/guidelines/faq.htm.

states that, having consulted the parties, the NCP *will* 'make publicly available the results of these procedures unless preserving confidentiality would be in the best interests of effective implementation of Guidelines.'[54] OECD Watch conclude in their twelve-month review up to June 2003: 'There is no consistent behaviour among the NCPs about informing parties of progress in handling cases; providing information to third parties; making public the fact that a case has been filed; issuing statements while a matter is still under consideration; making public the reasons for not proceeding with consideration of a case; and whether to name the parties in a specific instance.... a minority of NCPs seem determined to block the procedures entirely and most NCPs are reluctant to exchange information on specific issues.'[55] One can glean from the review carried out by OECD Watch of eleven NGO cases, raised with NCPs over twelve months, that human rights complaints under the Guidelines resulted in one case in a company withdrawing its threat of eviction, and in other cases, the NCP has brought the parties together for talks which might lead to agreements.

From the trade union perspective, John Evans, the General Secretary of the Trade Union Advisory Council to the OECD, has highlighted the utility of the procedures and has referred to a successful outcome following a complaint raised against Siemens before the Czech NCP, concerning the company's prevention of workers establishing a trade union.[56] Despite the failure of many governments to set up functioning NCPs which operate within reasonable delays, he points to other 'satisfactory outcomes' and suggests greater use of the OECD Guidelines in the context of: the receipt of public subsidies; access to export credit guarantees; the drafting of bilateral investment treaties; collective bargaining; and workers' pension and savings funds.

The second procedural possibility is recourse to the Committee on International Investment and Multinational Enterprises (CIME, now known as the 'Investment Committee'). This governmental Committee organizes exchanges of views on matters relating to the Guidelines and issues 'clarifications'. Although 'an individual enterprise will be given the opportunity to express its views either orally or in writing on issues concerning the Guidelines involving its interests', CIME 'shall not reach conclusions on the conduct of individual enterprises'.[57] NCPs can ask for assistance or guidance from CIME. More formally, CIME will consider a 'substantiated submission' by an adhering country, or either the trade union advisory body (TUAC), or the employers' advisory body (BIAC), on whether an NCP has correctly interpreted the Guidelines. This consideration could result in a 'clarification' being issued by CIME. Although the clarifications do not mention the name of the multinational, according to Jan Hunter from the Dutch Ministry of Economic Affairs: 'Successful requests for clarification, of which there have been

---

[54] Procedural Guidance, para. I.C. 4(b).
[55] OECD Watch No. 2 'Review of National Contact Points, June 2002–2003', at 6.
[56] J. Evans, 'OECD Guidelines—one tool for corporate social accountability' (2003), available at http://www.responsiblepractice.com/english/standards/tuac.
[57] Implementation Procedures II.4.

a dozen or so, were often seen as *de facto* condemnation of an MNE's behaviour in a particular case.'[58] Virginia Leary has highlighted the significance of the Guidelines in an early case. 'In the Badger case, a subsidiary of the U.S. Raytheon Corporation had refused to grant severance pay to employees because of its bankruptcy. The Guidelines provided that the parent corporation was responsible in such situations. . . . The case was resolved satisfactorily when Raytheon took care of the severance pay.'[59] Leary has suggested, in this context, that the traditional focus on *compliance* with binding accords is misplaced and that greater attention should be given to the *influence* and *effectiveness* of non-binding accords in this field.

Most requests for clarification have in the past concerned decisions by multinationals to close a subsidiary operation in an OECD country. (This is explained by the fact that the geographical scope of the Guidelines was assumed to be limited to OECD countries; as explained above, the revision in 2000 means that the Guidelines apply to OECD enterprises everywhere). The latest Commentary foresees that CIME may wish to call on experts to 'address and report on broader issues (e.g. child labour, human rights) or individual issues', but it understood 'that this will not become a panel to settle individual issues'.[60]

The impact of these two OECD procedures will depend on the use that is made of them by the recognized employer and union organizations, as well as by NGOs, governments, and other intergovernmental organizations such as the United Nations.[61] Critics of the arrangements point to the fact that the identities of the companies implicated have so far been kept secret and that the results are unenforceable.[62] But, as already highlighted, the new procedures presume that the NCPs will make publicly available the results of their procedures, and one can assume that some multinationals will be sensitive enough to such issues to enforce the application of the Guidelines for themselves as well as for subsidiaries under their control.[63] In the context of export credit guarantees, links are being explicitly made to the OECD Guidelines, and so one might expect to see increasing relevance for the OECD implementation procedures.[64]

---

[58] J. Hunter, 'The Multilateral Agreement on Investment and the Review of the OECD Guidelines for Multinational Enterprises' in M. Kamminga and S. Zia-Zarifi (eds) *Liability of Multinational Corporations Under International Law* (Hague: Kluwer, 2000) 197–205, at 202.

[59] V. Leary, 'Nonbinding Accords in the Field of Labor' in E. Brown Weiss (ed) *International Compliance with Nonbinding Accords* (Washington, DC: American Society of International Law, 1997a) 247–264, at 255.   [60] OECD (2001: 53).

[61] See, in particular, the reports by the Panel of Experts on the Illegal Exploitation of Natural Resources and Other Forms of Wealth of the Democratic Republic of the Congo, UN Doc. S/2002/1146, 16 October 2002; Addendum, S/2002/1146/Add.1, 20 June 2003; and S/2003/1027, 23 October 2003.   [62] ICHRP (2002: 101).

[63] Note the 'clarification' included in OECD (2001: 9): 'All entities, including parent companies, local subsidiaries, as well as intermediary levels of the organization, are expected to co-operate and assist, as necessary, in observing the Guidelines. To the extent that parent companies actually exercise control over the activities of their subsidiaries, they have a responsibility for observance of the Guidelines by those subsidiaries.'

[64] The UK Export Credit Guarantee Department website explicitly refers to the Guidelines: 'The OECD Guidelines for Multinational Enterprises (MNEs) are expectations of MNE behaviour

An unexpected trial for the OECD procedures has most recently resulted from the UN inquiry into the situation in the Eastern Part of the Democratic Republic of Congo. The 2002 report to the Security Council listed concerns with regard to eighty-five named corporations from OECD countries relating to compliance with the Guidelines, and recommended further action by the relevant governments.[65]

It is perhaps too early to come to any conclusions on the impact of the revised Guidelines and their implementation. One NGO that has followed these developments particularly closely is Rights and Accountability in Development (RAID). Its assessment is that: 'The good news is that most companies enter into the process and respond to the complaints.'[66] On the other hand, the performance of the NCPs is mixed, most of the criticism being targeted at a failure to properly deal with complaints in a transparent and participatory fashion. The OECD framework represents a potentially useful regime to hold corporations accountable for failure to respect the rights in the Universal Declaration of Human Rights and for any complicity in others' human rights violations. The prospects for success will depend in part on the attention that is given to ensuring that NCPs feel accountable beyond the business sector.[67]

6.4   THE TRIPARTITE DECLARATION OF PRINCIPLES CONCERNING MULTINATIONAL ENTERPRISES

The Tripartite Declaration of Principles concerning Multinational Enterprises and Social Policy was adopted by the Governing Body of the International Labour Office on 16 November 1977,[68] and amended in November 2000.[69] Like the

worldwide agreed by all OECD Governments. They are a framework of "principles of good conduct" for MNEs in their business activities and are designed to help them devise or revise their own codes of conduct.' Complaints against companies to the NCP are now increasingly in the public domain (due to the fact that the complainants often post them on their websites). It is likely that the fact of an unresolved complaint would most likely be taken into consideration when deciding export credit guarantees which, since 2000, are supposed to be screened for 'adverse or beneficial environmental, social or human rights aspects of relevant projects'. See ECGD Business Principles 2000.

[65] UN Doc. S/2002/1146, 16 October 2002, at paras 177–178: 'The Panel has drafted another list of business enterprises (annex III) which, in the view of the Panel, are in violation of the OECD Guidelines for Multinational Enterprises. Countries which are signatories to those Guidelines and other countries are morally obliged to ensure that their business enterprises adhere to and act on the Guidelines. The OECD Guidelines outline a procedure for bringing violations of the Guidelines to the attention of the Governments of the States where the business enterprises are registered. Home Governments have the obligation to ensure that enterprises in their jurisdiction do not abuse principles of conduct that they have adopted as a matter of law. They are complicit when they do not take remedial measures.'

[66] 'Review of the UK National Contact Point for the OECD Guidelines 2004' (mimeograph on file with the author).

[67] Some NGOs see the follow-up to the various UN Security Council reports on the Democratic Republic of the Congo as a litmus test for the effectiveness of the NCPs. Christian Aid (2004: 18), OECD Watch (2003:5).   [68] *Official Bulletin* 1978, vol. LXI, Series A, no. 1.

[69] *Official Bulletin* 2000, vol. LXXXIII, series A, No. 3.

OECD Guidelines, the Tripartite Declaration contains principles of relevance to both multinational and national enterprises.[70] In fact, the Declaration often addresses not only multinationals but also national enterprises specifically. Like the OECD Guidelines, the Declaration states that there is no need for a precise legal definition of a multinational enterprise (MNE). In order to 'facilitate the understanding of the Declaration', the Declaration gives examples of MNEs:

> Multinational enterprises include enterprises, whether they are of public, mixed or private ownership, which own or control production, distribution, services or other facilities outside the country in which they are based. The degree of autonomy of entities within multinational enterprises in relation to each other varies widely from one such enterprise to another, depending on the nature of the links between such entities and their fields of activity and having regard to the great diversity in the form of ownership, in the size, in the nature and location of the operations of the enterprises concerned. Unless otherwise specified, the term 'multinational enterprise' is used in this Declaration to designate the various entities (parent companies or local entities or both or the organization as a whole) according to the distribution of responsibilities among them, in the expectation that they will co-operate and provide assistance to one another as necessary to facilitate observance of the principles laid down in the Declaration.[71]

The Declaration sets out principles which governments, employers' and workers' organizations, and multinational enterprises 'are recommended to observe on a voluntary basis'.[72] The Declaration is therefore aimed at a wider target group than the OECD Guidelines: in addition to multinationals, the Declaration is addressed to governments and employers' and workers' organizations. Although the Declaration is expressed as a recommendation to be observed on a voluntary basis, it may also be seen as an authoritative interpretation of some of the International Labour Conventions and Recommendations on which it is based.[73] Seen together with the treaties and customary international law relevant to labour rights, the Declaration becomes a useful tool for determining the human rights obligations of non-state actors.[74] Rather than concentrating on the fact that the

---

[70] The Tripartite Declaration, para. 11 states: 'The principles laid down in this Declaration do not aim at introducing or maintaining inequalities of treatment between multinational and national enterprises. They reflect good practice for all. Multinational and national enterprises, wherever the principles of this Declaration are relevant to both, should be subject to the same expectations in respect of the their conduct in general and their social practices in particular.'   [71] Ibid, at para. 6.

[72] Ibid, at para. 7.

[73] According to Janelle Diller, Director of the Multinational Enterprises Department, ILO: 'As a document that links ILO standards with principles for good policy and practice, the MNE Declaration could be considered to be an articulation of existing principles underlying international labour law standards. In this regard, it may serve a function similar to the interpretations of UN human rights by treaty bodies.' Summary of remarks, Conference on Legal Dimensions of Corporate Responsibility, Royal Institute of International Affairs, 23 November 2001.

[74] Of course, such an argument assumes that we can transfer the customary obligations of states onto non-state actors such as corporations, and that corporations have the requisite capacity to be bound by such international duties. The theoretical framework for such a development is discussed in Ch 2, at 2.7, 2.8, and 2.9 above. See also the thoughtful and provocative analysis by Michelle Healy, 'Corporations, Legal Personality and Responsibility: A Consideration of Some Contemporary

principles are recommended on a voluntary basis, I shall examine first, how the principles are linked to binding obligations, and second, consider the methods developed by the ILO for their implementation.

6.4.1   The Tripartite Declaration's Links to Binding Obligations

The fact that the Declaration is stated to be voluntary can not detract from the normative value of those parts of it that reflect binding obligations;[75] where companies are already bound to respect certain legal obligations, their inclusion is declaratory and a reminder of those existing obligations.[76] The Declaration includes a number of general policies which are not necessarily related to questions of rights and obligations.[77] But there is a specific reference to human rights: 'All the parties concerned by this Declaration...should respect the Universal Declaration of Human Rights and the corresponding international Covenants adopted by the General Assembly of the United Nations.'[78] This injunction is a

Themes in International Law' in DEA mémoire (Geneva: Graduate Institute of International Studies, 2005). For considerations of the arguments concerning such an extension, see D. Kinley and S. Joseph, 'Multinational corporations and human rights: questions about their relationship' (2002) 27(1) *ALJ* 7–11; N. Jägers, *Corporate Human Rights Obligations: in Search of Accountability* (Antwerp: Intersentia, 2002); P. T. Muchlinski, 'Human rights and multinationals: is there a problem?' (2001a) 77 *International Affairs* 31–48; J. J. Paust 'Human Rights Responsibilities of Private Corporations' (2002) (35)3 *VJTL* 801–825; S. R. Ratner, 'Corporations and Human Rights: A Theory of Legal Responsibility' (2001) 111 *YLJ* 443–545; O. De Schutter, 'The Accountability of Multinationals for Human Rights Violations in European Law' in P. Alston (ed) *Non-State Actors and Human Rights* (Oxford: Oxford University Press, 2005) 227–314.

[75] Addendum I states: 'In keeping with the voluntary nature of the Declaration, all of its provisions, whether derived from ILO Conventions and Recommendations or other sources, are recommendatory, except of course for provisions in Conventions which are binding on the member States which have ratified them.' Addendum II deals with the adoption, in June 1998, of the Tripartite Declaration on Fundamental Principles and Rights at Work. The interpretation of the Tripartite Declaration on MNEs 'should fully take into account the objectives of the 1998 Declaration'. See also Leary (1997a: 260–261) for references to the possibility that the provisions of the Declaration may become customary international law and for the important finding by an ILO Fact-Finding and Conciliation Commission, in 1975, that freedom of association is a customary rule of international law. ILO, *The Trade Union Situation in Chile: Report of the Fact-Finding and Conciliation Commission on Freedom of Association*, at para. 466. Note also the way the OECD CIME used the Tripartite Declaration to interpret the OECD Guidelines in the *Hertz* case. In that case, Hertz in Denmark had imported workers from its branches outside the country to enable it to continue working during a strike by Danish workers. The resulting interpretation by CIME resulted in Hertz halting its use of outside workers. Furthermore the Guidelines were amended to prohibit the transfer of employees from component entities in other countries in order unfairly to influence negotiations or the exercise of the right to organize. See Principle IV.7, OECD 2001. For a general discussion of the cases, see Salzman (2000: 788).

[76] See I. Brownlie, 'Legal Effects of Codes of Conduct for MNEs: Commentary' in N. Horn (ed) *Legal Problems of Codes of Conduct for Multinational Enterprises* (Deventer: Kluwer, 1980) 39–43, at 41: 'certain paragraphs, certain bits of the various guidelines, do refer to already existing obligation: to take the most obvious example, the statement that multinational corporations are subject to the law within the jurisdiction of the host state'.

[77] For an overview of the Declaration and the way in which it has been applied and interpreted, see P. T. Muchlinski, *Multinational Enterprises and the Law* (Oxford: Blackwell, 1999) at 457–490.

[78] Tripartite Declaration, para. 8.

clear recognition by states, and employers' and workers' organizations (the members of the Governing Board that adopted the Declaration) that they should all take on human rights obligations as defined in the Universal Declaration and the two human rights Covenants of 1966. The fact that the Tripartite Declaration is a non-binding instrument which is not intended to create legal obligations itself should not blind us to the evidence that all parties consider that they should respect the human rights contained in the International Bill of Rights. In the elaboration of the draft UN Code of Conduct on Transnational Corporations, there is an echo of this injunction: 'Transnational corporations shall respect human rights and fundamental freedoms in the countries in which they operate.'[79] In this UN context, some governments were ready to move towards legally enforceable rules rather than a voluntary or non-mandatory code.[80]

Returning to the Declaration, the first paragraph of the Declaration, dealing with general policies, states that all parties 'should contribute to the realization of the ILO Declaration on Fundamental Principles and Rights at Work and its Follow-up adopted in 1998'.[81] This addition (in the amended Declaration) reminds us of the fundamental rights which are considered as international obligations for all ILO members. The 1998 Declaration refers to 'Conventions recognized as fundamental both inside and outside the Organization' and the 'the principles concerning the fundamental rights which are the subject of those Conventions'. In the words of the 1998 ILO Declaration these are:

(a) freedom of association and the effective recognition of the right to collective bargaining;
(b) the elimination of all forms of forced or compulsory labour;
(c) the effective abolition of child labour; and
(d) the elimination of discrimination in respect of employment and occupation.[82]

Although the Declaration does not list the Conventions 'recognized as fundamental both inside and outside the Organization',[83] today the core labour Conventions are considered to include at least eight: No. 29 concerning forced or compulsory labour; No. 87 concerning freedom of association and the right to organize; No. 98 concerning the application of the principles of the right to organize and bargain collectively; No. 100 concerning equal remuneration for men and women workers for work of equal value; No. 105 concerning the abolition of forced labour; No. 111 concerning discrimination in respect of employment and

---

[79] Draft Code of Conduct on Transnational Corporations, UN Doc. E/1990/94.

[80] In the 1983 draft, the relevant paragraph read '13. Transnational corporations should/shall respect human rights and fundamental freedoms in the countries in which they operate' UN Doc. E/1983/17/Rev.1 Annex II, ECOSOCOR Supplement 7. This was not a controversial article, see 'Outstanding issues in the draft code of conduct on transnational corporations' UN Doc. E/C.10/1984S/5, 29 May 1984; see also para. 91 concerning the use of shall/should in the draft.

[81] Tripartite Declaration, para. 8.

[82] ILO Declaration on Fundamental Principles and Rights at Work, adopted by the International Labour Conference in June 1998, para. 2.   [83] Ibid, para. 1.

occupation; No. 138 concerning the minimum age for admission to employment; and No. 182 concerning the prohibition and Immediate Action for the Elimination of the Worst Forms of Child Labour.[84]

I could offer the interim conclusion here that, despite the fact that the Tripartite Declaration contains only recommendations, the Declaration provides material evidence that the international labour law regime has come to include human rights obligations for national and multinational enterprises. These obligations include, at a minimum, respect for the principles in the Universal Declaration of Human Rights and duties to respect and promote the fundamental rights contained in the core labour conventions listed above. The importance of the place of the labour rights contained in the core conventions is underlined by the fact that, for many activist organizations working on corporate codes of conduct, the inclusion of the rights in these Conventions form part of the minimum floor of rights to be included in such codes.[85] There is still resistance among companies to explicit mention of these core labour standards by reference to the ILO texts. According to one study, only 3 per cent of company codes actually refer to the ILO core labour conventions.[86] On the other hand, 60 per cent of multistakeholder codes include these ILO conventions.[87] With initiatives such as the FTSE4Good including as criteria the option for companies to make a statement of commitment to 'all the ILO core labour standards globally',[88] and with some certification schemes stipulating respect for these international standards (in particular freedom of association and collective bargaining), the normative relevance of these standards could well become more entrenched for companies. Even though the Conventions might be seen as primarily addressed to states, their impact reaches well beyond those states that become contracting parties. As companies increasingly come within the reach of these Conventions, it will not be enough simply to avoid conduct that violates their terms. Positive obligations also accrue. In the words of Jill Murray: 'any firm which wishes to act consistently with the ILO schema has an active burden to secure the rights, freedoms, principles and standards enumerated by the ILO, and to set in place systems and procedures and

---

[84] The UK Foreign and Commonwealth Office, *Annual Report on Human Rights 2001* lists these eight conventions, stating (at 152) that they are 'considered to be *Core Labour Conventions*'.

[85] The Clean Clothes Campaign reports that its model code lists labour standards from the core conventions '(child labour, forced or bonded labour, discrimination, freedom of association and the right to collective bargaining) plus provisions on hours of work, living wage, health and safety, and job security. Today there is a high level of consensus among activists that these are our demands, and that company codes (and others) not mentioning these fall short of the mark'. N. Ascoly and I. Zeldenrust, 'Working with codes: perspectives from the Clean Clothes Campaign' in Jenkins, Pearson, and Seyfang (2002) 172–183, at 175.

[86] R. Jenkins, 'The political economy of codes of conduct' in Jenkins, Pearson, and Seyfang (2002) 13–30, at 19, based on an analysis of the OECD *Codes of Corporate Conduct: An Inventory* (1999).   [87] Ibid.

[88] Human Rights Criteria for the Global Resource Sector; Human Rights Criteria for Companies in Countries of Concern; see http://www.ftse.com/fstse4good.

internal guarantees which will overcome the power imbalance/s which exist in the status quo'.[89]

6.4.2 Implementing the Tripartite Declaration

There are three aspects to follow-up in the formal implementation of the Declaration to consider. The first is focused in the Sub-Committee on Multinational Enterprises.[90] This body conducts a periodic survey whereby member states, and national employers' and workers' organizations provide information on their experience in implementing the Declaration. This is compiled, analysed, and synthesized in a survey prepared for the ILO Governing Body. The last survey, covering 1996 to 1999, was completed in March 2001. From a human rights perspective, these surveys tell one very little about any concrete failure to respect the rights of workers. Although the responses of the organizations and govern-ments are neatly summarized, this is done is such a way, that when it comes to describing the reported behaviour of multinationals, the names of the multina-tionals concerned are deleted and the reference 'names of MNEs given' is inserted in brackets. This produces an almost comic effect. The entry from the National Confederation of Dominican Workers (CNTD) is summarized as follows under the heading Dominican Republic:

> CNTD further reports that participation by MNEs (names of MNEs given) in what were state industries but have now been privatized or deregulated has created labour problems. Unions were closed down before privatization (names of cases in utilities sector given), or liquidated after privatization (name of MNE and cases in agricultural manufacturing given). In addition, disputes will arise in future when the union headquarters try to promote the creation of trade unions in privatized companies since the new investors have warned that they will not allow it.[91]

The censorship is bizarre when one considers that most of the entries actually praise the efforts of specific multinationals, and often highlight the efforts made with regard to human rights and better working conditions. These doctored reports are then synthesized and analysed.

The analytical report is exquisitely balanced. So balanced, that it is hard to see this process ever evolving in a way that would satisfy human rights activists—or

---

[89] J. Murray, 'Labour rights/corporate responsibilities: the role of ILO labour standards' in Jenkins, Pearson, and Seyfang (2002) 31–42, at 38. Murray emphasizes that the obligations in the ILO Conventions have to be adapted by the corporations themselves 'to reflect the ways in which it is agreeing to self-limit its own power in order to respect the rights and uphold the obligations estab-lished by the ILO'.

[90] This is a sub-committee to the Committee on Legal Issues and International Labour Standards.

[91] See the Seventh Survey on the effect given to the Tripartite Declaration of principles concerning Multinational Enterprises and Social Policy: Summary of reports submitted by governments and by employers' and workers' organizations. Part II Summary of reports GB.280/MNE/1/2 March 2001, at 347.

indeed anyone interested in understanding the changes in this field. Consider the conclusion regarding export processing zones (EPZs):

> Overall, special incentives offered to investors in zones were perceived, in most cases, *not* to limit fundamental human rights or basic trade union rights, employment security, equality of treatment, safety and health standards or other rights of workers. However, some respondents, mainly workers' organizations, indicated that special incentives offered to investors in EPZs limited various rights of workers, particularly freedom of association and the right to collective bargaining.[92]

The recommendation of the Working Group of the Sub-Committee is simply that 'further study and consultations, combined with ongoing programmes in the Office, be conducted to promote the application of the Declaration by MNEs in the EPZs'.[93]

The second follow-up activity mirrors the OECD clarification procedure. There has been a procedure for interpretation of the provisions of the Declaration since 1981.[94] In order for this procedure to be applicable, there has to be a disagreement on the meaning of the Declaration which arises from an actual situation. The disagreement has to be between parties addressed by the Declaration. ('States members of the ILO, the employers' and workers' organizations concerned and the multinational enterprises operating in their territories.')[95] Requests can be made by governments and, where a government has refused to make a request on their behalf, by employers' and workers' organizations. The International Labour Office prepares a draft reply in consultation with the Sub-Committee, which is eventually considered by the Governing Body. According to Muchlinski, 'the procedure may involve the ascertainment of certain facts but not a resolution of disputes over facts and laws'.[96] The procedure is very restrictive in that it cannot be invoked 'in respect of national law and practice', or in respect of any international labour Convention/Recommendation, or in respect of matters falling under the freedom of association procedure.[97]

The third follow-up activity is promotion and studies. According to the replies received in the last survey, it would seem that the Declaration is still unknown in many countries and that many organizations feel unqualified to report on its

---

[92] Seventh Survey on the effect given to the Tripartite Declaration of Principles concerning Multinational Enterprises and Social Policy: Analytical report of the Working group on the reports submitted by governments and by employers' and workers' organizations, GB.280/MNE/1/1, March 2001, at para. 201. See also the Summary of reports GB.280/MNE/1/2, March 2001.

[93] Ibid, para. 203.

[94] The current procedure is contained in *Official Bulletin* 1986, vol. LXIX, Series A, no. 3, 196–197. For a detailed look at the pitfalls in the procedure as well as the outcome in four cases, see C. Scott (2001: 571–574), who reports (at 573) that the focus has been on job losses and the '*jurisprudence constante*' that has emerged is a 'principle that simultaneously censures unilateralism from within any one of the three sectors [labour, employers, state] and ungenerous interpretations of the interests protected by the Tripartite Declaration'.

[95] See preambular para. 10 of the Declaration.   [96] Muchlinski (1999: 459).

[97] See Art. 2 of the procedure.

implementation. Without some sort of grievance procedure with the possibility of reparation, or some other meaningful remedy, it seems unlikely that the Declaration will capture the imagination of those who are most affected by the breaches of its principles.

In sum, the Tripartite Declaration provides an important summary of the policies multinationals are expected to apply and contribute to. It covers not only human rights and core labour standards, but also the need for multinationals to increase employment opportunities and improve standards, to promote the advancement of nationals of the host country, the use of technologies that generate employment, equal opportunity and non-discrimination, the importance of providing reasonable notice of changes in operations, and the avoidance of arbitrary dismissal. When operating in developing countries, multinationals are to provide the best possible wages, benefits, and conditions of work; these are to be related to the economic position of the enterprise and should be 'at least adequate to satisfy basic needs of the workers and their families'.[98] But so far, little imagination has been expended in making this Declaration a tool in the hands of those claiming violations of their human rights by multinational enterprises. Perhaps, with the increased focus on ILO core labour rights as the minimum standard for inclusion in corporate codes of conduct, the Tripartite Declaration will take on a new life as its more detailed provisions become incorporated into collective bargaining agreements, contracts, tenders, and self-imposed sets of business principles. For present purposes, it is certainly evidence of states, employers' and workers' organizations (the members of the ILO) all expecting multinationals to respect the standards contained in the Universal Declaration of Human Rights.

6.5   THE UN GLOBAL COMPACT (2000) AND THE INCORPORATION OF RESPECT FOR HUMAN RIGHTS INTO BUSINESS AND UN PRACTICES

On 31 January 1999, at the World Economic Forum in Davos, Switzerland, the UN Secretary-General asked world business leaders to *embrace and enact* a Global Compact, both in their individual corporate practices and by supporting appropriate public policies. The Global Compact now includes ten principles. The first two refer to human rights. The Compact principles cover both the commission of human rights abuses and complicity in human rights abuses. On the one hand, companies are to make sure they do not themselves commit human rights abuses; on the other hand, companies are to support appropriate public policies and ensure they are not complicit in other people's human rights abuses. Under the Global Compact Principle 1, world business is asked to: 'support and respect the

---

[98]   See para. 34 of the Declaration.

protection of international human rights within their sphere of influence'. The UN Website originally explained the scope of these obligations in the following terms:

Companies committing themselves to human rights would ensure:

In the workplace

- safe and healthy working conditions;
- freedom of association;
- non-discrimination in personnel practices;
- no forced or child labour; and
- rights to basic health, education and housing (if operations are located in areas where these are not provided).

Outside the workplace

- respect for existing international guidelines and standards for the use of force (UN Code of Conduct for Law Enforcement Officials and UN Basic Principles on the Use of Force and Firearms by Law Enforcement Officials).

In the wider community

- prevent the forcible displacement of individuals, groups or communities;
- protect the economic livelihood of local communities; and
- contribute to the public debate. Companies interact with all levels of governing bodies in the countries where they operate. Within this context, they have the right and the responsibility to express their views on matters which affect their operations, their employees their customers and the communities of which they are part.

These examples still capture the thrust of Principle 1 of the Global Compact. The first element of this principle, as reflected in the first set of examples above, is the duty to respect human rights in the workplace. The corporate understanding of this element is fairly developed. Shell's *Management Primer* includes the following paragraphs:

The responsibilities of Shell companies, as articulated in the business principles, include the promotion of equal opportunity and non-discrimination in employment practices; ensuring that freedom of association and the right to organize are respected, guaranteeing that Shell companies do not use slave labour, forced labour or child labour; ensuring that healthy and safe working conditions are provided; that security of employment is created and that the rights of indigenous people and communities are respected.

The individual operating companies must, within their capacity to take action, ensure that these principles are implemented and respected. Within areas where it has control, such as on company sites or in defining employment conditions, the company has full responsibility for meeting human rights standards.[99]

The Global Compact described the second and third limbs of the principle as relating to 'outside the workplace' and 'in the wider community'. With regard to these other elements, Shell sees its responsibilities in spatial terms on a 'map', with

---

[99] Shell, *Business and Human Rights: A Management Primer* (1998) at 22, para. 3.12.

inner and outer orbits, and with performance harder to measure as one moves through the orbits. Shell includes a graphic with expanding spheres with the colours getting lighter. The darkest core relates to 'employee rights: health and safety, equal opportunity, freedom of association, pay and conditions, personal development and ILO Declaration'; the next refers to 'security policy: policy/standards/training'; the next is entitled 'community rights: indigenous people, local people, local HSE quality, social equity, right to development'; the next is listed as 'national rights: foreign direct investment/Sullivan principles, social equity/capital development, force for good by example'; the outer and lightest circle is 'advocacy: speaking out, silent diplomacy, education training, identifying and sharing issues, engaging shareholders'. 'It gets progressively more difficult to assign relevant performance measures (metrics) that can be verified as one moves from the inner to the outer orbits. This suggests that new approaches to measurement and verification are required here.'[100]

This 'spheres of influence' mapping also corresponds to some extent to three dimensions of human rights obligations. First, we see an obligation to *respect* human rights (for example in the workplace). Second, we can emphasize the duty to *protect* human rights (for example by controlling the use of force deployed by security forces outside the workplace). And last, there is an acknowledgement of the duty to *promote* human rights (for example by contributing to the wider debate on human rights).

The second Global Compact principle is, at first sight, also fairly uncomplicated: '2. The Secretary-General asked world business to make sure they are not complicit in human rights abuses.' The complicity concept extends the expectations on corporations beyond their immediate acts, and reaches activity where corporations contribute to someone else's illegal acts. But the notion of corporate complicity in human rights abuses is not confined to direct involvement in the immediate plotting and execution of illegal acts by others. Complicity has also been used to describe the corporate position *vis-à-vis* third-party abuses when the business *benefits* from human rights abuses committed by someone else.[101] The notion of complicity in the context of the Compact has been considered in a

---

[100] *Shell Report: People, planet and profits: An act of commitment* (1999) at 29.

[101] 'A company is beneficially complicit if it tolerates or knowingly ignores the human rights violations of one of its business partners, committed in furtherance of their common business objectives. Violations committed by security forces, such as the suppression of a peaceful protest against business activity or the use of repressive measures while guarding company facilities are often cited as examples of beneficial complicity. Examples of beneficial complicity could also include a company that receives financial incentives in an Export Processing Zone where the government prohibits unions; a company that purchases materials from a supplier that is committing gross human rights violations; and a company that tolerates working conditions detrimental to worker health in its supply chain.' A. P. Ewing, 'Understanding the Global Compact Human Rights Principles' in UN Global Compact Office & OHCHR, *Embedding Human Rights in Business Practice* (UN Global Compact Office: New York, 2004) 29–42, at 39; see also OHCHR, 'OHCHR Briefing Paper on the Global Compact and Human Rights: Understanding Sphere of Influence and Complicity', in the same publication at 14–26.

number of meetings and will continue to be debated and considered.[102] The UN High Commissioner for Human Rights, Mary Robinson, presented a threefold approach in her report to the UN General Assembly in 2001:

> In order to help define the responsibilities of business, I have suggested there are different degrees or types of complicity in this context: direct, beneficial and silent complicity.
>
> 109.   A corporation that knowingly assists a State in violating principles of international law contained in the Universal Declaration of Human Rights could be viewed as directly complicit in such a violation. For example, a company that promoted, or assisted with, the forced relocation of people in circumstances that would constitute a violation of international human rights could be considered directly complicit in the violation. The corporation could be responsible if it or its agents knew of the likely effects of their assistance.
>
> 110.   The notion of corporate complicity in human rights abuses is not confined to direct involvement in the execution of illegal acts by other parties. The complicity concept has also been used to describe the corporate position vis-à-vis government or rebel violations when business benefits from human rights abuses committed by another entity. Violations committed by security forces, such as the suppression of peaceful protest against business activities or the use of repressive measures while guarding company facilities, are often cited as examples of corporate complicity in human rights abuses. Where human rights violations occur in the context of a business operation, the business in question need not necessarily cause the violations for it to become implicated in the abuses.
>
> 111.   The notion of silent complicity reflects the contemporary expectation that companies should raise systematic or continuous human rights abuses with the appropriate authorities. Indeed, it reflects the growing acceptance within companies that there is something culpable about failing to exercise influence in such circumstances. Whether or not such silent complicity would give rise to a finding of a breach of a strict legal obligation against a company in a court of law, it has become increasingly clear that the moral dimension of corporate action (or inaction) has taken on significant importance.[103]

This categorization of complicity is now summarized on the Global Compact website as follows:[104]

Direct Complicity   Occurs when a company knowingly assists a state in violating human rights. An example of this is in the case where a company assists in the forced relocation of peoples in circumstances related to business activity.

Beneficial Complicity   Suggests that a company benefits directly from human rights abuses committed by someone else. For example, violations committed by security

---

[102] See in this context, J. Radon, ' "Hear No Evil, Speak No Evil, See No Evil" Spells Complicity', *Compact Quarterly* (online publication of the Global Compact) 5 April 2005.

[103] Report of the United Nations High Commissioner for Human Rights to the 56th Session of the General Assembly, UN Doc. A/56/36/2001, 28 September 2001.

[104] See http://www.unglobalcompact/AboutThe GC/TheNinePrinciples/prin2.htm; and see also M. McIntosh, R. Thomas, D. Leipziger, and G. Coleman, *Living Corporate Citizenship: Strategic routes to socially responsible business* (London: Prentice Hall, 2003) at 143.

forces, such as the suppression of a peaceful protest against business activities or the use of repressive measures while guarding company facilities, are often cited in this context.

Silent complicity Describes the way human rights advocates see the failure by a company to raise the question of systematic or continuous human rights violations in its interactions with the appropriate authorities. For example, inaction or acceptance by companies of systematic discrimination in employment law against particular groups on the grounds of ethnicity or gender could bring accusations of silent complicity.

This triptych of direct, beneficial, and silent complicity may now reflect the way corporate responsibility is developing through the corporate and UN manuals. Serious corporate social responsibility initiatives demand internal impact assessments, preventive action, and the avoidance of a wide range of types of complicity. Human rights organizations that monitor corporate behaviour against international human rights norms have adopted the complicity concept to explain the human rights grievances at the heart of their reports. Amnesty International's 'Human rights principles for companies' includes a policy recommendation that companies should establish procedures to ensure that all operations are examined for their potential impact on human rights and safeguards to ensure that company staff are never complicit in human rights abuses.[105] Human Rights Watch, in its report *Tainted harvest: Child labour and obstacles to organizing on Ecuador's banana plantations*, concluded: 'Human Rights Watch believes that when exporting corporations fail to use their financial influence to demand respect for labor rights on their supplier plantations, the exporting corporations benefit from, facilitate, and are therefore complicit in labor rights violations.'[106] Similarly, the Human Rights Watch Report report *Sudan, oil, and human rights* points to the failure of oil companies to voice human rights concerns regarding the Government's policy of forcibly displacing civilians from areas designated for oil extraction.[107] The report also charges that:

> Talisman's complicity in the government's abuses was not limited to its inaction in the face of the continued displacement campaign rolling through the oil areas. Its activities in some cases assisted forcible displacement and attacks on civilians. For example, it allowed government forces to use the Talisman/GNPOC airfield and road infrastructure in circumstances in which it knew or should have known that the facilities would be used to conduct further displacement and wage indiscriminate or disproportionate military attacks that struck and/or targeted civilians and civilian objects.[108]

[105] Amnesty International, *Human rights principles for companies*, AI Index 70/01/98 (1998).
[106] Human Rights Watch, *Tainted harvest: Child labor and obstacles to organizing on Ecuador's banana plantations* (2002b) at 5.
[107] 'From the beginning of its involvement in Sudan, Talisman resolutely refused to speak out against or to seriously investigate the Sudanese government's policy of forcibly displacing civilians from areas designated for oil extraction and the human rights abuses that have been an essential element of this policy. Yet, under modern concepts of corporate responsibility that Talisman claims to endorse, it had a responsibility to ensure that its business operations did not depend upon, or benefit from, gross human rights abuses such as those that have been committed by the government and its proxy forces in Sudan.' *Sudan, oil, and human rights* (2004) at 81–82.   [108] Ibid, at 88.

The focus on complicity has meant that corporate policies have been articulated which attempt to consider responsibilities with regard to possible human rights abuses directly committed by third parties rather than by the corporation itself. We can see an illustration of the complicity challenge if we return to the Shell *Management Primer*:

> In almost all circumstances the operating company will be able to respect and protect the human rights of its employees. When a third party takes an action which infringes on the human rights of a Shell employee, whether that action takes place on a company site or elsewhere, the operating company must take appropriate steps to remedy the situation.

> Where the operating company does not have complete control, that is, when the issue relates to incidents which did not take place on their site or where the company has limited legal or actual influence, the capacity to influence events is clearly diminished. However that does not mean that the issue can be ignored.

> In such cases, the company should tailor its approach according to its capacities and its view of how best to achieve policy aims. For example, the obligation to express support for fundamental human rights within the legitimate role of business does not necessarily mean public statements of support. It may be that expressions of view behind closed doors are more effective in achieving the desired goal. If, in the judgement of the responsible executives, that is the case, then that approach should be taken. The emphasis must be on achieving a result which upholds the human rights standards of the Group's business principles.[109]

The Shell Group's business principles include respect for the human rights of employees as well as promoting the application of such principles with regard to contractors and suppliers and in joint ventures. The same management primer also includes the following paragraph:

> A potentially serious problem exists when companies choose to operate in one of the few countries that do not allow independent human rights or humanitarian groups even to enter. In these cases there is no possibility of any legitimate monitoring, and as a result the public may suspect abusive practices. Corporations which choose to work in such countries will be scrutinized by human rights organizations in two main respects: that their presence is a measurable 'force for the good' in terms of human rights, and that the company does not seek to *benefit* from poor human rights laws on, for example, employment and health and safety.[110]

We find here the reflection of the beneficial complicity category. The principled approach seems simple when stated in abstract terms but the application is considered problematic by Shell. Shell's 'Training Supplement', *Human Rights Dilemmas*, highlights some practical challenges. For example, with regard to child labour, the supplement sets the following problem:

> You are the Purchasing Manager for Shell Select Shops in Europe. You approve contracts with suppliers of various consumer products. In these contracts suppliers must certify

---

[109] Shell (1998: 22–23) at para. 3.12.   [110] Shell (1998: 21) at para. 3.9 (emphasis added).

that no child labour is involved in their products. Your coffee supplier certifies every year that production does not involve child labour.

An NGO in Europe investigates conditions in Latin American coffee plantations where it grows beans for its coffee. This NGO is preparing to bring these concerns to the attention of major newspapers, stating that Shell is profiting from child labour.

You decide to investigate the practices of all of your major food and drinks suppliers. You find that many of your suppliers have systems to avoid child labour; however, it is very difficult to provide absolute assurances that no child has been used. Your supplier explains that the coffee beans sold in Shell Select Shops are grown on thousands of farms in more than 20 countries around the world, including places where it is seen as normal for children to work with their families in agriculture.

This example captures companies' concern that they not be seen to be profiting from human rights abuses committed by others: beneficial complicity. It also illustrates the practical obstacles to ensuring that a company and its employees avoid complicity in human rights abuses. But, most importantly for our purposes, the examples illustrate how companies have already taken on board the notion that they should respect, protect, and promote human rights (Principle 1); and that they have obligations to avoid assisting other's human rights abuses or benefiting from human rights abuses committed by their sub-contractors and business partners (Principle 2, the complicity principle).

With regard to the wider responsibilities, and what was referred to above as the silent complicity issue, Shell includes in its business principles recognition of responsibilities to society 'to express support for fundamental human rights in line with the legitimate role of business'.[111] BP, another company from the same sector, refers to its commitment to relationships and explains this as follows: 'We believe that long-term relationships founded on trust and mutual advantage are vital to BP's business success. Our commitment is to create mutual advantage in all our relationships so that others will always prefer to do business with BP. We will do this by:... demonstrating respect for human dignity and the rights of individuals.'[112] With regard to the complicity issue, BP states: 'We will seek partners whose policies are consistent with our own'; and they promise: 'We will make our contractors and suppliers aware of our own commitments and expectations, and their responsibilities in implementing them.' With regard to the wider expectation to raise human rights issues, even outside the context of relationships with subcontractors, the BP statement captures the notion:

> We recognize the changing public expectations of the extent to which companies should put pressure on governments on human rights issues and will seek, working in partnership with others, to resolve any tensions or conflicts arising between international expectations and national or local practices in a sensitive manner.

---

[111] Shell, *Statement of General Business Principles* (1997) 2. Responsibilities, para. (e).
[112] BP, *Business Policies* (2002). On dignity, see Ch 11 below.

This constitutes some evidence of practice that corporations proclaim the need to raise human rights issues with governments and avoid silent complicity. In the case of BP, the company is credited by (the usually critical) Christian Aid, with having developed 'a sophisticated understanding of human rights', and following non-governmental pressure to avoid complicity and issue public condemnation of human rights violations, such BP statements are said by Christian Aid to have had 'significant impact'.[113]

But patience is wearing out among such NGOs as it becomes clear that pressure on individual companies is difficult to sustain.[114] Christian Aid suggests that: 'In the long run, international NGOs may be more effective by throwing their collective weight behind the drive for international regulation than by tying up their scant resources in bilateral dialogues.'[115] Short of binding regulation, there are still concerns regarding the absence of effective monitoring for various sectoral schemes (for example, diamonds, timber, footwear), or even more generally, with regard to participation in the Global Compact. The mechanisms for monitoring the activity of those companies that have signed up for the Global Compact remain underdeveloped. It has been suggested that the UN efforts have in this context been used as a vehicle for companies and others to argue against a more regulatory approach with a clear normative framework. Several NGOs and scholars wrote to the Secretary-General expressing reservations about the Global Compact and asserted: 'Asking corporations, many of which are repeat offenders of both the law and commonly accepted standards of responsibility, to endorse a vague statement of commitment to human rights, labour and environmental standards draws attention away from the need for more substantial action to hold corporations accountable for their behaviour.'[116] Let us now turn to the most recent attempts to develop the substance of these human rights obligations.

6.6 INITIATIVES AT THE UN SUB-COMMISSION AND COMMISSION ON HUMAN RIGHTS AND THE GENERAL HUMAN RIGHTS OBLIGATIONS OF CORPORATIONS

The UN Sub-Commission on the Promotion and Protection of Human Rights is a body created to act as a 'think-tank'[117] to assist the UN Commission on Human

---

[113] Christian Aid, *Behind the mask: The real face of corporate social responsibility*, available at http://www.christian-aid.org.uk/indepth/0401csr/csr_behindthemask.pdf: (2004) at 12–13.

[114] Ibid, at 14. 'But the BP negotiations also demonstrated that NGOs lack the resources to maintain the level of lobbying, monitoring and scrutiny required to have a sustained impact on a multinational's operations.'

[115] Ibid, at 14, and for suggestions regarding regulation in the UK and at the EU level, see 57–59; see also the proposal presented by Friends of the Earth at the Johannesburg 2002 Summit, *Towards Binding Corporate Accountability*, January 2002.

[116] From the letter reproduced in part in S. Zadek, *The Civil Corporation: The New Economy of Corporate Citizenship* (London/Sterling, Virg.: Earthscan, 2001).

[117] OHCHR, 'Seventeen Frequently Asked Questions about United Nations Special Rapporteurs', Fact Sheet No. 27, at 17.

Rights (an inter-governmental body of fifty-three member states of the United Nations). Its twenty-six members are elected as independent experts by the inter-governmental Commission on Human Rights. In 2003, after four years of discussions and consultations, the Sub-Commission approved the 'Norms on the Responsibilities of Transnational Corporations and Other Business Enterprises with Regard to Human Rights' (the Norms).[118] The Sub-Commission decided to transmit to the Commission its Norms 'for consideration and adoption'. The Commission in turn decided to call for a study into the obligations on corporations, and determined that the Sub-Commission should not monitor the Norms contained in its 'draft proposal'.[119]

In the light of the subsequent study, prepared by the Office of the High Commissioner for Human Rights, the Commission decided, in April 2005, to request the Secretary-General to appoint a special representative on 'the issue of human rights and transnational corporations and other business enterprises'.[120] The special representative's mandate includes the identification and clarification of 'standards of corporate responsibility and accountability' with regard to human rights, as well as researching and clarifying 'the implications for transnational corporations and other business enterprises' of the concepts of 'complicity' and 'sphere of influence'. These concepts have been touched on above. At the time of writing, John Ruggie, the newly appointed Special Representative, had not yet reported to the Commission.[121]

In the present context, however, it is worth examining the Sub-Commission's text to see what it contributed to the initiatives already discussed. In contrast to the OECD and ILO texts, the Sub-Commission's text defines what is meant by a transnational corporation and draws a distinction between the responsibilities of transnationals and those of 'other business enterprises'. For the purposes of the Sub-Commission's text: 'The term "transnational corporation" refers to an economic entity operating in more than one country or a cluster of economic entities operating in two or more countries—whatever their legal form, whether in their home country or country of activity, and whether taken individually or collectively.'[122] The extension of the Norms to other business enterprises was

[118] UN Doc. E/CN.4/Sub.2/2003/12/Rev.2 (2003). Resolution 2003/16, 13 August 2003 contained in UN Doc. E/CN.4/2004/2, E/CN.4/Sub.2/2003/43, 20 October 2003, at 51. For a complete overview of the history and design of the Norms, see D. Weissbrodt and M. Kruger, 'Responsibilities of Transnational Corporations and Other Business Enterprises With Regard to Human Rights' in P. Alston (ed) *Non-State Actors and Human Rights* (Oxford: Oxford University Press, 2005).

[119] Decision 2004/116 of the UN Commission on Human Rights called for a report 'setting out the scope and legal status of existing initiatives and standards relating to the responsibility of transnational corporations and related business enterprises with regard to human rights'. The Decision also affirmed: 'that document E/CN.4/Sub.2/2003/12/Rev.2 has not been requested by the Commission and, as a draft proposal, has no legal standing, and that the Sub-Commission should not perform any monitoring function in this regard'. UN Doc. E/CN.4/2004/L.11/Add.7, 22 April 2004, at 82.

[120] UN Doc. E/CN.4/RES/2005/6, 20 April 2005.

[121] John Ruggie, Evron and Jeane Kirkpatrick Professor of International Affairs at the Center for Business and Government, Kennedy School of Government, Harvard University.

[122] At para. 20.

contentious during the drafting process, perhaps in part due to a fear that the Norms would eventually be applied to small companies in developing countries, and thereby place them at a competitive disadvantage compared to wealthy transnationals. The final text defines three situations in which the Norms are presumed to apply to: 'any business entity, regardless of the international or domestic nature of its activities, including a transnational corporation, contractor, subcontractor, supplier, licensee or distributor; the corporate, partnership, or other legal form used to establish the business entity; and the nature of the ownership of the entity'.[123] The Norms are 'presumed to apply, as a matter of practice' to these enterprises: where the business enterprise has any relation with a transnational corporation; where the impact of business enterprise is not entirely local; or where the activities involve violations of the right to security (as detailed in paragraphs 3 and 4 of the Norms).[124] We shall return to the 'right to security' provisions below. Although the Norms have this variegated application depending on the circumstances, the present discussion mainly refers to the addressees with the shorthand 'corporations' for the purposes of the following exposition.

The Norms start by recalling that the Universal Declaration of Human Rights was addressed to individuals and organs of society as well as governments. As we have seen, a close examination of the Declaration reveals that states are rarely mentioned as such, the Declaration being drafted to emphasize the rights of individuals rather than the duties of governments.[125] In 1948, the UN General Assembly proclaimed 'this Universal Declaration of Human Rights as a common standard of achievement for all peoples and all nations, to the end that every individual and every organ of society, keeping this Declaration constantly in mind, shall strive by teaching and education to promote respect for these rights and freedoms and by progressive measures, national and international, to secure their universal and effective recognition and observance'.[126] Moreover, the ILO Tripartite Declaration of 1977 called for corporations to respect the Universal Declaration and the Covenants.[127] The application of the Universal Declaration

---

[123] E/CN.4/Sub.2/2003/12/Rev.2 (the Norms), Section I. Definitions, para. 21.   [124] Ibid.

[125] J. J. Paust, 'The Other Side of Right: Private Duties Under Human Rights Law' 5 *Harv HRJ* (1992) 51–63, at 53.

[126] For the drafting history, see J. Morsink, *The Universal Declaration of Human Rights: Origins, Drafting, and Intent* (Philadelphia: University of Pennsylvania Press, 1999) at 324. See also GA Res. 53/144 'Declaration on the Right and Responsibility of Individuals, Groups and Organs of Society to Promote and Protect Universally Recognized Human Rights and Fundamental Freedoms' (1998), also known as the Declaration on Human Rights Defenders, which in the context of human rights organizations, implies duties for organs of society, see esp. paras 11 and 18. The Declaration is referred to in preambular para. 4 of the Norms. The Secretary-General's report 'Elements for a draft body of principles on the right and responsibility of individuals, groups and other organs of society to promote and protect human rights and fundamental freedoms', UN Doc E/CN.4/Sub.2/1982/12, 30 June 1982, contrasted organs of society with groups (at para. 9): 'Whereas all "organs of society" could enter into the broad category of "group", various groups do not reach the level of public acceptance and institutionalization which seems to be required to be considered "organs of society".'

[127] Tripartite Declaration of Principles concerning Multinational Enterprises and Social Policy (adopted by the Governing Body of the International Labour Office at its 204th Session (Geneva,

of Human Rights to corporate activity has been asserted by a number of organizations and authors. Lou Henkin sees multinationals as the addressees of the Declaration:

> At this juncture the Universal Declaration may also address multinational companies. This is true even though the companies never heard of the Universal Declaration at the time it was drafted. The Universal Declaration is not addressed only to governments. It is a 'common standard for all peoples and all nations.' It means that '*every individual and every organ of society* shall strive—by progressive measures . . . to secure their universal and effective recognition and observance among the people of the member states.' *Every individual* includes juridical persons. *Every individual* and *every organ of society* excludes no one, no company, no market, no cyberspace. The Universal Declaration applies to them all.[128]

Two UN High Commissioners for Human Rights, Mary Robinson and Sergio Vieira de Mello, both wrote that corporations were to be considered 'organs of society' in this context,[129] and such an interpretation is the basis of the approach of various NGOs, including Amnesty International.[130] By 2004, EU Governments conceded that 'such a provision could allocate responsibility to corporations', however, they go on to draw a distinction between 'responsibilities' and 'legal obligations'. For EU Governments, the legal obligations rest with states: 'The Covenants, Conventions and Declarations that lay the basis of human rights responsibilities have been negotiated, signed and ratified by States, which also bear prime responsibility for their implementation.'[131] This seems to admit a secondary responsibility (without *legal obligation*) for corporations.

November 1977) as amended at its 279th Session (Geneva, November 2000) para. 8, the relevant sentence of the paragraph reads: 'All the parties concerned by this Declaration should respect the sovereign rights of States, obey the national laws and regulations, give due consideration to local practices and respect relevant international standards. They should respect the Universal Declaration of Human Rights and the corresponding International Covenants adopted by the General Assembly of the United Nations as well as the Constitution of the International Labour Organization and its principles according to which freedom of expression and association are essential to sustained progress.'

[128] L. Henkin, 'The Universal Declaration at 50 and the Challenge of Global Markets' 25 *Brooklyn JIL* (1999) 24–25 (emphasis in the original). See also K. De Feyter, 'Corporate Governance and Human Rights' in Institut international des droits de l'homme, *Commerce mondial et protection des droits de l'homme: les droits de l'homme à l'épreuve de la globalisation des échanges economiques* (Brussels: Bruylant, 2001) 71–110, at 77. Amnesty International, 'The UN Human Rights Norms for Business: Towards Legal Accountability', IOR 42/001/2004 (2004) at 5 and 7.

[129] M. Robinson, 'The business case for human rights' in *Visions of Ethical Business*, Financial Times Management (London: Financial Times Professional, 1998) 14–17, at 14; S. Vieira de Mello, 'Human Rights: what role for business?' 2(1) *New Academy Review* (2003) 19–22, at 19.

[130] Amnesty International (UK), *Global trade, labour and human rights* (2000) at 7: 'Business interests and financial institutions are organs of society.'

[131] Para. 6. of the Austrian reply to the request by OHCHR for input from states regarding the report concerning 'Responsibilities of transnational corporation and related business enterprises with regard to human rights' (received 11 October 2004), see Decision of the Commission 2004/116, at 3. For all submissions to OHCHR regarding this issue, see: http://www.ohchr.org/english/issues/globalization/businness/contributions.htm.

The Sub-Commission's text starts by addressing those[132] who express concern that such an exercise distracts from focusing on the international responsibilities of states and could even start to undermine the scope of those obligations: 'States have the primary responsibility to promote, secure the fulfilment of, respect, ensure respect of and protect human rights recognized in international as well as national law, including ensuring that transnational corporations and other business enterprises respect human rights.'[133] The text also includes a savings clause which reinforces the point: 'Nothing in these Norms shall be construed as diminishing, restricting, or adversely affecting the human rights obligations of States under national and international law.'[134] The Norms contain detailed paragraphs which cover equal opportunity and non-discriminatory treatment, the security of persons, workers' rights, respect for national sovereignty, consumer protection, and environmental protection.

The text explains the different dimensions of the human rights responsibilities of corporations: 'Within their respective spheres of activity and influence, transnational corporations and other business enterprises have the obligation to promote, secure the fulfilment of, respect, ensure respect of and protect human rights recognized in international as well as national law, including the rights and interests of indigenous peoples and other vulnerable groups.' As discussed previously, these dimensions of human rights obligations have been addressed by companies and the Commentary to the Global Compact. When explicitly articulated in the form of the Sub-Commission's Norms, the responsibilities of corporations mirror the traditional dimensions of human rights obligations developed in the context of state obligations. The distinctions between the obligations to respect, protect, and secure fulfilment are well known and were explained with regard to states in the Maastricht Guidelines (a text adopted by an independent group of experts) in the following way:

> The obligation to respect requires States to refrain from interfering with the enjoyment of economic, social and cultural rights. Thus, the right to housing is violated if the State engages in arbitrary forced evictions. The obligation to protect requires States to prevent violations of such rights by third parties. Thus, the failure to ensure that private employers comply with basic labour standards may amount to a violation of the right to work or the right to just and favourable conditions of work. The obligation to fulfil requires States to take appropriate legislative, administrative, budgetary, judicial and other

---

[132] See, e.g. 'there is a serious risk that, if TNCs were given a responsibility of their own for ensuring the protection and promotion of human rights, States would find it easier to divert the blame, and the duty to take remedial action, from themselves'. Opinion prepared for the International Chamber of Commerce, 'In The Matter Of The Draft "Norms On The Responsibilities Of Transnational Corporations And Other Business Enterprises With Regard To Human Rights"'. Opinion of Professor Emeritus Maurice Mendelson QC, 4 April 2004, at para. 20. Annexed to the submission of the Confederation of British Industry to the Office of the High Commissioner for Human Rights, available at http://www.ohchr.org/english/issues/globalization/business/contributions.htm. See also the US submission quoted in part in Ch 1, at 1.4 above.

[133] UN Doc. E/CN.4/Sub.2/2003/12/Rev.2 (the Norms), General Obligations, Section A. para. 1.

[134] Ibid, General provisions on implementation, Section H, para. 19.

measures towards the full realization of such rights. Thus, the failure of States to provide essential primary health care to those in need may amount to a violation.[135]

How then do these obligations apply to corporations? The key to understanding the shift from state to non-state obligations in this text is, as we have seen, the qualifying phrase 'Within their respective spheres of activity and influence'. This limits the obligations of corporations so that a corporation engaged in further education would not necessarily be responsible for securing primary health care (as would a state). On the other hand, there would be obligations with regard to racial or other types of discrimination concerning employment and tuition. Several legal commentators, in developing their theories of the scope of the obligations of corporations, have highlighted the fact that the obligations vary according to the nexus[136] and the leverage[137] that companies have with regard to the abuse.

Applying the 'respect, protect, secure fulfilment, and promote' categories to corporations, I would suggest the following explanation in the present context. Corporations have to *respect* the human rights of everyone and refrain from any activity that represents an abuse of those rights; for example, using unnecessary lethal force against demonstrators would represent a breach of the obligation to respect human rights.[138]

The obligation to *protect* human rights means that corporations have some obligations to use their influence to protect all persons from threats to their

---

[135] 'The Maastricht Guidelines on Violations of Economic, Social and Cultural Rights' 20(3) *HRQ* (1998) 691–704. See in the context of the right to food, General Comment 12 of the UN Committee on Economic Social and Cultural Rights: 'The obligation to *respect* existing access to adequate food requires States parties not to take any measures that result in preventing such access. The obligation to protect requires measures by the State to ensure that enterprises or individuals do not deprive individuals of their access to adequate food. The obligation to *fulfil* (*facilitate*) means the State must proactively engage in activities intended to strengthen people's access to and utilization of resources and means to ensure their livelihood, including food security. Finally, whenever an individual or group is unable, for reasons beyond their control, to enjoy the right to adequate food by the means at their disposal, States have the obligation to *fulfil* (*provide*) that right directly.' General Comment 12 'the right to adequate food (art. 11)', adopted 12 May 1999, at para. 15, reproduced in UN Doc. HRI/GEN/1/Rev.7, 12 May 2004, at 63 (emphasis in the original).

[136] S. R. Ratner, 'Corporations and Human Rights: A Theory of Legal Responsibility' 111 *YLJ* (2001) 443–545, at 465.

[137] N. Jägers, *Corporate Human Rights Obligations: In Search of Accountability* (Antwerp: Intersentia, 2002) at 79.

[138] The example of forced evictions could also be used, as above. In such a situation, the corporation must not engage in an arbitrary forced eviction where the individuals have been denied the protection of a legal process that respects the right to adequate housing. In the words of the Commentary, corporations: 'shall not forcibly evict individuals, families and/or communities against their will from their homes and/or land which they occupy without having had recourse to, and access to, appropriate forms of legal or other protection pursuant to international human rights law'. UN Doc. E/CN.4/Sub.2/2003/38/Rev.2 (2003) at 12(c). The Resolution which approved the Norms, noted that 'the commentary may serve as a reference for the practical interpretation of the norms', preambular para. 3 of Res. 2003/16 adopted without a vote, 13 August 2003, contained in the Report of the Sub-Commission, UN Doc. E/CN.4/2004/2, E/CN.4/Sub.2/2003/43, 20 October 2003, at 51.

human rights, even if such threats do not emanate from the corporation itself. This means that corporations have a duty to ensure that the contractors with which they do business are complying with the Norms. Companies have a duty to use their influence to ensure protection. The Commentary suggests that corporations should 'initially work with [those that do not comply with the Norms] to reform or decrease violations, but if [those that do not comply with the Norms] will not change, the enterprise shall cease doing business with them'.[139] The protection obligation therefore imposes a duty of due diligence with regard to business partners. The scope of this obligation, which seems to include duties to inquire and to work with partners to 'decrease violations', will clearly vary according to the 'sphere of activity and influence' of the corporation.[140]

The obligation to *secure fulfilment* of human rights has to be related to the primary obligation of governments, and perhaps is best explained by the Commentary, which states that corporations: 'shall refrain from activities that would undermine the rule of law as well as governmental and other efforts to promote and ensure respect for human rights'.[141] This is an injunction which implies that companies inform themselves of the government's human rights obligations and respect the fact that there will be legal obligations on the government to ensure the enjoyment of rights, such as the right of trade unions to organize, freedom of expression, the right to privacy, the right to education, the right to adequate housing, through legislative, administrative, budgetary, judicial, and other measures. While corporations may feel it is in their interests to resist such measures, they have an obligation to do nothing to undermine the human rights of individuals who are owed those rights by their government under international law. The Norms combine the obligation to respect rights with an obligation to contribute to their realization by others. The Norms demand that corporations 'respect economic, social and cultural rights as well as civil and political rights and contribute to their realization'.[142] Corporations have already started to ask themselves what sort of spectrum of obligations this gives rise to. A leading participant and promoter of the Norms, the Swiss pharmaceutical company Novartis, has taken separate positions regarding civil and political rights as opposed to economic and social rights. After referring to the rights contained in the International Covenant on Civil and Political Rights of 1966 they state their position as follows:

> We respect and support civil and political rights within our sphere of influence and strive to ensure that we neither contribute directly or indirectly to human rights abuses nor knowingly benefit from such abuses . . .

---

[139] At para. 15 (c) of the Commentary (n 138 above).

[140] See UN Doc. E/CN.4/Sub.2/2003/12/Rev.2 (2003) A. General obligations, para. 1. The Commentary (n 138 above) para. 1(b), states that corporations: 'shall have the responsibility to use due diligence in ensuring that their activities do not contribute directly or indirectly to human abuses, and that they do not directly or indirectly benefit from abuses of which they were aware or ought to have been aware'. [141] At para. 1(b) of the Commentary (n 138 above).

[142] UN Doc. E/CN.4/Sub.2/2003/12/Rev.2 (2003) E. Respect for national sovereignty and human rights, para. 12.

Although all individuals and organs of society are expected to promote respect for the rights and freedoms by progressive measures, the duty to realise economic, social and cultural rights is the prime responsibility of the state. Business enterprises cannot on their own implement economic, social and cultural rights—they, however, contribute in many ways to economic welfare and the common good.[143]

Any sense of obligation to *promote* human rights is likely to be determined by the scope of activities and influence of the corporation. In 1998, the UN General Assembly Declaration on the responsibility to promote and protect human rights, stressed that 'the prime responsibility and duty to promote and protect human rights and fundamental freedoms lie with the State'.[144] The preamble continues with the recognition by member states of 'the right and the responsibility of individuals, groups and associations to promote respect for and foster knowledge of human rights and fundamental freedoms at the national and international levels'.[145] The duty on a corporation to promote human rights is perhaps less clear, in legal terms, than the duties to respect and protect human rights, and it is unlikely that this duty to promote human rights would translate into a concrete obligation giving rise to a remedy for its breach in a court of law. Nevertheless, NGOs have highlighted the failure of corporations to use their influence to deter states and rebel groups, as well as other corporations, from abusing human rights, and this approach has been explicitly based on the wording of the Norms.[146]

In addition to these four obligations, mention should be made of what is variously called secondary, indirect, or derivative responsibility. Any legal framework will have secondary rules that determine liability for assisting others to breach the primary rules, and rules determining what must be done to prevent breaches of the obligation. In the present context, while the strict secondary rules might be differentiated depending on the relevant legal order,[147] the broad principles can be gleaned from the Commentary to the Norms. First, corporations should ensure that they do not contribute to human rights abuses committed by others; second, corporations should not 'benefit from abuses of which they were aware or ought to have been aware';[148] and third, corporations are expected to 'inform themselves

---

[143] Novartis Foundation for Sustainable Development, The Prince of Wales, and International Business Leaders Forum, *Human Rights and the Private Sector: International Symposium Report* (Basel/London: Novartis Foundation/PWIBLF, 2004) at 17.

[144] GA Res. 53/144 'Declaration on the Right and Responsibility of Individuals, Groups and Organs of Society to Promote and Protect Universally Recognized Human Rights and Fundamental Freedoms', adopted 9 December 1998, preambular para. 7.   [145] Ibid, at preambular para. 8.

[146] See, e.g. Human Rights Watch, *The Curse of Gold* (2 June 2005) at 74. The report builds on AngloGold Ashanti's responsibilities as defined in the Sub-Commission's Norms, under the OECD Guidelines, under their participation in the Global Compact, the agreement signed with the International Federation of Chemical, Energy, Mine and General Workers' Union (ICEM) and the commitments made in the company's own business principles. Human Rights Watch concluded (at 75) that the 'considerable influence' of AngloGold Ashanti meant that it 'should have exercised its leverage to pursue local actors to respect human rights and should have conditioned its gold exploration activities on such commitments'.

[147] This is explored in more detail in 6.7 below, in the context of the *Unocal* case.

[148] Commentary 1(b) (n 138 above).

of the human rights impact of their principal activities and major proposed activities so that they can further avoid complicity in human rights abuses'.[149]

The general obligation regarding prevention is developed in more detail in one particular context. Where corporations take on security arrangements, the duty of due diligence with regard to prevention has been spelt out in the Commentary based on the universally applicable international standards: 'Transnational corporations and other business enterprises shall engage with due diligence in investigations of potential security guards or other security providers before they are hired and ensure that guards in their employ are adequately trained, guided by and follow relevant international limitations with regard, for example, to the use of force and firearms.'[150]

The question of implementation is dealt with briefly in the Norms. The most striking injunction is that: 'Each transnational corporation or other business enterprise shall apply and incorporate these Norms in their contracts or other arrangements and dealings with contractors, subcontractors, suppliers, licensees, distributors, or natural or other legal persons that enter into any agreement with the transnational corporation or business enterprise in order to ensure respect for and implementation of the Norms.'[151] Such an application of the Norms would create legally binding obligations through the contracts that are concluded. The obligations would be enforced under national contract law.

This review of the Norms, together with their Commentary, seeks to provide a constructive reading of the potential of the Sub-Commission's text. There is, however, concerted opposition to the Norms. Briefly summarized, the opposition suggests: that voluntary non-binding schemes are more effective than regulatory schemes; that the Norms inappropriately shift the focus of human rights away from the obligations of governments; that international human rights obligations apply in different countries in different ways; that the provisions which demand the payment of reparations are too burdensome; and that any UN implementation and monitoring system is unacceptable. A detailed attack on the text was published and circulated by the International Chamber of Commerce

---

[149] Ibid.

[150] Ibid, at 4(d). The relevant norms include in particular: 'the United Nations Basic Principles on the Use of Force and Firearms by Law Enforcement Officials; the United Nations Code of Conduct for Law Enforcement Officials; and emerging best practices developed by the industry, civil society and Governments', ibid, at 4(a). In this last category of best practices we should mention the Voluntary Principles on Security and Human Rights, 20 December 2000, available at http://www1.umn.edu/humanrts/links/volprinciples.html. These are discussed in more detail in Ch 7, at 7.7 below.

[151] At para. 15. This obligation is reinforced and developed in the Commentary (at 4(d)) with regard to security arrangements: 'If a transnational corporation or other business enterprise contracts with a State security force or a private security firm, the relevant provisions of these Norms (paragraphs 3 and 4 as well as the related commentary) shall be incorporated into the contract and at least those provisions should be made available upon request to stakeholders in order to ensure compliance.'

(ICC) and the International Organisation of Employers (IOE) which suggested that the Norms undermine human rights, the business sector, and the right to development.[152] They argued that 'the duties that the Sub-Commission wants to impose on private business persons constitute an extreme step towards the privatisation of human rights: its draft *Norms* has [sic] left the State out of the picture, even though the State is the duty-bearer'.[153] Referring to the 'enforcement' provisions in paragraphs 15 and 18, whereby the Norms are to be built into contracts and reparation is to be made through national legal remedies in the courts, the ICC and IOE complain that the Norms are lengthy and complex and that 'as a legal text that is to be directly enforced, it is an astonishingly vague document'.[154] The ICC/IOE publication goes on to complain that 'when the duties are as vague as those contained in the draft *Norms*, the private duty-bearer is given extraordinary power to determine the obligations of conduct. This is "privatisation" because it is the function of Government to define the do's and don'ts by enacting civil and criminal laws: it is not the prerogative of private actors'.[155] The publication complains that the balancing inherent in issues such as fulfilment of the right to water or the right to health, require legitimate government intervention, not a privatized decision. Lastly, the publication suggests that 'The promotion of business activity is a primary means for realizing the right to development'.[156] In this context, the ICC and IOE appeal to the Commission to contribute to the promotion of business, 'protecting the rights of business enterprises, and protecting the human rights of the people who manage, work for, and own businesses'.[157]

From another perspective, commentators, such as Daniel Litvin, have suggested the possibility that the Norms will deter transnationals from investing in developing countries for fear of being saddled with those governments' human rights problems and the threat of sanctions and reparations claims.[158]

> The long list of obligations, coupled with the threat of sanctions, suggests that even ethical firms could be held financially liable for myriad human rights abuses in countries in which they invest. Put another way, the 'Norms' potentially could deter responsible firms from investing in precisely those developing countries where governance and human rights problems are most acute—a perverse result, given that these countries are also most likely to be in urgent need of foreign capital and of integration with the global economy.

---

[152] See International Chamber of Commerce and International Organisation of Employers, *The Sub-Commission's Draft Norms* (March 2004) http://www.business-humanrights.org/Links/Repository/179848/jump. [153] Ibid, at 32.
[154] Ibid, at 22.   [155] Ibid, at 22.   [156] Ibid, at 40.   [157] Ibid, at 40.
[158] D. Litvin, 'Human Rights are Your Business', *Foreign Policy*, November–December 2003 (electronic version) and see also correspondence in the January number of *Foreign Policy* by J. G. Ruggie, G. Kell, J. W. Pitts, D. Litvin, and C. Hillemans, 'UN Norms on the Responsibilities of Transnational Corporations and Other Business Enterprises with Regard to Human Rights', *German Law Journal* (October 2003) (online journal): http:/www. germanlawjournal.com.

For Litvin, the other recent UN initiative is, by contrast, too soft:

> The 'Global Compact' has had various successes. For example, it has encouraged many fruitful local partnerships on development issues among companies, labor organizations and other groups. But the objection raised by NGOs—that the compact is toothless and allows multinationals to 'blue-wash' themselves (that is, to gain favorable publicity by associating themselves with the United Nations without actually improving their behavior)—has merit, too.
>
> Companies wishing to participate in this voluntary initiative face a relatively low set of hurdles: Their CEOs must write you a letter expressing support for the nine principles enunciated in the compact. The corporations must then 'set in motion changes to business operations so that the Global Compact and its principles become part of strategy, culture, and day-to-day operations.' But enforcement, such as it currently is, consists of a requirement that firms describe in their annual reports the ways in which they are fulfilling their commitments.
>
> Moreover, the two human rights provisions do little to define boundaries for companies in this area, merely declaring that firms should support human rights 'within their sphere of influence' and not be 'complicit' in abuses. The supporting literature on the compact's Web site offers some suggestions for possible actions by companies in this respect—for example, that they undertake a 'human rights assessment' of the situation in countries where they intend to do business. But obligations are not defined in any concrete fashion.[159]

One response could be that the human rights obligations in the Compact are now defined in a more concrete fashion through the Sub-Commission's elaboration and approval of the Norms.

In the end, the real effectiveness of the Norms will depend on their take-up by the business community. At the time of writing, a key group of companies had decided to 'road test' the Norms and included them in their operating practices,[160] and numerous NGOs have spoken out in support of the Norms.[161]

Simon Zadek, in his book *The Civil Corporation*, takes what he calls a 'sceptically optimistic' stance, concluding that the viability of 'civil' corporations achieving significant competitive advantage 'depends largely on two factors: the economic strength of adopting corporations, and the emergence of institutional arrangements that serve to guide and stabilize progressive market norms as they emerge'.[162] After reviewing a variety of corporate social responsibility initiatives, Zadek concluded that 'individual corporations acting alone will rarely be able to

---

[159] Litvin (2003).

[160] The Business Leaders' Initiative on Human Rights included in December 2003: ABB, Barclays, MTV Europe, National Grid Transco, Novartis, Novo Nordisk, and The Body Shop International (Christian Aid 2003: 51).

[161] See D. Weissbrodt and M. Kruger, 'Norms on the Responsibilities of Transnational Corporations and Other Business Enterprises with Regard to Human Rights' 97 *AJIL* (2003) 901–922; Statement of Support for the *UN Human Rights Norms for Business*, AI Index IOR 42/005/2004, 8 March 2004.　　　　　　　　　　　　　　　　　　　　[162] Zadek (2001: 216).

sustain *significantly* enhanced social and environmental performance for extended periods of time'.[163] He argues that the 'civil corporation will have to take a lead in creating collective processes, and codifying best practice and building adequate oversight to ensure implementation across the wider business community'. The inference he draws from his research is as follows:

> Such civil alliances and partnerships will over time seek to codify negotiated agreements into more formalized governance frameworks. The main reasons for this are to reduce transaction and other costs and increase the potential for replication by others. These new civil governance frameworks will in some instances promote public, statutory regulation and at other times seek to regulate through private standards. Those frameworks that fail to effectively codify agreements will, over time, fail and eventually collapse. Public bodies and private non-profit organizations, and indeed civil corporations, will withdraw their support and so remove a critical source of legitimacy as well as operational competences.[164]

It is too early to predict whether the Sub-Commission's Norms will enjoy sufficient take-up within the business community for them to achieve the sort of normative impact Zadek is describing. What is quite clear is that the Norms have some significance when coupled with other initiatives to determine the meaning and scope of corporations' human rights obligations. The Global Compact discussions foresee future work concerning UN procurement[165] and the Commentary to the Norms calls for a UN system-wide procurement policy using the Norms.[166] Although inclusion of human rights compliance in the procurement procedures remains a matter for ongoing discussion at the United Nations, there has in fact been an explicit inclusion of a requirement that companies comply with their human rights responsibilities in the context of UN cooperation with companies. The Guidelines for Cooperation between the United Nations and the Business

---

[163] Zadek (2001: 220).   [164] Ibid, at 221.

[165] According to the final report of the June 2004 Global Compact Leaders Summit (at 17): 'The United Nations Administration announced that the Global Compact's principles will be adopted throughout the UN in key areas, such as procurement, investment management (pension fund), facilities management and human resources.'

[166] See para. 16(c) of the Commentary to the Norms (n 138 above): 'The United Nations and its specialized agencies should also monitor implementation by using the Norms as the basis for procurement determinations concerning products and services to be purchased and with which transnational corporations and other business enterprises develop partnerships in the field.' With regard to the World Bank's sanctions committee, which monitors corruption by companies for the purposes of procurement, see A. Rigo Sureda, 'Process Integrity and Institutional Independence in International Organizations: the Inspection Panel and the Sanctions Committee of the World Bank' in L. Boisson de Chazournes, C. Romano, and R. Mackenzie (eds) *International Organizations and International Dispute Settlement: Trends and Prospects* (New York: Transnational Publishers, 2002) 165–193. There is no reason to believe that procurement decisions have to be directly dependent on the international *legal* obligations of companies. With regard to the WHO, the 'Guidelines on interaction with commercial enterprises to achieve health outcomes' EB107/20, Annex, states that in developing relationships with corporations, the WHO's reputation and values must be ensured. The aim is to avoid conflicts of interest and: 'Relationships should be avoided with commercial enterprises whose activities are incompatible with WHO's work, such as the tobacco or arms industries.' (at para. 9).

Community, issued by the Secretary-General on 17 July 2000, include paragraph 12(c), which states: 'Business entities that are complicit in human rights abuses, tolerate forced or compulsory labour or the use of child labour, are involved in the sale or manufacture of anti-personnel mines or their components, or that otherwise do not meet relevant obligations or responsibilities by the United Nations, are not eligible for partnership.'

In sum, the Norms are most likely to have an effect where they are incorporated into legal orders and effective procedures that give them 'teeth'. This may happen in a number of ways. First, where the Norms are included in contracts with subcontractors, they could be relied on in domestic courts, or in binding arbitration, in a claim for breach of contract. Second, adoption of a human rights policy based on the Norms by a business will give it a common language with which to communicate with investors, unions, employees, customers, and the local population.[167] To some extent, there may already be accountability mechanisms developed between the corporation and some of its stakeholders (for example, through a collective agreement with the union). Third, the Norms could become an interpretive device for the human rights conditions related to a procurement framework that screens out companies with poor human rights records. Whether or not the Norms develop in any of these directions, the stage has been set for the development of a normative framework that sets out the meaning of human rights obligations of corporations.[168] Any such exercise will have to, not only revisit the terrain covered by the Norms, but also consider how the international legal order has developed beyond an exclusive concern with state actors. As we shall see, evidence that international law is being used to hold corporations accountable for human rights violations is most prevalent in the United States under the Alien Tort Claims Act. Let us now turn to consider first, the role of international law, and second, the development of standards of corporate complicity under the Alien Tort Claims Act.

6.7 THE ROLE OF INTERNATIONAL LAW

National law usually applies to corporations in the country in which they operate (as we saw there may be exceptions regarding EPZs). National law may, however,

---

[167] As stated above, the Norms are being 'road-tested' by a number of corporations in a project coordinated by the Ethical Globalization Initiative. Other corporations, such as Vodaphone, have unilaterally taken on board the Norms in order to develop their own human rights policy. NGOs started using the Norms as a framework for recommendations even before their approval by the Sub-Commission, see Amnesty International, *Iraq: On Whose Behalf? Human Rights and the Economic Reconstruction Process in Iraq*, AI Index MDE 14/128/2003. See also, more recently, Amnesty International's recommendations to Caterpillar Inc in *Israel and the Occupied Territories: Under the rubble: House demolition and destruction of land and property*, AI Index MDE 15/033/2004.

[168] In 2005, after a consideration of the Norms, the Commission specifically mandated the Secretary-General's Special Representative to 'identify and clarify standards of corporate responsibility and accountability for transnational corporations and other business enterprises with regard to human rights'. UN Commission on Human Rights, Human rights and transnational corporations and other business enterprises, E/CN.4/RES/2005/69, 20 April 2005, at para. 1(a).

prove inadequate where the local authorities are unable or unwilling to penalize foreign investors for fear of losing them to less demanding sites for investment. Historically, foreign (or home) governments have had an interest in ensuring the fair treatment of 'their' multinationals when these multinational operate abroad. These governments may use their foreign policy to bring diplomatic pressure to bear on the host countries to respect the autonomy and competitiveness of multi-nationals. From the perspective of international law, this practice developed in the context of the international law of diplomatic protection for aliens abroad, and the attendant secondary rules of state responsibility which came to regulate this area. As we shall see in 6.7.1 below, with regards to state responsibility, rules were devel-oped in international law which set out when one state could claim that another state's treatment of the first state's company represented an internationally wrong-ful act giving rise to responsibility on the part of the second state. Such claims were usually brought by developed countries against developing countries in order to protect the former's companies from nationalization and discrimination under the laws of the latter. By contrast, developing countries sought to limit through law the extent to which multinationals might act in ways which they considered as con-stituting an interference in their internal affairs. In a study prepared for the UN General Assembly on the 'Progressive Development of the Principles and Norms of International Law Relating to the New International Economic Order', Georges Abi-Saab suggested that international law had to develop to create a duty on states to cooperate to control transnational corporations in this context:

> The Charter of Economic Rights and Duties, coming twelve years after resolution 1803, adds another provision (article 2, paragraph 2(b)) in this respect dealing with a particular form of private foreign investment which drew much attention in the mean-time, namely that of the transnational corporation. This provision, apart from affirming the legal power of the State to control and regulate activities of these entities with a view to ensuring their compliance with its laws and economic objectives and their non-inter-vention in its internal affairs (which is nothing but the reiteration of the power described above), prescribes a duty on all States to co-operate in rendering this control effective. Indeed as the activities of transnational corporations straddle several States, their effective control necessitates the co-operation of those States. But this is a different (positive) type of obligation than the ones usually attached to sovereign equality, and which are usually obligations of abstention or non-intervention with the exercise of the rights or powers of others.[169]

Although inter-state efforts to adopt a UN Code of Conduct for transnational corporations later ground to a halt,[170] the point remains that states will inevitably have to engage in cooperation to resolve issues relating to transnational corpora-tions. The revised OECD Guidelines, discussed above, represent an important example of such cooperation. The fact that this text is not adopted in the form of

---

[169] G. Abi-Saab, 'Progressive Development of the Principles and Norms of International Law Relating to the New International Economic Order. Report of the Secretary-General', UN Doc. A/39/504/Add.1. (1984) at 50.   [170] See Muchlinski (1999: 594).

an international treaty does not mean that there are no obligations on states with regard to corporate activity under international law. The existing public and private international law applies.

So, as we shall see in the next section, states may be, first, internationally responsible for the acts of entities which, even if they are not state organs, are actually empowered by the law of that state to exercise elements of governmental authority, and are acting in that capacity.[171] Second, where corporations are directed or controlled by a state in carrying out their conduct, the state will be internationally responsible for their acts.[172] Third, states are responsible for omissions which leave individuals devoid of human rights protection from non-state actors; the scope of these positive obligations depends on the relevant international human rights obligation and we deal with the treaty obligations in detail in Chapters 8 and 9.[173] Most of the focus in this last situation has been on the responsibilities of the state where the corporation is operating and where the harm occurs. Janet Dine, however, suggests that even the home state of a parent corporation (the state where the parent corporation is incorporated or has its headquarters) has a duty to ensure the protection of human rights through regulation of the 'way the parent exercises control over the subsidiary'.[174]

Turning to issues of jurisdiction, legal disputes concerning corporations may be resolved through binding judicial settlements. In such situations, the parties will have to rely on judges or arbitrators with jurisdiction over the dispute, and that jurisdiction may be governed by international law, as well as doctrines such as act of state and *forum non conveniens*.[175] One the one hand, international treaties may oblige states to ensure that they have jurisdiction over corporate offences. For example, the Convention for the Suppression of the Financing of Terrorism (1999) obligates states parties to 'take the necessary measures to enable a legal entity located in its territory or organized under its laws to be held liable when a person responsible for the management or control of that legal entity has, in that

---

[171] Art. 5 of the ILC's draft articles on responsibility of states for internationally wrongful acts, *Report of the ILC, 53rd Session*, adopted 10 August 2001, UN Doc. A/56/10. The UN General Assembly took note of the articles, 'commended them to the attention of Governments', and annexed the articles to its Res. 56/53, 12 December 2001; see also J. Crawford, *The International Law Commission's Articles on State Responsibility: Introduction, Text and Commentaries* (Cambridge: Cambridge University Press, 2002).

[172] See Art. 8 of the ILC's Articles on State Responsibility, discussed in detail in 6.7.1 below.

[173] With regard to obligations concerning economic, social and cultural rights, see Scott (2001).

[174] J. Dine, *Companies, International Trade and Human Rights* (Cambridge: Cambridge University Press, 2005) at 50. Dine pre-empts objections to extraterritorial legislation: 'Any objection on the grounds of imposition of different standards by the two jurisdictions could be met by a requirement that the parent should be under an obligation to require adherence *at least* to local standards and to report why it is necessary to depart from the standards of the home state.'

[175] An examination of the jurisdictional obstacles to holding corporations accountable in national courts is outside the scope of this book. For an overview of the conceptual problems and some useful suggestions for overcoming them, see C. Scott, 'Translating Torture into Transnational Tort: Conceptual Divides in the Debate on Corporate Accountability for Human Rights Harms' in C. Scott (ed) *Torture as Tort: Comparative Perspectives on the Development of Transnational Human Rights Litigation* (Oxford: Hart Publishing, 2001) 45–63.

capacity, committed an offence [set out in the treaty]'.[176] In addition, states parties must ensure that such legal entities are subject to effective sanctions.[177]

On the other hand, international treaties and institutions may create possibilities for corporations to sue for breach of investment contracts.[178] As we saw in Chapter 4, the Convention on the Settlement of Investment Disputes between States and Nationals of Other States (1965) established an International Centre for the Settlement of Investment Disputes (ICSID), whose seat is at the World Bank in Washington, DC. The facilities offered by this mechanism mean that in recent years investors have found a forum in which to submit disputes over whether their investment contracts have been breached. The ICSID Convention operates not only to facilitate conciliation or arbitration for disputes, but also ensures that awards can be enforced through the national courts of the contracting parties to the Convention. The concern of developed states to protect by law the investments of their transnational corporations is now being somewhat satisfied. Developing states are increasingly promising this sort of internationalized dispute resolution. In any event, the drive towards market liberalization has muted the voices of those governments which sought to contain and control transnational corporations; few governments want to be seen to present a hostile environment to potential investors.

Unlike the ICSID Convention (1965) and the Financing Terrorism Convention (1999), the three texts discussed in the previous sections, the OECD Guidelines, the ILO Tripartite Declaration, and the Sub-Commission's Norms, while they reflect to some extent existing international standards, cannot be described as treaties between states or between states and international organizations.[179] There is currently little appetite among states to develop new international treaties focused on the issue of human rights abuses facilitated or committed by corporations. Nor does it appear that the human rights treaty bodies are ready to interpret the UN human rights treaties to directly impose obligations on non-state actors or individuals.[180]

---

[176] Art. 5(1). Other crimes under international law may also give rise to jurisdictional questions: the on-going drafting of a Convention on Jurisdiction and Foreign Judgments in Civil and Commercial Matters has addressed the inclusion of an article which would ensure that national courts could continue to exercise their civil jurisdiction over acts which constitute serious crimes under international law. This could apply to human rights violations which constitute crimes, such as genocide committed abroad. See Special Commission of the Hague Conference on Private International Law, http://hcch.net/e/conventions/draft36e.html.   [177] Ibid, Art. 5(2).

[178] For a discussion of the way in which corporations may use the NAFTA procedures to bring states into compliance with their obligations, see G. Verhoosel, 'The Use of Investor-State Arbitration under Bilateral Investment Treaties to Seek Relief for Breaches of WTO Law' 6 *JIEL* (2003) 493–506.

[179] See the Vienna Convention on the Law of Treaties (1969) and the Vienna Convention on the Law of Treaties between States and International Organizations (1986) for definitions of treaties for the purposes of those instruments.

[180] See the UN Human Rights Committee's General Comment No. 31 (on Art. 2 of the Covenant: The Nature of the General Legal Obligation Imposed on States Parties to the Covenant) adopted 21 April 2004, UN Doc. CCPR/C/74/CRP.4/Rev.6, para. 8: 'The article 2, paragraph 1, obligations are binding on States parties and do not, as such, have direct horizontal effect as a matter of international law.'

Nevertheless, the recent treaties on corruption, financing terrorism, and trafficking by organized criminal groups show that international law treaties are indeed used to address the behaviour of legal entities such as corporations. In fact, based on the discussion in Chapter 5, concerning the obligations of non-state actors under the Treaty Establishing the European Community, it is accurate to say that at least one existing treaty already creates certain non-discrimination obligations for corporations. The extent to which European Community or other treaties are further interpreted to create obligations on non-state actors with direct effect will depend in part on the enthusiasm of the interpretive body for this sort of legal integration of international law and national enforcement. We saw in Chapter 4 that, so far, there is little evidence that ICSID panels would be receptive to human rights law. But in Chapter 5 we saw that the history of European integration has involved national courts (driven by the European Court of Justice) applying Community law with direct effect. This has involved the application of treaty provisions (not explicitly directed to non-state actors) against corporations. We shall examine, in Chapter 10, the extent to which national courts have applied human rights treaty provisions against private actors outside the EU law context. For the moment it suffices to note that treaty law has created direct obligations for corporations in the field of EU law.

6.7.1 State Responsibility for Corporations

There is a distinction in the law of state responsibility between responsibility for empowered entities and responsibility for entities under a state's control. We shall take each category in turn.[181]

The international law of state responsibility has been clearly developed to cover privatized state corporations which retain public or regulatory functions. In 2001, the draft articles on 'Responsibility of States for internationally wrongful acts' were finally adopted by the International Law Commission (ILC) and later annexed to a General Assembly Resolution.[182] Already in the early days of the process of drafting these articles, in the 1930s, the German Government was suggesting that the principles of state responsibility could apply exceptionally to situations where the state authorizes private organizations to carry out certain sovereign functions. The example given at that time was the situation where a

---

[181] We deal here only with state responsibility for corporations, and not the law on state responsibility for other entities such as 'armed bands'. The term 'armed bands' has a pedigree in the law of state responsibility and it is helpful to recall the state practice in this area when seeking to understand the emerging law with regard to what today would most likely be referred to as terrorist groups. For a historical overview of the law of state responsibility with regards to armed bands, see I. Brownlie, 'International Law and the Activities of Armed Bands' 7 *ICLQ* (1958) 712–735. The issue is summarized in the light of decisions by the International Court of Justice in the ILC's commentary to Art. 8, at pp 103–109. See also Ch 7, at 7.4 below, for a discussion of state responsibility for the acts of successful insurrectional movements who become the new government of the state, and of other movements that establish a new state.　　　　[182] A/Res/56/83, adopted 12 December 2001.

private railway company is permitted to maintain a police force. The ILC cited this example in 1974, in the context of the modern work on state responsibility. But today, in an age of privatized detention centres, prison transfers, airports, housing associations, and even water services, the image of private railway police is only a starting point.

The final ILC Commentary gives a wide scope to the sorts of entities that could fall within the scope of the relevant Article, Article 5 of the Articles on State Responsibility. This Article is aimed at attributing state responsibility for the activities of what the ILC label 'the increasingly common phenomenon of para-statal entities which exercise elements of governmental authority in place of State organs, as well as situations where former State corporations have been privatised but retain certain public or regulatory functions'.[183] Article 5 reads:

> The conduct of a person or entity which is not an organ of the State under article 4 but which is empowered by the law of that State to exercise elements of the governmental authority shall be considered an act of the State under international law, provided the person or entity is acting in that capacity in the particular instance.

The Commentary explains the intended scope of this Article:

> (2)   The generic term 'entity' reflects the wide variety of bodies which, though not organs, may be empowered by the law of a State to exercise elements of governmental authority. They may include public corporations, semi-public entities, public agencies of various kinds and even, in special cases, private companies, provided that in each case the entity is empowered by the law of the State to exercise functions of a public character normally exercised by State organs, and the conduct of the entity relates to the exercise of the governmental authority concerned. For example in some countries private security firms may be contracted to act as prison guards and in that capacity may exercise public powers such as powers of detention and discipline pursuant to a judicial sentence or to prison regulations.

An examination of the comments received from governments, and of the statements made at the General Assembly during the final debate on the articles, gives no reason to doubt that states do not consider these formulations as reflecting the current approach of international law to this topic. The state will be responsible at the international level for the acts and omissions of these privatized entities where such behaviour constitutes an internationally wrongful act, and the entity was 'acting in that capacity in the particular instance'.

We have then two cumulative tests, first, that the entity was empowered under internal law, and second, that the conduct concerned 'governmental activity and not other private or commercial activity in which the entity may engage'.[184] The state will be responsible for the acts of these empowered non-state actors where they carry out governmental activity, but not commercial activity. The example

---

[183] A/56/10, *Report of the ILC 53rd Session*, adopted 10 August 2001, Commentary to the draft articles, Art. 5, para. (1) of the Commentary, at p 92.   [184] Ibid, at para. 5.

given by the ILC is that the exercise of police powers granted to a railway company will be regarded as acts of state under international law, but activity unrelated to those powers, such as the sale of tickets, will not be attributable to the state.[185] The state is only responsible for the acts of non-state actors when they have been empowered to exercise governmental authority and are in fact acting in such a capacity.

The ILC has avoided trying to list what constitutes *elements of governmental authority*. Instead they simply state:

> Beyond a certain limit, what is regarded as 'governmental' depends on the particular society, its history and traditions. Of particular importance will be not just the content of the powers, but the way they are conferred on an entity, the purposes for which they are to be exercised and the extent to which the entity is accountable to government for their exercise. These are essentially questions of the application of a general standard to varied circumstances.[186]

Article 5 covers those entities that have been privatized or granted governmental powers by internal law. The commentary concludes in this way: 'The internal law in question must specifically authorize the conduct as involving the exercise of public authority; it is not enough that it permits activity as part of the general regulation of the affairs of the community. It is accordingly a narrow category.'[187]

When one applies this to particular contexts, the answers are not self-evident. Do corporations involved in health care come within the scope of Article 5? The answer will, it seems, depend on the 'history and traditions' of a particular society. Where health care has been considered 'governmental', and there is a degree of empowerment by internal law, then denial of the right to health could be considered an act directly attributable to the state under the law of state responsibility. This is the theoretical starting point for international lawyers.

There is, however, another category of situations which is not so narrow. Where a state actually controls or directs a company to act in a certain way, then there will be state responsibility for the acts of the company. Article 8 of the ILC Articles reads: 'The conduct of a person or group of persons shall be considered an act of a State under international law if the person or group of persons is in fact acting on the instructions of, or under the direction or control of, that State in carrying out the conduct.' The ILC Commentary specifically addresses the issue of state responsibility under international law for the acts of corporations:

> Questions arise with respect to the conduct of companies or enterprises which are State-owned and controlled. If such corporations act inconsistently with the international obligations of the State concerned the question arises whether such conduct is attributable to the State. In discussing this issue it is necessary to recall that international law acknowledges the general separateness of corporate entities at the national level, except in those cases where the 'corporate veil' is a mere device or a vehicle for fraud or evasion.

---

[185] Ibid.   [186] ILC Report (n 183 above) 2001, Commentary to Art. 5, para. 6, at p 94.
[187] Ibid, para. 7.

The fact that the State initially establishes a corporate entity, whether by a special law or otherwise, is not a sufficient basis for the attribution to the State of the subsequent conduct of that entity. Since corporate entities, although owned by and in that sense subject to the control of the State, are considered to be separate, prima facie their conduct in carrying out their activities is not attributable to the State unless they are exercising elements of governmental authority within the meaning of article 5. This was the position taken, for example, in relation to the de facto seizure of property by a State-owned oil company, in a case where there was no proof that the State used its ownership interest as a vehicle for directing the company to seize the property. On the other hand, where there was evidence that the corporation was exercising public powers, or that the State was using its ownership interest in or control of a corporation specifically in order to achieve a particular result, the conduct in question has been attributed to the State.[188]

There is a tendency to consider that the law of state responsibility exhausts the relevance of international law for corporate behaviour. This is not so. The law of state responsibility operates in a complementary way to the law that binds the corporations themselves. In addition to treaties, such as the Treaty Establishing the European Community, which may create obligations for corporations, customary international law may be seen as binding on corporations.

6.7.2   Customary International Law Obligations for Corporations

Customary international law binds all states. It is clear that where international law has criminalized certain acts, international law creates individual criminal responsibility for certain acts, now known as international crimes, such as: slavery, genocide, other crimes against humanity, certain war crimes, and torture. In an oft-quoted passage from the Nuremberg judgment, the International Tribunal determined that individuals have duties under both customary international law and under certain treaty law:

> Crimes against international law are committed by men, not by abstract entities, and only by punishing individuals who commit such crimes can the provisions of international law be enforced.[189]

For more than fifty years, governments and the International Law Commission (ILC) worked to develop a statute for an international criminal court that would have jurisdiction beyond the events of the Second World War. At different stages the issue was raised as to whether such a future court should have jurisdiction not only over individuals but over legal persons as well.[190] By 1998, the draft Statute for the International Criminal Court before the delegates at the start of the Rome Conference actually included, within the article on the jurisdiction of the Court, a

---

[188] Commentary to Art. 8, para. 6, at pp 107–108 (footnotes omitted).
[189] *Trial of Major War Criminals (Goering et al)*, International Military Tribunal (Nuremberg) Judgment and Sentence 30 September and 1 October 1946 (London: HMSO) Cmd 6964, at 41.
[190] For the details, see A. Clapham (2000: 146–172).

bracketed sentence (meaning that this was a proposal rather than a generally agreed text) which covered the possibility of trying 'legal persons, with the exception of States, when the crimes were committed on behalf of such legal persons or by their agents or representatives.'[191] This proposal was elaborated during the drafting process and the ultimate formulation read as follows:[192]

5. Without prejudice to any individual criminal responsibility of natural persons under this Statute[193] the Court may also have jurisdiction over a juridical person for a crime under this Statute.

Charges may be filed by the Prosecutor[194] against a juridical person, and the Court may render a judgement over a juridical person for the crime charged, if:

a) The charges filed by the Prosecutor against the natural person and the juridical person allege the matters referred to in subparagraphs (b) and (c); and

b) The natural person charged was in a position of control within the juridical person under the national law of the State where the juridical person was registered at the time the crime was committed; and

c) The crime was committed by the natural person acting on behalf of and with the explicit consent of that juridical person and in the course of its activities; and

d) The natural person has been convicted of the crime charged.

For the purpose of this Statute, 'juridical person' means a corporation whose concrete, real or dominant objective is seeking private profit or benefit, and not a State or other public body in the exercise of State authority, a public international body[195] or an organization registered, and acting under the national law of a State as a non-profit organization.

6. The proceedings[196] with respect to a juridical person under this article shall be in accordance with this Statute and the relevant Rules of Procedure and Evidence. The Prosecutor may file charges against the natural and juridical persons jointly or separately. The natural person and the juridical person may be jointly tried.[197]

If convicted, the juridical person may incur the penalties referred to in article 76.[198] These penalties shall be enforced in accordance with the provisions of article 99.[199]

---

[191] Draft Art. 23(5), UN Doc. A/CONF.183/2/Add.1, 14 April 1998.

[192] Working paper on Art. 23, paras 5 and 6, Conference Doc. A/Conf.183/C.1/WGGP/ L.5/Rev.2, 3 July 1998.

[193] Footnote in the original reads: 'This new phrase was inserted to replace former paragraph 6 of article 23 A/CONF.183/2/Add.1): "The criminal responsibility of legal persons shall not exclude the criminal responsibility of natural persons..."'.

[194] Footnote in the original reads: 'Language will have to be consistent with the eventual language in Part 5'.

[195] Footnote in the original reads: 'The applicable law under this Statute is defined in article 20'.

[196] Footnote in the original reads: 'Footnote 45 on page 41 of A/CONF.183/2/Add.1 states: "The terms 'proceedings' covers both investigations and prosecutions"'.

[197] Footnote in the original reads: 'N.B. The Rules of Procedure and Evidence of the International Tribunal for the Former Yugoslavia include rule 48, Joinder of accused: "Persons accused of the same or different crimes committed in the course of the same transaction may be jointly charged and tried." United Nations document IT/ 32/Rev.9, 5 July 1996. Rule 82 A reads: "In joint trials, each accused shall be accorded the same rights as if he were being tried separately"'.

[198] Footnote in the original reads: 'Once there is final agreement on articles 76 and 99, references to these articles could be deleted'.   [199] Footnote in the original reads: 'Ibid'.

These paragraphs for draft Article 23 did not survive the drafting process for the International Criminal Court in Rome. For present purposes it is sufficient to recall that, according to the Co-ordinator of the Working Group on General Principles at the Rome Diplomatic Conference 'Time was running out'.[200] The discussions had become bogged down in questions of how various national penal systems would accommodate, what was for them, the alien concept of corporate criminal responsibility.[201] The theoretical issue of the subjectivity of corporations in international law was not raised.[202] Of course, the individual responsibility of those who work for corporations remains covered by the eventual Statute of the International Criminal Court, and indeed the Prosecutor announced early on that he would be focusing on the financing of international crimes. He is reported as stating: 'Follow the trail of the money and you will find the criminals. If you stop the money then you stop the crime.'[203]

The failure in Rome to agree to bring corporations within the jurisdiction of the new Court has been seized on in the context of human rights litigation against Talisman Oil in the US Courts as evidence of a 'lack of any accepted rules or standards for corporate criminal responsibility under international law'.[204] Moreover, the explicit references in the Financing of Terrorism treaty were presented as evidence that: 'earlier criminal law conventions focusing on individual criminal responsibility are not intended to create a regime of corporate criminal responsibility'.[205] As already mentioned in Chapter 1, these arguments were rejected by Judge Schwartz, who held that 'corporations may also be held liable under international law, at least for gross human rights violations'.[206]

---

[200] P. Saland, 'International Criminal Law Principles' in R. S. Lee (ed) *The International Criminal Court, The Making of the Rome Statute* (The Hague: Kluwer, 1999) 189–216, at 199.

[201] K. Ambos, 'Article 25' in O. Triffterer (ed) *Commentary on the Rome Statute of the International Criminal Court* (Baden-Baden: Nomos, 1999) 475–493, at 478.

[202] For this debate see Ch 2, at 2.7 above.

[203] 'War Crimes Court Eyes Blood Diamond Buyers', *Reuters*, 23 September 2003.

[204] J. Crawford, *Declaration in The Presbyterian Church of Sudan et al v Talisman Energy Inc, Republic of the Sudan* Civil Action 01 CV 9882 (AGS), US District Court for the Southern District of New York, May 2002, (2002b) at para. 21. See also C. Greenwood (2002b) *Declaration in The Presbyterian Church of Sudan et al v Talisman Energy Inc, Republic of the Sudan* Civil Action 01 CV 9882 (AGS), US District Court for the Southern District of New York, 7 May 2002, filed 13 May 2002, at 8.   [205] Crawford (2002b) at para. 15.

[206] *The Presbyterian Church of Sudan et al v Talisman Energy Inc, Republic of the Sudan* Civil Action 01 CV 9882 (AGS), US District Court for the Southern District of New York at p 47 of the Order of 19 March 2003. The two expert declarations submitted by Talisman Oil argued against the suggestion that international law directly imposes responsibility or liability on corporations. The declarations requested by the Talisman Oil company were filed with the Court in May 2002. See the separate declarations of Crawford (2002b) and Greenwood (2002b). On 29 June 2004, the US Supreme Court decided in *Sosa v Alvarez Machain* that the Alien Tort Claims Act did not create a cause of action with regard to a short period of arbitrary detention. The opinion includes a footnote (fn 20) which simply states: 'A related consideration is whether international law extends the scope of liability for a violation of a given norm to the perpetrator being sued, if the defendant is a private actor such as a corporation or individual. Compare *Tel-Oren v. Libyan Arab Republic*, 726 F 2d 774, 791–795 (CADC 1984) (Edwards, J., concurring) (insufficient consensus in 1984 that torture by

It is possible to begin a new construction of corporate liability in international law. Celia Wells and Juanita Elias have highlighted how traditional assumptions about law have hampered progress in this field:

> ... it is not such an imaginative leap to conceive a corporation as the subject of international law. While the mind-set of the criminal lawyer is to think about individuals, that of the international lawyer was until the middle of the last century, to think about states. Yet the [International Criminal Court] and other war crimes tribunals finalize the break in that mould by addressing specifically the crimes of individual human agents. For the international lawyer to embrace a corporate entity is therefore less of a conceptual hurdle than for a domestic jurisdiction to move away from the individual. As people become more accustomed to conceiving of collective entities as wrongdoers, the conceptual gulf may become much less wide.[207]

Are we only talking then about a leap of imagination? In part yes, the imagined worlds of criminal and international law are hindering a vision whereby corporations are liable under international law. But, on the other hand, we are apparently faced with a dearth of evidence that international law seeks to ensure the liability of corporate actors. It is suggested here that we should look again at the purported absence of evidence to see if it really does point to a legal vacuum. Let us reconsider how international treaties address corporate behaviour.

6.7.3 International Treaties that Demand Action against Legal Persons

Let us first look at some international treaties that address criminal jurisdiction over 'legal persons' and 'corporations'. For example, Article 9 of the Council of Europe Convention on the Protection of the Environment Through Criminal Law (1998) provides that liability can flow for the corporation as a result of a finding of liability for a natural person or organ of the entity involved (Article 9).[208] The Explanatory Report states:

> Article 9 deals with the liability of legal persons. It is a fact that a major part of environmental crimes is committed within the framework of legal persons, while practice reveals serious difficulties in prosecuting natural persons acting on behalf of these legal persons.

---

private actors violates international law), with *Kadic v Karadžić*, 70 F 3d 232, 239–241 (CA2 1995) (sufficient consensus in 1995 that genocide by private actors violates international law).' Slip opinion, at 38.

[207] 'Catching the Conscience of the King: Corporate Players of the International Stage' in P. Alston (ed) *Non-State Actors and Human Rights* (Oxford: Oxford University Press, 2005) 141–175, at 155.

[208] Art. 9—Corporate liability: '1. Each Party shall adopt such appropriate measures as may be necessary to enable it to impose criminal or administrative sanctions or measures on legal persons on whose behalf an offence referred to in Articles 2 or 3 has been committed by their organs or by members thereof or by another representative.   2. Corporate liability under paragraph 1 of this article shall not exclude criminal proceedings against a natural person.   3. Any State may, at the time of signature or when depositing its instrument of ratification, acceptance, approval or accession, by a

For example, in view of the largeness of corporations and the complexity of structures of the organisation, it becomes more and more difficult to identify a natural person who may be held responsible (in a criminal law sense) for the offence. Furthermore, if an agent of management is sentenced, the sanction can easily be compensated by the legal person.

The international trend at present seems to support the general recognition of corporate liability in criminal law, even in countries which only a few years ago formally adopted the principle according to which corporations cannot commit criminal offences. Therefore, the present provision of the Convention is in harmony with these recent tendencies, e.g. the recommendations of international institutions (see 1994 AIDP Recommendations—Portland/Rio de Janeiro) and Recommendation No. R (88) 18 of the Committee of Ministers of the Council of Europe. The provision leaves, however, open to the States to impose 'criminal or administrative sanctions or measures on legal persons' corresponding to their legal traditions.

Article 9, paragraph 1 refers to corporate liability of legal persons. This type of liability necessitates clarification regarding its three conditions. The first condition is that an environmental criminal offence must have been committed, as specified in Article 2 (intentionally) or Article 3 (by negligence). The second condition is that the offence must have been committed 'on behalf of' the legal person. The third condition, which serves to limit this liability, requires the involvement of 'an organ, a member of its organs or other representatives' in the criminal offence, assuming that those physical persons referred to are legally or by fact in such position which may engage the liability of the legal person. Violations of the supervisorial duties are in this respect sufficient.

Article 9, paragraph 2 clarifies that corporate liability does not exclude individual liability. In a concrete case, different spheres of liability may be established at the same time, for example the responsibility of an organ etc. separately from the liability of the legal person as a whole. Individual liability may be combined with any of these categories of liability.

The explanatory report is cited *in extenso* to demonstrate that international definitions of corporate offences giving rise to corporate liability are seen as part of the effectiveness of international law. The argument is hardly very different from the way in which inter-state human rights treaties came to generate or reflect the offences of genocide or torture for individuals.

A similar approach with regard to *offences* by legal persons is taken in the Criminal Convention on Corruption adopted in the context of the Council of Europe (but open to other States such as Canada, Japan, Mexico, and the United States).[209] Article 1(d) of the Convention states: ' "legal person" shall mean any

declaration addressed to the Secretary General of the Council of Europe, declare that it reserves the right not to apply paragraph 1 of this article or any part thereof or that it applies only to offences specified in such declaration.'

[209] Art. 18 of the Convention reads: '1. Each party shall adopt such legislative and other measures as may be necessary to ensure that legal persons can be held liable for the criminal offences of active bribery, trading in influence and money laundering established in accordance with this Convention, committed for their benefit and by any natural person, acting either individually or as part of an organ of the legal person, who has a leading position within the legal person, based on: a power of representation of the legal person; or an authority to take decisions on behalf of the legal person; or an

entity having such status under the applicable national law, except for States or other public bodies in the exercise of State authority and for public international organizations.' This Convention is further evidence that international law has addressed behaviour by corporations and demanded, in the context of a treaty, that such legal persons are to be prosecuted for crimes defined in international treaties at the national level in different types of legal orders. Thus international treaties can overcome the comparative law problems of demanding trials against such legal persons by referring to the national law defining the status of the legal person. Moreover, this Council of Europe Corruption Convention seeks to address many of the concerns expressed by certain governments in the context of the Rome negotiations. It excludes both public bodies in the exercise of state authority, and public international organizations. The controversial problem of crimes of states is thereby expressly excluded and apparent practical difficulties related to holding corporations accountable for violations of international law are resolved through a construction of the 'nationality' of the corporation based on relevant domestic law.[210] The issue of corruption and the liability of legal persons is also the subject of a new UN Convention against Corruption (2003).[211] Here the treaty requires that legal persons be held liable, but states are left a choice of criminal, civil, or administrative methods to ensure liability.[212] Nevertheless, the method adopted must be dissuasive.

In the context of terrorism, a provision in the UN Convention on the Suppression of the Financing of Terrorism 1999 links corporate liability to a finding that an individual has committed the offence defined in the treaty.[213] The difficulties faced by

authority to exercise control within the legal person; as well as for involvement of such a natural person as accessory or instigator in the above mentioned offences.   2. Apart from the cases already provided for in paragraph 1, each Party shall take the necessary measures to ensure that a legal person can be held liable where the lack of supervision or control by a natural person referred to in paragraph 1 has made possible the commission of the criminal offences mentioned in paragraph 1 for the benefit of that legal person by a natural person under its authority.   3. Liability of a legal person under paragraphs 1 and 2 shall not exclude criminal proceedings against natural persons who are perpetrators, instigators of, or accessories to, the criminal offences mentioned in paragraph 1.'

[210] On the problem of the 'nationality' of corporations under international law, see Clapham (2000: 179–188).

[211] Adopted by the UN General Assembly, 31 October 2003, UN Doc. A/58/422.

[212] Art. 26—Liability of legal persons: '1. Each State Party shall adopt such measures as may be necessary, consistent with its legal principles, to establish the liability of legal persons for participation in the offences established in accordance with this Convention.   2. Subject to the legal principles of the State Party, the liability of legal persons may be criminal, civil or administrative.   3. Such liability shall be without prejudice to the criminal liability of the natural persons who have committed the offences.   4. Each State Party shall, in particular, ensure that legal persons held liable in accordance with this article are subject to effective, proportionate and dissuasive criminal or non-criminal sanctions, including monetary sanctions.'

[213] Art. 5. Offences of terrorism are defined by reference to the terrorism treaties contained in the annex as well as a general offence: '(a) An act which constitutes an offence within the scope of and as defined in one of the treaties listed in the annex; or (b) Any other act intended to cause death or serious bodily injury to a civilian, or to any other person not taking an active part in the hostilities in a situation of armed conflict, when the purpose of such act, by its nature or context, is to intimidate a population, or to compel a government or an international organization to do or to abstain from doing any act.' Art. 2(1).

states that do not know corporate *criminal* responsibility in their national legal orders
have led to recent criminal law treaties, such as the International Convention for
the Suppression of the Financing of Terrorism (1999), demanding that states take
measures to ensure the liability of legal entities with 'criminal, civil or administrative
sanctions'.[214] This approach is currently replicated in the UN draft comprehensive convention on international terrorism.[215] Building on this treaty-based
approach, the Security Council decided, in September 2001, that states shall:

[1] (a) Prevent and suppress the financing of terrorist acts;
(b) Criminalize the wilful provision or collection, by any means, directly or indirectly, of
funds by their nationals or in their territories with the intention that the funds should be
used, or in the knowledge that they are to be used, in order to carry out terrorist
acts; . . . [216]

Security Council Resolution 1373 goes on to create a number of other obligations
with regard to those who fund those who participate in terrorist acts. States shall:

[1] (d) Prohibit their nationals or any persons and entities within their territories from
making any funds, financial assets or economic resources or financial or other related
services available, directly or indirectly, for the benefit of persons who commit or
attempt to commit or facilitate or participate in the commission of terrorist acts, of entities owned or controlled, directly or indirectly, by such persons and of persons and entities acting on behalf of or at the direction of such persons; . . .

Note that the prohibition is aimed not only at natural persons but explicitly
includes 'entities'. Security Council Resolution 1373, as a decision which is binding on states,[217] creates an obligation for all states to prevent and suppress the
financing of terrorist acts. In addition, states must freeze without delay the funds
and assets of 'entities owned or controlled directly or indirectly by' persons who
commit, or attempt to commit, terrorist acts or participate in or facilitate the
commission of terrorist acts.

There is a similar approach in the related field of transnational criminal
organizations. Certain activity becomes an offence within the UN Convention

---

The annex lists the following treaties: 1. Convention for the Suppression of Unlawful Seizure of Aircraft
(1970). Convention for the Suppression of Unlawful Acts against the Safety of Civil Aviation (1971).
Convention on the Prevention and Punishment of Crimes against Internationally Protected Persons,
including Diplomatic Agents (1973). International Convention against the Taking of Hostages (1979).
Convention on the Physical Protection of Nuclear Material (1980). Protocol for the Suppression of
Unlawful Acts of Violence at Airports Serving International Civil Aviation, supplementary to the
Convention for the Suppression of Unlawful Acts against the Safety of Civil Aviation (1988).
Convention for the Suppression of Unlawful Acts against the Safety of Maritime Navigation (1988).
Protocol for the Suppression of Unlawful Acts against the Safety of Fixed Platforms located on the
Continental Shelf (1988). International Convention for the Suppression of Terrorist Bombings (1997).

[214] Art. 5(3).
[215] See draft Art. 9. Report of the Ad Hoc Committee established by General Assembly resolution
51/210 of 17 December 1996 Sixth session (28 January–1 February 2002) GAOR 57th Session,
Supplement No. 37 (A/57/37) at 10.   [216] Res. 1373 (2001) 28 September 2001.
[217] See Art. 25 of the UN Charter (1945).

against Transnational Organized Crime for the purposes of extradition and national jurisdiction over an extraterritorial crime. But the tendency is to go beyond the prosecution of individuals and to sanction legal persons. The legal persons targeted are not the criminal organizations as such, but those organizations which facilitate or participate in the criminal activities of the criminal organization. It is perhaps in this realm that one finds the most appropriate provisions on the regulation of corporate conduct with regard to international offences. The Convention criminalizes participation in the activities of an organized criminal group, as well as accomplice liability in the form of 'organizing, directing, aiding, abetting, facilitating or counselling'.[218] The liability of legal persons is specifically provided for in similar terms to the terrorism convention just discussed.[219]

In sum, there are numerous treaties that target corporate behaviour as offences under the particular treaty, and then leave it to states to determine an effective way to hold these corporations liable.[220] It is therefore arguable that international law has, in fact, developed regimes for ensuring the liability of corporations. It is true that most of these treaties do not actually criminalize corporate conduct in the same way that they demand a recognition of the criminal responsibility of the individual; but the treaties insist on liability nevertheless. The fact that treaties leave states a choice as to how to sanction a corporation does not undermine the aim of the international treaty, which is to outlaw the relevant corporate conduct. It is suggested that there is a temptation to make too much of the fact that some states prefer criminal sanctions while others focus on administrative sanctions. The fact that there is no uniform national method for holding corporations liable for offences defined in international treaties, should not necessarily lead to the conclusion that there is no liability in international law for corporations engaging in behaviour which violates international norms contained in treaties that specifically target legal persons.

We might conclude on this point by noting that, when the International Military Tribunal (IMT) in Nuremberg determined that individuals had obligations under international law, they had hardly any treaties in front of them that pointed to such individual liability under international law. Treaties dealing with the laws of war were silent on the need to criminalize violations of the international laws of war. The judges of the IMT went on to determine that this law applied directly to individuals. In the light of the plethora of provisions which address the behaviour of corporations, there is certainly room today to reverse the assumption that corporations have absolutely no liability under general international law. Although the jurisdictional possibilities are limited under existing international tribunals, where national law allows for claims based on violations of international law, it is becoming clear that international law obligates non-state actors. Claims against corporations for violations of international law have already

---

[218] See Art. 5.   [219] See Art. 10
[220] For further examples, see Clapham (2000: 172–178).

been the subject of a number of decisions in the federal courts of the United States. We now turn to look at some of these cases in order to understand the way corporate complicity for violations of international law has been developed by the US courts in recent years. The Alien Tort Claims Act is discussed more generally in Chapter 10.

6.8   THE ALIEN TORT CLAIMS ACT IN THE UNITED STATES

This vision that corporations can violate international law has been central to an interesting string of cases before the US courts under a piece of US legislation known as the Alien Tort Claims Act (ATCA) 1789 (also known as the Alien Tort Statute (ATS)).[221] The origins of this piece of legislation are misty and have been the subject of conjecture as legal scholars have applied their imaginations to events over 200 years ago.[222] In 2004, the Supreme Court stated that one can draw the following inference from the history:

> Congress intended the ATS to furnish jurisdiction for a relatively modest set of actions alleging violations of the law of nations. Uppermost in the legislative mind appears to have been offenses against ambassadors...violations of safe conduct were probably understood to be actionable...and individual actions arising out of prize captures and piracy may well have also been contemplated.[223]

Nevertheless, the effects of the Act today remain very real, as corporations find themselves in the role of defendants facing multi-million dollar lawsuits. The terms of the ATCA confer upon the Federal District Courts original jurisdiction over 'any civil action by an alien for a tort only, committed in violation of the law of nations'. A number of claims are currently pending or on appeal in relation to various oil companies accused of, among other things, forced labour, torture, and rape.[224] Other claims relate to detention facilities run by private corporations with regard to immigration centres, and most recently, claims against the private contractors responsible for the Abu Ghraib prison in Iraq.[225] We deal with wider issues concerning the ATCA in Chapter 10, in section 10.1.1.

The application of this statute to the activities of multinational corporations abroad is not without its critics.[226] Indeed, the US and other Governments have

---

[221]   28 US Code [USC] §1350.

[222]   A.-M. Burley, 'The Alien Tort Statute and the Judiciary Act of 1789: A Badge of Honor' 83(3) *AJIL* (1989) 461–493.

[223]   US Supreme Court, *Sosa v Alvarez Machain* Opinion of 29 June 2004, at 25 of slip opinion.

[224]   S. Zia-Zarifi, 'Suing Multinational Corporations in the U.S. for Violating International Law' 4(1) *UCLA JIL & FA* (1999) 81–148.

[225]   See 'Human right and the court' *International Herald Tribune*, 6 July 2004, at 6. Some of the cases concerning detention centres are discussed in Ch 10, at 10.1.2 below.

[226]   P. Z. Thadani, 'Regulating corporate human rights abuses: Is *UNOCAL* the answer?' 42(2) *William and Mary Law Review* (2002) 619–646.

filed objections in the Federal Courts objecting to the exercise of such jurisdiction.[227] But the evolving law on the application of the ATCA is affecting not only the cases before the courts but also the sense of the parameters of legal liability for companies more generally. In fact, the human rights claims against companies are not restricted to the ATCA. Other jurisdictional statutes include the Torture Victims Protection Act[228] and the Racketeer Influenced and Corrupt Organizations Act.[229] Both of these Acts are being used in the US courts against multinationals accused of participating in human rights violations outside the United States.[230]

The purpose of the following examination of one particular case, the *Unocal* case, is to understand the evolving judicial determination of the scope of corporate complicity in violations of international law. In the simple situation where a corporation's activities actually constitute genocide or slavery, the issue is clear. The corporation is said to have violated international criminal law and can, at present, apparently be held accountable in the US courts under the ATCA. The US courts have been gradually refining the list of violations of the 'law of nations' that directly attach in this way to non-state actors as such. Accordingly, recent rulings have determined that genocide, slave trading, slavery, forced labour, and war crimes are actionable even in the absence of any connection to state action.[231] In addition, according to the *Kadic v Karadžić* decision in the US courts, where rape, torture, and summary execution are committed (even in isolation)[232] these crimes 'are actionable under the Alien Tort Act, without regard to state action, to

---

[227] The complaint filed against Exxon Mobil regarding activity in Aceh, Indonesia in the US District Court for the District of Columbia on 11 June 2001, asks the Court to enjoin 'Defendants from further engaging in human rights abuses against Plaintiffs and their fellow villagers in complicity with the Indonesian Government and military.' For the full text of the complaint, see http://www. laborrights.org (last updated 31 August 2001). The US State Department argued that the case should not proceed as anti-terrorist efforts in Indonesia might be 'imperiled in numerous ways if Indonesia and its officials curtailed cooperation in response to perceived disrespect for its sovereign interests'. 'State Dept. opposes suit against Exxon over Indonesian venture' *International Herald Tribune*, 8 August 2002, 4. See also 'Human rights and terror' and K. Roth, 'U.S. hypocrisy in Indonesia', both in *International Herald Tribune*, 14 August 2002, 4. See also R. Verkaik, 'Ministers attempt to halt US human rights cases against British firms' *The Independent*, 11 February 2004, 2, regarding the *Sosa* case where the Governments of the UK, Australia, and Switzerland filed an *amicus* brief objecting to an interpretation of the ATCA that would permit the US courts to exercise jurisdiction over individuals and corporations where there was no significant link with the US. Brief in support of the Petitioner of 23 January 2004.   [228] 28 USC §1350.

[229] 18 USC §1961.

[230] See S. Joseph, *Corporations and Transnational Human Rights Litigation* (Oxford: Hart Publishing, 2004) at 61–63, who notes (at 61) that the courts have interpreted the term 'individual' in the Torture Victim Protection Act 'as encompassing an artificial person, including a corporation'. She refers to *Sinaltrainal v Coca-Cola* 256 F Supp 2d 1345 (SD Fla 2003) 1359 and *Estate of Rodrigues v Drummond* 256 Supp 2d 1250 (WD Al 2003) 1266–1267. On the Racketeer Influenced and Corrupt Organizations Act, see Joseph (2004: 78–81).

[231] *Wiwa v Royal Dutch Shell Petroleum (Shell)* US District Court for the Southern District of New York (28 February 2002) 39. See also *Doe I v Unocal Corp* (18 September 2002) paras 3ff.

[232] In other words, they need not be committed as part of a systematic or widespread attack so as to qualify as crimes against humanity.

the extent they were committed in pursuit of genocide or war crimes'.[233] According to *Kadic v Karadžić* an alien can sue in tort before the US Federal Courts under the ATCA with regard to any of these international crimes. In fact, the list need not be exclusive because international criminal law continues to evolve.[234]

However, cases of a corporation being sued under the ATCA in the US courts as the primary perpetrator of international crimes are rare and, in any event, would be likely to be settled out of court if the facts were clear. Most of the cases that have recently been contested before the US courts concern situations where corporations are alleged to have aided and abetted a state in governmental violations of international criminal law.[235] In other words, the cases turn on accomplice liability, or complicity.

6.8.1   Corporate Complicity in Violations of Human Rights Law

The corporate complicity cases before the US courts have coloured the general approach to the understanding of the scope of corporate responsibility and accountability. Although the scope of the legal liability under the Alien Tort Claims Act is not congruent with the expectations currently placed on corporations by the corporate responsibility movement, the evolving case-law at least points to a minimum standard that companies transgress at their peril, as there may be a group of plaintiffs ready to sue in the US courts. In fact, it may be precisely the prospect of multi-million dollar suits enforceable in the jurisdiction of the United States that is provoking the corporate backlash against moves to translate promises of corporate social responsibility into legally binding international norms.

In addition to the current cases before the US courts, reasoning based on the premise that companies have liabilities arising out of international law has been behind the claims and eventual settlements involving the Swiss banks and German industries, as well as litigation in the United States against Japanese companies in relation to issues of slave labour in the Second World War.[236]

---

[233] *Kadic v Karadžić* 70 F 3d 232 (2d Cir, 1995) pp 243–244, cited with approval in *Doe v Unocal* 2002, para. 3.

[234] See, e.g. with regard to non-state actor torture, *Prosecutor v Kunarac, Kovac and Vukovic* Cases IT–96–23 and IT–96–23/1–A, Judgment of the International Criminal Tribunal for the former Yugoslavia (Appeals Chamber), 12 June 2002, para. 148 (discussed in Ch 10, at 10.1.1 below).

[235] One recent case has suggested that the ATCA cannot be read as including aiding and abetting, see *Re South African Apartheid Litigation*, US District Court, Southern District of New York, 29 November 2004, Sprizzo, DJ. This conclusion was explicitly rejected by another judge in the Southern District of New York in *The Presbyterian Church of Sudan et al v Talisman Energy Inc* [2005] WL 1385326 (SDNY) Opinion and Order of 13 June 2005, at para. 6.

[236] M. J. Bazyler, 'Nuremberg in America: Litigating the Holocaust in United States Courts' 34 *URLR* (2000) 1–283; and A. Ramasastry, 'Corporate Complicity: From Nuremberg to Rangoon An Examination of Forced Labor Cases and Their Impact on the Liability of Multinational Corporations' 20 *Berkeley JIL* (2002) 91–159. The German Slave Labour Fund, jointly established by Germany and the firms, currently stands at US$5.2bn. These claims, together with similar claims made against the Swiss banks in the Holocaust Victims Assets Litigation (which have resulted in a

6.8.2   Corporate Complicity in the *Unocal* Ruling

There are various cases and rulings regarding the litigation concerning Unocal and its activity in Myanmar. The most important for present purposes is the ruling of the US Court of Appeals for the Ninth Circuit, filed 18 September 2002. This ruling no longer stands as the case was vacated,[237] and the Court of Appeals were due to deliver a new ruling when the case was suddenly settled for an undisclosed sum.[238] Even if the ruling no longer stands, the reasoning is worth examining; in the 2002 *Unocal* ruling, the Court of Appeals elaborated a number of approaches concerning the elements of corporate complicity as they apply in a suit under the Alien Tort Claims Act (ATCA) alleging corporate liability for violations of international law.

The plaintiffs (Burmese nationals) alleged that the Myanmar Military had subjected them to forced labour, murder, rape, and torture in connection with the construction of the Yadana gas pipeline project. There are factual disputes concerning: whether Unocal knew that the Myanmar Military were providing security for the project; the influence of Unocal over the Military; and whether Unocal knew that the Military were committing human rights violations in connection with the project. The Court of Appeals, however, clarified a number of issues. First, on the question of whether a private actor such as Unocal could be liable for the violations of international law at issue, the Court of Appeals reaffirmed earlier decisions by the US courts, which stated that some violations of international law require no state involvement and can be committed by private actors acting on their own.[239] Second, the Court concluded that forced labour is a modern form of slavery. In this way, forced labour falls among the international crimes that give rise to responsibility under international law, even in the absence of state action.

Swiss fund of US$1.25bn), are based on the law developed during the Nuremberg trials of the industrialists and its application in the US courts. In and around 1999, more than 30 cases were brought against US, German, and Swiss companies, alleging complicity in Nazi era crimes, based on the original trials of the industrialists in Nuremberg.

[237] See B. Stephens, 'Upsetting Checks and Balances: The Bush Administration's Efforts to Limit Human Rights Litigation' 17 *Harv HRJ* (2004) 170–205, at 184: 'The Ninth Circuit then voted to re-hear the case en banc, apparently to resolve this choice-of-law dispute; an order preceding oral argument stated that "the primary issue" the parties should address at oral argument was whether the federal courts should apply international law or federal common law to determine aiding-and-abetting liability.'

[238] Daphne Eviatar points to the fact that Unocal sued both its primary and re-insurers to suggest that Unocal's costs were significantly higher than the US$15m that the insurers would reimburse as an initial loss. 'A Big Win for Human Rights' *The Nation*, 9 May 2005 (internet version).

[239] 'Thus, under *Kadic*, even crimes like rape, torture, and summary execution, which by themselves require state action for ATCA liability to attach, do not require state action when committed in furtherance of other crimes like slave trading, genocide or war crimes, which by themselves do not require state action for ATCA liability to attach. We agree with this view and apply it below to Plaintiffs' various ATCA claims.' *John Roe III; John Roe VII; John VIII; John Roe X, v Unocal Corp; Union Oil Rswl Co of California* US Court of Appeals for the Ninth Circuit, filed 18 September 2002, at 14210, para. 3.

Third, turning to the allegations of complicity in the actual case, the ruling continued:

> We hold that the standard for aiding and abetting under the ATCA is, as discussed below, knowing practical assistance or encouragement that has a substantial effect on the perpetration of the crime. We further hold that a reasonable factfinder could find that Unocal's conduct met this standard.[240]

On this point, the Court of Appeals disagreed with the Court below, which had demanded a higher test, that of 'active participation' in the forced labour. What makes the case particularly interesting from an international perspective is that the tests have mostly been derived from the prosecutions for international crimes which followed the Second World War and the more recent international prosecutions by the *ad hoc* International Tribunals, established by the UN Security Council, with responsibility for prosecuting crimes committed in the former Yugoslavia and Rwanda. The complicity criteria adopted by the majority were based not on national law, but on international law.[241]

6.8.3   The *Actus Reus* of Complicity in the *Unocal* Case

The ruling gave an indication of the sort of *practical assistance* which will be evidence of the material element of the crime:

> The evidence also supports the conclusion that Unocal gave practical assistance to the Myanmar Military in subjecting Plaintiffs to forced labor.[242] The practical assistance took the form of hiring the Myanmar Military to provide security and build infrastructure along the pipeline route in exchange for money or food. The practical assistance also took the form of using photos, surveys, and maps in daily meetings to show the Myanmar Military where to provide security and build infrastructure.[243]

The Court found that this assistance had a *substantial effect* on the perpetration of the forced labour, and that the forced labour would most probably not have occurred in the same way 'without someone hiring the Myanmar Military to

---

[240] US Court of Appeals for the Ninth Circuit, at para. 4.

[241] The decision stated at para. 7: 'We find recent decisions by the International Criminal Tribunal for the former Yugoslavia and the International Criminal Tribunal for Rwanda especially helpful for ascertaining the current standard for aiding and abetting under international law as it pertains to the ATCA.'

[242] Footnote 29 in the original reads: 'The evidence further supports the conclusion that Unocal gave "encouragement" to the Myanmar Military in subjecting Plaintiffs to forced labor. The daily meetings with the Myanmar Military to show it where to provide security and build infrastructure, despite Unocal's knowledge that the Myanmar Military would probably use forced labor to provide these services, may have encouraged the Myanmar Military to actually use forced labor for the benefit of the Project. Similarly, the payments to the Myanmar Military for providing these services, despite Unocal's knowledge that the Myanmar Military had actually used forced labor to provide them, may have encouraged the Myanmar Military to continue to use forced labor in connection with the Project.'   [243] Ibid, at para. 11.

provide security, and without someone showing them where to do it'.[244] The Court noted that this conclusion:

> ... is supported by the admission of Unocal Representative Robinson that '[o]ur assertion that [the Myanmar Military] has not *expanded and amplified its usual methods* around the pipeline *on our behalf* may not withstand much scrutiny,' and by the admission of Unocal President Imle that '[i]f forced labor goes hand and glove with the military yes there will be *more forced labor.*' (Emphasis added [in original].)[245]

The Court applied a variation on a causation test. The participation by the company need not actually cause the violation of international law, but the assistance or encouragement has to be such that, without such participation, the violations *most probably* would not have occurred *in the same way*.

6.8.4   The *Mens Rea* Required for Complicity in the *Unocal* Case

The US Court of Appeals examined the evidence and applied a reasonable knowledge test. The requisite mental element for corporate complicity in these circumstances seems to be that the company knew or should have known that its acts assisted in the crime. The fact that a company benefits from the principal perpetrator's human rights violations has been emphasized and creates and important nexus:

> As for the *mens rea* of aiding and abetting, the International Criminal Tribunal for the former Yugoslavia held that what is required is actual or constructive (i.e., 'reasonabl[e]') 'knowledge that [the accomplice's] actions will assist the perpetrator in the commission of the crime.' *Furundžija* at para. 245. Thus, 'it is not necessary for the accomplice to share the *mens rea* of the perpetrator, in the sense of positive intention to commit the crime.' *Id.* In fact, it is not even necessary that the aider and abettor knows the precise crime that the principal intends to commit. *See id.* Rather, if the accused 'is aware that one of a number of crimes will probably be committed, and one of those crimes is in fact committed, he has intended to facilitate the commission of that crime, and is guilty as an aider and abettor.' *Id.* [footnote omitted]

> Similarly, for the *mens rea* of aiding and abetting, the International Criminal Tribunal for Rwanda required that 'the accomplice knew of the assistance he was providing in the commission of the principal offence.' *Musema* at para. 180. The accomplice does not have to have had the intent to commit the principal offense. *See id.* at para. 181. It is sufficient that the accomplice 'knew or had reason to know' that the principal had the intent to commit the offense. *Id.* at para.182.[246] ...

> [A] reasonable factfinder could also conclude that Unocal's conduct met the *mens rea* requirement of aiding and abetting as we define it today, namely, actual or constructive (i.e., reasonable) knowledge that the accomplice's actions will assist the perpetrator in the commission of the crime. The District Court found that '[t]he evidence does suggest that Unocal knew that forced labor was being utilized and that the Joint Venturers

---

[244] Ibid, at para. 12.   [245] Ibid, at para. 12.   [246] At para. 7.

benefitted from the practice.' *Doe/Roe II*, 110 F. Supp. 2d at 1310. Moreover, Unocal knew or should reasonably have known that its conduct—including the payments and the instructions where to provide security and build infrastructure—would assist or encourage the Myanmar Military to subject Plaintiffs to forced labor.[247]

This test puts companies on notice that they could be held liable for human rights abuses where they should have known that their conduct would encourage a government to commit certain human rights abuses, including forced labour. The reaction from the US business community has been to challenge the jurisdiction of the courts and the scope of the complicity test. On 5 April 2004, the *New York Times* printed on the op-ed page a notice entitled 'The Business of Human Rights', paid for by the National Foreign Trade Council. The subtitle asked: 'Suppose a foreign country engages in human rights abuses against its own people. Should corporations that happen to do business there be held liable?'[248] Various arguments were suggested for why the US Supreme Court should 'reign in' the use of the Alien Tort Claims Act.[249] The arguments presented against the use of the Act to hold companies liable included the following presentation. First, because it interferes with foreign affairs by requiring US courts to judge the actions of foreign governments. Second, because it discourages foreign investment in situations where companies could promote human rights through their economic and social contributions. Third, because it permits suits against 'bystander' companies. The complaint here is that the human rights abuses occur outside the control of the company:

> ... many of the suits challenge conduct that US corporations do not and cannot control. In fact often the suits do not even allege that the company directly committed any human rights abuses. Instead the companies often face legal actions simply because they relied upon the foreign government's security services to protect their workers in dangerous, war-torn regions.

Here we see the nub of the problem for some companies. Companies are indeed being accused of relying on security services that abuse human rights. The *Unocal* case established at a preliminary phase that, by failing to react to such abuses, companies can be considered under international law to have aided and abetted the human rights abuses. They can be considered complicit in specific violations.

---

[247] At para. 13.   [248] *New York Times*, 5 April 2004, at A19.

[249] The aim of the piece was to influence the Supreme Court in the *Sosa v Alvarez* case, mentioned above. See also the *amici curiae* brief filed by Australia, Switzerland, and the UK which argued that they were opposed to 'broad assertions of extraterritorial jurisdiction over aliens arising out of foreign disputes because such litigations can interfere with national sovereignty and impose legal uncertainty and costs', Brief of 23 January 2004, at 2. Later the brief concludes by stating: 'As global trading and investment nations, Australia, Switzerland and the United Kingdom are concerned not only about interference with their own domestic dispute resolution choices, but also that their enterprises and individuals are likely to be threatened with large damage claims because they have carried on normal business activities in a country that a US court believes has engaged in violations of the court's version of the "law of nations".' Brief of 23 January at 28. In the end the Supreme Court left open the issue of non-state actor accountability for violations of international law and the appropriate complicity criteria.

The logic can be be extended to certain crimes under international law including torture, crimes against humanity, and war crimes.

6.8.5 The Application in the *Unocal* Case of a Non-Criminal Law Test for Third-Party Liability for Violations of International Law

In a concurring opinion, Judge Reinhardt spelt out an alternative set of tests for determining the liability of Unocal in such a situation. Responding to the alternative pleadings of the plaintiffs, he examined three tests under US tort law. This examination of tort law is interesting, even if the majority opinion relied purely on international criminal law. Whatever the situation in US law, other jurisdictions may follow the international criminal law tests for accomplice liability when corporate complicity in violations of human rights arises under their criminal jurisdictions.[250] On the other hand, where corporate conduct cannot be described as criminal under any legal system, Judge Reinhardt's opinion may be quite helpful.

Judge Reinhardt's concurring opinion refers to three principles: joint venture, agency, and reckless disregard. In considering these principles we should bear in mind the extent to which such principles are common to major legal systems and therefore possibly applicable in international law as general principles of law. With regard to joint venture, Judge Reinhardt concludes, on the basis of an examination of a number of treaties and commentaries, that this principle is 'well established in international law and in other national legal systems'.[251] The opinion includes a footnote to the federal common law requirements for joint venture:

> It is well-accepted that joint liability will exist where (1) parties intended to form a joint venture; (2) parties share a common interest in the subject matter of the venture; (3) the parties share the profits and losses of the venture; and (4) the parties have joint control or the joint right of control over the venture. W. Keeton, *Prosser and Keeton on Torts*, § 72 at 518 (5th ed. 1984).[252]

Although in the *Unocal* case there was a factual dispute as to whether the Unocal subsidiary was independent of the joint venture and the military, the Judge

---

[250] Cases brought in Belgium with regard to allegations of corporate complicity in international crimes were filed as criminal cases, see 'Elf est poursuivie pour son soutien au président congolais Sassou Nguesso, Une palinte a été déposée à Bruxelles pour complicité de crimes' *Le Monde*, 18 October 2001 and 'Myanmar refugees seek Belgium trial for TotalFinaElf' *AFP*, 8 May 2002. See also the case against IBM in the Swiss courts (Geneva), *International Business Machines Corp (IBM) v Gypsy International Recognition and Compensation Action (GIRCA)* 4C.296/2004 /ech, Arrêt du 22 décembre 2004, Ire Cour civile. For a survey of the possibilities for corporate complicity suits (criminal and civil) alleging violations of international law in France, Norway, Canada, the UK, and the US, see International Peace Academy and Fafo AIS, *Business and International Crimes: Assessing the Liability of Business Entities for Grave Violations of International Law* (Oslo: Fafo-report 467, 2004). The report and the national survey are available at http://www.fafo.no.liabilities/index.htm.

[251] *Unocal* 2002 (n 239 above) at 14257.

[252] Ibid, at 14257, fn 11, and see, for another formulation, ICHRP (2002) 130, esp. fn 349.

pointed out that 'evidence in the record states that Unocal would share revenues and costs of both the drilling and transportation components of the Yadana project. In view of the above, I believe that plaintiffs ought to proceed to trial on their claim of joint venture liability'.[253]

Turning to the question of agency liability, the concurring opinion stated that 'an agency relationship may be express or implied; in addition, a jury may infer from the factual circumstances that apparent agency authority exists.... As is true of joint liability principles, agency liability principles are well-established in international law.... Principal-agent liability is also widely adopted by civil law and other common law systems'.[254] The Judge considered that the evidence suggested the existence of such a relationship:

> For instance, plaintiffs cite an internal Unocal briefing document regarding the Yadana Project, discussed by the majority, which states that '[a]ccording to our contract, the government of Myanmar is responsible for protecting the pipeline. There is military protection for the pipeline and, when we have work to do along the pipeline that requires security, the military people will, as a matter of course, be nearby.' They also point to memoranda by various Total and Unocal employees recounting that oil company officials requested specific battalions to perform various tasks, including the construction of helipads for the convenience of corporate executives. Plaintiffs argue that the record supports either an implied or express agency relationship, based on the conduct of the parties. As the majority has also pointed out, the record contains evidence of daily meetings between Total and Unocal executives and Myanmar military commanders, so that the corporations could instruct the military leaders regarding specific security or infrastructure projects that were required for the pipeline construction. Moreover, Unocal stated publicly on several occasions that it controlled the Myanmar military's actions in connection with the pipeline project. In response to accusations of human rights abuses occurring by the Myanmar military with respect to the Yadana project, Unocal denied the existence of such abuses, and stressed its ability to prevent any wrongdoing due to its control of the military. Unocal's alleged actions directing the Myanmar military create a triable question of fact as to whether an agency relationship existed between Unocal and the Myanmar armed forces.[255]

These passages are important, as they demonstrate that it is not any relationship with an abusive government that will give rise to agency liability for a company. There will have to be an employment situation whereby the company becomes responsible for the acts of its (government) agents. Where a company hires agents, or is in a position to influence the actual operations which are known to lead to human rights violations, the company will be liable for the acts of those agents who are the principal perpetrators. The opinion is clear that there is no need to show a contractual relationship:

> It is not essential that a formal contract have existed between Unocal and the Myanmar military in order for Unocal to be held liable for the government's actions under an

---

[253] *Unocal* 2002 (n 239 above) at 14259.   [254] Ibid, at 14261.   [255] Ibid, at 14262.

agency theory. Nevertheless, should plaintiffs prove their allegation that such a contract existed, a jury might have considerable difficulty in accepting Unocal's denial of an agency relationship.[256]

Lastly, Judge Reinhardt applied the principle of reckless disregard not only to acts that cause *direct* harm, but also to the situation where a company uses the services of an entity, which in turn, causes harm:

> I see no reason why the general principle that liability arises for one party's conscious disregard of unreasonable risks to another should not apply when a defendant consciously disregards the risks that arise from its decision to use the services of an entity that it knows or ought to know is likely to cause harm to another party.[257]

Under this common law theory the plaintiffs would have to prove that:

> Unocal had actual knowledge that the Myanmar military would likely engage in human rights abuses, including forced labor, if it undertook the functions Unocal and the other private parties desired it to perform in connection with the Yadana Pipeline Project. Nevertheless, according to plaintiffs, Unocal recklessly disregarded that known risk, determined to use and in fact did use the services of that military to perform pipeline-related tasks, and thereby set in motion international law abuses that were foreseeable to Unocal.[258]

6.8.6 Which Tests to Use for Corporate Human Rights Abuses under International Law: Criminal Law or Civil (Tort) Law?

Not every claim regarding corporate human rights abuses, or complicity in governmental violations of human rights, will involve international crimes. In such cases it seems inappropriate to use international criminal law or even national criminal law principles. For example, if the corporation is accused of denying political expression in the workplace, or assisting a government in restricting freedom of expression, neither the violation by the government, nor the action of the company is, on its own, an international crime. International law has not criminalized violations of freedom of expression as international crimes. Such a violation is, rather, an international tort, or delict, by the state. Such a concept is underdeveloped with regard to the responsibility of the corporation, but the issues are not totally theoretical. Although the focus in the *Unocal* case was on human rights abuses recognized as crimes under international law, other Alien Tort Claims Act cases have raised allegations outside the scope of international *criminal* law. In the *Wiwa v Shell* case, several of the complicity complaints against Shell concerned Shell's involvement in such international torts. Let us now turn to that case.

---

[256] Ibid, at 14263.   [257] Ibid, at 14265.   [258] Ibid, at 14263.

6.8.7   *Wiwa v Shell* and the Issue of Complicity in International Torts

In *Wiwa v Royal Dutch Petroleum (Shell)*[259] the plaintiffs alleged violations of international law in connection with the Nigerian Government's activities in the Ogoni region of Nigeria. The complaint was brought against the oil companies and a named managing director, for directing and aiding the Nigerian Government in violating the human rights of the complainants. The allegations focus on the suppression of the Movement for the Survival of the Ogoni People (MOSOP). It is alleged that Shell, operating through Shell Nigeria, recruited the Nigerian police and military to suppress MOSOP. The company is said to have:

> ... provided logistical support, transportation, and weapons to Nigerian authorities to attack Ogoni villages and stifle opposition to Shell's oil-excavation activities. Ogoni residents, including plaintiffs, were beaten, raped, shot, and/or killed during these raids. Jane Doe was beaten and shot during one raid in 1993, and Owens Wiwa was illegally detained.

> In 1995, Ken Saro-Wiwa and John Kpuinen were hanged after being convicted of murder by a special tribunal. Defendants bribed witnesses to testify falsely at the trial, conspired with Nigerian authorities in meetings in Nigeria and the Netherlands to orchestrate the trial, and offered to free Ken Saro-Wiwa in return for an end to MOSOP's international protests against defendants. During the trial, members of Ken Saro-Wiwa's family, including his elderly mother, were beaten.[260]

Although the claims include allegations that Shell's conduct violated international law, including the law on crimes against humanity and torture, part of the claims concern violations 'of the right to life, liberty and security of the person and peaceful assembly and association'.[261] To the extent that the complaint relies on the participation by Shell in violations of customary international law by Nigeria, such violations of international law would not all be international *crimes*, but might nevertheless be violations of international law by Nigeria. Assisting in such violations would not therefore be addressed by international criminal law, as no international crime has been committed. Nevertheless, the claims suggest that the corporate activity could involve individual or corporate 'civil responsibility' under international law.[262]

---

[259] US District Court for the Southern District of New York, decided 22 February 2002, filed 28 February 2002.

[260] From the ruling at Part IB, available at http://www.derechos.org/nizkor/econ/shell28feb02.html.

[261] At I.C.2 of the ruling, for the actual claims, see paras 121–126 of the Statement of Claim, available at http://www.ccr-ny.org.

[262] The Commentary to Art. 58 of the International Law Commission's Articles on State Responsibility deliberately leaves open the possibility that international law, having developed to encompass individual responsibility in the context of the Nuremberg and subsequent international criminal trials, might similarly develop in the field of 'individual civil responsibility'. Commentary to Art. 58 at para. 2, UN Doc. A/56/10, *Report of the ILC 53rd Session*, adopted 10 August 2001, at p 364. See further Ch 12, at 12.3 below.

Because international law has focused so far on *individual criminal* responsibility and *state 'civil'* responsibility, guidance on the international rules regarding international civil responsibility for non-state actors may most appropriately be sought in the developing law of state complicity as elaborated in the ILC's Articles on State Responsibility.

6.9   THE TEST FOR STATE RESPONSIBILITY FOR STATE COMPLICITY

In the law of state responsibility, the UN International Law Commission (ILC) has redefined the scope of complicity as it relates to assistance by one state in the violation of international law by another state. In the Articles adopted by the ILC in 2001, the relevant Article reads as follows:

Article 16   Aid or assistance in the commission of an internationally wrongful act

A State which aids or assists another State in the commission of an internationally wrongful act by the latter is internationally responsible for doing so if:

(a) That State does so with knowledge of the circumstances of the internationally wrongful act; and
(b) The act would be internationally wrongful if committed by that State.

The required connection between the aid and the wrongful act is explained in the final Commentary on Article 16. The Commentary states that it will be sufficient for the purposes of this complicity Article if the aid or assistance 'contributed *significantly* to that act'.[263]

It seems there are three factors determining responsibility for aiding and assisting in the commission of an internationally wrongful act. First, it is not necessary to show that the assisting state shared the intention of the assisted state. What is required is knowledge of the circumstances of the internationally wrongful act. Applying this rule, by analogy, to companies, one would not have to prove the intent of a company, one need merely show that the company knew the circumstances of the wrongful act. Second, to invoke the complicity of states in the wrongful acts of other states, it is necessary to show that the aid actually facilitated the wrongful act, and was given with a view to that purpose.[264] But one does not need to show that the aid was an essential contribution to a wrongful act. One does not have to show that, *but for* the corporate contribution, the wrongful act would not have been committed. The corporate contribution need only *actually facilitate the wrongful act*. And third, under the rules of state responsibility, the accomplice state must be bound by the same obligation to be held responsible in international law for complicity.

---

[263] At para. 5 of the Commentary to Art. 16 (emphasis added).
[264] Ibid.

Starting from the point that not all national legal systems make it a civil wrong for someone to assist someone else to breach their contractual obligations, Rapporteur James Crawford pointed out that any reading which would suggest state complicity for assisting in the breach of *any* internationally unlawful act would cover third-party assistance to a party to breach a bilateral treaty. This would mean that bilateral treaties could, in effect, be enforced on the rest of the world; states which were not parties to the bilateral treaties would be under an obligation not to assist the relevant states in breaching them. This was seen as a problem. The Rapporteur also concluded that problems would arise as to proof of the awareness of one state of another state's full range of bilateral and multilateral obligations.

As soon as one admits that the violations of customary international law at issue are violations of human rights law, and that the sorts of violations that are alleged represent actions that are clearly wrong, the defence of ignorance of the law seems less compelling. The human rights abuses which companies are accused of assisting in all relate to the fundamental human rights principles contained in the Universal Declaration of Human Rights. Commentators and human rights organizations increasingly suggest that all companies have to respect the Universal Declaration of Human Rights.[265] The Declaration is now regularly referred to by companies as part of their human rights policy statements. Chris Avery, who maintains a website on business and human rights, keeps track of company human rights policy statements that include explicit reference to the Universal Declaration of Human Rights. These include ABB, Ahold, Balfour Beatty, BG Group, The Body Shop, BP, BT Group, CGNU Group, Conoco, Co-operative Bank, Diageo, Freport-McMoRan, Ikea, National Grid, Norsk Hydro, Novo Group, Premier Oil, Reebok, Rio Tinto, Shell, Skanska, Stora Enso, Storebrand Group, Talisman Energy, TotalFinaElf, and Unocal.[266]

It is suggested that where the allegations of corporate complicity concern assistance to states in violation of the principles contained in the Universal Declaration of Human Rights, and these abuses cannot be described as crimes under international law, then it may be appropriate to apply the international state complicity (or international civil responsibility) test just described. The elements for responsibility are similar. It is possible to conclude that, even if the international law on criminal responsibility has focused on individuals, and the international law on civil responsibility has focused on states, the applicable rules can be adapted to the behaviour of corporations, depending on whether they are engaged in acts which constitute crimes or delicts under international law. Furthermore, as most allegations today turn on issues of complicity in governmental violations, the complicity tests developed in international law can be adapted to suit the allegations.

---

[265] E.g. Robinson (1998: 14), Vieira de Mello (2003: 19), Henkin (1999: 25), Amnesty International UK (2000: 7).

[266] http://business-humanrights.org/Company-policies-Examples.htm.

Where the allegations relate to assistance in the commission of acts which constitute international crimes, it makes sense to apply the appropriate international law on criminal complicity. Where the allegations relate to assistance in the commission of acts which constitute international delicts, the rules accepted by states for dealing with state complicity seem relevant.

There is a second, and separate, reason why it may make sense to focus, not only on criminal law, but also on tort law. Complaints of corporate complicity are aimed at achieving compensation rather than retributive criminal justice. In order to apportion damages, it will be essential in some circumstances to consider tort responsibility principles. The ILC Commentary states that 'in cases where the internationally wrongful act would clearly have occurred in any event, the responsibility of the assisting State will not extend to compensating for the act itself'.[267] The drive to hold corporations accountable for complicity in human rights abuses stems in part from the need to claim reparations from the accomplice company in situations where it is difficult, if not impossible, to claim reparations from the offending government. The complicity tests cannot substitute the corporation for the government. The corporation is responsible for its own act of assistance. In the context of state complicity with other state's illegal acts, the ILC Commentary suggests: 'By assisting another State to commit an internationally wrongful act, a State should not necessarily be held to indemnify the victim for all the consequences of the act, but only for those which, in accordance with the principles stated in Part Two of the articles, flow from its own conduct.'[268] By analogy with the law of state responsibility, corporations are liable for the damage caused by their assistance to others.

6.10 SUMMARY ON CORPORATE COMPLICITY IN HUMAN RIGHTS ABUSES UNDER INTERNATIONAL LAW

- Where a corporation assists another entity, whether it be a state, a rebel group, another company, or an individual, to commit an international crime, the rules for determining responsibility under international law will be the rules developed in international criminal law. The corporation will be responsible as an accomplice, whether or not it intended a crime to be committed, if it can be shown that (a) the corporation carries out acts specifically directed to assist, encourage or lend moral support to the perpetration of a certain specific international crime and this support has a substantial effect

[267] Report of the ILC (n 262 above) Commentary to Art. 16, para. 1, at 155.
[268] Ibid, Commentary to Art. 19, para. 10, at 159. See also Art. 31 and the Commentary thereto (at 223) for a discussion of foreseeability and remoteness of damage. The basic rule is contained in Art. 31(1): 'The responsible State is under an obligation to make full reparation for the injury caused by the internationally wrongful act.'

upon the perpetration of the crime; and (b) the corporation had the knowledge that its acts would assist the commission of a specific crime by the principal.

- Where a corporation is alleged to have assisted a government in violating customary international law rights in circumstances which do not amount to international crimes, but rather to international delicts or torts, the analogous rules for state responsibility suggest that the corporations must be (a) aware of the circumstances making the activity of the assisted state a violation of international human rights law; (b) the assistance must be given with a view to facilitating the commission of such a violation and actually contribute significantly to the violation; and (c) the company itself should have an obligation not to violate the right in question.

6.11   FINAL COMMENTS ON CORPORATE RESPONSIBILITY UNDER INTERNATIONAL LAW

States have adopted international texts which are addressed to corporations themselves and which specifically call for human rights to be respected by transnational corporations (or indeed by any sort of business entity).[269]

Individuals were recognized as having duties and rights under international law as international tribunals came to exert jurisdiction over such rights and duties. Although there are only rare instances of an international tribunal where a corporation could be the respondent in a dispute,[270] corporations can still be the bearer

---

[269] See the discussion above with regard to the different approaches adopted by the OECD, the ILO, and the UN Sub-Commission on the Promotion and Protection of Human Rights.

[270] Such as a case before the Seabed Disputes Chamber of the Law of the Sea Tribunal; see Art. 291(2) of the Law of the Sea Convention of 1982, and Art. 187, which states that the Chamber shall have jurisdiction over certain 'disputes between parties to a contract, being States Parties, the Authority or the Enterprise, state enterprises and natural or juridical persons referred to in article 153, paragraph 2(b)'. Art. 153(2) reads: 'Activities in the Area shall be carried out as prescribed in paragraph 3: (a) by the Enterprise, and (b) in association with the Authority by States Parties, or state enterprises or natural or juridical persons which possess the nationality of States Parties or are effectively controlled by them or their nationals, when sponsored by such States, or any group of the foregoing which meets the requirements provided in this Part and in Annex III.' Annex III details the 'Basic Conditions of Prospecting, Exploring and Exploitation' and makes it clear that applicant contractors undertake to accept as enforceable and comply with the obligations under Part XI of the Convention (which includes settlement of disputes). Although a contractor has to be sponsored by a Contracting State; these are not state entities and there is no state responsibility for their actions: 'A sponsoring State shall not, however, be liable for damage caused by any failure of a contractor sponsored by it to comply with its obligations if that State Party has adopted laws and regulations and taken administrative measures which are, within the framework of its legal system, reasonably appropriate for securing compliance by persons under its jurisdiction.' Art. 4(4) of Annex III. The Press Release from the inauguration of the Court gives an indication of the range of ways in which the Tribunal may eventually act outside the inter-state context: ITLOS/Press 3, 23 October 1996: 'States parties to the Convention can bring their disputes for resolution to the Tribunal. In addition, the Tribunal can resolve disputes amongst States, the International Seabed Authority, companies and private individuals, arising out of the exploitation of the deep seabed.'

of international duties. Lack of international jurisdiction to try a corporation does not mean that a corporation is under no international legal obligation. Clearly, if the Nuremberg judgment is to make legal sense, the individuals tried in Nuremberg must have been under some international obligation before the Nuremberg Tribunal was created to try them. This view is reinforced by the reasoning of the International Criminal Tribunal for the former Yugoslavia (ICTY) in the *Tadić* decision of the Appeals Chamber.[271] International legal obligations can exist independently of any international institution to enforce them, and the ICTY has been at pains to demonstrate that the individuals were bound by existing international law and not due to any law-making exercise by the Security Council itself. According to Christian Tomuschat the Security Council could not have created new substantive rules establishing offences for which individuals could 'directly incur criminal responsibility under international law. Such legislative authority would not have been covered by Article 41 [of the UN Charter]'.[272] In addition, any retrospective creation of individual criminal offences would violate the *nullum crimen sine lege* principle in human rights law.[273] It makes sense to speak of the separation between the obligation under international law and international jurisdiction to try the alleged offender (the jurisdictional filter). There are clearly violations of international criminal law that exist in the absence of any international jurisdiction to try them. The absence of an international jurisdiction to try corporations does not mean that transnational corporations cannot break international law.

The various treaties that address the behaviour of legal persons with regard to financing terrorism, corruption, environmental crimes, and trafficking, demonstrate that states can be bound in international law to ensure that corporations respect particular obligations defined in international instruments. The Bamako Convention on the Ban of the Import into Africa and the Control of Transboundary Wastes within Africa goes further than most treaties discussed above and actually explicitly demands national legislation 'for imposing criminal penalties on all persons who have planned, committed, or assisted in such illegal imports. Such penalties shall be sufficiently high to both punish and deter such conduct'.[274] The Convention defines 'person' as meaning 'any natural or legal person'. Of course, any prosecution would take place through the prism of national law, but the possibility exists that a treaty could create international obligations not only for the state parties, but for those entities identified as having obligations

---

[271] *Prosecutor v Dusko Tadić* Decision on the Defence Motion for Interlocutory Appeal on Jurisdiction (Appeals Chamber), 2 October 1995, (IT–94–1), esp. paras 94 and 143.

[272] *Human Rights: Between Idealism and Realism* (Oxford: Oxford University Press, 2003) at 287.

[273] See Art. 11(2) of the Universal Declaration of Human Rights and Art. 15(1) of the International Covenant on Civil and Political Rights. Similar provisions appear in the regional human rights treaties.

[274] 29 January 1991, reproduced in 30 *ILM* (1991) at 773. See esp. Arts 1(16), (definition); 4(1) 'Such import shall be deemed illegal and a criminal act'; and 9(2) (Obligation on States parties to introduce criminal penalties on all persons guilty of illegal imports.)

under the treaty.[275] There is, of course, the option of developing a new treaty to set out what states must do to ensure that 'their' corporations abide by international human rights law. Such a treaty could be modelled on the corruption treaties, now widely understood and accepted. There are recurring suggestions that such an exercise would present an opportunity to clarify the scope of the obligations on companies and provide a boost to the corporate social responsibility movement by introducing fairer conditions for competition.[276]

Nevertheless, it is suggested here that overly focusing on the jurisdictional possibilities for holding corporations accountable has obscured the important notion that international law already applies to corporations and is developing the scope of their obligations not to commit or assist in human rights abuses. In an important review of the development of corporate responsibility for human rights violations, Steven Ratner reminds us:

> Some norms based on the principles of international responsibility will be incorporated by business themselves under economic pressure from interested shareholders and consumers, who serve as private enforcers of the law. Some claims will be addressed in domestic fora as legislators and government officials draft statutes, regulations, or government policy. Some prescription and application of law will take place in international arenas as diplomats, perhaps prodded by NGOs, prepare treaties or non-binding legal instruments. And both domestic and international courts and other dispute resolution bodies may play a role. But excessive focus on the activities of courts diverts attention from the principal venues in which international legal argumentation is made and matters.[277]

The massive settlements with regards to Nazi-era conduct (stolen assets and slave labour, Swiss banks, German industries) have been followed by a new round of claims in the American courts concerning reparations for slavery from US companies.[278] The common theme in all of these legal complaints is that the language of

---

[275] Cf *Tadić* (n 271 above) at paras 94 and 143. The theoretical basis for this argument is discussed in Ch 7 below.

[276] N. Jägers, *Corporate Human Rights Obligations: in Search of Accountability* (Antwerp: Intersentia, 2002) at 258. See also the proposal presented by Friends of the Earth at the Johannesburg 2002 Summit, *Towards Binding Corporate Accountability*, January 2002, http://www.foe.co.uk/resource/briefings/corporate_accountability.pdf.

[277] S. R. Ratner, 'Corporations and Human Rights: A Theory of Legal Responsibility' 111 *YLJ* (2001) 443–545, at 451.

[278] See 'The guilt of a nation' *The Economist*, 13 April 2002, at 15, and 'Time and punishment' at 47. Note the way in which these claims become part of a political campaign to garner government funds. *The Economist* refers to the compensation fund for the victims of 11 September 2001. Note also the US$1.6bn paid by the government to 80,000 Japanese Americans interned during the Second World War. For the litigation concerning the Swiss banks and the Holocaust Victims Assets Litigation, see A. Ramasastry, 'Corporate Complicity: From Nuremberg to Rangoon An Examination of Forced Labor Cases and Their Impact on the Liability of Multinational Corporations' 20 *Berkeley JIL* (2002) 91–159; A. Ramasastry, 'Secrets and Lies? Swiss Banks and International Human Rights' 31 *Van JTL* (1998) 325–456; and for the Holocaust litigation generally see M. J. Bazyler, *Holocaust Justice: The Battle for Restitution in America's Courts* (New York: New York University Press, 2003) and M. J. Bazyler, 'Nuremberg in America: Litigating the Holocaust in United States Courts' 34 *URLR* (2000) 1–283.

7

Non-State Actors in Times of
Armed Conflict

7.1 REBELS, INSURGENTS, AND BELLIGERENTS

Rebels, insurgents and belligerents are sometimes depicted by international lawyers as being positioned on a sliding scale according to degrees of control over territory and recognition by governments.[1] International law originally only considered rebels as having international rights and obligations from the time they graduate to insurgency. Traditionally, insurgents were considered to have international rights and obligations with regard to those states that recognized them as having such a status. According to Antonio Cassese, to be eligible for such recognition, insurgents need only satisfy minimal conditions:

> International law only establishes certain loose requirements for eligibility to become an international subject. In short, (1) rebels should prove that they have effective control over some part of the territory, and (2) civil commotion should reach a certain degree of intensity and duration (it may not simply consist of riots, or sporadic and short-lived acts of violence). It is for States (both that against which the civil strife breaks out and other parties) to appraise—by granting or withholding, if only implicitly, *recognition of insurgency*—whether these requirements have been fulfilled.[2]

With regard to an insurrectional group recognized as such by the relevant state, it is clear that there are certain international rights and obligations that flow from this status, depending on the terms of the recognition.[3] Under this traditional international law, insurgents, who were recognized by the state against which they were fighting, not only as insurgents, but also expressly as *belligerents*, became assimilated to a state actor with all the attendant rights and obligations which flow

---

[1] E.g. H. A. Wilson, *International Law and the Use of Force by National Liberation Movements* (Oxford: Oxford University Press, 1988) at 24. See also L. Oppenheim and H. Lauterpacht (eds) *International Law: a Treatise (Disputes, War and Neutrality)*, vol. II (London: Longman, 7th edn, 1952) at 209–116; R. Jennings and A. Watts (eds) *Oppenheim's International Law (Peace)*, vol. I, part 1, (London: Longman, 9th edn, 1996) at 161–183.

[2] A. Cassese, *International Law* (Oxford: Oxford University Press, 2nd edn, 2005) at 125. See also A. Cassese, *International Law in a Divided World* (Oxford: Oxford University Press, 1986) at 81–85.

[3] E. H. Reidel, 'Recognition of Insurgency' in R. Bernhardt (ed) *Encyclopedia of Public International Law*, vol. IV (Amsterdam: Elsevier, 2000b) 54–56.

from the laws of *international* armed conflict.[4] Today, these recognition regimes have been replaced by compulsory rules of international humanitarian law which apply when the fighting reaches certain thresholds. Commentators such as Ingrid Detter, have suggested that the idea that the application of the rules of armed conflict are related to the recognition of belligerency has been 'abandoned';[5] and Heather Wilson has claimed that, since the First World War, the old law is 'more theoretical than real' as recognition has hardly occurred since that time.[6]

Although the theoretical possibilities remain for states to bestow rights and obligations on rebels by recognizing them as either insurgents or belligerents, it makes more sense today to consider rebels (unrecognized insurgents) simply as addressees of international obligations under contemporary international humanitarian law, especially the obligations contained in Common Article 3 to the four Geneva Conventions of 1949, in Protocol II of 1977 to the Geneva Conventions, and in Article 19 of the Hague Convention on Cultural Property of 1954. These obligations are considered in more detail below. Today, international law imposes obligations on certain parties to an internal armed conflict irrespective of any recognition granted by the state they are fighting against or by any third state. The problem is that governments are often loath to admit that the conditions have been met for the application of this customary international law; for to admit such a situation is seen as an admission that the government has lost a degree of control, and an 'elevation' of the status of the rebels.

In some cases, written agreements have been entered into during and after armed conflicts. These may contain mutual commitments, not only to respect the laws of armed conflict, but human rights as well.[7] Such agreements are less focused on the old questions of recognition and simply aim to build confidence; placing the protection of the individual at the centre of such measures. Such agreements are nevertheless sometimes predicated on the actual capacity of the rebels to fulfil the obligations in question. The preamble to the San José Agreement on Human Rights, between El Salvador and the *Frente Farabundo Martí para la Liberación Nacional* (FMLN), included the following paragraph: '*Bearing in mind* that the Frente Farabundo Martí para la Liberación Nacional has the capacity and the will and assumes the commitment to respect the inherent attributes of the human person.'[8] In this case, the agreement was also signed by the Representative of the UN Secretary-General (Alvaro de Soto) and this fact, together with the arrangements for UN monitoring, suggests that this would constitute an agreement governed by international law between an entity recognized as having the requisite international status to assume rights and obligations under

---

[4] See further E. H. Reidel, 'Recognition of Belligerency' in R. Bernhardt (ed) *Encyclopedia of Public International Law*, vol. IV (Amsterdam: Elsevier, 2000a) 47–50.

[5] I. Detter, *The Law of War* (Cambridge: Cambridge University Press, 2nd edn, 2000) at 43.

[6] Wilson (1988: 27).

[7] See the San José agreement between El Salvador and the *Frente Farabundo Martí para la Liberación Nacional* (FMLN) signed by both sides on 26 July 1990. UN Doc. A/44/971–S/21541 of 16 August 1990, Annex.   [8] Ibid, at 2.

international law.[9] This example shows how international law has moved beyond recognition of insurgency during armed conflict to a new type of recognition for human rights purposes. The obligations of the non-state actor in such situations stretch beyond both the duration of armed conflict and the laws of armed conflict.

7.2 NATIONAL LIBERATION MOVEMENTS

An additional category of international actor to be considered in this context is the national liberation movement (NLM). In some ways it is clumsy to list NLMs as non-state actors. Their representatives may reject the label of non-state actor as, not only may they wish to stress their putative state-like aspirations and status, but they may sometimes already be recognized as a state member in certain regional inter-governmental organizations. One difference between such groups and the recognized belligerents and insurgents discussed above is that such NLMs may be able to claim rights, and will be subject to international obligations, even in the absence of control of territory or express recognition by their adversaries. Article 1(4) of the 1977 Protocol I to the Geneva Conventions classifies three types of war of national liberation as international armed conflict, so that all the rules applicable to those conflicts apply. It covers 'armed conflicts in which peoples are fighting against colonial domination and alien occupation and against racist régimes in the exercise of their right to self-determination'.[10] Under Article 96(3) of Protocol I, the authority representing the people struggling against the colonial, alien, or racist party to the Protocol can undertake to apply the Conventions and the Protocol by making a declaration to the depository (the Swiss Federal Council).[11]

Furthermore, such a liberation authority could make a declaration under the Convention on Prohibitions or Restrictions on the Use of Certain Conventional Weapons Which May be Deemed to be Excessively Injurious or to Have Indiscriminate Effects.[12] Such a declaration can bring into force, not only the Weapons Convention and its protocols, but also the Geneva Conventions, even where the state against which the liberation movement is fighting is not a party to

---

[9] See L. Zegveld, *Accountability of Armed Opposition Groups in International Law* (Cambridge: Cambridge University Press, 2002) at 49–51; see more generally with regard to all agreements witnessed by the UN, E. Roucounas, 'Non-State Actors: Areas of International Responsibility in Need of Further Exploration' in M. Ragazzi (ed) *International Responsibility Today: Essays in Memory of Oscar Schachter* (Leiden: Brill, 2005) 391–404, esp. at 397. For a discussion of other agreements which may not have such a status, see P. H. Kooijmans, 'The Security Council and Non-State Entities as Parties to Conflicts' in K. Wellens (ed) *International Law: Theory and Practice* (The Hague: Martinus Nijhoff, 1998) 333–346.   [10] See also GA Res. 3103(XXVIII), 12 December 1973.
[11] A number of declarations of this kind have been deposited with the ICRC by groups such as the ANC, SWAPO, the PLO, and the Eritrean People's Liberation Front. See also the other examples given by M. Veuthey, *Guérilla et droit humanitaire* (Geneva: ICRC, 1983) at xxvi.
[12] 10 October 1980, see Art. 7(4).

Protocol I.[13] In the absence of any declarations having been accepted, however, attention has turned to the customary status of these rules.[14]

Suffice it to say that no government faced with a liberation movement accepts that it is colonial, racist, or in alien occupation. Arguments before South African and Israeli judges that liberation movements are entitled to privileges under international law have not met with success,[15] although the thrust of the ideas expressed in Article 1(4) of Protocol I seemed at one point to be relevant when it came to sentencing certain SWAPO fighters in Namibia.[16] Attempts by the Red Army Faction and the Republic of New Afrika to invoke the rule as customary also failed before the courts of the Netherlands and the United States respectively.[17] The category of NLMs highlights the fact that non-state actors can become bound by international law pursuant to the terms of international humanitarian law treaties. It also leads us to consider below more closely the situation where armed groups are bound by the laws of internal armed conflict and where they make declarations or enter into agreements to abide by certain international standards.

---

[13] Art. 7(4)(b).

[14] Although certain declarations have been sent to the ICRC, the procedure demands a communication with the Swiss authorities. The table of ratifications compiled by the ICRC contains the following note: 'Palestine: On 21 June 1989, the Swiss Federal Department of Foreign Affairs received a letter from the Permanent Observer of Palestine to the United Nations Office at Geneva informing the Swiss Federal Council "that the Executive Committee of the Palestine Liberation Organization, entrusted with the functions of the Government of the State of Palestine by decision of the Palestine National Council, decided, on 4 May 1989, to adhere to the Four Geneva Conventions of 12 August 1949 and the two Protocols additional thereto". On 13 September 1989, the Swiss Federal Council informed the States that it was not in a position to decide whether the letter constituted an instrument of accession, "due to the uncertainty within the international community as to the existence or non-existence of a State of Palestine".' This was not a declaration under either Art. 96(3) of Protocol I or Art. 7 of the Conventional Weapons Convention 1980, so the issue was not whether the PLO represented an authority which represented an NLM, but whether it could be considered a state. For full discussion of the state practice and the history of the these provisions, see A. Cassese, 'Wars of National Liberation' in C. Swinarski (ed) *Studies and Essays in International Humanitarian Law and Red Cross Principles: Essays in Honour of Jean Pictet* (The Hague: Martinus Nijhoff, 1984) 314–324; L. R. Penna, 'Customary International Law and Protocol I: An Analysis of Some Provisions' in Swinarski (1984) 201–225; G. Abi-Saab, 'Wars of National Liberation in the Geneva Conventions and Protocols' (1979) 165 *RCADI* (1979) 357–455. See also Zegveld (2002: 14) for further references regarding failed attempts to adhere to the Conventions by the Provisional Revolutionary Government of Algeria and the Smith Government in Rhodesia.

[15] *S v Mogoerane* (unreported) Transvaal Provincial Division of the South African Supreme Court, 6 August 1982, discussed by C. Murray, 'The 1977 Geneva Protocols and Conflict in Southern Africa' 33 *ICLQ* (1984) 462–470; *S v Petane* [1988] 3 SALR 51; see also the rejection of combatant status for members of the Organisation of the Popular Front for the Liberation of Palestine caught in military uniform in *Military Prosecutor v Kassem and ors* [1971] 42 ILR 470.

[16] See C. Murray, 'The Status of the ANC and SWAPO in International Humanitarian Law' 100 *South African Law Journal* (1983) 402; *S v Sagarius* [1983] 1 SA 833 (SWA).

[17] *Public Prosecutor v Folkerts* [1987] 74 ILR 695; *US v Marilyn Buck* US District Court for the Southern District of New York, [1988] 690 F Supp 1291; both excerpted and discussed in M. Sassòli and A. A. Bouvier, *How Does Law Protect in War?* (Geneva: ICRC, 1999) 1435–1448.

7.3   REBEL GROUPS, UNRECOGNIZED INSURGENTS, ARMED OPPOSITION GROUPS, PARTIES TO AN INTERNAL ARMED CONFLICT, ETC.

Where there is no recognition of insurgency or belligerency, and the group in question is not a national liberation movement (NLM) that has successfully triggered the application of the rules of international armed conflict, one is left with an internal armed conflict involving rebels or what are sometimes termed 'armed opposition groups'. The humanitarian law which applies during internal armed conflict gives rise to certain duties for these rebels.[18] The minimum protection offered by Common Article 3 to the four Geneva Conventions of 1949 contains obligations for 'each Party to the conflict'. These obligations are to 'Persons taking no active part in the hostilities' as well as to the 'wounded and sick'. The actual prohibitions include: murder; violence to the person; cruel treatment; the taking of hostages; humiliating and degrading treatment; and sentences or executions without judicial safeguards. Lastly, the Article includes a positive obligation to collect and care for the sick and wounded.

The designation of a situation as 'an armed conflict not of an international character', so as to trigger the application of Common Article 3 to the Geneva Conventions of 1949, is obviously an act of considerable political importance for all sides to the conflict. The rebels will often welcome the designation of their attacks as constituting armed conflict as this confers a curious sort of international recognition on them;[19] and the applicability of Common Article 3 reinforces the special role of the International Committee of the Red Cross (ICRC).[20] On the other hand, as already noted, the government may be less willing to acknowledge the situation as one of armed conflict, preferring instead to portray it as a fight against criminals and terrorists. To be clear, the application of the obligations does not depend on any acceptance by the government that the threshold for the applicability of humanitarian law has been reached. In some cases the situation is put beyond doubt by UN Resolutions stating that the humanitarian rules contained in Common Article 3 are to be respected by both sides in a particular conflict.[21]

---

[18] See Zegveld (2002); L. Moir, *The Law of Internal Armed Conflict* (Cambridge: Cambridge University Press, 2002); T. Meron, *Human Rights and Humanitarian Norms as Customary Law* (Oxford: Clarendon Press, 1989); Y. C. Sandoz, C. Swinarski, and B. Zimmerman (eds) *Commentary on the Additional Protocols of 8 June 1977 to the Geneva Conventions of 12 August 1949* (Geneva: Martinus Nijhoff, 1987); T. Meron, *Human Rights in Internal Strife: Their International Protection* (Cambridge: Grotius, 1987).

[19] This is despite the fact that Common Art. 3 ends with the sentence: 'The application of the preceding provisions shall not affect the legal status of the Parties to the conflict.'

[20] Common Art. 3 includes the paragraph: 'An impartial humanitarian body, such as the International Committee of the Red Cross, may offer its services to the Parties to the conflict.'

[21] See, e.g. the UN Commission on Human Rights Resolution on El Salvador, 1991/71, preambular para. 6 and operative para. 9. See also GA Res. 45/172 and 46/133 on El Salvador.

Human rights organizations, such as Amnesty International and Human Rights Watch, have avoided determining whether the Geneva Conventions are, strictly speaking, applicable, and starting in the 1990s, began reporting on abuses by 'armed opposition groups' in ways that were guided by the *humanitarian law principles* contained in Common Article 3.[22] This reporting now goes beyond principles gleaned from Common Article 3 and covers human rights such as those related to the recruitment of child soldiers. Moreover, the need to rely on principles of international humanitarian law may now be diminished due to the recognition that human rights law obligations apply to non-state actors engaged in disturbances short of armed conflict. The Resolution adopted by the distinguished expert body, the Institute of International Law, at its Berlin session in 1999 (discussed with regard to the United Nations in Chapter 4 at 4.1.1) stated that: 'All parties to armed conflicts in which non-State entities are parties, irrespective of their legal status ... have the obligation to respect international humanitarian law as well as fundamental human rights.'[23] With regard to disturbances short of armed conflict, the Resolution includes an Article X to similar effect concerning fundamental human rights: 'To the extent that certain aspects of internal disturbances and tensions may not be covered by international humanitarian law, individuals remain under the protection of international law guaranteeing fundamental human rights. All parties are bound to respect fundamental rights under the scrutiny of the international community.'[24]

---

[22] In 1992, the oral intervention of Amnesty International at the UN Commission on Human Rights (Item 12) explained their approach at that time in the following terms: 'In times of internal armed conflict not only do governments remain bound by international human rights law: both governments and their opponents should observe minimum standards laid down by humanitarian law. Amnesty International has long condemned the torture and killing of prisoners by armed opposition groups; as part of the continuing development of our work we will now oppose a wider range of abuses by such groups, guided by the protection of the individual enshrined in Common Article 3 of the Geneva Conventions. We will oppose other deliberate and arbitrary killings in addition to the execution of prisoners. Deliberate killings of people not taking part in the conflict are in this sense always arbitrary whether the victim was targeted individually or the object of an indiscriminate attack. We will also oppose the taking or holding of hostages, condemning absolutely the arbitrary threat to life, liberty and security implicit in the condition of a hostage. We will document patterns of such abuses, and seek opportunities to bring pressure to bear on the perpetrators.' At the time, the introduction to the *Amnesty International Report: 1992* (London: AI Publications, 1992) mentioned some of the groups who were alleged to have carried out such abuses in 1991 including: the Mozambique National Resistance, the Sudan People's Liberation Army, Revolutionary Armed Forces of Colombia and the National Liberation Army in Colombia, Shining Path in Peru, Afghanistan's Mujahidin opposition groups, Sikh separatist groups in Punjab, the Tamil Tigers in Sri Lanka, the IRA, the Ulster Volunteer Force (UVF), the Ulster Freedom Fighters (UFF), the Basque separatist organization Basque Homeland and Liberty (ETA), the Kurdish Workers' Party in Turkey, and Palestinian armed groups in the Israeli-Occupied Territories. According to the Human Rights Watch Annual Report of 1998: 'Controversial as well was our decision to break from the human rights movement's exclusive focus on governments, and to address atrocities that rebel forces commit. We saw these steps as necessary to protect those most vulnerable to harm.'

[23] 'The Application of International Humanitarian Law and Fundamental Human Rights, in Armed Conflicts in which Non-State Entities are Parties', resolution adopted at the Berlin Session, 25 August 1999, Art. II.

[24] Ibid, Art. X. According to the Commentary, fundamental rights are assimilated to those rights that are applicable in states of emergency. Institute of International Law, *L'application du droit international humanitaire et des droits fondamentaux de l'homme dans les conflits armés auxquels prennent*

The protection offered by Protocol II to the Geneva Conventions goes beyond the minimum standards contained in Common Article 3, although the minimum standards contained in Common Article 3 remain in effect even when Protocol II is applicable. The Protocol supplements these standards with extra protection for civilians, children, and medical and religious personnel. It also details the procedural guarantees that must be afforded to people interned or detained. The important point in the present context is that it applies this wide range of duties to both sides fighting the internal armed conflict.

However, in order to trigger the application of Protocol II, the intensity of fighting has to be greater than that traditionally required for the application of Common Article 3. According to Article 1(2) of the Protocol, the Protocol does not apply to situations of internal disturbances, riots, and sporadic acts of violence. In addition, Article 1(1) of the Protocol requires that the dissident armed groups are under responsible command and exercise such control over part of the territory that they are in a position to carry out military operations and implement the guarantees in the Protocol. This is generally considered to constitute a higher threshold for applicability than Common Article 3. It also suggests that the rebels themselves become bound through their willingness to apply the Protocol.[25] As will be discussed, various theories have been advanced in the past to explain how the rebels, as such, become bound under the Protocol. Some of these are today less relevant as the key provisions come to be seen as customary international law for the purposes of individual prosecutions. For the moment, it suffices to note that in 2004, the Appeals Chamber of the Sierra Leone Special Court simply held that 'it is well settled that *all* parties to an armed conflict, whether states or non-state actors, are bound by international humanitarian law, even though only states may become parties to international treaties'.[26]

A crucial difference between international armed conflict and internal armed conflicts is that, in an international conflict, prisoners of war are 'released and repatriated after the cessation of active hostilities' (Article 118 of Geneva Convention III); on the other hand, in an internal armed conflict, the Government will have a degree of discretion under Protocol II with regard to the release of captured rebels. This distinction has been outlined by the Constitutional Court of Colombia in the context of their constitutional review of Protocol II as approved by Law 171 of 16 December 1994 and their decision to declare it applicable:

> Now, as already stated in this Ruling, one of the essential characteristics of prisoner-of-war status is that prisoners may not be punished simply for having taken up arms and

---

part des entités non étatiques: résolution de Berlin du 25 août 1999—The application of international humanitarian law and fundamental human rights in armed conflicts in which non-state entities are parties: Berlin resolution of 25 August 1999 (commentaire de Robert Kolb) Collection 'résolutions' n° 1, (Paris: Pedone, 2003) at 43.

[25] A. Cassese, 'The Status of Rebels under the 1977 Geneva Protocol on Non-International Armed Conflicts' 30 *ICLQ* (1981) 416–439, at 424–426.

[26] *Prosecutor v Sam Hinga Norman* (Case SCSL–2004–14–AR72(E)) Decision on preliminary Motion Based on Lack of Jurisdiction (Child Recruitment), Decision of 31 May 2004, at para. 22.

having participated in hostilities; indeed, if States are at war, the members of their respective armed forces are considered to have the right to serve as combatants. The party that captures them may retain them only in order to limit the enemy's potential to wage war, but it may not punish them for having fought. Consequently, as a prisoner-of-war has not violated humanitarian law, he must be released and repatriated without delay after the cessation of active hostilities, as stated in Article 118 of the Third Geneva Convention. Any prisoner who has violated humanitarian law should be punished as a war criminal in the instance of a grave breach, or could be subject to other penalties for other violations, but he may in no case be punished for having served as a combatant.

It is thus unnecessary for States to grant reciprocal amnesty after the end of an international war, because prisoners-of-war must be automatically repatriated. In internal armed conflicts, however those who have taken up arms do not in principle enjoy prisoner of war status and are consequently subject to penal sanctions imposed by the State, since they are not legally entitled to fight or to take up arms. In so doing they are guilty of an offence, such as rebellion or sedition, which is punishable under domestic legislation . . .

In situations such as those of internal conflict, where those who have taken up arms do not in principle enjoy prisoner-of-war status, it is easy to understand the purpose of a provision designed to ensure that the authorities in power will grant the broadest possible amnesty for reasons related to the conflict, once hostilities are over, as this can pave the way towards national reconciliation.[27]

This represents a rare instance of a state applying humanitarian law in the context of an internal armed conflict. It illustrates how delicate such an application can be. It does not, however, assist in clarifying how such international humanitarian law becomes applicable against the rebel group itself. At the time of the drafting of Protocol II to the Geneva Conventions, several states explained their conviction that insurgents engaged in a civil war were simply criminals, and that the protocol conferred no international legal personality on them.[28]

However, this treaty is today assumed to contain obligations for rebels who ful-fil the criteria in the Protocol and where the fighting has passed the Protocol's threshold. Various theories have been suggested to explain how a treaty, such as Protocol II, entered into by states, can create international duties for the rebel group as such.[29] Today, even in the absence of a consensus on a theoretical justification, it has become clear that, not only are rebels bound as parties to the conflict by Common Article 3 to the Geneva Convention, but they are also bound by the provisions of Protocol II. Indeed, from early on the ICRC Commentary to the Protocol simply asserted this to be the case:

The deletion from the text of all mention of 'parties to the conflict' only affects the drafting of the instrument, and does not change its structure from a legal point of

---

[27] Ruling No. C–225/95, Re File No. L.A.T.–040, unofficial translation in Sassòli and Bouvier (1999: 1370). See also *The Azanian Peoples Organization (AZAPO) v The President of the Republic of South Africa* Constitutional Court of South Africa, Case CCT 17/96, 25 July 1996, in Sassòli and Bouvier (1999: 970) esp. paras 30–31.   [28] Cassese (1981).
[29] Ibid.

view. All the rules are based on the existence of two or more parties confronting each other.

These rules grant the same rights and impose the same duties on both the established government and the insurgent party, and all such rights and duties have a purely humanitarian character.[30]

The Commentary highlights the theories which allow for the imposition of international duties on individuals and groups and asserts that the fact of application is not challenged by states in practice.

The question is often raised how the insurgent party can be bound by a treaty to which it is not a High Contracting Party. It may therefore be appropriate to recall here the explanation given in 1949 ... the commitment made by a State not only applies to the government but also to any established authorities and private individuals within the national territory of that State and certain obligations are therefore imposed upon them. The extent of rights and duties of private individuals is therefore the same as that of the rights and duties of the State. Although this argument has occasionally been questioned in legal literature, the validity of the obligation imposed upon insurgents has never been contested.[31]

More recently this approach has been endorsed by Zegveld in her review of international practice: 'International bodies have generally considered the ratification of the relevant norms by the territorial state to be sufficient legal basis for the obligations of armed opposition groups. These bodies thereby establish the conception of international law as a law controlled by states, under which states can simply decide to confer rights and impose obligations on armed opposition groups.'[32] While this approach is considered legitimate for humanitarian law, Zegveld does not consider it appropriate for human rights law due to an assumption that: 'The main feature of human rights is that these are rights that people hold against the state only.'[33] I questioned the continuing validity of this assumption in Chapter 1 and will not reiterate the arguments here. Suffice to add that where the problem has arisen as a practical problem, as with the Guatemalan Clarification Clarification Commission,[34] it was determined that at times when

---

[30] Y. Sandoz, C. Swinarski, and B. Zimmermann (eds) *Commentary on the Additional Protocols of 8 June 1977 to the Geneva Conventions of 12 August 1949* (Geneva/Dordrecht: ICRC/Nijhoff, 1987) at para. 4442. [31] Ibid at 4444, footnotes omitted.

[32] Zegveld (2002: 17). [33] Ibid, at 53.

[34] See the discussion by Christian Tomuschat: 'For a long time it seemed to be an unassailable axiom that it is incumbent upon governments only to respect and ensure human rights, so that it was inconceivable that groups without any official position could also violate human rights. Here again, the argument of reciprocity is of great weight. Not to subject insurgent movements to any obligation owed to the international community before an armed conflict may be found to exist would leave them exclusively under the authority of domestic law, favouring them, but also discriminating against them at the same time. It was one of the great challenges of the Guatemalan Clarification Commission to determine the legal yardstick by which conduct of the different guerrilla groups could be measured even in times when one could hardly speak of an armed conflict.' C. Tomuschat, *Human Rights: Between Idealism and Realism* (Oxford: Oxford University Press, 2003) at 261. He goes on to refer to the paragraphs cited below.

there was no armed conflict, the insurgents were bound by certain international law principles common to human rights and humanitarian law. A rough translation would mean that these included the prohibition on torture, inhuman and degrading treatment, a prohibition on hostage-taking, guarantees of fair trial, and physical liberty for the individual.[35] In short, the assumption that human rights law only applies to governments and not to insurgents is no longer a universally shared assumption.

It may be useful to consider the existing legal arguments for the application of these obligations to armed opposition groups under four headings. First, private individuals and groups are bound as nationals of the state that has made the international commitment. Second, where a group is exercising government-like functions it should be held accountable as far as it is exercising the *de facto* governmental functions of the state.[36] Third, the treaty itself directly grants rights and imposes obligations on individuals and groups. Fourth, obligations such as those in Common Article 3 are aimed at rebel groups, and it has been argued by Theodor Meron that the effective application of these rules should not depend on the incorporation of duties under national law. In Meron's words: 'Therefore, it is desirable that Article 3 should be construed as imposing direct obligations on the forces fighting the government.'[37]

---

[35] See the full Report of the Commission, only available in Spanish, at paras 1698–1700: '1698. La prohibición de la tortura en todas sus formas, la defensa de la integridad física, la ilicitud de todo trato cruel, inhumano o degradante de la dignidad de la persona, la toma de rehenes, la violación de las garantías a un proceso justo, la defensa de la libertad del individuo, por señalar algunos de los más preciados derechos que la conciencia del mundo civilizado defiende bajo cualquier circunstancia, constituyen algunos de los principios comunes del derecho internacional humanitario como del derecho internacional de los derechos humanos.   1699. En consecuencia, ambos órdenes jurídicos, aún siendo diversos, se integran de modo armónico en defensa de la superior dignidad humana. La violación de cualquiera de estos órdenes normativos, implica la infracción de los principios comunes a ambos.   1700. Una expresión de esa comunidad de principios, se encuentra contenida en el Preámbulo de la Declaración Universal de Derechos Humanos de 1948, que proclama dicho instrumento como "ideal común por el que todos los pueblos y naciones deben esforzarse, a fin de que tanto los individuos como las instituciones, inspirándose constantemente en ella, promuevan mediante la enseñanza y la educación, el respeto a estos derechos y libertades, y aseguren, por medidas progresivas de carácter nacional e internacional, su reconocimiento y aplicación universales y efectivos…".' Available from http://shr.aaas.org/guatemala/ceh/mds/spanish/.

[36] R. Wolfrum and C. E. Philipp, 'The Status of the Taliban: Their Obligations and Rights under International Law '6 *Max Planck Yearbook of United Nations Law* (2002) 559–601, who recall that *de facto* regimes exercising effective control over parts of territory may enjoy limited rights and duties under international law (at 585). Their inquiry concerns the rights and obligations regarding the use of force and they conclude that as a *de facto* regime (albeit unrecognized) the Taliban are considered an international subject, and their complicity with the terrorist group Al Qaeda, meant they could be targeted in order to bring them into compliance with their international law obligations (at 601).

[37] T. Meron, *Human Rights in Internal Strife: Their International Protection* (Cambridge: Grotius, 1987) at 39. For a discussion of the other approaches, see Meron, ibid, at 33–40, Zegveld (2002: 15–16), and R. Baxter, 'Jus in Bello Interno: the Present and Future Law' in J. Moore (ed) *Law and Civil War in the Modern World* (Baltimore: Johns Hopkins University Press, 1974) 518–536.

While these theories could all justify the application to individuals and non-state actors of certain human rights obligations found in treaties,[38] the focus has remained on international humanitarian law.[39] The theoretical basis for the application of the laws of internal armed conflict remain misty. Such theories have rarely been articulated by governments or international organizations in their application of international law to rebel groups. For example, in 1998 with regard to Afghanistan, the UN Security Council simply reaffirmed that 'all parties to the conflict are bound to comply with their obligations under international humanitarian law and in particular under the Geneva Conventions' of 1949.[40] Interestingly, the resolution goes on to state that 'persons who commit or order the commission of breaches of the Conventions are individually responsible in respect of such breaches'. This confirms at the highest level that individual responsibility attaches to violations of international humanitarian law in internal armed conflicts (even outside the contexts of Yugoslavia, Rwanda, and the regime of the International Criminal Court). It is also of interest that Council Resolutions in this context demand that 'Afghan factions' put an end to violations of human rights. In the context of Afghanistan, the demand was focused on discrimination against girls and women, but the resolution also demands that the factions 'adhere to the international norms and standards in this sphere'.[41] Moreover, the Security

---

[38] See Meron (1987: 34–35), who highlights direct obligations imposed on individuals by Arts 5(1) and 20 of the International Covenant on Civil and Political Rights; under the heading 'human rights instruments' he highlights the international individual criminal responsibility under the International Convention on the Suppression and Punishment of *Apartheid* (1973) and the Convention on the Prevention and Punishment of the Crime of Genocide (1948).

[39] Zegveld (2002: 52) questions whether: 1. there indeed exists a protection gap which is not addressed by humanitarian law,   2. human rights principles would lead to a different result from the application of humanitarian law principles, and   3. the threshold for the application of humanitarian law is arguably not as high as is presumed so that efforts should concentrate on the application of humanitarian law. Zegveld concludes (at 151) that: 'There is widespread international practice demonstrating that armed opposition groups can be held accountable for violations of international law.' But she wishes to minimize the application of human rights law to these groups. With regard to the practice she concludes (ibid): 'International practice is thus ambiguous on the question of conditions for accountability of armed opposition groups for violations of human rights law. There is some authority for the proposition that human rights instruments could govern armed opposition groups exercising governmental functions. However, this conclusion is mitigated by practice holding armed opposition groups apparently lacking any effectiveness accountable for human rights violations.' Her recommendation (at 152) points towards a cautious application of human rights law: 'since the accountability of armed opposition groups is a direct consequence of their status as parties to the conflict, there should be a close link between their accountability and their status. This is also why international bodies are and should be very cautious about holding armed opposition groups accountable for violations of human rights norms. These norms presume the existence of a government, or at least, an entity exercising governmental functions. Armed opposition groups rarely function as de facto governments'. The present book is asking the reader to reassess whether it is really true that these questions should depend on the idea that human rights norms 'presume the existence of a government'.   [40] Resolution 1214 (1998), 8 December 1998, preambular para. 12.

[41] Ibid; in full the paragraph reads: '12. *Demands* that the Afghan factions put an end to discrimination against girls and women and other violations of human rights, as well as violations of international humanitarian law, and adhere to the international norms and standards in this sphere'. See also S/RES/1193 (1998) para. 14 which '*Urges* the Afghan factions to put and end to

Council went on to suggest that local authorities that did not respect human rights should be denied reconstruction assistance.[42]

In the context of Guinea Bissau, the Security Council called on 'all concerned' to respect relevant provisions of humanitarian law and human rights, as well as to ensure unimpeded access by humanitarian organizations.[43] With regard to Liberia, the demand first mentions the use of child soldiers and then simply demands 'that all parties cease all human rights violations and atrocities against the Liberia population, and stresses the need to bring to justice those responsible'.[44] The negotiations over the former Yugoslavia involved the participation of the various parties and the formulae used by the Council in the Resolutions with regard to the former Yugoslavia included demands on various parties to, *inter alia*, facilitate humanitarian assistance and cease 'ethnic cleansing', leading Theo van Boven to conclude: 'The responsibility of Non-State Actors and their duties to respect and to comply with international law, must be regarded as inherently linked with the claim that they qualify as acceptable parties in national and international society.'[45]

---

discrimination' and other violations of human rights. Following the attack on the Taliban by the US and others, the Security Council stated that it was '*Deeply concerned* by the grave humanitarian situation and the continuing serious violations by the Taliban of human rights and international humanitarian law' (preambular para. 10 of S/RES/1378 (2001)); whereas it *called* 'on all Afghan forces to refrain from acts of reprisal, to adhere strictly to their obligations under human rights and international humanitarian law'. (Operative para. 2.) See also S/RES/1528 (2004) preambular para. 6, which called on the parties and the Government 'to prevent further violations of human rights and international humanitarian law and to put an end to impunity'. Although the Council's Resolution on weapons of mass destruction and non-state actors offers a definition of non-state actor for the purposes of the resolution, it does not address the non-state actors as such, but calls on states to take certain measures, S/RES/1540 (2004). A non-state actor is defined 'for the purpose of this resolution only' as an 'individual or entity, not acting under the lawful authority of any State in conducting activities which come within the scope of this resolution'.

[42] S/1471 (2003) at para. 4: 'Stresses also, in the context of paragraph 3 above, that while human-itarian assistance should be provided wherever there is a need, recovery or reconstruction assistance ought to be provided, through the Transitional Administration, and implemented effectively, where local authorities demonstrate a commitment to maintaining a secure environment, respecting human rights and countering narcotics.'

[43] S/RES/1216 (1998) para. 5: 'Calls upon all concerned, including the Government and the Self-Proclaimed Military Junta, to respect strictly relevant provisions of international law, including humanitarian and human rights law, and to ensure safe and unimpeded access by international humanitarian organizations to persons in need of assistance as a result of the conflict'.

[44] S/RES/1509 (2003) para. 10. See also, regarding Côte d'Ivoire, S/RES/1479 (2003) para. 8: 'Emphasizes again the need to bring to justice those responsible for the serious violations of human rights and international humanitarian law that have taken place in Côte d'Ivoire since 19 September 2002, and reiterates its demand that all Ivorian parties take all the necessary measures to prevent further violations of human rights and international humanitarian law, particularly against civilian populations whatever their origins.'

[45] T. van Boven, 'Non-State Actors; Introductory Comments [1997]' in F. Coomans, C. Flinterman, F. Grünfeld, I. Westendorp, and J. Willems (eds) *Human Rights from Exclusion to Inclusion; Principles and Practice: An Anthology from the Work of Theo van Boven* (The Hague: Kluwer, 2000) 363–369. See esp. the compilation of parties addressed by the Security Council and list of demands made at 368; cf P. Gaeta, 'The Dayton Agreements and International Law' 7 *EJIL* (1996) 147–163.

The human rights demands regarding the treatment of girls and women, access to humanitarian assistance, the use of child soldiers, and respect for the civilian population are situation specific; but the Security Council presumes that non-state actors have international obligations under the international humanitarian law of armed conflict and human rights law. The alternative explanations: that the Security Council is itself recognizing the non-state actor as a belligerent,[46] or 'creating' the obligations for the factions, seem unconvincing and unworkable. The idea that the Security Council *creates* the obligation for the actual non-state actor being targeted has been specifically dismissed by Christian Tomuschat who, having reviewed the practice of the Security Council with regard to the former Yugoslavia, Afghanistan, the Sudan, Sierra Leone, Ivory Coast, the Democratic Republic of the Congo, Angola, Liberia, and Somalia, concluded that:

> When pronouncing on the duty of parties to armed conflict to respect human rights standards, the Security Council does not intend to create new obligations. It just draws the attention of the addressees to the obligations incumbent upon them under international human rights law, as interpreted by it. For that purpose, no specific order is necessary.[47]

For Christian Tomuschat, the non-state actors are bound by international human rights law, whether or not they have consented to the relevant human rights rule:

> A movement struggling to become the legitimate government of the nation concerned is treated by the international community as an actor who, already at his embryonic stage, is subject to the essential obligations and responsibilities every State must shoulder in the interest of a civilized state of affairs among nations. The rule that any obligation requires the consent of the party concerned has long been abandoned. The international community has set up a general framework of rights and duties which every actor seeking to legitimize himself as a suitable player at the inter-State level must respect.[48]

But Tomuschat's underlying rationale for this approach is based on a recognition that 'elements of governmental authority have fallen into the hands of a rebel movement'.[49] This leaves open the possibility that, where rebels are not seen as exercising government authority, they may avoid international human rights obligations. It is well known that neither governments nor international organizations will readily admit that rebels are operating in ways which are akin to governments. Linking rebel obligations to their government-like status is likely to result in there being few situations where human rights obligations can be unequivocally

---

[46] This question is examined by Wolfrum and Philipp (2002: 583–584) with regard to the Taliban; they conclude that Security Council statements concerning the application of humanitarian law were declaratory rather than constitutive and that no recognition as belligerents by the Security Council can be implied.

[47] C. Tomuschat, 'The Applicability of Human Rights Law to Insurgent Movements' in H. Fischer, U. Froissart, W. Heintschel von Heinegg, and C. Raap (eds) *Krisensicherung und Humanitärer Schutz—Crisis Management and Humanitarian Protection: Festschrift für Dieter Fleck* (Berlin: Berliner Wissenschafts-Verlag, 2004) 573–591, at 586.　　　　[48] Ibid, at 587.

[49] Ibid, at 588.

applied to insurgents. One effectively returns to the position of those commentators who dismiss the applicability of human rights obligations for insurgents on the grounds that non-state actors rarely operate as *de facto* governments,[50] and in any event are incapable of protecting human rights. Lindsay Moir accepts the full application of humanitarian obligations for insurgents but is adamant that such non-state actors have no human rights obligations:

> Human rights obligations are binding on governments only, and the law has not yet reached the stage whereby, during internal armed conflict, insurgents are bound to observe the human rights of government forces, let alone of opposing insurgents. Non-governmental parties are particularly unlikely to have the capacity to uphold certain rights (e.g. the right to due process, being unlikely to have their own legal system, courts, etc.).[51]

Rather than focusing on the obligations that insurgents cannot fulfil (fair trial with legal aid and interpretation, progressive implementation of access to university education) it is preferable to stress that the obligations apply to the extent appropriate to the context. As discussed in Chapter 6, it is now understood that more is expected of larger corporations with an extended sphere of influence than might be expected of small family firms. Even conventional human rights law demands that a state take steps 'to the maximum of its available resources' to fulfil progressively its human rights obligations in the context of economic and social rights.[52] It might therefore be more realistic to accept that there may be a fifth theory, which could be called a 'presumptive' theory.[53] It will be presumed that rebel groups have international humanitarian law obligations when the fighting rises to the threshold level foreseen in the treaties and the corresponding customary rules.

  With regard to human rights obligations we have seen that these are currently presumed by the United Nations to apply when they are being flagrantly denied by a faction, party to a conflict, or armed opposition group.[54] For Dieter Fleck it is simply 'logical' that if the insurgents can have obligations under humanitarian law they should also be able to bear human rights obligations.[55] From here it is a small step to suggest that such international human rights obligations apply at all times to all armed opposition groups (even before the appeals of the Security Council).

---

[50] Zegveld (2002: 152) discussed at n 39 above.   [51] Moir (2002: 194).

[52] Art. 2(1) International Covenant on Economic, Social and Cultural Rights.

[53] Cf J. Klabbers, 'Presumptive Personality: The European Union in International Law' in Koskenniemi (ed) *International Law Aspects of the of the European Union* (The Hague: Kluwer, 1998) 231–253.

[54] Zegveld (2002: 48) highlights the Security Council Afghanistan Resolution 1193 (1998) and also mentions the Resolution on Angola (S/RES1213 (1998)) which is addressed not only to the Government of Angola but also to UNITA.

[55] According to Dieter Fleck: 'If non-state actors have human rights, it appears logical that they also must have responsibilities, no different from the obligations insurgents have under international humanitarian law. There is a clear trend to subject non-state actors to human rights law.' D. Fleck, 'Humanitarian Protection Against Non-State Actors' in *Verhandeln für den Frieden—Negotiating for Peace: Liber Amicorum Tono Eitel* (Berlin: Springer, 2003) 69–94, at 79.

To those who would prefer to rely simply on humanitarian law I would respond as follows: first, this branch of international law does not apply in the absence of protracted armed conflict, and second, the added value of the human rights framework allows for a wider range of accountability mechanisms, including monitoring by the Special Rapporteurs of the UN Commission of Human Rights.

7.4   SUCCESSFUL INSURRECTIONAL AND OTHER MOVEMENTS

The International Law Commission (ILC) articles on 'Responsibility of States for Internationally Wrongful Acts'[56] stipulate that the conduct of an insurrectional movement, which succeeds in becoming the new government, is conduct which gives rise to state responsibility under international law.[57] In addition to insurrectional movements, 'other' movements that succeed in establishing a new *state* will also be held responsible, as a state, for their unlawful acts committed while they were a non-state actor.[58] There is no need in such cases for any recognition until the insurgency succeeds. The new government is obviously recognized in the context of the eventual claim made against it. At that point the insurrectional (or other) movement's behaviour is treated as if it were a government at the time of its internationally wrongful acts.[59] The obligations at the time would include, not only the rules of international humanitarian law, briefly referred to above, but also general rules of international law including, it is now suggested, international human rights law.[60]

The history of this rule of attribution in the context of state responsibility reflects state practice concerning claims made regarding 'damage caused to foreigners by an insurrectionist party which has been successful'.[61] The background to the rule of attribution involves the substantive law concerning the protection of aliens rather than the laws of armed conflict (which historically were rather underdeveloped

---

[56] See UN Doc. A/Res/56/83, adopted 12 December 2001. The Commentary is found in A/56/10, Report of the ILC, adopted at its 53rd session, 2001. The Commentary is also reproduced together with a helpful introduction and appendices in J. Crawford, *The International Law Commission's Articles on State Responsibility: Introduction, Text and Commentaries* (Cambridge: Cambridge University Press, 2002a).

[57] Art. 10(1): 'The conduct of an insurrectional movement which becomes the new government of a State shall be considered an act of that State under international law.'

[58] Art. 10(2): 'The conduct of a movement, insurrectional or other, which succeeds in establishing a new State in part of the territory of a pre-existing State or in a territory under its administration shall be considered an act of the new State under international law.'

[59] It has been suggested that this responsibility arises 'as from the beginning of the revolution', C. F. Amerasinghe, *State Responsibility for Injuries to Aliens* (Oxford: Clarendon, 1967) at 54.

[60] D. Matas, 'Armed Opposition Groups' 24 *Manitoba Law Journal* (1997) 621–634.

[61] See para. 13 of Art. 10, the ILC Commentary (n 56 above) at p 117 citing a document prepared for the 1930 Preparatory Committee for the Codification Conference.

with regard to internal armed conflict). Today the substantive law on the protection of aliens has been overtaken by the international law of human rights,[62] and it makes sense simply to apply the law of human rights to the successful insurgents.

The definition of 'dissident armed forces' is said to capture the 'essential idea of an "insurrectional movement" '.[63] The ILC Commentary suggests that a guide to the sort of groups which are covered by this rule can be found in the threshold criteria contained in Protocol II to the Geneva Conventions. Protocol II covers armed conflicts which take place between the forces of a party to the treaty and 'dissident armed forces or other organized armed groups which, under responsible command, exercise such control over a part of its territory as to enable them to carry out sustained and concerted military operations and to implement this Protocol'. The ILC identifies certain situations that are not covered, with the result that groups engaged in such activity would not count as insurrectional movements.[64] Article 1(2) states: 'This Protocol shall not apply to situations of internal disturbances and tensions, such as riots, isolated and sporadic acts of violence and other acts of a similar nature, as not being armed conflicts.' The Commentary excludes from the article's reference to 'other movements', 'the actions of a group of citizens advocating separation or revolution where these are carried out within the framework of the predecessor State'.[65]

Unsuccessful insurrectional movements fall outside the application of the rules of state responsibility, but the International Law Commission is careful to state that an unsuccessful insurrectional movement may be held responsible for their own breaches of international law.[66] In other words, unsuccessful movements may have international human rights obligations, but they are not detected when one examines them through the state responsibility filter.

7.5 PRACTICAL STEPS TAKEN TO ENSURE RESPECT FOR HUMAN RIGHTS BY NON-STATE ACTORS IN TIMES OF ARMED CONFLICT

It would be tempting to leave the issue here: international humanitarian law applies to all sides, in accordance with the thresholds outlined in that branch of

---

[62] See John Dugard, Special Rapporteur, ILC, First report on diplomatic protection, UN Doc. A/CN.4/506, 7 March 2000, at para. 32: 'Contemporary international human rights law accords to nationals and aliens the same protection, which far exceeds the international minimum standard of treatment for aliens set by Western Powers in an earlier era.'

[63] ILC Commentary (n 56 above) para. 9 to Art. 10, at 115.   [64] Ibid.

[65] Ibid, para. 10 of Art. 10, at 115.

[66] Ibid, para. 16 of Art. 10, at 118: 'A further possibility is that the insurrectional movement may itself be held responsible for its own conduct under international law, for example for a breach of international humanitarian law committed by its forces. The topic of the international responsibility of unsuccessful insurrectional or other movements, however, falls outside the scope of the present Articles, which are concerned only with the responsibility of States.'

law, and human rights obligations can be discerned from the practice of the Security Council and applied more generally. Where an insurgent or other movement succeeds in becoming a new government or creating a new state, that new government will be internationally responsible for the violations of international law committed by the movement. But serious practical problems remain; the theory does not work in practice.

First, as mentioned above, by relying on the threshold criteria, such as those found in Protocol II,[67] one is in reality asking a government to accept that rebels have control of territory and have achieved some sort of authority. Governments have been reluctant to do this or even recognize the arguably lower threshold in Common Article 3, i.e. that that there is an 'armed conflict not of an international character occurring within the territory of one of the High Contracting Parties'.[68] Although the treaties are at pains to point out that the application of the rules confers no recognition or status on the rebels, governments nevertheless often deny the applicability of these norms. Does such a denial really matter? As Christopher Greenwood has emphasized, 'the acceptance by a government that an armed conflict exists is not a legal prerequisite', the obligations in Common Article 3 and Protocol II 'are stated to be applicable provided that certain objective criteria are met'.[69] So if the law applies should we worry about the attitude of the government? The attitude of the government is, of course, relevant as it obviously becomes harder to convince the rebels that they should comply with rules that the government is refusing to acknowledge as the appropriate framework for their own troops. Despite the fact that the rules are designed to protect the victims of war, rather than create a level playing field, the reciprocity between government

[67] The Protocol applies to 'all armed conflicts which are not covered by Article 1 of the Protocol Additional to the Geneva Conventions of 12 August 1949, and relating to the Protection of Victims of International Armed Conflicts (Protocol I) and which take place in the territory of a High Contracting Party between its armed forces and dissident armed forces or other organized armed groups which, under responsible command, exercise such control over a part of its territory as to enable them to carry out sustained and concerted military operations and to implement this Protocol. (2) This Protocol shall not apply to situations of internal disturbances and tensions, such as riots, isolated and sporadic acts of violence and other acts of a similar nature, as not being armed conflicts.' Art. 1(1) and (2). The Protocol has been applied in Russia (Chechnya), Colombia, El Salvador, and Rwanda.

[68] With regard to Art. 3, the International Criminal Tribunal for the former Yugoslavia's definition of an armed conflict is increasingly applied. In *Prosecutor v Tadić* (jurisdiction) Case IT–94–1–AR72, 2 October 1995, the Appeals Chamber posited a definition of the meaning of armed conflict and the scope of the obligations (at para. 70): 'an armed conflict exists whenever there is a resort to armed force between States or protracted armed violence between governmental authorities and organized armed groups or between such groups within a State. International humanitarian law applies from the initiation of such armed conflicts and extends beyond the cessation of hostilities until a general conclusion of peace is reached; or, in the case of internal conflicts, a peaceful settlement is achieved. Until that moment, international humanitarian law continues to apply in the whole territory of the warring States or, in the case of internal conflicts, the whole territory under the control of a party, whether or not actual combat takes place there'.

[69] C. Greenwood, 'International Humanitarian Law (Laws of War)' in F. Kalshoven (ed) *The Centennial of the First International Peace Conference* (The Hague: Kluwer Law International, 2000) 161–259, at 231.

and rebels remains important—and that very suggestion of parity is part of the problem.

Second, turning to the rebels, theories concerning why they should comply with these norms are of more than academic interest. Arguments that rest on national commitments or international custom may be rejected by rebels who have neither participated in the process, nor been allowed to adhere to the treaty.[70] Reliance on the binding nature of national law (even where this merely implements international law) may be met with a frosty response in situations where the rebels seek to challenge the legitimacy of the regime to adopt any law at all. While some rebel groups seeking to become the government of a state may be looking for international legitimacy, and could perhaps be convinced of the need to accept the application of norms accepted by the international community of states, other groups may have no such aspirations, being content with control of certain natural resources and the opportunity to run organized criminal activity.[71]

Perhaps it is time for a radical rethink. As discussed in Chapter 1, human rights organizations, such as Amnesty International, are reporting on armed groups and demanding respect for human rights obligations outside the framework of humanitarian law obligations (recruitment of under-eighteens, abuses of humanitarian workers, denial of freedom of expression through restrictions on journalists, etc.).[72] Human Rights Watch have reported on the forced divorces and physical abuses inflicted by an armed opposition group on their own fighters.[73] In short, human rights monitors are expanding the traditional normative framework beyond humanitarian law. An interesting development in this field is the adoption of

---

[70] See generally M. Sassòli, 'Possible Legal Mechanisms to Improve Compliance by Armed Groups with International Humanitarian Law and International Human Rights Law', Conference Paper, University of Quebec in Montreal, available at http://www.ihlresearch.org/ihl/ (2000); Zegveld (2002: 17, fn 27).

[71] See the discussion by C. Bruderlein, 'The role of non-state actors in building human security: the case of armed groups in intra-state wars' (Geneva: Centre for Humanitarian Dialogue, 2000) at 11.

[72] See *Israel and the Occupied Territories and the Palestinian Authority: Without distinction—attacks on civilians by Palestinian armed groups*, AI Index MDE 02/003/2002; regarding armed groups in Algeria, *Algeria: Steps towards change or empty promises?*, MDE 28/005/2003 (to immediately stop targeting civilians and respect the most fundamental human right, the right to life; to immediately stop the practice of abducting women and girls and subjecting them to rape and other forms of torture). Regarding armed political groups in the Democratic Republic of Congo, see *DRC: On the precipice: the deepening human rights and humanitarian crisis in Ituri*, AI Index AFR 62/006/2003 (armed political groups should immediately cease unlawful killings and other human rights abuses against civilians and combatants who have ceased to take part in hostilities; all forces should immediately cease harassment of and human rights abuses against humanitarian NGO staff and human rights activists and ensure unhindered and safe access for humanitarian agencies to all areas under their control; all armed groups should end the recruitment into their forces of child soldiers under the age of 18 and cooperate with MONUC and other appropriate agencies for the disarmament, demobilization, and reintegration of these children.) See also *DRC: Addressing the present and building a future*, AI Index AFR 62/050/2003; and *Haiti: Abuse of human rights: political violence as the 200th anniversary of independence approaches*, AI Index AMR 36/007/2003. See also *Iraq: In cold blood: abuses by armed groups*, AI Index MDE 14/009/2005.

[73] Human Rights Watch, *No Exit: Human Rights Abuses Inside the MKO Camps* (May 2005).

commitments, declarations, codes of conduct, and memoranda of understanding by the armed groups themselves. Such texts increasingly refer to human rights standards and have been tailored to the particularities of the situation. The preliminary empirical work done in this area 'suggests that where armed groups do commit themselves to written codes of conduct, this encourages them to respect human rights'.[74] Another study of eleven such codes with regard to Burundi, Liberia, Somalia, Sierra Leone, Afghanistan, Sudan, the Democratic Republic of the Congo, Angola, East and West Timor, the Democratic People's Republic of Korea, and the Russian Federation revealed that 'for non-State actors, the agreements refer to international human rights customary law'.[75] This study also notes that all of the agreements state that the beneficiaries of humanitarian aid are to enjoy the following rights: 'the right to live in security and dignity, the right to basic needs, the right to receive humanitarian assistance without discrimination and according to basic needs, the right to be involved in humanitarian activities of concern to them, the right to legal and effective human rights protection, and the right to protection against forced population transfer'.[76] In addition to these rather generic codes of conduct, two particular initiatives are highlighted below.

7.5.1   The Special Representative of the Secretary-General for Children and Armed Conflict

The Special Representative of the Secretary-General for children and armed conflict has obtained commitments from over sixty armed groups. His report to the General Assembly explained:

> In Sri Lanka in 1998, the Liberation Tigers of Tamil Eelam committed not to use children under 18 years of age in combat and not to recruit those under 17 years of age.... In Sierra Leone in 1999, the Special Representative secured commitments from the Revolutionary United Front to allow humanitarian access and the release of abducted children and child soldiers, while the Civil Defence Force committed to the non-recruitment and the demobilization of child soldiers. These commitments were successfully monitored and followed through by UNAMSIL and UNICEF; In the Democratic Republic of the Congo in June 2001, the Special Representative obtained the commitment of all political and military leaders to a five-point plan of action for ending child soldiering. The United Nations Organization Mission in the Democratic Republic of the Congo and UNICEF have followed up on this commitment. Altogether, the Special Representative has received some 60 commitments from 15 parties. Although they have all become important advocacy benchmarks, a number of these

---

[74] International Council on Human Rights Policy, *Ends and Means: human rights approaches to armed groups* (Versoix: ICHRP, 2000) at 52.

[75] J.-D. Vigny and C. Thompson, 'Fundamental Standards of Humanity: What Future?' 20 *NQHR* (2002) 185–199, at 193.   [76] Ibid, at 194.

commitments remain unobserved. As with other standards, the challenge is to ensure systematic monitoring and the application of pressure for enforcement.[77]

The monitoring of such commitments may sound as though it is devoid of any enforcement mechanism, but the interest of the UN Security Council in this field means that legally enforceable sanctions have been envisaged to ensure compliance more generally. The Secretary-General proposed that the Security Council consider measures such as the imposition of travel restrictions on leaders and the exclusion of such leaders from any governance structures and amnesty provisions to bring armed groups into compliance with their obligations.[78] The Security Council initially has responded by noting its concern with regard to the continued recruitment and use of children by parties mentioned in the Secretary-General's report 'in violation of applicable international law relating to the rights and protection of children'[79] and expressed an 'intention to consider imposing targeted and graduated measures, through country-specific resolutions, such as, inter alia, a ban on the export or supply of small arms and light weapons and of other military equipment and on military assistance, against these parties if they refuse to enter into dialogue, fail to develop an action plan or fail to meet the commitments included in their action plan, bearing in mind the Secretary-General's report'.[80] More recently, the Security Council decided to establish a working group to review progress by relevant parties and make recommendations to the Council and other UN bodies.[81]

Armed groups anxious to be taken seriously in the context of any peace initiatives organized by the United Nations will watch the pronouncements of the Security Council with particular attention. The Special Representative's list for 'naming and shaming' parties for non-cooperation, failure to cease recruitment of child soldiers, and for committing other 'abuses and violations' shows how far the United Nations has come in holding non-state actors accountable for human rights abuses.[82] With regard to the actual commitments entered into by the non-state actors, the Security Council called on 'all parties concerned to abide by the international obligations applicable to them relating to the protection of children affected by armed conflict, *as well as the concrete commitments they have made to the Special Representative of the Secretary-General for Children and Armed Conflict, to UNICEF and other United Nations agencies,* and to cooperate fully with the UN peace-keeping missions and UN country teams, where appropriate, in the context

---

[77] UN Doc. A/58/328, 29 August 2003, paras 21–22. The status of the commitments and the compliance record are available at http://www.un.org/special-rep/children-armed-conflict/English/Commitments.html.

[78] 'Report of the Secretary-General: Children and Armed Conflict' UN Doc. A/58/546–S/2003/1053, 10 November 2003, at para. 105(g); see further A/59/695–S/2005/72, 9 February 2005.   [79] SC Res. 1539 (2004), 22 April 2004, para. 5.

[80] Ibid, para. 5(c).   [81] S/Res/1612 (2005), 26 July 2005.

[82] 'Report of the Secretary-General: Children and Armed Conflict' UN Doc. A/59/695–S/2005/72, 9 February 2005, Annexes I and II.

of the cooperation framework between the United Nations and the concerned government, in the follow-up and implementation of these commitments.[83]

7.5.2   Geneva Call

'Geneva Call is an international humanitarian organisation dedicated to engaging armed non-state actors (NSAs) to respect and to adhere to humanitarian norms, starting with the ban on antipersonnel (AP) mines.'[84] The centre-piece of its approach involves the relevant non-state actors signing a 'Deed of Commitment for Adherence to a Total Ban on Anti-Personnel Mines and for Cooperation in Mine Action'. Non-state actors are not currently entitled to sign the Ottawa Convention on the Prohibition of the Use, Stockpiling, Production and Transfer of Anti-Personnel Mines and on their Destruction. In fact, unlike the provisions of the 1977 Protocol I to the Geneva Conventions[85] and the 1980 Convention on Prohibitions or Restrictions on the Use of Certain Weapons Which May be Deemed to be Excessively Injurious or to Have Indiscriminate Effects,[86] the Ottawa Convention contains no provision for a declaration expressing a willingness to be bound from even the narrow category of authorities representing a people 'fighting against colonial domination and alien occupation and against racist regimes in the exercise of their right of self-determination'.[87]

During the negotiations for the Ottawa Convention it was in fact proposed by Colombia that the treaty include a provision regulating armed opposition groups, however, no provision was included in the main body of the treaty. Similarly, nothing came of the proposal by the International Campaign to Ban Landmines to bind all parties to a conflict involving a state party, as well as all persons and entities in the territory of a state party during peacetime.[88] It has been suggested

---

[83] Ibid, para. 4 (emphasis added). The Commitments to the SRSG are listed together with comments concerning compliance at http://www.un.org/special-rep/children-armed-conflict/English/Commitments.html. As of 20 July 2005, the following commitments from non-state actors were listed: The Sudan People's Liberation Movement gave its commitment not to use anti-personnel Landmines in the southern conflict zone; During the 1998 visit to Sierra Leone, the Civil Defense Forces committed itself to stop recruiting children under the age of 18. This commitment was reiterated in the Lomé Peace Accord and in the Human Rights Manifesto; the Revolutionary United Front committed itself to stop recruitment of children under the age of 18; in Sri Lanka the Liberation Tigers of Tamil Eelam (LTTE) leadership made a commitment not to use children below 18 in combat, and not to recruit children below the age of 17; the LTTE pledged not to impede the return to their homes of Muslim populations displaced by previous outbreaks of hostilities; the Revolutionary Armed Forces of Colombia announced that they would no longer recruit young persons under 15.

[84] From the website: http://www.genevacall.org/home.htm. In the interests of transparency, it should be pointed out that the present author has been a member of the Board of Geneva Call since 2004.   [85] See Arts 96(3) and I(4).

[86] See Art. 7(4).

[87] Art. 1(4) of Additional Protocol I of 1977 to the Geneva Conventions of 1949.

[88] S. Maslen, *Commentaries on Arms Control Treaties, Volume I, The Convention on the Prohibition of the Use, Stockpiling, Production, and Transfer of Anti-Personnel Mines and on their Destruction* (Oxford: Oxford University Press, 2004) at 53, 64, and 74–75.

that disarmament treaties can be distinguished from humanitarian law treaties where 'purported legal applicability to "all parties to the conflict" is no stranger'.[89] But non-state actors may in fact already be bound under weapons treaties. As Kathleen Lawand from the International Committee of the Red Cross (ICRC) has pointed out, as regards states parties to amended Protocol II to the Convention on Certain Conventional Weapons, non-state actors 'would be bound to respect the Protocol's restrictions on the use of anti-personnel mines, without prejudice to them unilaterally adhering to a total ban on use of these weapons'.[90] Moreover, the amended Convention itself (which entered into force on 18 May 2004) has a similar reach, as its Article 1 replicates the obligation on non-state actors engaged in armed conflict with a state party and extends this obligation with regard to the other protocols: 'In case of armed conflicts not of an international character occurring in the territory of one of the High Contracting Parties, each party to the conflict shall be bound to apply the prohibitions and restrictions of this Protocol.'[91] One should not therefore assume that today, weapons treaties are somehow in a different category of the laws of war and thus unable to fix obligations on non-state actors.

Returning to the Ottawa Convention on Anti-Personnel Mines, it is clear that, despite the proposals mentioned above, the treaty does not explicitly bind non-state parties to an internal conflict, nor does it make a specific reference to the possibilities of declarations by national liberation movements. This omission has led to alternative methods of encouraging armed groups to abandon the use of anti-personnel mines. Addressing a wide spectrum of armed groups (and not relying on the concept of self-determination struggles referred to above) Geneva Call has invited armed groups to sign a 'Deed of Commitment' for 'Adherence to a total ban on anti-personnel mines and for cooperation in mine action'. As of 20 November 2004, Deeds of Commitment had been signed by twenty-six armed groups from Africa, Asia, and the Middle East.[92] Three aspects of this initiative are worth highlighting in the current context: the possible extension of such deeds to

---

[89] Maslen (2004: 64).

[90] K. Lawand, 'Reviewing the Legal Regime' in *Looking Back, Looking Forward—Workshop on Engaging Non-State Actors in a Landmine Ban*, International Campaign to Ban Landmines and Geneva Call, 13 September 2003, Bangkok at 3; the paper contains the usual disclaimer that the views do not necessarily reflect the position of the ICRC.

[91] Although the amended Convention allows for future Protocols to avoid this extension to non-state actors, Protocol V on Explosive Remnants of War does refer back to the amended Art. 1 of the Convention.

[92] See from Burundi: Conseil National pour la Défense de la Démocratie—Forces pour la Défense de la Démocratie (CNDD-FDD) (Hussein Radjabu), signed 15 December 2003; from Somalia all signed 11 November 2002: Banidiri (Mohamed Osman Maye); Hiran Patriotic Alliance (HPA)/Somali Reconciliation and Restoration Council (SRRC) (Hasan Abdulle Qalad); Jowhar Administration (Mohamed Omar Habeb 'Dhere') Puntland State of Somalia (Abdullahi Yusuf), Rahanweyn Resistance Army (RRA)/SRRC (faction of Hassan Mohamed Nur 'Shatigudud' and faction of Sheikh Adan Madobe); Somali African Muki Organisation (SAMO)/SRRC/Nakuru (Mowlid Ma'ane Mohamud); Somali National Front (SNF)/SRRC (Mohamed Sayid Aden); Somali Patriotic Movement (SPM)/SRRC (Aden Abdullahi Nur, 'Gabyow'); Southern Somali National Movement (SSNM)/BIREM (Abdullahi Sheikh Ismail); Southern Somali National Movement

cover human rights abuses; the commitment to go beyond the scope of the equivalent governmental treaty obligations; and the plurality of accountability mechanisms. Let us deal with each of these in turn.

7.5.2.1   The Commitment as a Step towards Recognizing the Human Rights Obligations of Non-State Actors

Article 5 in the standard Deed includes a commitment:

> TO TREAT this commitment as one step or part of a broader commitment in principle to the ideal of humanitarian norms, particularly of international humanitarian law and human rights, and to contribute to their respect in field practice as well as to the further development of humanitarian norms for armed conflicts.

An annotated commentary, prepared by Soliman Santos, stated that, in addition to the obligation to contribute to the development of humanitarian law, the Deed of Commitment reflects the fact that future work of Geneva Call may use human rights as the basis for future commitments regarding: 'torture, use of child soldiers, civilian targeted bombings and "acts of threats of violence the primary purpose of which is to spread terror among the civilian population" '.[93] The preamble to the standard Deed contains two clear references to human rights obligations that suggest that, even though human rights are not the specific subject of the commitments in the Deed and its implementation/accountability mechanisms, *it is recognized that armed groups have human rights obligations.*[94]

> *Reaffirming* our determination to protect the civilian population from the effects or dangers of military actions, and to respect their rights to life, to human dignity, and to development...

(SSNM)/SNA/SRRC (Abdulaziz Sheikh Yusuf); Transitional National Government (Hassan Abshir and Abdalla Derow Isak); United Somali Congress (USC)/Somali National Alliance (SNA)/(SRRC) (Hussein Farah Aideed); USC/North Mogadishu/SRRC (Hilowle Imam Omar); USC/SNA/SRRC/ Nakuru (Osman Hassan Ali 'Ato'); USC/Somali Salvation Army (SSA) (Omar Mohamoud Mohamed 'Finish'). From Sudan: Sudan People's Liberation Movement and Sudan People's Liberation Army (SPLM/A) (Nhial Deng Nhial), signed 4 October 2001. From Burma/Myanmar: Arakan Rohingya National Organisation (ARNO) (Nurul Islam, Salim Ullah), signed 2003; National United Party of Arakan (NUPA) (Khing Maung, Khaing Zaw), signed 2003; From India: National Socialist Council of Nagalim (NSCN) (Thuingaleng Muivah), signed 17 October 2003. From the Philippines: Moro Islamic Liberation Front (MILF) (Al Haj Murad), signed 7 April 2002; Revolutionary Proletarian Army—Alex Boncayao Brigade (RPA-ABB) (Arturo Tabara, Nilo de la Cruz), signed 10 September 2002; Revolutionary Workers Party of Mindanao (RPM-M) (Harry Tubongbanwa), 11 September 2003. From Iraq: Kurdistan Regional Government—Erbil, Democratic Party of Kurdistan (Shawkat Sheikhyezdin), signed 11 August 2002; Kurdistan Regional Government—Sulaimanyia, Patriotic Union of Kurdistan (Adnan Mufti), signed 10 August 2002.

[93] S. M. Santos, 'Geneva Call's Deed of Commitment for Armed Groups: An Annotation' in *Seeking Rebel Accountability: Report of the Geneva Call Mission to the MILF in the Philippines, 3–8 April 2002* (Geneva: Geneva Call, 2002) 82–91, at 88. The quotation regarding acts of terror is from Protocol 1, Art. 51(2) and Protocol II, Art. 13(2).

[94] Recall also the Berlin Resolution of the International Law Institute 1999, discussed in Ch 2 above: 'The Application of International Humanitarian Law and Fundamental Human Rights, in Armed Conflicts in which Non-State Entities are Parties'.

Accepting that international humanitarian law and human rights apply to and oblige all parties to armed conflicts;

Such explicit recognition by the groups themselves helps to transform the debate about the human rights obligations of non-state actors. If armed groups are prepared to take on these human rights obligations, arguments about their non-applicability under international law lose much of their force. States may fear the legitimacy that such commitments seem to imply—but from a victim's perspective such commitments may indeed be worth more than the paper they are written on. If the language of human rights obligations becomes the medium for the protection of human dignity, this should be welcomed rather than dismissed as legally illiterate. The extension beyond the issue of anti-personnel mines into human rights obligations for non-state actors is foreseen in the Statute of Geneva Call, which states that its aim is to be 'dedicated to engaging armed non-State actors to adhere to a ban on landmines and to respect humanitarian and human rights norms, in particular, through the signing of deeds of commitment to a total ban on:—the use of anti-personnel mines;—the enrolment and/or the use of child soldiers;—the practice of torture and other cruel, inhuman or degrading treatment'.[95]

Lastly, it should be recalled that claims regarding any sort of legal status accruing from the Deed are explicitly renounced in Article 6: 'This Deed of Commitment shall not affect our legal status, pursuant to the relevant clause in common article 3 of the Geneva Conventions of August 12, 1949.' The commentary by Santos states that this 'simply means that signing it does not add to or subtract from the existing legal status of the concerned armed group. In particular, there is no grant here of belligerency status, after all an obsolete concept in international law'.[96] It cannot be denied, however, that a partial effect of the Deed is to endow the non-state actor with some sort of enhanced moral status; by eclipsing the traditional legal approach, whereby the focus is on international recognition by governments and inter-governmental organizations, Geneva Call has opened the door to a new accountability mechanism for armed opposition groups. Rather than depending on the internationally legally significant Swiss Government (the depositary of the Geneva Conventions), the Republic and Canton of Geneva as 'custodian' of the Deed achieves the symbolism of Geneva law,[97] without running

---

[95] Art. 3.   [96] Santos (2002: 89). See also Riedel (2000a) and (2000b).

[97] According to the official website of the Etat de Genève, the Geneva Conseil d'Etat wrote to the Swiss Federal Government drawing its attention to the problems associated with anti-personnel mines and their use by non-state actors; the Conseil has asked the Federal authorities to take the necessary *démarches* to include a provision inspired by Art. 96(3) of Protocol I so that such an authority representing a people fighting for liberation against a state party could make a declaration and become bound under the amended treaty. Accepting that such a *démarche* will take time, the Geneva Government decided to act as custodian for the unilateral declarations renouncing the use of anti-personnel mines collected by Geneva Call. ('[L]e gouvernement genevois a décidé de conserver, à titre intérimaire, par sa chancellerie d'Etat, des déclarations unilatérales par lesquelles les groupes non-étatiques s'engagent à renoncer à l'utilisation des mines antipersonnel qui sont recueillies par

into the usual obstacles that international law has placed on the participation of non-state actors. In this way, the armed opposition groups have been able to go beyond the limiting inter-state framework and make humanitarian commitments beyond their obligations under a formal reading of international humanitarian law.

7.5.2.2   The Scope of the Obligations in the Commitment

Turning to the scope of the obligations, it is clear that the theory regarding the application of treaty rights to the inhabitants of a state is of no relevance to the assumption of obligations through these deeds of commitment. Deeds of commitment are entered into, not only in situations where the state has ratified the Ottawa treaty, but also where the government is not bound by international law under that treaty. Furthermore, the substance of the obligations undertaken by the non-state actors goes beyond the obligations contained in the treaty. Anti-personnel mines are defined by their *impact or effect*, rather than with regard to the *design intention*. Article 1 of the standard Deed of Commitment defines the objects of the ban as: 'those devices which effectively explode by the presence, proximity or contact of a person, including other victim-activated explosive devices and anti-vehicle mines with the same effect whether with or without anti-handling devices'. In addition, there are no exceptions permitted under the Deeds of Commitment, unlike the Ottawa treaty, where as governments have ensured exceptions for themselves with regard to training in detection and destruction techniques.

7.5.2.3   Accountability and Monitoring

The possibilities for ensuring accountability might be considered to pose the biggest problems. Nevertheless, if one reflects for a moment, the accountability of states for their commitments made under international treaties is also less than perfect. Inter-state complaints before the International Court of Justice are rare. Reprisals in the form of trade sanctions have proven to be blunt instruments, and are difficult to implement in the light of commitments undertaken in the context of the WTO.[98] Under the Ottawa treaty, the specific accountability mechanism is the state reporting obligation. Self-reporting by states is seen as central to account-ability. An innovative aspect of Geneva Call's project has been the demand for compliance reports from the non-state actor signatories to Geneva Call's Deeds of

l'Appel de Genève.') Point de presse 29 March 2000, available at http://www.geneve.ch/chancellerie/conseil/1997–2001. One might point out that any amendment to the Ottawa Convention which would be limited to recognized liberation movements would severely restrict the legal applicability under the treaty to non-state actors of the type currently engaged in the Geneva Call initiative. As the formula under Protocol I has led to no recognized declaration in 25 years, it seems likely that the political problems with regard to admitting the existence of a category of liberation movements would remain. See further D. Matas, 'The law: a tool to engage non-state actors in a landmine ban' in M. Foster (ed) *Engaging non-state actors in a landmine ban: a pioneering conference*, Conference held in Geneva, 24–25 March 2000, Quezon City (Philippines: Conference Organizers, 2001) 130–135.

   [98] See Ch 5, at 5.1.1.3 above.

Commitment. Among the details requested are reports on the disciplinary regime put in place for sanctions by the non-state actors themselves against commanders or others who allow the use of anti-personnel mines. In addition, the report is to give details of actual sanctions taken.

The accountability mechanism also includes an obligation on the part of the non-state actor to allow for monitoring and verification.[99] So far, some verification has predictably proven problematic for political and security reasons, although certain issues have been clarified through monitoring in the field.[100] One concrete sanction foreseen in the Deed is the possibility of publicity for non-compliance.[101] One might ask why rebel groups should care about publicity concerning a breached commitment? The reasons are the same as the motivations that affect the willingness to make the commitment in the first place.

First, such a commitment is a step towards increased legitimacy within the international community, and thus to political support for demands related to human rights or political autonomy. Second, such a commitment makes it easier to argue that the government forces should give up the use of landmines. Where a government is refusing to enter into an international commitment, such as the Ottawa treaty, this can be used to present the rebelling party as more humanitarian than the regime it is fighting. Third, in some cases, by 'getting ahead' of other non-state actors, the committed group can present themselves as a superior partner for a variety of entities in the international community (observer states, international organizations, and non-governmental organizations (NGOs) may all feel more comfortable working with a group committed (even in part) to upholding international norms). Fourth, signing the commitment opens the way for Geneva Call to facilitate mine action in rebel-held areas. Finally, some representatives of some non-state actors may be genuinely moved by a sense of 'humanitarianism'. At least one negotiation and signing took place in the Alabama Room in Geneva—the room where the first Geneva Convention was signed in 1864—and a symbolic room in the history of international arbitration and the peaceful settlement of disputes. One cannot rule out that some sentiments permeating the international law of dispute settlement and humanitarian law might play a role. In this vein, some parallel unilateral statements issued by armed non-state actors

---

[99] See generally para. 3 of the Deed of Commitment.

[100] See Geneva Call, *Seeking Rebel Accountability: Report of the Geneva Call Mission to the MILF in the Philippines, 3–8 April 2002* (Geneva: Geneva Call, 2002); see also Santos, who has referred to the opportunity during that mission to verify and clarify 'admitted use of "string-pulled" improvised APMs and on the correct concept of "command detonation" ', 'A Critical Reflection on The Geneva Call Instrument and Approach in Engaging Armed Groups on Humanitarian Norms: A Southern Perspective', paper for the Conference, Curbing Human Rights Violations by Non-State Armed Groups, 13–15 November 2003, The Armed Groups Project, Centre for International Relations, Liu Institute—University of British Columbia, at 11.

[101] Para. 7 states: 'We understand that Geneva Call may publicize our compliance or non-compliance with this Deed of Commitment.'

make preambular references to religious beliefs and teachings.[102] Other similar statements refer in a secular way to the dignity of the people whose support the non-state actors are hoping to secure.[103] Motivations will always be mixed, and however difficult these commitments are to monitor, the Deeds of Commitment do illustrate an interesting regime for holding non-state actors to account for abuses of rules based on international law.

Do such commitments contribute to the elaboration of international obligations for the non-state actors themselves? It is suggested that we can discern a hardening of the obligations in the context of this process. First, the unilateral commitment made towards, not only an NGO (Geneva Call), but also towards a 'territorial unit of a state'[104] (the Republic and Canton of Geneva) could be seen as generating, in itself, expectations and even obligations. In some cases the signing has been in the presence, not only of a representative of the Republic and Canton of Geneva, but also of an Ambassador from the state against which the rebels are fighting. The process is evidently more than a simple bilateral arrangement with an NGO.

It is uncontroversial that where a rebel group enters into an agreement with a state to respect human rights or humanitarian principles, as foreseen in Common Article 3 to the Geneva Convention, such an agreement would be legally binding on the non-state actor[105] and could give rise to individual international criminal responsibility.[106] While the Deeds of Commitment may be legally distinguishable

---

[102] See, e.g. with regard to kidnap-for-ransom activities, the Moro Islamic Liberation Front's pre-ambular statement that: 'Whereas, more than 1,400 years ago before the [Four] Geneva Conventions were adopted by the community of nations on August 12, 1949, Islam had already prescribed that non-combatants such as children, women, old people, monks or priests and the like are not the objects of war; and also it prohibited the destruction of properties, orchards, mutilation of the dead and other cruelties during war.' Reproduced in Geneva Call, *Seeking Rebel Accountability: Report of the Geneva Call Mission to the MILF in the Philippines, 3–8 April 2002* (Geneva: Geneva Call, 2002) at 48; see also the declaration of the Taliban on landmines of 6 October 1998, reproduced in 'Statements By Non-State Armed Actors—NSAs Under International Humanitarian Law-IHL—Some Historical Precedents', available from Geneva Call.

[103] Consider the statement made to the ICRC by the African National Congress on 28 November 1980, which starts: 'It is the conviction of the African National Congress of South Africa that international rules protecting the dignity of human beings must be upheld at all times.' Reproduced in 'Statements by Non-State Armed Actors' (n 102 above).

[104] This is the expression used in the International Law Commission's Articles on State Responsibility (n 56 above), Art. 4, conduct of organs of a state.

[105] See Zegveld (2002: 28–30 and 50). Note the Deeds of Commitment are not 'deposited' with the Swiss Federal Authorities; rather, the Canton and Republic of Geneva acts as the 'custodian' of the Deed. We might add here that the ICRC has succeeded in encouraging armed non-state actors to adopt unilateral declarations and bilateral agreements with governments in numerous situations of internal armed conflict.

[106] See ICTY Appeals Chamber, *Prosecutor v Tadić* (jurisdiction) IT–94–1–AR72, 2 October 1995, at para. 143: 'Before both the Trial Chamber and the Appeals Chamber, Defence and Prosecution have argued the application of certain agreements entered into by the conflicting parties. It is therefore fitting for this Chamber to pronounce on this. It should be emphasised again that the only reason behind the stated purpose of the drafters that the International Tribunal should apply customary international law was to avoid violating the principle of *nullum crimen sine lege* in the event that a party to the conflict did not adhere to a specific treaty. (Report of the Secretary-General,

from such agreements, there is no reason to believe that their impact in curbing behaviour is somehow consequently diminished. Moreover, should the procedure surrounding adoption come formally to include states or inter-governmental organizations such as the United Nations, the legal status of these commitments may yet come to be seen as generating international legal obligations, as opposed to quasi-contractual obligations under national law.

Secondly, the states parties to the Ottawa Treaty seem now to suggest that the norms contained in the treaty should indeed extend to non-state actors and that the commitments made by non-state actors should provide an accountability mechanism. The Fourth meeting of states parties to the Ottawa Treaty included the following conclusion:

> 12. We reaffirm that progress to free the world from anti-personnel mines would be promoted by the commitment by non-State actors to cease and renounce their use in line with the international norm established by this Convention. We urge all non-State actors to cease and renounce the use, stockpiling, production and transfer of anti-personnel mines according to the principles and norms of International Humanitarian Law.[107]

At the fifth meeting, the European Union encouraged non-state actors to enter into Deeds of Commitment with Geneva Call:

> The European Union expresses the hope that all non-state actors will cease the use of anti-personnel landmines and will sign the deed of commitment for adherence to a total ban on anti-personnel mines and for cooperation in mine action, as provided for by Geneva Call.[108]

The final Declaration of the Fifth Meeting of the states parties stated:

> 12. We reaffirm that progress to free the world from anti-personnel mines will be enhanced if non-State actors embrace the international norm established by this Convention. We urge all non-State actors to cease and renounce the use, stockpiling, production and transfer of anti-personnel mines according to the principles and norms of international humanitarian law, and to allow mine action to take place. We welcome the efforts of non-governmental organizations, the International Committee of the Red Cross and the United Nations in engaging non-State actors on a ban on anti-personnel mines and express our appreciation for the work of these organizations . . . as well as our desire that individual States parties that are in a position to do so facilitate this work.[109]

---

at para. 34.) It follows that the International Tribunal is authorised to apply, in addition to customary international law, any treaty which: (i) was unquestionably binding on the parties at the time of the alleged offence; and (ii) was not in conflict with or derogating from peremptory norms of international law, as are most customary rules of international humanitarian law.' Discussed by Zegveld (2002: 30), who concludes: 'It may be inferred that the Tribunal referred to agreements concluded by both states and armed groups.'

[107] Declaration of the Fourth Meeting of States Parties, adopted by the plenary meeting on 20 September 2002, APLC/MSP.42002/1, at 10 para. 12.

[108] Statement by Amb. C. Trezza, Bangkok, 15–19 September 2003.

[109] Bangkok Declaration, adopted by the plenary meeting 19 September 2003, APLC/MSP.5/2003/5, at 2, para. 12.

This encouragement to renounce the use, stockpiling, production, and transfer of anti-personnel mines 'according to the principles and norms of international humanitarian law' could be read as evidence that states consider that such behaviour can now represent a violation of humanitarian law for non-parties to the Ottawa treaty.

Third, it is clear that the commitments regime developed by Geneva Call has encouraged governments and inter-governmental organizations to incorporate such an approach into their own missions. The UN Mine Action Advocacy Strategy includes Goal 4, which reads:

> Armed non-state actors adhere to and comply with commitments and obligations to halt immediately and unconditionally new deployments of anti-personnel mines and to comply with relevant international human rights and humanitarian norms and standards.
>
> 4.1 Elicit commitments from armed non-state actors to comply with international norms regarding landmines or ERW [explosive remnants of war].
> 4.2 Elicit commitments from armed non-state actors to comply with international norms regarding the rights of persons affected by landmines or ERW.
> 4.3 Monitor and report on relevant commitments by armed non-state actors in the appropriate forums.

Such action is not dependent on the legal status of the groups or the nature of the commitments entered into. Whatever the legal obligation of the non-state actors under international humanitarian law, the use of 'commitments' provides a clear set of obligations and nascent compliance mechanisms which could develop into something at least as effective as the treaty regime for ensuring state compliance. In fact, the prospect of continual verification and monitoring through field missions means that, in terms of detecting non-compliance, the commitments regime has the potential to become even more effective than the formal treaty regime.

7.6 PRIVATE SECURITY FIRMS AND THE ISSUE OF MERCENARIES

An immediate response to the issue of private security firms in the context of armed conflict is to label them mercenaries and hence suggest that they are tainted with illegality and illegitimacy. The modern international definition of a mercenary is problematic and operates in international humanitarian law simply to deprive captured individuals of any right to claim prisoner of war status in an international armed conflict.[110] Outside international humanitarian law, attempts to criminalize mercenary activity flounder on a series of definitions which are easy to evade. While the label of 'mercenary' will continue to be applied to express the speaker's disapproval, rather than to describe an individual satisfying the

---

110 See Art. 47 of Protocol I to the Geneva Conventions of 1949.

specific criteria under international law, it is suggested that human rights concern in this area is less likely to be about whether an individual fulfils the criteria for being a mercenary, and more likely to be focused on issues of corporate accountability, contract law, and individual criminal responsibility under the laws of armed conflict. Let us briefly examine the international legal regime concerning mercenaries before looking at the modern phenomenon of the private security firm (PSF).

Although treaty crimes concerning mercenaries have been in force for some time with regard to Africa,[111] prosecutions for the crime of mercenarism as defined in the Convention for the Elimination of Mercenarism in Africa treaty are rare, even if some quite well-known trials of 'mercenaries' have taken place based on violations of national law.[112] The OAU treaty was adopted against the background of private fighters being recruited to undermine or overthrow newly liberated African governments in the 1960s and 1970s.[113] The definition in this treaty (as in others) starts from the premise that the mercenary is 'specially recruited' to fight in an armed conflict. It is far from clear that the sorts of private armed forces employed by governments over the last ten years would fall within the various definitions of mercenaries found in such treaties, as such persons are usually recruited, not for armed conflict, but for training and security reasons.

---

[111] Convention of the OAU for the Elimination of Mercenarism in Africa of 3 July 1977, which entered into force on 22 April 1985, and the International Convention against the Recruitment, Use, Financing and Training of Mercenaries Mercenary Convention of 4 December 1989, which entered into force on 20 October 2001. The African treaty contains the following: 'Article 1 DEFINITION: 1. A mercenary is any person who: a) is specially recruited locally or abroad in order to fight in an armed conflicts; b) does in fact take a direct part in the hostilities; c) is motivated to take part in the hostilities essentially by the desire for private gain and in fact is promised by or on behalf of a party to the conflict material compensation; d) is neither a national of a party to the conflict nor a resident of territory controlled by a party to the conflicts; e) is not a member of the armed forces of a party to the conflict; and f) is not sent by a state other than a party to the conflict on official mission as a member of the armed forces of the said state.   2. The crime of mercenarism is committed by the individual, group or association, representative of a State or the State itself who with the aim of opposing by armed violence a process of self-determination stability or the territorial integrity of another State, practises any of the following acts: a) Shelters, organises, finances, assists, equips, trains, promotes, supports or in any manner employs bands of mercenaries; b) Enlists, enrols or tries to enrol in the said bands; c) Allows the activities mentioned in paragraph (a) to be carried out in any territory under its jurisdiction or in any place under its control or affords facilities for transit, transport or other operations of the above mentioned forces.   3. Any person, natural or juridical who commits the crime of mercenarism as defined in paragraph 1 of this Article commits an Offence considered as a crime against peace and security in Africa and shall be punished as such.' Note that the crime against peace and security in Africa can be committed by a 'juridical' person, i.e. a corporation.

[112] The trials in 2004 of those accused of plotting a coup in Equatorial Guinea did not mention mercenarism. See Amnesty International, *Equatorial Guinea: Trial of alleged coup plotters seriously flawed*, AI Index AFR 24/017/2004, 30 November 2004, similarly the charges in Zimbabwe with regard to the same plot were focused on firearms and immigration infractions: ' "Mercenaries" ' appeal in Zimbabwe', BBC News, 9 December 2004, details accessed at http://news.bbc.co.uk/1/hi/world/africa/4082481.stm.

[113] See further E. David, *Mercenaires et volontaires internationaux en droit des gens* (Brussels: Editions de L'Université de Bruxelles, 1978) at 229–263. For a table depicting the various firms and their objectives with regards to various African countries see Appendix I 'Mercenaries: Africa's Experience 1950s–1990' in A.-F. Musah and J. 'Kayode Fayemi (eds) *Mercenaries: An African Security Dilemma* (London: Pluto, 2000) at 265–274.

Outside armed conflict, the International Convention against the Recruitment, Use, Financing and Training of Mercenaries extends the definition of mercenary to those specially recruited to participate 'in a concerted act of violence' aimed at overthrowing a government or undermining the constitutional order or territorial integrity of a state.[114] Mercenaries fighting against a state would fall foul of these definitions and could be prosecuted under relevant national laws.

Although there remains considerable unease among some African states that mercenaries continue to escape legal control, there was insufficient support for the inclusion of a crime of 'mercenarism' in the jurisdiction of the International Criminal Court.[115] Some states have continued to press for further international rules on mercenaries and the UN Human Rights Commission has mandated expert meetings on this subject.[116] Although this process resulted in suggestions to expand the definition of mercenaries, these have been met with the response that ways should be found to protect the legitimacy of private security companies when they are called on by governments, the United Nations, and multinationals. In this regard, the focus may be shifting from criminalization to new forms of regulation and accountability.

7.6.1   Recent Controversies Concerning the Use of Private Military/Security Firms

In 1998, the United States tendered out to private companies their participation in the unarmed verification mission of the Organization for Security and

---

[114] The UN Convention differs from the OAU treaty in some respects: 'For the purposes of the present Convention, 1. A mercenary is any person who: (a) Is specially recruited locally or abroad in order to fight in an armed conflict; (b) Is motivated to take part in the hostilities essentially by the desire for private gain and, in fact, is promised, by or on behalf of a party to the conflict, material compensation substantially in excess of that promised or paid to combatants of similar rank and functions in the armed forces of that party; (c) Is neither a national of a party to the conflict nor a resident of territory controlled by a party to the conflict; (d) Is not a member of the armed forces of a party to the conflict; and (e) Has not been sent by a State which is not a party to the conflict on official duty as a member of its armed forces.   2. A mercenary is also any person who, in any other situation: (a) Is specially recruited locally or abroad for the purpose of participating in a concerted act of violence aimed at: (i) Overthrowing a Government or otherwise undermining the constitutional order of a State; or (ii) Undermining the territorial integrity of a State; (b) Is motivated to take part therein essentially by the desire for significant private gain and is prompted by the promise or payment of material compensation; (c) Is neither a national nor a resident of the State against which such an act is directed; (d) Has not been sent by a State on official duty; and (e) Is not a member of the armed forces of the State on whose territory the act is undertaken. Article 2 Any person who recruits, uses, finances or trains mercenaries, as defined in article 1 of the present Convention, commits an offence for the purposes of the Convention. Article 3(1). A mercenary, as defined in article 1 of the present Convention, who participates directly in hostilities or in a concerted act of violence, as the case may be, commits an offence for the purposes of the Convention.'

[115] See the proposal by Comoros and Madagascar, UN Doc. A/CONF.183/C.1/L.46, 3 July 1998.

[116] See, e.g. Report of the Third Meeting of Experts on Traditional and New Forms of Mercenary Activities as a Means of Violating Human Rights and Impeding the Exercise of the Right of Peoples to Self-Determination, Geneva, 6–10 December 2004.

Co-operation in Europe (OSCE) in Kosovo. Dyncorp beat another company, Military Professional Resources, for the contract. The privatization of this sort of activity came as a shock to many. One expert, Mary Kaldor, is reported as saying: 'It is extraordinary that a country with a highly paid volunteer army should turn to a private company of mercenaries. This is not the sort of task that should be done for profit.'[117]

Private military companies might be considered modern 'mercenaries', but could also be described as agents of the state,[118] and in this way, the normal rules for state responsibility would apply where the firm's activity is controlled by the state.[119] But this legal analysis fails to capture the full picture. The use of private military companies by states with existing armies has proved politically unacceptable in situations such as Bougainville and Sierra Leone, where the respective governments came under heavy pressure to abandon their use of such private forces. The instances of the involvement of the private military companies Sandline International and Executive Outcomes in such situations represent well-known recent examples of corporate military forces being used beyond ensuring the security of ministers and buildings; in these cases the forces were used to fight armed conflicts.[120] Apart from resentment and suspicion from the regular members of the armed forces, and questions regarding the appropriate use of scarce resources, there is also a concern that the eventual fragmentation of the companies into smaller units may mean assistance, not only for governments, but also for rebels and mining operations in rebel-held territory. At this point the accountability of the firm collapses, the government is weakened and the private forces become part of the problem rather than part of the solution. In addition, as private security firms gravitate to the private entities that can best afford their services, this may leave the poorest sections of society most vulnerable to violence and insecurity.[121] One commentator sees the world of private security firms in the following way:

> When Executive Outcomes became politically unpopular in South Africa, and the government began to pass national laws to control PMF's [private military firms], the

---

[117] Quoted in 'US gives Kosovo monitoring job to mercenaries' *Guardian*, 31 October 1998, 1, and 'Peacekeeping Inc flies in', ibid, 6.

[118] See generally D. Shearer, 'Outsourcing War' *Foreign Policy* (1998) (Fall) 68–81. Consider also Art. 47 of the 1977 Protocol I to the 1949 Geneva Conventions. For an explanation of the background political debates at the UN and the OAU on the issue of mercenaries and the eventual adoption of Art. 47, see A. Cassese, 'Mercenaries: Lawful Combatants or War Criminals?' 40 *ZaöRV* (1980) 1–30.　　　[119] See Ch 6, at 6.7.1 above.

[120] See T. McCormick, 'The "Sandline Affair": Papua New Guinea Resorts to Mercenarism to End the Bougainville Conflict' 1 *Yearbook of International Humanitarian Law* (1998) 292–300. For an examination of issue in Sierra Leone, see D. J. Francis, 'Mercenary intervention in Sierra Leone: providing national security or international exploitation?', *Third World Quarterly* (1999) 319–338. With regards to Sierra Leone, the role of Executive Outcomes was considered in the Report of the Sierra Leone Truth and Reconciliation Commission, vol. two, ch two, at paras 401–404.

[121] See P. W. Singer, *Corporate Warriors: The Rise of the Privatized Military* (Ithaca, NY: Cornell University Press, 2004) Ch 14.

company simply dissolved and reconstituted itself as several smaller companies in other countries. At the level of its organizational DNA, a private military firm has more in common with that other non-state actor that flourished in the post-cold war environment—al Qaeda—than it does with the United States military.[122]

P. W. Singer has pointed out that, not only can such firms take on a new name and corporate structure when they are challenged, but attempts to eliminate the firms through national legislation 'tend only to drive them and their clients further underground, away from public oversight'.[123]

7.6.2 Accountability for Human Rights Abuses

What then should the human rights response be? Singer has suggested that a 'body of international experts, with input from all stakeholders (governments, the academy, nongovernmental organizations, and the firms themselves) could establish the parameters of the issues, build an internationally recognized database of the firms in the industry, and lay out potential forms of regulation, evaluation tools, and codes of conduct that public-decision makers could then weigh and decide upon'.[124] Singer foresees that the process would involve audits that would 'include subjecting PMF personnel data bases to appraisal for past violations of human rights'.[125] In addition, such a body could not only monitor compliance with international norms but also have 'certain powers to suspend payments'.[126] The idea is that an approved and monitored firm could work for the United Nations and be in a position to win tenders from multinationals 'concerned about their image'.[127]

It may seem strange to consider that the murky world of mercenarism could be made accountable through market pressures, but two factors make this approach worthy of serious consideration. First, because these firms may be forced to rely on their contractual arrangements with governments to ensure payment, including respect for certain human rights and humanitarian law standards as 'essential elements' of any contract would permit governments to withhold part-payment under certain conditions in order to compensate victims for harm done. The international arbitration under UNCITRAL rules and subsequent litigation concerning Sandline International and the Government of Papua New Guinea ended in a settlement of US$13.3 million. Although this contract did mention 'conformance with the Geneva Convention',[128] a properly drafted contract term

---

[122] P. R. Keefe, 'Iraq: America's Private Armies' *New York Review of Books*, 12 August 2004, 48–50, at 50 (review of P. W. Singer, *Corporate Warriors: The Rise of the Privatized Military* (Ithaca, NY: Cornell University Press, 2004)).

[123] P. W. Singer, 'War, profits, and the Vacuum of Law: Privatized Military Firms and International Law' 42 *Col JTL* (2004) 521–549, at 535.

[124] P. W. Singer, *Corporate Warriors: The Rise of the Privatized Military* (Ithaca, NY: Cornell University Press, 2004) at 241.   [125] Ibid.

[126] Ibid.   [127] Ibid.

[128] Contract of 31 January 1997, the contract was made available on the Sandline International website: http://www.sandline.com/site/. It is also reproduced in Singer's book, *Corporate Warriors* (n 124 above) at 245.

demanding *full respect for international humanitarian law and internationally recognized human rights* as well as guarantees regarding *careful recruitment and discipline for human rights abuses* would provide a real incentive to comply with international human rights law due to the prospect of future disputes and settlements.[129] Second, private security firms themselves may be coming to see the advantages of human rights monitoring in order to enter the mainstream and the lucrative possibilities it offers.

Tim Spicer's autobiography, *An Unorthodox Soldier: Peace and War and the Sandline Affair*, contains multiple references to human rights in its opening Chapter. Some of these are worth reproducing here for what they reveal about how respect for human rights is presented as part of the solution from the perspective of a non-state actor:

> Given that a PMC [private military company] is a business, it is acknowledged that a fundamental law of successful business is that the supplier is only as good as his last contract. Ethical businesses first build a reputation and then work hard to protect it. If a particular PMC performed badly or unethically, exploited the trust placed in it by a client, changed sides, violated human rights or sought to mount a coup, then the company and its principals would find that their forward order book was decidedly thin. Discarding ethical and moral principles can therefore only be a one time opportunity. The chance will not recur and the company's prospects would disappear.[130]

One hears here echoes of the corporate social responsibility embrace of human rights. The difference may be that, in the context of armed conflict, the abuse of human rights quickly translates into international criminal responsibility for the individuals concerned. There is no need to formulate elaborate arguments about conspiracy and complicity in the present context; the individuals themselves may be accused of the direct commission of international crimes. Many of those concerned are nationals of states parties to the Rome Statute of the International Criminal Court. Furthermore, several countries with internal armed conflicts have ratified the Rome Statute including, the Democratic Republic of Congo, Afghanistan, and Columbia. The prospect of criminal prosecution before an international tribunal has been registered by Tim Spicer as part of the incentive for private military companies to comply with the Geneva Conventions.

Spicer goes on to suggest field-based monitoring of the behaviour of private military companies (PMCs). He suggests that observer teams be deployed

---

[129] Françoise Hampson has suggested that the agreement between a company and a government should include, *inter alia*, 'the circumstances in which they can open fire in defence of property and /or in defence of life' as well as obligations to cooperate in any investigation into the unlawful use of force. With regard to contracts between security companies and corporations she has suggested that the security company should be required to provide its personnel with training in the relevant domestic law and that it should be stipulated in the contract that security personnel will be subject to the domestic criminal law of the country in which they are operating. 'The problem with mercenary activity', working paper for the UN meeting of the Group of Experts, Geneva, 13–17 May 2002, at 3.

[130] *An Unorthodox Soldier: Peace and War and the Sandline Affair* (Edinburgh: Mainstream Publishing, 1999) at 25–26.

alongside the company; operating 'in the same way as a referee at a football match' (but without the power to send players off, a task which should be left to local commanders). In this way 'the PMC will be fully cognisant of the fact that their actions are being monitored and will not want to be banned from "playing in another game" in the future, or to find themselves in front of an international tribunal'.[131] The threat of criminal sanctions may well be an effective form of regulation from a human rights perspective. Yet while many will be subject to the potential jurisdiction of the International Criminal Court or the prospect of national trials for crimes contained in the Rome Statute for the International Criminal Court, others will fail to come within the scope of any effective criminal law. The problem has been highlighted in the context of the United States due to lacunae in the US legal order. Singer recounts the situation in the following terms:[132]

> Under the Neutrality Act, U.S. law prohibits only the recruitment of mercenaries within the United States but not the sale of military services. In turn, the Uniform Code of Military Justice only covers transgressions committed by members of the U.S. military, but not any civilians accompanying the force overseas. The 2000 Military Extraterritorial Jurisdiction Act was intended to fill in the gap, by applying the code to civilians serving in U.S. military operations outside the United States. However, it only applies to civilian contractors working directly for the U.S. Department of Defense on U.S. military facilities, not to contractors working for another U.S. agency, such as the Central Intelligence Agency, nor to U.S. nationals working overseas for a foreign government or organization. Moreover, Major Joseph Perlak, a Judge Advocate with the U.S. Marine Corps, writes that the law itself still is not fleshed out and no one is quite sure how and when to apply it. 'There is a dearth of doctrine, procedure, and policy on just how this new criminal statute will affect the way the military does business with contractors.'[133]
>
> Thus, if an American PMF [private military firm] employee commits any offense abroad, under the frequent conditions that do not meet the above standards, only the host nation may prosecute. However, for many likely areas of activity prosecution against a PMF or its individual employee is unlikely to occur. This result might be because the host state is unwilling to challenge the PMF, as was the case in Colombia (where the firm was carrying out the state's dirty work). Or, the host state may be unable to challenge the PMF, as was the case in the failed states of Bosnia and Sierra Leone (where the legal system has simply crumbled). Or finally, the host government may have no control over the PMF because the PMF is fighting against the government. For example, during the Iraq war, an American PMF working on Iraqi soil could hardly have been expected to turn its employees over to the government of Saddam Hussein, if any were suspected of individual criminal activity. The result is 'an environment where civilians are untouchable despite commission of what would be serious crimes within the

---

[131] Ibid, at 26.

[132] P. W. Singer, 'War, Profits, and the Vacuum of Law: Privatized Military Firms and International Law' 42 *Col JTL* (2004) 521–549, at 537–538 (some footnotes omitted).

[133] The footnote in the original reads: 'Joseph R. Perlak, The Military Extraterritorial Jurisdiction Act of 2000: Implications for Contractor Personnel, 169 *Mil. L. Rev.* 92, 95 (2001).'

United States.... A contractor, there to support the U.S. national interest, could murder, rape, pillage and plunder with complete, legal unaccountability.'[134]

The Abu Ghraib scandal has been addressed in various US official reports. Major General Taguba's Investigation recommended that Steven Stephanowicz, a Contract US Civilian Interrogator, from Consolidated Analysis Centers Inc (CACI), 205th Military Intelligence Brigade, 'be given an Official Reprimand to be placed in his employment file, termination of employment, and generation of a derogatory report to revoke his security clearance for the following acts' which included the fact that he 'Allowed and/or instructed MPs, who were not trained in interrogation techniques, to facilitate interrogations by "setting conditions" which were neither authorized and [*sic*]˙in accordance with applicable regulations/policy. He clearly knew his instructions equated to physical abuse'.[135] The Schlesinger Report mentions a finding of inadequate training among 35 per cent of private contractors used for interrogation and suggests that future contracts should specify the experience and qualifications needed.[136] From a human rights perspective, the response to the participation in abuse by private contractors has been rather feeble. There is no sense that any of the companies involved will suffer any disadvantage or have any new incentive to tighten their procedures to avoid future abuse and exclude those already implicated from any future contact with detainees.

A series of expert reports have argued for new regulation for this sector at the national, regional, and international levels.[137] Part of the concern stems from perceived ambiguities in international law with regard to the status of the personnel:[138] When can they be considered combatants entitled to prisoner of war status on capture? When can they be prosecuted under military law? When does their activity amount to mercenarism? Concern stems in part from the fact that so few prosecutions have been brought in home countries (such as the United States) for human rights abuses committed in Iraq,[139] given that it is impossible for the Iraqi national authorities to prosecute those working for the Coalition. Concern also

---

[134] The footnote in the original reads: 'Gordon Campbell, Contractors on the Battlefield: The Ethics of Paying Civilians to Enter Harm's Way and Requiring Soldiers to Depend upon Them, Presentation at the Joint Services Conference on Professional Ethics, Springfield, VA (Jan. 27–28, 2000).'

[135] *Article 15–6 investigation of the 800th Military Police Brigade*, at 48, available at http://www.globalpolicy.org/security/issues/iraq/attack/law/2004/2004tagubareport.pdf.

[136] Final Report of the Independent Panel to Review DoD Operations, at 69, available at http://www.defenselink.mil/news/Aug2004/d20040824finalreport.pdf.

[137] See, e.g. C. Holmqvist, 'Private Security Companies: The Case for Regulation', Stockholm: Stockholm International Peace Research Institute Policy Paper No. 9 (2005); F. Schreier and M. Caparini, 'Privatising Security: Law, Practice and Governance of Private Military and Security Companies', Geneva: Geneva Centre for the Democratic Control of Armed Forces Occasional Paper No. 6 (2005); P. W. Singer, 'The Private Military Industry and Iraq: What Have We Learned and Where to Next?', Geneva: Geneva Centre for the Democratic Control of Armed Forces (2004).

[138] E.g. Schreir and Caparini (2005: ii), Singer, n 137 above (2004: 11–14).

[139] Singer, n 137 above (2004: 13).

comes from a more general suspicion that those engaged in armed conflict and interrogation should be democratically accountable in the public sphere.

So far, the international response has resulted in a dual mandate for the United Nations' Working Group on the use of Mercenaries. On the one hand, the Working Group is to monitor the effects of 'private companies offering military assistance' on the 'enjoyment of human rights', and on the other hand, the Working Group is to 'prepare draft international principles that encourage respect for human rights on the part of those companies in their activities'.[140] At the time of writing, this Working Group had not yet reported back to the UN Commission on Human Rights.

7.6.3   The Incorporation of Human Rights Obligations into National Licensing Regimes

In considering the impact of human rights law on various regimes for licensing private security companies, one may begin with the regulation of the private security companies by the Coalition Provisional Authority in Iraq. To comply with Iraqi Ministry of Interior vetting standards, employees of private security companies must: 'Be willing to respect the law and all human rights and freedoms of all Iraqi citizens.'[141] Note that companies have to submit a minimum refundable bond of US$25,000 and that 'any breaches of Iraq or other applicable law by employees or companies may result in forfeiture of the bond'.[142] Prompt action with respect to 'individual violations' is to be taken into account by the Ministry in determining whether the bond should be forfeited in whole or in part. This arrangement should be seen in the context of the situation in Iraq, where contractors are 'immune from Iraqi legal process with respect to acts performed by them pursuant to the terms and conditions of a Contract or any sub-contract thereto'.[143] Although there is obviously a risk that a US$25,000 bond could be written off as an operating cost, this sum represents a minimum and one could imagine larger sums, proportionate to the actual contract, which could be used to compensate the victims of any human rights abuses committed by the company.

A further example is provided by the South African Regulation of Foreign Military Assistance Act which states that government approval may not be granted if it would 'result in the infringement of human rights and fundamental freedoms in the territory in which the foreign military assistance is to be rendered'.[144] This clause is less about accountability after the fact than about seeking to force a consideration of the human rights implications into the approval process. A poor record on human rights issues would surely render unlikely the

---

[140] Commission on Human Rights Resolution 2005/2.

[141] CPA/MEM/26 June 2004/17, s 2(6)(b).

[142] Ibid, s 3(3). I am grateful to James Stewart from the legal office of the ICRC for bringing this to my attention.   [143] CPA/ORD/27 June 2004/17, s 4(3).

[144] S. 7(1)(b).

approval of any agreement to offer private military services. Operating without approval is a criminal offence which applies not only to natural persons but also to juristic persons, in other words, to the companies themselves.[145]

The UK Green Paper, entitled *Private Military Companies: Options for Regulation*,[146] sets out various regulatory options, ranging from an outright ban, through registration and licensing, to a voluntary code of conduct. Human rights obligations figure explicitly in the discussion of a Voluntary Code of Conduct. The Green Paper foresees that such a code would cover respect for human rights, as well as respect for international law including international humanitarian law and the laws of war.[147] It is suggested that a trade association, such as the British Security Industry Association, would police compliance with the code. It is also suggested that the code would include a provision allowing for external monitoring. For many observers, any regulation in this field must take into consideration international human rights obligations and ensure that the companies themselves abide by these obligations. According to Beyani and Lilley: 'The UK Government should ensure that national legislation reflects relevant international human rights and humanitarian law, so UK mercenaries and private military companies do not violate these laws.'[148]

It is, however, the voluntary code model which is currently most influential. In the field of security for companies in the extractive sector, the process which led to the adoption of the Voluntary Principles on Security and Human Rights involved representatives from human rights organizations, trade unions, the oil companies, and the Governments of the United States and the United Kingdom.[149] In normative terms, the Principles are helpful in outlining the international standards with which private security companies are expected to comply, and the human rights obligations for which the extractive industry companies should

---

[145] S. 8(1).

[146] HC 577, 12 February 2002. For an overview of the situation in other countries, see Annex B to the Green Paper. Apart from South Africa and the United States regulation is almost entirely limited to outlawing mercenarism. For the United States see the US Arms Export Control Act 1968; licences have to be obtained from the State Department under the International Transfer of Arms Regulations and exports of defence services over $50m have to be notified to Congress.

[147] Ibid, at para. 76.

[148] C. Beyani and D. Lilley, *Regulating private military companies: options for the UK Government* (London: International Alert, 2001) at para. 61.

[149] Voluntary Principles on Security and Human Rights, 20 December 2000, available at http://www1.umn.edu/humanrts/links/volprinciples.html. Secretary of State Madeleine Albright listed those entities that had been involved: 'I wouldn't usually take the time to list all the entities involved, but I will today because their breadth and caliber is revealing. The companies are Texaco, Chevron, BP, Conoco, Freeport MacMoran, Rio Tinto and Shell. The NGOs are Amnesty International, Human Rights Watch, Business for Social Responsibility, Fund for Peace, International Alert, Prince of Wales Business Leaders Forum, Council on Economic Priorities and the Lawyers Committee for Human Rights. The labor side is represented by the International Federation of Chemical, Energy, Mine and General Workers Unions.' Available at http://secretary.state.gov/ www/statements/2000/001220.html. The Netherlands, Norway, BG Group, Newmont Mining Exxon-Mobil, Occidental Petroleum Marathon Oil, and Anglo American, have since joined the process.

ensure respect when engaging such private security companies. For instance, the Guidelines state that:

Private security should act in a lawful manner. They should exercise restraint and caution in a manner consistent with applicable international guidelines regarding the local use of force, including the UN Principles on the Use of Force and Firearms by Law Enforcement Officials and the UN Code of Conduct for Law Enforcement Officials, as well as with emerging best practices developed by Companies, civil society, and governments. . . .

Private security should (a) not employ individuals credibly implicated in human rights abuses to provide security services; (b) use force only when strictly necessary and to an extent proportional to the threat; and (c) not violate the rights of individuals while exercising the right to exercise freedom of association and peaceful assembly, to engage in collective bargaining, or other related rights of Company employees as recognized by the Universal Declaration of Human Rights and the ILO Declaration on Fundamental Principles and Rights at Work.

This seems to represent an appropriate translation of human rights standards to the private sector.[150] With regard to the role of the extractive industry company itself, the Guidelines state:

In cases where physical force is used, private security should properly investigate and report the incident to the Company. Private security should refer the matter to local authorities and/or take disciplinary action where appropriate. Where force is used, medical aid should be provided to injured persons, including to offenders. . . .

Where appropriate, Companies should include the principles outlined above as contractual provisions in agreements with private security providers and ensure that private security personnel are adequately trained to respect the rights of employees and the local community. To the extent practicable, agreements between Companies and private security should require investigation of unlawful or abusive behavior and appropriate disciplinary action. Agreements should also permit termination of the relationship by Companies where there is credible evidence of unlawful or abusive behavior by private security personnel.

The Principles may be included in contracts in a manner which would render them legally enforceable (under the law governing the contract) and there is some evidence that companies are seeking to give the Principles a place, not only in their training schemes and 'discussions with stakeholders',[151] but also in their contractual relations.[152]

---

[150] On the concept of human rights 'translation' see C. Scott, 'Translating Torture into Transnational Tort: Conceptual Divides in the Debate on Corporate Accountability for Human Rights Harms' in C. Scott (ed) *Torture as Tort: Comparative Perspectives on the Development of Transnational Human Rights Litigation* (Oxford: Hart Publishing, 2001) 45–63.

[151] C. Batruch, 'Oil and conflict: Lundin Petroleum's experience in Sudan' in A. J. K. Bailes and I. Frommelt (eds) *Business and Security: Public-Private Sector Relationships in a New Security Environment* (Oxford: Oxford University Press, 2004) 148–160, at 154–155.

[152] See, e.g. BP's *Sustainablility Report* 2003, at 32.

7.7   THE ROLE OF HUMANITARIAN ORGANIZATIONS

There has been considerable critical commentary regarding the role that humanitarian organizations play in conflict situations. As with the commentary on the World Bank (discussed in Chapter 4), there is often a confusion of two separate questions. On the one hand, there is the question of which organizations should be mandated to carry out human rights work (training, monitoring, reporting, denouncing, and so on). On the other hand, there is the question of how to ensure that humanitarian organizations do not actually encourage or contribute to human rights violations. Both questions have been confused through the fashionable mantra that all organizations should take a 'rights-based approach'. Organizations that did not see themselves as involved with human rights have now come to embrace the importance of human rights in their work. The invocation of rights in this manner has forced a degree of reflection concerning human rights obligations in the context of humanitarian operations. The first question that will be considered below is the humanitarian organizations and their role as human rights defenders.

7.7.1   The Question of Human Rights Denunciations by Humanitarian Organizations

If humanitarian agencies are to take a rights-based approach, this presumably means that they should act to prevent and denounce human rights violations. This is said by some to make their work unviable in certain situations. How can one ask military commanders to grant humanitarian access if the humanitarians are going to fuel the propaganda against that side by reporting on human rights violations? From another perspective, once concentration camps, such as the one in Banja Luka in Bosnia, are discovered by an agency such as the International Committee of the Red Cross, should the agency then denounce the treatment and risk losing access to the detainees? These are real dilemmas that have been highlighted in a number of recent books which examine the role of humanitarian actors in conflict situations.[153] But the question of whether to denounce the conditions of detainees is too complex to be reduced to a question of legal obligation. The question whether or not to denounce can only be answered according to the precise context. Much will depend on the predictions as to the immediate reaction

---

[153] See esp. D. Rieff, *A Bed for the Night: Humanitarianism in Crisis* (London: Vintage, 2002) at 148–149, 221–222, 314 who notes the dangers of mixing human rights reporting with a humanitarian mission; and M. Ignatieff, *Empire Lite: Nation-building in Bosnia, Kosovo and Afghanistan* (London: Vintage, 2003) 54–56. For a historical perspective which examines the debate within the ICRC concerning atrocities committed by the German government during in the period up to an including the Second World War, see C. Moorehead, *Dunant's Dream: War Switzerland and the History of the Red Cross* (London: Harper Collins, 1998) xv–xxxi, 342–356, 420–426.

of the perpetrators. If a denunciation is likely to result in danger or death for the agency's workers in the region it can hardly be countenanced at such a time. If denunciation by another agency with no presence in the area can have a beneficial effect there may be an argument for a division of labour. Organizations such as Amnesty International, that focus on public reports and campaigns on human rights violations, tend not to have an extensive field presence. On the other hand, organizations such as *Médecins sans frontières* (MSF), have forged a path in the humanitarian sector by insisting that they will combine a medical assistance role in the field with a determination to bear witness; in MSF's terms, a founding principle was *témoignage*.[154] It points out the difficulty of cooperating with human rights organizations due to the politicization of human rights in the contemporary world:

> ... humanitarian organizations that witness massive crimes need only convey the information to human rights organizations, thereby avoiding the difficult choice between denunciation (at the risk of expulsion) and silence (at the risk of complicity).

> However, this kind of approach blurs the nature of each organization's responsibility. Public statements made by humanitarian NGOs address not only violations of human rights, but also (and more importantly) the quality of relief actions, and the obstacles placed in their way. This discreet cooperation between humanitarian and human rights organizations is not necessarily synonymous with security.

> Indeed, in a context in which human rights are an element of international diplomacy, giving confidential information to human rights groups might be regarded by the authorities as clandestine, suspicious and subversive. Passing on information this way hardly ensures the safety of humanitarian staff working in the field. Moreover, it may make protection of the populations concerned subject to the specific agenda of human rights diplomacy.[155]

Nevertheless, the decision to make a public denunciation cannot simply be based on a human rights obligation, or the avoidance of complicity; such a decision is a policy choice for the organization determined for a particular time and place. The divisions which such a policy choice can create are evident and still define the nature and reputation of different organizations. As discussed in Chapter 6, this dilemma is not confined to humanitarian organizations working in the field. Corporations are developing their own guidelines to determine whether they should raise human rights issues when working in countries with serious problems.[156] Again, it makes little sense to present advocacy and denunciation as a

---

[154] From the MSF website: 'Témoignage is a French term that encompasses the MSF commitment to testimony, open advocacy and outright denunciation when working with endangered populations throughout the world.'

[155] 'The principles and practices of "rebellious humanitarianism"' by Françoise Bouchet-Saulnier *MSF 2000 International Activity Report*, reproduced on the website: http://web.archive.org/web/2001/041/7231/036/www.msf.org/publications/activ-rep/2000/law.htm.

[156] Cf the discussion in Ch 6 above regarding the avoidance of silent complicity by BP and Shell where their publications describe the importance of knowing how to choose between 'speaking out' and 'silent diplomacy' in the fifth sphere.

human rights obligation under international law. The duties and expectations depend entirely on the involvement and capacity of the non-state actor in question. As an entity becomes more involved with those committing human rights violations, the question of complicity becomes clearer, not only in the sense of placing the humanitarian organization in a moral dilemma, where those who remain silent feel themselves to be complicit in the violations, but also in a strict legal sense where activity or even mere presence assists or encourages the commission of international crimes. The next section considers this second question: When may the activity of a humanitarian organization actually violate international human rights obligations?

7.7.2 The Human Rights Obligations of Humanitarian Organizations

Awareness of the human rights obligations of humanitarian organizations has been enhanced due to two developments. First is the move towards denunciation and 'témoignage'. This awareness has been articulated as part of a renewed approach to protection. According to one manual: 'A protective approach requires that humanitarian workers go beyond an aid-only approach and also focus on ensuring respect for humanitarian and human rights norms.'[157] From the perspective of these humanitarian workers: 'Violations of legal rights impose clear humanitarian, military or political duties on governments, non-state actors, individuals and humanitarian agencies.'[158] Second, humanitarian organizations have looked inwards in the wake of a widely-publicized scandal concerning sexual favours in return for humanitarian assistance with regard to refugee children in Guinea, Liberia, and Sierra Leone. This scandal and related concerns thrust the issue of accountability of humanitarian agencies into the spotlight. The assessment team sent in response by the UN High Commissioner for Refugees and Save the Children UK 'received allegations of abuse and exploitation against 67 individuals based in a range of agencies responsible for the care and protection of refugee and IDP communities. The agencies that are possibly implicated in some way include UN peacekeeping forces, international and local NGOs, and government agencies responsible for humanitarian response'.[159] The findings cover the whole range of agencies and are distressing:

> In all three countries, agency workers from international and local NGOs as well as UN agencies were reportedly the most frequent sex exploiters of children, often using the very humanitarian aid and services intended to benefit the refugee population as a tool

[157] H. Slim and E. Eguren, *Humanitarian Protection: A Guidance Booklet* (London: ALNAP, 2004) at 64.   [158] Ibid.
[159] UNHCR/Save the Children UK, note for implementing and operational partners, 'Sexual Violence and Exploitation: the experience of refugee children in Liberia, Guinea and Sierra Leone', February 2002, at 2.

of exploitation. Most of the allegations involved male national staff, trading humanitarian commodities and services, including oil, bulgur wheat, tarpaulin or plastic sheeting, medicines, transport, ration cards, loans, education courses, skills training and other basic services, in exchange for sex with girls under 18. The practice appeared particularly pronounced in locations with large established aid programmes. From the assessment report there appears to be a pattern of this type of abuse in refugee camps in Guinea and Liberia in particular: 'It's difficult to escape the trap of those (NGO) people; they use the food as bait to get you to sex with them' (adolescent in Liberia).[160]

It is possible to distinguish four types of humanitarian organization, as the route for understanding their international human rights obligations depends in part on an understanding of their formal status in international law. First, governmental agencies are clearly organs of governments and their acts and omissions will trigger state responsibility in the normal way. The state will have all the human rights obligations that flow from general international law as well treaties to which that state is a party. The agency may adhere to various sectoral codes of conduct, thereby clarifying and developing its obligations. Second, are agencies established by two or more governments. These are generally part of an international organization, such as the United Nations or the European Union, and the rules concerning the attribution of acts or omissions to international organizations will apply.[161] It is fairly uncontroversial that the United Nations and the European Union are bound by the customary international law of human rights, as found, for example, in the Universal Declaration of Human Rights. Again, these intergovernmental organizations may be adherents to the various codes of conduct that have been elaborated for humanitarian agencies. Third, is the International Committee of the Red Cross, which has a *sui generis* status due to its recognition as an entity with certain privileges under general international law, as well as the specific rights granted to it by treaties such as the Four Geneva Conventions of 1949.[162] So far, the ICRC has tended to avoid formal participation in the different accountability initiatives.[163] Fourth, are non-governmental organizations

---

[160] Ibid, at 4.

[161] See the relevant draft Article on the responsibility of international organizations adopted on first reading by the International Law Commission: 'Article 4 General rule on attribution of conduct to an international organization   1. The conduct of an organ or agent of an international organization in the performance of functions of that organ or agent shall be considered as an act of that organization under international law whatever position the organ or agent holds in respect of the organization.   2. For the purposes of paragraph 1, the term "agent" includes officials and other persons or entities through whom the organization acts.   3. Rules of the organization shall apply to the determination of the functions of its organs and agents.   4. For the purpose of the present draft article, "rules of the organization" means, in particular: the constituent instruments; decisions, resolutions and other acts taken by the organization in accordance with those instruments; and established practice of the organization.' UN Doc. A/CN.4/L.648, 27 May 2004.

[162] *Prosecutor v Šimić*, Decision of 27 July 1999, at para. 35, discussed in more detail in Ch 5 above.

[163] But see the Code of Conduct for the International Red Cross and Crescent Movement and NGOs in Disaster Relief, reproduced in Sphere Project, *Humanitarian Charter and Minimum Standards in Disaster Response* (Oxford: Oxfam Publishing, 2000) at 312–322.

(NGOs). To the extent that an entity is a legal person, the NGO is in a similar position to the corporation.[164] Although there are no equivalents to the texts discussed in Chapter 6 (OECD Guidelines and ILO Tripartite Declaration), some guidelines such as those prepared by the Special Representative of the Secretary General on Internal Displacement, and the UN High Commissioner for Human Rights on Trafficking,[165] are directly addressed to humanitarian organizations. Furthermore, the NGOs have developed their own accountability mechanism for ensuring that NGOs live up to their own Humanitarian Charter (based on international human rights obligations).

Humanitarian organizations have for some time been considering the sort of accountability to which they themselves should be subject.[166] One initiative, entitled the 'Sphere' project, resulted in a Humanitarian Charter which set out three broad fields of responsibilities. Each field is based on international legal obligations that apply to governments and other non-state actors.[167] The Humanitarian Charter affirmed the fundamental importance of the following principles:

1. The right to life with dignity

This right is reflected in the legal measures concerning the right to life, to an adequate standard of living and to freedom from cruel, inhuman or degrading treatment or punishment. We understand an individual's right to life to entail the right to have steps taken to preserve life where it is threatened, and a corresponding duty on others to take

---

[164] For an argument that the 'community acceptances' and international recognition given to the rights and role of NGOs leads to the conclusion that they are 'bound by the norms of the international legal order applicable to them', see K. Nowrot, 'Legal Consequences of Globalization: The Status of Non-Governemental Organizations Under International Law' 6 *Global Legal Studies Journal* (1999) 579–645, at 635.

[165] The Introduction and scope of the Guidelines on Internal Displacement explain that they are designed to give guidance to, *inter alia*: 3(d) 'Intergovernmental and non-governmental organizations when addressing internal displacement.' UN Doc. E/CN.4/1998/53/Add.2, 11 February 1998. The 'Recommended Principles and Guidelines on Human Rights and Human Trafficking', Guideline 1 is addressed to inter-governmental and non-governmental organizations 'where applicable' UN Doc. E/2002/68/Add.1, Report of the High Commissioner for Human Rights, 20 May 2002.

[166] This Chapter focuses on responsibilities of humanitarian organizations in situations of armed conflict and humanitarian crisis. For a review of the responsibilities of human rights NGOs generally, see International Council on Human Rights Policy, *Deserving Trust: Issues of Accountability for Human Rights NGOs (Draft Report)* (Versoix: ICHRP, 2003). The report suggests that human rights NGOs should not practice discrimination on any basis listed in Art. 2 of the Universal Declaration of Human Rights, but notes that there are complications as NGOs must 'select' their priorities (at 41–45). With regard to personal behaviour the draft report found that, with the exception of children's rights organizations, which tend to have codes of conduct or regulations covering what staff may and may not do with regard to children in their care, few human rights NGOs have similar rules governing staff behaviour (at 117). Issues with regard to the treatment of domestic workers, sexual, and racial discrimination are discussed at 117–118.

[167] 'The Humanitarian Charter expresses agencies' commitment to these principles and to achieving the Minimum Standards. This commitment is based on agencies' appreciation of their own ethical obligations, and reflects the rights and duties enshrined in international law in respect of which states and other parties have established obligations.' Sphere Project, *Humanitarian Charter and Minimum Standards in Disaster Response* (Oxford: Oxfam Publishing, 2000) at 6.

such steps. Implicit in this is the duty not to withhold or frustrate the provision of life-saving assistance. In addition, international humanitarian law makes specific provision for assistance to civilian populations during conflict, obliging states and other parties to agree to the provision of humanitarian and impartial assistance when the civilian population lacks essential supplies.

2. The distinction between combatants and non-combatants

This is the distinction which underpins the 1949 Geneva Conventions and their Additional Protocols of 1977. This fundamental principle has been increasingly eroded, as reflected in the enormously increased proportion of civilian casualties during the second half of the twentieth century. That internal conflict is often referred to as 'civil war' must not blind us to the need to distinguish between those actively engaged in hostilities, and civilians and others (including the sick, wounded and prisoners) who play no direct part. Non-combatants are protected under international humanitarian law and are entitled to immunity from attack.

3. The principle of non-refoulement

This is the principle that no refugee shall be sent (back) to a country in which his or her life or freedom would be threatened on account of race, religion, nationality, membership of a particular social group or political opinion; or where there are substantial grounds for believing that s/he would be in danger of being subjected to torture.

Each of these principles is referenced back to the international treaties which are binding on states in this area. In addition to a connected set of Minimum Standards which are aimed at assisting in understanding the process for implementing these principles, the agencies have developed an accountability mechanism to hold them to their commitment to respect the Humanitarian Charter. This was known as the Humanitarian Accountability Project.

The origins of the Humanitarian Accountability Project can be traced to the 1996 Joint Evaluation of the International Response to the Genocide in Rwanda. A preliminary set of pilot studies led to the establishment by major humanitarian agencies of the Humanitarian Accountability Partnership (HAP) International in Geneva in January 2003.[168] The purpose of the Partnership, according to Article 4 of its statute, is 'to achieve and promote the highest principles of accountability through self-regulation by members linked by common respect for the rights and dignity of beneficiaries'. The rights of the beneficiaries are essentially understood as those outlined in the Humanitarian Charter quoted above. Member agencies are subjected to monitoring by HAP International and are obliged to report on their own self-monitoring. Article 22 of the HAP International Statute states that:

Member organisations agree to: (a) Self-monitor and self-report on their implementation of the HAP International Accountability Principles at least annually (b) Follow up

---

[168] Full members of HAP International as of November 2004: CAFOD, CARE International, Danish Refugee Council (DRC), Medical Aid for Palestinians (MAP), Medair, Norwegian Refugee Council (NRC), Office Africain pour le Développement et la Coopération (OFADEC), Oxfam GB, Tearfund, Women's Commission for Refugee Women and Children (WCRWC), World Vision International (WVI). See generally http://www.hapinternational.org/en/.

concerns brought to their attention and report back to HAP International (c) Monitoring by HAP International as part of an agreed schedule and agreed terms of reference (d) By common agreement only, cooperate in peer review process either as reviewee or reviewer.

The reporting process mirrors the reporting by states under the UN human rights treaties. Article 23(1) requires that: 'Members submit a report to HAP International each year on their implementation of the accountability principles. If and when applicable, reports about complaints handling, external monitoring and/or peer review are considered.' Ultimately an agency could be expelled from HAP International. Article 23.2 states that reports are to be reviewed by the Board which can take decisions regarding membership which might include a request for more information, a suspension or renewal.

The motivation for such an initiative comes from a need to ensure credibility and transparency with donors, a wish to identify and isolate organizations that trample the rights of beneficiaries, and from a genuine desire to practice what one preaches. As with corporations, similar concerns arise with regard to the danger of implying that governments' obligations are being somehow reduced, or that humanitarian agencies are to be considered substitutes for governments with duties to provide education, food, and health care. Nevertheless the initiatives described above do illustrate that non-state actors can be held accountable for human rights obligations without necessarily displacing the simultaneous and complementary obligations that exist on the relevant states.

8

Selected UN Human Rights Treaties

There is a temptation among international lawyers to see the question of the responsibility of the state with regard to private encroachments on human rights as a matter to be resolved through the rules on state responsibility.[1] This is understandable when one considers the state-centric nature of views about international law and the history of the protection of the individual under international law. As we have seen, the international regime for the protection of individuals evolved against the background of the diplomatic protection of nationals abroad.[2] This inter-state regime elaborated specific requirements for attributing acts to states and at the same time a substantive due diligence standard evolved with respect to state omissions. These rules were binding as rules of customary international law outside any particular treaty regime.[3] What a state is expected to do to protect foreigners on its territory under these customary standards of diplomatic protection may not be congruent with what a state is now expected to do under human rights treaty obligations with regard to everyone within its jurisdiction. Indeed, according to John Dugard, the International Law Commission's Special Rapporteur on diplomatic protection: 'Contemporary international human rights law accords to nationals and aliens the same protection, which far exceeds the international minimum standard of treatment for aliens set by Western Powers in an earlier era.'[4] This higher level of protection will have effects on the standard of due diligence required of states regarding human rights protection from non-state actors. In other words, human rights treaty law contains a higher level of protection than the standards developed in the context of the protection of aliens abroad in the nineteenth and twentieth centuries. Furthermore, even the rules for attribution of acts to the state may be different in the context of human rights treaties, as the aim of the treaty is the protection of the individual, rather than a mutual arrangement for

---

[1] These rules are codified and developed in the International Law Commission's articles on responsibility of states for internationally wrongful acts, *Report of the ILC, 53rd Session*, adopted 10 August 2001, UN Doc. A/56/10 (discussed further in Ch 6, at 6.7.1 above). The UN General Assembly took note of the articles, 'commended them to the attention of Governments', and annexed the articles GA Res. 56/83, 12 December 2001. For an explanation of the evolution of the Articles, see J. Crawford, *The International Law Commission's Articles on State Responsibility: Introduction, Text and Commentaries* (Cambridge: Cambridge University Press, 2002).

[2] See C. F. Amerasinghe, *State Responsibility for Injuries to Aliens* (Oxford: Clarendon Press, 1967).

[3] For the background, see John Dugard, Special Rapporteur, ILC, First report on diplomatic protection, UN Doc. A/CN.4/506, 7 March 2000.　　　　　　　　　　　　　　[4] Ibid, at para. 32.

resolving inter-state obligations concerning obligations owed to each other's nationals abroad. In short, I would suggest that human rights law has developed a set of state obligations that cannot be understood by the application of the primary rules of diplomatic protection of foreigners and the secondary rules of state responsibility.[5]

In fact, the history of Article 55 of the ILC's Articles on State Responsibility highlights the specific example that human rights treaties may diverge from the general rules set out in the Articles.[6] Furthermore, it is necessary not only to consider the specific human rights treaty to see if it contains better protection than the general rules of diplomatic protection and state responsibility, but we also have to examine specific human rights to gauge the extent of the obligation to protect the beneficiaries of the treaty from non-state actors. This chapter will provide a truncated overview of the contribution of some of the UN bodies charged with monitoring respect for such treaties.[7] (Full scale examination would require a whole book.) The texts produced by the these bodies mostly concentrate on the treaty obligations of states to protect the beneficiaries of human rights from infringements of their rights by non-state actors. These duties are variously referred to as responsibilities for 'omissions', 'positive obligations', 'duties to protect', and 'duties of due diligence'.[8] This overview seeks to give a flavour of how

---

[5] Cf R. Lawson, 'Out of Control. State Responsibility and Human Rights: Will the ILC's Definition of the "Act of State" meet the Challenges of the 21st Century?' in M. Castermans, F. van Hoof, and J. Smith (eds) *The Role of the Nation-State in the 21st Century* (The Hague: Kluwer, 1998) 91–116.

[6] Art. 55, entitled *'Lex specialis'*, reads: 'These articles do not apply where and to the extent that the conditions for the existence of an internationally wrongful act or the content or implementation of the international responsibility of a State are governed by special rules of international law.' The Commentary refers to the restrictive definition of the state in the Convention Against Torture and the wider rules for attribution that would probably follow from the rules in the Articles. (at para. 3 to the Commentary on Art. 55, Report of the ILC, GAOR Supp. No. 10), UN Doc. A/56/10, 358, fn 865. It is not being suggested that human rights treaties represent a 'strong' form of *lex specialis* and constitute self-contained regimes. Rather, in the expression of the Commentary, they may contain provisions, or have been interpreted, so that they differ from the scope of general obligations under the law of state responsibility. As the Commentary puts it, Art. 55 covers self-contained regimes as well as '"weaker" forms such as specific treaty provisions on a single point' (para. 5 to the Commentary on Art. 55).

[7] The Convention on the Prevention and Punishment of the Crime of Genocide is seen by many as a human rights treaty, it does not, however, have a comparable UN body to the treaty bodies examined here. See further W. Schabas, *Genocide in International Law: The Crime of Crimes* (Cambridge: Cambridge University Press, 2000). The International Convention on the Protection of the Rights of All Migrant Workers and Members of Their Families has entered into force but, at the time of writing, the monitoring body has only just begun its work: 'Report of the Committee on the Protection of the Rights of All Migrant Workers and Members of Their Families', First session, 1–5 March 2004, GAOR Supp. No. 48, UN Doc. A/59/48. See further R. Cholewinski, *Migrant Workers in International Human Rights Law: Their Protection in Countries of Employment* (Oxford: Clarendon Press, 1997).

[8] In national law, the terminology used to describe the requirements for the application of human rights law in the field of relations between non-state actors includes: *Drittwirkung*, horizontality, the state action requirement, and horizontal effect. Because national courts often interpret and apply the same human rights as those found in the international treaties, the terminology migrates from the

the UN treaty bodies have managed to develop simultaneously the primary obligations of states to protect individuals from infringements by non-state actors, and to give some guidance as to what is expected from non-state actors in the context of these different treaties.

8.1   INTERNATIONAL CONVENTION ON THE ELIMINATION OF ALL FORMS OF RACIAL DISCRIMINATION

The Racial Discrimination Convention highlights the concern that international law might demand that states regulate private behaviour and that this very regulation could in turn impinge on established private freedoms. On ratification of the treaty, the United States formulated a reservation which foresees a clash between the demand that governments regulate private conduct and the freedom of individuals in the private sphere.[9]

The wording of the treaty is confusing. Article 1 includes a reference to discrimination 'in the political, economic, social, cultural or any other field of public life', but Article 2(d) demands that 'Each State Party shall prohibit and bring to an end, by all appropriate means, including legislation as required by circumstances, racial discrimination by any persons, group or organization'. There is now, however, little doubt that the state has a duty to ensure that non-state actors in the private sector do not engage in direct or indirect discrimination. This interpretation is illustrated by a complaint against Denmark, brought under the optional complaints procedure established by Article 14. The Committee considered the scope of the Convention with regard to a complaint by Ziad Ben Ahmed Habassi, a Moroccan, who was refused a bank loan. The Committee concluded:

> In the present case the author was refused a loan by a Danish bank on the sole ground of his non Danish nationality and was told that the nationality requirement was motivated

national to the international level and *vice versa*. I have referred to this elsewhere, with apologies to Jochen Frowein, as a 'dialectical development'. See A. Clapham, *Human Rights in the Private Sphere* (Oxford: Clarendon Press, 1993) at 270–271, 347. The situation in different national legal orders is dealt with in Ch 10 below.

[9] The reservation reads: '(2) That the Constitution and laws of the United States establish extensive protections against discrimination, reaching significant areas of non-governmental activity. Individual privacy and freedom from governmental interference in private conduct, however, are also recognized as among the fundamental values which shape our free and democratic society. The United States understands that the identification of the rights protected under the Convention by reference in article 1 to fields of "public life" reflects a similar distinction between spheres of public conduct that are customarily the subject of governmental regulation, and spheres of private conduct that are not. To the extent, however, that the Convention calls for a broader regulation of private conduct, the United States does not accept any obligation under this Convention to enact legislation or take other measures under paragraph (1) of article 2, subparagraphs (1) (c) and (d) of article 2, article 3 and article 5 with respect to private conduct except as mandated by the Constitution and laws of the United States.'

by the need to ensure that the loan was repaid. In the opinion of the Committee, however, nationality is not the most appropriate requisite when investigating a person's will or capacity to reimburse a loan. The applicant's permanent residence or the place where his employment, property or family ties are to be found may be more relevant in this context. A citizen may move abroad or have all his property in another country and thus evade all attempts to enforce a claim of repayment. Accordingly, the Committee finds that, on the basis of article 2, paragraph (d), of the Convention, it is appropriate to initiate a proper investigation into the real reasons behind the bank's loan policy vis-à-vis foreign residents, in order to ascertain whether or not criteria involving racial discrimination, within the meaning of article 1 of the Convention, are being applied.[10]

The Danish authorities had been informed of the refusal, and were found to have failed to investigate properly the alleged discrimination by the non-state actor. The Committee found that Denmark had violated the Convention. The complaint is particularly interesting as it illustrates that, not only does the Convention extend to the private sector, but that the discrimination obligations for the non-state actor also extend to indirect discrimination. The bank did not discriminate on grounds of race as such; their policy related to nationality. Nevertheless, the complaint demanded that the bank and the authorities examine the indirect effect of the policy to ascertain whether there was racial discrimination. The complaint admits that the policy might be justified, but that it was for the private body and the public authorities to properly ensure that there were no unintended effects that would amount to racial discrimination. The communication highlighted these points:

3.1 Counsel claims that the facts stated above amount to violations of article 2, paragraph 1 (d), and article 6 of the Convention, according to which alleged cases of discrimination have to be investigated thoroughly by the national authorities. In the present case neither the police department of Skive nor the State Prosecutor examined whether the bank's loan policy constituted indirect discrimination on the basis of national origin and race. In particular, they should have examined the following issues: first, to what extent persons applying for loans were requested to show their passports; second, to what extent Sparbank Vest granted loans to non-Danish citizens; third, to what extent Sparbank Vest granted loans to Danish citizens living abroad.

3.2 Counsel further claims that in cases such as the one under consideration there might be a reasonable justification for permanent residence. However, if loans were actually granted to Danish citizens who did not have their permanent residence in Denmark, the criterion of citizenship would in fact constitute racial discrimination, in accordance with article 1, subparagraph 1, of the Convention. It would be especially relevant for the police to investigate whether an intentional or an unintentional act of discrimination in violation of the Convention had taken place.

[10] Communication No. 10/1997: Denmark, 6 April 1999, UN Doc. CERD/C/54/D/10/1997, at para. 9.3.

The failure of the authorities to follow up the complaints made to them led to a finding of a violation of the Convention for action taken in the private sphere by a non-state actor.[11]

The Convention is quite specific in demanding that states parties prohibit racial discrimination in all its forms and guarantee a right of access to 'transport, hotels, restaurants, cafés, theatres and parks'.[12] In addition, there is an explicit obligation in Article 5(b) to guarantee: 'The right to security of person and protection by the State against violence or bodily harm, whether inflicted by government officials or by any individual group or institution.'

The oblique and contradictory mention of 'public life' in Article 1 of the Convention has been the subject of academic commentary in the past,[13] but the above-mentioned opinion regarding the bank in Denmark and the Committee's General Recommendation 20 (see below) make it clear that states have obligations to deal with racism and racial discrimination perpetrated by non-state actors in the public and private spheres. The obligation therefore covers all forms of employment, housing, commercial, and financial arrangements. Because the arrangements made by private institutions could contribute to racism, or have effects which disadvantage racial groups, governments are required to introduce legislation to ensure that private individuals and institutions avoid all forms of racial discrimination. If they fail to introduce effective methods for investigation and enforcement mechanisms, they risk being found in violation of the Convention.

General Recommendation 20, adopted in 1996, states:

> The rights and freedoms referred to in article 5 of the Convention and any similar rights shall be protected by a State party. Such protection may be achieved in different ways, be it by the use of public institutions or through the activities of private institutions. In any case, it is the obligation of the State party concerned to ensure the effective implementation of the Convention and to report thereon under article 9 of the Convention. To the extent that private institutions influence the exercise of rights or the availability of

[11] For a complaint concerning dismissal by a private employer on racist grounds, see *Yilmaz-Dogan v The Netherlands*, Opinion adopted on 10 August 1988 at the 36th Session of the Committee, GAOR 43rd Session, Supp. No. 18, UN Doc. A/43/18, Report of the Committee on the Elimination of Racial Discrimination, annex iv, Communication 1/1984.

[12] Art. 5: 'In compliance with the fundamental obligations laid down in article 2 of this Convention, States Parties undertake to prohibit and to eliminate racial discrimination in all its forms and to guarantee the right of everyone, without distinction as to race, colour, or national or ethnic origin, to equality before the law, notably in the enjoyment of the following rights . . . (f) The right of access to any place or service intended for use by the general public, such as transport, hotels, restaurants, cafes, theatres and parks.'

[13] It has been suggested that in conflicts between the reference to 'public life' in Art. 1(1) and the operative provisions of Art. 5, the latter should prevail. E. Schwelb, 'The International Convention on the Elimination of All Forms of Racial Discrimination' 15 *ICLQ* (1966) 996, at 1005–1006, see also T. Meron, 'The Meaning and Reach of the International Convention on the Elimination of All Forms of Racial Discrimination' 79 *AJIL* (1985) 283, at 293–295; K. Boyle and A. Baldaccini, 'A Critical Evaluation of International Human Rights Approaches to Racism' in S. Fredman (ed) *Discrimination and Human Rights, The Case of Racism* (Oxford: Oxford University Press, 2001) at 159: 'CERD practice has made it clear that these guarantees extend to employment in private enterprises, to housing provided by private owners, or admission to private clubs.'

opportunities, the State party must ensure that the result has neither the purpose nor the effect of creating or perpetuating racial discrimination.[14]

More recently, General Recommendation 30 on the rights of non-citizens offers particular examples of non-state actors that states should control. States are recommended to: 'Take resolute action to counter any tendency to target, stigmatize, stereotype or profile, on the basis of race, colour, descent, and national or ethnic origin, members of "non-citizen" population groups, especially by politicians, officials, educators and the media, on the Internet and other electronic communications networks and in society at large.'[15] Furthermore, states should: 'Ensure the right of non-citizens, without discrimination based on race, colour, descent, and national or ethnic origin, to have access to any place or service intended for use by the general public, such as transport, hotels, restaurants, cafés, theatres and parks.'[16]

8.2   CONVENTION ON THE RIGHTS OF THE CHILD

The UN General Assembly's 1959 Declaration of the Rights of the Child called 'upon parents, upon men and women as individuals, and upon voluntary organizations, local authorities and national Governments to recognize these rights and strive for their observance by legislative and other measures progressively taken in accordance with the [principles set out in the Declaration]'.[17] Thirty years later, the Convention on the Rights of the Child included a specific reference to the need for certain non-state actors to respect the principle of decision-making in accordance with the best interests of the child. Article 3(1) states: 'In all actions concerning children, whether undertaken by public or private social welfare institutions, courts of law, administrative authorities or legislative bodies, the best interests of the child shall be a primary consideration.' The Committee on the Rights of the Child has held discussions on the role of the private sector, and in its General Comment on implementation, the Committee speaks of 'indirect obligations' for non-state actors under the Convention: 'The Committee emphasizes that States parties to the Convention have a legal obligation to respect and ensure the rights of children as stipulated in the Convention, which includes the obligation to

---

[14] Recommendation 20, 48th Session (1996), at para. 5. The Recommendation is reproduced in 'Compilation of General Comments and General Recommendations Adopted by Human Rights Treaty Bodies', UN Doc. HRI/GEN/1/Rev.7, 12 May 2004, at 211 (hereinafter document references for printed versions of Comments and Recommendations are to this 'UN Compilation'). Note also General Recommendation 14 on Art. 1, para. 1, 42nd Session (1993), which states in its para. 3: 'Article 1, paragraph 1, of the Convention also refers to the political, economic, social and cultural fields; the related rights and freedoms are set up in article 5.' 'UN Compilation' at 206. There is no reference to the phrase 'other field of public life' and it seems not to limit in any way the scope of the Convention to acts of public institutions.

[15] 'Discrimination against non-citizens', UN Doc. CERD/C/64/Misc.11/Rev. 3, 64th Session (23 February–12 March 2004), at para. 12.   [16] Ibid, at para. 38.

[17] Proclaimed by GA Res. 1386(XIV) of 20 November 1959.

ensure that non-State service providers operate in accordance with its provisions, thus creating indirect obligations on such actors.'[18] The Committee is very clear that, in the context of privatization, states cannot diminish their obligation to ensure the full recognition of all Convention rights for all children within the jurisdiction.[19] The Committee has therefore proposed: 'that there should be a permanent monitoring mechanism or process aimed at ensuring that all State and non-State service providers respect the Convention'.[20]

The Committee is demanding here that states ensure respect for the Convention by non-state actors. But the Committee has gone further and directly addressed non-state actors and detailed the sorts of steps it expects non-state actors to take in the context of respect for children's human rights. This rather unusual step from a UN Human Rights Treaty Body is excerpted here in its entirety:

Recommendations to non-State service providers

16.   The Committee calls on all non-State service providers to respect the principles and provisions of the Convention on the Rights of the Child. It further recommends that all non-State service providers take into account the provisions of the Convention when conceptualizing, implementing and evaluating their programmes, including when sub-contracting other non-State service providers, in particular the four general principles set out in the provisions concerning non-discrimination (art. 2), the best interests of the child (art. 3), the right to life, survival and development (art. 6), and the right of the child to express his or her views freely and have those views be given due weight in accordance with the age and maturity of the child (art. 12).

17.   To that end, the Committee encourages non-State service providers to ensure that service provision is carried out in accordance with international standards, especially those of the Convention. It further encourages non-State service providers to develop self-regulation mechanisms which would include a system of checks and balances. To that end, the Committee recommends that, when developing self-regulation mechanisms, the following criteria be included in the process:

(i) The adoption of a code of ethics, or similar document, which should reflect the principles of the Convention and which should be developed jointly by the various stakeholders and in which the four general principles of the Convention should figure prominently;

(ii) The establishment of a system for monitoring the implementation of such a code, if possible by independent experts, as well as the development of a system of transparent reporting;

(iii) The development of indicators/benchmarks as a prerequisite for measuring progress and establishing accountability;

(iv) The inclusion of a system enabling the various partners to challenge each other regarding their respective performance in implementing the code;

---

[18] General Comment No. 5, 'General measures of implementation of the Convention on the Rights of the Child (arts. 4, 42 and 44, para. 6)', 27 November 2003, at para. 43; 'UN Compilation', at 332.   [19] Ibid, at para. 44.
[20] Ibid, at para. 44.

(v) The development of an effective complaints mechanism with a view to rendering self-regulation more accountable, including to beneficiaries, particularly in the light of the general principle that provides for the right of the child to express his or her views freely and have those views be given due weight in accordance with the age and maturity of the child (art. 12).

18.   Furthermore, the Committee encourages non-State service providers, particularly for profit service providers, as well as the media, to engage in a continuing process of dialogue and consultation with the communities they serve and to create alliances and partnerships with the various stakeholders and beneficiaries in order to enhance transparency and involve community groups in decision-making processes and, where appropriate, in service provision itself. Service providers should collaborate with communities, particularly in remote areas, or with communities composed of minority groups, in order to ensure that services are provided in compliance with the Convention, and in particular in a manner that is culturally appropriate and in which availability, accessibility and quality are guaranteed for all.[21]

This blueprint for non-state actor behaviour to ensure respect for the human rights in the Convention could well be adapted for use in other contexts.

8.3   INTERNATIONAL COVENANT ON ECONOMIC, SOCIAL AND CULTURAL RIGHTS

The Committee on Economic, Social and Cultural Rights has focused on the impact of non-state actors in a series of General Comments. In the context of gender equality, the Committee is clear that this obligation extends to the private sphere and that states have an obligation to protect women from non-state actor discrimination. According to General Comment 16, states' obligations include 'the adoption of legislation to eliminate discrimination and to prevent third parties from interfering directly or indirectly with the enjoyment of this right'.[22] The introduction of legislation is not, however, sufficient. States are obligated to monitor non-state actor behaviour: 'States parties have an obligation to monitor and regulate the conduct of non-state actors to ensure that they do not violate the equal right of men and women to enjoy economic, social and cultural rights. This obligation applies, for example, in cases where public services have been partially or fully privatized.'[23]

---

[21] Recommendations following the 'Day of General Discussion on "The private sector as service provider and its role in implementing child rights" ', Report on its 31st Session, September–October 2002, UN Doc. CRC/C/121, 11 December 2002, at para. 653.

[22] General Comment 16, 'Article 3: the equal right of men and women to the enjoyment of all economic, social and cultural rights', UN Doc. E/C.12/2005/3, 13 May 2005 (unedited text) at para. 19.

[23] Ibid, at 20. For more detail with regard to monitoring specific rights in the private sector, see paras 22–31.

With regard to the right to food, the Committee stated:

Violations of the right to food can occur through the direct action of States or other entities insufficiently regulated by States. These include: the formal repeal or suspension of legislation necessary for the continued enjoyment of the right to food; denial of access to food to particular individuals or groups, whether the discrimination is based on legislation or is proactive; the prevention of access to humanitarian food aid in internal conflicts or other emergency situations; adoption of legislation or policies which are manifestly incompatible with pre-existing legal obligations relating to the right to food; and failure to regulate activities of individuals or groups so as to prevent them from violating the right to food of others, or the failure of a State to take into account its international legal obligations regarding the right to food when entering into agreements with other States or with international organizations.[24]

The Committee here suggests that non-state actors are capable of 'violating the right to food'. It refers to the 'responsibilities' of non-state actors and then concentrates on the steps that states must take to ensure that non-state actors are prevented from committing such violations:

While only States are parties to the Covenant and are thus ultimately accountable for compliance with it, all members of society—individuals, families, local communities, non-governmental organizations, civil society organizations, as well as the private business sector—have responsibilities in the realization of the right to adequate food. The State should provide an environment that facilitates implementation of these responsibilities. The private business sector—national and transnational—should pursue its activities within the framework of a code of conduct conducive to respect of the right to adequate food, agreed upon jointly with the Government and civil society.[25]

A similar approach has been taken with regard to the right to water, with the Committee focusing on the steps that states have to take to protect the right to water from interference by non-state actors in this sector:

23.   The obligation to *protect* requires States parties to prevent third parties from interfering in any way with the enjoyment of the right to water. Third parties include individuals, groups, corporations and other entities as well as agents acting under their authority. The obligation includes, inter alia, adopting the necessary and effective legislative and other measures to restrain, for example, third parties from denying equal access to adequate water; and polluting and inequitably extracting from water resources, including natural sources, wells and other water distribution systems.

24.   Where water services (such as piped water networks, water tankers, access to rivers and wells) are operated or controlled by third parties, States parties must prevent them from compromising equal, affordable, and physical access to sufficient, safe and acceptable water. To prevent such abuses an effective regulatory system must be established, in conformity with the Covenant and this general comment, which

---

[24] General Comment 12, 'the right to adequate food (art. 11)', adopted 12 May 1999, at para. 19; 'UN Compilation', at 63.   [25] Ibid, at para. 20.

includes independent monitoring, genuine public participation and imposition of penalties for non-compliance.[26]

The right to health operates in a sector where the role of non-state actors can hardly be ignored. The Committee's General Comment on 'the right to the highest attainable standard of health' clarifies the nature and the content of such a right. The Comment explains that the reference in Article 12.1 to 'the highest attainable standard of physical and mental health' is not confined to the right to health care: 'On the contrary, the drafting history and the express wording of article 12.2 acknowledge that the right to health embraces a wide range of socio-economic factors that promote conditions in which people can lead a healthy life, and extends to the underlying determinants of health, such as food and nutrition, housing, access to safe and potable water and adequate sanitation, safe and healthy working conditions, and a healthy environment.'[27]

The General Comment applies the Committee's approach to the duty to 'protect' in the context of non-state actor interferences with the right to health:

> Obligations to *protect* include, *inter alia*, the duties of States to adopt legislation or to take other measures ensuring equal access to health care and health-related services provided by third parties; to ensure that privatization of the health sector does not constitute a threat to the availability, accessibility, acceptability and quality of health facilities, goods and services; to control the marketing of medical equipment and medicines by third parties; and to ensure that medical practitioners and other health professionals meet appropriate standards of education, skill and ethical codes of conduct. States are also obliged to ensure that harmful social or traditional practices do not interfere with access to pre- and post-natal care and family-planning; to prevent third parties from coercing women to undergo traditional practices, e.g. female genital mutilation; and to take measures to protect all vulnerable or marginalized groups of society, in particular women, children, adolescents and older persons, in the light of gender-based expressions of violence. States should also ensure that third parties do not limit people's access to health-related information and services.[28]

The General Comment also addresses itself directly to non-state actors, setting out the *responsibilities* of non-state actors with regard to the right to health:

> While only States are parties to the Covenant and thus ultimately accountable for compliance with it, all members of society—individuals, including health professionals, families, local communities, intergovernmental and non-governmental organizations, civil society organizations, as well as the private business sector—have responsibilities regarding the realization of the right to health. State parties should therefore provide an environment which facilitates the discharge of these responsibilities.

---

[26] General Comment 15, 'the right to water (arts. 11 and 12)' adopted 26 November 2002; 'UN Compilation', at 106.

[27] Committee on Economic, Social and Cultural Rights, General Comment 14 'the right to the highest attainable standard of health (art. 12)', adopted 11 August 2000, at para. 4, 'UN Compilation', at 86.   [28] Ibid, at para. 35.

In a recent book, Nicola Jägers has taken the right to health as elaborated by the Committee and sought to determine the responsibilities of corporations with regard to the realization of this right. She follows the approach of the Committee and breaks the rights down into the familiar separate obligations to respect, protect, and fulfil the right. The following paragraphs contain her conclusions:[29]

> For a corporation the duty to respect the right to health may require that the corporation abstains from operations that may cause environmental problems that are detrimental to the health of employees and the people residing on the land where the corporation operates. Moreover where corporations knowingly market unhealthy products, a violation of the obligation to respect the right to health will occur. An example of the latter is the aggressive marketing of powdered milk by multinationals in developing States....
>
> For corporations the duty to protect the right to health will come into play especially with regard to the 'underlying determinants' of the right to health, such as food and nutrition, housing, access to safe and potable water and adequate sanitation, safe and healthy working conditions, and a healthy environment. The duty to protect may require a corporation to adopt guidelines in order to ensure that the activities of business partners will not lead to violations of other individuals' right to health. For example, a corporation should ensure that their subcontractors promote healthy working conditions....
>
> It is conceivable that the obligation to fulfil comes into play when a corporation operates in a remote part where the state is not capable of providing for health facilities. In such a case a corporation may be under the obligation to fulfil the right of its employees to health by providing for health care services and hospitals.

The evolving understanding of the obligations of corporations was discussed in some detail in Chapter 6. The present discussion illustrates how the work of the human rights treaty bodies is catalytic to the thinking on what human rights obligations corporations should bear. The answer lies not so much in the wording of the treaty, but rather in a sophisticated understanding of the context. As Jägers illustrates, the responsibilities of corporations may depend on the role they have assumed, as well as their capacity to bear the burden in question.

The Committee has not confined its attention to the corporate sector. It has been careful to draw attention to *obligations* of international organizations, including the World Bank and the IMF. Remaining in the context of the right to health, General Comment 14 includes a part entitled 'Obligations of Actors Other Than States Parties'. The relevant paragraphs set out the Committee's approach to UN agencies,[30] the International Committee of the Red Cross, and non-governmental organizations. In the light of the examination of the international financial institutions in Chapter 4, one might highlight the following sentence: 'In particular, the international financial institutions, notably the World Bank and the International Monetary Fund, should pay greater attention to the

---

[29] N. Jägers, *Corporate Human Rights Obligations: in Search of Accountability* (Antwerp: Intersentia, 2002) at 87 (footnote omitted).

[30] The particular connection between certain UN agencies and the Covenant is explained in detail in P. Alston, 'The United Nations' Specialized Agencies and Implementation of the International Covenant on Economic, Social, and Cultural Rights' 18 *Col JTL* (1979) 79–118.

protection of the right to health in their lending policies, credit agreements and structural adjustment programmes.'[31] Similar injunctions exist under the heading 'Obligations of Actors Other Than States Parties' in the context of the right to education,[32] and the right to water.[33]

8.4   INTERNATIONAL COVENANT ON CIVIL AND POLITICAL RIGHTS

The Human Rights Committee has recently articulated its appreciation of the scope of the Covenant with regard to non-state actors. In General Comment 31, the Committee states:

> . . . the positive obligations on States parties to ensure Covenant rights will only be fully discharged if individuals are protected by the State, not just against violations of Covenant rights by its agents, but also against acts committed by private persons or entities that would impair the enjoyment of Covenant rights insofar as they are amenable to application between private persons or entities. There may be circumstances in which a failure to ensure Covenant rights as required by article 2 would give rise to violations by States parties of those rights, as a result of States parties' permitting or failing to take appropriate measures or to exercise due diligence to prevent, punish, investigate or redress the harm caused by such acts by private persons or entities. States are reminded of the interrelationship between the positive obligations imposed under article 2 and the need to provide effective remedies in the event of breach under article 2, paragraph 3. The Covenant itself envisages in some articles certain areas where there are positive obligations on States parties to address the activities of private persons or entities. For example, the privacy-related guarantees of article 17 must be protected by law. It is also implicit in article 7 that States parties have to take positive measures to ensure that private persons or entities do not inflict torture or cruel, inhuman or degrading treatment or punishment on others within their power. In fields affecting basic aspects of ordinary life such as work or housing, individuals are to be protected from discrimination within the meaning of article 26.[34]

The Committee has, at the same time, taken a very restrictive approach to the actual responsibilities of non-state actors under the Covenant. In contrast to the other treaty bodies examined above, the Human Rights Committee goes out of its way to suggest that the Covenant does not create direct international obligations for non-state actors: 'The article 2, paragraph 1, obligations are binding on States parties and do not, as such, have direct horizontal effect as a matter of

---

[31]   Committee on Economic, Social and Cultural Rights, General Comment 14, at para. 64.

[32]   General Comment 13, 'the right to education, art. 13', 8 December 1999, at para. 60; 'UN Compilation', at 71. And see also General Comment 2, 'International technical assistance measures (art. 22)', 2 February 1990; 'UN Compilation', at 12.

[33]   See General Comment 15, 'the right to water (arts. 11 and 12)' adopted 26 November 2002, at para. 60; 'UN Compilation', at 106.

[34]   General Comment No. 31,'(art. 2) the nature of the general legal obligation imposed on states parties to the Covenant', 29 March 2004, at para. 8; 'UN Compilation', at 192.

international law.'[35] The careful phrasing suggests that the Committee has left open the suggestion that international human rights obligations may be binding on non-state actors under general international law. It is just that the treaty itself does not generate these rights and obligations; the treaty, as such, merely generates obligations for the states parties.[36] What is clear, however, is that these obligations extend into the private sphere.[37]

Various General Comments have, over the years, tackled the scope of state obligations with regard to protection of individuals from non-state actors. The following discussion will only touch on a few. With respect to the right to life, the Committee referred to a number of private actions threatening human rights and the state's duty to deter such activity: the duty to prevent propaganda for war and incitement to violence (referring to the connection with Article 20); the duty to prevent and investigate disappearances; and the desirability of taking all possible measures to reduce infant mortality and increase life expectancy through the adoption of measures which eliminate malnutrition and epidemics.[38] The Committee has also mentioned in passing that the state should take measures to prevent and punish deprivation of life by criminal acts.[39]

With regard to the prohibition on torture, or cruel, inhuman, or degrading treatment or punishment, the Committee's General Comment 20 states that the Covenant covers such behaviour whether it is inflicted by a state or non-state actor. The Committee explains that it is the 'duty of the State party to afford everyone protection through legislative and other measures as may be necessary against the acts prohibited by article 7, whether inflicted by people acting in their official capacity, outside their official capacity or in a private capacity'.[40] The General Comment also extends the prohibition to corporal punishment in terms which suggest that the prohibition spans the public/private divide.[41] In addition, the Comment also demands that states should indicate the provisions of their criminal law which penalize breaches of the prohibition and specify the applicable penalties for such acts 'whether committed by public officials or other persons

---

[35] Ibid, at 192.
[36] See the discussion of the right to equality as an obligation with 'third party effects' by the Inter-American Court of Human Rights in Ch 9, at 9.2.3 below.
[37] For an examination of the drafting history of the Covenant on this point, see A. Clapham, 'Revisiting *Human Rights in the Private Sphere*: Using the European Convention on Human Rights to Protect the Right of Access to the Civil Courts' in C. Scott (ed) *Torture as Tort: Comparative Perspectives on the Development of Transnational Human Rights Litigation* (Oxford: Hart Publishing, 2001) 513–535, esp. at 516–517.
[38] General Comment 6, 'the right to life (art. 6)', 30 April 1982; 'UN Compilation', at 128.
[39] Ibid, at para.3.
[40] General Comment 20, 'prohibition of torture and cruel treatment or punishment (art. 7)', 10 March 1992, at para. 2; 'UN Compilation', at 150.
[41] Ibid, at para. 7: the prohibition in Art. 7 'must extend to corporal punishment, including excessive chastisement ordered as punishment for a crime or as an educative or disciplinary measure. It is appropriate to emphasize in this regard that article 7 protects, in particular, children, pupils and patients in teaching and medical institutions'.

acting on behalf of the State, or by private persons'.[42] The references in this General Comment to 'private capacity' and 'private persons' leave no doubt that Article 7 of the Covenant covers acts committed by non-state actors.

The 1982 General Comment on Article 10 (Humane treatment of persons deprived of their liberty) referred to 'all institutions where persons are lawfully held against their will, not only in prisons but also, for example, hospitals, detention camps or correction institutions'.[43] The 1992 General Comment on the same subject was deliberately designed to cover private institutions.[44] The wording 'under their jurisdiction' was specifically rejected by the Chairman as it would have excluded private institutions. 'Within their jurisdiction' was held to cover those detained by non-state actors in the private sphere.[45] In a complaint concerning treatment in a privately run prison in Australia, the Committee explicitly took up the scope of the state's obligations towards private prisons:

> Prior to considering the admissibility of the individual claims raised, the Committee must consider whether the State party's obligations under the Covenant apply to privately-run detention facilities, as is the case in this communication, as well as State-run facilities. While this is not an argument put forward by the State party, the Committee must consider ex officio whether the communication concerns a State party to the Covenant in the meaning of article 1 of the Optional Protocol. It recalls its jurisprudence in which it indicated that a State party 'is not relieved of its obligations under the Covenant when some of its functions are delegated to other autonomous organs.' The Committee considers that the contracting out to the private commercial sector of core State activities which involve the use of force and the detention of persons does not absolve a State party of its obligations under the Covenant, notably under articles 7 and 10 which are invoked in the instant communication. Consequently, the Committee finds that the State party is accountable under the Covenant and the Optional Protocol of the treatment of inmates in the Port Philip Prison facility run by Group 4.[46]

The Committee went on to treat the complaint as if it had been brought against state agents and found that the complaint concerning the holding of the two detainees 'for an hour in a triangular "cage"' justified a finding of a violation of Article 10(1).[47]

---

[42] General Comment 20, 'Prohibition of torture and cruel treatment or punishment (art. 7)', at para. 13.

[43] General Comment 21, 'Article 10 (Humane treatment of persons deprived of their liberty)', 10 April 1992, at para 1; 'UN Compilation', at 131.

[44] The author witnessed the debate during the open session of the Committee on this Comment during its 44th Session.

[45] The full paragraph reads: 'Article 10, paragraph 1, of the International Covenant on Civil and Political Rights applies to anyone deprived of liberty under the laws and authority of the State who is held in prisons, hospitals—particularly psychiatric hospitals—detention camps or correctional institutions or elsewhere. States parties should ensure that the principle stipulated therein is observed in all institutions and establishments within their jurisdiction where persons are being held.' At para. 2; 'UN Compilation', at 152.

[46] *Cabal and Pasini Bertran v Australia* (Communication 1020/2001) 19 September 2003, at para. 7.2, UN Doc. CCPR/C/78/D/1020/2001 (footnote omitted).   [47] Ibid, at para. 8.3.

With regard to freedom of expression, the Committee has simply called on states to provide further information as to steps they are taking to protect freedom of expression in the context of private mass media.[48]

Turning to the right to privacy, the Committee's view is that 'this right is required to be guaranteed against all such interferences and attacks whether they emanate from State authorities or from natural or legal persons'.[49] Concerning the rights of children, the Committee has stated that every possible measure should be taken to prevent children 'from being exploited by means of forced labour or prostitution, or by their use in the illicit trafficking of narcotic drugs, or by other means'.[50] Furthermore: 'In cases where the parents and the family seriously fail in their duties, ill-treat or neglect the child, the State should intervene to restrict parental authority and the child may be separated from his family when circumstances so require.'[51]

With regard to non-discrimination, the Committee has asked states to provide information on discrimination by non-state actors:

> When reporting on Articles 2(1), 3 and 36 of the Covenant, States Parties usually cite provisions of their constitution or equal opportunity laws with respect to equality of persons. While such information is of course useful, the Committee wishes to know if there remain any problems of discrimination in fact, which may be practised either by public authorities, by the community, or by private persons or bodies. The Committee wishes to be informed about legal provisions and administrative measures directed at diminishing or eliminating such discrimination.[52]

[48] 'Not all States parties have provided information concerning all aspects of the freedom of expression. For instance, little attention has so far been given to the fact that, because of the development of modern mass media, effective measures are necessary to prevent such control of the media as would interfere with the right of everyone to freedom of expression in a way that is not provided for in paragraph 3.' General Comment 10 'Article 19 (Freedom of opinion)', 29 June 1983, at para. 2; 'UN Compilation', at 133.

[49] General Comment 16, 'Article 17 (Right to privacy)', 8 April 1988, at para. 1; 'UN Compilation', at 142. The Comment continues (at para. 10): 'The gathering and holding of personal information on computers, data banks and other devices, whether by public authorities or private individuals or bodies, must be regulated by law. Effective measures have to be taken by States to ensure that information concerning a person's private life does not reach the hands of persons who are not authorized by law to receive, process and use it, and is never used for purposes incompatible with the Covenant. In order to have the most effective protection of his private life, every individual should have the right to ascertain in an intelligible form, whether, and if so, what personal data is stored in automatic data files, and for what purposes. Every individual should also be able to ascertain which public authorities or private individuals or bodies control or may control their files. If such files contain incorrect personal data or have been collected or processed contrary to the provisions of the law, every individual should have the right to request rectification or elimination.' For a discussion of a complaint concerning a hotel development in Tahiti, see *Francis Hopu and Tepoaitu Bessert v France* Communication 549/1993, UN Doc. CCPR/C/60/D/549/1993/Rev.1, 29 December 1997. For a detailed analysis, see C. Scott, 'Multinational Enterprises and Emergent Jurisprudence on Violations of Economic, Social and Cultural Rights' in A. Eide, C. Krause, and A. Rosas (eds) *Economic, Social and Cultural Rights: A Textbook* (Dordrecht: Martinus Nijhoff, 2nd edn, 2001) 563–595, at 584–586.

[50] General Comment 17 'Rights of the child (Art. 24)', 7 April 1989, at para. 3; 'UN Compilation', at 144.   [51] Ibid, at para. 6.

[52] General Comment 18, 'Non-discrimination' 10 November 1989, at para. 9; 'UN Compilation', at 146.

With regard to private discrimination, the Committee has had occasion to express its concern with regard to Switzerland that 'legislation protecting individuals against discrimination in the private sector does not exist in all parts of the State party's territory. The State party should ensure that legislation exists throughout its territory to protect individuals against discrimination in the private field, pursuant to articles 2 and 3 of the Covenant'.[53]

The Committee has also examined in some detail the need to protect individuals from non-state actors in the context of the protection of minority rights:

> Although article 27 is expressed in negative terms, that article, nevertheless, does recognize the existence of a 'right' and requires that it shall not be denied. Consequently, a State party is under an obligation to ensure that the existence and the exercise of this right are protected against their denial or violation. Positive measures of protection are, therefore, required not only against the acts of the State party itself, whether through its legislative, judicial or administrative authorities, but also against the acts of other persons within the State party.[54]

The Committee has even focused on the need to prevent non-state actors from interfering with freedom of movement under the Covenant. The Committee drew particular attention to the need for states to tackle the actions of relatives who might prevent women from exercising this right:

> The State party must ensure that the rights guaranteed in article 12 are protected not only from public but also from private interference. In the case of women, this obligation to protect is particularly pertinent. For example, it is incompatible with article 12, paragraph 1, that the right of a woman to move freely and to choose her residence be made subject, by law or practice, to the decision of another person, including a relative.[55]

---

[53] Concluding observations, Switzerland, UN Doc. CCPR/CO/73/CH, 12 November 2001, at para. 10.

[54] General Comment 23, 'The rights of minorities (Art. 27)', 8 April 1994, at para. 6.1; 'UN Compilation', at 158. For a discussion of how the state is implicated through its legislation in disputes within indigenous communities, see *Kitok v Sweden* Communication 197/1985, Views of the Human Rights Committee, adopted 27 July 1988, esp. at para. 9.4: 'With regard to the State party's argument that the conflict in the present case is not so much a conflict between the author as a Sami and the State party but rather between the author and the Sami community (see para. 4.3 above), the Committee observes that the State party's responsibility has been engaged, by virtue of the adoption of the Reindeer Husbandry Act of 1971, and that it is therefore State action that has been challenged. As the State party itself points out, an appeal against a decision of the Sami community to refuse membership can only be granted if there are special reasons for allowing such membership; furthermore, the State party acknowledges that the right of the County Administrative Board to grant such an appeal should be exercised very restrictively.' See further Scott (2001).

[55] General Comment 27, 'Article 12 (Freedom of movement)', at para. 6; 'UN Compilation', at 173.

8.5   CONVENTION ON THE ELIMINATION OF ALL FORMS OF DISCRIMINATION AGAINST WOMEN

The Committee on the Elimination of Discrimination against Women has been at the forefront of efforts to develop international human rights law to make it clear that states have positive duties to protect individuals from the violent acts of other individuals or groups. In its General Recommendation 19, the Committee addressed the issue of 'Violence against women'. Paragraph 9 of that General Recommendation builds on the concept of due diligence under 'general international law' to protect individuals from non-state actors, and makes it clear that the state has an obligation to prevent and punish private discrimination:

> It is emphasized, however, that discrimination under the Convention is not restricted to action by or on behalf of Governments (see articles 2 (e), 2 (f) and 5). For example, under article 2 (e) the Convention calls on States parties to take all appropriate measures to eliminate discrimination against women by any person, organization or enterprise. Under general international law and specific human rights covenants, States may also be responsible for private acts if they fail to act with due diligence to prevent violations of rights or to investigate and punish acts of violence, and for providing compensation.[56]

The Committee recommends that: 'States parties should take appropriate and effective measures to overcome all forms of gender-based violence, whether by public or private act.'[57] The Recommendation tackles a series of obligations under the Convention which are particularly relevant to the behaviour of non-state actors. These include sexual harassment at work,[58] and family violence.[59] Subsequent Recommendations have referred to the obligations of states to tackle 'violations' by non-state actors with regard to access to health care,[60] and that in this sector states have positive obligations even where health care is provided by

---

[56] General Recommendation 19, 'Violence against women', 29 January 1992, at para. 9; 'UN Compilation', at 248.   [57] Ibid, at para. 24(a).

[58] 'Sexual harassment includes such unwelcome sexually determined behaviour as physical contact and advances, sexually coloured remarks, showing pornography and sexual demands, whether by words or actions. Such conduct can be humiliating and may constitute a health and safety problem; it is discriminatory when the woman has reasonable ground to believe that her objection would disadvantage her in connection with her employment, including recruitment or promotion, or when it creates a hostile working environment.' Ibid, at para. 18.

[59] 'Family violence is one of the most insidious forms of violence against women. It is prevalent in all societies. Within family relationships women of all ages are subjected to violence of all kinds, including battering, rape, other forms of sexual assault, mental and other forms of violence, which are perpetuated by traditional attitudes. Lack of economic independence forces many women to stay in violent relationships. The abrogation of their family responsibilities by men can be a form of violence, and coercion. These forms of violence put women's health at risk and impair their ability to participate in family life and public life on a basis of equality.' Ibid, at para. 23.

[60] 'The obligation to protect rights relating to women's health requires States parties, their agents and officials to take action to prevent and impose sanctions for violations of rights by private persons and organizations.' General Recommendation 24, 'Article 12 of the Convention (women and health)' at para. 15; 'UN Compilation', at 274.

the private sector.[61] Furthermore, the Committee is clear that discrimination is prohibited in the public and private spheres, and this requires legislation which covers discrimination by state and non-state actors.[62]

This interpretation of women's human rights has been reflected outside the context of states parties' obligations under the treaty. For evidence of developments in the current state of general international law in this area, one might refer to the UN Declaration on Violence against Women:

> States should condemn violence against women and should not invoke any custom, tradition or religious consideration to avoid their obligations with respect to its elimination. States should pursue by all appropriate means and without delay a policy of eliminating violence against women and, to this end, should: . . . (c) Exercise due diligence to prevent, investigate and, in accordance with national legislation, punish acts of violence against women, whether those acts are perpetrated by the State or by private persons;[63]

The references in these two texts to *due diligence* have been used to develop a set of positive obligations for states with regard to violence by non-state actors.[64] The due diligence notion has even been applied in non-governmental monitoring to the expectations on a non-state actor, the international peace-keeping force in Kosovo (UNMIK).[65]

The influence of demands for women's rights has permeated the attitude of all monitoring bodies with regard to the state/non-state actor divide. One area which has been rapidly evolving is the scope of refugee protection for women fleeing non-state actor violence.

[61] 'States and parties cannot absolve themselves of responsibility in these areas by delegating or transferring these powers to private sector agencies. States parties should therefore report on what they have done to organize governmental processes and all structures through which public power is exercised to promote and protect women's health. They should include information on positive measures taken to curb violations of women's rights by third parties and to protect their health and the measures they have taken to ensure the provision of such services.' Ibid, at para. 17.

[62] 'Firstly, States parties' obligation is to ensure that there is no direct or indirect discrimination against women in their laws and that women are protected against discrimination—committed by public authorities, the judiciary, organizations, enterprises or private individuals—in the public as well as the private spheres by competent tribunals as well as sanctions and other remedies.' (Footnote omitted.) General Recommendation 25, 'Article 4, paragraph 1, of the Convention (temporary special measures)', at para. 7. See also 'Relevant legislation on non-discrimination and temporary special measures should cover governmental actors as well as private organizations or enterprises.' para 31; 'UN Compilation', at 282.

[63] Art. 4, Res. 48/104, adopted by consensus by the UN General Assembly, 20 December 1993.

[64] See Amnesty International, *Making Rights a Reality: The Duty of States to Address Violence against Women*, AI Index ACT 77/049/2004. Amnesty International, *Respect, protect, fulfil—Women's human rights: State responsibility for abuses by 'non-state actors'*, AI Index IOR 50/01/00.

[65] In the context of trafficking of women and children in Kosovo, Amnesty applies the due diligence obligation to show that states have obligations under the Convention on the Elimination of All Forms of Discrimination against Women 'to, for example, introduce measures to criminalize trafficking (as UNMIK has done in Kosovo), effectively enforce this prohibition, provide legal assistance and remedies for victims, and take preventative action to address the underlying causes of trafficking.' Amnesty International, *Kosovo (Serbia and Montenegro): 'So does that mean I have rights?' Protecting the human rights of women and girls trafficked for forced prostitution in Kosovo*, AI Index EUR 70/010/2004, at 5.

8.6   REFUGEE LAW

Under the 1951 Convention relating to the Status of Refugees, the basic definition of a refugee covers those who: 'owing to well-founded fear of being persecuted for reasons of race, religion, nationality, membership of a particular social group or political opinion, is outside the country of his nationality and is unable, or owing to such fear, is unwilling to avail himself of the protection of that country; or who, not having a nationality and being outside the country of his former habitual residence as a result of such events, is unable or, owing to such fear, is unwilling to return to it.'[66]

Refugee law is seen to require a degree of individual persecution. For this reason, women who flee internal armed conflict for fear of being raped have often found themselves unprotected by refugee law. However, the development of temporary regimes for the duration of the armed conflict has ameliorated the harshness of a strict interpretation of 'refugee' in this context. The state of persecution may be found to be unwilling or unable to protect the women concerned. Although there is a divergence of state practice, the better view is that the Refugee Convention is about protection and not about accountability or state responsibility in the country of origin.[67] Nowhere is this more important than with regard to obligations to protect individuals from the conduct of non-state actors. The UN High Commissioner for Refugees explains the obligations of receiving states to non-state agents of persecution in the following terms:

(g) Agents of persecution

65.   Persecution is normally related to action by the authorities of a country. It may also emanate from sections of the population that do not respect the standards established by the laws of the country concerned. A case in point may be religious intolerance, amounting to persecution, in a country otherwise secular, but where sizeable fractions of the population do not respect the religious beliefs of their neighbours. Where serious discriminatory or other offensive acts are committed by the local populace, they can be considered as persecution if they are knowingly tolerated by the authorities, or if the authorities refuse, or prove unable, to offer effective protection.[68]

---

[66] Art. 1A(2).

[67] See the conclusions of the 'Expert Workshop on Human Rights and Refugees: Human rights violations, persecution and non-state agents', UNHCR, Athens, 17–20 December 1998: 'the accountability view does not sufficiently take into account that the 1951 Refugee Convention already recognizes the linkage between refugee protection and human rights by referring in its preamble to the Charter of the United Nations and the Universal Declaration of Human Rights as well as to endeavours "to assure refugees the widest possible exercise of these fundamental rights and freedoms". In this regard it is important to note that human rights case law on the prohibition of inhuman return also recognises that persons cannot be returned to situations where they are risk of very serious harm, irrespective of the source of this harm'.

[68] *Handbook on Procedures and Criteria for Determining Refugee Status under the 1951 Convention and the 1967 Protocol relating to the Status of Refugees*, HCR/IP/4/Eng/Rev.1 re-edited, Geneva, January 1992, UNHCR 1979.

This formulation builds in a requirement of state inaction in the country of persecution. One could question whether 'persecution' really requires such an additional passive role by the state where the persecution took place.[69] The UN High Commissioner for Refugees' Guidance may be increasingly accepted in the application of the Refugee Convention, but its requirement that there be a corresponding failure by the authorities is not coherent with the developing notion of persecution in international criminal law.[70] In that context, the international crime of persecution as a crime against humanity can attach to non-state actors (irrespective of the capacity of the state to protect the victims). If the perpetrator can be considered as a persecutor in international criminal law, why should the victim of persecution have to show a failure of a state to fall within the protected category of a victim of persecution for purposes of refugee law and the protection that offers? The answer is, of course, that states wish to limit who can claim to be a victim of persecution for the purposes of granting the individual the protection of refugee status. The logic is that states should step in when individuals have lost the 'usual benefits of nationality', in that they are not receiving the necessary level of protection in the state where the persecution is taking place.[71] The problem with this approach, however, is that it inevitably forces the authorities of the receiving state to make judgments about the capacities and good faith of the state of origin, and this is at variance with the need to prioritize protection over responsibility and accountability. Karen Landgren, a former Chief of Standards and Legal Advice at UNHCR, makes the point:

> Refugee protection is not concerned with attributing international responsibility for persecution. It implies no prospect of redress or reparation, and refugee law does not engage those responsible for the wrong. This would be at odds with the sensitivity to

---

[69] For a well-argued critique of the bias towards state responsibility in this context, see D. Wilshire, 'Non-State Actors and the Definition of a Refugee in the United Kingdom: Protection, Accountability or Culpability?' 15 *IJRL* (2003) 68–112.

[70] See Art. 7(1)(h) of the Statute of the International Criminal Court (1998), and for a further definition of persecution as a crime against humanity, see *Prosecutor v Kupreskić and ors* Case IT–95–16–T, Judgment of the International Criminal Tribunal for the former Yugoslavia, 14 December 2000, para. 621.

[71] J. C. Hathaway, *The Law of Refugee Status* (Ontario: Butterworths, 1991) at 124ff. See also G. Goodwin-Gill, *The Refugee in International Law* (Oxford: Oxford University Press, 2nd edn, 1996), who notes that the law of state responsibility provides illustrations of situations where a state may be internationally responsible regarding harm committed by private groups and that these circumstances would also provide a basis for fear of persecution, but states (at 73): 'The correlation is coincidental, however, not normative.' For a comparison of states that take a 'restrictive view', which requires that the state tolerates or encourages persecution, and an 'expansive view', whereby it is sufficient that the state of origin is unable to offer protection, see J.-Y. Carlier, 'The Geneva refugee definition and the "theory of the three scales"' in F. Nicholson and P. Twomey (eds) *Refugee Rights and Realities: Evolving International Concepts and Regimes* (Cambridge: Cambridge University Press, 1999) 37–54, at 47–48. Carlier suggests (at 48) that 'whoever the agent of persecution may be and whatever the situation of the authorities in the country of origin, it is sufficient, once the risk of persecution has been established, to conclude that no adequate national protection exists in order to substitute international protection'.

national sovereignty which prevailed at its drafting, and with its emphasis on the social and humanitarian nature of the problem of refugees. . . . The confusion between the individual's need for protection, and the concept of attributability as it relates to state responsibility, is unfortunate, and deprives of international protection persons unable to obtain protection in their own country. There is a great deal of supportive case-law and analysis, however, which needs to be disseminated and reinforced.[72]

The UNHCR Guidance quoted above is today more than a guideline. According to the UNHCR legal adviser:

> An essential element necessary to qualify for refugee status is the absence of effective national protection, irrespective of the reasons for it. In such cases, it needs to be demonstrated that the State was either unwilling or unable to provide effective protection against persecutory acts stemming from non-State agents. Such an interpretation is in line with the letter, object and purpose of the 1951 Refugee Convention. In short it is an appropriate interpretation of its Article 1.[73]

The issue of non-state actor persecution has arisen before the English courts in three contexts: women fleeing private violence, flight from a war-torn or collapsed state, and minorities fleeing racist violence. The interpretation of the Refugee Convention by the House of Lords may help to put the issue in context and highlight the dilemmas faced by national authorities with regard to those fleeing non-state actor persecution.

From the point of view of a woman fleeing threats to her safety and life, it makes no difference whether the violence emanates from the State security apparatus or from her family. To generate a state/non-state actor divide around this issue would be unfair and would itself be discriminatory against women, as they may be more likely to be the victims of private violence than are men. In situations of armed conflict, not only are societies fragmented, but people are set against each other in a cycle of violence, where civilians and women in particular may be primary targets. Furthermore, there has been a tendency in some jurisdictions to focus on the way women are seen rather than the dangers they face.[74]

---

[72] 'The Future of Refugee Protection: Four Challenges' 11 *Journal of Refugee Studies* (1998) 416–432, at 420.

[73] V. Türk, 'Non-State Agents of Persecution' in V. Chetail and V. Gowlland-Debbas (eds) *Switzerland and the International Protection of Refugees* (The Hague: Kluwer, 2002) 95–110, at 97–98.

[74] See further S. Kneebone, 'Women within the Refugee Construct: "Exclusionary Inclusion" in Policy and Practice – The Australian Experience' 17 *IJRL* (2005) 7–42, who concludes: 'the jurisprudence on the Refugee Convention shows that in relation to Refugee Woman the definition is narrowly interpreted so that she is defined by her "exclusionary inclusion". First, many harms are not recognised as coming within the meaning of "persecution". Second, the grounds are narrowly construed as relating to civil or political status. Thus it will often be decided that Refugee Woman is not persecuted "for reasons" related to Refugee Convention grounds. The tendency is to use the social group ground to construct Refugee Woman, but to use it narrowly. If she is defined into a social group it is likely to be as a Woman at Risk in a patriarchal power relationship. It is rare for her claims to be recognised as political or as overlapping with the other grounds. In particular, decision-makers fail to define the family as a political/social group and Refugee Woman as a person with an imputed

In 1999, the House of Lords ruled in the *Islam* case that it would be contrary to the United Kingdom's international obligations under the Refugee Convention for Mrs Islam to be required to leave the United Kingdom. Mrs Islam had fled her violent husband in Pakistan. She was a teacher in Pakistan and had intervened to break up a fight in the school where she was teaching. The boys involved were from rival political factions and one faction made allegations of infidelity against her. The allegations were made to her husband who was a supporter of the same faction. He assaulted her and she had to go to hospital on two occasions. She left her husband and tried to stay with her brother. However her brother was threatened and she eventually sought asylum in the United Kingdom. The case was heard together with another appeal and set an important precedent. The judges who heard the case were at pains to draw a line between women fleeing domestic violence, and women who should qualify as refugees under the 1951 Convention Relating to the Status of Refugees. The speech of Lord Steyn contains a neat explanation of how they saw the dilemma:

> Notwithstanding a constitutional guarantee against discrimination on the grounds of sex a woman's place in society in Pakistan is low. Domestic abuse of women and violence towards women is prevalent in Pakistan. That is also true of many other countries and by itself it does not give rise to a claim to refugee status. The distinctive feature of this case is that in Pakistan women are unprotected by the state: discrimination against women in Pakistan is partly tolerated by the state and partly sanctioned by the state. Married women are subordinate to the will of their husbands. There is strong discrimination against married women, who have been forced to leave the matrimonial home or have simply decided to leave. Husbands and others frequently bring charges of adultery against such wives. Faced with such a charge the woman is in a perilous position. Similarly, a woman who makes an accusation of rape is at great risk. Even Pakistan statute law discriminate[s] against such women.[75]

The House of Lords judgment builds on Canadian, Australian, and US decisions and, although it is restricted to the facts in the relevant case, has opened the door for a feminization of the concept of persecution for reasons of membership of a particular social group. The speech of Lord Hoffman explained why this concept of persecution remains linked to a requirement to find the state of origin at fault. According to him, a situation where women could not be protected because marauding men are assaulting women would not qualify as persecution within the Convention: 'The distinguishing feature of the present case is the evidence of

---

political opinion. Instead her status is often described as "private". The social group ground is applied to construct her socially or culturally in denial of the power relationships involved. The irony of this situation is that under the umbrella of human rights protection, Refugee Woman is construed from a culturally relative perspective'. At part 5 of the online version.

[75] *R v Immigration Appeal Tribunal and another, ex p Shah (United Nations High Commissioner for Refugees intervening) Islam and ors v Secretary of State for the Home Department (United Nations High Commissioner for Refugees intervening)* [1999] 2 All ER 545, at 548.

institutionalised discrimination against women by the police, the courts and the legal system, the central organs of the State.'[76]

This teleological interpretation of the Convention was criticized by the Secretary of State for the Home Department (Jack Straw) who felt this went beyond the intentions of the drafters of the Convention.[77] The challenge of adapting the refugee regime to meet threats to individuals from non-state actors has met with different responses in different jurisdictions and is still in a state of flux.[78]

It is becoming clear that effective protection demands that the interpretation of persecution as meaning direct persecution by the state, has given way to an interpretation that recognizes that people are fleeing life-threatening violence in situations where the state apparatus is unable or unwilling to protect the victim. This is relevant not only in the context of private violence against women but also in the context of all persons persecuted in civil wars or by racists.[79] Again, different jurisdictions have approached this question in different ways and a full discussion is beyond the scope of this book. What is important in the present context is the way in which refugee law has come to influence the application of human rights treaty law.

The House of Lords has more recently taken a restrictive approach to the scope of the European Convention on Human Rights in a case concerning a married

---

[76] Ibid, at 566.

[77] 'Straw wants curb on liberal judges' *The Guardian*, 12 October 1999, at 4. The report quotes the Home Secretary: 'for good or ill, our courts interpret our obligations under the 1951 convention to a much more liberal degree than almost any other European country . . . One example is the case in which it has been held that women who are in fear of domestic violence in Pakistan may come under terms of the convention. Now I am concerned about women in fear of domestic violence in Pakistan, but there is no way it can be realistically argued that was in contemplation when the convention was put in place.'

[78] For a comparative overview, see B. Vereulen, T. Spijkerboer, K. Zwaan, and R. Ferhour, 'Persecution by Third Parties'(research paper), University of Nijmegen (1998). See also A. Macklin 'Refugee Women and the Imperative of Categories' 17 *HRQ* (1995) 213–277. A recent case in the Court of Appeal refused to extend protection to girls fearing female genital mutilation: 'although female circumcision in Sierra Leone may be condemned as a violation of Article 3 [of the ECHR] and to constitute persecution of young uncircumcised girls on that account, its practice in that country's society is not discriminatory or one that results from society having set them apart, other than by the persecution itself. There is, therefore, no factual basis upon which the Court could have resort to insufficiency of state protection against discriminatory conduct to qualify the general rule that, for the purpose of the Refugee Convention, a "particular social group" cannot be defined solely by reference to the persecution.' *Fornah v Secretary of State for the Home Department* [2005] EWCA Civ 680, at para. 44.

[79] See also *R v Secretary of State for the Home Department, ex p Adan* [1998] UKHL 15, where it was found, in the context of the clan warfare in Somalia, that it will not be enough for an asylum-seeker to show that he or she would be at risk if returned. The asylum-seeker must be able to show fear of persecution for Convention reasons beyond the risks inherent in the conflict. See also *R v Secretary of State for the Home Department, ex p Adan* and *R v Secretary of State for the Home Department ex p Aitseguer* [2000] UKHL 67. For a case looking at non-state actor violence by racist gangs, outside the situation of armed conflict, see *R v Home Secretary, ex p Horvath* [2001] 1 AC 489, where it was held that, although such non-state actor violence did not preclude the initial application of the Convention, the protection offered to Roma by Slovakia was satisfactory, and so the asylum-seekers were not entitled to protection as refugees.

Lithuanian couple. The husband and wife claimed that their human rights would be violated if they were returned to Lithuania. The husband was of Roma ethnic origin and the couple had been subjected to violence at the hands of the wife's brother and associates, due to the fact that the brother objected to his sister having married a man of Roma origin.[80] The issue of non-state actor persecution was dealt with as raising similar questions under refugee law and human rights law. The judgment recalled that, under the Refugee Convention, a degree of protection from non-state violence is granted where the home state is unable or unwilling to provide reasonable protection from the conduct of non-state actors. But the judgment pointedly remarked: 'not all those party to the Refugee Convention recognise even the concept of persecution by non-state agents'.[81] The judgment suggests that the courts apply the approach developed under refugee law when faced with complaints alleging inhuman and degrading treatment under Article 3 of the European Convention on Human Rights. In this way, the judgment noted that: 'in the great majority of cases an article 3 claim to avoid expulsion will add little if anything to an asylum claim'.[82]

This tidy result bears closer inspection. The couple were denied their claim that they were at risk of human rights violations because they had failed to show that the state of Lithuania would fail to provide them with sufficient protection. It was not enough to show that they were at serious risk of harm from a non-state actor. The reasoning relies on a strict state/non-state actor divide which may make sense in the context of transfer from one Council of Europe member state to another, but breaks down outside this context. The judgment states that:

> In cases where the risk 'emanates from intentionally inflicted acts of the public authori-ties in the receiving country' (the language of para 49 of *D v United Kingdom* 24 EHRR 423, 447) one can use those terms interchangeably: the intentionally inflicted acts would without more constitute the proscribed treatment. Where, however, the risk emanates from non-state bodies, that is not so: any harm inflicted by non-state agents will not constitute article 3 ill-treatment unless in addition the state has failed to provide reasonable protection.[83]

The conceptual point is reiterated later: 'Non-state agents do not subject people to torture or the other proscribed forms of ill-treatment, however violently they treat them: what, however, would transform such violent treatment into article 3 ill-treatment would be the state's failure to provide reasonable protection against it.'[84] But this is not really the approach of human rights treaty bodies (even if it is a dominant theory in refugee law). Imagine a deportation to a country which is not a party to a human rights treaty; it would not be fair to say that the factor on

---

[80] *R v Secretary of State for the Home Department, ex p Bagdanavicius* [2005] UKHL 38, at para. 14.
[81] *Per* Lord Brown, at para 29.   [82] Ibid, at para. 30.   [83] Ibid, at para. 24.
[84] Ibid, at para. 24.

which the legality of the deportation depends is whether the receiving state will fulfil positive obligations contained in Article 3. First, it would be odd to judge the situation in terms of international treaty obligations to which the receiving state is not subject, and second, the state that has to fulfil Article 3 obligations is the sending state that is party to the human rights treaty. The behaviour of the receiving state is relevant in assessing the need to protect the individual in the sending state; assessing the receiving state's compliance with international positive obligations is a near impossible task. In many cases, the receiving state will not allow for complaints to an international treaty body, and knowledge of the scope of what protection can reasonably be expected in the receiving state under general international law will be guesswork. It would be difficult for the European Court of Human Rights to divine what are the positive obligations of a developing country under the African Charter of Human and Peoples' Rights. If the receiving state has ratified no relevant human rights treaty, its obligations fall to be determined under customary international law. What can reasonably be expected in terms of protecting an individual from criminal gangs, terrorists, or rebels will depend on the resources available to the state in question. The whole ethos of humanitarian protection argues against such a judgmental approach with regard to the receiving state. It is suggested that the only criterion under human rights treaty law is whether the person will be subject to a substantial risk of harm from the non-state actor.[85] If there is such a risk, the human rights treaty obligations on the sending state should prevent such a state from sending individuals into harm's way.

---

[85] See, e.g. the Concluding Observations of the Human Rights Committee with regard to France in 1997: 'The Committee is particularly concerned by the restrictive definition of the concept of "persecution" of refugees used by the French authorities as it does not take into account possible persecution by non-State actors. Therefore: the Committee recommends that the State party adopt a wider interpretation of "persecution" to include non-State actors.' UN Doc. CCPR/C/79/Add.80, 4 August 1997, at para. 21. See also the discussion in 8.4 above, regarding the interpretation of the prohibition on torture in the International Covenant on Civil and Political Rights, which suggests that private actors can engage in torture and inhuman and degrading treatment and that it is the state's duty to protect individuals from such harm. The Human Rights Committee has not suggested that this rule does not apply in the context of deportations or extradition. Of course, everyone is covered by customary international law, which prohibits not only torture, inhuman and degrading treatment, but also *refoulement*. This rule has been summarized as follows: 'No person shall be rejected, returned or expelled in any manner whatever where this would compel them to remain in or return to a territory where substantial grounds can be shown for believing that they would face a real risk of being subjected to torture, cruel, inhuman or degrading treatment or punishment. This principle allows of no limitation or exception.' See E. Lauterpacht and D. Bethlehem, 'The Scope and Content of the Principle of *Non-refoulement*: Opinion' (Geneva: UNHCR, 2001) at para. 252. Note the extension of torture under customary international law to non-state actors by the Appeals Chamber of the ICTY: 'The Trial Chamber in the present case was therefore right in taking the position that the public official requirement is not a requirement under customary international law in relation to the criminal responsibility of an individual for torture outside of the framework of the Torture Convention.' *Prosecutor v Kunarac, Kovać and Vuković* Case IT–96–23 and IT–96–23/1–A, Judgment of the International Criminal Tribunal for the former Yugoslavia (Appeals Chamber), 12 June 2002, para. 148.

8.7   CONVENTION AGAINST TORTURE AND OTHER CRUEL, INHUMAN OR DEGRADING TREATMENT OR PUNISHMENT

This Convention defines torture in a way that demands a nexus to the state. Article 1 reads:

(1) For the purposes of this Convention, the term 'torture' means any act by which severe pain or suffering, whether physical or mental, is intentionally inflicted on a person for such purposes as obtaining from him or a third person information or a confession, punishing him for an act he or a third person has committed or is suspected of having committed, or intimidating or coercing him or a third person, or for any reason based on discrimination of any kind, when such pain or suffering is inflicted by or at the instigation of or with the consent or acquiescence of a public official or other person acting in an official capacity. It does not include pain or suffering arising only from, inherent in or incidental to lawful sanctions.

(2) This article is without prejudice to any international instrument or national legislation which does or may contain provisions of wider application.

The first point to note is that the definition of torture in this treaty is not confined to state actors. A non-state actor inflicting torture at the instigation of, or with the consent or acquiescence of, a state actor falls within the scope of the Convention. Moreover, the state will have all the obligations under the Convention with regard to preventing, prohibiting, and punishing such acts.[86]

The question of whether a non-state actor had the requisite *de jure* or *de facto* official capacity to be prosecuted for torture under the Convention arose in the *Zardad* case, the English criminal trial of Faryadi Zardad, chief commander of Hezb-I-Isla, concerning allegations of torture in Afghanistan. A preliminary question before the judge was whether at the time of the alleged torture, Zardad could be considered to have been acting in an official capacity for the purposes of the Convention and the implementing legislation. The judge found that there was insufficient evidence to show that Zardad was a *de jure* public official; Zardad was actually found to be leading campaigns against the government. With reference to the claim that Zardad was a *de facto* official, the judge decided that there was enough evidence for this issue to be eventually determined by the jury, but he made the following interesting comments in coming to that decision:

It seems to me that what needs to be looked at is the reality of any particular situation. Is there sufficient evidence that Hezb-I-Islami had a sufficient degree of organisation, a sufficient degree of actual control of an area and that it exercised the type of functions

---

[86] States may therefore refer to the arrangements they have made with regard to the private management of prisons in the context of periodic reviews under this Treaty, e.g. UN Doc. CAT/C/SR.607, 18 May 2004, at paras 21–22 (New Zealand).

which a government or governmental organisation would exercise? It seems to me that I have to take care not to impose Western ideas of an appropriate structure for government, but to be sensitive to the fact that in countries such as Afghanistan different types of structure may exist, but which may legitimately come within the ambit of an authority which wields power sufficient to constitute an official body.[87]

Zardad was eventually found guilty of torture at the Old Bailey in London and sentenced to twenty years in prison. The case represents a concrete application of the international law of human rights to a non-state actor (here an anti-state actor). It may also have consequences for those seeking to claim protection from expulsion to countries where they fear torture from non-state actors.

In addition to the prohibition on torture and other inhuman and degrading treatment carried out in connection with officials, the Convention includes a prohibition against the transfer of individuals to other countries where they may face torture. Article 3 reads:

(1) No State Party shall expel, return ('refouler') or extradite a person to another State where there are substantial grounds for believing that he would be in danger of being subjected to torture.

(2) For the purpose of determining whether there are such grounds, the competent authorities shall take into account all relevant considerations including, where applicable, the existence in the State concerned of a consistent pattern of gross, flagrant or mass violations of human rights.

The issue which has tested the scope of the Convention concerns protection from non-state actors in other countries, either where there is no state nexus (as the risk of torture comes from a non-state actor fighting the state rather than working with the approval of the state), or where there may be no obvious form of government.

The Committee Against Torture was faced early on with a claim concerning return to Peru, where the complainant feared torture at the hands of a non-state actor (the complainant had been abducted and raped by members of *Sendero Luminoso*). The Committee gave a restrictive reading to the protection offered by the Convention, holding: 'that the issue whether the State party has an obligation to refrain from expelling a person who might risk pain or suffering inflicted by a non-governmental entity, without the consent or acquiescence of the Government, falls outside the scope of article 3 of the Convention'.[88] Critics of this approach have pointed to the fact that the complaint alleged that the rape had been reported to the authorities but that they 'did not show any interest in the matter';[89] it was therefore, according to McCorquodale and La Forgia, open to

---

[87] *R v Zardad*, 7 April 2004, Central Criminal Court (Treacy J) at para. 33.
[88] *G.R.B. v Sweden* UN Doc. CAT/C/20/D/83/1997, 15 May 1998, at para. 6.5. Cf the protection offered against the risk of non-state actor violence under the European Convention on Human Rights: *Ahmed v Austria* Judgment of the European Court of Human Rights of 27 November 1996, discussed in Ch 9, at 9.1.4.2 below.
[89] *G.R.B. v Sweden* UN Doc. CAT/C/20/D/83/1997, 15 May 1998, at para. 2.3.

the Committee to see this as a case of state acquiescence. 'This approach would have required the Committee against Torture to decide whether the government of Peru had properly investigated the rape, how many rapes reported had not been investigated and whether non-State actors were able to rape due to lack of State action.'[90]

The Committee's General Comment has slightly clarified its approach. The Committee stated that the obligation in Article 3 'is confined in its application to cases where there are substantial grounds for believing that the author would be in danger of being subjected to torture as defined in article 1 of the Convention'.[91] With respect to the risk which engages the obligation, the Committee said that this should be 'personal and present',[92] to an extent that goes 'beyond mere theory or suspicion', but need not 'meet the test of being highly probable'.[93] The Committee also stressed the need for a state nexus: 'Pursuant to article 1, the criterion, mentioned in article 3, paragraph 2, of "a consistent pattern [of] gross, flagrant or mass violations of human rights" refers only to violations by or at the instigation of or with the consent or acquiescence of a public official or other person acting in an official capacity.'

This approach of the Committee was further tested in an application brought by Mr Elmi against Australia, concerning a feared return to Somalia. The Committee was conscious of the fact that the case was seen as potentially setting a precedent: 'the independent expert of the Commission on Human Rights on the situation of human rights in Somalia has appealed in the author's case and made reference to it both in her report to the Commission on Human Rights and in oral statements, indicating that "[a] case currently pending in Australia concerning a forced return to Mogadishu of a Somali national is particularly alarming, due to the precedent it will create in returning individuals to areas undergoing active conflict" '.[94]

The applicant alleged that, if returned to Somalia, he would be in danger of torture at the hands of armed factions. The Committee said that where, in the absence of a central government, armed factions are exercising *de facto* some of the functions normally exercised by a legitimate government, members of those factions can in this context be considered 'public officials or other persons acting in an official capacity'. Part of their reasoning was based on the particular status of the clan leaders on the international stage. The Committee stated that:

> 5.5   In relation to Somalia, there is abundant evidence that the clans, at least since 1991, have, in certain regions, fulfilled the role, or exercised the semblance, of an

---

[90] R. McCorquodale and R. La Forgia, 'Taking off the Blindfolds: Torture by Non-State Actors' 1 *Human Rights Law Review* (2001) 189–218, at 209–210.

[91] General Comment 1 'Article 3', 21 November 1997, para. 1; 'UN Compilation', at 291.

[92] Ibid, para 7.   [93] Ibid, para. 6.

[94] *Elmi v Australia* UN Doc. CAT/C/22/D/120/1998, 25 May 1999, at para. 5.11. The Committee refers earlier, at footnote 9, to the 'Report of the independent expert of the Commission on Human Rights, Ms. Mona Rishmawi, on the situation of human rights in Somalia, E/CN.4/1999/103, 23 December 1998, para. 154', and later to 'Oral statement on the situation of human rights in Somalia, delivered on 22 April 1999 before the Commission on Human Rights'.

authority that is comparable to government authority. These clans, in relation to their regions, have prescribed their own laws and law enforcement mechanisms and have provided their own education, health and taxation systems. The report of the independent expert of the Commission on Human Rights illustrates that States and international organizations have accepted that these activities are comparable to governmental authorities and that '[t]he international community is still negotiating with the warring factions, who ironically serve as the interlocutors of the Somali people with the outside world'.[95]

The Committee continued with an approach that highlights the governmental-like qualities of the clans rather than the need for protection and takes into account the UN Independent Expert's reports of gross human rights violations in the country (even in the absence of obvious state actors):

6.5   The Committee does not share the State party's view that the Convention is not applicable in the present case since, according to the State party, the acts of torture the author fears he would be subjected to in Somalia would not fall within the definition of torture set out in article 1 (i.e. pain or suffering inflicted by or at the instigation of or with the consent or acquiescence of a public official or other person acting in an official capacity, in this instance for discriminatory purposes). The Committee notes that for a number of years Somalia has been without a central government, that the international community negotiates with the warring factions and that some of the factions operating in Mogadishu have set up quasi-governmental institutions and are negotiating the establishment of a common administration. It follows then that, de facto, those factions exercise certain prerogatives that are comparable to those normally exercised by legitimate governments. Accordingly, the members of those factions can fall, for the purposes of the application of the Convention, within the phrase 'public officials or other persons acting in an official capacity' contained in article 1.

6.6   The State party does not dispute the fact that gross, flagrant or mass violations of human rights have been committed in Somalia. Furthermore, the independent expert on the situation of human rights in Somalia, appointed by the Commission on Human Rights, described in her latest report[96] the severity of those violations, the situation of chaos prevailing in the country, the importance of clan identity and the vulnerability of small, unarmed clans such as the Shikal, the clan to which the author belongs.

6.7   The Committee further notes, on the basis of the information before it, that the area of Mogadishu where the Shikal mainly reside, and where the author is likely to reside if he ever reaches Mogadishu, is under the effective control of the Hawiye clan, which has established quasi-governmental institutions and provides a number of public services. Furthermore, reliable sources emphasize that there is no public or informal agreement of protection between the Hawiye and the Shikal clans and that the Shikal remain at the mercy of the armed factions.

---

[95] Footnote 9 in the original reads: '9. Report of the independent expert of the Commission on Human Rights, Ms. Mona Rishmawi, on the situation of human rights in Somalia, E/CN.4/1999/103, 23 December 1998, para. 154.'

[96] Footnote 13 in the original refers to Rishmawi's report of 18 February 1999 (UN Doc. of E/CN.4/1999/103/Add 1).

6.8   In addition to the above, the Committee considers that two factors support the author's case that he is particularly vulnerable to the kind of acts referred to in article 1 of the Convention. First, the State party has not denied the veracity of the author's claims that his family was particularly targeted in the past by the Hawiye clan, as a result of which his father and brother were executed, his sister raped and the rest of the family was forced to flee and constantly move from one part of the country to another in order to hide. Second, his case has received wide publicity and, therefore, if returned to Somalia the author could be accused of damaging the reputation of the Hawiye.

6.9   In the light of the above the Committee considers that substantial grounds exist for believing that the author would be in danger of being subjected to torture if returned to Somalia.

In sum, the Committee has been careful not to stretch the Convention beyond acts with a state nexus or where the direct perpetrators have a quasi-governmental function. The reticence of the Committee not to stray beyond these categories is explained by the history and wording of the Convention, which suggests a restrictive approach. Indeed, the *travaux préparatoires* were referred to by Australia to suggest that the *Elmi* case fell outside the Convention, as the Somali clans could not be accommodated in the concept of public authority as agreed at the time of the drafting.[97] The Committee's extension of the Convention's protection to people fleeing non-state actor violence in Somalia may nevertheless be seen as a crucial admission that non-state torture is covered by this Convention and, more generally, that non-state actor abuses can rise to the level of a 'consistent pattern of gross, flagrant or mass violations of human rights'. Note, however, that the Committee subsequently described the situation in the *Elmi* case as exceptional, and found that three years later the situation in Somalia had changed, so that a later complainant was not protected by the Convention.[98]

The restrictive wording of the Convention that demands a finding of official control or acquiescence is not mirrored in the regional human rights treaties. These treaties guarantee most rights, such as the right not to be tortured, without qualifications concerning the status of the perpetrator. It is to these regional Conventions that we now turn.

---

[97] *Elmi v Australia*, UN Doc. CAT/C/22/D/120/1998, 25 May 1999, at paras 4.6–4.8.

[98] Communication No. 177/2001, *H.M.H.I. v Australia*, UN Doc. CAT/C/28/D/177/2001, 1 May 2002, at para. 6.4: 'The Committee considers that, with three years having elapsed since the *Elmi* decision, Somalia currently possesses a State authority in the form of the Transitional National Government, which has relations with the international community in its capacity as central Government, though some doubts may exist as to the reach of its territorial authority and its permanence. Accordingly, the Committee does not consider this case to fall within the exceptional situation in *Elmi*, and takes the view that acts of such entities as are now in Somalia commonly fall outside the scope of article 3 of the Convention.'

9

Regional Human Rights Bodies

Regional human rights bodies have been faced with a number of cases where the direct perpetrator of the human rights abuse was a non-state actor. The jurisdiction of these bodies is confined to complaints against states. In a series of developments, these regional bodies have developed approaches to defining the extent of a state's positive obligation to protect individuals from human rights abuses committed by non-state actors. Some of these decisions illustrate how human rights apply in the private sphere; they explain how the treaties take effect on a horizontal plane in the sphere of relations between private individuals or organizations. This Chapter examines the jurisprudence of the regional human rights bodies. The case-law has, for example, required states: to set in place policies to prevent and punish private violence; to ensure adequate protection from forced labour in the context of trafficked domestic help; to ensure that press freedom does not disproportionately infringe on respect for private life; to regulate properly entities that pollute and infringe rights to enjoy one's home and family life; to prevent employers from engaging in anti-union practices; and to ensure that concessions given to corporations do not undermine the enjoyment of rights to food, housing, and a safe environment. In each regional regime, attention will be drawn to the evolving understanding of the obligations of the state as well as the clarification of what is expected of non-state actors under human rights law.

The secondary rules of state responsibility are engaged, not only through acts directly attributable to the state, but also through omissions by the state.[1] Whether or not an omission gives rise to a violation of international law depends on the primary substantive international obligation in question. The rules on state responsibility have developed in the context of the customary international law, which obligates states to exercise due diligence in the treatment of foreigners within their jurisdiction. The scope of the international human rights obligations of states and their potential state responsibility for omissions builds, in part, on the 'due diligence' test developed in the context of the law of diplomatic protection,

---

[1] See Ch 6 at 6.7.1. See also Art. 2 of the International Law Commission's Articles on State Responsibility, which refers to an act or 'omission'. Note also the ILC's Commentary which states that: 'In the English text, it is necessary to maintain the expression "internationally wrongful act", since the French "fait" has no exact equivalent; nonetheless, the term "act" is intended to encompass omissions, and this is made clear in article 2.' UN Doc. A/Res/56/83, adopted 10 December 2001. See *Report of the ILC 53rd Session*, adopted 10 August 2001, UN Doc. A/56/10, at 68.

but is further influenced by the evolving jurisprudence surrounding the separate substantive rights in the various human rights treaties.

The extent to which human rights law should be seen as encompassing obligations in the private sphere was already being debated at the time of the drafting of the International Covenant on Civil and Political Rights. The rights contained in that Covenant are now firmly established as creating possible positive obligations for states where the threat to the enjoyment of those rights emanates from non-state actors.[2] With regard to economic, social, and cultural rights, the UN Committee has developed its approach to remind states of the importance of ensuring that privatized services do not deprive individuals of the enjoyment of their rights to water, housing, or education. Furthermore, the Committee on the Elimination of Discrimination Against Women, has developed the due diligence concept in the context of its Convention, and elaborated specific duties on states to prevent and punish non-state actor violence against women.[3] The complementary approach of the regional institutions is worth studying in the present context as, although it is now uncontroversial that states have obligations to protect human rights from encroachments by non-state actors, the regional case-law illustrates which international human rights are 'amenable to application between private persons or entities',[4] and, in particular, how the human rights of these other persons/entities are also to be taken into consideration. It is only through a detailed examination of the cases that we can begin to understand the process through which these rights are applied in the context of threats from non-state actors.[5]

---

[2] '[T]he positive obligations on States Parties to ensure Covenant rights will only be fully discharged if individuals are protected by the State, not just against violations of Covenant rights by its agents, but also against acts committed by private persons or entities that would impair the enjoyment of Covenant rights in so far as they are amenable to application between private persons or entities.' Human Rights Committee, General Comment 31 (art. 2, the nature of the general legal obligation imposed on states parties to the Covenant), 29 March 2004, at para. 8. See Ch 8, at 8.4 above.

[3] See General Recommendation 19 (violence against women), 29 January 1992, Ch 8, at 8.5 above. See further, Amnesty International: *Making Rights a Reality: The Duty of States to Address Violence Against Women*, AI Index ACT 77/049/2004, *Respect, protect, fulfil—Women's human rights—State responsibility for abuses by 'non-state actors'*, AI Index IOR 50/01/00, and *Kosovo (Serbia and Montenegro): 'So does that mean I have rights?' Protecting the human rights of women and girls trafficked for forced prostitution in Kosovo*, AI Index EUR 70/010/2004.

[4] General Comment 31 (n 2 above) at para. 8.

[5] The European Social Charter and its complaints mechanism will not be examined here. In its current form, the mechanism hardly develops the obligations of non-state actors but rather it focuses on the failure of states to legislate. See R. R. Churchill and U. Khaliq, 'The Collective Complaints System of the European Social Charter: An Effective Mechanism for Ensuring Compliance with Economic and Social Rights' 15 *EJIL* (2004) 417–456, esp. at 441–451. Note, however, how the Charter and its interpretation plays an important role in determining the scope of, *inter alia*, Art. 11 of the European Convention on Human Rights; see particularly the *Gustafsson* and *Wilson* cases discussed in 9.1.11.2. below.

9.1 THE EUROPEAN COURT OF HUMAN RIGHTS

In a number of cases, the European Court of Human Rights has addressed the issue of the obligations of states to take action to protect human rights from interferences by non-state actors. This case-law, usually analysed under the rubric of the 'positive obligations' of the state, has given rise to attempts in the doctrine to differentiate positive obligations according to the context and the appropriate margin of appreciation that states should enjoy with regard to the application of the Convention.[6] So far, the Court has demonstrated a reluctance to develop a general theory of positive obligations. The question of the positive obligations of states under the Convention is often discussed in conjunction with the direct horizontal effect of the Convention. That is to say, the extent to which the Convention itself can create obligations for individuals and private entities (non-state actors) which may be justiciable in the internal legal orders of the states parties to the Convention.[7] There is some ambiguity about the extent to which the Convention creates duties not only for states but for private parties (non-state actors) as well. It has been suggested that, even though a complaint against a non-state actor will be declared inadmissible before the European Court of Human Rights, a national judge will not be bound by these conditions for admissibility. Fédéric Sudre points out in this context that the French Cour de Cassation tends to apply the Convention in cases between private parties.[8]

Sudre and Dean Spielmann quote approvingly Vincent Coussirat-Coustère's contention that the Convention is part of the legal order that the national judge is bound to ensure is respected, and consequently, the rights have direct effect against not only public authorities (vertical effect) but also in cases between

[6] For two analyses see F. Sudre, 'Les "obligations positives" dans la jurisprudence européenne des droits de l'homme' in P. Mahoney, F. Matscher, H. Petzold, and L. Wildhaber (eds) *Protecting Human Rights: The European Perspective—Studies in memory of Rolv Ryssdal* (Cologne: Carl Heymanns, 2000) 1359–1376; and K. Starmer, 'Positive Obligations Under the Convention' in J. Jowell and J. Cooper (eds) *Understanding Human Rights Principles* (Oxford: Hart Publishing, 2001) 139–159.

[7] D. Spielmann, 'Obligations positives et effet horizontal des dispositions de la Convention' in F. Sudre (ed) *L'interpretation de la Convention européenne des droits de l'homme* (Brussels: Nemesis, 1998) 133–174. See also A. Drzemczewski, *European Human Rights Convention in Domestic Law* (Oxford: Clarendon Press, 1983).

[8] Sudre (2000: 1369). See also *Société Nikon France SA v M. Féderic O.* Cour de Cassation (Chambre sociale), Judgment no. 4164 of 2 October 2001, which concerned a complaint in which an employee was dismissed after his employer looked at his personal e-mails written on the computer provided for him by his employer. The Cour de Cassation quashed the decision of the Cour d'appel, which had upheld the dismissal. The reasoning referred to Art. 8 ECHR and stated: 'Attendu que le salarié a droit, même au temps et au lieu de travail, au respect de l'intimité de sa vie privée; que celle-ci implique en particulier le secret des correspondances; que l'employeur ne peut dès lors sans violation de cette liberté fondamentale prendre connaissance des messages personnels émis par le salarié et reçus par lui grâce à un outil informatique mis à sa disposition pour son travail et ceci même au cas où l'employeur aurait interdit une utilisation non professionnelle de l'ordinateur'.

private parties (horizontal effect).[9] This contention may well be correct for judges in the French or Luxembourg national legal orders; in other states, the ability of the national judge to apply the Convention in disputes between private parties may depend on the terms of the incorporating legislation. Commentators such as Ovey and White therefore prefer to see the binding effect of the Convention on private parties in terms of national law:

> Consideration of positive obligations has led to suggestions that Convention rules can in some circumstances bind private parties. The better—and certainly more orthodox— view is that the Convention only impacts upon the conduct of private parties adjectivally when action is taken by the State to secure the rights protected by the Convention which requires or prohibits certain conduct by individuals. A formal analysis of the situation would, accordingly, lead to the conclusion that the duties imposed on individuals would flow from the national law implementing the State's obligations under the Convention rather than from the Convention itself. This is, of course, reflected in the fact that applications complaining of violations can only be made against Contracting Parties to the Convention, that is, against States.[10]

Such an analysis is again heavily influenced by the jurisdictional filter of the European Court of Human Rights and dualist national legal orders. On the other hand, van Dijk and van Hoof note that in some national legal orders, the Convention is applied so that an individual can enforce his or her rights against another individual; while in other countries this is not possible. They remain open-minded as to whether Article 1 of the Convention actually obliges states to ensure that such direct horizontal effect is possible: 'In fact one can not deduce from Article 1 whether the Contracting States are obliged to secure the rights and freedoms only in relation to the public authorities or also in relation to other individuals.'[11]

---

[9] 'Le juge interne n'est pas du tout dans la même position que les organs de Strasbourg, sa compét-ence d'appliquer la Convention n'est pas assujettie aux restrictions ci-dessus indiquées et par conséquent rien ne s'oppose à ce qu'il appliqué la Convention dans les contentieux inter-individuels. Cela résulte de ce que la Convention fait partie de la légalité que le juge doit faire respecter et, par conse-quent, l'effet direct des droits guarantis est autant vertical (contentieux de droit public) qu'horizontal (contentieux de droit privé).' V. Coussirat-Coustère, 'Convention européenne des droits de l'homme et droit interne: Primauté et effet direct' in L.-E. Pettiti *et al* (eds) *La Convention européenne des droits de l'homme* (Brussels: Nemesis, 1992) at 14, cited in full in Spielmann (1998: 164). On the direct horizontal effect of the Convention, see further Spielmann, esp. 164–168, who suggests three types of approach by national courts: categorical rejection (with the example of a Belgian case concerning freedom of religion); implicit acceptance (the Court of Appeal in Luxembourg); and explicit accep-tance of direct horizontal effect (the French Cour de Cassation's Judgment of 6 March 1996 which concerned the use of Art. 8 of the Convention to condemn a housing organization that had prohib-ited tenants from living with relatives. *Opac de Paris c Mme Mel Yedei*, Cass. 3rd civ. J.C.P., éd. G (1996) IV, 973.)

[10] C. Ovey and R. C. A. White, *Jacobs & White, The European Convention on Human Rights* (Oxford: Oxford University Press, 3rd edn, 2002) at 30.

[11] P. van Dijk and G. J. H. van Hoof, *Theory and Practice of the European Convention on Human Rights* (The Hague: Kluwer, 3rd edn, 1998) at 24. See also E. A. Alkema, 'The Third-Party Applicability or "Drittwirkung" of the European Convention on Human Rights' in F. Matscher and H. Petzold (eds) *Protecting Human Rights: The European Dimension (Studies in Honour of Gérard J. Wiarda)* (Cologne: Carl Heymanns, 1988) 33–45.

It is suggested that the way to understand the obligations of states in this field is to look closely at the contexts in which positive obligations have been determined by the Court, and specifically to examine the rights at issue, to see which have been found amenable to such a horizontal application. Commentators are increasingly identifying the fact that any examination of the positive obligations of states reveals the scope of the duty to protect individuals' Convention rights from infringements by non-state actors. They articulate the idea that human rights can actually be *infringed* by non-state actors. Alastair Mowbray concludes his book-length study as follows: 'One of the most prevalent types of positive obligation is the duty upon states to take reasonable measures to protect individuals from infringement of their Convention rights by other private persons.'[12] In her book on *Tort Law & Human Rights*, Jane Wright explains that states' positive obligations under the Convention derive in part from 'the recognition by Strasbourg of state obligations to act in the private sphere to regulate the relationships of non-state actors'.[13] Wright connects this with the fact that in England, under Article 6(3) of the Human Rights Act 1998, the courts are explicitly bound to act in a manner compatible with Convention rights. For her, this fact:

> . . . suggests that the Act will be of indirect horizontal effect, so that in the development of the common law (in the broadest sense, including the doctrines of equity) the courts will be obliged to accommodate Convention principles, regardless of the identity of the defendant. The substantive development of English principles in private litigation will then be shaped by the extent to which Strasbourg has required obligations to be implemented in the private sphere.[14]

The European Court of Human Rights has clearly stated that the right to private life in the Convention create obligations for states which involve 'the adoption of measures designed to secure respect for private life *even in the sphere of the relations of individuals between themselves*'.[15] This principle has also been affirmed by the Court beyond the context of respect for private life. The Court articulated the principle in the context of the right to counter-demonstrate: 'Like Article 8, Article 11 sometimes requires positive measures to be taken, even in the sphere of relations between individuals, if need be.'[16]

It is suggested that statements by the Court, that the Convention covers the sphere of relations between private individuals, have had important consequences beyond the scope of state responsibility for positive obligations as determined in that Court. First, the extension of the scope of human rights into the private sphere has meant that, where national courts have had occasion to deal with a

---

[12] A. Mowbray, *The Development of Positive Obligations under the European Convention on Human Rights by the European Court of Human Rights* (Oxford: Hart Publishing, 2004) at 225.

[13] J. Wright, *Tort Law & Human Rights* (Oxford: Hart Publishing, 2001) at 17, fn 6.

[14] Ibid, at 23.

[15] *Case of X and Y v The Netherlands* Judgment of 26 March 1985, para. 23 (emphasis added).

[16] *Case of Plattform 'Ärzte für das Leben'* Judgment of 21 June 1988, para. 32.

complaint against a private actor, such a national court may consider that a private actor has human rights obligations which stem from the European Convention. This is sometimes known as the horizontal, third-party, or *Drittwirkung* effect of the relevant Convention article.[17] The precedence given to Convention rights in national law will depend on the national legal order, but the applicability of a human rights obligation will depend in part on the interpretation that has been given to that right by the European Court regarding the application of the right to relations between private parties.[18] Second, the extension into the private sphere implicitly demands consideration of the actual obligations of these private actors between themselves. In the absence of an international or national jurisdiction, such an exercise could be considered by some as 'academic'. But there are multiple mechanisms for attempting to ensure the accountability of non-state actors. For example, procurement, investment, and credit guarantee arrangements may require that companies respect human rights.[19] The case-law of the European Court of Human Rights regarding human rights in the private sphere may provide useful indications of what the scope of these human rights obligations might be.

9.1.1   Article 1 Obligation to Secure Human Rights to Everyone within the Jurisdiction

Article 1 of the Convention reads:

> The High Contracting Parties shall secure to everyone within their jurisdiction the rights and freedoms defined in Section I of this Convention.

Dean Spielmann has contrasted the strong injunction in the English text—'shall secure', with the weaker French '*reconnaître*', and concluded that the English version, rather than the French version of the Convention, is more suggestive that the Convention applies between private parties.[20] This may be pertinent, but the Court has not overly relied on a textual reading of the Convention in its case-law concerning the application of the Convention to the private sphere. In *Young, James and Webster v United Kingdom*, the Court focused on the absence of legislation to

---

[17] R. Brinktrine, 'The Horizontal Effect of Human Rights in German Constitutional Law: The British debate on horizontality and the possible role model of the German doctrine of "*mittelbare Drittwirkung der Grundrechte*"' *EHRLR* (2001) 421–432. See also A. Clapham, 'The "Drittwirkung" of the European Convention' in R. St J. Macdonald, F. Matscher, and H. Petzold (eds) *The European System for the Protection of Human Rights* (Dordrecht: Martinus Nijhoff, 1993) 163–206.

[18] For the influence of the Court's case-law on a case between private parties at the national level, see the English Court of Appeal judgment in *Michael Douglas, Catherine Zeta-Jones, Northern & Shell plc v Hello Ltd, Hola SA, Eduardo Sanchez Junco* [2005] EWCA Civ 595, at para. 150. Discussed in detail in Ch 10, at 10.3.3.1 below.

[19] See Ch 6, see also S. R. Ratner, 'Corporations and Human Rights: A Theory of Legal Responsibility' (2001) 111 *YLJ* 443–545, at 465.   [20] Spielmann (1998: 157).

protect workers from being obliged to join a certain union. The judgment discussed Article 1 in the following terms:

Under Article 1 of the Convention, each Contracting State 'shall secure to everyone within [its] jurisdiction the rights and freedoms defined in...[the] Convention'; if a violation of one of those rights and freedoms is the result of non-observance of that obligation in the enactment of domestic legislation, the responsibility of the State for that violation is engaged. Although the proximate cause of the events giving rise to this case was the 1975 agreement between British Rail and the railway unions, it was the domestic law in force at the relevant time that made lawful the treatment of which the applicants complained. The responsibility of the respondent State for any resultant breach of the Convention is thus engaged on this basis. Accordingly, there is no call to examine whether, as the applicants argued, the State might also be responsible on the ground that it should be regarded as employer or that British Rail was under its control.[21]

The Court therefore attributed the omission by the legislature to the state, rather than focusing on an attribution of the behaviour of the employer to the state. The conclusion that must be drawn is that the state is obliged to protect, through law, freedom of association under Article 11, both with regard to employment in the state sector and in the private sector. Put another way, the Convention's Article 11 covers employment in the private sphere. The recourse to Article 1 is in part explained by the Government's argument that the acts of British Rail (then a nationalized industry) could not be attributed to the state, as British Rail was not an organ of the state nor was British Rail under the control of the state.[22] Nevertheless, this case opened the way for the conclusion that states have (in addition to the obligation to protect individuals' rights from arbitrary interference by public authorities) 'positive obligations to secure the effective enjoyment' of rights to association in trade unions, even where the direct infringement is not by the state.[23] Indeed, as we shall see, the logic is not restricted to rights connected to the right to join a trade union. The Court in *Cyprus v Turkey* was faced, not only with allegations regarding the activities of the local authorities of the Turkish Republic of Northern Cyprus (which gave rise to state responsibility for Turkey), but also those of private individuals. The Court was seized with the allegation that 'Greek Cypriots living in northern Cyprus were racially harassed by Turkish settlers with

---

[21] European Court of Human Rights, Judgment of 26 June 1981, at para. 49.

[22] For a detailed discussion, see A. Clapham, *Human Rights in the Private Sphere* (Oxford: Clarendon Press, 1993) 234–236. Here the state was responsible by *omission* (Art. 2 of the ILC's Articles on State Responsibility) for failing to have a law which protected individuals from such infringements on their right to freedom of association (whether by the state or by non-state actors). State responsibility arises because the state has failed through an omission to protect a human right from infringement by a non-state actor and that omission is an internationally unlawful act due to the treaty obligation entered into by the state to secure to everyone the rights in the Convention. Compare Arts 4 and 8 of the International Law Commission's Articles on State Responsibility (n 1 above) reproduced in Ch 7, at 7.7.2 and Ch 6, at 6.7.1 respectively.

[23] See *Wilson and ors v UK* Judgment of the European Court of Human Rights, 2 July 2002, at para. 41, discussed below.

the connivance and knowledge of the "TRNC" authorities for whose acts Turkey was responsible'.[24] The Court noted that: 'the acquiescence or connivance of the authorities of a Contracting State in the acts of private individuals which violate the Convention rights of other individuals within its jurisdiction may engage that State's responsibility under the Convention. Any different conclusion would be at variance with the obligation contained in Article 1 of the Convention'.[25]

The scope of the positive obligations of the state to tackle such 'acts of private individuals which violate the Convention rights of other individuals' will depend on the right in question. In response to the Court's expansive interpretation of the positive obligations under the Convention, new protections developed in Protocol 12 to the Convention (concerning discrimination) have been expressly limited in order to avoid creating an extensive set of positive obligations. Nevertheless, even in such contexts, the drafters of the new anti-discrimination rights recognized that certain contexts require special attention. In the debate over Protocol 12, the drafters and the Committee of Ministers of the Council of Europe adopted an Explanatory Report which addresses the question of the positive obligations of the state to secure the right to non-discrimination from non-state actors. The Protocol is drafted with an emphasis on non-discriminatory enjoyment of rights granted under national law, as well as discrimination by public authorities. The Protocol will be examined in detail later in this Chapter. The Report emphasizes, however, that the new rights protected by Article 1 of the Protocol are not intended to address the issue of discrimination by non-state actors:

> The Article is not intended to impose a general positive obligation on the Parties to take measures to prevent or remedy all instances of discrimination in relations between private persons. An additional protocol to the Convention, which typically contains justiciable individual rights formulated in concise provisions, would not be a suitable instrument for defining the various elements of such a wide-ranging obligation of a programmatic character.[26]

But the Report carves out the following exception:

> ... any positive obligation in the area of relations between private persons would concern, at the most, relations in the public sphere normally regulated by law, for which the state has a certain responsibility (for example, arbitrary denial of access to work, access to restaurants, or to services which private persons may make available to the public such as medical care or utilities such as water and electricity, etc). The precise form of the response which the state should take will vary according to the circumstances. It is

---

[24] Judgment of 10 May 2001, at para. 73.

[25] Ibid, at para. 81, note the Judgment's use of Art. 1 in the context of the obligation of the state to investigate killings by non-state actors, at para. 131.

[26] At para. 25 of the Explanatory Report to Protocol No. 12 to the European Convention on Human Rights, prepared by the Steering Committee for Human Rights, and adopted by the Committee of Ministers of the Council of Europe on 26 June 2000. The Report states that it 'does not constitute an instrument providing an authoritative interpretation of the text of the Protocol although it may facilitate the understanding of the Protocol's provisions'.

understood that purely private matters would not be affected. Regulation of such matters would also be likely to interfere with the individual's right to respect for his private and family life, his home and his correspondence, as guaranteed by Article 8 of the Convention.[27]

The report uses the expression 'public sphere' to cover not only relations with state authorities but also relations with non-state actors in fields such as employment, access to restaurants, and medical care, as well as to utilities such as water and electricity. The excluded area is an intimate sphere of 'purely private matters' where non-discrimination claims might have to give way to claims of respect for private life. While the states of the Council of Europe may have attempted to isolate this intimate sphere from anti-discrimination provisions in the Protocol, the Court has been prepared to enter in where the threats from non-state actors involve violence and exploitation. In short, protection of human rights in the private sphere falls within the scope of the Convention and the jurisdiction of the Court.

A second example of the Court's reliance on Article 1 is *Costello-Roberts v United Kingdom*. The case concerned corporal punishment in a private school. The Judgment stated:

26. The Court has consistently held that the responsibility of a State is engaged if a violation of one of the rights and freedoms defined in the Convention is the result of non-observance by that State of its obligation under Article 1 to secure those rights and freedoms in its domestic law to everyone within its jurisdiction . . . Indeed, it was accepted by the Government for the purposes of the present proceedings that such an obligation existed as regards securing the rights guaranteed by Articles 3 and 8 to pupils in independent schools. Notwithstanding this, they argued that the responsibility of the United Kingdom was not in fact engaged because the English legal system had adequately secured the rights guaranteed by Articles 3 and 8 of the Convention by prohibiting the use of any corporal punishment which was not moderate or reasonable.

27. The Court notes first that, as was pointed out by the applicant, the State has an obligation to secure to children their right to education under Article 2 of Protocol No. 1. It recalls that the provisions of the Convention and its Protocols must be read as a whole . . . Functions relating to the internal administration of a school, such as discipline, cannot be said to be merely ancillary to the educational process . . .

Secondly, in the United Kingdom, independent schools co-exist with a system of public education. The fundamental right of everyone to education is a right guaranteed equally to pupils in State and independent schools, no distinction being made between the two . . .

Thirdly, the Court agrees with the applicant that the State cannot absolve itself from responsibility by delegating its obligations to private bodies or individuals . . .

28. Accordingly, in the present case, which relates to the particular domain of school discipline, the treatment complained of although it was the act of a headmaster of an independent school, is none the less such as may engage the responsibility of the

---

[27] Ibid, at para. 28.

United Kingdom under the Convention if it proves to be incompatible with Article 3 or Article 8 or both.[28]

The passage illustrates a different logic concerning the positive obligations of states with regard to infringements by non-state actors. As is clear from the beginning of the passage, it was accepted that states had to protect individuals from non-state actors that might subject people to inhuman treatment (Article 3) or attacks on their physical integrity (Article 8). Nevertheless, perhaps because the Court would find that the beating did not constitute the sort of treatment that was covered by Articles 3 and 8, it developed an approach that focused on the fact the case arose in the context of education, and that education is an area in which the state is assumed to have certain responsibilities. The Court then held that the state 'cannot absolve itself' from these responsibilities by delegating to non-state actors.[29]

It has been suggested by Harris, O'Boyle, and Warbrick that it is 'likely that the approach in the *Costello-Roberts* case was particular to its facts and does not signal a departure from the earlier precedents concerning positive obligations'.[30] They do, however, suggest that this approach could be used by the Court with regard to private prisons. I would suggest that the Court does seem to be putting down a marker that, in certain contexts, there are expectations in human rights law that the state has obligations which may go beyond the minimal obligation to secure the rights in the Convention through law. The fields of education and detention are clearly two such areas. There are some parallels here with the rule on state responsibility which attributes to the state the conduct of persons or entities empowered by the law of the state to exercise elements of governmental authority.[31] But this rule simply attributes the action of the non-state entity to the state and should not affect the question of the positive obligations of the state under the human rights treaty. Nor does it help to define this category of contexts where there will be increased scrutiny. Education, for example, would not necessarily always be considered a governmental function under the rules of state responsibility.[32]

The Court has supplemented its reasoning in *Costello-Roberts* in the later case of *A v United Kingdom*.[33] This case concerned a child who had been beaten by his stepfather. The stepfather escaped criminal justice by successfully relying on the defence of 'reasonable chastisement' at his criminal trial. With regard to the positive obligations of the state which stem from Article 1, the Court stated:

> 22.   It remains to be determined whether the State should be held responsible, under Article 3, for the beating of the applicant by his stepfather.

---

[28] Judgment of 25 March 1993.   [29] Ibid, at para. 27 (quoted above).

[30] D. Harris, M. O'Boyle, and C. Warbrick, *Law of the European Convention on Human Rights* (London: Butterworths, 1995) at 21.

[31] See Art. 5 of the ILC's Articles on State Responsibility (n 1 above) discussed in Ch 6, at 6.7.1 above.

[32] As we saw in Ch 6, at 6.7.1 above, the ILC's Commentary (n 1 above) simply states: 'Beyond a certain limit, what is regarded as "governmental" depends on the particular society, its history and traditions.' UN Doc. A/56/10, at 94.   [33] Judgment of 23 September 1998.

> The Court considers that the obligation on the High Contracting Parties under Article 1 of the Convention to secure to everyone within their jurisdiction the rights and freedoms defined in the Convention, taken together with Article 3, requires States to take measures designed to ensure that individuals within their jurisdiction are not subjected to torture or inhuman or degrading treatment or punishment, including such ill-treatment administered by private individuals...Children and other vulnerable individuals, in particular, are entitled to State protection, in the form of effective deterrence, against such serious breaches of personal integrity...

The Court goes on to refer to Articles 19 and 37 of the UN Convention on the Rights of the Child. The suggestion is that children, and other vulnerable individuals, are owed a duty of special protection by the state, and the Court will be particularly demanding in its supervision of a state's existing measures designed to protect these individuals from private violence. In other words, the Court will allow states a narrower margin of appreciation regarding the adequacy of the measures taken in such contexts.

One can conclude that Article 1 has been interpreted to ensure, first, a general rule; and second, a principle that some contexts will trigger expectations that a state has more extensive obligations and that its conduct will be subject to a greater level of scrutiny by the Court. The general rule requires that certain rights are protected from infringements by private actors and that the state is obliged to ensure that the legal system provides effective remedies for individuals who want to claim that non-state actors are infringing on their enjoyment of their rights. In the words of Harris, O'Boyle, and Warbrick, the basis for the state's responsibility under the Convention for such obligations 'is that contrary to Article 1, it has failed to "secure" to individuals within its jurisdiction the rights guaranteed in the Convention by not rendering unlawful the acts of private persons that infringe them'.[34] The special principle is that there are expectations that, with regard to the protection of children and other vulnerable individuals, a state's obligations will extend beyond providing an effective remedy and there will be an increased level of scrutiny of state conduct to ensure that the state fulfils its responsibility to protect these individuals from private violence.

The following section considers in more detail some of the actual rights protected under the Convention, and the extent to which the Court has held that these rights must be protected where the direct source of the infringement is a non-state actor rather than a public authority.

9.1.2 Article 13 Right to an Effective Remedy

Article 13 reads: 'Everyone whose rights and freedoms as set forth in this Convention are violated shall have an effective remedy before a national authority notwithstanding that the violation has been committed by persons acting in an

---

[34] Harris, O'Boyle, and Warbrick (1995: 21–22).

official capacity.' The extension of this guarantee into the private sphere, in order to provide a remedy for infringements of rights by non-state actors, is accepted by Jacobs and White in the second edition of *The European Convention on Human Rights*:

> What is clear is that the State must provide for a remedy for any violation, whether committed by it or by a private individual. For Article 13, by providing in effect that it should not be a defence that a violation was committed by a person acting in an official capacity, presupposes that it cannot be a defence that it was committed by a private individual.[35]

It is suggested that the Court and Commission's case-law tends to suggest that national courts are obliged to ensure respect for the guarantees in the Convention when deciding private law disputes. Of course, the actual operation of directly effective Convention rights in national law will depend on the nature and manner of that State's reception of the Convention into national law. (We consider the United Kingdom situation in Chapter 10.) However, the lack of an effective remedy before a national authority to ensure respect by a private person of a Convention right (such as Article 3 or 8) could give rise to a violation of Article 13, and could be sanctioned at the international level.[36]

9.1.3   Article 2 Right to Life

Article 2 reads:

(1)   Everyone's right to life shall be protected by law. No one shall be deprived of his life intentionally save in the execution of a sentence of a court following his conviction of a crime for which this penalty is provided by law.

(2)   Deprivation of life shall not be regarded as inflicted in contravention of this article when it results from the use of force which is no more than absolutely necessary:
(a) in defence of any person from unlawful violence;
(b) in order to effect a lawful arrest or to prevent the escape of a person lawfully detained;
(c) in action lawfully taken for the purpose of quelling a riot or insurrection.

---

[35] (Oxford, Clarendon Press, 1996) at 19. The third edn (2002) by C. Ovey and R. C. A. White, rephrases this (at 19): 'If the violation is by a private individual...a State may have fulfilled its obligations if its law adequately protects the rights guaranteed and provides for an effective remedy in the event of a violation.' On the early doctrine surrounding the scope of Art. 13, see Clapham (1993: 125, 240–244).
[36] See, e.g. the Judgment in *Costello-Roberts v UK* (discussed in 9.1.1 above) esp. para. 40, which considered the civil remedy for assault against a teacher working in a private school. The Court found the remedy adequate and hence there was no violation of Art. 13. See also the finding of a violation of Art. 13 by the Court in *Hatton and ors v UK* Judgment of 8 July 2003, paras 137–142 (although the Grand Chamber did not apparently address the issue of whether the absence of a remedy for nuisance or trespass led to a violation of Art. 13, preferring instead to look at the question of judicial review of the governmental policy. See also the Judgment of the Chamber (Third Section) in that case, 2 October 2001, paras 108–116.

9.1.3.1   The Commission Finds that Non-State Actor Killings Come within the Scope of Article 2

Early applications before the European Commission on Human Rights demanded physical protection from terrorist attacks. Although none of these cases were successful, they effectively led to a determination that the state has a positive obligation under the Convention to protect individuals from terrorist killings. In an application brought against Ireland in 1973, the applicant stated that in 1969, he had been shot in the back and leg by the Irish Republican Army (IRA), and although this led to the conviction of one man, two suspects remained free at the time of the application. For three years following the attack, the applicant was provided with special police protection in the form of a personal armed escort and a 24-hour uniformed officer stationed at his home. He was informed in 1973 that he would no longer be provided this protection and he complained to the European Commission of Human Rights. The Commission addressed the Article 2 point in terms which came to be used by both sides in future applications:

> It is true that Art. 2 provides that everyone's right to life shall be protected by law. However, the applicant has not even suggested that there are no laws in Ireland protecting the right to life, his complaint being simply that he personally has been refused a constant personal bodyguard.
>
> The Commission finds that Art. 2 cannot be interpreted as imposing a duty on a State to give protection of this nature, at least not for an indefinite period of time, which is what in effect the applicant requests.[37]

This ambiguous dismissal of the application developed into a general acceptance by the Commission that Article 2 included a duty on the part of the state to offer protection from attacks by non-state actors such as terrorists.

In parallel applications, *Mrs W v Ireland*[38] and *Mrs W v United Kingdom*,[39] another applicant complained about the failure to protect the lives of her husband and brother killed in Ireland and Northern Ireland respectively. Mrs W's husband was shot at a cattle auction in Ireland and the Provisional IRA claimed responsibility. In a separate incident, Mrs W's brother was shot when three or more gunmen burst into a bar, shot out the lights, and then shot Mrs W's brother in the head several times. Mrs W was considered by the Commission in the application brought against the United Kingdom as not entitled to bring the complaints as a victim affected by the death of her husband, as her husband was not 'within the jurisdiction' of the United Kingdom at the time of his death; on the other hand, she was entitled to bring applications as a next-of-kin victim affected by the death of her brother in Northern Ireland, and as a victim of a continuing situation in respect of

---

[37] *X v Ireland* App. 6040/73, 44 *Collection of Decisions* (1974) 121, at 122.
[38] App. 9360/81, 32 D & R 211.   [39] App. 9348/81, 32 D & R 190.

her own security.[40] Mrs W made the case that the right to life guaranteed in the Convention,

> ... interpreted in the light of the phrase 'The High Contracting Parties shall secure ... the right and freedoms defined in Section 1' in Article 1 of the Convention, requires the United Kingdom, in the emergency situation prevailing in Northern Ireland, to protect the right to life not only by criminal prosecution of offenders but also by such preventive control, through deployment of its armed forces, as appears necessary to protect persons who are considered to be exposed to the threat of terrorist attacks.[41]

In response, the Commission baulked at a detailed security review of the situation with the obvious political implications this would entail:

> 14.   The Commission does not find that it can be its task, in the examination of the present applicant's complaint under Article 2, to consider in detail, as she appears to suggest, the appropriateness and efficiency of the measures taken by the United Kingdom to combat terrorism in Northern Ireland.
>
> 15.   The Commission cannot find that the United Kingdom was required under the Convention to protect the applicant's brother by measures going beyond those actually taken by the authorities to shield life and limb of the inhabitants of Northern Ireland against attacks from terrorists.
>
> 16.   Nor can it find that the applicant can under Article 2 require such further measures as regards her own protection. In this connection the Commission notes from the applicant's submission that, while the peace-time army strength in Northern Ireland was 4,000 men, it currently stands at about 10,500 and that, between August 1969 and December 1981, several hundred members of the armed and security forces lost their lives there combating terrorism.[42]

In a later application, concerning a similar killing by non-state actors, the applicant sought to highlight more specifically the state policies which could be criticized. In an application brought against Ireland and the United Kingdom, the widow of a part-time corporal in the Ulster Defence Regiment complained of 'the degree of training offered to the police force regarding large scale man-hunts, failures of security regarding a break-out from the Maze prison, and security problems regarding certain frontier crossings'.[43] The Commission recalled its previous approach and found that the United Kingdom was not required to take measures going beyond those it had already taken 'to shield life and limb of the inhabitants of Northern Ireland against attacks from terrorists'.[44] With regard to the specific allegations concerning the Maze prison break-out and the attempts to block border crossings, the Commission found that these could not be said to lead to a violation of Article 2.[45]

---

[40] At para. 8 of *Mrs W v UK*, App. 9348/81, 32 D & R 190, 199.

[41] Ibid, at 199–200, para. 11.

[42] Ibid, at 200. With regard to the application against Ireland, the part concerning the husband was rejected as having been lodged out of time. The other claims were rejected as not falling within the jurisdiction of Ireland. See App. 9360/81, 32 D & R 211, at 213–216.

[43] App. 10018/82, 7 March 1982, unreported.   [44] Ibid, at para. 21.   [45] Ibid.

9.1.3.2   The Court Develops Criteria for the Duty to Protect the Right to Life from Non-State Actors

It then fell to the Court, almost fifteen years later, to offer a clearer set of criteria for what is expected of the state in terms of the prevention, protection, investigation, and punishment of killings by non-state actors. The details of *Osman v United Kingdom* were complex and are only sketched here.[46] In brief, Ahmet Osman's teacher, Paul Paget-Lewis, developed an attachment to Ahmet, who was at the time, a fifteen-year-old British citizen living in London. The teacher was transferred to another school. Over the following three months, there followed a number of attacks on the Osman family's property. There was also a collision between the teacher's car and a car carrying Ahmet Osman's friend, Leslie Green. During this time, there were various interviews between the teacher and the local authorities, as well as between the police and the teacher. The car accident involving the teacher and Leslie Green was investigated by the police. Following an attempt to arrest the teacher for criminal damage, the teacher disappeared from his new school and travelled around England hiring cars under his newly-adopted name of Osman. The teacher had changed his name by deed poll from Paul Paget-Lewis to Paul Ahmet Yildirim Osman. The teacher stole a shotgun and returned to London where he was spotted by Ahmet's friend Leslie Green near the Osmans' house. In the words of the European Court, the situation culminated as follows:

> The Government accept that, on 5 March 1988, Detective Sergeant Boardman received a message which stated 'phone Mrs Green' but since there was no phone number on the note he did not connect the message with the mother of Leslie Green...
>
> On 7 March 1988 Paget-Lewis was seen near the applicants' home by a number of people. At about 11.00 pm Paget-Lewis shot and killed Ali Osman and seriously wounded Ahmet. He then drove to the home of Mr Perkins [the deputy head teacher] where he shot and wounded him and killed his son. Early the next morning Paget-Lewis was arrested. On being arrested he stated 'why didn't you stop me before I did it, I gave you all the warning signs?'[47]

For present purposes, two points of interpretation under the European Convention on Human Rights are relevant. First, the Court stated clearly that

---

[46] Judgment of 28 October 1998. The present author participated as a member of the Osmans' legal team; as far as possible references have been made to the Court's appreciation of the facts.

[47] At paras 55–57. The Judgment continues: '58. Later that day Paget-Lewis was interviewed by the police. According to the record of the interview, Paget-Lewis said that he had been planning the attacks ever since he lost his job, and for the previous two weeks he had been watching the Osmans' house. Although he considered Mr Perkins as his main target, he also regarded Ali and Ahmet Osman as being responsible for his losing his position at Homerton House. Paget-Lewis stated that he had been hoping in the back of his mind that the police would stop him. He admitted holding the family at gunpoint as they returned to the house, making Ali and Ahmet Osman kneel down in the kitchen, turning out the light and shooting at them. He denied that on earlier occasions he had damaged the windows of the Osmans' house but admitted that he had let down the tyres of their car as a prank.'

there were positive obligations on the state even where the violence emanates from a private individual:

> It is thus accepted by those appearing before the Court that Article 2 of the Convention may also imply in certain well-defined circumstances a positive obligation on the authorities to take preventive operational measures to protect an individual whose life is at risk from the criminal acts of another individual.[48]

The majority of the Commission and the Court held, however, that there was no violation of Article 2 in the particular circumstances of this case. The Commission found by ten votes to seven that there had been no violation of Article 2. The majority considered that: 'The failings to take additional investigative steps do not, in the Commission's view, disclose any seriously defective response by the police to the threat posed by Paget-Lewis as perceived at the time.'[49] The majority suggested a test which required wilful disregard of duties required by law. The key passage reads:

> 92.   The extent of the obligation to take preventive steps may however increase in relation to the immediacy of the risk to life. Where there is a real and imminent risk to life to an identified person or group of persons, a failure by State authorities to take appropriate steps may disclose a violation of the right to protection of life by law. In order to establish such a failure, it will not be sufficient to point to mistakes, oversights or that more effective steps might have been taken. In the Commission's view, there must be an element of gross dereliction or wilful disregard of the duties imposed by law such as to conflict fundamentally with the essence of the guarantee secured by Article 2 of the Convention.[50]

The minority, led by the President of the Commission, Stefan Trechsel, proposed an alternative new test to determine the liability of the State where its duty to protect human rights is under examination: the 'increase of risk test'. 'Responsibility is established, under this test, as soon as it can be said that the action called for would have considerably diminished the risk of the result, in other words, if the omission considerably increased the risk.'[51] He rejected the majority approach, which he categorized as a 'causation' test, pointing out that it is difficult to establish a link between omission and result. Trechsel's opinion helpfully described the preventive positive steps that the authorities could have taken and applies a reasoning which evokes a proportionality test and looks at what could have been expected, rather than what would definitely have prevented the loss of life:

> I accept that it was not possible to set up a permanent protection of the endangered persons by body-guards. I am quite aware that such a protection necessitates an enormous effort and is also very costly. However, it would have been possible, in the present case,

---

[48] Judgment of 28 October 1998, at para. 115.
[49] Report of the Commission, 1 July 1997, at para. 99.   [50] Ibid, at para. 92.
[51] Partially dissenting opinion of Mr S. Trechsel, joined by Messrs E. Busuttil, A. Weitzel, J.-C. Geus, I. Cabral Barreto, and I. Békés, attached to report of 1 July 1997.

to concentrate on the source of the danger, a single person who does not seem to have shrewdly attempted to conceal his whereabouts.

The question then arises as to whether seriously watching over, probably also arresting Paget-Lewis would have saved the applicants. The majority, without making it explicitly clear, apply a test of causation which I cannot follow.[52]

The Court for its part found by seventeen votes to three that there had been no violation of Article 2. The Court's majority judgment did not follow the approach of the majority of the Commission; the Court set out a test which focused on the proportionality of the burden on the authorities and the knowledge which the authorities had, or ought to have had, of the danger posed to the actual eventual victim. The test emerges from two long paragraphs in the judgment:

115. The Court notes that the first sentence of Article 2 §1 enjoins the State not only to refrain from the intentional and unlawful taking of life, but also to take appropriate steps to safeguard the lives of those within its jurisdiction.... It is common ground that the State's obligation in this respect extends beyond its primary duty to secure the right to life by putting in place effective criminal-law provisions to deter the commission of offences against the person backed up by law-enforcement machinery for the prevention, suppression and sanctioning of breaches of such provisions. It is thus accepted by those appearing before the Court that Article 2 of the Convention may also imply in certain well-defined circumstances a positive obligation on the authorities to take preventive operational measures to protect an individual whose life is at risk from the criminal acts of another individual. The scope of this obligation is a matter of dispute between the parties.

116. For the Court, and bearing in mind the difficulties involved in policing modern societies, the unpredictability of human conduct and the operational choices which must be made in terms of priorities and resources, such an obligation must be interpreted in a way which does not impose an impossible or disproportionate burden on the authorities. Accordingly, not every claimed risk to life can entail for the authorities a Convention requirement to take operational measures to prevent that risk from materialising. Another relevant consideration is the need to ensure that the police exercise their powers to control and prevent crime in a manner which fully respects the due process and other guarantees which legitimately place restraints on the scope of their action to investigate crime and bring offenders to justice, including the guarantees contained in Articles 5 and 8 of the Convention.

In the opinion of the Court where there is an allegation that the authorities have violated their positive obligation to protect the right to life in the context of their above-mentioned duty to prevent and suppress offences against the person (see paragraph 115 above), it must be established to its satisfaction that the authorities knew or ought to have known at the time of the existence of a real and immediate risk to the life of an identified individual or individuals from the criminal acts of a third party and that they failed to take measures within the scope of their powers which, judged reasonably, might have been expected to avoid that risk. The Court does not accept the Government's view that the failure to perceive the risk to life in the circumstances known at the time or to

---

[52] Ibid.

take preventive measures to avoid that risk must be tantamount to gross negligence or wilful disregard of the duty to protect life (see paragraph 107 above). Such a rigid standard must be considered to be incompatible with the requirements of Article 1 of the Convention and the obligations of Contracting States under that Article to secure the practical and effective protection of the rights and freedoms laid down therein, including Article 2 . . . For the Court, and having regard to the nature of the right protected by Article 2, a right fundamental in the scheme of the Convention, it is sufficient for an applicant to show that the authorities did not do all that could be reasonably expected of them to avoid a real and immediate risk to life of which they have or ought to have knowledge. This is a question which can only be answered in the light of all the circumstances of any particular case . . .

After evaluating the various versions of events and the evidence available to the police the Court concluded:

121.   In the view of the Court the applicants have failed to point to any decisive stage in the sequence of the events leading up to the tragic shooting when it could be said that the police knew or ought to have known that the lives of the Osman family were at real and immediate risk from Paget-Lewis. While the applicants have pointed to a series of missed opportunities which would have enabled the police to neutralise the threat posed by Paget-Lewis, for example by searching his home for evidence to link him with the graffiti incident or by having him detained under the Mental Health Act 1983 or by taking more active investigative steps following his disappearance, it cannot be said that these measures, judged reasonably, would in fact have produced that result or that a domestic court would have convicted him or ordered his detention in a psychiatric hospital on the basis of the evidence adduced before it. As noted earlier (see paragraph 116 above), the police must discharge their duties in a manner which is compatible with the rights and freedoms of individuals. In the circumstances of the present case, they cannot be criticised for attaching weight to the presumption of innocence or failing to use powers of arrest, search and seizure having regard to their reasonably held view that they lacked at relevant times the required standard of suspicion to use those powers or that any action taken would in fact have produced concrete results.

The conclusion that there was no violation of Article 2 in this case was ameliorated by a finding that there had been a violation of Article 6, as the Osmans had been unable to have access to court to sue the police for negligence in the domestic courts.[53] The Court awarded Ahmet Osman and his mother £10,000 each in damages.

---

[53] This aspect of the case has been the object of much commentary due to its possible implications for the English law of negligence and the public policy exception with regard to suits against public bodies such as the police. See, e.g. J. Wright, *Tort Law & Human Rights* (Oxford: Hart Publishing, 2001) and B. Markesinis, J.-B. Auby, C. Waltjen, and S. Deakin (eds) *The Tortious Liability of Statutory Bodies* (Oxford: Hart Publishing, 1999). The Court revised its approach to suits in negligence against public authorities in the case of *Z and ors v UK* Judgment of 10 May 2001, where it was held that the inability to sue the local authority in fact stemmed from the substantive law and not from any immunity (at para. 100), with the result that Art. 6 was not applicable. As it had been conceded that there was a lack of effective remedies regarding Art. 3, the Court held there had been a violation of Art. 13. The Court noted the Government's point that in the future, victims would be able to bring complaints against such authorities under the Human Rights Act 1998.

It is worth highlighting here one aspect of the reasoning of the Court in paragraph 116, quoted above. The Court emphasized that, in designing its criteria for determining the scope of the positive obligation to protect individuals from private actors, the human rights of the private actor have to be taken into account. It is this balancing act that usually distinguishes determinations of simple direct human rights violations by the state from those where the direct perpetrators are non-state actors that are themselves the holders of human rights. In the *Osman* case, the Court highlighted the due process, privacy, and arbitrary detention rights of the non-state actor involved. As will become apparent in relation to Article 10 below, this balancing operation by the Court becomes even more marked when rights to freedom of expression are weighed against privacy or property rights of the non-state actor hindering that freedom.

It was not long before the Court was faced again with claims of a state's failure to protect individuals from private violence. Mahmut Kaya complained that Turkey had failed to protect individuals from non-state violence in the context of the instability in the Kurdish areas of Turkey. In *Mahmut Kaya v Turkey* the failures to investigate either the counter-guerrilla groups established outside the formal framework of the state, or the involvement of the state security forces, led to the Court's finding that 'the authorities failed to take reasonable measures available to them to prevent a real and immediate risk to the life of [the deceased]'.[54] The case nevertheless applied the tests developed in the *Osman* case and focused in part on the specific risk to the deceased, which was not only real and immediate, but of which the authorities were held to be aware.[55]

A second case concerning Turkey presents an even clearer picture of a situation where the state failed to protect the right to life from non-state violence. Having recalled the *Osman* criteria at length, the Court again found that these were satisfied, even in the absence of evidence of state collusion or acquiescence:

> 79. In the present case, it has not been established beyond reasonable doubt that any State agent or person acting on behalf of the State authorities was involved in the killing of Zübeyir Akkoç (see paragraphs 248–59 of the Commission's report). The question to be determined is whether the authorities failed to comply with their positive obligation to protect him from a known risk to his life.
>
> 80. The Court notes that the applicant's husband [Zübeyir Akkoç], who was a teacher of Kurdish origin, had been involved with the applicant in the trade union Eğit-Sen, which was regarded as unlawful by the authorities. He had been detained a number of times by the police. Following a demonstration in October 1992, in which teachers had claimed that police officers had assaulted and abused them and eleven had been taken into custody, the applicant and her husband had received telephone calls in

---

[54] Judgment of 28 March 2000, at para. 101. For helpful discussion of the case-law concerning positive obligations under Art. 2, see Mowbray (2004) Ch 2.

[55] 'The Court is satisfied that Hasan Kaya, as a doctor suspected of aiding and abetting the PKK, was at that time at particular risk of falling victim to an unlawful attack. Moreover, this risk could in the circumstances be regarded as real and immediate.' Ibid, at para. 89.

which it was threatened that they would be killed next. These had been reported to the public prosecutor in petitions.

81.   The Government have claimed that Zübeyir Akkoç was not at more risk than any other person, or teacher, in the south-east region. The Court notes the tragic number of victims to the conflict in that region. It recalls, however, that in 1993 there were rumours current alleging that contra-guerrilla elements were involved in targeting persons suspected of supporting the PKK. It is undisputed that there were a significant number of killings—the 'unknown perpetrator killing' phenomenon—which included prominent Kurdish figures such as Musa Anter as well as other persons suspected of opposing the authorities' policies in the south-east... The Court is satisfied that Zübeyir Akkoç, as a Kurdish teacher involved in activities perceived by the authorities as being unlawful and in opposition to their policies in the south-east, was at that time at particular risk of falling victim to an unlawful attack. Moreover, this risk could in the circumstances be regarded as real and immediate.

82.   The Court is equally satisfied that the authorities must be regarded as being aware of this risk. Although the Government disputed the seriousness of the threatening telephone calls, the Court finds it rather significant that the public prosecutor took no steps in response to the petitions lodged by the applicant and her husband.[56]

The detailed judgment highlighted the failure of the authorities to respond effectively to killings in the region and concluded 'that in the circumstances of this case the authorities failed to take reasonable measures available to them to prevent a real and immediate risk to the life of Zübeyir Akkoç'.[57] Having seen what is expected of states with regard to preventing immediate risks to life, let us now turn to the measures which states are expected to adopt with regard to procedural steps that should be taken to minimize loss of life and properly investigate all killings.

9.1.3.3   *The Court Develops a Duty to Prevent, Investigate, and Ensure Accountability for Killings by Non-State Actors*

The cases on preventive protection have been supplemented by a jurisprudence which states that the state's obligations concerning the right to life include an obligation to investigate properly and punish killings by non-state actors.[58] In *Ergi v Turkey*, the Court found that the government's counter-terrorism ambush had not been planned in a way to minimize the risk of civilian casualties. The fact that it had not been proven that the bullet which killed the applicant's sister, Havva Ergi, came from a gun used by the state forces, did not prevent the Court from finding a violation of Article 2:

> ... the responsibility of the State is not confined to circumstances where there is significant evidence that misdirected fire from agents of the State has killed a civilian. It may also be engaged where they fail to take all feasible precautions in the choice of means and

[56] *Akkoç v. Turkey* Judgment of 10 October 2000.   [57] Ibid, at para. 94.
[58] *Ergi v Turkey* Judgment of 28 July 1998; *Yaşa v Turkey* Judgment of 2 September 1998; and *Tanrıkulu v Turkey* Judgment of 8 July 1999, at paras 101–111.

methods of a security operation mounted against an opposing group with a view to avoiding and, in any event, to minimising, incidental loss of civilian life.

Thus, even though it has not been established beyond reasonable doubt that the bullet which killed Havva Ergi had been fired by the security forces, the Court must consider whether the security forces' operation had been planned and conducted in such a way as to avoid or minimise, to the greatest extent possible, any risk to the lives of the villagers, *including from the fire-power of the PKK members caught in the ambush.*[59]

The Court recalled its case-law, which determined that Articles 1 and 2, read together, imply an obligation to carry out 'some form of effective official investigation when individuals have been killed as a result of the use of force', and confirmed that:

> ... contrary to what is asserted by the Government... this obligation is not confined to cases where it has been established that the killing was caused by an agent of the State. Nor is it decisive whether members of the deceased 's family or others have lodged a formal complaint about the killing with the relevant investigatory authority. In the case under consideration, the mere knowledge of the killing on the part of the authorities gave rise *ipso facto* to an obligation under Article 2 of the Convention to carry out an effective investigation into the circumstances surrounding the death.[60]

The Court went on to find that there had been a violation of Article 2 'on account of the defects in the planning and conduct of the security forces' operation and the lack of an adequate and effective investigation'.[61] This reasoning was followed in further cases and extended to attempted killings.[62]

Moving away from the context of terrorism and counter-terrorism, brief mention should be made of the case of *Paul and Audrey Edwards v United Kingdom*.[63] The case concerned the killing of Christopher Edwards by his cellmate Richard Linford while they were in police custody. The Court applied the *Osman* criteria of knowledge and real risk and found that there had been a breach of Article 2. The force of the obligation is considered more intense when someone is already in police custody. At this point, one comes within the Court's category of vulnerable persons:

> 56. In the context of prisoners, the Court has had previous occasion to emphasise that persons in custody are in a vulnerable position and that the authorities are under a duty to protect them. It is incumbent on the State to account for any injuries suffered in custody, which obligation is particularly stringent where that individual dies. ...
>
> 57. Christopher Edwards was killed while detained on remand by a dangerous, mentally ill prisoner, Richard Linford, who was placed in his cell. As a prisoner he fell under the responsibility of the authorities who were under a domestic-law and Convention obligation to protect his life. The Court has examined, firstly, whether the

---

[59] *Ergi v Turkey* Judgment of 28 July 19, at para. 79 (emphasis added).   [60] Ibid, at para. 82.
[61] Ibid, at para. 86.
[62] See *Yaşa v Turkey* Judgment of 2 September 1998, at paras 100 and 107 regarding an attempted murder; see also *Tanrıkulu v Turkey* Judgment of 8 July 1999, para.103.
[63] Judgment of 14 March 2002.

authorities knew or ought to have known of the existence of a real and immediate risk to the life of Christopher Edwards from the acts of Richard Linford and, secondly, whether they failed to take measures within the scope of their powers which, judged reasonably, might have been expected to avoid that risk.

...

64.   The Court concludes that the failure of the agencies involved in this case (medical profession, police, prosecution and court) to pass information about Richard Linford on to the prison authorities and the inadequate nature of the screening process on Richard Linford's arrival in prison disclose a breach of the State's obligation to protect the life of Christopher Edwards.

The Court went on to find a further violation of the procedural obligations in Article 2: 'the lack of power to compel witnesses and the private character of the proceedings from which the applicants were excluded, save when they were giving evidence, failed to comply with the requirements of Article 2 of the Convention to hold an effective investigation into Christopher Edwards's death'.[64]

These cases have extended the international law of human rights into new realms. First, the right to life in the Convention covers situations where the killer was a private or non-state actor, as well as situations where it is not clear whether the killing was carried out by state agents or others. In short, it is not necessary to show who carried out the killing to come within the protective scope of Article 2. Second, the Court has extended the procedural guarantees in Article 2 to situations where the killing is not necessarily attributed to state actors. Third, the positive obligations of the state have been articulated and applied in ways that seek to ensure that states put in place procedures at the national level which will avoid the need for the European Court of Human Rights to investigate the facts of each loss of life.[65] These developments have radically changed the way in which one thinks about the right to life in human rights law. The next question is whether the Court has given any clues as to the actual obligations of the non-state actors themselves.

9.1.3.4   *The Scope of the Human Rights Obligations of Non-State Actors with Regard to the Right to Life*

The issue of the obligations of the non-state actor as regards the right to life hardly arises in practice. Taking a life is clearly illegal under national law and there would normally be no reason to raise this before a national court in terms of human rights law. As discussed in Chapter 1, the issue does arise with regard to reporting on human rights violations by international and non-governmental organizations. It was suggested earlier that such reporting has now been recast as reporting on violations of principles of humanitarian law, or international criminal law, so that in the context of killings by non-state actors, the reporting is likely to be framed in

---

[64] Judgment of 14 March 2002, at para. 87.
[65] For this insight, see further Mowbray (2004: 30).

terms of genocide, crimes against humanity, or war crimes. It is also possible that terrorist crimes, such as those defined in the Terrorist Bombing Convention of 1997, will be of more relevance than claims regarding violations of the right to life as such,[66] as framing the killing as a terrorist offence will trigger further obligations under the Convention. The issue does arise, however, in relation to whether non-state actors might themselves have positive obligations to protect life, and the parallel obligations of the state to ensure that the non-state actor fulfils these obligations with regard to everyone within the state's jurisdiction.

The issue of the positive obligations expected of individuals with regard to the right to life emerged in the hardly noticed admissibility decision of the European Commission on Human Rights in *H v United Kingdom*.[67] The applicant's husband had been employed at Manchester High School (a private school); he had taken time off work as he was suffering from chest pains, but returned to the school to collect his wages. At 16.10 hrs he was discovered collapsed. 'Several people, including teachers with some first aid training, saw him and decided he was dead. The school called an ambulance at 17.25 hrs and it took the applicant's husband to the hospital nearby where he was pronounced dead by doctors at 18.05 hrs. A post mortem conducted revealed that her husband had died of a coronary occlusion.'[68]

The applicant first complained that not all necessary measures which might have saved her husband's life were taken, and secondly that English law 'appears to condone such negligence by not imposing a specific obligation to take prompt emergency steps in such circumstances and by not awarding compensation to the victims or their families'. The Commission dismissed the first part of the claim, stating that they could not accept complaints against private individuals. The Commission indulged the argument that English law seemed to condone the negligence of the teachers by not imposing an obligation to take prompt action and considered that, even if the Convention could be said to create an obligation on states to ensure that private individuals are under an express obligation to take immediate action to save lives, in this case the existence or absence of such an obligation would not have made any difference. The Commission recalled:

> ... that the medical evidence established that the death was inevitable as a result of the massive coronary damage, that the staff of the school, who were unskilled in cardiac resuscitation, would have been unable to resuscitate him even if they had tried and that even if an ambulance had been summoned it could not have arrived in time. In these tragic circumstances, the existence of any express obligation to take prompt emergency action would not have been of any avail to the applicant's husband. Therefore, even assuming Article 2 of the Convention can be said to impose an obligation on States to protect individuals by such legal measures, the Commission finds that an examination

[66] An exceptional reference to terrorists violating the right to life can be seen in Report of the Policy Working Group on the United Nations and Terrorism established by the Secretary-General, UN Doc. A/57/273–S/2002/875, 6 August 2002, at para. 26, quoted in Ch 1, at 1.3.

[67] App. 11590/85, Decision of 18 July 1986, 48 D & R 258.   [68] Ibid.

of this complaint as it has been submitted does not disclose any appearance of a violation of the above Article (Art. 2).

The issue remains open as to whether the Convention requires states to ensure that individuals are under a 'duty to rescue' in order to save lives.[69] With respect to the need for a civil liability rule or a tort, Jane Wright concludes: 'in view of the range of responses on the part of states and the lack of a European consensus on the issue, it is unlikely that any duty to rescue on the part of a private actor found by the Strasbourg Court would take the form of mandatory civil liability'.[70] Nevertheless Wright observes that the Court's approach to Article 8 suggests that 'in the context of rescue, arguably, effective respect for private life could be achieved through the imposition of criminal sanctions'.[71] The Court has indeed demanded that states criminalize certain behaviour to ensure an effective protection of physical integrity.[72] It would be strange to limit the positive obligations of non-state actors to the realm of invasions of private life and not include obligations to protect life. As Wright points out: 'However, there is something distinctly unattractive about a legal system which denies redress where it can be shown that physical injury or death could have been avoided through the provision of assistance which would have involved no risk to the rescuer.'[73]

Perhaps the most that can be said at the moment is that the scope of the positive obligations on the state with regard to the right to life is greater than the duties that individuals and other non-state actors may have to protect the right to life. Individuals are not expected to mount armed protection or ensure effective investigations of killings. But what of the obligation of powerful private entities with the capacity to develop life-saving drugs? Could they be said to be under a positive obligation to do everything in their power to ensure life-saving drugs for all? Perhaps once it is admitted that there are some positive obligations on non-state actors, then the next exercise is to try to determine what should be expected of each non-state actor in the relevant context.

Alastair Mowbray has highlighted an interesting case concerning the role of the private sector in health care.[74] In *Calvelli and Ciglio v Italy* a Grand Chamber of the Court dealt with the scope of Article 2 in relation to suits against a doctor from a private hospital. According to the judgment: 'Immediately following its birth in a private clinic, "La Madonnina", in Cosenza the applicant's new-born baby was admitted to the intensive care unit of Cosenza Hospital suffering from serious respiratory and neurological post-asphyxia syndrome induced by the position in which it had become lodged during delivery. The baby died on 9 February 1987, two days after birth.' The applicants lodged a complaint and the prosecutor's office immediately started an investigation. The case turned on the application of

---

[69] See the discussion by Wright (2001: 115–145).   [70] Ibid, at 142–143.
[71] Ibid, at 143.
[72] See *X and Y v The Netherlands* Judgment of 26 March 1985, discussed below.
[73] Wright (2001: 143).   [74] Mowbray (2004: 26).

Italian law and the competing priorities of the prosecutor. What is of interest in the present context is the way that the Court highlights health care as an area where states have a particular responsibility with regard to the public and private sectors.

> The aforementioned positive obligations therefore require States to make regulations compelling hospitals, whether public or private, to adopt appropriate measures for the protection of their patients' lives. They also require an effective independent judicial system to be set up so that the cause of death of patients in the care of the medical profession, whether in the public or the private sector, can be determined and those responsible made accountable . . .[75]

Turning to the measures which have to be put in place by the state, the Court left states a wide range of choices. Article 2 does not necessarily demand that criminal sanctions be imposed on private parties; civil, administrative, or disciplinary sanctions may be appropriate. What is clear is that states are obliged to ensure that non-state actors are made accountable for acts which infringe the right to life:

> . . . if the infringement of the right to life or to personal integrity is not caused intentionally, the positive obligation imposed by Article 2 to set up an effective judicial system does not necessarily require the provision of a criminal-law remedy in every case. In the specific sphere of medical negligence the obligation may for instance also be satisfied if the legal system affords victims a remedy in the civil courts, either alone or in conjunction with a remedy in the criminal courts, enabling any liability of the doctors concerned to be established and any appropriate civil redress, such as an order for damages and for the publication of the decision, to be obtained. Disciplinary measures may also be envisaged.[76]

The majority of the Grand Chamber determined that, even though the criminal prosecution had become time-barred, the acceptance of compensation by the applicants meant that they could no longer claim to be victims of a violation of Article 2.[77]

In a later case, *Vo v France*, the majority of the Grand Chamber again found that the absence of a criminal remedy against a doctor for unintentional homicide against a foetus did not result in a violation of Article 2, due to the adequacy of the remedy available to the applicant through the administrative courts (for the fault of the public servant). Again the Grand Chamber highlighted that Article 2 does, however, demand that regulations are introduced that compel hospitals 'whether private or public, to adopt appropriate measures for the protection of patients' lives'.[78] For present purposes, the important point is that negligence by private individuals in the medical profession which results in death falls within the scope of Article 2. The state has to ensure that the cause of death is investigated and that individuals are held accountable. One could imagine future complaints which

---

[75] Ibid, at para. 49.   [76] Ibid, at para. 51.
[77] See the criticism by Mowbray (2004: 27) and the minority.
[78] Judgment of 8 July 2004, at para. 89.

demand that, where merely holding individuals accountable is unsatisfactory, it should be possible to hold the private medical institution itself accountable. Where this is impossible under national law, a case could arise under Article 2 before the European Court of Human Rights.

9.1.3.5 Summary Concerning Article 2

The Court's jurisprudence concerning Article 2 is complex and the findings set out above could be summarized in the following form:

- Killings and attempted killings by non-state actors come within the scope of Article 2.

- The duty of the state to prevent such killings and offer protection depends on the knowledge by the authorities, including what they ought to have known, about the real and immediate nature of the risk. The possible measures to be taken will depend on what is proportionate in the circumstances. Where protection from terrorists could entail an expansion of military presence or questioning sensitive political policies, human rights bodies are likely to be cautious with regard to what they will demand of states.

- The obligation to protect is heightened when individuals enter the custody of the authorities. As vulnerable individuals, they enjoy special protection and the authorities are under an obligation to inform themselves about the risk to individuals that other individuals may pose. Where death results from violence by a private individual in a custody situation, Article 2 includes procedural obligations that include a right for close relatives to participate in the eventual inquiry.

- The duty to investigate a killing in the context of counter-terrorism applies whether or not the killing had been shown to be the work of the state authorities. The state cannot avoid the duty to investigate in the context of counter-terrorism operations by blaming deaths on the terrorists. There is even a duty to arrange operations to minimize the chance of death whether the direct cause of death emanates from state or non-state actors.

- In some circumstances, non-state actors will have obligations concerning the right to life which go beyond the injunction not to kill. Although it is unclear whether there is a general duty on everyone to rescue those in danger of their lives, in the context of health care workers Article 2 has been interpreted as demanding that the state put in place an effective system for ensuring investigations into deaths, as well as ensuring accountability for the persons concerned.

9.1.4 Article 3 Prohibition of Torture

Article 3 reads as follows: 'No one shall be subjected to torture or to inhuman or degrading treatment or punishment.'

9.1.4.1   Protection of Children and the Prosecution of Rape

This prohibition has been interpreted to cover corporal punishment in private schools,[79] a beating by a step-father,[80] and parental neglect.[81] The state was determined to have obligations to prevent, protect, and punish in such situations. These cases could be seen as falling within a special category, as the Court has emphasized the special responsibilities of the state with regard to children in general, and the educational sphere in particular. In such cases, the role of the state has been examined with the benefit of hindsight. It had been argued before the Court that applicants need to show that the abuse would *definitely* have been prevented if the state had taken the specific steps which could have been reasonably expected of it at the time. In the Case of *E and ors v United Kingdom* the Court recalled this argument and rejected it:

> 99.   The Court recalls that the Government argued that notwithstanding any acknowledged shortcomings it has not been shown that matters would have turned out any differently, in other words, that fuller co-operation and communication between the authorities under the duty to protect the applicants and closer monitoring and supervision of the family would not necessarily have either uncovered the abuse or prevented it. The test under Article 3 however does not require it to be shown that 'but for' the failing or omission of the public authority ill-treatment would not have happened. A failure to take reasonably available measures which could have had a real prospect of altering the outcome or mitigating the harm is sufficient to engage the responsibility of the State.
>
> 100.   The Court is satisfied that the pattern of lack of investigation, communication and co-operation by the relevant authorities disclosed in this case must be regarded as having had a significant influence on the course of events and that proper and effective management of their responsibilities might, judged reasonably, have been expected to avoid, or at least, minimise the risk or the damage suffered.[82]

This standard would seem to apply to the special category of children and other vulnerable persons, such as those in the custody of the state's authorities. In sum, the rule is that in such cases, the authorities have to manage their responsibilities effectively and in such a way that one could expect that events could have been avoided, or the risk at least minimized. The Court has also developed the substantive obligations with respect to the definition of crimes and the burden of proof. Again, the Court is not seeking to determine how certain acts should be punished, but rather to develop the scope of the state's obligation to prevent and protect.

In *MC v Bulgaria* the Court found a violation of Article 3 due to the fact that the authorities dropped a rape investigation because of the perceived lack of evidence that the applicant was 'compelled', as understood in the national law definition of the crime of rape.[83] The national law imposed a two-step approach

---

[79] *Costello-Roberts v UK* (n 28 above).   [80] *A v UK* (n 33 above).
[81] *Z and ors v UK* (n 53 above).   [82] Judgment of 26 November 2002.
[83] Judgment of 4 March 2004.

which required showing that the person raped was first threatened with force and then violated. The Court referred to comparative European practice, General Recommendation 19 of the UN Committee on the Elimination of Discrimination against Women (discussed in Chapter 7), and cases from the International Criminal Tribunal for the former Yugoslavia, as well as a brief on comparative law from the non-governmental organization Interights. The Court's judgment reiterated its general approach that Article 3 'requires States to take measures designed to ensure that individuals within their jurisdiction are not subjected to ill-treatment, including ill-treatment administered by private individuals'.[84] Although the applicant was aged fourteen years and ten months at the time of the events, the Court looked at the issue in general terms of protection of everyone from rape, and focused on the sensibilities of young women with regard to proof of consent. In determining the scope of the state's positive obligations regarding the investigation and prosecution of rape, the Court was careful to allow states a certain margin of appreciation, but the general obligations concerning discrimination against women, and the need for the Convention to be effective, meant that the Court was prepared to go beyond a comparative approach which fixes on the lowest common denominator:

154. In respect of the means to ensure adequate protection against rape States undoubtedly enjoy a wide margin of appreciation. In particular, perceptions of a cultural nature, local circumstances and traditional approaches are to be taken into account.

155. The limits of the national authorities' margin of appreciation are nonetheless circumscribed by the Convention provisions. In interpreting them, since the Convention is first and foremost a system for the protection of human rights, the Court must have regard to the changing conditions within Contracting States and respond, for example, to any evolving convergence as to the standards to be achieved...

156. The Court observes that, historically, proof of physical force and physical resistance was required under domestic law and practice in rape cases in a number of jurisdictions. The last decades, however, have seen a clear and steady trend in Europe and some other parts of the world towards abandoning formalistic definitions and narrow interpretations of the law in this area...

157. Firstly, it appears that a requirement that the victim must resist physically is no longer present in the statutes of European countries.

158. In common-law jurisdictions, in Europe and elsewhere, any reference to physical force has been removed from legislation and/or case-law ...

163. In international criminal law, it has recently been recognised that force is not an element of rape and that taking advantage of coercive circumstances to proceed with sexual acts is also punishable. The ICTY has found that in international criminal law any sexual penetration without the victim's consent constitutes rape and that consent must be given voluntarily, as a result of the person's free will, assessed in the context of the surrounding circumstances... While the above definition was formulated in the particular context of rapes committed against the population in the conditions of an

[84] Judgment of 4 March 2004 at para. 149.

armed conflict, it also reflects a universal trend towards regarding lack of consent as the essential element of rape and sexual abuse.

164. As submitted by the intervener [Interights], the evolving understanding of the manner in which rape is experienced by the victim has shown that victims of sexual abuse—in particular, girls below the age of majority—often provide no physical resistance because of a variety of psychological factors or because they fear violence on the part of the perpetrator . . .

. . .

181. The Court considers that while in practice it may be sometimes difficult to prove lack of consent in the absence of 'direct' proof of rape, such as traces of violence or direct witnesses, the authorities must nevertheless explore all the facts and decide on the basis of an assessment of all the surrounding circumstances. The investigation and its conclusions must be centred on the issue of non-consent.

182. That was not done in the applicant's case. The Court finds that the failure of the authorities in the applicant's case to investigate sufficiently the surrounding circumstances was the result of them putting undue emphasis on 'direct' proof of rape. Their approach in the particular case was restrictive, practically elevating 'resistance' to the status of the defining element of the offence.

183. The authorities may also be criticised for having attached little weight to the particular vulnerability of young persons and the special psychological factors involved in cases concerning the rape of minors . . .

. . .

185. In sum, the Court, without expressing an opinion on the guilt of P. and A., finds that the effectiveness of the investigation of the applicant's case and, in particular, the approach taken by the investigator and the prosecutors in the case fell short of the requirements inherent in the States' positive obligations—viewed in the light of the relevant modern standards in comparative and international law—to establish and apply effectively a criminal-law system punishing all forms of rape and sexual abuse.

186. As regards the Government's argument that the national legal system provided for the possibility of a civil action for damages against the perpetrators, the Court notes that this assertion has not been substantiated. In any event, as stated above, effective protection against rape and sexual abuse requires measures of a criminal-law nature . . .

187. The Court thus finds that in the present case there has been a violation of the respondent State's positive obligations under both Articles 3 and 8 of the Convention.

This judgment is interesting as it indirectly elaborates the standard to which the non-state actor is to be held accountable. First, this type of behaviour constitutes inhuman or degrading treatment under the Convention. Second, the non-state actor has to be subject to the criminal law. Third, the non-state actor cannot rely on a defence of non-resistance. Fourth, by relying on judgments in the field of international individual criminal responsibility, it becomes even clearer that the Court is, in effect, establishing a human rights standard which states have to apply to prevent and punish such acts by individuals. Although rape, such as occurred in the case outlined above, is not justiciable before an International Criminal

Tribunal,[85] the European Court of Human Rights is insisting on a sort of human rights complementarity between national prosecutions and international accountability of the state. If the national criminal system is unable or unwilling to prosecute certain acts of violence, it becomes a matter for the European Court of Human Rights, which will hold the state responsible for failing to protect individuals from non-state actor violence by ineffectively securing their human rights.

9.1.4.2   Protection from Violent Non-State Actors Abroad

Another line of cases demonstrates the development of a duty to protect individuals from violence emanating from non-state actors abroad. This means that deportation or extradition to a situation where the individual faces a threat of violence from a non-state actor can be challenged as giving rise to a potential violation of the Convention. The Commission's decision in the *Altun v Federal Republic of Germany* application stated that:

> ... only the existence of an objective danger to the person to be extradited may be considered. The finding that such a danger exists does not necessarily involve the liability of the Government of the State requesting extradition. The Commission moreover has taken account, in cases of expulsion, of a danger not arising out of the authorities of the State receiving the person concerned ... [86]

In fact, in this application, the issue of non-state actor violence was not developed, as the threat essentially concerned the prospect of proper treatment by the receiving state in the event of an extradition. In the end, the applicant committed suicide before he could be extradited to Turkey, and the Commission struck the application from its list. The prospect of the Convention covering protection

---

[85] It is worth highlighting here how the importance of protecting human dignity has driven an interpretation of rape as a war crime or crime against humanity before international criminal tribunals. In one case before the International Criminal Tribunal for the former Yugoslavia, a claim was made that a wider definition of rape ran counter to the principle of *nullum crimen sine lege*. This was met in part with the response: 'Thus the notion that a greater stigma attaches to a conviction for forcible vaginal or anal penetration than to a conviction for forcible oral penetration is a product of questionable attitudes. Moreover any such concern is amply outweighed by the fundamental principle of protecting human dignity, a principle which favours broadening the definition of rape.' *Prosecutor v Furundžija* Case IT–95–17/1–T, Judgment of 10 December 1998, at para. 184. See also the discussion in 9.1.7 below, and more generally regarding human dignity Ch 11.

[86] At para. 5 of the decision on admissibility of 3 May 1983, appended to the Report of 7 March 1984. The Commission refers to two of its own earlier decisions where the point had been raised although not decided: *App. 7216/75 v FRG* 5 D & R 137, 20 May 1976, where the applicant alleged plots by Palestinian commandos in Lebanon; and *App. 8581/79 v UK* 29 D & R 48, 6 March 1980, concerning the extradition to Turkey of a political activist. In the latter case, however, the applicant had been a member of the MHP (Milliyetei Haraket Partisi), an extreme right-wing party which had been feuding with an extreme left-wing party, the THKO (Turk Halk Kurtukus Ordusu). The applicant's main involvement had been as an informer and, according to the Commission's decision: 'the applicant fears for his safety if he is returned to Turkey as he is not confident in view of the many sectarian murders which have already occurred that the Turkish authorities can adequately protect him'. Neither decision came to a conclusion on the applicability of Art. 3 to such threats of non-state actor violence.

from private violence in the context of deportation remained unresolved until the cases of *Ahmed v Austria* and *HLR v France* came before the Commission and Court.

In *Ahmed v Austria* the applicant complained that expulsion to Somalia would put him at risk of treatment which infringed his rights under Article 3. By the time of the application in 1994, Somalia was in a state of internal armed conflict, and the threat to the applicant could not be said to come from the authorities of a state. The fact that the threat came from a non-state actor (the faction of General Aideed) was said by the Government of Austria to take the case outside the scope of the Human Rights Convention. The Commission disagreed:

> The position of the Austrian authorities that there is no substantial risk for the applicant since the State authority had ceased to exist in Somalia cannot be accepted. It is sufficient that those who hold substantial power within the State, even though they are not the Government, threaten the life and security of the applicant. That is clearly the situation in the present case, given the powerful position of General Aideed.[87]

The Commission found unanimously that the applicant's expulsion would be in violation of Article 3. The Court emphasized the lack of any authority to protect the applicant in Somalia and upheld the Commission's approach, stating that the Commission's conclusion was not invalidated by the lack of any state authority in Somalia.[88]

In *HLR v France* the Strasbourg organs were not faced with a non-state actor operating as a substitute for a state authority, but rather with threats from a criminal organization involved in drug trafficking. The applicant, who was in transit through Roissy Airport (France) from Colombia to Italy, was arrested for being in possession of 580 grammes of cocaine. He cooperated with the investigators and supplied them with information concerning those who had recruited him in Colombia. This information enabled Interpol to identify a certain HB, who was subsequently arrested in Frankfurt, sentenced to prison, and under a year later, deported to Colombia. The applicant was also convicted and sentenced to prison. The terms of his sentence included an exclusion order from France, and he was threatened with deportation at the end of his prison sentence. He argued that his return to Colombia would put him at risk from the criminal organization on which he had informed. The French Government argued that such private acts were outside the scope of Article 3 of the Convention, and that, in any event, the risk to the applicant was as great in France as in Colombia. The majority of the Commission rejected these arguments, recalled its decision in *Altun* and its report in *Ahmed*,[89] and found by nineteen votes to ten that there would be a violation of Article 3 if the applicant were to be returned to Colombia. Several members of the

---

[87] Report of the Commission, 5 July 1995, at para. 68.
[88] Judgment of 27 November 1996, at para. 46.
[89] Report of 7 December 1995, at para. 41.

minority were not convinced that the scope of Article 3 should be extended in this way to cover criminal threats of inhuman or degrading treatment abroad.[90] The Court sided with the majority of the Commission regarding the extension of the Convention to threats by non-state actors abroad, but found that, in the circumstances of the case, the real risk of violence had not been proven:

> 39.   It is therefore necessary to examine whether the foreseeable consequences of H.L.R.'s deportation to Colombia are such as to bring Article 3 into play. In the present case the source of the risk on which the applicant relies is not the public authorities. According to the applicant, it consists in the threat of reprisals by drug traffickers, who may seek revenge because of certain statements that he made to the French police, coupled with the fact that the Colombian State is, he claims, incapable of protecting him from attacks by such persons.
>
> 40.   Owing to the absolute character of the right guaranteed, the Court does not rule out the possibility that Article 3 of the Convention may also apply where the danger emanates from persons or groups of persons who are not public officials. However, it must be shown that the risk is real and that the authorities of the receiving State are not able to obviate the risk by providing appropriate protection.
>
> 41.   Like the Commission, the Court can but note the general situation of violence existing in the country of destination. It considers, however, that this circumstance would not in itself entail, in the event of deportation, a violation of Article 3.
>
> 42.   The documents from various sources produced in support of the applicant's memorial provide insight into the tense atmosphere in Colombia, but do not contain any indication of the existence of a situation comparable to his own. Although drug traffickers sometimes take revenge on informers, there is no relevant evidence to show in H.L.R.'s case that the alleged risk is real. His aunt's letters cannot by themselves suffice to show that the threat is real. Moreover, there are no documents to support the claim that the applicant's personal situation would be worse than that of other Colombians, were he to be deported...
>
> 43.   The Court is aware, too, of the difficulties the Colombian authorities face in containing the violence. The applicant has not shown that they are incapable of affording him appropriate protection.
>
> 44.   In the light of these considerations, the Court finds that no substantial grounds have been established for believing that the applicant, if deported, would be exposed to a real risk of being subjected to inhuman or degrading treatment within the meaning of Article 3. It follows that there would be no violation of Article 3 if the order for the applicant's deportation were to be executed.

The Court therefore concluded by a majority of fifteen votes to six that there would be no violation in the event of a deportation. The minority felt that the majority judgment set too high a burden on the applicant to prove that he was subject to a real risk from the non-state actor concerned. They

---

[90] See the dissenting opinion of K. Herndl, joined by Messrs E. Busuttil, A. Weitzel, D. Sváby, G. Ress, A. Perenic, and C. Bîrsan, at para. 6: 'En l'absence de précédent valable, la simple possibilité qu'un requérant soit victime d'un crime de droit commun, par vengeance ou non, dans le pays d'accueil, son pays natal, ne peut pas justifier l'application de l'article 3.'

suggested that with regard to such threats, the Court needs to apply a more generous test:

> The real evidence showing that H.L.R.'s life would be at risk if he were deported is, admittedly, quite meagre. But that is only to be expected: killers seldom give advance warning before striking. In my view to demand more concrete evidence from an applicant who has been shown to be an 'informer' is to impose an unrealistic burden on him. For 'informers' to meet such a fate is not unknown in Colombia.[91]

A separate dissent by Judge Jambrek made the point that for him the issue is the risk to the victim, rather than an objective nexus with the receiving government. The projected failure of the receiving government is simply an issue which goes to the evaluation of the risk:

> For me, the danger or degree of risk run by the applicant, if deported to Colombia, of suffering treatment proscribed by Article 3 is the most important criterion. I agree that such a risk is more predictable when the State authorities are involved. However, in my view, a clear distinction cannot be made in abstracto between situations where the danger comes from the State, or where there is complicity on the part of the Government, or even where the State is non-existent and the applicant cannot be protected. Therefore, an assessment must be made in the light of the particular circumstances of each case.[92]

Even though HLR was unsuccessful on the facts, the Judgment represents an important step forward in understanding the scope of the Convention. Protection under the Convention is now extended to those who fear deportation or extradition to countries where they face threats from non-state actors. In another deportation application, a Chamber of the Court, referring to the *HLR* case, put the point as follows:

> The Court's case-law further indicates that the existence of this obligation is not dependent on whether the source of the risk of the treatment stems from factors which involve the responsibility, direct or indirect, of the authorities of the receiving country. Having regard to the absolute character of the right guaranteed, Article 3 may extend to situations where the danger emanates from persons or groups of persons who are not public officials.[93]

Although the issue of threats from non-state actors abroad has so far arisen before the Court mostly in the context of Articles 2 and 3, one can imagine complaints

---

[91] Dissenting opinion of Judge Pekkanen, joined by Judge Thór Vilhjálmsson, Judge Lopes Rocha, and Judge Lohmus, at para. 1.　　[92] Attached to the judgment, no paragraph numbers.
[93] App. 43844/98, *TI v UK* Decision of 7 March 2000, at 17. The case was declared inadmissible, as the German procedures (the applicant was about to be deported to Germany from where he feared deportation to Sri Lanka) provided sufficient protection from deportation even where the threat came from non-state agents. The Court was not determining conformity with international obligations under the Refugee Convention; it accepted that these may be narrower than the protection offered by the Convention: 'the fact that the German authorities exclude from consideration of asylum claims non-State agent sources of risk of ill-treatment and ill-treatment from individual officers prohibited by the laws of the country is not directly relevant. The Court's primary concern is whether there are effective procedural safeguards of any kind protecting the applicant from being removed from Germany to Sri Lanka'. At 20.

regarding deportation based on unchecked non-state actor interferences with the enjoyment of the right to manifest religion or enjoy private life.[94] After a review of decisions by the Strasbourg organs, the House of Lords recognized in its judgment in *R v Special Adjudicator, ex p Ullah* that the Convention's protection in the context of deportation and extradition could extend beyond Article 3. According to Lord Steyn's Opinion, the Convention could protect individuals from potential violations of Articles 2, 4, 5, 6, 7, 8, 9, 10, 11, and 14, although in such cases, 'a high threshold test will always have to be satisfied. It will be necessary to establish at least a real risk of a flagrant violation of the very essence of the right before [these] other articles could become engaged'.[95]

9.1.5   Article 4 Prohibition of Slavery and Forced Labour

Article 4 reads as follows:

(1) No one shall be held in slavery or servitude.

(2) No one shall be required to perform forced or compulsory labour.

(3) For the purpose of this article the term 'forced or compulsory labour' shall not include:
    (a) any work required to be done in the ordinary course of detention imposed according to the provisions of Article 5 of this Convention or during conditional release from such detention;
    (b) any service of a military character or, in case of conscientious objectors in countries where they are recognised, service exacted instead of compulsory military service;
    (c) any service exacted in case of an emergency or calamity threatening the life or well-being of the community;
    (d) any work or service which forms part of normal civic obligations.

This Article has obvious scope for application to the behaviour of non-state actors. Slavery is considered a violation of international law even when conducted by non-state actors, and enslavement can rise to the level of a crime against humanity for the individual perpetrator.[96] In the context of such criminal prosecutions, the International Criminal Tribunal for the former Yugoslavia has

---

[94] The extent to which an expelling state has an obligation to ensure that Convention rights can still be enjoyed abroad is unclear. In one decision, the Court seems to suggest that Sweden would not have to ensure the full guarantees of Art. 9 in the context of an expulsion to Iran of a Christian who feared future violations of his rights to religious freedom: 'As regards the applicant's right to freedom of religion, the Court observes that, in so far as any alleged consequence in Iran of the applicant's conversion to Christianity attains the level of treatment prohibited by Article 3 of the Convention, it is dealt with under that provision. The Court considers that the applicant's expulsion cannot separately engage the Swedish Government's responsibility under Article 9 of the Convention.' App. 64599/01, *Razaghi v Sweden* Decision of 11 March 2003, discussed in *R v Special Adjudicator, ex p Ullah* [2004] UKHL 26.

[95] *R v Special Adjudicator, ex p Ullah* [2004] UKHL 26, at para. 50. The issue of protection under human rights law from non-state actor threats abroad is likely to become entangled with the issue of protection under refugee law from non-state actor persecution; see Ch 8, at 8.6 above and *R v Secretary of State for the Home Department, ex p Bagdanavicius* [2005] UKHL 38.

[96] See Trial Chamber *Prosecutor v Kunarac and ors* Case IT–96–23 and IT–96–23/1, Judgment of the ICTY, 22 February 2001. The Trial Chamber judgment defined enslavement for these purposes

highlighted factors to be taken into account to determine whether or not there is such enslavement: 'control of someone's movement, control of physical environment, psychological control, measures taken to prevent or deter escape, force, threat of force or coercion, duration, assertion of exclusivity, subjection to cruel treatment and abuse, control of sexuality and forced labour'.[97]

The European Court of Human Rights has only very rarely dealt with Article 4 complaints. Many applications have been lodged concerning prison labour. In an early set of applications, concerning the fact that certain detainees in Germany were working for private companies contracted by the state-run prison, the Commission dismissed the applications by reference to a United Nations study which showed that, at the time of the drafting of the Convention, prison labour on behalf of private enterprise was quite common.[98]

With regard to rules developed by the professional association of lawyers in Belgium that demanded that lawyers provide their services for clients who cannot afford the normal fees, the Court has held that the state has a positive obligation to ensure that such non-state actors do not infringe an individual's rights under this provision. In the case of *Van Der Mussele v Belgium*, a young lawyer complained that the scheme which obliged him to represent individuals for reduced fees represented a violation of his rights under Article 4. The scheme was imposed by the *Ordre des avocats* and the Government claimed that it could not be held responsible for the acts of such an organization. The Judgment stated:

> 28.   Before the Commission and in their memorial to the Court, the Government submitted that there was no primary or subordinate legislation that obliged avocats to accept work entrusted to them by a Legal Advice and Defence Office: their duty to act for indigent persons was said to derive solely from professional rules freely adopted by the Ordres des avocats themselves. According to the Government, the Belgian State did not prescribe either how appointments were to be made or their effects; it was therefore not answerable for any infringements of the Convention's guarantees that might be occasioned by implementation of the professional rules.

The court was not convinced by the Government's argument and stated that:

> Under the Convention, the obligation to grant free legal assistance arises, in criminal matters, from Article 6 §3 (c); in civil matters, it sometimes constitutes one of the means

at para. 540: 'that the *actus reus* of the violation is the exercise of any or all of the powers attaching to the right of ownership over a person. The *mens rea* of the violation consists in the intentional exercise of such powers'.

[97] *Prosecutor v Kunarac and ors* Case IT–96–23 and IT–96–23/1–A, Judgment of the ICTY (Appeals Chamber), 12 June 2002, at para. 119.

[98] *Twenty-One Detained Persons v Federal Republic of Germany*, Apps 3134/67, 3172/67, 3188–3206/67, 27 *Collection* 97: 'whereas it appears from this study that in 1955 the systems of prison labour described as "lease", "contract", and "piece-price", each of which entails the presence of private enterprise interests, were still found in a number of states; whereas, within Europe, these systems appeared to provide employment for substantial proportions of prisoners, for example in Austria (21.4 per cent), Belgium (about 70 per cent), France (nearly 50 per cent of all prisoners assigned to work) and Sweden'. For a case which came before the Court concerning prison labour, see *Van Droogenbroeck v Belgium* Judgment of 27 May 1982, at paras 58–60.

of ensuring a fair trial as required by Article 6 §1 . . . This obligation is incumbent on each of the Contracting Parties. The Belgian State—and this was not contested by the Government—lays the obligation by law on the Ordres des avocats, thereby perpetuating a state of affairs of long standing; under Article 455, first paragraph, of the Judicial Code, the Councils of the Ordres are to make provision for the assistance of indigent persons by setting up Legal Advice and Defence Offices . . . As was pointed out by the applicant, the Councils have 'no discretion as regards the principle itself': legislation 'compels them to compel' members of the Bar to 'defend indigent persons'. Such a solution cannot relieve the Belgian State of the responsibilities it would have incurred under the Convention had it chosen to operate the system itself.[99]

It has been suggested that this approach mirrors the Court's approach in the *Costello-Roberts* case (discussed above), which focuses on an existing area of international responsibility and the impossibility of delegating this to a private entity.[100] In *Costello-Roberts* the issue was discipline in schools; here it was the provision of a fair trial. Harris, O'Boyle, and Warbrick suggest that there should be room for a broader view which looks beyond such a narrow realm and covers forced labour in general. So far, there have been few applications regarding the labour market more generally. Harris *et al* refer to a decision by the Commission concerning the rules for the transfer of professional footballers. The Commission's decision recalled the Court's judgment in the *Young, James and Webster* case and stated that 'it could be argued that the responsibility of the Netherlands Government is engaged to the extent that it is its duty to ensure that the rules, adopted, it is true, by a private association, do not run contrary to the provisions of the Convention, in particular where the Netherlands courts have jurisdiction to examine their application'.[101] This assertion brought the application within the scope of the Convention, but the Commission dismissed the complaint as being outside the scope of forced labour. The facts can be summarized as follows: the football player wanted to leave his club and had been accepted by another club. However, under the rules, the transfer fee demanded by the old club meant he was unable to take up his job with the new club. He complained that he was in effect being forced to work for the old club. The Commission recalled its jurisprudence that 'forced or compulsory labour' comprises basically two elements: first, the labour must be performed against the person's will, and second, the obligation to perform the services must be either unjust or oppressive, or the service itself constitutes an avoidable hardship.[102] With regard to the first element the

---

[99] Judgment of 27 October 1983, at para. 29. In the end, the Court held there was no violation of Art. 4.   [100] Harris, O'Boyle, and Warbrick (1995: 94).

[101] *X v The Netherlands* App. 9322/81, 32 D & R 180, at 182.

[102] Ibid, at 182–183, cf the Court's approach in *Van Der Mussele* (at para. 34): 'It remains to be ascertained whether there was "forced or compulsory" labour. The first of these adjectives brings to mind the idea of physical or mental constraint, a factor that was certainly absent in the present case. As regards the second adjective, it cannot refer just to any form of legal compulsion or obligation. For example, work to be carried out in pursuance of a freely negotiated contract cannot be regarded as falling within the scope of Article 4 on the sole ground that one of the parties has undertaken with the other to do that work and will be subject to sanctions if he does not honour his promise.'

Commission found that prior consent was a decisive factor and that the applicant 'freely chose to become a professional football player knowing that he would in entering the profession be affected by the rules governing the relationship between his future employers'.[103] The Commission did not consider the arrangement oppressive and noted that the fees paid by one club to another do not affect the player's contractual freedom. The fee did not, in fact, oblige the player legally to continue to play from a club he wished to leave, and, indeed, in this case, the player did not renew his contract with his old club.

The Commission did not embrace the idea of judging employment contracts against the guarantees of Article 4. A series of complaints alleged that Austria's labour law meant that termination of contracts in the context of bankruptcy meant that the applicants were obliged to work for less than full pay or lose their lump sum entitlement. In response, the Commission recalled its approach to compulsory or forced labour in its decision in the footballer's application and found that:

> ... the applicants entered freely into their contracts of employment. Moreover it appears that, according to S. 20 para. 4 of the Employees' Act, they were free to terminate them with one month's notice. Moreover, the applicants failed to show that the financial losses they would suffer from terminating their contracts of employment, would be such as to amount to a restriction of their contractual freedom. Therefore, it cannot be said that they had to perform their work against their will. In any event, there is no indication that the performance of their work can be considered as unjust or oppressive or as constituting avoidable hardship.[104]

Lastly, it should be noted that domestic staff, who work without proper pay or conditions, may be able to complain that their Article 4 rights have not been properly protected by the state. The Court found a violation of Article 4 in an application brought by a Toglese national who was 15 years old at the time of her arrival in France, and who worked as a 'maid without pay' until the *comité contre l'esclavage moderne* intervened, with the result that the couple for whom the applicant worked were prosecuted and ordered to pay compensation, including for the services rendered over three years. The applicant's complaint focused on the argument that the state failed to fulfil its positive obligations by having in place a penal law system which could effectively prevent, prosecute, and punish those non-state actors involved in such a form of trafficking and slavery.[105]

---

[103] Ibid, at 183.

[104] *Ilse Baumgartner and ors v Austria* App. 23085/93, Decision of 15 May 1996; and see the friendly settlement on the basis of Art. 6, report of 16 May 1996.

[105] See *Siliadin v France* Judgment of 26 July 2005, 'la Cour estime que, conformément aux normes et aux tendances contemporaines en la matière, il y a lieu de considérer que les obligations positives qui pèsent sur les Etats membres en vertu de l'article 4 de la Convention commandent la criminalisation et la répression effective de tout acte tendant à maintenir une personne dans ce genre de situation (voir m*utatis mutandis MC c* Bulgarie, préctié, §166).' The judgement appeared too late for a detailed consideration in the present book. Note the Court's interpretation of 'forced or compulsory labour' and the use of the concept of '*esclavage domestique*'. See Recommendation 1663 (2004) of the Parlimentary Assembly of the Council of Europe: 'Domestic slavery: servitude, au pairs and "mail-order brides".'

9.1.6   Article 6 and the Right to Fair Trial

Article 6 reads, in part, as follows: '(1) In the determination of his civil rights and obligations or of any criminal charge against him, everyone is entitled to a fair and public hearing within a reasonable time by an independent and impartial tribunal established by law.' This suggests that in complaints brought against non-state actors at the national level, there is an obligation on the state to ensure fair proceedings. To be clear, the Strasbourg Court has actually excluded certain public law disputes from the scope of this Article; public employment involving teachers, policemen, and clergymen does not necessarily give rise to 'civil rights'.[106]

The protection of Article 6(1) implies an existing substantive right in domestic law.[107] A dispute over a private right may be determined by a non-state actor such as a professional association. Where the dispute results in a determination of the civil rights (rather than a simple disciplinary sanction), Article 6 will be in play. It is not that the tribunal itself has to conform to Article 6, but there must be the possibility of an appeal from the original decision, and the procedure at appeal will then have to conform with the guarantees in Article 6. This was clearly stated by the Court in *Albert and Le Compte*:

> Nonetheless, in such circumstances the Convention calls for at least one of the following systems: either the jurisdictional organs themselves comply with the requirements of Article 6(1), or they do not comply but are subject to subsequent control by a judicial body that has full jurisdiction and does provide the guarantees of Article 6(1).[108]

This case concerned the right to practise medicine as determined by the *Ordre des médecins*. Not every decision concerning access to a profession will necessarily count as a 'dispute'. In a case concerning competence for admission as an accountant, the Court held that the procedure did not constitute a dispute (*contestation*) and stated: 'An assessment of this kind, evaluating knowledge and experience for carrying on a profession under a particular title, is akin to a school or university examination and is so far removed from the exercise of the normal judicial function that the safeguards in Article 6 cannot be taken as covering resultant disagreements.'[109]

---

[106] The Court's approach is to balance the public and private rights involved in, say, proceedings concerning a widow's supplementary pension under industrial accident insurance, and if the private rights predominate then Art. 6(1) is applicable. See *Deumeland v FRG* Judgment of 26 May 1986, and *Feldbrugge v The Netherlands* Judgment of 29 May 1986 (health insurance allowance—predominantly private rights). See also *Pellegrin v France* Judgment of 18 December 1999. For a careful examination of the drafting of this part of the Article, see P. van Dijk, 'The Interpretation of "Civil Rights and Obligations" by the European Court of Human Rights: One More Step to Take' in F. Matscher and H. Petzold (eds) *Protecting Human Rights: The European Dimension (Studies in Honour of Gérard J. Wiarda)* (Cologne: Carl Heymanns, 1988) 134–143.

[107] See, e.g. *Z and ors v UK*, discussed above, as well as the explanation provided by Lord Bingham in *Matthews v Ministry of Defence* [2003] UKHL 4, at para. 3, who suggests that the line separating the scope of substantive rights and procedural bars is not that bright.

[108] *Albert and Le Compte v Belgium* Judgment of 10 February 1983, at para. 29.

[109] *Van Marle and ors v The Netherlands* Judgment of 26 June 1986, at para. 36.

Article 6(2) guarantees that: 'Everyone charged with a criminal offence shall be presumed innocent until proved guilty according to law.' In a case concerning a criminal defamation suit, which had been pursued by a company against a journalist, the European Court of Human Rights found a violation of Article 6(2) due to the fact that the national court had awarded costs against the journalist, even though the case never went to trial.[110] National law may therefore have to protect everyone from criminal prosecutions brought by non-state actors that do not actually provide the proof of guilt.

Article 6 provides not only for these guarantees to an independent tribunal and the presumption of innocence, but has also been interpreted as requiring that states provide the means for individuals to respond properly in disputes concerning civil rights and obligations. When two campaigners from London Greenpeace were successfully sued by McDonald's, they complained that the lack of legal aid available to them meant that they had not been able to deal properly with the legal and factual points at trial. The freedom of expression aspect of this case is dealt with below. With regard to the absence of legal aid, the Court found that this lack of assistance had 'deprived them of the opportunity to present their case effectively before the court and contributed to an unacceptable inequality of arms with McDonald's'.[111]

9.1.7 Article 7 Non-Retroactivity of Criminal Law for Individual Offences

Article 7 reads as follows:

(1) No one shall be held guilty of any criminal offence on account of any act or omission which did not constitute a criminal offence under national or international law at the time when it was committed. Nor shall a heavier penalty be imposed than the one that was applicable at the time the criminal offence was committed.

(2) This article shall not prejudice the trial and punishment of any person for any act or omission which, at the time when it was committed, was criminal according to the general principles of law recognised by civilised nations.

In the case of *SW v United Kingdom* the European Court of Human Rights was faced with a claim that a man convicted of raping his wife was the victim of a violation of Article 7. He argued that, at the time of his trial, English common law did not recognize that a man could rape his wife. The English courts had indeed recognized a form of immunity for husbands based on the fictional consent to sexual intercourse which the wife was deemed to have given at the time of the marriage.[112] The European Court held that, in any system of law, there is an 'inevitable element of judicial interpretation'[113] and a 'need for elucidation of

---

[110] *Minelli v Switzerland* Judgment of 25 March 1983.
[111] *Steel and Morris v UK* Judgment of 15 February 2005, at para. 72.
[112] Judgment of 22 November 1995, at para. 22.   [113] Ibid, at para. 36.

doubtful points and for adaptation to changing circumstances'.[114] The development of the law does not violate Article 7 provided that such a development is 'consistent with the essence of the offence and could reasonably be foreseen'.[115] The interesting aspect of the judgment in the present context is the Court's reference, not only to the right of a state to elucidate and develop its criminal law rules, but also to the evolving nature of the rights of women: 'In particular, given the recognition of women's equality of status with men in marriage and outside it and of their autonomy over their own bodies, the adaptation of the ingredients of the offence of rape was reasonably foreseeable, with appropriate legal advice, to the applicant.'[116]

The point is developed by the Grand Chamber of the Court in the case concerning the East German border and the use of mines and automatic firing equipment. In response to the applicants' complaint, concerning their conviction by the German courts after reunification in breach of Article 7(1), the Court referred to the international obligations of the German Democratic Republic, with regard to human rights, and held that it could be assumed that the individuals realized that participation in such violations of international law would expose them to the possibility of prosecution:

> The State practice in issue was to a great extent the work of the applicants themselves, who, as political leaders, knew—or should have known—that it infringed both fundamental rights and human rights, since they could not have been ignorant of the legislation of their own country. Articles 8 and 19 §2 of the 1968 Constitution already provided, respectively: 'The generally recognised rules of international law intended to promote peace and peaceful cooperation between peoples are binding on the State and every citizen' and 'Respect for and protection of the dignity and liberty of the person are required of all State bodies, all forces in society and every citizen'... Furthermore, as early as 1968 the first chapter of the Special Part of the Criminal Code included an introduction that provided: 'The merciless punishment of crimes against... humanity and human rights... is an indispensable prerequisite for stable peace in the world, for the restoration of faith in fundamental human rights and the dignity and worth of human beings, and for the preservation of the rights of all'... Similarly,... the applicants could not have been ignorant of the international obligations entered into by the GDR or of the repeated international criticism of its border-policing regime.[117]

The Grand Chamber did not found its judgment on international criminal law, but rather, the violations of human rights law by the state and the offences this generated under national law. The Court left open whether the individual

---

[114] Judgment of 22 November 1995, at para. 36.   [115] Ibid, at para. 36.
[116] Ibid, at para. 40.
[117] *Streletz, Kessler and Krenz v Germany* Judgment of 22 March 2001, para. 103. Discussed by P. Sardaro, 'The right to reparation for gross and systematic violations from the perspective of general international law', *Expert Seminar on Reparation for Victims of Gross and Systematic Human Rights Violations in the Context of Political Transitions* (Antwerp: University of Antwerp, 10 March 2002) 15–24.

offences might themselves have been violations of international law, and thus covered by Article 7(2).[118]

9.1.8   Article 8 Right to Respect for Private and Family Life

Article 8 reads as follows:

(1) Everyone has the right to respect for his private and family life, his home and his correspondence.

(2) There shall be no interference by a public authority with the exercise of this right except such as is in accordance with the law and is necessary in a democratic society in the interests of national security, public safety or the economic well-being of the country, for the prevention of disorder or crime, for the protection of health or morals, or for the protection of the rights and freedoms of others.

9.1.8.1   *Protection from Violence to the Person and the Home*

The facts of *X and Y v The Netherlands* were dramatic.[119] The Court's judgment opens with the following details:

During the night of 14 to 15 December 1977, Miss Y was woken up by a certain Mr. B, the son-in-law of the directress [of a privately-run home for mentally handicapped children]; he lived with his wife on the premises of the institution although he was not employed there. Mr. B forced the girl to follow him to his room, to undress and to have sexual intercourse with him.

This incident, which occurred on the day after Miss Y's sixteenth birthday, had traumatic consequences for her, causing her major mental disturbance.[120]

There existed a gap in Dutch law, so that an effective criminal prosecution could not be brought by the father of the girl (Mr X), and Miss Y (the victim of the assault) could not file a complaint which could lead to a criminal prosecution. Civil remedies were available, but it was claimed that the procedure was lengthy, traumatic for the victim, and not sufficiently preventive to constitute adequate protection.

The European Court of Human Rights recalled that 'there may be positive obligations inherent in an effective respect for private or family life', and it then went on to state: 'These obligations may involve the adoption of measures designed to secure respect for private life *even in the sphere of the relations of individuals between themselves.*'[121]

This approach was followed in *MC v Bulgaria* (discussed above) and the Court in this later case referred to the state's positive obligations in the following terms:

Positive obligations on the State are inherent, in the right to effective respect for private life under Article 8; these obligations may involve the adoption of measures even in the

---

[118] Ibid, at paras 106 and 108.   [119] Judgment of 27 February 1985.
[120] Ibid, at para. 8   [121] Ibid, at para. 23 (emphasis added).

sphere of the relations of individuals between themselves. While the choice of the means to secure compliance with Article 8 in the sphere of protection against acts of individuals is in principle within the State's margin of appreciation, effective deterrence against grave acts such as rape, where fundamental values and essential aspects of private life are at stake, requires efficient criminal-law provisions. Children and other vulnerable individuals, in particular, are entitled to effective protection.[122]

Other types of private violence have also been considered to fall within the scope of Article 8. In the *Costello-Roberts* case, concerning corporal punishment in private schools, the Court held that the case fell to be considered primarily under Article 3, and that the punishment had not reached sufficient severity to bring it within that Article. But with regard to Article 8, the Court declared that it:

> ... does not exclude the possibility that there might be circumstances in which Article 8 could be regarded as affording in relation to disciplinary measures a protection which goes beyond that given by Article 3. Having regard, however, to the purpose and aim of the Convention taken as a whole, and bearing in mind that the sending of a child to school necessarily involves some degree of interference with his or her private life, the Court considers that the treatment complained of by the applicant did not entail adverse effects for his physical or moral integrity sufficient to bring it within the scope of the prohibition contained in Article 8. While not wishing to be taken to approve in any way the retention of corporal punishment as part of the disciplinary regime of a school, the Court therefore concludes that in the circumstances of this case there has also been no violation of that Article 8.[123]

The attacks on the Osman's house were considered by the Court to be within the scope of Article 8, yet on the facts, the Court decided that the authorities had done everything that could reasonably have been expected of them.[124] Similarly, a complaint that the law did not properly protect an individual from someone who was stalking her was held by the Commission to come within the scope of the positive obligations of the state under Article 8.[125] In the event, the Commission found that the applicant had not exhausted her domestic remedies; but the implication has been drawn by Wright that 'there is a positive obligation under Article 8 of the Convention to protect a person against harassment by a non-state actor in their home'.[126]

---

[122] Judgment of 4 December 2003, at para. 150.

[123] Judgment of 25 March 1993, at para. 36

[124] *Osman v UK* Judgment of 28 October 1998, at para. 128.

[125] 'On the facts of this case, the alleged harassment of the applicant by Mr. B. is of a level which could arguably constitute an interference with the applicant's right to respect for her private life and the enjoyment of her home. The Commission notes the persistent and distressing nature of the alleged conduct of Mr. B. and the consequent effect which it has had on the applicant and the way in which she leads her life. In these circumstances, the Commission finds that the responsibility of the State is engaged and that it is under a positive obligation to secure the applicant's rights by providing adequate protection against this type of deliberate persecution.' App. 20357/92, *Marina Whiteside v UK*, 7 March 1994.

[126] Wright (2001: 117), who goes on to suggest that the UK's Protection from Harassment Act 1997 'would arguably fulfil that obligation rather than the common law'.

9.1.8.2 Protection from Pollution

The approach of the European Court of Human Rights in the early case of *Powell and Rayner* is instructive as to how this Court deals with more difficult questions.[127] In this case, the complaints under Article 8 concerned noise from Heathrow Airport. The UK Government attempted to rely on the private nature of the ownership of the aircraft. According to the Judgment, the Government submitted that:

> ... the facts disclosed no 'interference by a public authority' with the applicants' right under Article 8, Heathrow Airport and the aircraft using it not being and never having been owned, controlled or operated by the Government or any agency of the Government. It was, [the Government] contended, not the negative but the positive obligations of the State under Article 8 which were in reality in issue; and there was no arguable ground for establishing any failure on the part of the Government to secure the right of either applicant to respect for his private life and his home.[128]

The Court avoided developing separate approaches to the right depending on whether one is dealing with direct interference by the state, or whether the issue is the positive obligations of the state to protect people from interferences by others.[129] The Court determined that 'the existence of large international airports, even in densely populated urban areas, and the increasing use of jet aircraft have without question become necessary in the interests of a country's economic well-being',[130] and found that the Government had achieved a fair balance of interests as required under Article 8.[131]

Incidents of pollution by non-state actors came before the Court in two further cases concerning Spain and Italy. In *López Ostra v Spain* the local authorities had failed to regulate the operation of a tannery waste-treatment plant, resulting in interference with respect to the applicants' home, private, and family life.[132] The Spanish courts accepted that the applicant's quality of life had been impaired but did not accept that there was an infringement of fundamental rights. The European Court of Human Rights found that the case came within the scope of Article 8 and noted that: 'Naturally, severe environmental pollution may affect individuals' well-being and prevent them from enjoying their homes in such a way as to affect their private and family life adversely, without, however, seriously endangering their health.'[133] With regard to the issue of state responsibility, the Court acknowledged that the state was not the polluter: 'Admittedly, the Spanish authorities, and in particular the Lorca municipality, were theoretically not directly responsible for the emissions in question. However, as the Commission pointed out, the town allowed the plant to be built on its land and the State subsidised the plant's construction.'[134] But the Court went on to recall its position

---

[127] Judgment of 21 February 1990.   [128] Ibid, at para. 39.   [129] Ibid, at para. 41.
[130] Ibid, at para. 42.   [131] Ibid, at para. 45.
[132] *López Ostra v Spain* Judgment of 9 December 1994.   [133] Ibid, at para. 51.
[134] Ibid, at para. 52.

in *X and Y v The Netherlands* that the state has to take the necessary measures to protect everyone's private life,[135] and did not overly focus on the state nexus with the waste plant. In the end, the Court found that Spain had not struck a fair balance between the town's economic well-being and Mrs Lopes Ostra's effective enjoyment of her right to respect for her home and her private and family life.[136]

In the *Guerra* case, Italy was held to have violated the Convention where it failed to provide effective protection for the applicants with regard to toxic substances released from a factory. The failure to provide the relevant information about pollution from the plant to the applicants resulted in a violation of their rights to privacy.[137]

Pollution by non-state actors was one of the first cases to be heard under the new arrangements for a full-time Court. The application in *Hatton and ors v United Kingdom* was deposited on the first day of the new regime. The final judgment of the Grand Chamber gives an indication of how far the Court is prepared to go in holding states accountable for protecting individuals from pollution by non-state actors. It also provides some sense of the measures which states need to take to ensure that victims of pollution have an effective remedy even where the pollution stems from a non-state actor.[138] At first instance, a Chamber of the Court (in a majority finding) distinguished the case before it from *Powell and Rayner* by pointing to the fact that the present applications to the Court related to an increase in night noise since the lifting of certain restrictions on night flights. The Chamber recalled the previous jurisprudence concerning the balancing role to be played by the Court even in the case of positive obligations. It then developed a proportionality test with regard to the prevention of pollution; and found that the Government had not sought to minimize the interference with private life. It underlined 'that in striking the required balance, States must have regard to the whole range of material considerations. Further, in the particularly sensitive field of environmental protection, mere reference to the economic well-being of the country is not sufficient to outweigh the rights of others'.[139] The judgment imposed a burden on states to find alternatives, as well as conducting full investigations into how to achieve the correct balance with regard to a particular project.[140]

---

[135] *López Ostra v Spain* Judgment of 9 December 1994, at para 55.

[136] Ibid, at para. 58.

[137] *Guerra v Italy* Judgment of 19 February 1998, at para. 60. The Court rejected the proposal that Art. 10 created a positive obligation in this context (at para. 54). It has been noted that the Court did not in this case rely on the margin of appreciation doctrine (Spielmann 1998: 148); compare the *Hatton* case discussed below.

[138] Judgment of 2 October 2001 (Chamber), Judgment of 8 July 2003 (Grand Chamber). See also *Baggs v UK*, the report of the Commission, 8 July 1987, this last case ended in a 'friendly settlement' and it is worth noting that Heathrow Airport was actually a nationalized body at the start of the proceedings and privatized by the time of the 'friendly settlement'.

[139] Chamber Judgment of 2 October 2001, at para. 97.

[140] Ibid. 'It considers that States are required to minimise, as far as possible, the interference with these rights, by trying to find alternative solutions and by generally seeking to achieve their aims in

Under the arrangements which had just come into force in connection with Protocol 11, it was possible for the Government to ask for the case to be referred to the Grand Chamber. The argument was that this judgment represented a departure from previous case-law and so should exceptionally be heard by a Grand Chamber. This request was granted, and a Grand Chamber eventually delivered a judgment which found there had been no violation of Article 8; however, the Grand Chamber did find that the applicants had been denied a remedy which would allow them to raise the Article 8 issues at the national level, and so the Grand Chamber found a violation of Article 13.

The Judgment has reiterated the approach of the Court to the positive obligations of the state concerning pollution. The expectations under the Convention now have the stamp of the Grand Chamber. First, the Judgment explains how, in the context of pollution by non-state actors, the state may be held responsible for a violation of the right to respect for private life under the Convention either through the implementation of its actual regulation, or through its failure to regulate. Second, with regard to the role of the Court in determining whether the balance has been correctly determined, the Grand Chamber eventually stepped back from an attempt to engage in complex policy decisions, and found that the state needed to be given a fairly wide margin of appreciation in this context:[141]

> 119.   It is clear that in the present case the noise disturbances complained of were not caused by the State or by State organs, but that they emanated from the activities of private operators. It may be argued that the changes brought about by the 1993 Scheme are to be seen as a direct interference by the State with the Article 8 rights of the persons concerned. On the other hand, the State's responsibility in environmental cases may also arise from a failure to regulate private industry in a manner securing proper respect for the rights enshrined in Article 8 of the Convention. As noted above (paragraph 98), broadly similar principles apply whether a case is analysed in terms of a positive duty on the State or in terms of an interference by a public authority with Article 8 rights to be justified in accordance with paragraph 2 of this provision. The Court is not therefore required to decide whether the present case falls into the one category or the other. The question is whether, in the implementation of the 1993 policy on night flights at Heathrow airport, a fair balance was struck between the competing interests of the individuals affected by the night noise and the community as a whole.
>
> 120.   The Court notes at the outset that in previous cases in which environmental questions gave rise to violations of the Convention, the violation was predicated on a

the least onerous way as regards human rights. In order to do that, a proper and complete investigation and study with the aim of finding the best possible solution which will, in reality, strike the right balance should precede the relevant project.'

[141] For an analysis of the way the Court grants a 'margin of appreciation' to states in such circumstances, see R. St J. Macdonald, 'The Margin of Appreciation in the Jurisprudence of the European Court of Human Rights' in *Collected Courses in European Law*, vol. I, book 2 (Dordrecht: Martinus Nijhoff, 1990) 95–161; see also H. C. Yourow, *The Margin of Appreciation Doctrine in the Dynamics of the European Court of Human Rights Jurisprudence* (The Hague: Martinus Nijhoff, 1996); Y. Arai-Takahashi, *The margin of appreciation doctrine and the principle of proportionality in the jurisprudence of the ECHR* (Antwerp: Intersentia, 2002).

failure by the national authorities to comply with some aspect of the domestic regime. Thus, in *López Ostra* the waste-treatment plant at issue was illegal in that it operated without the necessary licence, and it was eventually closed down (*López Ostra* judgment, pp. 46, 47, §§ 16–22). In *Guerra*, too, the violation was founded on an irregular position at the domestic level, as the applicants had been unable to obtain information that the State was under a statutory obligation to provide (*Guerra* judgment p. 219, §§ 25–27). This element of domestic irregularity is wholly absent in the present case . . .

. . .

125.   Whether in the implementation of that regime the right balance has been struck in substance between the Article 8 rights affected by the regime and other conflicting community interests depends on the relative weight given to each of them. The Court accepts that in this context the authorities were entitled, having regard to the general nature of the measures taken, to rely on statistical data based on average perception of noise disturbance. It notes the conclusion of the 1993 Consultation Paper that due to their small number sleep disturbances caused by aircraft noise could be treated as negligible in comparison to overall normal disturbance rates (cf. paragraph 40 above). However, this does not mean that the concerns of the people affected were totally disregarded. The very purpose of maintaining a scheme of night flight restrictions was to keep noise disturbance at an acceptable level for the local population living in the area near the airport. Moreover, there was a realisation that in view of changing conditions (increase of air transport, technological advances in noise prevention, development of social attitudes, etc.) the relevant measures had to be kept under constant review.

126.   As to the economic interests which conflict with the desirability of limiting or halting night flights in pursuance of the above aims, the Court considers it reasonable to assume that those flights contribute at least to a certain extent to the general economy. The Government have produced to the Court reports on the results of a series of inquiries on the economic value of night flights, carried out both before and after the 1993 Scheme. Even though there are no specific indications about the economic cost of eliminating specific night flights, it is possible to infer from those studies that there is a link between flight connections in general and night flights. In particular, the Government claim that some flights from far-east destinations to London could arrive only by departing very late in the night, giving rise to serious passenger discomfort and a consequent loss of competitiveness. One can readily accept that there is an economic interest in maintaining a full service to London from distant airports, and it is difficult, if not impossible, to draw a clear line between the interests of the aviation industry and the economic interests of the country as a whole. However, airlines are not permitted to operate at will, as substantial limitations are put on their freedom to operate, including the night restrictions which apply at Heathrow. The Court would note here that the 1993 Scheme which was eventually put in place was stricter than that envisaged in the 1993 Consultation Paper, as even the quietest aircraft were included in the quota count system. The Government have in addition resisted calls for a shorter night quota period, or for the lifting of night restrictions . . .

. . .

128.   On the procedural aspect of the case, the Court notes that a governmental decision-making process concerning complex issues of environmental and economic

policy such as in the present case must necessarily involve appropriate investigations and studies in order to allow them to strike a fair balance between the various conflicting interests at stake. However, this does not mean that decisions can only be taken if comprehensive and measurable data are available in relation to each and every aspect of the matter to be decided. In this respect it is relevant that the Government have consistently monitored the situation, and that the 1993 Scheme was the latest in a series of restrictions on night flights which stretched back to 1962. The position concerning research into sleep disturbance and night flights is far from static, and it was the Government's policy to announce restrictions on night flights for a maximum of five years at a time, each new scheme taking into account the research and other developments of the previous period. The 1993 Scheme thus had been preceded by a series of investigations and studies carried out over a long period of time. The particular new measures introduced by that scheme were announced to the public by way of a Consultation Paper which referred to the results of a study carried out for the Department of Transport, and which included a study of aircraft noise and sleep disturbance. It stated that the quota was to be set so as not to allow a worsening of noise at night, and ideally to improve the situation. This paper was published in January 1993 and sent to bodies representing the aviation industry and people living near airports. The applicants and persons in a similar situation thus had access to the Consultation Paper, and it would have been open to them to make any representations they felt appropriate. Had any representations not been taken into account, they could have challenged subsequent decisions, or the scheme itself, in the courts. Moreover, the applicants are, or have been, members of HACAN [Heathrow Association for the Control of Aircraft Noise], and were thus particularly well-placed to make representations.

129.   In these circumstances the Court does not find that, in substance, the authorities overstepped their margin of appreciation by failing to strike a fair balance between the right of the individuals affected by those regulations to respect for their private life and home, and the conflicting interests of others and of the community as a whole, nor does it find that there have been fundamental procedural flaws in the preparation of the 1993 regulations on limitations for night flights.

With regard to Article 13, the Grand Chamber felt that the existing possibilities for judicial review did not allow the applicants to challenge the scheme as an arguable infringement on their right to privacy. The Judgment also notes that the Government's scheme meant that there was no possibility of bringing a claim against the non-state actors for nuisance or trespass over the lawful night flights.[142] Again, the Court seems to prefer to demand that procedural reforms allow for proper ventilation of the issues at the national level, rather than inviting the possibility of having to make delicate determinations itself regarding the competing interests of private individuals, commercial non-state actors, and the general public. The question of how to ensure that individuals are protected from other individuals is left ambiguous. It is clear that before national authorities draw up regulations concerning pollution, there will need to be meaningful consultation with those affected. One could also infer from this judgment that states have

---

[142] Grand Chamber Judgment of 8 July 2003, at para. 139.

to ensure that there are 'horizontal' remedies at the national level that allow for tort claims against the direct source of the pollution. The Court will be loath to suggest exactly what form of national remedy has to be put in place in this context. The issue is, however, developed further in the context of claims of invasion of privacy by the press.

9.1.8.3   Invasions of Privacy by Photographers and the Media

In the wake of the death of Diana, Princess of Wales, there was considerable concern about the pursuit of certain figures by photographers, known in this context as *paparazzi*. The Council of Europe's Parliamentary Assembly convened special hearings and adopted a resolution which included the following paragraphs:

> 6.   The Assembly is aware that personal privacy is often invaded, even in countries with specific legislation to protect it, as people's private lives have become a highly lucrative commodity for certain sectors of the media. The victims are essentially public figures, since details of their private lives serve as a stimulus to sales. At the same time, public figures must recognise that the special position they occupy in society—in many cases by choice—automatically entails increased pressure on their privacy.
>
> 7.   Public figures are persons holding public office and/or using public resources and, more broadly speaking, all those who play a role in public life, whether in politics, the economy, the arts, the social sphere, sport or in any other domain.
>
> 8.   It is often in the name of a one-sided interpretation of the right to freedom of expression, which is guaranteed in Article 10 of the European Convention on Human Rights, that the media invade people's privacy, claiming that their readers are entitled to know everything about public figures.
>
> 9.   Certain facts relating to the private lives of public figures, particularly politicians, may indeed be of interest to citizens, and it may therefore be legitimate for readers, who are also voters, to be informed of those facts.
>
> 10.   It is therefore necessary to find a way of balancing the exercise of two fundamental rights, both of which are guaranteed by the European Convention on Human Rights: the right to respect for one's private life and the right to freedom of expression.
>
> 11.   The Assembly reaffirms the importance of every person's right to privacy, and of the right to freedom of expression, as fundamental to a democratic society. These rights are neither absolute nor in any hierarchical order, since they are of equal value.
>
> 12.   However, the Assembly points out that the right to privacy afforded by Article 8 of the European Convention on Human Rights should not only protect an individual against interference by public authorities, but also against interference by private persons or institutions, including the mass media.
>
> 13.   The Assembly believes that, since all member states have now ratified the European Convention on Human Rights, and since many systems of national legislation comprise provisions guaranteeing this protection, there is no need to propose that a new convention guaranteeing the right to privacy should be adopted.
>
> 14.   The Assembly calls upon the governments of the member states to pass legislation, if no such legislation yet exists, guaranteeing the right to privacy containing the

following guidelines, or if such legislation already exists, to supplement it with these guidelines:

(i) the possibility of taking an action under civil law should be guaranteed, to enable a victim to claim possible damages for invasion of privacy;

(ii) editors and journalists should be rendered liable for invasions of privacy by their publications, as they are for libel;

(iii) when editors have published information that proves to be false, they should be required to publish equally prominent corrections at the request of those concerned;

(iv) economic penalties should be envisaged for publishing groups which systematically invade people's privacy;

(v) following or chasing persons to photograph, film or record them, in such a manner that they are prevented from enjoying the normal peace and quiet they expect in their private lives or even such that they are caused actual physical harm, should be prohibited;

(vi) a civil action (private lawsuit) by the victim should be allowed against a photographer or a person directly involved, where paparazzi have trespassed or used 'visual or auditory enhancement devices' to capture recordings that they otherwise could not have captured without trespassing;

(vii) provision should be made for anyone who knows that information or images relating to his or her private life are about to be disseminated to initiate emergency judicial proceedings, such as summary applications for an interim order or an injunction postponing the dissemination of the information, subject to an assessment by the court as to the merits of the claim of an invasion of privacy;

(viii) the media should be encouraged to create their own guidelines for publication and to set up an institute with which an individual can lodge complaints of invasion of privacy and demand that a rectification be published.[143]

The Resolution is cited here *in extensu* for two reasons: first, the Assembly clearly considers that Article 8 already includes extensive protection from invasions of privacy by non-state actors and, in this sense, calls on states to ensure that there is a civil remedy to enable people to protect their privacy against such invasions (paragraph 14(i)). Second, the Resolution was cited in its entirety and relied on by the judges of the European Court of Human Rights in a key judgment concerning the scope of protection from photographers and publishers.

In the case of *von Hannover v Germany*, Princess Caroline of Monaco complained to the European Court of Human Rights about the failure of the German courts to protect her private life with regard to certain photographs which appeared in German publications.[144] These photographs showed her; respectively, with the actor Vincent Lindon in a restaurant, tripping over at a swimming pool in Monte Carlo, on a skiing holiday in Austria, playing tennis with Prince

---

[143] Resolution on the Protection of Privacy, 1196 (1998) 26 June 1998.

[144] Judgment of 24 June 2004, a number of different photographs are discussed in the judgment, the key photographs are detailed in para. 49.

Ernst August von Hannover (before they were married), and out shopping on her own.

After lengthy legal proceedings in Germany, which included a 'landmark' decision of the Constitutional Court, the case eventually came before the European Court of Human Rights. The Strasbourg Court, of course, could not deal with the publisher's behaviour as such, but only with the complaint concerning 'the lack of adequate State protection of [the applicant's] private life and her image'.[145] Nevertheless, it is worth noting here that the Court allowed for written interventions from one of the magazines concerned; Hubert Burda Media, as well as from the Association of German Magazine Publishers.

The Court found that there was no doubt that the publication of the photographs by the German magazines fell within the scope of the protection of the Princess' private life. In this respect the approach differed from that of the German courts, which had had focused on protection of the free development of the personality under the German Basic Law (section 2(1)), emphasizing:

> ... the general right to protection of personality rights, of allowing the individual a sphere, including outside the home, in which he does not feel himself to be the subject of permanent public attention—and relieves him of the obligation of behaving accordingly—and in which he can relax and enjoy some peace and quiet. This criterion does not excessively restrict press freedom because it does not impose a blanket ban on pictures of the daily or private life of figures of contemporary society, but allows them to be shown where they have appeared in public. In the event of an overriding public interest in being informed, the freedom of the press can even, in accordance with that case-law authority, be given priority over the protection of the private sphere...[146]

The European Court reiterated its jurisprudence that Article 8 involves positive obligations for states that 'may involve the adoption of measures designed to secure respect for private life even in the sphere of relations of individuals between themselves'.[147] The Court recalled that both negative and positive obligations under Article 8 demand a fair balance between the competing interests of the individual and the community as a whole. And the Court recalled the existence of a margin of appreciation for the state in this context. The Court then turned to the competing interests of the publishers and the general public to freedom of expression and information under Article 10. Here again, the European Court differed in its approach from the German courts. The Constitutional Court had emphasized the role of entertainment in freedom of expression and information and appears to have elevated entertaining material to the level of constitutionally protected speech:

> The formation of opinions and entertainment are not opposites. Entertainment also plays a role in the formation of opinions. It can sometimes even stimulate or influence

---

[145] Judgment of 24 June 2004, at para. 56: 'In the present case the applicant did not complain of an action by the State, but rather of the lack of adequate State protection of her private life and her image.'
[146] As quoted at para. 26 of the European Court of Human Rights Judgment.
[147] Ibid, at para. 57.

the formation of opinions more than purely factual information. Moreover, there is a growing tendency in the media to do away with the distinction between information and entertainment both as regards press coverage generally and individual contributions, and to disseminate information in the form of entertainment or mix it with entertainment ('infotainment'). Consequently, many readers obtain information they consider to be important or interesting from entertaining coverage...

Nor can mere entertainment be denied any role in the formation of opinions. That would amount to unilaterally presuming that entertainment merely satisfies a desire for amusement, relaxation, escapism or diversion. Entertainment can also convey images of reality and propose subjects for debate that spark a process of discussion and assimilation relating to philosophies of life, values and behaviour models. In that respect it fulfils important social functions... When measured against the aim of protecting press freedom, entertainment in the press is neither negligible nor entirely worthless and therefore falls within the scope of application of fundamental rights...[148]

With regard to information about celebrities, the German Constitutional Court explained why such information needs a protected status:

The same is true of information about people. Personalization is an important journalistic means of attracting attention. Very often it is this which first arouses interest in a problem and stimulates a desire for factual information. Similarly, interest in a particular event or situation is usually stimulated by personalised accounts. Additionally, celebrities embody certain moral values and lifestyles. Many people base their choice of lifestyle on their example. They become points of crystallisation for adoption or rejection and act as examples or counter-examples. This is what explains the public interest in the various ups and downs occurring in their lives.[149]

By contrast, the European Court of Human Rights started from the perspective of the applicant, seeing the photographs in the larger context of continual harassment, and placing very little weight on the value of such information:

Although freedom of expression also extends to the publication of photos, this is an area in which the protection of the rights and reputation of others takes on particular importance. The present case does not concern the dissemination of 'ideas', but of images containing very personal or even intimate 'information' about an individual. Furthermore, photos appearing in the tabloid press are often taken in a climate of continual harassment which induces in the person concerned a very strong sense of intrusion into their private life or even of persecution.[150]

The European Court contrasted the photographs in this case with 'information', which it had valued in other cases, and found that preventing the publication constituted a violation of Article 10. These cases concerned: photographs of an accused on trial for a mail bombing campaign,[151] a photograph of a politician accused of unlawful earnings,[152] and a book about President Miterrand's illness

---

[148] Ibid, reproduced at para. 25.   [149] Ibid.   [150] Ibid, at para. 59.
[151] *News Verlags GmbH & Co KG v Austria* Judgment of 11 January 2000.
[152] *Krone Verlag GmbH & Co KG v Austria* Judgment of 26 February 2002.

written by his doctor.[153] For the European Court, the photographs in Princess Caroline's case showed her engaged in activities of a 'purely private nature'.[154] The European Court considered:

> . . . that a fundamental distinction needs to be made between reporting facts—even controversial ones—capable of contributing to a debate in a democratic society relating to politicians in the exercise of their functions, for example, and reporting details of the private life of an individual who, moreover, as in this case, does not exercise official functions. While in the former case the press exercises its vital role of 'watchdog' in a democracy by contributing to 'impart[ing] information and ideas on matters of public interest['] (*Observer and Guardian*, cited above, ibid.) it does not do so in the latter case . . .[155]

The Court concluded that:

> . . . the public does not have a legitimate interest in knowing where the applicant is and how she behaves generally in her private life even if she appears in places that cannot always be described as secluded and despite the fact that she is well known to the public. Even if such a public interest exists, as does a commercial interest of the magazines in publishing these photos and these articles, in the instant case those interests must, in the Court's view, yield to the applicant's right to the effective protection of her private life.[156]

This case has been examined in detail as, although it is formally about the positive obligations of the state, the Court is in fact delimiting the human rights obligations of publishers and photographers under the Convention (and the judgment eventually had a considerable impact on the attitude of domestic judges to developing the law of privacy applicable against the media).[157] The European Court is even explicit in this regard when it recalls that 'the press plays an essential role in a democratic society', and then goes on to state 'it must not overstep certain bounds, in particular in respect of the reputation and rights of others, its duty is nevertheless to impart—*in a manner consistent with its obligations and responsibilities*—information and ideas on all matters of public interest'.[158] The Court is determining the scope of these obligations under the Convention, both for the purposes of Article 8 claims, and for claims by the press regarding Article 10. Of course, the Court cannot hold the publishers directly accountable, but the effect of the judgment is to delimit the scope of these obligations and eventually generate a common European understanding of the obligations of the press under the Convention.[159]

---

[153] *Plon (Société) v France* Judgment of 18 May 2004.

[154] *Von Hannover v Germany* Judgment of 24 June 2004, at para. 61.　　　[155] Ibid, at para. 63.

[156] Ibid, at para. 77.

[157] See Ch 10, at 10.3.3.1 below. and the discussion in *Michael Douglas, Catherine Zeta-Jones, Northern & Shell plc v Hello Ltd, Hola SA, Eduardo Sanchez Junco* [2005] EWCA Civ 595, at para. 150.　　　[158] Ibid, at para. 58 (emphasis added).

[159] Sudre (2000: 1376) has suggested more generally that 'La notion prétorienne d'obligation positive participe ansi pleinement de la construction d'un ordre juridique commun.'

This is the most developed judgment of the Court concerning the protection of private life from such celebrity journalism. In an earlier admissibility decision the French magazine *Voici* had published six photographs of a television actress in her swimming costume, with a male friend, looking affectionate, beside a swimming pool in Tunisia.[160] The title of the article ran '*Elle semble bien accroché'*. The actress sued the magazine for a breach of her right to respect for her private life. The French courts awarded the actress FFr150,000 (about US$25,000) in damages and ordered the magazine to print the details of the award together with an admission that it had treated with scorn the actress's right to respect for her image and private life. The magazine complained that the requirement to publish the announcement was a sanction that violated the magazine's rights to freedom of expression and information under Article 10 of the Convention. The European Court of Human Rights quoted in full the Parliamentary Assembly's resolution and highlighted in particular the sentence in paragraph 6: 'people's private lives have become a highly lucrative commodity for certain sectors of the media'. The award by the French courts was held to be proportionate to the aim: the protection of private life. The boundaries of freedom of expression for this sort of information/entertainment are circumscribed by obligations to respect private life that are becoming clearer and clearer with each case before the European Court of Human Rights.

A separate issue has arisen with regards to closed-circuit television cameras. In *Peck v United Kingdom* a complaint arose over the use of images filmed by these cameras. The local authorities had installed a system of closed circuit television cameras (CCTV) whose images were monitored and, in the event of a suspected crime, could be switched through to the local police. Mr Peck was suffering from depression; he walked to the town centre and attempted to commit suicide by cutting his wrists with a kitchen knife. He was caught on camera holding the knife and the police were alerted. The police arrived at the scene and administered medical assistance. The local authorities released the pictures in the context of publicity about the utility of CCTV. Subsequent articles in the newspapers, as well as different television programmes, revealed images of the applicant that meant he was recognized by people who knew him. Although the suicide attempt was not caught on film, the period immediately afterwards was captured. The Court found that the local authorities had not done everything possible to protect Mr Peck's right to privacy. The situation with regard to the press and television companies is more complex. The Court left open whether the BBC or Anglia Television could be considered a state agent so that their actions could be directly attributed to the state. It did, however, go on to examine the remedies that Mr Peck could rely on directly against the media. The Court found that these were insufficient under the Article 13 of the Convention. The various media commissions, which allowed for complaints against the TV companies and the

---

[160] *Societé Prisma v France* App. 66910/01, Decision of 1 July 2003.

newspapers,[161] were found by the Court to fall short of what was required to provide a remedy for Mr Peck. The Court stated that 'the lack of legal power of the commissions to award damages to the applicant means that those bodies could not provide an effective remedy to him. It notes that the [Independent Television Commission's] power to impose a fine on the relevant television company does not amount to an award of damages to the applicant'.[162]

This judgment illustrates the developing jurisprudence which demands that contracting states put in place meaningful remedies for infringements of private life by various non-state actors, including newspapers,[163] magazines, television companies, and even private detectives.[164]

9.1.9 Article 9 Freedom of Thought, Conscience, and Religion

Article 9 reads as follows:

(1) Everyone has the right to freedom of thought, conscience and religion; this right includes freedom to change his religion or belief and freedom, either alone or in community with others and in public or private, to manifest his religion or belief, in worship, teaching, practice and observance.

(2) Freedom to manifest one's religion or beliefs shall be subject only to such limitations as are prescribed by law and are necessary in a democratic society in the

---

[161] The Broadcasting Standards Commission (for the BBC), the Independent Television Commission (for Anglia Television), and the Press Complaints Council (for the *Yellow Advertiser*).

[162] Ibid, at para. 109.

[163] See also the important decision by the European Commission of Human Rights in *Earl and Countess Spencer v UK* Apps 28851/95 and 28852/95, Decision of 16 January 1998, referred to by the Court in the *Peck* case with regard to the scope of a possible breach of confidence action. The Commission admitted the possibility that the newspaper articles reporting the Countess's admittance to a private clinic for an eating disorder and alcoholism could be considered to have interfered with her private life and that there had to be a remedy for this at the national level. The decision is explicit about the responsibilities of the press: 'On the facts as presented by the parties, the Commission would not exclude that the absence of an actionable remedy in relation to the publications of which the applicants complain could show a lack of respect for their private lives. It has regard in this respect to the *duties and responsibilities* that are carried with the right of freedom of expression guaranteed by Article 10 of the Convention and to Contracting States' obligation to provide a measure of protection to the right of privacy of an individual affected by others' exercise of their freedom of expression.' (Emphasis added).

[164] In *Verlière v Switzerland* App. 41953/98, Decision of 28 June 2001, the Court recalled its jurisprudence that Art. 8 applies even in the sphere of relations between individuals, noting that Swiss law provided for both civil and criminal suits against those who invade private life. The applicant had failed in her civil suit against the private detectives and the insurance company as the Court had applied the law which allowed for surveillance where there were overriding public or private interests involved. The Court distinguished the *X and Y* case, pointing to the existence of these domestic remedies (at p 5): 'The domestic courts had thus found that the insurer had an overriding interest that made the interference with the applicant's personality rights lawful. In the light of the foregoing, the Court considers that Switzerland has complied with its positive obligation inherent in the notion of effective respect for family life, at both the legislative and judicial levels.' See also the friendly settlement in *Raymond and Sheila Arnott v UK* App. 44866/98, Decision of the Court, 3 October 2000. The application concerned the lack of a remedy for protection of private life. The Government agreed to pay £1,000 in full and final settlement of all claims (including legal costs).

interests of public safety, for the protection of public order, health or morals, or for the protection of the rights and freedoms of others.

The case-law concerning non-state actors' obligations with regard to freedom of religion as protected under Article 9 has given rise to disagreements within the Court and among commentators. The issue has arisen in the context of prohibitions on films and books which have been deemed offensive to those with religious convictions. The question is to what extent do private individuals and other non-state actors have duties to avoid offending others' religious beliefs? The issue raises an explicit obligation of the non-state actor concerned, due to the inclusion in Article 10(2) (concerning freedom of expression) of a reference to the exercise of freedom of expression carrying 'with it duties and responsibilities'. It is possible to contrast some of the claims that have been brought under the Convention.

Abdul Hussain Choudhury brought a case for judicial review of the failure of the Magistrates' Court in England to grant an application for a summons against Salman Rushdie and Viking Penguin Publishing Co Ltd (Penguin) alleging the commission of the offences of blasphemous libel and seditious libel at common law.[165] Choudhury had sought summonses alleging that the author and publishers of *The Satanic Verses* had unlawfully and wickedly published or caused to be published 'a blasphemous libel concerning Almighty God (Allah), the Supreme Deity common to all the major religions of the world, the Prophet Abraham and his son Ishmael, Muhammad (Pbuh) the Holy Prophet of Islam, his wives and companions and the religion of Islam and Christianity, contrary to common law'.[166]

The main question for the High Court was whether the offence of blasphemy was restricted to the Christian religion. After an extensive review of the authorities the Court stated: 'We have no doubt that as the law now stands it does not extend to religions other than Christianity.'[167] Nevertheless the applicant suggested that the courts should extend it to cover other religions. The Court considered the policy arguments against extending it in this way. First, such action would create a criminal offence retroactively. Second, attempts in Parliament to extend the law to religious feeling generally had failed. Third, the Law Commission had recommended abolition of the offence of blasphemy. Fourth, it was deemed 'virtually impossible' to set limits to the offence. Defining religion is difficult and to expect juries or even authors to decide whether 'material scandalised one sect and not another' was too demanding. An application was then made to Strasbourg, alleging violations of Articles 9 and 14 of the Convention.

The Commission dismissed the application in a brief decision that simply found the application to be outside the scope of the Commission's jurisdiction.

---

[165] *R v Bow Street Court, ex p Choudhury* [1990] 3 WLR 986. See Clapham (1993: 313–322) for a detailed consideration of the judgment, see further M. Tregilgas-Davey, '*Ex Parte Choudhury*: An Opportunity Missed', *MLR* (1991) 294–299.   [166] From the judgment, ibid, at 989.   [167] At 999.

The Commission first focused on the fact that no state body had interfered with the applicant's right to manifest his religion. The decision then declared that there was no right not to be offended in one's religious sensitivities:

> The question in the present case is therefore whether the freedom of Article 9 of the Convention may extend to guarantee a right to bring any specific form of proceedings against those who, by authorship or publication, offend the sensitivities of an individual or of a group of individuals. The Commission finds no indication in the present case of a link between freedom from interference with the freedoms of Article 9 para. 1 of the Convention and the applicant's complaints.[168]

Having found that there was no arguable claim with regard to Article 9, the Commission then dismissed the complaint concerning non-discrimination with regard to the enjoyment of rights under Article 9 as also being outside the scope of the Convention.[169] The Commission read freedom of religion in a narrow negative obligations sense; the Commission did not consider whether there may be positive obligations for the state under Article 9 which might include protection from discriminatory laws or from attacks on one's religion. This decision has been roundly criticized in a leading commentary on the Convention. Harris, O'Boyle, and Warbrick have suggested that there might 'be grounds for reconsidering the decision in *Choudhury v United Kingdom* that the absence of a criminal sanction in English law against publications which offended against the religious beliefs of non-Christians was not a violation of Article 9. This conclusion as surprising as it is regrettable, is out of line with the general practice of European states'.[170]

This decision can be contrasted with the approach of the Court in *Otto-Preminger-Institut v Austria*.[171] The applicant Institute was a non-profit making organization with the aim of promoting creativity, communication, and entertainment through audio-visual media. The Institute announced to its 2,700 members screenings of a film *Das Liebeskonzil*. The announcement was also posted in various windows in Innsbruck. The announcement explained that the film was a satire set in Heaven and filmed from a theatrical performance in Rome based on Oska Panizza's 1895 trial and conviction for blasphemy. The announcement further stated that:

> Panizza starts from the assumption that syphilis was God's punishment for man's fornication and sinfulness at the time of the Renaissance, especially at the court of the Borgia Pope Alexander VI. In Schroeter's film, God's representatives on Earth carrying the insignia of worldly power closely resemble the heavenly protagonists.

---

[168] *Choudhury v UK* App. 17439/90, Decision of 5 March 1991, reproduced in 12 *HRLJ* (1991) 172.

[169] For a further discussion of whether such an instance of discrimination as regards blasphemy could be considered in conformity with Art. 14, see the concurring opinion of Judge Pettiti as well as the dissenting opinions in *Wingrove v UK* Judgment of 25 November 1996.

[170] Harris *et al* (1995: 360).   [171] Judgment of 20 September 1994.

Trivial imagery and absurdities of the Christian creed are targeted in a caricatural mode and the relationship between religious beliefs and worldly mechanisms of oppression is investigated.[172]

It was also announced that persons under seventeen years old would not be admitted to the film. The Innsbruck diocese of the Roman Catholic Church successfully requested the Public Prosecutor to bring charges of 'disparaging religious doctrines' against the manager of the Institute. Following a private showing of the film before a judge, the film was seized and the scheduled screenings could not take place. An appeal by the distributor of the film failed, as the Austrian Court of Appeal held that freedom of expression was necessarily limited by the rights of others to freedom of religion.[173] The Court of Appeal further held that the criminal code applied where the material would offend the religious feelings of an average person with normal religious sensitivity.[174] The criminal proceedings against the manager of the Institute were later dropped, but proceedings were brought under the Media Act in order to suppress the film and the Regional Court ordered the forfeiture of the film.

The European Commission on Human Rights found violations of Article 10 with regard to the seizure of the film (by nine votes to five) and with regard to the forfeiture of the film (by thirteen votes to one).[175] The European Court of Human Rights in contrast, found by six votes to three, that there had been no violation of Article 10.

The judgment of the Court is interesting in the present context for what it said about the positive obligations of the state to ensure the effective enjoyment of freedom of religion, as well as for its *dicta* concerning the responsibilities of those who seek to exercise freedom of expression. The Court was quite expansive on the scope of Article 9:

> Those who choose to exercise the freedom to manifest their religion, irrespective of whether they do so as members of a religious majority or a minority, cannot reasonably expect to be exempt from all criticism. They must tolerate and accept the denial by others of their religious beliefs and even the propagation by others of doctrines hostile to their faith. However, the manner in which religious beliefs and doctrines are opposed or denied is a matter which may engage the responsibility of the State, notably its responsibility to ensure the peaceful enjoyment of the right guaranteed under Article 9 to the holders of those beliefs and doctrines. Indeed, in extreme cases the effect of particular methods of opposing or denying religious beliefs can be such as to inhibit those who hold such beliefs from exercising their freedom to hold and express them.[176]

The Court then went beyond these positive obligations of the state to consider that Article 9 includes a right to respect for religious feeling and that certain

---

[172] A summary description of the film is appended to the European Commission on Human Rights Report of 14 January 1993.

[173] Decision of 30 July 1985, as explained in the Judgment of the European Court of Human Rights of 20 September 1994, at para. 13.   [174] Ibid.

[175] Report of 14 January 1993.   [176] Judgment of 20 September 1994, at para. 47.

portrayals of religion can violate this right: 'The respect for the religious feelings of believers as guaranteed in Article 9 can legitimately be thought to have been violated by provocative portrayals of objects of religious veneration; and such portrayals can be regarded as malicious violation of the spirit of tolerance, which must also be a feature of democratic society.'[177] The Court then recalled that Article 10(2) refers to 'duties and responsibilities' for those exercising freedom of expression and, according to the Court, among these duties and responsibilities: 'may legitimately be included an obligation to avoid as far as possible expressions that are gratuitously offensive to others and thus an infringement of their rights, and which therefore do not contribute to any form of public debate capable of furthering progress in human affairs'.[178]

Here is an explicit statement by the Court that Article 9 may be violated by provocative portrayals of religion, and that individuals, and other non-state actors seeking to exercise freedom of expression, have an *obligation* to avoid gratuitous offence which would constitute an infringement of rights under Article 9.

The majority of the Court weighed the right to impart and receive information on the one hand, and 'the right of other persons to proper respect for their freedom of thought, conscience and religion, on the other hand'.[179] The majority gave particular weight to the fact that Roman Catholicism is the religion of 97 per cent of Tyroleans, and they considered that the Austrian authorities were acting to ensure 'religious peace in that region and to prevent that some people should feel the object of attacks on their religious beliefs in an unwarranted and offensive manner'.[180] They decided that the national judges were better placed to assess the need for such measures, and they found that the Austrian authorities could not be considered to have overstepped their margin of appreciation. There had therefore been no violation of Article 10.

The minority took a different approach, first with regard to the necessity of the restriction on freedom of expression, and second by stating quite clearly that: 'The Convention does not, in terms, guarantee a right to protection of religious feelings. More particularly, such a right cannot be derived from the right to freedom of religion, which in effect includes a right to express views critical of the religious opinions of others.'[181] The minority accepted that it may be legitimate to set limits to freedom of expression, and that 'the democratic character of a society will be affected if violent and abusive attacks on the reputation of a religious group are allowed'.[182] The minority, however, set out a different duty for the non-state actor:

> The duty and the responsibility of a person seeking to avail himself of his freedom of expression should be to limit, as far as he can reasonably be expected to, the offence that his statement may cause to others. Only if he fails to take necessary action, or if such action is shown to be insufficient, may the State step in.[183]

---

[177] Judgment of 20 September 1994, at para. 47.   [178] Ibid, at para. 49.
[179] Ibid, at para. 55.   [180] Ibid, at para. 56.   [181] At para. 6 of the dissent.
[182] Ibid.   [183] Ibid, at para. 7.

In assessing the need for prevention of freedom of expression, the minority suggested that the 'need for repressive action amounting to complete prevention of the exercise of freedom of expression can only be accepted if the behaviour concerned reaches so high a level of abuse, and comes so close to a denial of the freedom of religion of others, as to forfeit for itself the right to be tolerated by society'.[184] In this case, the minority concluded, there was little likelihood of anyone being confronted with the material unwittingly, and the applicant association had acted responsibly in limiting the harmful effects of the film.

The Court's judgment has been described as 'mistaken' by van Dijk and van Hoof.[185] They argue that: 'The screening of this film in no way would have limited or inhibited Roman Catholics in manifesting their religion, and therefore did not restrict their rights under Article 9. The Court has unjustifiably extended the right (flowing from Article 9) to be protected against vicious attacks of fellow citizens on a religion or belief that could endanger the actual enjoyment of the freedom to manifest this religion or belief—particularly relevant for minorities— to a general right—even for dominant minorities—not to be insulted in one's religious or non-religious views.'[186] They suggest that such a right is actually inconsistent with the pluralism that the Court has said is 'indissociable from a democratic society'.[187] This criticism may have led the Court to change tack and avoid similar explicit wide-ranging references to the scope of Article 9 in a subsequent case concerning a banned video intended to represent St Teresa.[188] Nevertheless, in this subsequent case (*Wingrove v United Kingdom*) the Court recalled its approach in the *Otto-Preminger* case, and with regard to the responsibilities of non-state actors seeking to enjoy freedom of expression, referred to 'a duty to avoid as far as possible an expression that is, in regard to objects of veneration, gratuitously offensive to others and profanatory'.[189]

9.1.10 Article 10 Freedom of Expression and the Role of Article 17

Article 10 reads as follows:

> (1) Everyone has the right to freedom of expression. This right shall include freedom to hold opinions and to receive and impart information and ideas without interference by public authority and regardless of frontiers. This article shall not prevent States from requiring the licensing of broadcasting, television or cinema enterprises.

---

[184] Ibid.   [185] van Dijk and van Hoof (1998: 551).   [186] Ibid.

[187] Ibid, referring to the Court's Judgment of 25 May 1993, *Kokkinakis v Greece*, at para. 31.

[188] See *Wingrove v UK* Judgment of 25 November 1996; the concurring opinion of Judge Pettiti stated: 'Article 9 is not in issue in the instant case and cannot be invoked. Certainly the Court rightly based its analysis under Article 10 on the rights of others and did not, as it had done in the Otto-Preminger-Institut judgment combine Articles 9 and 10, morals and the rights of others, for which it had been criticised by legal writers.'

[189] Ibid, at para. 52, the *duty* is among the 'duties and responsibilities' that come with the exercise of freedom of expression as stated in Art. 10(2) of the Convention.

(2) The exercise of these freedoms, since it carries with it duties and responsibilities, may be subject to such formalities, conditions, restrictions or penalties as are prescribed by law and are necessary in a democratic society, in the interests of national security, territorial integrity or public safety, for the prevention of disorder or crime, for the protection of health or morals, for the protection of the reputation or rights of others, for preventing the disclosure of information received in confidence, or for maintaining the authority and impartiality of the judiciary.

Freedom of expression is recognized as essential to a democracy as it ensures that new ideas are debated and possibilities for change are canvassed. The ideal speech situation which allows for arguments to flourish and be properly considered, however, has limits. Patrick Birkenshaw explains this as follows: 'Information is necessary to make sensible choice or wise judgment. Moral and ethical evaluation depends on information acquired through our own and our predecessors' experience. Information in the form of facts constitutes the basis of order in our lives, of community, regularity and knowledge.'[190] Nevertheless, Birkenshaw points to the converse side of freedom of information:

> ... there are spheres of our personal and private lives that are a legitimate object of secrecy. Without adequate protection for justifiable secrets our integrity can be compromised, our identity shaken, our security shattered. Details of legitimate, intimate relationships, medical facts, of prolonged sensitive negotiations, investigations in the public interest, development of strategic or commercial plans, often require secrecy, likewise the long-term development of products requiring constant experimentation and creative thought or the protection of ideas.[191]

This is a situation where state and non-state actor obligations are obviously rather different. When one challenges the state to provide information, the state can respond with the argument that the information must remain secret for reasons of national security or because it is necessary to protect the rights of others. When one demands that a private individual provide information, the individual may be able to rely on their right to privacy and the intimacy of certain medical details.

In fact, the Convention grants not only individuals, but also corporate non-state actors, the right to respect for their place of business. In the case of *Société Colas Est and ors v France* the Court recognized that a raid on company premises in the context of anti-competition proceedings could amount to a violation of the right to respect for the company's 'home'.[192] But the Court may have accepted the French Government's contention, in that case, that interference might be

---

[190] P. Birkenshaw, *Freedom of Information: The Law, the Practice and the Ideal* (London: Weidenfeld and Nicolson, 1988) at 11.   [191] Ibid, at 12–13.

[192] 'Building on its dynamic interpretation of the Convention, the Court considers that the time has come to hold that in certain circumstances the rights guaranteed by Article 8 of the Convention may be construed as including the right to respect for a company's registered office, branches or other business premises.' Judgment of 16 April 2002, at para. 41.

legitimately more extensive in the case of a company's commercial premises than for an individual's professional 'domicile'.[193] One can surmise that, with regard to infringements by non-state actors on a company's premises, the human rights obligations will be diminished as compared to invasions of an individual's residence. As a general rule corporations, churches, trades unions, and other non-state actors will often be able to rely on rights in human rights treaties,[194] but the scope of any particular right will depend on the wording of the treaty and the context in which it is invoked.[195]

The question has been raised as to whether private bodies have an obligation to issue corrections or to impart information. As we saw above with regard to the case concerning *Voici*, the Court has held that requiring a magazine to publish details of a judicial finding does not necessarily contravene its freedom of expression. This is, however, not quite the same as suggesting that the Convention includes first, a positive obligation on states to ensure that information is made available, and, second, an obligation on non-state actors to publish certain material including corrections. Van Dijk and van Hoof have highlighted the early

---

[193] Ibid, at paras 30 and 42.

[194] Local government councils are excluded but political parties and politicians in their personal capacity are entitled to bring complaints. L. J. Clements, *European Human Rights: Taking a case under the Convention* (London: Sweet & Maxwell, 1994) at 18. H. C. Krüger and C. A. Nørgaard have explained that in the jurisprudence of the European Commission 'legal persons come under the concept of "non-governmental organizations".' Furthermore they state in the same article that: 'The "non-governmental" character of the organizations concerned means that they must not be public corporations participating in the exercise of State power.' 'The Right of Application' in R. St. J. Macdonald, F. Matscher, and H. Petzold (eds) *The European System for the Protection of Human Rights* (Dordrecht: Martinus Nijhoff, 1993) 657–675, at 666. See further Ch 2 at 2.8 for a discussion of religious organizations recognized as public law corporations and the European Court of Human Rights' Judgment in *The Holy Monasteries v Greece* Judgment of 9 December 1994.

[195] See Art. 34 ECHR: 'The Court may receive applications from any person, non-governmental organization or group of individuals claiming to be the victim of a violation by one of the High Contracting Parties of the rights...' According to Ovey and White (2002: 405), 'The term 'person' (*personne physique* in the French text) appears to include only natural persons but an application may be brought by any corporate or unincorporated body. Thus applications have been brought by companies, trade unions, churches, political parties, and numerous other types of body. A corporate body has some but not all of the rights of individuals; thus it has the right to fair trial under Article 6, to protection of its correspondence under Article 8, and is expressly granted property rights under Article 1 of the First Protocol, but it does not have the right to education under Article 2 of Protocol No. 1.' Note that complaints under the ICCPR are limited to individuals under the First Protocol. This does not mean that peoples and organizations are not rights-holders, it only means they cannot complain under the particular mechanism established by the Protocol. Petitions under the Inter-American Convention are allowed as followed: 'Any person or group of persons, or any nongovernmental entity legally recognized in one or more member states of the Organization, may lodge petitions with the Commission containing denunciations or complaints of violation of this Convention by a State Party.' Art. 44. However, the rights are only held by 'human beings'; see Art. 1(2) ACHR. Under the African Charter, most rights are protected for the individual. 'Peoples' enjoy rights under the African Charter and others can petition the Commission on their behalf: R. Murray, *The African Commission on Human and Peoples' Rights and International Law* (Oxford: Hart Publishing, 2000) at 110.

resolution of the Consultative (now Parliamentary) Assembly of the Council of Europe on the right to freedom of expression which refers to a 'corresponding duty for the public authorities to make available information on matters of public interest within reasonable limits and a duty for mass communications media to give complete and general information on public affairs'.[196] They further ask whether 'the right to receive information calls for pluriformity in imparting information, which then has to be guaranteed by the authorities, for instance by making grants to persons and institutions imparting information, where this is necessary for such pluriformity'.[197] We can go some way to answering these question through a careful examination of the case of *VgT Verein gegen Tierfabriken v Switzerland*.[198]

The VgT association works for the protection of animals with a special focus on animal experiments and the conditions in which animals are kept with regard to industrial meat production. The association wished to respond to television adverts produced by the meat industry. VgT prepared a 55-second television commercial with two scenes. The Judgment explained:

> The first scene of the film showed a sow building a nest for her piglets in the forest. Soft orchestrated music was played in the background, and the accompanying voice referred, *inter alia*, to the sense of family which sows had. The second scene showed a noisy hall with pigs in small pens, gnawing nervously at the iron bars. The accompanying voice stated, *inter alia*, that the rearing of pigs in such circumstances resembled concentration camps, and that the animals were pumped full with medicaments. The film concluded with the exhortation: 'eat less meat, for the sake of your health, the animals, and the environment!'.[199]

In order to have the commercial shown on Swiss national television the association sent the video-cassette to the Commercial Television Company (now called *Publisuisse*) responsible for television advertising. The Company refused to broadcast the commercial due to its 'clear political character'. The Swiss Government submitted that such a refusal 'did not bring about the responsibility of the Swiss authorities. The latter exercised no supervision over the Commercial Television Company which was a company established under and governed by private law, and they did not prevent the Company from broadcasting commercials'.[200] The Court took particular notice of the submission by the Government that the Company 'when deciding on whether or not to acquire advertising, was acting as a private party enjoying contractual freedom'.[201] The Court did not therefore attribute the acts of the Company to the state. The Court recalled its jurisprudence with regard to Article 1, and stated that 'in addition to the primarily negative

---

[196] Res. 428 (1970) 21st Ordinary Session (Third Part) 22–30 January 1970, van Dijk and van Hoof (1998: 566), compare van Dijk and van Hoof's first edition of the same book (1990: 418).

[197] Ibid, at 566.   [198] Judgment of 28 June 2001.   [199] Ibid, at para. 10.

[200] Ibid, at para. 40.   [201] Ibid, at 44.

undertaking of a State to abstain from interference in Convention guarantees, "there may be positive obligations inherent" in such guarantees. The responsibility of a State may then be engaged as a result of not observing its obligation to enact domestic legislation'.[202]

Unfortunately, the Court eschews the chance to explain the scope of such legislation and the breadth of the responsibilities that should be placed on non-state actors in national law in order to bring the state into compliance with its obligation to enact such domestic legislation. In a bout of judicial restraint, the Court simply stated that it 'does not consider it desirable, let alone necessary, to elaborate a general theory concerning the extent to which the Convention guarantees should be extended to relations between private individuals *inter se*'.[203]

In addition to the situation where a private entity interferes with another entity's freedom of expression, one finds the situation where the applicant is *denied a remedy* due to a duty to respect other people's rights. This sort of indirect enforcement of non-state actor obligations is often overlooked, as it is not presented as a violation of human rights. For example, consider an application concerning a violation of freedom of expression brought by a teacher for dismissal following published racist remarks in the school's newspaper. The European Court of Human Rights declined to allow such a claim, invoking the responsibilities owed by individuals.[204] Even beyond the context of state schools, the logic applies to deny individuals the right to rely on freedom of expression when their actions are aimed at the destruction of other people's rights under Article 17.[205] In *Garaudy v France* the Court dismissed a claim regarding freedom of expression on the grounds that Article 17 overrode Article 10:

> There can be no doubt that denying the reality of clearly established historical facts, such as the Holocaust, as the applicant does in his book, does not constitute historical research akin to a quest for the truth. The aim and the result of that approach are completely different, the real purpose being to rehabilitate the National-Socialist regime and, as a consequence, accuse the victims themselves of falsifying history. Denying crimes against humanity is therefore one of the most serious forms of racial defamation of Jews and of incitement to hatred of them. The denial or rewriting of this type of historical fact undermines the values on which the fight against racism and anti-Semitism are based and constitutes a serious threat to public order. Such acts are incompatible

---

[202] Ibid, at para. 45. Cf para. 49 of *Young, James and Webster v UK* cited in Ch 8, at 8.1.1 above.
[203] *VgT* (n 198 above) at para. 46.
[204] *Seurot v France* App. 57383/00 of 18 May 2004, at para. 9: 'Le contenu revêt incontestablement un caractère raciste, est incompatible avec les devoirs et responsabilités particuliers qui incombaient au requérant.' See also *Lehideux and Isorni v France* Judgment of 23 September 1998, where it was suggested (at para. 47) that Holocaust negation or revision would 'be removed from the protection of Article 10 by Article 17'.
[205] Art. 17 reads: 'Nothing in this Convention may be interpreted as implying for any state, group or person any right to engage in any activity or perform any act aimed at the destruction of any of the rights and freedoms set forth herein or at their limitation to a greater extent than is provided for in the Convention.' For a review of some of the earlier cases, see Clapham (1993: 184–186).

with democracy and human rights because they infringe the rights of others. Its proponents indisputably have designs that fall into the category of aims prohibited by Article 17 of the Convention.

The Court considers that the main content and general tenor of the applicant's book, and thus its aim, are markedly revisionist and therefore run counter to the fundamental values of the Convention, as expressed in its Preamble, namely justice and peace. It considers that the applicant attempts to deflect Article 10 of the Convention from its real purpose by using his right to freedom of expression for ends which are contrary to the text and spirit of the Convention. Such ends, if admitted, would contribute to the destruction of the rights and freedoms guaranteed by the Convention.

Accordingly, the Court considers that, in accordance with Article 17 of the Convention, the applicant cannot rely on the provisions of Article 10 of the Convention regarding his conviction for denying crimes against humanity.[206]

This approach was also used with regard to a claim by a regional organizer for the British National Party, who placed in his window a poster which, according to the judgment, had 'a photograph of the Twin Towers in flame, the words "Islam out of Britain—Protect the British People" and a symbol of a crescent and star in a prohibition sign'.[207] He was prosecuted for 'displaying, with hostility towards a racial or religious group, any writing, sign or other visible representation which is threatening, abusive or insulting, within the sight of a person likely to be caused harassment, alarm or distress by it'. He claimed this breached his rights to freedom of expression under the Convention. The Court dismissed his claim concluding: 'The applicant's display of the poster in his window constituted an act within the meaning of Article 17, which did not, therefore, enjoy the protection of Articles 10 or 14'.[208]

Lastly, one can refer to the importance attached to freedom of expression by the Court in the 'Mclibel' case. The longest running case in English legal history[209] resulted in two campaigners being successfully sued by McDonald's for defamation. The damages awarded were eventually fixed at £36,000 for Ms Steel and £40,000 for Mr Morris. As noted previously, the European Court of Human Rights found a violation of the fair trial guarantees in Article 6, due to the denial of legal aid to the applicants. With regard to freedom of expression, the Court held that, even though domestic law could legitimately demand that a defendant in libel proceedings bear the burden of proving on the balance of probabilities that the defamatory statements were true,[210] and even considering that the company has a legitimate interest in protecting its reputation, and that the state has a margin of appreciation to determine how this should be done,[211] in this case, the absence of fairness, and the inequality between the campaigners and McDonald's, meant that

---

[206] Decision of 23 June 2003 at p 23 of the translation.
[207] *Norwood v UK* Decision of 16 November 2004, at 2.   [208] Ibid, at 4.
[209] The case ran in the High Court from 28 June 1994 to 13 December 1996, with 313 days in Court.   [210] *Steel and Morris v UK* Judgment of 15 February 2005, at para. 93.
[211] Ibid, at para. 94.

the interference with freedom of expression could not be justified as proportionate to the aim of protecting the commercial interests of McDonald's.[212] Furthermore, the Court found that the amount of damages awarded was disproportionate to the aim which was supposed to be served.[213] States are obliged under the European Convention to ensure that libel suits guarantee, not only equality of arms between the parties, but that any award of damages is proportionate to the situation. Non-state actors may not use the law to stifle freedom of expression in ways that go beyond what is proportionate to the protection of their interests. The Court was clear that:

> ... in a democratic society even small and informal campaign groups, such as London Greenpeace, must be able to carry on their activities effectively and that there exists a strong public interest in enabling such groups and individuals outside the mainstream to contribute to the public debate by disseminating information and ideas on matters of general public interest such as health and the environment...[214]

9.1.11   Article 11 Rights to Assembly and Association

Article 11 reads as follows:

> (1) Everyone has the right to freedom of peaceful assembly and freedom of association with others, including the right to form and join trade unions for the protection of his interests.
> (2) No restrictions shall be placed on the exercise of these rights other than such as are prescribed by law and are necessary in a democratic society in the interests of national security or public safety, for the prevention of crime, for the protection of health or morals or for the protection of the rights and freedoms of others. This Article shall not prevent the imposition of lawful restrictions on the exercise of these rights by members of the armed forces, of the police or of the administration of the State.

9.1.11.1   Freedom of Assembly

Freedom of assembly is being threatened in new ways by non-state actors. An example of modern challenges to the enjoyment of this right is illustrated by the

---

212 'The inequality of arms and the difficulties under which the applicants laboured are also significant in assessing the proportionality of the interference under Article 10. As a result of the law as it stood in England and Wales, the applicants had the choice either to withdraw the leaflet and apologise to McDonald's, or bear the burden of proving, without legal aid, the truth of the allegations contained in it. Given the enormity and complexity of that undertaking, the Court does not consider that the correct balance was struck between the need to protect the applicants' rights to freedom of expression and the need to protect McDonald's rights and reputation. The more general interest in promoting the free circulation of information and ideas about the activities of powerful commercial entities, and the possible "chilling" effect on others are also important factors to be considered in this context, bearing in mind the legitimate and important role that campaign groups can play in stimulating public discussion.' Ibid, at para. 95.

213 Ibid, at para. 97. For another case where the Court held that libel damages were disproportionate and that there had been a violation of Art. 10, see *Tolstoy Miloslavsky v the UK* Judgment of 13 July 1995, where an award by a jury for £1,500,000 was found to be not 'necessary in a democratic society', thereby resulting in a violation by the state of Art. 10.

214 *Steel and Morris v UK* Judgment of 15 February 2005, at para. 89.

case of *Appleby v United Kingdom*.[215] This case concerned a group of citizens who were worried by a decision by the local Council to grant planning permission to a College to build on part of a green park, which according to the judgment was 'the only playing field in the vicinity of Washington town centre which is available for use by the local community'.[216] The town centre of the town of Washington had been sold by a governmental body to a private company. The town centre, now known as 'The Galleries', includes a shopping mall, careers' office, the public library, the health centre, post office, and police station. The concerned citizens set up two stands at the entrance to the Galleries to inform the public of the probable loss of their playing fields as open space for leisure. They sought signatures to present to the Council to demonstrate the extent of local opposition. In time, security guards prevented the protestors from collecting signatures on land owned by the company that owned 'The Galleries'. The right to protest was pitched against the right to property enjoyed by the company which owned the Galleries and the town centre. The Court sought to strike a fair balance 'between the general interest of the community and the interests of the individual'. They found that the protestors' rights had not been violated. The European Court suggested that, where there is no other way to protest, the right to freedom of expression may override rights to private property. This would be so where 'the bar on access to property has the effect of preventing any effective exercise of freedom of expression or it can be said that the essence of the right has been destroyed, the Court would not exclude that a positive obligation could arise for the State to protect the enjoyment of Convention rights by regulating property rights'.[217] As discussed in Chapter 10, in the United States, the Supreme Court did actually uphold freedom of expression in the context of a company town. The European Court referred to this precedent:

46.   The Court would observe that, though the cases from the United States in particular illustrate an interesting trend in accommodating freedom of expression to privately-owned property open to the public, the U.S. Supreme Court has refrained from holding that there is a federal constitutional right of free speech in a privately owned shopping mall. Authorities from the individual states show a variety of approaches to the public and private law issues that have arisen in widely differing factual situations. It cannot be said that there is as yet any emerging consensus that could assist the Court in its examination in this case concerning Article 10 of the Convention.

47.   That provision, notwithstanding the acknowledged importance of freedom of expression, does not bestow any freedom of forum for the exercise of that right. While it is true that demographic, social, economic and technological developments are changing the ways in which people move around and come into contact with each other, the Court is not persuaded that this requires the automatic creation of rights of entry to private property, or even, necessarily, to all publicly-owned property (Government offices and ministries, for instance). Where however the bar on access to property has the effect of preventing any effective exercise of freedom of expression or it can be said

---

[215] Judgment of 6 May 2003.   [216] Ibid, at para. 13.   [217] Ibid, at para. 47.

that the essence of the right has been destroyed, the Court would not exclude that a positive obligation could arise for the State to protect the enjoyment of Convention rights by regulating property rights. The corporate town, where the entire municipality was controlled by a private body, might be an example (see *Marsh v. Alabama*, cited at paragraph 26 above).

48.   In the present case, the restriction on the applicants' ability to communicate their views was limited to the entrance areas and passageways of the Galleries. It did not prevent them from obtaining individual permission from businesses within the Galleries (the manager of a hypermarket granted permission for a stand within his store on one occasion) or from distributing their leaflets on the public access paths into the area. It also remained open to them to campaign in the old town centre and to employ alternative means, such as calling door-to-door or seeking exposure in the local press, radio and television. The applicants do not deny that these other methods were available to them. Their argument, essentially, is that the easiest and most effective method of reaching people was in using the Galleries, as shown by the local authority's own information campaign (see paragraph 21). The Court does not consider however that the applicants can claim that they were, as a result of the refusal of the private company, Postel, effectively prevented from communicating their views to their fellow citizens. Some 3,200 people submitted letters in their support. Whether more would have done so if the stand had remained in the Galleries is speculation which is insufficient to support an argument that the applicants were unable otherwise to exercise their freedom of expression in a meaningful manner.

49.   Balancing therefore the rights in issue and having regard to the nature and scope of the restriction in this case, the Court does not find that the Government failed in any positive obligation to protect the applicants' freedom of expression.[218]

Although there are innovative, exciting ways to influence public debate through the use of new public spheres, such as the internet, the mass media, etc., simple protest to assert different opinions on local issues is evidently under threat from the privatization of public spaces. This issue is dealt with again in the context of some of the national decisions taken under US constitutional law in Chapter 10, in section 10.2.2.3. For the moment it suffices to highlight that the European Court recognized that where the 'essence' of the right to freedom of expression was extinguished, there would be a failure on the part of the state to protect human rights. In *Appleby v United Kingdom* the Court felt that the protestors had other effective avenues of protest open to them.

9.1.11.2   Freedom of Association

The *Young, James and Webster* judgment confirmed that the state has to ensure the protection of freedom of association rights in the context of a private employment relationship. In that case, the right not to join a trade union was upheld on the grounds of personal conviction. Since that time, the Court has distinguished *Young, James and Webster* in a case where a trade union official resigned from a

---

[218]   Ibid. at paras 46–49.

union (the TGWU) over an alleged slander and insisted on joining another union. He was transferred by his employer to another depot and considered this to amount to constructive dismissal. His claims failed at the national level. Although the UK Government had argued that the applicant's employer was a private body and therefore not the responsibility of the Government, the Commission declared the application admissible. The Commission noted 'that actions leading to the dismissal of the applicant were primarily the responsibility of the applicant's employer and trade union. Where, however, the domestic law makes lawful the treatment complained of, the Commission finds that the responsibility of the respondent State may be engaged in particular cases'.[219] The Court reiterated its formula that although the action was not attributable to the state, the state might have an obligation to ensure its law protected the applicant.[220] It went on to hold that:

> ...the facts of the present case are such that it can...be distinguished from that of Young, James and Webster. It notes in the first place that, unlike Mr Young, Mr James and Mr Webster...Mr Sibson did not object to rejoining TGWU on account of any specific convictions as regards trade union membership (and he did in fact join another union instead). It is clear that he would have rejoined TGWU had he received a form of apology acceptable to him...and that accordingly his case, unlike theirs, does not also have to be considered in the light of Articles 9 and 10 of the Convention. Furthermore, the present case is not one in which a closed shop agreement was in force...Above all, the applicants in the earlier case were faced with a threat of dismissal involving loss of livelihood...whereas Mr Sibson was in a rather different position: he had the possibility of going to work at the nearby Chadderton depot, to which his employers were contractually entitled to move him...; their offer to him in this respect was not conditional on his rejoining TGWU; and it is not established that his working conditions there would have been significantly less favourable than those at the Greengate depot...

> Having regard to these various factors, the Court has come to the conclusion that Mr Sibson was not subjected to a form of treatment striking at the very substance of the freedom of association guaranteed by Article 11.[221]

In a further case the Court upheld a complaint by a taxi driver who was obliged by law to join a private taxi drivers association.[222] The Court noted the fact that the applicant's licence had been revoked on one occasion for failure to pay his dues, and considered this sanction grave enough to trigger Article 11.[223] The Court also

---

[219] *Sibson v UK* Report of 10 December 1991, para. 28.

[220] 'The present case involves no direct interference on the part of the State. If the matters complained of by Mr Sibson constituted an infringement of his rights under Article 11 of the Convention, the responsibility of the United Kingdom would nevertheless be engaged if that infringement resulted from a failure on its part to secure those rights to him in its domestic law.' *Sibson v UK* Judgment of 20 April 1993, at para. 27.					[221] Ibid, at para. 29.

[222] *Sigurdur A Sigurjónsson v Iceland* Judgment of 30 June 1993.

[223] 'Such a form of compulsion, in the circumstances of the case, strikes at the very substance of the right guaranteed by Article 11 and itself amounts to an interference with the right.' Ibid, at para. 36.

took note of the ideological opposition to joining the association articulated by the applicant:

> What is more, Mr Sigurdur A. Sigurjónsson objected to being a member of the association in question partly because he disagreed with its policy in favour of limiting the number of taxicabs and, thus, access to the occupation; in his opinion the interests of his country were better served by extensive personal freedoms, including freedom of occupation, than State regulation. Therefore, the Court is of the view that Article 11 can, in the circumstances, be considered in the light of Articles 9 and 10, the protection of personal opinion being also one of the purposes of the freedom of association guaranteed by Article 11... The pressure exerted on the applicant in order to compel him to remain a member of Frami contrary to his wishes was a further aspect going to the very essence of an Article 11 right; there was an interference too in this respect.
>
> The Government's argument that Frami was a non-political association is not relevant in this regard.[224]

Two further cases merit attention in this context. The first concerned a Swedish restaurant owner.[225] Mr Gustafsson owned a summer restaurant and youth hostel on the island of Gotland. He was not a member of an employers' association and was not therefore bound to enter into an agreement with the relevant union. He refused to enter into a substitute agreement with the Hotel and Restaurant Workers' Union (HRF), referring to his objections of principle regarding the system of collective bargaining. He also 'emphasised that his employees were paid more than they would have been under a collective agreement and that they themselves objected to his signing a substitute agreement on their behalf.'[226] According to the Judgment, the HRF union placed the restaurant under a 'blockade' and declared a boycott against it; industrial action in sympathy was taken by other trade unions, and deliveries to the restaurant were stopped. Gustafsson maintained before the Court 'that the unions' boycott and blockade of his business had affected his right to negative freedom of association'.[227] The Court found that the case fell within the ambit of freedom of association:

> The Court considers that although the extent of the inconvenience or damage caused by the union action to the applicant's business may be open to question, the measures must have entailed considerable pressure on the applicant to meet the union's demand that he be bound by a collective agreement. He had two alternative means of doing so: either by joining an employers' association, which would have made him automatically bound by a collective agreement, or by signing a substitute agreement... The Court accepts that, to a degree, the enjoyment of his freedom of association was thereby affected.[228]

The Court draws a careful distinction between being pressured into joining an association and being pressured into signing a substitute agreement. Because Gustafsson had the latter option open to him, the Court did not feel it was

---

[224] Ibid, at para. 37.   [225] *Gustafsson v Sweden* Judgment of 25 April 1996.
[226] Ibid, at para. 11.   [227] Ibid, at para. 43.   [228] Ibid, at para. 44.

appropriate to upset the Swedish model for encouraging collective bargaining,[229] particularly as international human rights law and relevant ILO Conventions recognize the importance of collective bargaining.[230] The interference with Mr Gustafsson's ideological beliefs was not held to violate his human rights as he had not been forced to join an association as such. His objection was to the effect of being bound to enter into collective bargaining, and the Court held that the Convention did not protect the right not to enter into collective bargaining arrangements, and consequently the state had no positive obligations in this regard.[231]

The second case concerned the use by employers of financial incentives offered to employees to get them to surrender certain union rights. In the *Wilson* case, eleven individuals and two trade unions complained that the state had failed to protect their freedom of association from action taken by their non-state actor employer.[232] The facts vary between the separate applications, but it is convenient to start with Wilson himself. Mr Wilson, a journalist with the *Daily Mail*, received a letter informing him that the employer did not intend to negotiate a new collective bargaining agreement with the local branch of the National Union of Journalists, and that the Union would not be recognized as a negotiating body. Wilson was asked to sign a new contract providing for an annual review of salaries on an annual individual basis and was promised that signature would result in a backdated wage increase of 4.5 per cent. Wilson refused to sign the new contract on the grounds that he objected to the provisions prohibiting trade union activity during working hours and the removal of his trade union rights. Although his salary increased in subsequent years it 'was never raised to the same level as that of employees who had accepted personal contracts'.[233] Similar situations arose for the other applicants who were offered personal contracts with promises of wage increases in return for relinquishing rights to trade union recognition and representation.

[229] *Gustafsson v Sweden* Judgment of 25 April 1996, at para. 52.

[230] Ibid, at para. 53: 'It should also be recalled in this context that the legitimate character of collective bargaining is recognised by a number of international instruments, in particular Article 6 of the European Social Charter, Article 8 of the 1966 International Covenant on Economic, Social and Cultural Rights and Conventions nos. 87 and 98 of the International Labour Organisation (the first concerning freedom of association and the right to organise and the second the application of the principles of the right to organise and to bargain collectively).'

[231] 'In reality the applicant's principal objection to the second alternative was, as in relation to the first alternative, of a political nature, namely his disagreement with the collective-bargaining system in Sweden. However, Article 11 of the Convention does not as such guarantee a right not to enter into a collective agreement (see the above-mentioned *Swedish Engine Drivers' Union* judgment, pp 15–16, paras 40–41). The positive obligation incumbent on the State under Article 11, including the aspect of protection of personal opinion, may well extend to treatment connected with the operation of a collective-bargaining system, but only where such treatment impinges on freedom of association. Compulsion which, as here, does not significantly affect the enjoyment of that freedom, even if it causes economic damage, cannot give rise to any positive obligation under Article 11.' Ibid, at para. 52.

[232] *Wilson, the National Union of Journalists and ors v UK* Judgment of 2 July 2002.

[233] Ibid, at para. 11.

The Court recalled its approach that states have positive obligations to secure the effective enjoyment of Article 11 rights.[234] It further recalled its consistent position that 'although collective bargaining may be one of the ways by which trade unions may be enabled to protect their members' interests, it is not indispensable for the effective enjoyment of trade union freedom'.[235] The judgment explains that: 'Compulsory collective bargaining would impose on employers an obligation to conduct negotiations with trade unions. The Court has not yet been prepared to hold that the freedom of a trade union to make its voice heard extends to imposing on an employer an obligation to recognise a trade union.'[236]

As with the *Appleby, Sigurjónsson,* and *Gustafsson* cases, the judgment distils the essence of the essential elements of the Article 11 rights in question. First:

> The Court agrees with the Government that the essence of a voluntary system of collective bargaining is that it must be possible for a trade union which is not recognised by an employer to take steps including, if necessary, organising industrial action, with a view to persuading the employer to enter into collective bargaining with it on those issues which the union believes are important for its members' interests.[237]

Second:

> . . . it is of the essence of the right to join a trade union for the protection of their interests that employees should be free to instruct or permit the union to make representations to their employer or to take action in support of their interests on their behalf. If workers are prevented from so doing, their freedom to belong to a trade union, for the protection of their interests, becomes illusory. It is the role of the State to ensure that trade union members are not prevented or restrained from using their union to represent them in attempts to regulate their relations with their employers.[238]

The Court focused on the fact that employers could, under the law, offer substantial pay increases to those employees who acquiesced in the termination of collective

---

[234] 'The Court observes at the outset that although the essential object of Article 11 is to protect the individual against arbitrary interference by public authorities with the exercise of the rights protected, there may in addition be positive obligations to secure the effective enjoyment of these rights. In the present case, the matters about which the applicants complain—principally, the employers' de-recognition of the unions for collective-bargaining purposes and offers of more favourable conditions of employment to employees agreeing not to be represented by the unions—did not involve direct intervention by the State. The responsibility of the United Kingdom would, however, be engaged if these matters resulted from a failure on its part to secure to the applicants under domestic law the rights set forth in Article 11 of the Convention.' Ibid, at para. 41.   [235] Ibid, at para. 44.
[236] Ibid, at para. 44.   [237] Ibid, at para. 46.
[238] Ibid, at para. 46. The concurring opinion of Judge Gaukur Jörundsson provides further clarification of the Court's approach to the rights inherent or essential to Art. 11's promise that everyone has the right to form and join trade unions for the 'protection of his interests'. He pointed out that the Court had 'underlined that the members of a trade union have a right "in order to protect their interests, that the trade union should be heard"'. He emphasized the 'right to be heard' as a minimum right to be protected by Art. 11 (and other relevant treaties: see following footnote). For him, the UK legal situation at issue in *Wilson* 'stripp[ed] the trade union of effective power to protect members' interests. It permitted employers to ignore all representation by trade unions on behalf of their members and, furthermore, to use financial incentives to induce employees to surrender important union rights'.

bargaining and deny such increases to those that refused to sign. The Court went on to state that: 'The corollary of this was that United Kingdom law permitted employers to treat less favourably employees who were not prepared to renounce a freedom that was an essential feature of union membership. Such conduct constituted a disincentive or restraint on the use by employees of union membership to protect their interests.'[239] The Court concluded that the United Kingdom had failed in its positive obligation to secure the enjoyment of these union rights under Article 11.

9.1.12 Other Rights under the Convention and its Protocols

This review of the case-law of the European Court of Human Rights has not exhausted the possibilities for finding that a state has failed to protect a victim from human rights abuses committed by a non-state actor. Nearly all of the Articles of the Convention and its Protocols could be implicated with regard to the application of human rights in the private sphere. Commentators have suggested at various times that the Convention's reach into the private sphere covers: the right to marry under Article 12;[240] the right to peaceful enjoyment of possessions under Article 1 of Protocol 1;[241] denial of the right to education under Article 2 of Protocol 1;[242] and the right of spouses to equality under domestic law under Article 5 of Protocol 7.[243]

Finally, mention should be made of the complex wording of Protocol 12 on non-discrimination. This Protocol was drafted with the positive obligations of states regarding abuses by non-state actors very much in mind, and the drafters sought to focus on discrimination by public authorities.

Article 1—General prohibition of discrimination

(1) The enjoyment of any right set forth by law shall be secured without discrimination on any ground such as sex, race, colour, language, religion, political or other opinion, national or social origin, association with a national minority, property, birth or other status.

(2) No one shall be discriminated against by any public authority on any ground such as those mentioned in paragraph 1.

---

[239] *Wilson, the National Union of Journalists and ors v UK* Judgment of 2 July 2002, at para. 47. Note also the Court's reference to criticism of this aspect of the law by other international bodies in charge of monitoring separate international treaties: 'Under United Kingdom law at the relevant time it was, therefore, possible for an employer effectively to undermine or frustrate a trade union's ability to strive for the protection of its members' interests. The Court notes that this aspect of domestic law has been the subject of criticism by the Social Charter's Committee of Independent Experts and the ILO's Committee on Freedom of Association (see paragraphs 32–33 and 37 above).' Ibid, at para. 48.
[240] See van Dijk and van Hoof (1990: 446), who raise the question of private employers discriminating against employees on grounds of their married status.
[241] J. Raymond, 'L'Article 1 du Protocole additionnel et les rapports entre particuliers' in Matscher and Petzold (1988) 531–538.   [242] Van Dijk and van Hoof (1990: 473).
[243] S. Trechsel, 'Das Verflixte Siebente? Bemerkungen zum 7. Zusatzprotokoll zur EMRK' in M. Nowak, D. Steurer, and H. Tretter (eds) *Progress in the Spirit of Human Rights* (Kehl am Rhein: Engel, 1988) 195–211.

The possibility remains, however, of complaints concerning discrimination by non-state actors alleging a failure by the state to secure non-discrimination rights opposable against non-state actors in domestic law. According to the Explanatory Report:

24. The wording of Article 1 reflects a balanced approach to possible positive obligations of the Parties under this provision. This concerns the question to what extent Article 1 obliges the Parties to take measures to prevent discrimination, even where discrimination occurs in relations between private persons (so-called 'indirect horizontal effects'). The same question arises as regards measures to remedy instances of discrimination. While such positive obligations cannot be excluded altogether, the prime objective of Article 1 is to embody a negative obligation for the Parties: the obligation not to discriminate against individuals.

25. On the one hand, Article 1 protects against discrimination by public authorities. The Article is not intended to impose a general positive obligation on the Parties to take measures to prevent or remedy all instances of discrimination in relations between private persons. An additional protocol to the Convention, which typically contains justiciable individual rights formulated in concise provisions, would not be a suitable instrument for defining the various elements of such a wide-ranging obligation of a programmatic character. Detailed and tailor-made rules have already been laid down in separate conventions exclusively devoted to the elimination of discrimination on the specific grounds covered by them (see, for example, the Convention on Elimination of All Forms of Racial Discrimination and the Convention on the Elimination of All Forms of Discrimination against Women, which were both elaborated within the United Nations). It is clear that the present Protocol may not be construed as limiting or derogating from domestic or treaty provisions which provide further protection from discrimination...

26. On the other hand, it cannot be totally excluded that the duty to 'secure' under the first paragraph of Article 1 might entail positive obligations. For example, this question could arise if there is a clear lacuna in domestic law protection from discrimination. Regarding more specifically relations between private persons, a failure to provide protection from discrimination in such relations might be so clear-cut and grave that it might engage clearly the responsibility of the State and then Article 1 of the Protocol could come into play (see, *mutatis mutandis*, the judgment of the Court of 26 March 1985 in the case of *X and Y v. the Netherlands*, Series A, No 91, paragraphs 23–24, 27 and 30).[244]

9.1.13 Concluding Remarks on the European Convention

The obligation on states under this treaty is, according to Article 1, to secure all rights, and this gives rise to positive obligations to protect potential and actual

---

[244] The Report explains that it was prepared by the Steering Committee for Human Rights (which drafted the Protocol) and was adopted by the Committee of Ministers of the Council of Europe on 26 June 2000. The Report states that it 'does not constitute an instrument providing an authoritative interpretation of the text of the Protocol although it may facilitate the understanding of the Protocol's provisions'. At para. II. The Report is available at http://conventions.coe.int/Treaty/EN/Reports/Html/177.htm.

victims from infringements by non-state actors where this results from a failure to enact legislation.[245] In addition, even where the non-state actor behaviour is outlawed under national law, there may be positive obligations to ensure the enjoyment of Convention rights through, for example, the deployment of law enforcement officers. The limits to these obligations may depend on what is reasonably foreseeable and the steps that can be reasonably expected in such a situation.[246] Where the human right in question has explicit limitations, the limits to these positive obligations can also be deduced by considering the very 'essence' or 'substance' of the particular Article in conjunction with its limitation clause.[247]

In some cases legislation may be enacted but be inadequate to protect properly the Convention right from non-state actors who enjoy power in the relevant sector. This was the case with regards to the control of television advertising we encountered in the Swiss vegetarians case.[248] In such a situation the state will be held to have violated the Convention due to the failure of its courts to balance correctly (according to the Strasbourg Court) the human rights of the private parties to the dispute.

Lastly, we have seen that Article 13 protects the right to a national remedy even when the threat emanates from a non-state actor. This protection operates at two levels. First, one can complain that there is no avenue to effectively review the governmental policy which has led to interference with the right by the non-state actor.[249] Second, it is suggested, one can complain that the absence of an effective remedy in private law against the non-state actor may result in a violation of Article 13 by the state.[250]

---

[245] See *Young, James and Webster v UK* at para. 49 (9.1.1 above).

[246] See, e.g. *Osman v UK* at para. 116 (9.1.3.2 above) and *Plattform 'Ärzte für das Leben' v Austria* Judgment of 21 June 1988.

[247] For the Court's use of the notion of the 'very essence' (or 'substance') of rights when interference comes directly from non-state actors see, e.g. *Osman v UK* at para. 92 (9.1.3.2 above), *Appleby v UK* at para. 47 (9.1.11.1 above), *Sigurdur A Sigurjónsson v Iceland* at para. 37 (9.1.11.2 above), *Powell and Rayner v UK* at para. 41 (9.1.8 above), *Wilson and ors v UK* at para. 46 (9.1.11.2 above), *Gustafsson v Sweden* at para. 45 (Art. 11) 59–60, (Prot 1, Art. 1) and cf partly dissenting opinion of Judge Jambrek, para. 1, and dissenting opinion of Judge Martens, joined by Judge Matscher, para. 8. (9.1.11.2 above). Note the evaluation of Overy and White (2002: 19): 'The precise extent to which a State may be liable for the conduct of a private individual must ultimately depend on the terms of the individual articles and must be examined separately in relation to each of the rights guaranteed.' It is suggested that in order to understand what the Court means by the essence of the right, one must take into account the aim of the right in question in the light of the Court's desire to protect the values of dignity and democracy; see further Ch 11 below.

[248] *VgT Verein gegen Tierfabriken v Switzerland* (9.1.10 above).

[249] See, e.g. with regard to aircraft noise *Hatton and ors v UK* Judgment of 8 July 2003, at paras 131–142 (9.1.8.2 above).

[250] See the discussion by the Court in *Costello-Roberts v UK* para. 40 (above). It should be noted that Art. 13 'does not go so far as to guarantee a remedy allowing a Contracting State's laws as such to be challenged before a national authority on the ground of being contrary to the Convention' (at para. 40). See also the discussion in *Hatton and ors v UK* (9.1.2 and 9.1.8.2 above).

9.2   THE INTER-AMERICAN SYSTEM

9.2.1   The Inter-American Commission on Human Rights and its Action with Regard to Acts of Violence by 'Irregular Armed Groups'

The Inter-American Commission on Human Rights differs from the European Commission of Human Rights in that it has a role outside the action it takes upon receipt of communications under the relevant regional human rights instrument.[251] It has promotional and reporting functions with regard to all the member states of the Organization of American States (OAS). Since the entry into force of the Protocol of Buenos Aires, the Commission is also formally a Charter organ of the OAS with an extra-consultative role to the Organization.

One particular aspect of the Commission's work is the production of country reports. These may include discussions of the failure of a state to regulate oil companies, such as the report prepared on Ecuador, which stemmed from a complaint about toxic waste and the effects on the right to health of the people living in the Ecuadorian Amazon.[252] But the more controversial issue has been the Commission's approach to political violence by armed groups.

As early as 23 April 1970, the Commission adopted a Resolution condemning 'acts of political terrorism and urban or rural guerrilla terrorism, as they cause serious violations of the rights to life, personal security and physical freedom, freedom of thought, opinion and expression, and the rights to protection, upheld in the American Declaration and other international instruments'. Over the years there has been a tendency for governments to seek to justify repression by reference to the need to tackle terrorism and the Commission was faced with a request to concern itself with 'the human rights of the victims of terrorism'.[253] By 1993, the Commission was clear that a focus on armed groups would distract it from its main task:

> It need hardly be said that under no circumstances should a sensitivity toward the activities of armed irregular groups leading to violations of human rights be used as a

---

[251] See Art. 41 of the American Convention on Human Rights (ACHR) for the functions of the Commission with regard to States Parties to the Convention; Art. 18 of the Statute of the Commission with respect to all Member States of the OAS; Art. 19 of the Commission's Statute for States Parties to the Convention; and Art. 20 of the Commission's Statute for OAS Member States that are not parties to the Convention. See generally T. Buergenthal, R. Norris, and D. Shelton, *Protecting Human Rights in the Americas* (Kehl am Rhein: Engel, 3rd edn, 1990).

[252] Inter-American Commission on Human Rights, Report of the Situation of Human Rights in Ecuador, OAS Doc. OEA/Ser.L/V/II.96 (1997), discussed in C. Scott, 'Multinational Enterprises and Emergent Jurisprudence on Violations of Economic, Social and Cultural Rights' in A. Eide, C. Krause, and A. Rosas (eds) *Economic, Social and Cultural Rights: A Textbook* (Dordrecht: Martinus Nijhoff, 2nd edn, 2001) 563–595 at 577–578, see also N. Jägers, *Corporate Human Rights Obligations: In Search of Accountability* (Antwerp: Intersentia, 2002) at 155–156.

[253] See the Annual Report of the Inter-American Commission on Human Rights 1990–1991, 504–514. Discussed in greater detail in Clapham (1993: 120–124).

justification for the violations of human rights by governments themselves. One should bear in mind that the primary function of the Commission is 'to promote respect for and defense of' human rights which members of the OAS have undertaken to respect in the terms set forth in the American Declaration of the Rights and Duties of Man, and the American Convention on Human Rights. Though the Commission is willing and anxious to expand its focus, when relevant, to deal with any violation of human rights, nothing may be done that could possibly minimize its primary function.[254]

The issue resurfaced in the wake of the September 11 attacks in the United States and the Commission set out its approach to human rights and terrorism at some length:

> It is also pertinent to observe that the human rights framework established by member states of the OAS is one that speaks generally to the obligations and responsibilities of states, which are obliged to refrain from supporting, tolerating or otherwise acquiescing in acts or omissions that fail to conform with their international human rights commitments. Consistent with this premise, the Commission's mandate is to promote the observance and protection of human rights by states and their agents rather than non-state actors.
>
> This does not mean, however, that the conduct of non-state actors, including terrorists and terrorist groups, bears no relevance to the evaluation of states' obligations concerning human rights protections in the Hemisphere. Throughout its history, the Commission has, for example, referenced the atrocities committed by armed dissident groups in its press releases, in communications with governments, and in its reports on the situation of human rights in the various member states of the OAS. The Commission has considered violence of this nature to constitute a relevant component of the environment in which states' general compliance with human rights standards must be evaluated, and as a justification that may potentially be invoked by states as grounds for temporarily suspending the exercise of certain rights.[255]

One country report will suffice to illustrate the legal framework applied. The 1999 report on Colombia set out the approach as follows:[256]

> 2. Before discussing its concerns and other matters relating to the violence and ongoing hostilities in Colombia, the Commission believes it useful to clarify various issues concerning its competence to investigate and condemn acts of violence. In accordance with the legal framework established by member states of the Organization of American States (the 'OAS'), the Commission is expressly charged with monitoring and promoting respect for and defense of fundamental human rights by each of those states. The Commission's duty, therefore, is to apply human rights instruments to cases and situations involving State responsibility.
>
> 3. Under the individual petition procedure set forth in its Statute and the American Convention on Human Rights, the Commission's jurisdiction extends only to situations

---

[254] Annual Report 1992–1993, 'Activities of Armed Groups', Ch V, Pt II.
[255] OAS Doc. OEA/Ser.L/V/II.116, Doc. 5 rev. 1 corr., 22 October 2002, at paras 47–48 (footnotes omitted).
[256] Colombia report 1999, Ch IV, Pt B, available at http://www.cidh.org/countryrep/Colom99en/chapter-4.htm (footnotes omitted).

where the international responsibility of a member State is at issue. Thus, the IACHR is authorized to receive, investigate and decide cases lodged against member States for the acts or omissions of their agents and organs that allegedly violate the human rights guaranteed in the American Convention or the American Declaration of the Rights and Duties of Man (the 'Declaration'). The Commission's jurisdiction also encompasses cases of transgressions of these same rights by private persons or groups who are, in effect, State agents or when such transgressions by private actors are acquiesced in, tolerated, or condoned by the State.

4. The Commission as well as the Court have also consistently pointed out that the State has a duty under the American Convention and the Declaration to prevent and to investigate acts of violence committed by private parties and to prosecute and punish the perpetrators accordingly. The Commission thus may process individual cases alleging the failure of a State to comply with this duty. At the same time, the Commission recognizes that in situations of civil strife the State cannot always prevent, much less be held responsible for, the harm to individuals and destruction of private property occasioned by the hostile acts of its armed opponents.

5. As noted in its two previous country reports on Colombia, OAS member States opted deliberately not to give the Commission jurisdiction to investigate or hear individual complaints concerning illicit acts of private persons or groups for which the State is not internationally responsible. If it were to act on such complaints, the Commission would be in flagrant breach of its mandate, and, by according these persons or groups the same treatment and status that a State receives as a party to a complaint, it would infringe the sovereign rights and prerogatives of the State concerned.

6. This limitation on its competence to process individual complaints does not mean that the Commission has been indifferent or silent in the face of atrocities and other violent acts committed by dissident armed groups, drug traffickers and other private actors in Colombia and other OAS member States. Outside of the context of individual cases, the Commission has frequently referenced the atrocities committed by armed dissident groups in its press releases, in communications with governments and in its reports on the situation of human rights in the various member States of the OAS. In this regard, for example, the Commission stated in its 'Second Report on the Situation of Human Rights in Colombia':

'[T]he Commission is . . . emphatic in its condemnation of the terrible aggression perpetrated against the Colombian people by irregular armed groups. The Commission considers the use of terrorism, whatever its form, to be utterly reprehensible as are blackmail, extortion, kidnapping, torture and assassination.'

7. A relatively recent expression of the Commission's condemnation of illicit acts committed by an armed dissident group in Colombia is found in the following text of an official press release issued by the Commission on April 1, 1998:

The Inter-American Commission on Human Rights has learned that the Revolutionary Armed Forces of Colombia ("Fuerzas Armadas Revolucionarias de Colombia"—FARC), on March 23, set up a roadblock for almost eight hours on the highway which connects Bogotá to the western plains of Colombia. During the period which the roadblock was in place, the armed dissident group halted the movement of those who traveled on this highway, many of whom were returning to Bogotá after an extended weekend, and detained several persons. The FARC subsequently freed some individuals but continued to hold others under its control. According to information received by the Commission, the FARC have threatened to execute the persons who remain in captivity.

The Commission has indicated, on other occasions, that international norms absolutely prohibit, in any armed conflict, executions and any other act of violence against members of the civilian population who do not participate directly in the hostilities. These norms also prohibit the taking of hostages and arbitrary deprivation of liberty. The Commission reaffirms its prior statements on this occasion and energetically repudiates any violation of these international law norms committed against any individual.

The IACHR again emphasizes that the most diverse lines of thought recognize essential values which require respect for human dignity, even in conflict situations. The IACHR, with absolute independence and objectivity, has consistently and uniformly expressed this same position in a coherent manner, in respect of the States in this hemisphere and, in appropriate cases, in reference to the actions of non-State groups. This has occurred, as is public knowledge, in situations which have taken place in various member States of the Organization, including Colombia.

For these reasons, the Inter-American Commission on Human Rights, through this press release, exhorts the group which holds under its control several persons kidnapped in the roadblock which the FARC put in place on March 23 to respect the lives, security and health of those individuals and to proceed to liberate them immediately.

In short, the Commission, through press releases and its public reports, appeals directly to rebel non-state actors in specific situations to respect lives, security, and health. It also condemns in general terrorism, blackmail, extortion, kidnapping, torture, and assassination.

9.2.2   Petitions to the Inter-American Commission and the Jurisprudence of the Court of Human Rights

The Inter-American Court and Commission have both considered the obligations of the state with regard to protecting people from non-state actors. The Inter-American Commission on Human Rights clearly stated in 1981, in the context of violent attacks in Guatemala, that 'the governments must prevent and suppress acts of violence, even forcefully, whether committed by public officials or *private individuals*, whether their motives are political or otherwise'.[257] One particular petition brought against Guatemala related to the Coca-Cola bottling plant. The communication described murders that the local company had paid for and, in addition, it alleged that the company had organized an advertising campaign in the newspapers to defame and denigrate the union leader so that there would be no outcry when he was murdered.[258] The Government of Guatemala did not

---

[257] IACHR, 'Report on the Situation of Human Rights in the Republic of Guatemala', OAS Doc. OEA/Ser.L/V/II.53, Doc. 21, rev. 2, 13 October 1981, para. 10 (emphasis added).

[258] Res. 38/81, Case No. 4425 (Guatemala) 25 June 1981, para. 1. Case available from http://www.cidh.oas.org/annualrep/80.81eng/Guatemala4425.htm.

reply to the Commission's requests for information and the Commission proceeded on the presumption that the facts were true. The Commission declared that the state had violated various rights in the American Convention on Human Rights, including the rights to life, humane treatment, personal liberty, fair trial, assembly, association, and judicial protection. This approach, in which the Convention is seen as outlining positive obligations for the state to protect individuals from non-state violence, was developed by the Court in an early case.

This early Judgment of the Inter-American Court of Human Rights concerned the positive obligations of states under the American Convention on Human Rights with regard to the investigation and punishment of 'disappearances'. The Court highlighted that states have a 'duty to ensure' all rights in the treaty and declared that it did not need to establish whether the actual act of kidnapping took place at the hands of state or non-state actors. Whatever the identity of the direct perpetrator, the state has an obligation of 'due diligence' under the Convention:

> 172.   Thus, in principle, any violation of rights recognized by the Convention carried out by an act of public authority or by persons who use their position of authority is imputable to the State. However, this does not define all the circumstances in which a State is obligated to prevent, investigate and punish human rights violations, nor all the cases in which the State might be found responsible for an infringement of those rights. An illegal act which violates human rights and which is initially not directly imputable to a State (for example, because it is the act of a private person or because the person responsible has not been identified) can lead to international responsibility of the State, not because of the act itself, but because of the lack of due diligence to prevent the violation or to respond to it as required by the Convention.[259]

It is the illegal act by the non-state actor that is seen here as a *violation* of human rights. State responsibility follows where the state has failed in its due diligence obligations under the Convention. The Court went on to detail what those due diligence obligations entail:

> 173.   Violations of the Convention cannot be founded upon rules that take psychological factors into account in establishing individual culpability. For the purposes of analysis, the intent or motivation of the agent who has violated the rights recognized by the Convention is irrelevant—the violation can be established even if the identity of the individual perpetrator is unknown. What is decisive is whether a violation of the rights recognized by the Convention has occurred with the support or the acquiescence of the government, or whether the State has allowed the act to take place without taking measures to prevent it or to punish those responsible. Thus, the Court's task is to determine whether the violation is the result of a State's failure to fulfill its duty to respect and guarantee those rights, as required by Article 1(1) of the Convention.

> 174.   The State has a legal duty to take reasonable steps to prevent human rights violations and to use the means at its disposal to carry out a serious investigation of

---

[259]   *Velásquez Rodriguez v Honduras* Judgment of 29 July 1988, at para. 172.

violations committed within its jurisdiction, to identify those responsible, to impose the appropriate punishment and to ensure the victim adequate compensation.

175.   This duty to prevent includes all those means of a legal, political, administrative and cultural nature that promote the protection of human rights and ensure that any violations are considered and treated as illegal acts, which, as such, may lead to the punishment of those responsible and the obligation to indemnify the victims for damages. It is not possible to make a detailed list of all such measures, since they vary with the law and the conditions of each State Party. Of course, while the State is obligated to prevent human rights abuses, the existence of a particular violation does not, in itself, prove the failure to take preventive measures. On the other hand, subjecting a person to official, repressive bodies that practice torture and assassination with impunity is itself a breach of the duty to prevent violations of the rights to life and physical integrity of the person, even if that particular person is not tortured or assassinated, or if those facts cannot be proven in a concrete case.

176.   The State is obligated to investigate every situation involving a violation of the rights protected by the Convention. If the State apparatus acts in such a way that the violation goes unpunished and the victim's full enjoyment of such rights is not restored as soon as possible, the State has failed to comply with its duty to ensure the free and full exercise of those rights to the persons within its jurisdiction. The same is true when the State allows private persons or groups to act freely and with impunity to the detriment of the rights recognized by the Convention.

177.   In certain circumstances, it may be difficult to investigate acts that violate an individual's rights. The duty to investigate, like the duty to prevent, is not breached merely because the investigation does not produce a satisfactory result. Nevertheless, it must be undertaken in a serious manner and not as a mere formality preordained to be ineffective. An investigation must have an objective and be assumed by the State as its own legal duty, not as a step taken by private interests that depends upon the initiative of the victim or his family or upon their offer of proof, without an effective search for the truth by the government. This is true regardless of what agent is eventually found responsible for the violation. Where the acts of private parties that violate the Convention are not seriously investigated, those parties are aided in a sense by the government, thereby making the State responsible on the international plane.

The language of the judgment speaks of private parties *violating* the Convention. At the same time, the state is to be held responsible where it has failed to ensure that violations of the Conventions are considered illegal acts under national law and properly investigated and punished (whether the direct perpetrator is a public or a private actor). This approach, which sees transgressions of the Convention by non-state actors as simultaneously violations of international law, and as acts which the state has an obligation to make illegal under national law, is developed in the Court's Advisory Opinion on migrant workers, discussed below.

The Court went on to find that the disappearance had been carried out by 'agents who acted under cover of public authority',[260] but was careful to add that, even if this fact had not been proven, the 'failure of the State apparatus to act' was

---

[260]   *Velásquez Rodríguez v Honduras* Judgment of 29 July 1988, at para. 182.

a failure on the part of Honduras to fulfil its duties under Article 1(1) of the Convention 'to ensure Manfredo Velásquez the free and full exercise of his human rights'.[261] Subsequent cases concerning disappearances have reinforced the Court's approach, which does not insist on direct attribution, but rather on the failure of the state to react.[262] With regard to the murder and disappearance of street children, the Court also found a violation by Guatemala of its obligation to ensure the welfare of children, with some judges highlighting the positive obligation on the state to ensure the right to a life with dignity.[263]

In another context the Court has suggested that, although the state has an obligation to protect the security of everyone within its jurisdiction, 'this duty is more evident with respect to persons detained in a State detention center, in which case the responsibility of the State must be presumed regarding what happens to those who are under its custody'.[264]

With regard to the acts of paramilitary groups, even where such groups were already outlawed by the state, the Commission has held that where private individuals, acting as paramilitaries, carry out joint operations with the army, such individuals act as agents of the state and the state is directly liable for violations of the Convention resulting from the acts of these private individuals.[265]

Turning away from the issue of murder and disappearances, the Inter-American bodies have also considered the positive obligations of the state with regard to indigenous peoples and the activities of corporations and private individuals. In *Yanomami v Brazil* the Commission considered a series of complaints brought under the American Declaration of the Rights and Duties of Man with regard to the behaviour of corporate and other non-state actors. The focus of the decision was on the action of the Brazilian Government first, in authorizing the exploitation of the resources of the Indian territories, and second 'permitting the massive

---

[261] Ibid at para. 182.

[262] See, e.g. *Paniagua-Morales et al v Guatemala* Judgment of 8 March 1998, at para. 91: 'Unlike domestic criminal law, it is not necessary to determine the perpetrators' culpability or intentionality in order to establish that the rights enshrined in the Convention have been violated, nor is it essential to identify individually the agents to whom the acts of violation are attributed. The sole requirement is to demonstrate that the State authorities supported or tolerated infringement of the rights recognized in the Convention. Moreover, the State's international responsibility is also at issue when it does not take the necessary steps under its domestic law to identify and, where appropriate, punish the authors of such violations.'

[263] See, *Villagran Morales et al v Guatemala* Judgment of 19 November 1994, at paras 178–198. See also Joint Concurring Opinion of Judges A. A. Cançado Trindade and A. Abreu-Burelli (at para. 4): 'The duty of the State to take positive measures is stressed precisely in relation to the protection of life of vulnerable and defenseless persons, in situation of risk, such as the children in the streets. The arbitrary deprivation of life is not limited, thus, to the illicit act of homicide; it extends itself likewise to the deprivation of the right to live with dignity. This outlook conceptualizes the right to life as belonging, at the same time, to the domain of civil and political rights, as well as economic, social and cultural rights, thus illustrating the interrelation and indivisibility of all human rights.'

[264] *Case of Urso Branco Prison*, Provisional Measures with Respect to Brazil, order of 18 June 2002, at para. 8.

[265] Report No. 62/01, Case 11.654, *Riofrío Massacre*, Colombia, 6 April 2001, at paras 48–52 available from http://www.cidh.oas.org/annualrep/2001eng/Colombia12266.htm.

penetration into the Indians' territory of outsiders carrying various contagious diseases'.[266] The Commission found:

a. That on account of the beginning, in 1973, of the construction of highway BR-210 (the Northern Circumferential Highway), the territory occupied for ages beyond memory by the Yanomami Indians was invaded by highway construction workers, geologists, mining prospectors, and farm workers desiring to settle in that territory;

b. That those invasions were carried out without prior and adequate protection for the safety and health of the Yanomami Indians, which resulted in a considerable number of deaths caused by epidemics of influenza, tuberculosis, measles, venereal diseases, and others;

c. That Indian inhabitants of various villages near the route of highway BR-210 (the Northern Circumferential Highway) abandoned their villages and were changed into beggars or prostitutes, without the Government of Brazil's taking the necessary measures to prevent this; and

d. That after the discovery in 1976 of ores of tin and other metals in the region where the Yanomamis live, serious conflicts arose that led to acts of violence between prospectors and miners of those minerals, on one side, and the Indians, on the other. Such conflicts, which occurred especially in the areas of the Serra dos Surucucus, Couto de Magalhäes, and Furo de Santa Rosa, affected the lives, security, health, and cultural integrity of the Yanomamis.

11. That from the facts set forth above a liability of the Brazilian Government arises for having failed to take timely and effective measures to protect the human rights of the Yanomamis.[267]

The Commission went on to find violations of the right to life, liberty, and personal security, the right to residence and movement, and the right to the preservation of health and to well-being under the American Declaration of the Rights and Duties of Man.

Turning to the Inter-American Court of Human Rights, threats to indigenous peoples have arisen in the context of a case brought against Nicaragua. The Court's Judgment covers important ground, especially with regard to the judicial protection of rights under national and international law, as well as the rights to property for indigenous peoples under the Convention. On this last aspect, it is worth quoting an excerpt from the Judgment:

... it is the opinion of this Court that article 21 of the Convention protects the right to property in a sense which includes, among others, the rights of members of the indigenous communities within the framework of communal property, which is also recognized by the Constitution of Nicaragua.

Given the characteristics of the instant case, some specifications are required on the concept of property in indigenous communities. Among indigenous peoples there is a communitarian tradition regarding a communal form of collective property of the land, in the sense that ownership of the land is not centered on an individual but rather on the

---

[266] Res. 12/85, Case 7615, 5 March 1985, available from http://www.cidh.oas.org/annualrep/84.85eng/Brazil7615.htm.　　　　　[267] Ibid, at paras 10–11.

group and its community. Indigenous groups, by the fact of their very existence, have the right to live freely in their own territory; the close ties of indigenous people with the land must be recognized and understood as the fundamental basis of their cultures, their spiritual life, their integrity, and their economic survival. For indigenous communities, relations to the land are not merely a matter of possession and production but a material and spiritual element which they must fully enjoy, even to preserve their cultural legacy and transmit it to future generations.[268]

The Court held that the failure of the state to delimit the territory belonging to the indigenous Community gave rise to an obligation not to allow 'third parties' to interfere with the enjoyment of the property located in the area where the members of the Community live.[269] In the instant case, there had been problems relating to a logging concession granted (and subsequently withdrawn) by the authorities. The Court found that the concessions amounted to an interference with property rights and that there had been a violation of the rights to property under Article 21 of the Convention in connection with Articles 1 and 2 of the Convention.[270] A further finding of the Court related to a violation of the Article 25 right to judicial protection from acts that violate 'fundamental rights recognized by the constitution or laws' of the state concerned or of the Convention. The Court decided, *inter alia*, that the State 'must abstain from any acts that might lead the agents of the State itself, or third parties acting with its acquiescence or its tolerance, to affect the existence, value, use or enjoyment of the property located in the geographic area where the members of the Mayagna (Sumo) Awas Tingni Community live and carry out their activities'.[271]

Other contentious cases before the Court have reminded states that, in the context of freedom of expression, the media are required to discharge their social functions responsibly,[272] and that Article 11 of the Convention establishes that everyone has the right to have his honour respected and his dignity recognized. This implies that there are limits on individual freedom, and that an individual who considers his honour affected should have recourse to protection by judicial mechanisms established by the state.[273]

9.2.3 The Advisory Opinion on the Rights of Migrant Workers

In 2003, the Court set out clear obligations for the state to prevent discrimination by private employers in an advisory opinion on the rights of migrant workers.

---

[268] *The Mayagna (Sumo) Awas Tingni Community v Nicaragua* Judgment of 31 August 2001, at paras 148–149. [269] Ibid, at para. 153.
[270] Ibid, at paras 153–155. [271] Ibid, at para. 173.
[272] *Herrera Ulloa v Costa Rica* Judgment of 2 July 2004, at para. 117. I am grateful to Jo Pasqualucci for identifying this issue before the Court for me and more generally for the helpful references to several other cases (discussed above) in her book: *The Practice and Procedure of the Inter-American Court of Human Rights* (Cambridge: Cambridge University Press, 2003).
[273] *Ricardo Canese v Paraguay* Judgment of 31 August 2004, at para. 101.

Interestingly, the Court determined that equality was a principle of customary international law (even a *jus cogens*/peremptory principle).

> Indeed, this principle [of non-discrimination] may be considered peremptory under general international law, inasmuch as it applies to all States, whether or not they are party to a specific international treaty, and gives rise to effects with regard to third parties, including individuals. This implies that the State, both internationally and in its domestic legal system, and by means of the acts of any of its powers *or of third parties who act under its tolerance, acquiescence or negligence*, cannot behave in a way that is contrary to the principle of equality and non-discrimination, to the detriment of a determined group of persons.[274]

The effect on third parties is referred to later as an *erga omnes* obligation: 'The effects of the fundamental principle of equality and non-discrimination encompass all States, precisely because this principle, which belongs to the realm of *jus cogens* and is of a peremptory character, entails obligations *erga omnes* of protection that bind all States and give rise to effects with regard to third parties, including individuals.'[275] These effects, according to the Court, create human rights obligations for non-state actors:

> In this way, the obligation to respect and ensure human rights, which normally has effects on the relations between the State and the individuals subject to its jurisdiction, also has effects on relations between individuals. As regards this Advisory Opinion, the said effects of the obligation to respect human rights in relations between individuals is defined in the context of the private employment relationship, under which the employer must respect the human rights of his workers.[276]

After a review of the relevant law, the Court summarized its opinion with regard to state responsibility for discrimination by non-state actors:

> In summary, employment relationships between migrant workers and third party employers may give rise to the international responsibility of the State in different ways. First, States are obliged to ensure that, within their territory, all the labor rights stipulated in its laws—rights deriving from international instruments or domestic legislation—are recognized and applied. Likewise, States are internationally responsible when they tolerate actions and practices of third parties that prejudice migrant workers, either because they do not recognize the same rights to them as to national workers or because they recognize the same rights to them but with some type of discrimination.[277]

The Court recalled a *pro hominem* principle, whereby the rights which are most favourable to the worker, whether under national or international law, must be respected.[278] For the Court, the purpose of the protection of a worker's rights is ultimately the protection of human dignity, and the Court gives an indication of

---

[274] OC–18/03 of 17 September 2003, *Juridical Condition and Rights of the Undocumented Migrants*, at para. 100 (emphasis added).   [275] Ibid, at para. 110.
[276] Ibid, at para. 146, and see at n 282 below, the reference to the concurring opinion of the President of the Court, Judge Antônio A. Cançado Trindade.   [277] Ibid, at para. 153.
[278] Ibid, at para. 156.

the sorts of rights at risk, giving us a useful checklist of rights to be respected by non-state and state actors alike.

> In the case of migrant workers, there are certain rights that assume a fundamental importance and yet are frequently violated, such as: the prohibition of obligatory or forced labor; the prohibition and abolition of child labor; special care for women workers, and the rights corresponding to: freedom of association and to organize and join a trade union, collective negotiation, fair wages for work performed, social security, judicial and administrative guarantees, a working day of reasonable length with adequate working conditions (safety and health), rest and compensation. The safeguard of these rights for migrants has great importance based on the principle of the inalienable nature of such rights, which all workers possess, irrespective of their migratory status, and also the fundamental principle of human dignity embodied in Article 1 of the Universal Declaration, according to which '[a]ll human beings are born free and equal in dignity and rights. They are endowed with reason and conscience and should act towards one another in a spirit of brotherhood.'[279]

The Court highlighted the behaviour of the employers themselves: 'On many occasions, undocumented migrant workers are not recognized [as having] the said labor rights. For example, many employers engage them to provide a specific service for less than the regular remuneration, dismiss them because they join unions, and threaten to deport them.'[280] In the final part of the opinion the Court decided:

> That the State has the obligation to respect and guarantee the labor human rights of all workers, irrespective of their status as nationals or aliens, and not to tolerate situations of discrimination that are harmful to the latter in the employment relationships established between private individuals (employer-worker). The State must not allow private employers to violate the rights of workers, or the contractual relationship to violate minimum international standards.[281]

This is a rare authoritative judicial ruling on the obligations of states to ensure respect for rights by non-state actor employers. For the President of the Court, Judge Antônio Augusto Cançado Trindade, the use of the concept of *erga omnes* obligations by the Court highlights that the inherent rights belonging to workers are opposable, not only against the state, but also against non-state actors: 'the obligations *erga omnes* of protection bind both the organs and agents of (State) public power, and the individuals themselves (in the inter-individual relations)'.[282] He later reinforced the point as follows: 'The fundamental rights of the migrant workers, including the undocumented ones, are opposable to the public power and likewise to the private persons or individuals (e.g., employers), in the inter-individual relations.'[283] The Advisory Opinion marks a breakthrough in

---

279 Ibid, at para. 156.   280 Ibid, at para. 159.
281 Ibid, at para. 173, resolutory point 9.
282 Concurring Opinion at para. 77, see also on this point, para. 78.   283 Ibid, at para. 85.

human rights law by building on the concepts of third-party effects and *erga omnes* obligations to suggest that human rights obligations under general international law are binding on non-state actors (in this case employers and individuals).[284]

9.3   THE AFRICAN APPROACH UNDER THE OAU HUMAN RIGHTS TREATIES

Rachel Murray has suggested that traditional Western assumptions about the division between public/private and state/non-state actors have less resonance in Africa. She states that in the African context: 'the notion of a state detached from the individual is not the same as in the West. The precolonial structure emphasised the community rather than the individual, and thus did not see a divide between the individual and the state. As a result the division between the public and the private is less apparent'.[285] Murray considers that colonialism imported some aspects of the public/private divide with its imposed concepts of the liberal state, but she suggests: 'An African stance may take into account a wider range of violations involving non-state actors.'[286] Of particular note is the focus on violence against women in the private sphere, and protection from traditions and cultural practices, as well as the protection of rights in the workplace.[287] Such an approach is, in part, assisted by the African Charter's emphasis on duties owed by the individual.[288]

The concept of individual duties as part of the human rights agenda has given rise to some misgivings, as Barney Pityana explains: there is 'a preponderance of opinion which suggests that the mere provision of "duties" creates a reactionary environment for the protection of human rights'.[289] But Pityana counters this and

---

[284]   This aspect of the Opinion is emphasized in the concurring opinion of Judge Hernán Salgado-Pesantes: 'I consider that an extremely important point in this Advisory Opinion is that of establishing clearly the effectiveness of human rights with regard to third parties, in a horizontal conception. These aspects, as is acknowledged, have been amply developed in German legal writings (*Drittwirkung*) and are contained in current constitutionalism. It is not only the State that has the obligation to respect human rights, but also individuals in their relationships with other individuals. The environment of free will that prevails in private law cannot become an obstacle that dilutes the binding effectiveness *erga omnes* of human rights.' At paras 17 and 18. On *Drittwirkung*, see Ch 10, at 10.3.4 below.

[285]   R. Murray, *The African Commission on Human and Peoples' Rights and International Law* (Oxford: Hart Publishing, 2000) at 38, and see generally 37–47.   [286]   Ibid, at 39.

[287]   See the Protocol to the African Charter on Human and Peoples' Rights on the Rights of Women in Africa, which explicitly extends its provisions on violence to the private sphere as well as ensuring that certain employment rights are protected in the private sector. See esp. Arts 1(f)(j), 2(2), 3(4), 4(2)(a), 5, 12, 13, 14, 18, 21, and 23. See also the African Charter on the Rights and Welfare of the Child, esp. Arts 1(3), 15, 16, 21, 27, and 29.

[288]   See Arts 27–29; see also Art. 31 of the African Charter on the Rights and Welfare of the Child.

[289]   N. B. Pityana, 'The Challenge of Culture for Human Rights in Africa: the African Charter in a Comparative Context' in M. D. Evans and R. Murray (eds) *The African Charter on Human and Peoples' Rights; The System in Practice, 1986–2000* (Cambridge: Cambridge University Press, 2002) 219–245 at 229.

suggests: 'Far from duties creating an environment for a gratuitous invasion of rights, duties should be understood as reinforcing rights. Secondly, it becomes necessary to make reference to duties because, in the modern global environment, the key performers are not necessarily the States but non-State actors. To focus solely on States as providers and protectors of rights would be to leave out of consideration a large part of social commerce where rights are exercised.'[290]

These duties under the Charter include a duty on the individual 'to respect and consider his fellow beings without discrimination, and to maintain relations aimed at promoting, safeguarding and reinforcing mutual respect and tolerance'.[291] Although Pityana sees the duties as moral duties rather than legal duties,[292] Cristof Heyns sees the Charter as generating duties for individuals which may affect the enjoyment of their rights: 'Traditionally, international treaties bind only states. The African Charter, however, also imposes duties on individuals.[293] These duties have the potential to limit the rights recognised in the Charter.'[294] As discussed above, with regard to Article 17 of the European Convention, the idea that individuals may have their rights limited where their actions unduly impinge on the rights of others is already quite developed. One important aspect of the inclusion of duties, such as the duty not to discriminate, quoted above, is that this emphasizes the extension of the Charter into the private sphere. With reference to non-discrimination, Heyns states that 'Article 28 applies to relations on the horizontal plane and deals with discrimination between individuals.'[295]

Commentators have highlighted the Commission's willingness to look at the protection of human rights, not only in terms of refraining from action, but also in terms of obligations to take action to secure the enjoyment of all rights.[296] Two decisions of the Commission might be highlighted. First, as regards the general obligation to secure the right to life, the Charter provides an obligation to investigate murder even where the perpetrators of murder were not proven to be state agents. In a communication against Chad, a human rights organization complained that: 'journalists are harassed, both directly and indirectly. These attacks are often by unidentified individuals who the complainants claim to be security service agents of the Government'. They also complained of 'the assassination of Bisso Mamadou, who was attacked by armed individuals. The Minister responsible was warned of the danger to Mr. Bisso, but he refused to issue protection.

---

[290] Ibid, at 230.   [291] Art. 28.   [292] Pityana (2002: 231).
[293] The footnote in the original reads: 'These are secondary as their existence depends upon the State having assumed the primary duty to be bound by the treaty.'
[294] C. Heyns, 'Civil and Political Rights in the African Charter' in Evans and Murray (2002: 137–177, at 140). Cf Murray (2000: 87) who concludes 'although individual duties may not be enforceable on the international level, that individuals have duties that derive from international law is clear'.   [295] Heyns (2002: 146).
[296] See Murray (2000: 37–47); F. Ouguerouz, *The African Charter on Human and Peoples' Rights: A Comprehensive Agenda for Human Dignity and Sustainable Democracy in Africa* (The Hague: Martinus Nijhoff, 2003) esp. at 98–99, 398–399, footnotes 361–363 and accompanying text.

Subsequently, the Minister did not initiate investigation into the killing'.[297] The Commission rejected the Government's argument that it could not control what happened in a state of civil war, and held that the state party had a duty to protect individuals from state and non-state actors:

> In the present case, Chad has failed to provide security and stability in the country, thereby allowing serious and massive violations of human rights. The national armed forces are participants in the civil war and there have been several instances in which the Government has failed to intervene to prevent the assassination and killing of specific individuals. Even where it cannot be proved that violations were committed by government agents, the Government had a responsibility to secure the safety and the liberty of its citizens, and to conduct investigations into murders. Chad therefore is responsible for the violations of the African Charter.[298]

The main point was reiterated in general terms in a later Communication:

> The Commission would also like to reiterate a fundamental principle proclaimed in Article 1 of the Charter that not only do the States Parties recognise the rights, duties and freedoms enshrined in the Charter, they also commit themselves to respect them and to take measures to give effect to them. In other words, if a State Party fails to ensure respect of the rights contained in the African Charter, this constitutes a violation of the Charter. Even if the State or its agents were not the perpetrators of the violation.[299]

A second decision demonstrates how economic, social, and cultural rights can be threatened by non-state actors. The African Commission went into some detail on this issue with regard to a complaint focused on the behaviour of an oil consortium comprising the state oil company and Shell in Nigeria.[300] According to the summary of the facts:

> The Communication alleges that the oil consortium has exploited oil reserves in Ogoniland with no regard for the health or environment of the local communities, disposing toxic wastes into the environment and local waterways in violation of applicable international environmental standards. The consortium also neglected and/or failed to maintain its facilities causing numerous avoidable spills in the proximity of villages. The resulting contamination of water, soil and air has had serious short and long-term health impacts, including skin infections, gastrointestinal and respiratory ailments, and increased risk of cancers, and neurological and reproductive problems.[301]

The Commission looked at the harm caused by the consortium and concluded that the Government of Nigeria had failed in its obligation to protect the rights to

---

[297] Comm. 74/92, *Commission Nationale des Droits de l'Homme et des Libertés v Chad*, at paras 2 and 5, available at http://hei.unige.ch/humanrts/africa/comcases/74–92.html.

[298] Ibid, at para. 22.

[299] Comm. 204/97, *Mouvement Burkinabé des Droits de l'Homme et des Peuples v Burkina Faso*, available at http://hei.unige.ch/humanrts/africa/comcases/204–97.html.

[300] Comm. 155/96, *The Social and Economic Rights Action Center and the Center for Economic and Social Rights v Nigeria*, at 31, available at http://hei.unige.ch/~clapham/hrdoc/docs/ achprseracase.pdf.

[301] Ibid, at para. 2.

health and a healthy environment as guaranteed by the Charter. The decision goes on to consider the violation of the right to natural resources under Article 21 of the Charter:

> The Commission notes that in the present case, despite its obligation to protect persons against interferences in the enjoyment of their rights, the Government of Nigeria facilitated the destruction of the Ogoniland. Contrary to its Charter obligations and despite such internationally established principles, the Nigerian Government has given the green light to private actors, and the oil Companies in particular, to devastatingly affect the well-being of the Ogonis. By any measure of standards, its practice falls short of the minimum conduct expected of governments, and therefore, is in violation of Article 21 of the African Charter.[302]

With regard to the right to housing, the Commission was explicit concerning the need to protect individuals from non-state actors:

> [The state's] obligations to protect obliges it to prevent the violation of any individual's right to housing by any other individual or non-state actors like landlords, property developers, and land owners, and where such infringements occur, it should act to preclude further deprivations as well as guaranteeing access to legal remedies. The right to shelter even goes further than a roof over ones head. It extends to embody the individual's right to be let alone and to live in peace—whether under a roof or not.[303]

In relation to the right to food, the Commission found that the right was implicit in the Charter: 'The right to food is inseparably linked to the dignity of human beings and is therefore essential for the enjoyment and fulfilment of such other rights as health, education, work and political participation.'[304] The Commission held that the right to food gives rise to an obligation with regard to protection from certain non-state actors holding that the Nigerian Government 'should not allow private parties to destroy or contaminate food sources, and prevent peoples' efforts to feed themselves'.[305] The Commission also referred to violations by private actors in the context of its finding of a violation of the right to life by the state.[306] The Commission concluded by appealing to the Government to 'ensure protection of the environment, health and livelihood of the people of Ogoniland by:

> — Ensuring that appropriate environmental and social impact assessments are prepared for any future oil development and that the safe operation of any further oil development is guaranteed through effective and independent oversight bodies for the petroleum industry; and
> — Providing information on health and environmental risks and meaningful access to regulatory and decision-making bodies to communities likely to be affected by oil operations.[307]

---

[302] Ibid, at para. 58.   [303] Ibid, at para. 61, footnotes omitted.   [304] Ibid, at para. 65.
[305] Ibid, at para. 65.
[306] 'Given the wide spread violations perpetrated by the Government of Nigeria and by private actors (be it following its clear blessing or not), the most fundamental of all human rights, the right to life has been violated.' Ibid, at para. 67.   [307] Ibid, at p 44.

9.4   FINAL REMARKS ON THE APPROACH OF THE REGIONAL BODIES

There is a temptation to try to distinguish the approaches of the regional bodies by focusing on textual differences in the instruments they are applying. This would be a mistake. What an analysis of the case-law shows is that the complaints have thrown up a variety of threats from non-state actors and that the regional bodies have taken the opportunity to develop human rights law according to the cases presented before them. There has even been a degree of cross-fertilization over the question of the extent to which human rights treaties oblige states to take positive steps to protect people from non-state actors.[308] These developments can be summarized as follows:

- Faced with an open-ended set of responsibilities to protect people from private violence, the European Court has focused on what is reasonably foreseeable for the authorities.

- Faced with competing human rights claims such as freedom of expression versus privacy, or freedom of association versus the enjoyment of private property, the European Court has focused on what might be considered the 'essence' of the rights in question and sought a solution that protects this essence.

- Faced with disappearances and murder perpetrated by unknown agents, the Inter-American Court has focused on the obligation of the state to prevent, investigate, and punish such violence by whomsoever committed.

- Faced with corporate exploitation of lands inhabited by indigenous peoples, the Inter-American Court has focused on judicial protection of fundamental rights and respect for the right to property.

- Faced with complaints about economic, social, and cultural rights in the context of commercial activity by non-state actors, the African Commission demonstrated that the state can be found to have violated its human rights obligations where it fails to protect the rights to life, food, and housing from the actions of non-state actors. Its approach highlighted how non-state actors can be expected to respect internationally defined economic, social and cultural rights.

- Faced with environmental damage through oil extraction activities, the African Commission focused on the 'green light' given to the companies, and appealed for new procedures involving both greater participation in decision-making by the people affected and external human rights impact assessments.

---

[308] See, e.g. Comm. 155/96, *The Social and Economic Rights Action Center and the Center for Economic and Social Rights v Nigeria* (n 300 above) at para. 57.

10

National Legal Orders

The human rights obligations of non-state actors under national law are as complex and variable as the various national legal orders themselves.[1] Several attempts have been made to classify the different models of constitutional protection against private actors. The scholarship in this area is rich and I have greatly benefited from a number of recent scholarly writings.[2] Analysis has recently focused on finding models to describe the different ways that human/constitutional rights apply to private actors in various national legal orders in the world. It has been suggested that at one extreme one sees the 'vertical' model, whereby constitutional rights only apply against the state and its actors. At the other extreme we find constitutional rights directly enforceable against private persons in the so-called 'horizontal' model. In between, there are variants (sometimes referred to as 'diagonal' models) which allow judges to apply conditional protection in a suit between private parties where one party relies on law which is unconstitutional (known as strong indirect horizontal effect); another variant merely allows judges to read in constitutional *values* when deciding cases between private parties (known as weak indirect horizontal effect).

Various writings have canvassed the arguments for and against such models.[3] Often the appropriateness of a particular model derives from a rather fundamentalist approach to the constitutional text in question. Parsing the exact meaning of the national text and the presumed intentions of the drafters is presented as the appropriate and most convincing constitutional approach, thus leading to the labelling of a particular constitutional order as inevitably falling within the vertical, horizontal, or indirectly horizontal model. In reality, the extent to which any

---

[1] For an early set of papers on this subject, see International Institute of Human Rights, *René Cassin Amicorum discipulorumque liber* (4 vols) (Paris: Pedone, 1969) vol. iii.

[2] At this stage we should mention S. Gardbaum, 'The "Horizontal Effect" of Constitutional Rights' 102 *Mich LR* (2003) 387–459; M. Hunt, 'The Horizontal Effect of the Human Rights Act', *Public Law* (1998) 423–443; B. Markesinis, 'Privacy, Freedom of Expression, and the Horizontal Effect of the Human Rights Bill: Lessons from Germany' 115 *LQR* (1999) 47–88; M. Tushnet, 'The issue of state action/horizontal effect in comparative constitutional law' 1 *International Journal of Constitutional Law* (2003) 79–98.

[3] See, e.g. A. Barak, 'Constitutional Human Rights and Private Law' in D. Friedmann and D. Barak-Erez (eds) *Human Rights in Private Law* (Oxford: Hart Publishing, 2001) 13–42; and K. Markus, 'What is Public Power: The Courts' Approach to the Public Authority Definition Under the Human Rights Act' in J. Jowell and J. Cooper (eds) *Delivering Rights: How the Human Rights Act is Working* (Oxford: Hart Publishing, 2003) 77–114.

constitutional or national legal order should extend human rights protection into the private sphere is a struggle over who chooses the values that should dictate the direction the polity is supposed to take. The problem with geometric metaphors, as Murray Hunt has pointed out, is that not only do they mislead and conceal the complexities of the debate, they may also frustrate the purpose of making 'fundamental human rights pervade our law in order to give them genuine, practical effectiveness'.[4]

At this point it is worth pausing to ask why this issue is so divisive and what are the stakes at issue. The answer is that the extension of human/constitutional rights into the private sphere is perceived as destabilizing the current order, which protects private autonomy and private power. In contrast to the restriction of the state through fundamental rights, it is thought that restricting private action is itself an unacceptable encroachment on entrenched fundamental freedoms concerning respect for, among other things, privacy, property, and the right to do business. Fear of human rights encroachment on the established order of things has come not only from interests such as the media, employers, and religious organizations. The trade union movement in the United Kingdom and Sweden have been suspicious that human rights law would be applied to undermine the closed shop and invoked to prevent secondary industrial action in response to anti-union practices.[5] Indeed some analysts see human rights and their judicial enforcement as generally inimical to collective action for the protection of workers' interests.[6]

Each country will have its own set of tensions. For instance, in South Africa, the issue concerns the importance of ensuring that private entities are not free to discriminate on racial or other grounds in any sphere of life. In the United States, the tension revolves in part around the fear of judicial legislation over private law matters that ought to remain the preserve of the different states that make up the

---

[4] M. Hunt, 'The "Horizontal Effect" of the Human Rights Act: Moving beyond the Public-Private Distinction' in J. Jowell and J. Cooper (eds) *Understanding Human Rights Principles* (Oxford: Hart, 2001) 161–178 at 173.

[5] See the discussion with regard to English law in A. Clapham, *Human Rights in the Private Sphere* (Oxford: Clarendon Press, 1993) at 308–313. See also the decision in Sweden in Case A–238–1997, of 11 February 1998, whereby a company, Kurt Kellerman, brought an action in the Industrial Tribunal based on Art. 11 of the European Convention, arguing the negative right to association when faced with industrial action in response to its refusal to enter into a collective agreement. See also the arguments in *Gustafsson v Sweden*, Judgment of the European Court of Human Rights, discussed in Ch 9 above. The minority of eight judges argued that that there had been a violation of the negative right of association; i.e. they found a right of an employer not to deal with a union had been violated. For the situation in Ireland, where constitutional rights may be directly invoked against trade unions and companies, see A. S. Butler, 'Constitutional Rights in Private Litigation: A Critique and Comparative Analysis' 22 *Anglo-American Law Review* (1993) 1–41, at 28–31.

[6] G. Mundlak, 'Human Rights and the Employment Relationship: A Look Through the Prism of Juridification' in D. Friedmann and D. Barak-Erez (eds) *Human Rights in Private Law* (Oxford: Hart Publishing, 2001) 297–328; but see S. Fredman, 'Scepticism under Scrutiny: Labour Law and Human Rights' in T. Campbell, K. D. Ewing, and A. Tomkins (eds) *Sceptical Essays on Human Rights* (Oxford: Oxford University Press, 2001) 197–213.

United States as a federal entity. Similarly, in South Africa there may be some reticence on the part of the judges to resolve delicate issues of legislated private law through Constitutional interpretation, due to the hierarchy of norms in the legal order: once the law has been determined in this way, it will be difficult for the democratically elected legislature to recalibrate the balance that was achieved by the court.

Despite these contextual differences, and the variations in the texts that enshrine human rights in national law, one should also be alert to the influential ideological positions that permeate this debate. At one extreme, those who wish to confine human rights to the relationship between the individual and the state are usually concerned, not only with fidelity to the text and historical traditions, but also to conserve a distinct space for economic and personal freedom. For Murray Hunt, these 'verticalists' insist that 'legal relations between private individuals must remain outside the reach of such law in order to preserve the sanctity of the private sphere from officious meddling by the State'.[7] On the other hand, those who wish to extend human rights protection to the private sphere start from the point that: 'The private sphere itself is constituted by the State in the sense that it is dependent on the State for the provision and enforcement of the norms which regulate relations within that sphere.'[8] Those who want to extend human rights protection in this way highlight the illusory distinction between public and private in order to bring certain issues within the scope of human rights protection. These issues, as encountered throughout this book, are: the behaviour of certain corporations with regard to their workforce and the local communities in which they operate; the discriminatory treatment of workers, tenants, and job seekers; domestic violence; denial of freedom of expression by commercial interests in formerly public spaces; abuse in privately run places of detention; and the behaviour of privatized entities that have taken over the functions of formerly 'public' bodies dealing with water, electricity, and gas, as well as telephone services and access to broadcasting possibilities.

The question is no longer really only about an extension of human rights into the private sphere; rather the question is now being asked: should human rights law continue to apply when the government chooses to move activity out of the public sphere? When a town centre becomes a privately-owned commercial shopping centre, should freedom of expression be deemed irrelevant, as the pretended violation regards a non-state actor and human rights 'traditionally' only apply against the state?[9] Many would accept that freedom of expression should continue to apply; the key to understanding the complications involved in this shift is that, in moving activity into this so-called private sphere, one encounters a different

---

[7] M. Hunt, 'The Effect on the Law of Obligations' in B. S. Markesinis (ed) *The Impact of the Human Rights Bill on English Law: The Clifford Chance Lectures, Volume 3* (Oxford: Oxford University Press, 1998) 159–180, at 161. [8] Ibid.

[9] See the discussion of *Appleby v UK* in Ch 9 above.

sort of clash of rights. The shopping mall owner has private property rights, arguably—for some—as important as the free speech rights in question.[10]

This Chapter, rather than presenting the arguments as to why rights should be extended into the private sphere, or given a degree of 'horizontal effect', will seek to demonstrate that courts are likely to develop their approach in the future. Our focus continues to be those international human rights that belong to individuals and organizations under international law. The issue is the different ways in which the national legal order might protect these rights against non-state actors. It is suggested that we might consider four ways in which this can happen:

(1) the national legal order allows for human rights complaints against non-state actors even when they have no public function or connection to government;

(2) the national court determines that the non-state actor is fulfilling a public function, or acting under 'colour of law', and so the non-state actor is deemed to have to comply with human rights law;

(3) the national court, in applying the law to the case involving the non-state actor, interprets/develops the law to ensure respect for international human rights—in some cases this may be because the court considers itself a state actor and thus bound to ensure respect for human rights; and

(4) the court considers the positive obligations of the state to protect people from the actions of non-state actors which are impeding the enjoyment of human rights by others.

Litigants may well rely on a combination of these possibilities; they are not mutually exclusive routes to ensuring the accountability of non-state actors for human rights violations in the national legal order. Indeed there are instances where different judges may favour different routes even within the same judgment. Moreover, different jurisdictions may shift between these routes or combine them to form their own jurisprudence.[11] The relevance of any one route will depend in

---

[10] For a creative solution to this problem, see J. Rowbottom, 'Property and Participation: A Right of Access for Expressive Activities', *EHRLR* (2005) 186–202. He suggests the development of a right of access to private property for the purposes of freedom of expression. He reminds us that although 'many public spaces have been transferred into private hands' in fact the issue may be just as important with regard to property that was never owned by the state.

[11] For the shifting focus of the German Constitutional Court, see R. Brinktrine, 'The Horizontal Effect of Human Rights in German Constitutional Law: The British debate on horizontality and the possible role model of the German doctrine of "*mittelbare Drittwirkung der Grundrechte*"', *EHRLR* (2001) 421–432. Craig Scott, in the context of suits against corporations for torture, suggests that we consider the different routes by which a judge might hold a corporation liable in terms of 'simultaneous multiplicity'. C. Scott, 'Translating Torture into Transnational Tort: Conceptual Divides in the Debate on Corporate Accountability for Human Rights Harms' in C. Scott (ed) *Torture as Tort: Comparative Perspectives on the Development of Transnational Human Rights Litigation* (Oxford: Hart Publishing, 2001) 45–63, at 63.

part on the position of the relevant court in the overall legal order, the relationship between the judiciary and the legislature, and the wording of the national provisions. No one can hope to offer a comprehensive review of how this issue is dealt with in every jurisdiction in the world. This examination will concentrate on three jurisdictions where recent cases have forced the courts to grapple with these problems: the United States, South Africa, and the United Kingdom. Some brief references will draw on the situation in Canada, New Zealand, Hong Kong, Japan, Germany, and Ireland.

10.1 HUMAN RIGHTS COMPLAINTS AGAINST NON-STATE ACTORS ACTING IN A NON-GOVERNMENTAL WAY

Some legal orders allow for a human rights complaint to be brought against a non-state actor where the right in question can appropriately be said to generate an obligation on the non-state actor concerned. The right can be vindicated irrespective of any nexus to the state or public function. Under Irish constitutional law the Constitution can be used to found a cause of action against non-state actors; for some commentators such an action is best understood as a 'constitutional tort'.[12] In other national legal orders, such as that of Sweden, the European Convention on Human Rights, having been incorporated into national law, has been said to apply in disputes between private individuals where those rights are of significance.[13] Some new constitutional arrangements in Eastern and Central Europe seem also to encompass non-state actor obligations. The Constitutions of Poland and Hungary can both be read as providing protection from private discrimination.[14] Other

---

[12] See Butler (1993: 20–22).

[13] See Case A–238–1997, of 11 February 1998: 'The industrial tribunal is of the opinion that, as a result of the incorporation of the Convention which may be of significance in the relation between individuals may also be applied in disputes between them.' Unofficial translation. The case concerned a complaint by a company concerning industrial action against it in response to its failure to enter into a collective agreement. The Tribunal held that the industrial action did not violate Art. 11 ECHR and relied on the *Gustafsson v Sweden* judgment (discussed in Ch 9 above).

[14] Art. 77(2) of the Hungarian Constitution reads: 'This Constitution and laws and statutes established in accordance with this Constitution are equally binding for everybody of the country.' There is some discussion as to whether such binding obligations on individuals are really to be seen as giving rise to direct legal obligations; see also Art. 70K: 'Claims arising from infringement on fundamental rights, and objections to the decisions of public authorities regarding the fulfillment of duties may be brought before a court of law.' In Hungary there has even been a decision of the City Court of Monor applying the Constitutional provision on discrimination in a horizontal way in a case where an employer advertised for a man not younger than 35: Monor Városi Bírósag 3.P.21.321/1997/13.Szám. See further Kovács Krisztina and Lehoczkyné Kollonay Csilla, both in 4 *Fundamentum* (1998) 85–90 and 91–95, see http://157.181.181.13/dokuk/98-4-10.PDF and http://157.181.181.13/dokuk/98-4-11.PDF (both in Hungarian). The 1997 Constitution of Poland includes Art. 32, which seems to outlaw private discrimination in political social or economic life: '1. All persons shall be equal before the law. All persons shall have the right to equal treatment by public authorities. 2. No one shall be discriminated against in political, social or economic life for any reason whatsoever.'

Constitutions, such as those of Bulgaria and Romania, simply impose the obligations of the Constitution on their citizens.[15]

In the United States, although some parts of the Bill of Rights in the Constitution may be applied as constitutional torts against individual prison guards, the Supreme Court has declined to allow equivalent suits against a private corporation running a prison, citing the availability of alternative remedies and the limited dissuasive effect on the company itself.[16] The scope of constitutional torts depends on whether the Supreme Court feels these are necessary in the case at hand; the present Court is reluctant to expand the existing constitutional remedies. With the exception of the Thirteenth Amendment, concerning slavery,[17] the US Constitution has not yet been seen as extending to relations between parties in the absence of state action. Section 10.2 considers the situation where there is the requisite 'state action' involved for a non-state actor to be liable for a breach of the US Bill of Rights.

[15] See Art. 26 of the 1991 Bulgarian Constitution: '1. Irrespective of where they are, all citizens of the Republic of Bulgaria shall be vested with all rights and obligations proceeding from this Constitution.' And Art. 58: '1. Citizens shall observe and implement the Constitution and the laws. They shall respect the rights and the legitimate interests of others.' Art. 15 of the 1991 Romanian Constitution: '1. All citizens enjoy the rights and freedoms granted to them by the Constitution and other laws, and have the duties laid down thereby.' Both English versions are those found in *The rebirth of democracy: 12 constitutions of central and eastern Europe* (Strasbourg: Council of Europe, 1995).

[16] In a majority judgment (5 votes to 4) the Supreme Court decided that no constitutional tort (in this case cruel and unusual punishments (Eighth Amendment to the US Constitution)) could lie against a private corporation. *Correctional Serv. Corp v Malesko* 534 US 61 (2001) at 66.

[17] For an essay on the possibilities in this field, see T. D. Rakhoff, 'Enforcement of Employment Contracts and the Anti-Slavery Norm' in D. Friedmann and D. Barak-Erez (eds) *Human Rights in Private Law* (Oxford: Hart Publishing, 2001) 283–295. See also the US Supreme Court opinion in *Civil Rights Cases* 109 US 3 (1883), which is seen as suggesting that the prohibition of slavery 'applied to individual citizens, as well as the states'. J. E. Nowak and R. D. Rotunda, *Constitutional Law* (St Paul, Minn: West Group, 6th edn, 2000) at 1038, see also 502. The right granted by the US Constitution meant that any law interfering with that right was invalid. In this way, any attempt by a state or non-state actor to use the law to interfere with the right would be unenforceable: 'It is true that slavery cannot exist without law any more than property in lands and goods can exist without law, and therefore the thirteenth amendment may be regarded as nullifying all state laws which establish or uphold slavery.' 109 US 3 (1883) at 20. The Court did not, however, accept that discrimination with regard to access to inns was a form of prohibited slavery and struck down the civil rights legislation passed by Congress. It is of interest that Justice Harlan, in his dissent, assimilated individuals and corporations operating in this field to those with a public function: 'I agree that government has nothing to do with social, as distinguished from technically legal, rights of individuals. No government ever has brought, or ever can bring, its people into social intercourse against their wishes. Whether one person will permit or maintain social relations with another is a matter with which government has no concern. I agree that if one citizen chooses not to hold social intercourse with another, he is not and cannot be made amenable to the law for his conduct in that regard; for no legal right of a citizen is violated by the refusal of others to maintain merely social relations with him, even upon grounds of race. What I affirm is that no state, nor the officers of any state, nor any corporation or individual wielding power under state authority for the public benefit or the public convenience, can, consistently either with the freedom established by the fundamental law, or with that equality of civil rights which now belongs to every citizen, discriminate against freemen or citizens, in their civil rights, because of their race, or because they once labored under disabilities imposed upon them as a race.' 109 US 3 (1883) at 59.

The US legal order, however, does include a separate possibility for suits against non-state actors for violations of human rights: The Alien Tort Statute (ATS) or Alien Tort Claims Act (ATCA). It is to such claims that we now turn.

10.1.1 The Alien Tort Claims Act in the United States

Claims that non-state actors, including individuals and corporations, have violated international law have led to an interesting string of cases before the US courts under a piece of US legislation known as the Alien Tort Claims Act (or Alien Tort Statute) 1789.[18] The history of this Act was considered in Chapter 6 at section 6.7.[19] The effects of the Act today are very real as non-state actors find themselves as defendants facing multi-million dollar suits.[20] These claims have attracted considerable attention and have led the US Administration,[21] and the Governments of the United Kingdom, Switzerland, and Australia to submit briefs to the US courts in various Alien Tort Statute (ATS) cases urging a restrictive jurisdiction.[22] The stance of these governments has led to consternation by human rights groups, and suggests that the biggest obstacles to ensuring human rights accountability for corporations are not really philosophical but governmental.[23]

The ATS confers upon the federal district courts original jurisdiction over 'any civil action by an alien for a tort only, committed in violation of the law of nations'.[24] The US Supreme Court has recently considered the meaning and scope of this provision. In a case concerning a Mexican doctor (Alvarez-Machain), who sued the US Government and Mexican individuals for his kidnap and detention, the Supreme Court clarified that, once the ATS granted jurisdiction to

---

[18] This Chapter, in contrast to Ch 6 above, uses the abbreviation ATS rather than ATCA. This is because we will focus on the approach of the Supreme Court, whose judgment uses ATS rather that ATCA.

[19] See further B. Stephens and M. Ratner, *International Human Rights Litigation in U.S. Courts* (Irvington-on-Hudson, NY: Transnational, 1996) 12–18.

[20] Cases against individuals have resulted in multi-million awards of damages in at least ten cases, but enforcing these judgments has proved almost impossible. According to one account, the victims had recovered only US$300 by the end of 2003. I. Bottigliero, *Redress for Victims of Crimes Under International Law* (Leiden: Martinus Nijoff, 2004) at 63–65. At the time of writing, no awards had been made against corporate actors, however, the incentive to settle is obviously far greater for a corporate non-state actor as their assets will be much more evident and their reputational loss much more significant. The settlement in the *Unocal* case is discussed in Ch 6 above, suffice it to add here that the sum involved was said by the parties to provide 'substantial assistance to people who may have suffered hardships in the region' and Katherine Redford, one of the initiators of the suit, said she was 'thrilled' with the outcome. See Robert Horn, 'Paying For It: Doing business with regimes may cost American companies cash as well as goodwill' *Time (Asia)*, 27 December 2004.

[21] B. Stephens, 'Upsetting Checks and Balances: The Bush Administration's Efforts to Limit Human Rights Litigation' 17 *Harv HRJ* (2004) 170–205.

[22] See, e.g. Brief of Australia, Switzerland and the United Kingdom, dated 23 January 2003, addressed to the Supreme Court in *Sosa v Alvarez-Machain et al* (the judgment is discussed below).

[23] R. Verkaik, 'Ministers attempt to halt US human rights cases against British firms' *The Independent*, 11 February 2004, at 2, see further Ch 1, at 1.4 above.

[24] 28 United States Code [USC] §1350.

the federal courts, those courts could entertain claims 'because torts in violation of the law of nations would have been recognized within the common law of the time'.[25] For the Supreme Court the drafters had in mind:

> ... a sphere in which these rules binding individuals for the benefit of other individuals overlapped with the norms of state relationships. Blackstone referred to it when he mentioned three specific offenses against the law of nations addressed by the criminal law of England: violation of safe conducts, infringement of the rights of ambassadors, and piracy. [4 Commentaries 68.] An assault against an ambassador, for example, impinged upon the sovereignty of the foreign nation and if not adequately redressed could rise to an issue of war. [See Vattel 463–464.] It was this narrow set of violations of the law of nations, admitting of a judicial remedy and at the same time threatening serious consequences in international affairs, that was probably on minds of the men who drafted the ATS with its reference to tort.[26]

The pertinent issue then became the extent to which the common law has incorporated more contemporary violations of international law (including the law of human rights) and whether the content of this customary international law can be said to include the torts complained of by Dr Alvarez-Machain. The Supreme Court started its consideration of this issue with a long list of reasons why the judiciary should proceed with extreme caution in this context: first, today the common law is no longer considered as being 'discovered' by judges—it is well-understood that judges are engaging in law-making. Second, a general practice has therefore been 'to look for legislative guidance before exercising innovative authority over substantive law'.[27] Third, the creation of a *private* cause of action raises the problem that enforcement would be permitted 'without the check imposed by prosecutorial discretion'.[28] Fourth, the implication for the foreign relations of the United States suggests a 'high bar to new private causes of action for violating international law'.[29] For the Supreme Court, such actions could mean that US courts would decide claims for 'a limit on the power of foreign governments over their own citizens, and to hold that a foreign government or its agent has transgressed those limits'.[30] Therefore, attempts by 'the federal courts to craft remedies for the violation of new norms of international law ... should be undertaken, if at all, with great caution'.[31] Lastly the Supreme Court felt that, not

---

[25] *Sosa v Alvarez-Machain et al* 542 US_(2004) at 19 of the slip opinion.

[26] Ibid, at 20–21.   [27] Ibid, at 32.

[28] Ibid, at 33. This reason may have played a significant role, as the human rights violation at the centre of the claim, i.e. arbitrary arrest and detention, was argued by Alvarez to include: 'a general prohibition of "arbitrary" detention defined as officially sanctioned action exceeding positive authorization to detain under the domestic law of some government, regardless of the circumstances' (at 42). For the Court, this rule, if translated into a cause of action, would be unmanageable: 'for its implications would be breathtaking. His rule would support a cause of action in federal court for any arrest, anywhere in the world, unauthorized by the law of the jurisdiction in which it took place ... It would create an action in federal court for arrests by state officers who simply exceed their authority; and for the violation of any limit that the law of any country might place on the authority of its own officers to arrest' (at 43).   [29] Ibid, at 33.

[30] Ibid, at 33.   [31] Ibid, at 33.

only did they have 'no congressional mandate to seek out and define new and debatable violations of the law of nations',[32] they also considered that Congress had done nothing to promote ATS suits, and concerning human rights law:

> ... the Senate has expressly declined to give the federal courts the task of interpreting and applying international human rights law, as when its ratification of the International Covenant on Civil and Political Rights declared that the substantive provisions of the document were not self-executing.[33]

All of these reasons explain why the US judiciary is cautious with regard to this particular jurisdiction and the attendant causes of action. They also explain the cautious approach to the interpretation of what constitutes customary international law with regard to arbitrary detention. The Court found that there was insufficient evidence to show that arbitrary detention had the 'definite content' and 'acceptance among civilized nations' that the three 'historical paradigms' had in 1789.[34] The claim of Alvarez-Machain therefore failed.[35]

Two further passages from the judgment are of interest. First, the Supreme Court envisages 'a policy of case-specific deference to the political branches'.[36] The first example that the Supreme Court gives is that of the class action suits against corporations for complicity in the *apartheid* regime in South Africa.[37] In the light of the South African Government's statement that such claims interfere with the policy of its Truth and Reconciliation Commission, the Supreme Court considered that: 'In such cases, there is a strong argument that federal courts should give serious weight to the Executive Branch's view of the case's impact on foreign policy.'[38] Second, the Supreme Court hints at the necessity of a non-state actor test which would determine whether the international norm in question binds not only states but also non-state actors.[39]

Let us now turn to see how the lower courts have determined whether an international norm binds non-state actors. Claims under the ATS have met with the

---

[32] Ibid, at 34.   [33] Ibid, at 34.   [34] Ibid, at 38.

[35] The concurring opinion of Scalia J, joined by Rehnquist CJ and Thomas J, suggests that there is almost no scope for judicial recognition that international law norms have become common law causes of action enforceable in federal court: 'American law—the law made by the people's democratically elected representatives—does not recognize a category of activity that is so universally disapproved by other nations that it is automatically unlawful here, and automatically gives rise to a private action for money damages in federal court.' At 14 of the Opinion of Scalia J (slip opinion).

[36] *Sosa v Alvarez-Machain et al* 542 US_(2004) at 39 of the slip opinion (footnote 21).

[37] The subsequent opinion and order in *Re South African Apartheid Litigation* US District Court Southern District of New York, 29 November 2004, Sprizzo DJ is discussed below.

[38] *Sosa v Alvarez-Machain et al* 542 US_(2004) at 39 of the slip opinion (footnote 21).

[39] See ibid, footnote 20, which points to the question of 'whether international law extends the scope of liability for a violation of a given norm to the perpetrator being sued, if the defendant is a private actor such as a corporation or individual' and goes on to compare cases *Tel-Oren v Libyan Arab Republic* 726 F 2d 774 (CADC 1984) (torture) and *Kadic v Karadžić* 70 F 3d 232 (CA2 1995) (genocide). We deal with these cases in more detail below. The judgment also alludes to a 'broader rule' in the event that Sosa (the alleged perpetrator) was not shown to be 'acting on behalf of a government when he made the arrest' (at 43 of the slip opinion). See also the concurring opinion of Breyer J at 1 of the slip opinion.

response that the international law at issue is only binding on states. In some cases, this argument has been accepted, and in others the US courts have determined that the international norm in question binds non-state actors. As discussed in Chapter 6, genocide, slave trading, slavery, forced labour, and war crimes have been said by the US courts to be actionable even in the absence of a state nexus.[40] And the *Kadic v Karadžić* decision stated that where rape, torture, and summary execution are committed in isolation, these crimes 'are actionable under the Alien Tort Act, without regard to state action, to the extent they were committed in pursuit of genocide or war crimes'.[41] The Supreme Court in the *Alvarez-Machain* case pointed to a 1984 decision of the Court of Appeals for the District of Columbia Circuit that there was 'insufficient consensus in 1984 that torture by private actors violates international law'.[42] However, the assumption that the crime of torture is confined to state officials has now been rebutted; as the Appeals Chamber of the International Criminal Court for the former Yugoslavia has more recently confirmed, there is no need for a public official to be involved in order for a private individual to be responsible under international law for the international crime of torture.[43]

As to whether obligations can extend beyond states and individuals to corporations, this has been presumed in the cases pending in the US federal courts,[44] and was examined in some detail in at least one case. The determination in that case was that corporations do have obligations under international human rights law. In the preliminary stages of the case against Talisman Energy Inc, concerning human rights abuses in Sudan, Judge Schwartz concluded:

> . . . substantial international and United States precedent indicates that corporations may also be held liable under international law, at least for gross human rights violations. Extensive Second Circuit precedent further indicates that actions under the ATCA [Alien Tort Claims Act] against corporate defendants for such substantial

---

[40] *Wiwa v Royal Dutch Shell Petroleum (Shell)* US District Court for the Southern District of New York, 28 February 2002, at 39. See also *Doe I v Unocal Corp*, 18 September 2002, paras 3ff.

[41] *Kadic v Karadžić* 70 F 3d 232 (2d Cir, 1995) at 243–244.

[42] Referring to *Tel-Oren v Libyan Arab Republic* 726 F 2d 774 (CADC 1984) at footnote 20.

[43] 'The Trial Chamber in the present case was therefore right in taking the position that the public official requirement is not a requirement under customary international law in relation to the criminal responsibility of an individual for torture outside of the framework of the Torture Convention.' *Prosecutor v Kunarac, Kovać and Vuković* Case IT–96–23 and IT–96–23/1–A, Judgment of the ICTY (Appeals Chamber), 12 June 2002, para. 148.

[44] In addition to the case mentioned in n 45 below, see also the following cases pending under this legislation at the time of writing: *Wiwa v Royal Dutch Petroleum Co et al* Case 96–CIV–8386 (KMW) (SDNY 2002); *Villeda et al v Fresh Del Monte Produce Inc et al* Case 01–CIV–3300 (SD Fla 2001); *Bowoto et al v Chevron et al* Case C99–2506 (ND Cal 2000); *Arias et al v DynCorp et al* Case 01–01908 (DDC 2001); *John Doe I et al v Exxon Mobil Corp et al* Case 01–CV–01357 (DDC 2001); *Sinaltrainal et al v Coca-Cola et al* 256 F Supp 2d 1345 (SD Fla 2003); *Estate of Rodrigues et al v Drummond Company Inc et al* Case CV–02–0665–W (ND Ala 2002). For a detailed discussion of all of the decisions concerning corporations up to July 2004, see S. Joseph, *Corporations and Transnational Human Rights Litigation* (Oxford: Hart Publishing, 2004).

violations of international law, including *jus cogens* violations, are the norm rather than the exception.[45]

10.1.1.1 The US Courts' Application of the ATS Subsequent to the Supreme Court's Judgment in Sosa

But what of the reaction of the US courts since the Supreme Court's call for caution? In the *South African Apartheid Litigation* case, Judge Sprizzo considered the claims against the defendant corporations under three heads: first, that the corporations 'engaged in state action by acting under color of law in perpetrating these international law violations'; second, that the 'defendants aided and abetted the apartheid regime'; and third, that the 'defendants' business activities alone are sufficient to make out an international law violation'.[46] The first claim was said to fail on the facts, the second claim was dismissed after recalling the Supreme Court's policy reasons for judicial caution in *Sosa* and through a finding that 'the ATCA presently does not provide for aider and abettor liability'.[47]

With regard to the third head which is of particular interest, Judge Sprizzo declared that no liability for violation of the norms in the Genocide and Torture Conventions would apply due to the fact that the United States had declared the treaties not to be self-executing: 'Therefore there is no private liability under the treaties in United States Courts.'[48] A similar approach was taken to obligations contained in the International Covenant on Civil and Political Rights. The Apartheid Convention, the UN Charter, and the Universal Declaration of Human Rights were all dismissed as insufficient to 'create binding international law actionable under the ATCA'.[49] With regard to General Assembly resolutions calling for an end to business activities in South Africa, Judge Sprizzo held that 'the opinions expressed by these resolutions never matured into customary international law actionable under the ATCA'.[50] The Judge then reiterated the foreign policy reasons for not extending jurisdiction over such cases and concluded that 'doing business in apartheid South Africa is not a violation of international law that would support jurisdiction in federal court under ATCA'.[51]

---

[45] *The Presbyterian Church of Sudan et al v Talisman Energy Inc, Republic of the Sudan* Civil Action 01–CV–9882 (AGS), US District Court for the Southern District of New York, at 47 of the Order of 19 March 2003. This case and the arguments are discussed in detail in Ch 6, at 6.7.1 above.

[46] *Re South African Apartheid Litigation* US District Court Southern District of New York, 29 November 2004, Sprizzo DJ, at 15–16 of the transcript.

[47] Ibid, at 21. Judge Sprizzo deferred to both the Supreme Court and Congress stating (at 21) that the refusal to write aider and abettor liability into the ACTA statute 'to be heedful of the admonition in *Soso* that Congress should be deferred to with respect to innovative interpretations of that statute'. The question of the appropriate aider and abettor regime in the context of the ATS was at the kernel of the decision to rehear the *Unocal* case *en banc* (discussed in Ch 6, at 6.8 above). See Stephens (2004: 184). Note that Judge Cote, ruling on a subsequent request in the *Talisman* case explicitly refused to follow this line of reasoning: *The Presbyterian Church of Sudan et al v Talisman Energy Inc* [2005] WL 1385326 (SDNY) Opinion and Order of 13 June 2005, at para. 6.   [48] Ibid. at 24.

[49] Ibid, at 25. See also similar findings in *Flores v Southern Peru Copper Corp* 343 F 3d 140 (2d Cir 2003) (which concerned questions of pollution and rejected claims based on the right to life and the right to health) referred to by Sprizzo at 24–26.   [50] Ibid, at 27.

[51] Ibid, at 29.

In *Jama v Esmor* the Supreme Court's *Sosa* test was applied by the District Court dealing with claims made by asylum-seekers against individual guards and the company for which they worked (Esmor). Senior District Judge Dickenson R. Debevoise quoted the Supreme Court's test and found that the individual allegations of sexual harassment and other mistreatment did not meet the rigorous threshold set by the Supreme Court.

> A federal court applying the ATCA 'should not recognize private claims under federal common law for violations of any international law norm with less definite content and acceptance among civilized nations than the historical paradigms when §1350 was enacted.' [*Sosa* at 2765.[52]] None of the claims against the individual Esmor Guards can meet the rigorous *Sosa* requirements. Compare the conduct in which each individual Esmor Guard is alleged to have engaged with the torture and murder which was the subject of *Filartiga v. Pena-Irala* [630 F. 2d 876 (CA 6 1980)].[53]

The context of the claims is quite shocking, however, and the Judge's Opinion sets out the facts under twenty-one headings in relation to claims against the officers of the corporation and the possibility that the corporation will be bound by the acts of its officers, in this case the detention facility Administrator. According to the Judge's Opinion:

> There is testimony or other evidence to support each of the following allegations: i) For a period of time shackles were used when detainees had contact visits or court appearances; ii) shackles were used when detainees were placed in segregation; iii) during and after the June 18, 1995 riot detainees were abused by deprivation of food, beatings and other physical abuse—some of this abuse was inflicted by Esmor guards and some may have been inflicted by police and INS employees; iv) detainees were beaten; v) inmates were subject to verbal abuse including racial epithets and remarks; vi) inmates were sexually harassed, for example, by guards watching women take showers, ridiculing inmates's genitals, touching a male inmate's penis, sexually assaulting a female inmate in the laundry room; vii) unnecessary searches and pat-downs, particularly at night by the SERT team; viii) spoiled, under cooked, rotten and inadequate food, ix) physical facilities were unlighted and toilet and shower facilities lacked privacy; x) filthy clothing was provided and frequently inadequate or inappropriate clothing was provided; xi) toilets and showers remained in disrepair and inadequate cleaning supplies were provided, leading to unsanitary living quarters; xii) heating was defective and the cold of the winter was accentuated by inadequate clothing and the allocation of only one blanket to each detainee; xiii) lights were kept on for 24 hours of the day or night in dormitory areas, and sleep was further disrupted by loud talking and TV playing by the guards and middle of the night headcounts; xiv) there was virtually no outdoor recreation; xv) inmates were deprived of hygiene supplies such as sanitary napkins, toothpaste and tooth brushes; xvi) conditions in segregation were even more intolerable—cells soiled with faeces, blocked toilets, lack of sheets or blankets; xvii) inadequate medical care and medication were provided; xviii) segregation was imposed on inmates without notice

---

[52] The Court's reference is to the reported version *Sosa v Alvarez-Machain* 124 S Ct 2739 (2004).
[53] *Jama v Esmor* Civ No. 97–3093(DRD), 10 November 2004, at 33 of the published transcript.

or hearings; xix) in a variety of ways detainees were denied access to counsel and the courts, e.g., limiting or denying phone calls to lawyers, guards remaining present during visits with lawyers, inadequate or non-existent law libraries or materials; loss or destruction of legal papers; xx) the property of detainees was taken from them and not returned; xxi) the inmates' right to exercise their religions was interfered with, whether Muslim, Hindu or Christian.[54]

The Opinion determines that the ATS case against the corporation Esmor itself could not be dismissed in a summary judgment, and that the *Sosa* strict requirements were satisfied in terms of customary international human rights law, in particular the right not to be subjected to inhuman and degrading treatment. The Judge carefully took into account the Supreme Court's reference to consider whether there might be alternative remedies to an alien tort claim under the ATS. In the present case, normal routes of complaint were closed off, either because the private corporation was not bound by the Constitutional and public law protections or because the aliens were ineligible to invoke certain remedies.[55]

As for the argument that ATS cases have to be strictly contained to avoid a flood of cases complaining of infringements of various laws concerning arrest and detention around the United States, or indeed all over the world, the Judge distinguished general prison conditions from the complaints of Jama and the other detainees:

> The present case is different. It involves the alleged gross mistreatment, not of criminals or persons accused of crime, but rather of persons who have committed no crime but are awaiting a decision on their applications for asylum. The law of nations as evidenced in the various conventions, treaties, declarations and other sources cited by the *Jama* plaintiffs can be said to have reached a consensus that the inhumane treatment of a huge number of persons accused of no crime and held in confinement is a violation of the law of nations. Further, the remedies available to those who are held in penal institutions may not be available to detainees such as the plaintiffs in the instant case.[56]

This case, represents a clear finding that proceedings may continue under the ATS against a non-state actor for violations of human rights law. It represents a stark example of why it makes sense to speak of human rights obligations of non-state actors; not only because the Opinion illustrates how such claims might be 'justiciable' and enforceable in Court, but also because to deny that human rights

[54] Ibid, at 66–67.

[55] In a case concerning a Federal prison run by a private company, the Supreme Court decided that no constitutional tort for cruel and unusual punishments (Eighth Amendment to the US Constitution) could lie against a private corporation (even though it can lie against individual federal guards where there is no other remedy). *Correctional Serv Corp v Malesko* 534 US 61 (2001).

[56] Ibid, at 34. The Opinion goes on to point out that because there is an absence of state action, there is no remedy under 43 USC para. 1983, and that the Supreme Court had been unwilling to extend Constitutional protection against entities acting 'as a private corporation operating a halfway house under contract with the Bureau of Prisons'; see further the judgment of the Supreme Court *Correctional Serv Corp v Malesko* 534 US 61 (2001).

have been violated in the absence of any other remedy is incomprehensible for the victims of these abuses, and for any corporation to escape liability for such human rights abuses seems unconscionable. The case shows that we have to look beyond arguments about 'trivialization' and the 'traditional meaning' of human rights and face up to the roles assumed, and power exercised, by non-state actors today.

10.1.2 The South African Constitution

The debate in South Africa concerning the applicability of the Constitution to private (or non-state) actors was, and remains, divisive. The arguments of the 'verticalists' (rights only to be applied against the state) and 'horizontalists' (rights protection to cover the acts of private persons) re-run many of the oppositions we have encountered throughout this book. But the South African context has thrown the dilemmas into sharp relief, and some of the solutions offered are extremely helpful in transcending the antagonisms and finding workable solutions.[57] One newspaper commentator sets out the doomsday scenario which is said by him to follow from the horizontal application of human rights under the Constitution:

> Miss Milosevic, a deaf Serbian immigrant, applies to the Good Hope Bank for a loan to purchase a flat in Hillbrow. The Good Hope Bank, however, has unhappy experiences of bond defaulters in Hillbrow and refuses Miss Milosevic a loan. On being requested reasons for such refusals under section 32(2) of the final constitution, the Bank responds that it has a policy of not advancing loans to applicants in areas that are unsanitary, overpopulated and in a state of major urban decay.
>
> Miss Milosovic, assisted by the Greater Johannesburg Transitional Metropolitan Council, the Society for the Deaf and Gauteng department of housing institutes urgent proceedings for a mandatory interdict to compel the Good Hope Bank to grant her a housing loan. Miss Milosovic relies on sections 8(3) and (4) of the bill of rights, as well as the fact that the Bank's redlining policy is grossly discriminatory.
>
> The Good Hope Bank is ordered to grant Miss Milosovic a loan and is subsequently faced with a class action by the Community Law Centre, on behalf of 5,000 applicants for loans, most of whom later default.
>
> In the face of pending proceedings for curatorship by the SA Reserve Bank, the bank is faced with a liquidity crisis and decides to abandon the home loan market.
>
> The one beneficiary would, undoubtedly, be the legal profession, as no business would be able to take any decision affecting anyone, never mind simply an employee, without seeking advice from a constitutional lawyer.[58]

---

[57] Some of the most useful commentary includes: H. Cheadle and D. Davis, 'The Application of the 1996 Constitution in the Private Sphere' 13 *SAJHR* (1997) 44–66; S. Woolman, 'Application (Revison Service 3)' in M. Chalskalson, J. Kentridge, J. Klaaren, G. Marcus, D. Spitz, and S. Woolman (eds) *Constitutional Law of South Africa* (Kenwyn: Juta, 1998) Ch 10.1-68; J. de Waal, I. Currie, and G. Erasmus, *The Bill of Rights Handbook* (Lansdowne: Juta, 4th edn, 2001); W.-J. van der Wolf, *The Future and Futurity of the Public-Private Distinction in the View of the Horizontal-Application of Fundamental Rights* (Nijmegen: Wolf Legal Productions, 2002).

[58] P. Leon, 'Nanny or nightwatchman? It's not an academic argument when common law is under threat' *The Sunday Independent*, 31 March 1996, at 23.

The idea that the application of human rights to the business sector will paralyse decision-making is a recurring claim. In this example it is linked with the idea that human rights and economic sense are irreconcilable, and that, in the long run, only sound economics can bring access to resources and justice for all. The debate in South Africa has been intense, as the interim Constitution left some room for ambiguity over this question, and the Constitutional Court had delivered a majority judgment in favour of a textual interpretation and a vertical application of the Bill of Rights, so that private power would not be subject to such obligations under the Constitution. This judgment is considered in detail below.

10.1.2.1 *The Constitutional Court's Approach in* Du Plessis v De Klerk

The Constitutional Court's discussion in *Du Plessis v De Klerk* of the indirect horizontal effect of the interim constitution provides plenty of hints as to the legal philosophy of the judges, as well as how competing rights might be weighed in the future (now that the Constitution does indeed allow for direct horizontal effect).

In *Du Plessis v De Klerk* the Constitutional Court had to consider an appeal by the *Pretoria News* concerning defamation actions brought against the newspaper by Mr Gert de Klerk and his company. According to the judgment:

> During February and March, 1993, the newspaper published a series of six articles dealing with the supply by air of arms and other material to the Angolan rebel movement, UNITA. The tenor of the articles was that South African citizens were engaged in these operations, that the operations were covert, and that they entailed the evasion of South African air control regulations. The flights were described in the articles as 'illegal' and as 'pirate flights.' The articles suggested that those responsible for the flights were 'fuelling the war in Angola', and were doing so for motives of personal gain, notwithstanding the disastrous effect of the Angolan civil war on the inhabitants of that country.[59]

The newspaper had sought to add a defence based on the freedom of speech section in the interim Constitution of South Africa (1993) and the plaintiffs had objected, *inter alia*, that the interim Constitution did not apply horizontally, and that, alternatively, it did not apply to disputes of this nature. The judge at first instance ruled that Chapter 3 of the interim Constitution had no horizontal effect and submitted a point of general public importance to the Constitutional Court. That Court decided to ask for arguments on the question: '(b) Are the provisions of Chapter 3 of the Constitution—and more particularly section 15—capable of application to any relationship other than that between persons and legislative or executive organs of state at all levels of government?' The judgment of Kentridge AJ focused on the text of the interim Constitution but cast a glance at other constitutional orders:

> 33.   There can be no doubt that the resolution of the issue must ultimately depend on an analysis of the specific provisions of the Constitution. It is nonetheless illuminating

---

[59] Case CCT 8/95, 7 November 1995, at para. 1.

to examine the solutions arrived at by the courts of other countries. The Court was referred to judgments of the courts of the United States, Canada, Germany and Ireland. I would not presume to attempt a detailed description, or even a summary, of the relevant law of those countries, but in each case some broad features are apparent to the outside observer. A comparative examination shows at once that there is no universal answer to the problem of vertical or horizontal application of a Bill of Rights. Further, it shows that the simple vertical/horizontal dichotomy can be misleading. Thus under the Constitution of the United States the First to Tenth Amendments (the 'Bill of Rights') and the Fourteenth Amendment, insofar as they confer rights on individuals, would at first sight appear to be vertical, in the sense of being directed only against state power.[60] Yet the courts of that country have in some cases at least reached what is effectively a horizontal application of constitutional rights by holding that the judicial power is a state power against which constitutional protections may invoked.

The approach which considers courts as state actors is considered, in section 10.3.2 below. On the question of direct horizontal effect in the Constitution, Kentridge AJ continued:

> 62.   What I conclude is that Chapter 3 does not have a general direct horizontal application but that it may and should have an influence on the development of the common law[61] as it governs relations between individuals. I insert the qualification 'general' because it may be open to a litigant in another case to argue that some particular provision of Chapter 3 must by necessary implication have direct horizontal application. Section 15(1) is not such a provision. No such implication is necessary. One of the purposes of the section is to give protection against far-reaching censorship laws and other statutes restricting free speech which were common under the regime of Parliamentary supremacy. Accordingly, my response to the second issue referred to this Court by the learned judge would be that Chapter 3 of the Constitution does not in general have direct horizontal application, and more particularly that section 15(1) does not have direct horizontal application. On the other hand, the values which it embodies can and must be taken into account in the development of the common law of defamation.

Kriegler J wanted to take the horizontal effect further and suggested that it covered 'all law, including that applicable to private relationships'.[62] However, he considered that law is only involved if a party seeks to enforce a particular law against a victim of discrimination. For Kriegler J, there would be no direct horizontal effect where a victim tried to obtain redress by simply relying on the Constitution on its own (in the absence of separate law). According to Kriegler J the Constitution did not supply a cause of action, there would be no constitutional tort against a private party. The Constitution can be used as a shield in a private action to attack a private action as unconstitutional, but the Constitution

---

[60] Footnote 46 in the original reads: 'The Thirteenth Amendment (outlawing slavery and involuntary servitude) has by reason of its language been held to impose direct obligations on individuals in private law relationships'.

[61] Footnote 105 in the original reads: 'Including, of course, customary law. The development of customary law in accordance with section 35(3) must be one of the major tasks facing the judiciary'.

[62] Ibid, at para. 135.

may not be used as a sword to attack a private violation of human rights or an act of private discrimination.[63]

> Unless and until there is a resort to law, private individuals are at liberty to conduct their private affairs exactly as they please as far as the fundamental rights and freedoms are concerned. As far as the Chapter is concerned a landlord is free to refuse to let a flat to someone because of race, gender or whatever; a white bigot may refuse to sell property to a person of colour; a social club may black-ball Jews, Catholics or Afrikaners if it so wishes. An employer is at liberty to discriminate on racial grounds in the engagement of staff; a hotelier may refuse to let a room to a homosexual; a church may close its doors to mourners of a particular colour or class. But none of them can invoke the law to enforce or protect their bigotry. One cannot claim rescission of a contract or specific perform-ance thereof if such claim, albeit well-founded at common law, infringes a Chapter 3 right. One cannot raise a defence to a claim in law if such defence is in conflict with a protected right or freedom. The whole gamut of private relationships is left undis-turbed. But the state, as the maker of the laws, the administrator of laws and the inter-preter and applier of the law, is bound to stay within the four corners of Chapter 3. Thus, if a man claims to have the right to beat his wife, sell his daughter into bondage or abuse his son, he will not be allowed to raise as a defence to a civil claim or a criminal charge that he is entitled to do so at common law, under customary law or in terms of any statute or contract.[64]

But other Justices were not convinced that guaranteeing 'liberty' to conduct one's private affairs would properly protect the interests of South Africans. According to Mahomed DP:

> There is force in this approach but I have difficulties with it. The premise is and must be that private persons falling within the examples referred to in this quotation, who perform acts otherwise inconsistent with the rights specified in Chapter 3, are not doing so in terms of law. I think this is an incorrect premise. All the acts performed by such private persons are acts performed in terms of what the common law would allow. A landlord who refuses to let to someone because of his race is exercising a right which is incidental to the rights of the owner of property at common law; this applies equally to the white bigot who refuses to sell property to a person of colour. A social club which black-balls Jews, Catholics or Afrikaners acts in terms either of its own constitution or

---

[63] See the article by M. Hunt, who suggests that this indirect horizontal approach would be appropriate under the UK's Human Rights Act 1998: 'The Horizontal Effect of the Human Rights Act', *Public Law* (1998) 423–443, at 435. See also the treatment of this issue by B. Dickson, 'The Horizontal Application of Human Rights Law' in A. Hegarty and S. Leonard (eds) *Human Rights: An Agenda for the 21st Century* (London: Cavendish, 1999) 59–78, who argues (at 78) for 'the use of human rights standards to govern not just inter-State or State-personal relationships, but also inter-personal relationships'. He mentions (at 74) the South African Constitution of 1996 as a quite suc-cessful incorporation into constitutional law of the principle that judges should 'have regard to international obligations which a country undertakes—whether or not they have been incorporated into domestic law—for the purposes of removing ambiguity or uncertainty from national constitu-tions, legislation or common law [Bangalore Principles of 1988]'. The Bangalore Principles concern the domestic judicial application of international human rights norms. They are reproduced in M. Hunt, *Using Human Rights Law in the English Courts* (Oxford: Hart Publishing, 1998) App. III.

[64] *Du Plessis v De Klerk* (n 59 above) at para. 135.

the common law pertaining to voluntary associations or freedom of contract. I am not persuaded that there is, in the modern State, any right which exists which is not ultimately sourced in some law, even if it be no more than an unarticulated premise of the common law and even if that common law is constitutionally immunized from legislative invasion. Whatever be the historical origins of the common law and the evolutionary path it has taken, its continued existence and efficacy in the modern State depends, in the last instance, on the power of the State to enforce its sanction and its duty to do so when its protection is invoked by the citizen who seeks to rely on it. It is, I believe, erroneous to conclude that the law operates for the first time only when that sanction is invoked. The truth is that it precedes it and is indeed the ultimate source for the legitimation of any conduct. Freedom is a fundamental ingredient of a defensible and durable civilization, but it is ultimately secured in modern conditions, only through the power, the sovereignty and the majesty of the law activated by the State's instruments of authority in the protection of those prejudiced through its invasion by others. Inherently there can be no 'right' governing relations between individuals *inter se* or between individuals and the State the protection of which is not legally enforceable and if it is legally enforceable it must be part of law.[65]

He found that a fairer result could be found by using the general provision concerning the obligation on the court to have regard to the spirit of the Chapter in the application and development of the common law:

> on that interpretation most of the common law rules, upon which reliance would have to be placed by private persons seeking to perpetuate unfair privilege or discrimination, would themselves be vulnerable to invasion and re-examination in appropriate circumstances. What contracts and actions public policy would permit or enforce in the future will have to be re-examined.[66]

The nub of the Court's reticence is revealed in the concurring opinion of Sachs J. To understand the problem, recall that this is a jurisdiction where the Constitutional Court has the final say on such issues to the detriment of both the legislator and the normal courts within the national legal order. Sachs J's hypothetical scenario elegantly illuminates the dilemmas for judges in such a court when faced, as here, with a defamation case:

> If we followed the indirect or 'diagonal' approach to applicability, the Appellate Division would remain in the picture. Say, for purposes of argument, it decided to uphold the approach adopted in the carefully articulated judgment by Cameron J in terms of which the plaintiff would have to prove negligence on the part of the publisher. Parliament could then examine the Appellate Division's decision, decide to refer the matter to the Law Commission for investigation, and finally opt for a completely different approach.
>
> Say that Parliament eventually came to the conclusion that a better approach would be that when publishing defamatory material about someone in the public domain, the media must take reasonable steps to verify the accuracy of the statements, and that the more injurious to the personal as opposed to the political reputation of the person

---

[65] *Du Plessis v De Klerk* (n 59 above) at para. 79.　　　　[66] Ibid, at para. 86.

concerned the more stringent should the investigation be; say that the legislators felt that when there is a manifest invasion of the privacy of someone in public life, it is not for the plaintiff to prove negligence or absence of justification on the part of the publishers, but for the publishers to establish that the invasion of privacy was in all the circumstances justified in the interest of the public knowing about the lives of such figures. Legislation could then be adopted to these effects, and if any publishers felt aggrieved, they could approach this Court and ask us to strike down the offending provisions. We would then weigh up the matter, decide whether the legislation conforms to the principles of free speech and respect for dignity and privacy and make an appropriate ruling, bearing in mind a number of factors, such as the powers of reading down, severance and total invalidation subject to the discretionary power granted to us in section 98(5). Furthermore, in determining the justifiability of the legislation in terms of section 33, we would decide whether the path followed by Parliament was one of many reasonably permissible options, not whether we thought it the best one.

Assume, on the other hand, that the matter was regarded as one of direct, self-enforcing horizontal application, with the result that the Appellate Division was excluded, and our Court came to the very same conclusion as that posited above for the Appellate Division. Parliament would no longer be able to pass the legislation it thought appropriate, unless it was willing to amend the Constitution for this purpose, or, unless, possibly, it could come up with an alternative proposal that met constitutional criteria and did not conflict with the ratio of the Constitutional Court's judgment. Whatever position we adopted when confronted with the issue, our dilemma would be profound. If we made no reformulation whatsoever and simply left the matter open, the Appellate Division would be out of the picture, and each Division of the Supreme Court could develop its own rulings, with the result that a plaintiff could win in one part of the country and lose in another, the publication being exactly the same in both. If, on the other hand, we reformulated the common law ourselves in the manner we thought most consonant with the Constitution, we would solve the problem of divided decisions, but tie the hands of Parliament until death or a constitutional amendment did us part. There would be little or no scope for Law Commission enquiry, little chance for subsequent amendments in the light of experience and public opinion. Parliament would have to defer to our discretion in the matter, seeking to find some margin of appreciation left in our judgment within which it could dot i's, cross t's and seek alternative, not incompatible, solutions.[67]

For Sachs J, the Constitution clearly spoke to the attacks on dignity meted out through racial discrimination in the private sphere. He simply doubted that there should be a remedy for such indignities under the Constitution:

> People are denied access to jobs, facilities and accommodation on a daily basis purely because of the colour of their skin. It would be a strange Constitution indeed that had nothing to say about such flagrant denials of dignity and equality. I have no doubt that the Constitution speaks to such issues. Yet in my opinion it would be quite inappropriate to say that each and every violation of personal rights in such a situation raised a constitutional question for ultimate determination by our Court. The appropriate

---

[67] Ibid, at paras 183–185.

manner for such issues to be dealt with would be through legislation pioneered perhaps by the Human Rights Commission.[68]

Sachs J went on to invoke the familiar clash between non-discrimination and freedom of choice regarding employees in small and intimate employment situations:

> Widespread research and consultation would be needed to decide precisely where to establish the cut-off point in each situation: in many countries, persons employing only a handful of workers in a close and intimate work environment, or a landlady letting one room in her house, or social activities of a genuinely private character, are expressly excluded from antidiscrimination legislation.[69]

For other Justices, the democratic balance between the legislature and the judiciary weighed less heavily than concerns for a justice system which recognizes human dignity. For Madala J, the South African context was fundamental to understanding the challenge faced by the Court:

> Ours is a multi-racial, multi-cultural, multi-lingual society in which the ravages of apartheid, disadvantage and inequality are just immeasurable. The extent of the oppressive measures in South Africa was not confined to government/individual relations but equally to individual/individual relations. In its effort to create a new order, our Constitution must have been intended to address these oppressive and undemocratic practices at all levels. In my view our Constitution starts at the lowest level and attempts to reach the furthest in its endeavours to restructure the dynamics in a previously racist society.[70]

Madala J's dissenting judgment on the question of direct applicability of the Bill of Rights envisaged obligations for non-state actors: 'On the question of horizontality, I am of the view that some of the rights in Chapter 3 lend themselves to direct horizontality while in respect of others, Chapter 3 is indirectly horizontally applicable.'[71]

The significance of the Justices' findings is diminished by the wording of the new Constitution, which introduces direct horizontal effect. However, there is still scope for considerable judicial discretion with regard to which rights are applied and to what extent. The judicial philosophy revealed in these passages will continue to exert an influence. In other words, there will be judicial caution where issues can be better dealt with through the legislature, and there will be continuing consideration of how to safeguard personal choice and privacy. This private sphere will remain protected, to a certain extent, and private matters will not easily become constitutional cases. In a way, there is a parallel between the reticence of a constitutional court to consider private inter-individual disputes and the resistance in the international legal order to acknowledge the subjectivity of private persons. In the constitutional context, the highest court would rather the issue was dealt with at a lower level through the medium of normal national law (in this

---

[68] *Du Plessis v De Klerk* (n 59 above) at para. 186.   [69] Ibid, at para. 186.
[70] Ibid, at para. 163.   [71] Ibid, at para. 165.

case the legislation or common law). At the international level, the issue is seen as better dealt with at the national level through domestic law.

10.1.2.2 The 1996 Constitution of the Republic of South Africa

Section 8 of the new 1996 Constitution of the Republic of South Africa reads:

> *8 Application*
>
> (1) The Bill of Rights applies to all law and binds the legislature, the executive, the judiciary and all organs of state.
>
> (2) A provision of the Bill of Rights binds a natural or a juristic person if, and to the extent that, it is applicable, taking into account the nature of the rights and of any duty imposed by the right.
>
> (3) When applying a provision of the Bill of Rights to a natural or juristic person in terms of subsection (2), a court—
>
> > (a) in order to give effect to a right in the Bill, must apply, or if necessary develop, the common law to the extent that legislation does not give effect to that right; and
> >
> > (b) may develop rules of the common law to limit the right, provided that the limitation is in accordance with section 36(1).
>
> (4) A juristic person is entitled to the rights in the Bill of Rights to the extent required by the nature of the rights and of that juristic person.

Section 36(1) reads:

> The rights in the Bill of Rights may be limited only in terms of law of general application to the extent that the limitation is reasonable and justifiable in an open and democratic society based on human dignity, equality and freedom, taking into account all relevant factors, including—
>
> (a) the nature of the right;
>
> (b) the importance of the purpose of the limitation;
>
> (c) the nature and extent of the limitation;
>
> (d) the relation between the limitation and its purpose; and
>
> (e) less restrictive means to achieve the purpose.

Other provisions similarly aim to cover the private sphere,[72] but we shall concentrate here on Section 8(2) and (3) and the extent to which these provisions may lead to human rights obligations for non-state actors.

The Constitutional Court has now had occasion to clarify that non-state actors may indeed have obligations under section 8(2) of the Constitution. The first question for the Court, in response to a claim of horizontal effect, is to see whether the right in question should be 'applicable' in the context of the case before it. In *Khumalo v Holomisa* the Court left no doubt that, where a media entity is sued for defamation, freedom of expression is of 'direct horizontal application'.[73] The

---

[72] E.g. s 12(1) sets out that 'Everyone has the rights to freedom and security of the person which includes the right—... (c) to be free from all forms of violence from either public or private sources.'

[73] Case CCT 53/01, 14 July 2002, O' Reagan J, at para. 33.

reason for such applicability was: 'the intensity of the constitutional right in question, coupled with the potential invasion of that right which could be occasioned by persons other than the state or organs of state'.[74] Beyond this sentence there is, so far, little more to guide us as to when the Constitutional Court will apply the Bill of Rights to horizontal relations or, in other words, consider human rights obligations for non-state actors.

The wording of section 8(2) means that some provisions will not be enforced against non-state actors. Commentators have set out a number of suggestions for delimiting the scope of this horizontal effect. For Im Rautenbach: '*The rule merely involves asking whether a provision of the bill of rights is capable of being applied to the particular private relation.* In most instances, even with respect to so-called socio-economic rights, the answer may be positive. In this respect, the qualification in section 8(2) may have very little practical effect.'[75] He argues against the compilation of lists, suggesting that everything will turn on the context.[76] Ironically, those commentators opposed to the courts directly enforcing the Bill of Rights against private parties similarly counsel against any distinction between rights which are capable of horizontal application and those that are not. Chris Sprigman and Michael Osborne are in favour of judicial restraint generally, and against the judicial enforcement of individual rights in 'purely private disputes', as this can lead to 'a constitutional ruling that strikes the balance once and for all, with no opportunity for revision by the legislature outside of amending the constitution'.[77] They suggest that section 8(2) 'may represent a grant to the courts of the discretion to apply provisions of the Bill of Rights horizontally wherever the court believes that the vindication of a right demands horizontal application ... [T]he drafters have created an open text with respect to application, and they have invited the courts to fill it in; the drafters have decided to let the courts decide'.[78]

Other commentators have been ready to separate out appropriate rights from inappropriate rights in this context. Halton Cheadle and Dennis Davis argue that section 8(2) 'points to an interpretative process that goes beyond the strict construction of the text alone and to whether the right is capable of being applied

[74] Case CCT 53/01, 14 July 2002, O' Reagan J, at para. 33. The Judgment then went on to apply s 8(3) and enquire whether the common law should be developed. The common law application of human rights in the private sphere is touched on in 10.3.3.2 below. The relationship between South African constitutional adjudication and the development of the common law has attracted considerable commentary in this context: J. van der Walt, 'Progressive Indirect Horizontal Application of the Bill of Rights: Towards a Co-operative Relation Between Common-Law and Constitutional Jurisprudence' 17 *SAJHR* (2001) 341–363; A. Fagan, 'Determining the Stakes: Binding and Non-Binding Bills of Rights' in D. Friedmann and D. Barak-Erez (eds) *Human Rights in Private Law* (Oxford: Hart Publishing, 2001) 73–96; M. du Plessis and J. Ford, 'Developing the Common Law Progressively—Horizontality, the Human Rights Act and the South African Experience', *EHRLR* (2004) 286–313.

[75] 'The bill of rights applies to private law and binds private persons', *Journal of South African Law (TSAR)* (2000) 296–316, at 313 (footnote omitted, emphasis in the original).

[76] Ibid, at 314.

[77] C. Sprigman and M. Osborne, 'Du Plessis is *not* Dead: South Africa's 1996 Constitution and the Application of the Bill of Rights to Private Disputes' 15 *SAJHR* (1999) 25–51 at 41–42.

[78] Ibid, at 36.

or whether the right is suitable for horizontal application'.[79] In their view, this means that 'the rights of arrested detained and accused persons are neither capable of being applied to natural or juristic persons nor suitable for horizontal application'. More generally, they suggest that an inquiry into the 'nature' of the right and duty involved may reveal that the right is 'capable' of being applied to private persons, due to the existence of equivalent common law recognition: injury, defamation, delict, and nuisance. This capability (capacity) suggests that the right is 'suitable' for application to private persons. They point to a further indicator of suitability for horizontal application:

> The fact that legislation is commonly used to give effect to a right as between private persons may also assist in this enquiry. Anti-discrimination legislation is common in many democratic societies. Typically that legislation prohibits discrimination by private persons. Accordingly the right to equality can be, and often is, applied horizontally. Labour relations rights and environmental rights are often given effect to as between private persons by legislation.[80]

This is a relatively generous approach, but Cheadle and Davis go on to introduce a suitability filter to prevent duties that would be 'particularly onerous on a private person'.[81] They seem to suggest that the rights to life and access to housing may go beyond existing duties, and that, even where the rights themselves refer to private persons, the sense of the provisions may suggest that it is for the legislature to regulate these spheres.[82] They are even more restrictive with regard to socio-economic rights (such as the rights to housing, health care services, food, and water) and emphasize the Constitution's reference to state duties to take measures 'to achieve the progressive realization of each of these rights'.[83] They conclude: 'Given the potentially onerous nature of such a duty on private persons the likely outcome of the analysis must be that these rights are not suitable for horizontal application.'[84]

Johan de Waal, Iain Currie, and Gerhard Erasmus have emphasized the distinction between rights and 'provisions'. In this way, they argue, the courts can find that some aspects of some rights may be seen as inapplicable to private persons, while the rest of the rights may indeed be applied:

> Section 8(2) states that a 'provision' may apply to private conduct. It does not say that a 'right' may apply to private conduct. It is therefore possible, and quite reasonable, that some provisions of the Bill of Rights may apply to the conduct of a private person or juristic person while other provisions in the same section (and pertaining to the same right) will not apply to such conduct. For example, the right to access to health care services (s 27(1) and (2)) probably does not apply horizontally.[85] However, the right not

---

[79] H. Cheadle and D. Davis, 'The Application of the 1996 Constitution in the Private Sphere' 13 *SAJHR* (1997) 44–66, at 57.   [80] Ibid, at 58.

[81] Ibid, at 58.

[82] See, e.g. the discussion with regard to ss 26(2), (4), 12(1c), 15(2), 23, 28, and 31(1)(b).

[83] See ss 27(2) and 26(2).   [84] Cheadle and Davis (1997: 60).

[85] Footnote 58 in the original reads: 'The reason is that the duty imposed by the right is too burdensome to impose on private individuals.'

to be refused emergency medical treatment (s 27(3)) probably does apply horizontally. Also the freedom to make political choices (s 19(1)) and the right to vote (s 19(3)) may be violated by private conduct, but the right to free, fair and regular elections only placed duties on states.[86]

De Waal, Currie, and Erasmus rightly stress that everything depends in the end on context: although the right to be informed of the reasons for arrest might not generally be a duty imposed on private persons, one can imagine situations where it could be (a security officer making a private arrest). With regard to the right to peaceful assembly, De Waal *et al* suggest that this 'generally applies on the horizontal level', so that the 'right to assemble in, for example shopping malls and on the property of an employer is therefore guaranteed. But in some circumstances it may be inappropriate to apply the right horizontally. For example, it is unlikely that the right to assemble can be relied on to justify demonstrations in or in front of someone's private home'.[87]

I suggest that one looks at the balancing exercise as simply an extension of the exercise that is used with regard to vertical application,[88] when a court considers a government's justification for infringing human rights based on the legitimate aim of protecting the rights of others, the judge in effect is balancing the competing human rights.[89] Perhaps the best guide at this point is that judges will concentrate on whether the claim actually extinguishes the enjoyment of the rights or simply interferes with it. To reprise the vocabulary of the European Court of Human Rights (examined in Chapter 9 above), judges will be concerned that the *essence* of the right is protected. So, for example, there may be a difference between protesting outside a private house and access to the only meeting place in town.

10.2   NON-STATE ACTORS WITH A PUBLIC FUNCTION OR STATE NEXUS

As we saw in Chapters 6 and 7 above, the rules of state responsibility attribute the acts of non-state actors to the state where that entity is empowered by the law of the state to exercise elements of governmental authority; where the non-state actor was acting on the instructions of, or under the direction or control of the state; where the non-state actor is in fact exercising elements of government authority due to defaulting government authorities; where the non-state actor becomes the new government of a state; and lastly, where the state acknowledges and adopts

---

[86] J. de Waal, I. Currie, and G. Erasmus, *The Bill of Rights Handbook* (Lansdowne: Juta, 4th edn, 2001) at 55.   [87] Ibid, at 55.

[88] We saw this approach developed in Ch 9 above, in the context of the approach of the European Court of Human Rights, *Lopez Ostra v Spain* Judgment of 9 December 1994, at para. 51.

[89] See the discussion in Ch 11, at 11.3 below, regarding the rights of parents to respect for their religious beliefs in the context of corporal punishment in private schools.

the conduct of the non-state actors as its own.[90] This international set of secondary rules is essential to understanding the international responsibility of states with regard to their negative obligations (we saw the scope of their positive obligations in Chapter 9 above).

There is no reason that these rules should be congruent with national rules that determine which acts will count as public acts for the purposes of national human rights legislation. The New Zealand Bill of Rights Act[91] and the Canadian Charter of Rights and Freedoms[92] have been interpreted in ways which bring

[90] See Arts 5, 8, 9, 10, and 11 of the Articles on State Responsibility adopted by the ILC on 10 August 2001, the General Assembly took note of the Articles, 'commended them to the attention of Governments', and annexed them to its Res. 56/53 of 12 December 2001.

[91] The New Zealand Bill of Rights Act 1990 applies: 'only to acts done (a) By the legislative, executive, or judicial branches of the government of New Zealand; or (b) By any person or body in the performance of any public function, power, or duty conferred or imposed on that person or body by or pursuant to law'. The Government's explanation extends the duties to bodies such as professional associations for doctors and the Gaming Commission, bodies which would not normally be considered as exercising governmental authority under the international law of state responsibility. According to the Government publication 'The Guidelines on the New Zealand Bill of Rights Act 1990: A Guide to the Rights and Freedoms in the Bill of Rights Act for the Public Sector': 'Section 3(b) provides that the Bill of Rights Act applies to non-government bodies, but only in respect of their public functions. At present the scope of section 3(b) is not completely certain, because the courts have not settled the precise margins of the "public function" test. However, the fact that a particular organisation is essentially private in nature does not, by itself, mean that it is never performing a "public function, power or duty". For example, a privately-funded non-statutory industry self-regulating body has been held to fall within the scope of public sector activity because of the public nature of its functions. An organisation may be subject to the Bill of Rights Act on some occasions but not others. For example, a school board of trustees may at times be performing functions more traditionally associated with the commercial operations of a private company, and at other times may make decisions relating to the delivery of state-sponsored education programmes...Examples of these activities may include (but are not limited to): 1. The administration of a public welfare regulatory framework: Organisations that regulate the media (Press Council, Advertising Standards Authority, Films and Videos Labelling Body) Organisations that administer liquor licensing laws (Alcohol Liquor Advisory Council) 2. The delivery of social services/government programmes to the community: Organisations that deliver health or education services (District Health Boards, School Boards of Trustees, Tertiary Institutions) 3. The regulation of professional bodies: Professional bodies that have responsibility for regulating the professional activities of members and for taking disciplinary action (Medical Council, District Law Societies). So what does "conferred or imposed by or pursuant to law" mean? Although an organisation may be performing a "public function", the Bill of Rights Act may not apply if the function is not "conferred or imposed pursuant to law". While this term has not received extensive consideration by the courts, it is clear that section 3(b) applies in respect of a broader range of activities than just those imposed by legislation. Section 3(b) applies where a body voluntarily assumes obligations under a set of legal rules as well as an organisation that operates under legal rules conferred or imposed on it.' Footnotes omitted, available at http://www.justice.govt.nz/pubs/reports/2004/bill-of-rights-guidelines/index.html. See also *R v H* [1994] 2 NZLR 143 (government instigation for a private individual passing on information to them brought the information within the scope of the Bill of Rights Act (s 21)).

[92] Although the Canadian Charter is usually assumed to apply only to government actors, note the reasoning of the Supreme Court in *Eldridge v British Columbia (Attorney General)* [1997] 3 SCR 624, *per* La Forest J, at paras 50–51: 'The structure of the Hospital Insurance Act reveals, therefore, that in providing medically necessary services, hospitals carry out a specific governmental objective. The Act is not, as the respondents contend, simply a mechanism to prevent hospitals from charging for their services. Rather, it provides for the delivery of a comprehensive social program. Hospitals are merely the vehicles the legislature has chosen to deliver this program. It is true that

non-state actors within the scope of those with human rights obligations. Yet judges in every legal order will be aware of the limits on including non-state actors as prescribed by the legislature; differences between the Canadian[93] and Hong Kong[94] rights instruments allow for different results as to whether a state-funded university has human rights obligations in the national legal order.

The UN Human Rights Committee, in the context of its examination of the situation in Hong Kong, has criticized the fact that governments have sought to incorporate international human rights texts in ways that limit the remedies to governmental violations of rights. Section 7 of the Hong Kong ordinance reads:

> Binding effect of Ordinance
>
> i. This Ordinance binds only—
>   a) the Government and all public authorities; and
>   b) any person acting on behalf of the Government or a
>   c) public authority.
> ii. In this section—'person' includes any body of persons, corporate or unincorporate.

hospitals existed long before the statute, and have historically provided a full range of medical services. In recent decades, however, health care, including that generally provided by hospitals, has become a keystone tenet of governmental policy. The interlocking federal-provincial medicare system I have described entitles all Canadians to essential medical services without charge. Although this system has retained some of the trappings of the private insurance model from which it derived, it has come to resemble more closely a government service than an insurance scheme . . . in the present case there is a "direct and . . . precisely-defined connection" between a specific government policy and the hospital's impugned conduct. The alleged discrimination—the failure to provide sign language interpretation—is intimately connected to the medical service delivery system instituted by the legislation. The provision of these services is not simply a matter of internal hospital management; it is an expression of government policy. Thus, while hospitals may be autonomous in their day-to-day operations, they act as agents for the government in providing the specific medical services set out in the Act. The Legislature, upon defining its objective as guaranteeing access to a range of medical services, cannot evade its obligations under s. 15(1) of the Charter to provide those services without discrimination by appointing hospitals to carry out that objective. In so far as they do so, hospitals must conform with the Charter.'

[93] See, e.g. the Supreme Court of Canada with regard to a claim brought by professors and staff concerning mandatory retirement age against a University. The majority held that: 'The exclusion of private activity from the Charter was not a result of happenstance. It was a deliberate choice which must be respected. We do not really know why this approach was taken, but several reasons suggest themselves. Historically, bills of rights, of which that of the United States is the great constitutional exemplar, have been directed at government. Government is the body that can enact and enforce rules and authoritatively impinge on individual freedom. Only government requires to be constitutionally shackled to preserve the rights of the individual. Others, it is true, may offend against the rights of individuals. This is especially true in a world in which economic life is largely left to the private sector where powerful private institutions are not directly affected by democratic forces. But government can either regulate these or create distinct bodies for the protection of human rights and the advancement of human dignity.' *McKinney v University of Guelph* [1990] 3 SCR 229, at 262, *per* La Forest J.

[94] See the discussion of the Hong Kong case, *Hong Kong Polytechnic University, Poon Chung-kwong and Yiu Tung-wah v Next Magazine* (1997) by S. Ping-Fat, 'Universities and Public Authorities' 167 *Justice of the Peace* (2003) 91–95. For further discussion of what constitutes 'Government' and what constitutes a 'public authority' under the Hong Kong Bill of Rights, see J. Chan, *The Annotated Ordinances of Hong Kong: Hong Kong Bill of Rights Ordinance* (Chapter 383) (Hong Kong: Butterworths Asia, 1999) at paras 7.02 and 7.03.

In response to the United Kingdom's 1995 report on Hong Kong the Human Rights Committee emphasized that:

> ... under the Covenant a State party does not only have an obligation to protect individuals against violations by Government officials but also by private parties. It thus notes with deep concern the absence of legislation providing effective protection against violations of Covenant rights by non-governmental actors.[95]

The report submitted to the Human Rights Committee by China in 1999 with regard to Hong Kong explained that, although the Bill of Rights only bound the Government and did not regulate relations between private individuals, this was because it was felt that it was better to introduce such protection through specific legislation. Such legislation had been introduced, for example, in 1995 in the fields of sex and disability discrimination through the enactment of specific ordinances.[96]

The UN Human Rights Committee reacted in its concluding observations by stating that it remained 'concerned that no legislative remedies are available to individuals in respect of discrimination on the grounds of race or sexual orientation. Necessary legislation should be enacted in order to ensure full compliance with article 26 of the Covenant'.[97]

In the United Kingdom, national protection of human rights is seen as a simple national application of what happens at the international level, not by reference to the observations of the Human Rights Committee, but rather in terms of what happens before the European Court of Human Rights. Because the Human Rights Act in the United Kingdom was said to 'bring rights home',[98] so that the victim does not have to 'traipse off to Strasbourg to claim their rights',[99] the international test (which determines which acts are attributable to a government for the purposes of its negative obligations under the European Convention on Human Rights) has been applied at the national level to exclude some claims from the scope of the Human Rights Act 1998. The situation is different in other countries, such as the United States, where constitutional rights are considered more or less independently of any international obligations or international monitoring mechanism.

---

[95] UN Doc. CCPR/C/79/Add.57, 9 November 1995, at para. 10.

[96] See UN Doc. CCPR/C/HKSAR/99/1, 16 June 1999, at para. 487.

[97] UN Doc. CCPR/C/79/Add.117, 12 November 1999, at para. 15. On some of the issues in this context, see A. Byrnes, 'Equality and Non-Discrimination' in R. Wacks (ed) *Human Rights in Hong Kong* (Hong Kong: Oxford University Press, 1992) 225–263.

[98] For details of the Labour Party's proposal for incorporation made whilst in opposition, see J. Straw and P. Boateng 'Bringing Rights Home: Labour's Plans to Incorporate the European Convention on Human Rights in U.K. Law', *EHRLR* (1997) 71–80. The Human Rights Bill [HL], HL Bill 38 was presented to Parliament along with a White Paper 'Rights Brought Home: the Human Rights Bill' (London: HMSO, Cm. 3782, October 1997).

[99] See Secretary of State for the Home Department, Jack Straw, House of Commons, 17 June 1998, Col. 412.

10.2.1   The Human Rights Act 1998 in the United Kingdom

The United Kingdom was one of the original signatories to the European Convention on Human Rights on 5 November 1950, and, on 8 March 1951, was the first state to ratify the Convention. The story of the various attempts made to incorporate the Convention is well known, and culminated in the Human Rights Act 1998.[100] Although the Convention was not incorporated into domestic law until the Human Rights Act 1998 entered into force on 2 October 2000, the Convention had already had an enormous impact on the reasoning and outcomes of cases decided in the domestic courts of the United Kingdom even before incorporation,[101] with different jurisdictions adopting separate approaches.[102] Views differ on whether the Act has been as successful as some had hoped.[103] Many observers, however, did not anticipate the effect that that the Human Rights Act would have across the legal culture and among the general public. Lord Browne-Wilkinson (a former Law Lord), speaking in 2005, expressed amazement at how the Act 'has percolated its way into every facet of our life'.[104] Let us now consider the extent to which human rights obligations have filtered through the public/private divide.

10.2.1.1   *Parliamentary Debates and Ministerial Statements*

Sections 6 to 9 of the Human Rights Act 1998 come under the heading 'Public authorities' and the scope of these provisions has been subjected to considerable scholarly scrutiny.[105]

Section 6 reads:

> 6.—(1) It is unlawful for a public authority to act in a way which is incompatible with a Convention right.

[100] See, e.g. J. Wadham, H. Mountfield, and A. Edmundson, *Blackstone's Guide to the Human Rights Act 1998* (London: Blackstone Press, 3rd edn, 2003); F. Klug, *Values for a Godless Age: The Story of the UK's New Bill of Rights* (Harmondsworth: Penguin, 2000); M. Zander, *A Bill of Rights?* (London: Sweet & Maxwell, 4th edn, 1996).

[101] A detailed discussion can be found in Clapham (1993: 1–66 and 298–342) (with particular emphasis on cases applying the norms in the Convention against non-state actors). See also the extensive treatment in M. Hunt, *Using Human Rights Law in English Courts* (Oxford: Hart Publishing, 1997) at 127–206 and see his Appendix of 473 cases in which judicial reference was made to unincorporated international human rights law between 1964 and 1996.

[102] See M. J. Beloff and H. Mountfield, 'England and Wales; Unconventional Behaviour?'; B. Dickson, 'The Convention in Northern Irish Courts'; A. Grotian 'The European Convention: A Scottish Perspective', all in *EHRLR* (1996) at 467–495, 496–510, and 511–523, respectively.

[103] See K. D. Ewing, 'The Futility of the Human Rights Act', *Public Law* (2004) 829–852, and the response by A. Lester, 'The Utility of the Human Rights Act: A Reply to Keith Ewing', *Public Law* (2005) 249–258.   [104] BBC Radio 4, 'Unreliable Evidence', 12 April 2005.

[105] See, e.g. the series of articles by Dawn Oliver, 'Functions of a Public Nature under the Human Rights Act', *Public Law* (2004) 329–351; 'Comment: Chancel Repairs and the Human Rights Act', *Public Law* (2001) 651–653; 'The Frontiers of the State: Public Authorities and Public Functions under the Human Rights Act', *Public Law* (2000) 476–493. Ch 5 of *The Law of Human Rights (Volume 1)* (Oxford: Oxford University Press, 2000) by Richard Clayton and Hugh Tomlinson has also been particularly influential.

(2) Subsection (1) does not apply to an act if—

    (a) as the result of one or more provisions of primary legislation, the authority could not have acted differently; or

    (b) in the case of one or more provisions of, or made under, primary legislation which cannot be read or given effect in a way which is compatible with the Convention rights, the authority was acting so as to give effect to or enforce those provisions.

(3) In this section 'public authority' includes—

    (a) a court or tribunal, and

    (b) any person certain of whose functions are functions of a public nature, but does not include either House of Parliament or a person exercising functions in connection with proceedings in Parliament.

(4) In subsection (3) 'Parliament' does not include the House of Lords in its judicial capacity.

(5) In relation to a particular act, a person is not a public authority by virtue only of subsection (3)(b) if the nature of the act is private.

(6) 'An act' includes failure to act but does not include a failure to—

    (a) introduce in, or lay before, Parliament a proposal for legislation; or

    (b) make any primary legislation or remedial order.

Section 6(1) corresponds, in some ways, to the simple attribution test found in the context of the law of state responsibility. It distinguishes government bodies (state actors) from bodies carrying out functions of a public nature (non-state actors). Government bodies are always liable, whatever the nature of their act. On the other hand, non-state actors are only liable under the Act when their functions are of a public nature and the nature of the act is not private (section 6(3)(b) and (5)). Non-state actors do therefore have a limited liability under the Act. The intended difference between the liability of these two categories was explained by the Lord Chancellor, Lord Irvine, during the debates in the House of Lords:

> Clause 6(1) refers to a 'public authority' without defining the term. In many cases it will be obvious to the courts that they are dealing with a public authority. In respect of government departments, for example, or police officers, or prison officers, or immigration officers, or local authorities, there can be no doubt that the body in question is a public authority. Any clear case of that kind comes in under Clause 6(1); and it is then unlawful for the authority to act in a way which is incompatible with one or more of the convention rights. In such cases, the prohibition applies in respect of all their acts, public and private. There is no exemption for private acts such as is conferred by Clause 6(5) in relation to Clause 6(3)(c) [later 6(3)(b)].
>
> Clause 6(3)(c) [later 6(3)(b)] provides further assistance on the meaning of public authority. It provides that 'public authority' includes, 'any person certain of whose functions are functions of a public nature'. That provision is there to include bodies which are not manifestly public authorities, but some of whose functions only are of a public nature. It is relevant to cases where the courts are not sure whether they are looking at a public authority in the full-blooded Clause 6(1) sense with regard to those bodies which fall into the grey area between public and private. The Bill reflects the decision to

include as 'public authorities' bodies which have some public functions and some private functions.

Perhaps I may give an example that I have cited previously. Railtrack would fall into that category because it exercises public functions in its role as a safety regulator, but it is acting privately in its role as a property developer. A private security company would be exercising public functions in relation to the management of a contracted-out prison but would be acting privately when, for example, guarding commercial premises. Doctors in general practice would be public authorities in relation to their National Health Service functions, but not in relation to their private patients.

The effect of Clause 6(5) read with Clause 6(3)(c) [later 6(3)(b)] is that all the acts of bodies with mixed functions are subject to the prohibition in Clause 6(1) unless—I emphasise this—in relation to a particular act, the nature of which is private.

Clause 6 accordingly distinguishes between obvious public authorities, all of whose acts are subject to Clause 6, and bodies with mixed functions which are caught in relation to their public acts but not their private acts. In so far as the noble Lord is concerned with obvious public authorities such as those I have described, Clause 6 already does the job which his amendment is designed to do. In so far as he is concerned with bodies in the second category, I would contend that it is right to exempt from Clause 6 their private acts. In relation to employment matters, for example, I do not see a distinction between a private security company which has a contracted-out prison in its portfolio and one which does not. There is no reason to make the first company liable under Clause 6 in respect of its private acts and the second one not liable simply because the first company is also responsible for the management of a prison. As far as acts of a private nature are concerned, the two private security companies are indistinguishable; nor do I see a distinction in this area between Railtrack and other property developers or between doctors with NHS patients and those without.[106]

This definition of public authority is differently worded from the attribution test found under the rules of state responsibility. One can compare, however, the International Law Commission's direct attribution test to the 'clear cases' of public authority (government departments, the police, etc).[107] One can compare the non-private acts of 'bodies with mixed functions' with the International Law Commission's attribution test for entities 'exercising elements of governmental authority'.[108] But this does not necessarily fully cover what Parliament seemingly

---

[106] House of Lords, Committee, 24 November 1997, Cols 811–812. All debates on the Act (House of Commons and House of Lords) are available at http://www.dca.gov.uk/hract/lawlist2.htm.

[107] See Art. 4 of the ILC's Articles on the Responsibility of States for Internationally Wrongful Acts: 'Article 4 Conduct of organs of a State: 1. The conduct of any State organ shall be considered an act of that State under international law, whether the organ exercises legislative, executive, judicial or any other functions, whatever position it holds in the organization of the State, and whatever its character as an organ of the central government or of a territorial unit of the State.' Annexed to GA Res. 56/83, 12 December 2001.

[108] See ibid, Art. 5 Conduct of persons or entities exercising elements of governmental authority: 'The conduct of a person or entity which is not an organ of the State under article 4 but which is empowered by the law of that State to exercise elements of the governmental authority shall be considered an act of the State under international law, provided the person or entity is acting in that capacity in the particular instance.'

intended. It seems from the White Paper, which is the explanatory document that accompanied the introduction of a Bill into Parliament, that the intention was to ensure that privatized utilities are covered. So, for example, electricity boards, British Gas, Railtrack, and British Telecom would probably be covered where they carry out public functions. The White Paper stated:

> The definition of what constitutes a public authority is in wide terms. Examples of persons or organizations whose acts or omissions it is intended should be able to be challenged include central government (including executive agencies); local government; the police; immigration officers; prisons; courts and tribunals themselves; and, to the extent that they are exercising public functions, companies responsible for areas of activity which were previously within the public sector, such as the privatised utilities. The actions of Parliament however are excluded.[109]

The fact of having previously been in the public sector does not necessarily equate with the concept of 'elements of governmental authority' under international law. Transport by rail is not necessarily a governmental function, and before nationalization, was indeed in the private sector (albeit regulated). The example given in the Parliamentary debates was a privatized railway company which could be liable for breach of public duties with regard to safety under its statutory duties, but would not be responsible under the act for a property sale as this would be considered a private act.[110] In some ways this evokes the attribution rule in the law of state responsibility concerning 'entities exercising elements of governmental authority', as the example is carefully limited to safety regulation, as opposed to general functioning of the railways. But it will be suggested here that 'functions of a public nature' may go further than the analogous concept of governmental authority. For example, human rights law generates obligations for states in the field of education; as we have seen, the European Court of Human Rights has taken a broad approach, holding the state responsible for discipline in state and private schools, holding that 'the State cannot absolve itself from responsibility by delegating its obligations to private bodies or individuals'.[111] From the perspective of the European Convention on Human Rights, the issue may not be whether something has been privatized,[112] or was once in the public sector, but rather

---

[109] At para. 2.2.

[110] 'For example, Railtrack has statutory public powers and functions as the safety regulatory authority; but equally, it may well carry out private transactions, such as the disposal of, the acquisition of, or the development of property. If one follows the scheme through, we suggest that it is perfectly capable of being understood.' Lord Williams of Mostyn, 24 November 1997, House of Lords, Hansard Col. 758.

[111] See *Costello-Roberts v UK* Judgment of 25 March 1993, at para. 27, discussed in Ch 9, at 9.1 above.

[112] The Parliamentary Notes on Clauses in both the House of Commons and the House of Lords deal with bodies which are 'clearly public authorities' such as Government departments, Ministers of the Crown, and local authorities) and state, with regard to the bodies with functions of a public nature, that the subsections 'bite upon other bodies (for example certain privatized companies) which have a mix of public and private functions'.

whether a human rights obligation has been apparently passed on to a non-state actor. It is arguable whether privatized companies providing access to water or telephone communication are exercising 'elements of governmental authority' (perhaps they are with regard to safety, but some might argue not regarding billing or disconnection). On the other hand, many would argue that such companies are, fulfilling a public function essential to the enjoyment of human rights. Access to water remains a human right. Using a mobile phone, by contrast, cannot necessarily be considered on the same plane. The fact that the provider is a privatized company, or the activity is something that was formerly exclusively in the public sector, does not really help to determine the scope of the entities exercising 'elements of governmental authority' for the purposes of state responsibility under human rights treaties.

A case against a privatized water company arose early on before the English courts. The complaint was brought by a house-owner claiming compensation for the flooding of a garden with dirty water. It was accepted by both parties that the water company was 'a public authority within the meaning of the Human Rights Act' even though the House of Lords eventually rejected the human rights claim on the grounds that there was a separate statutory scheme for resolving such disputes.[113]

It seems the public authority need not be carrying out a *governmental* function for it to be considered public under the Human Rights Act 1998. It is therefore suggested that the scope of the Act covers more bodies than would be covered by the state responsibility test developed by the International Law Commission, but such an extension is fully warranted as it means that issues which would be covered by the European Court of Human Rights (albeit in cases brought against a state for failure to legislate or act to ensure compensation) can be dealt with in the national courts directly against the responsible non-state actor. The drafters of the legislation clearly foresaw that human rights obligations would be extended beyond the organs of the state to a plethora of different entities. After the adoption of the 1998 Act, but before its entry into force, the then Home Secretary, Jack Straw, gave a keynote speech at a conference organized to prepare charities and

---

[113] *Marcic v Thames Water Utilities Ltd* Case 1998 TCC 224, 14 May 2001, at para. 59; [2002] EWCA Civ 65 (Court of Appeal); [2003] UKHL 66 (House of Lords). The House of Lords rejected Marcic's claims on the ground that the statutory scheme placed the decision-making in the hands of the regulator and not in the hands of the Courts: 'Whether the system adopted by a sewerage undertaker is fair is a matter inherently more suited for decision by the industry regulator than by a court. And the statutory scheme so provides.' *Per* Lord Nicholls, at para. 38. Note Lord Hoffman's speech (at para. 71) which, after referring to the European Court of Human Rights judgment in *Hatton* (discussed in Ch 8 above) shifted the focus from the water company to the regulator: 'National institutions, and particularly the national legislature, are accorded a broad discretion in choosing the solution appropriate to their own society or creating the machinery for doing so. There is no reason why Parliament should not entrust such decisions to an independent regulator such as the Director. He is a public authority within the meaning of the 1998 Act and has a duty to act in accordance with Convention rights. If (which there is no reason to suppose) he has exceeded the broad margin of discretion allowed by the Convention, Mr Marcic will have a remedy under section 6 of the 1998 Act.'

companies for the impact of the Act. The following excerpt sets out the Home Secretary's understanding of the scope of the legislation just adopted:

> A key term in the Human Rights Act is 'public authority'. The Act gives a wide meaning to 'public authority'. There is quite a bit of background and law to this but the basic effect is that a court can treat you, or a part of you, as a public authority even if you are outside the central or local government machine. What matters is what you do and how that affects people's rights.
>
> And I guess that what most of you here today do includes some public authority function. Charities like the NSPCC [National Society for the Prevention of Cruelty to Children], who prosecute. Regulators, looking after public services independently of government. Nursing homes. Housing associations. Bodies like Group 4, though a private, not nationalised concern, with both private and public authority functions. For some of you, giving a fair hearing to people may be the issue. For others there may be issues about privacy. For all of you, discrimination is something you will want to avoid. It's a question of sorting out the relevant human rights and understanding what it means for your work.[114]

The second leg of the International Law Commission test for indirect state responsibility involves finding internal law which has empowered the non-state actor.[115] In the United Kingdom, the form of empowerment seems not to be considered particularly relevant.[116] During the Parliamentary debates on the Human Rights Bill, the then Home Secretary, Jack Straw, had a further example to illustrate a private (non-state actor) that would be considered as exercising functions of a public nature and therefore be saddled with human rights obligations under the Act:

> The best example involves regulation in the City: the Takeover Panel was not established by statute and, as far as I am aware, none of its members is appointed by Ministers, but it plays a crucial role in the regulation of markets and competition policy and has been regarded by our domestic courts as susceptible to judicial review. Although they have not used that language, the courts have effectively said that the Takeover Panel, which may be entirely private in its composition, exercises a public function. That is one of the complexities with which we have had to deal in trying to draft the Bill.[117]

---

[114] Institute for Public Policy Research (IPPR) Conference, 29 March 2000, 'Human Rights Act—Standing up for Britain and for Corporate Citizenship', at 4, Keynote address' (mimeograph on file with the author). See also an article written explaining the aims of the conference by Sarah Spencer 'A hard Act to follow' *The Times*, 28 March 2000, law supplement, at 5. Spencer quotes from a Group 4 (private security company) manual which advises staff: 'You will need to fit everything you do into the new framework created by the Act. If it does not fit there is no place for it in this company.'

[115] See Art. 5: 'The conduct of a person or entity which is not an organ of the State under article 4 but which is empowered by the law of that State to exercise elements of the governmental authority shall be considered an act of the State under international law, provided the person or entity is acting in that capacity in the particular instance'. Annexed to GA Res. 56/83, 12 December 2001.

[116] Note that ILC Art. 4(2) states, with regard to state organs: '2. An organ includes any person or entity which has that status in accordance with the internal law of the State.' The word 'includes' means that the designation by internal law is not essential in this context.

[117] House of Commons, 17 June 1998, Col. 407 (Home Secretary, Jack Straw).

He also developed the question of privatized services:

> For example, between 1948 and 1993, a public authority—the British Railways Board—was responsible for every aspect of running the railway. Now, Railtrack plc does that, but it also exercises the public function of approving and monitoring the safety cases of train operating companies. Railtrack acts privately in its functions as a commercial property developer. We were anxious—I make this point to the right hon. Member for Sutton Coldfield in particular—that we should not catch the commercial activities of Railtrack—or, for example, of the water companies—which were nothing whatever to do with its exercise of public functions.[118]

He then turned to the second thorny question, private security companies:

> Private security firms contract to run prisons: what Group 4, for example, does as a plc contracting with other bodies is nothing whatever to do with the state, but, plainly, where it runs a prison, it may be acting in the shoes of the state. The effect of clause 6(7) is that those organisations, unlike the 'obvious' public authorities, will not be liable in respect of their private acts. The third category is organisations with no public functions—accordingly, they fall outside the scope of clause 6.[119]

Taken together, these speeches from these Government Ministers suggest that they wanted to exclude employment matters as matters which are 'private acts' as well as property development. The logic is based on the idea that there should be equality of treatment between entities competing in the market-place—even when one of them has some public functions some of the time. The public acts that would seem to trigger human rights accountability are the health and safety aspects of the railways and the actual running of a prison. This presents a new conception of the private and public spheres. Human rights obligations turn not on the body as such, but on its function at any given moment.

The private security company that has on its portfolio both running a prison and security for a supermarket could, arguably, be said to be liable under the Human Rights Act only for abuse or discrimination in the context of its public function in running the prison. This company and any other company engaged in security for shops and other 'private' arrangements is then apparently excluded from the scope of the Human Rights Act with regard to these activities in the 'private sphere'. A better approach would be to see such security arrangements as a form of 'privatization of the public function of ensuring security and the rule of law'. It is suggested that wherever security guards operate, they should be liable as performing a public function under the Human Rights Act. The idea that a guard and the company would be liable for mistreatment in prison but immune under the Human Rights Act for mistreatment at the supermarket seems indefensible from the viewpoint of the victim, and therefore arguably from a human rights point of view.

---

[118] House of Commons, 17 June 1998, at Col. 409.   [119] Ibid, at Cols 409–110.

A further consideration is that, in the past, a state-owned company such as British Rail would attract state responsibility before the European Court of Human Rights in Strasbourg, not only for health and safety issues but also with regard to employment relations.[120] Similarly, Home Office employment of prison guards would attract state responsibility for an issue of employment, say a policy of excluding people on grounds of sexual orientation or trade union membership. Now it seems as though the same sector will be immune from human rights challenges as the employment relationship is seen as an act of a 'private nature'.

Of course, in both examples, violence in defence of a supermarket and discrimination by an employer, there would probably be other remedies available under national law, and in the application of the Human Rights Act the judge would be obligated to take into account other remedies granted in relation to the act in question.[121] But in the event that no remedy were available, recourse would still lie in Strasbourg, not necessarily because these security companies would be considered public authorities by the European Court of Human Rights, but because the state had failed to secure effective protection for human rights, thus failing to fulfil its positive obligations under the Convention. As discussed in Chapter 9 above, the failure to provide protection from a private employer who engaged in anti-union discrimination was found to be a violation of the Convention. The Human Rights Act may not therefore preclude the tiring trip to Strasbourg where the immediate violator is a non-state actor.

The debate in the House of Commons engendered considerable speculation on the nature of a number of institutions which do not obviously fall on one side or the other of the public/private line. The Home Secretary stated:

> To take a topical example, the courts have said that the Football Association is not such a public body as to be susceptible to judicial review, so they are used to drawing a line, and, up to now, the line which they have drawn has been sensible. The Takeover Panel plainly performs a public function—there can be no argument about that, even though it is a private body—and even though the public enjoy football, it is highly debatable whether the functions of the FA are public functions. The same is true of the Jockey Club and its functions. The courts have been careful in holding susceptible to judicial review bodies which are not plainly agents of the state.
>
> The courts will consider the nature of a body and the activity in question. They might consider whether the activities of a non-statutory body would be the subject of statutory regulation if that body did not exist, which covers the point about the Takeover Panel; whether the Government had provided underpinning for its activities; and whether it exercised extensive or monopolistic powers.[122]

---

[120] See *Young, James and Webster v UK* Judgment of 26 June 1981, discussed in Ch 9, at 9.1.1 above.

[121] See s 8(3)(a). The UK's Equality Bill (Bill 72) as introduced in March 2005 includes private discrimination in employment and housing on grounds such as religion, age, and sexual orientation.

[122] House of Commons, 17 June 1998, at Col. 410.

So we see here that the Panel on Take-Overs and Mergers would be considered a public authority (even though it is not a state actor) due to its public functions, but it was suggested that the Football Association and Jockey Club would not be considered public authorities. The distinction so far turns on whether the Government has delegated some sort of power or authority (by whatever legal route).

The discussion regarding television companies is more confusing. By the end of the debates, the opinion was characterized by the opposition that the 'BBC would be a public authority, that Channel 4 might be one, and that commercial television might not be'.[123] The Home Secretary explained the discussion within the Government:

> I shall be quite open about the fact that we discussed the BBC and the press. The BBC is plainly performing a public function, and the House has long accepted that it should be the subject of much greater regulation than the press. We have ended up with a mixed economy: the BBC has clear injunctions on it about balance, while the press rightly have no such injunctions on them, except those which they impose on themselves through the PCC [Press Complaints Commission]. That is entirely right in a free society.[124]

With regard to British Board of Film Classification he continued:

> That is a very interesting body. As I know all too well, following the interesting discussions in which I have had to engage with the board to get it to do the job that is expected of it, it is an entirely private organisation. It is not regulated by statute. It has a curious connection with the Video Recordings Acts, but hon. Members on both sides of the House—on behalf of the public—are pressurising it to do a job on behalf of the public, and classify films properly. In any other jurisdiction, a state body would probably do the work. Here, it is done by a self-regulating body that clearly has a public function. I believe—and I think the public would believe—that that body should be seen as exercising public functions.[125]

The key debates in the House of Commons and House of Lords ranged over a number of non-state actors that were seen to be almost certainly caught as public authorities in that their functions were of a public nature. One the whole, it was assumed by most, but not all, that the BBC, Channel 4, and ITV would be considered by the courts as public, in these circumstances, while there were doubts about individual ITV companies and 'private television stations'.[126]

---

[123] Debate in the House of Commons, 2 July 1998, Col. 544 (Sir Norman Fowler).

[124] House of Commons, 17 June 1998 (Home Secretary, Jack Straw), Col. 411.

[125] Ibid, at Col. 413.

[126] Ibid, at Col. 401, Sir Norman Fowler, referring to Home Office Minister Lord Williams of Mostyn, House of Lords debate of 3 November 1997, at Col. 1309 who had said: 'The noble and learned Lord, Lord Simon of Glaisdale, asked what would or would not be a public body. He rightly conjectured that we would anticipate the BBC being a public authority and that Channel 4 might well be a public authority, but that other commercial organisations, such as private television stations, might well not be public authorities. I stress that that is a matter for the courts to decide as the jurisprudence develops. Some authorities plainly exercise wholly public functions; others do not.

The Press Complaints Commission (PCC) was at one stage considered as outside the scope of the Human Rights Bill, but, following a legal opinion by David Pannick for the PCC, it was suggested by the Lord Chancellor that the PCC might well be considered by the courts as a public authority carrying out functions of a public nature.[127] Newspapers were seen by Lord Williams of Mostyn, Minister for the Home Office, as outside the definition of public authority,[128] although they would be made indirectly more accountable should the PCC become liable. There was an assumption that professional organizations,[129] chambers of commerce, churches,[130] and charities could fall within the scope of the Act where they are carrying out a public function, and the following entities were all mentioned by name in the House of Commons debate of 17 June 1998: the Royal Society for the Prevention of Cruelty to Animals;[131] the General Medical

There is no difficulty here.' See also: Miss Julie Kirkbride at Col. 401; Mr Jack Straw (Secretary of State for the Home Office) at Cols 411 (discussed above) and 414; cf Mr Edward Leigh at Col. 419: 'Today, we have debated the BBC. The Home Secretary originally said that the BBC would be a public authority, but ITV would not. I am advised by Professor Ian Leigh of Durham university, who has helped me with the drafting of my amendments . . . He is professor of law at Durham university and he has advised me that the BBC would not be a public authority.'

[127] Lord Chancellor, House of Lords, 27 November 1997, Col. 786: 'I tend to believe that the important function of the PCC to adjudicate on complaints from the public about the press may well be held to be a function of a public nature, so that, as I said in my letter, the PCC might well be held to be a public authority under the Human Rights Bill.' For the background, see House of Commons Library Research Paper 98/25, '*The Human Rights Bill [HL]*', Bill 119 of 1997–98: privacy and the press', 13 February 1998, available at http://www.parliament.uk/commons/lib/research/rp98/rp98-025.pdf.

[128] House of Lords, 3 November 1997, Col. 1310: 'subject to the cautious proviso that this is a matter for the courts to determine in due time, it is our belief that a newspaper is not a public authority'.

[129] House of Commons, 17 June 1998, Col. 412: 'Mr. Grieve: Surely any body that regulates a profession of any kind must be a public body for the purpose of that regulation. Mr. Straw: That is true.'

[130] House of Lords, 29 October 1998, Col. 2091. Following the inclusion of s 13 (see below) the Bishop of Oxford saw the following scenario: 'Let me give one brief example. Let us suppose that there is a voluntary aided school—either Jewish, Moslem or Christian—and the head teacher of that school decides to convert to another religion. If he claims a right to freedom of speech, and therefore the right to remain in his position, what would happen to the particular ethos of that voluntary aided school? Under the amendment which the Government have incorporated into this Bill, it is said that if the matter comes to court then the court must have particular regard to the importance of the right of the institution.' Lord Lester explained (at Col. 2091) how human rights obligations would attach to churches: 'there are situations in which the Church is part of the state or exercises public functions; for example, in maintaining voluntary schools. In such a case the law already intervenes; for example, by forbidding racial discrimination in providing education in all schools, including voluntary schools. Even religious bodies are capable of breaching convention rights and cannot be above the law of the convention; and no one disputes that'. He seems to imagine that there would be times when the Church would not be exercising a public function. He continued: 'it seems to us that this provision does not in any way seek to immunise religious bodies from the convention but respects freedom of conscience, belief and religion, drawing attention to the importance of that and maintaining the distinction between the public sphere and the private sphere'.

[131] House of Commons, 17 June 1998, Col. 427 Mr Grieve: 'For example, the Royal Society for the Prevention of Cruelty to Animals has charitable status, but also has the task of prosecuting for the purposes of animal welfare. It is a charitable body, which has been granted quite extensive powers by Parliament. It clearly falls within the ambit of an extension of the state because it is tolerated in the functions that it exercises. Therefore, the idea that we have to extend to public authorities the discipline of the convention should not be a matter of dispute.'

Council;[132] the Law Society;[133] and the Royal National Lifeboat Institution.[134] In sum, the Home Secretary stressed that the test referred to the 'substance and nature of the act, and not to the form and legal personality'.[135]

The debates illustrate the scope of the concern regarding certain non-state actors and their inclusion as possible defendants under litigation based on the Human Rights Act. The Court of Appeal and House of Lords, however, have rejected recourse to these debates under the *Pepper v Hart* exception in order to determine what Ministers meant by 'public authority' in this context.[136] Lord Nicholls explained: 'it is not the ministers' words, uttered as they were on behalf of the executive, that must be referred to in order to understand what Parliament intended. It is the words used by Parliament that must be examined in order to understand and apply the legislation that it has enacted'.[137]

10.2.1.2 Cases before the UK courts

Since the adoption of the Human Rights Act the question of what constitutes a public authority in this context has come before the lower courts, the Court of Appeal, and the House of Lords. The early cases suggest that the boundaries are yet to be clearly established. Judges have sometimes come to opposite conclusions with regard to the same body. The Parliamentary Joint Committee on Human Rights found that:

> The tests being applied by the courts to determine whether a function is a 'public function' within the meaning of section 6(3)(b) of the Human Rights Act are, in human rights terms, highly problematic. Their application results in many instances where an organisation 'stands in the shoes of the State' and yet does not have responsibilities under the Human Rights Act. It means that the protection of human rights is dependent not on the type of power being exercised, nor on its capacity to interfere with human rights, but on the relatively arbitrary (in human rights terms) criterion of the body's administrative links with institutions of the State. The European Convention on Human Rights provides no basis for such a limitation, which calls into question the capacity of the Human Rights Act to bring rights home to the full extent envisaged by those who designed, debated and agreed the Act . . .[138]
>
> The gaps and inconsistencies in human rights protection arising from this situation are likely to mean that the UK falls short of its international obligations (under Articles 1 and 13 ECHR) to secure the effective protection of Convention rights and to provide an effective remedy for their breach . . .[139]

---

[132] House of Commons, 17 June 1998, at Col. 412 (Mr Straw, Secretary of State).

[133] Ibid, at Col. 412 (Mr Garnier).

[134] Ibid, at Col. 407 (Mr Grieve), at Col. 430 (Mr Lansley).   [135] Ibid, at Col. 433.

[136] *Pepper v Hart* [1993] AC 593.

[137] *Aston Cantlow and Wilmcote with Billesley Parochial Church Council v Wallbank* [2003] UKHL 37, at para. 37.

[138] House of Lords, House of Commons, Joint Committee on Human Rights, *The Meaning of Public Authority under the Human Rights Act, Seventh Report of Session 2003–04*. HL Paper 39, HC Paper 382, 3 March 2004, accessible at http://heiwww.unige.ch/~clapham/hrdoc/docs/ukpublicauthorityreport.pdf, at para. 41 (para. 1 of the Conclusions and recommendations).

[139] Ibid, at para. 73 (para. 7 of the Conclusions and recommendations).

The disparities in human rights protection that arise from the current case law on the meaning of public authority are unjust and without basis in human rights principles. Unless other avenues of redress can be found, this situation is likely to deprive individuals of redress for breaches of their substantive Convention rights incorporated under the Human Rights Act. The situation created by the current state of the law is unsatisfactory, unfair, and inconsistent with the intention of Parliament...[140]

The application of the functional public authority provision in section 6(3)(b) of the Human Rights Act leaves real gaps and inadequacies in human rights protection in the UK, including gaps that affect people who are particularly vulnerable to ill-treatment. We consider that this deficit in protection may well leave the UK in breach of its international obligations to protect the Convention rights of all those in the jurisdiction and to provide mechanisms for redress where those rights are breached.[141]

The case-law is elegantly summarized in the Joint Committee Report and will not be rehearsed here.[142] It has covered: housing associations, care homes, mental health care facilities, organizations managing public markets, local councils, and the governing bodies of sports associations.[143] The Report was written against a background of concern that the courts were suggesting that the Human Rights Act does not apply against private housing associations and charities where housing and health care functions have been contracted out by local authorities.[144] The Report concluded with its own explanation as to why there should be no difference between, on the one hand, a body set up by statute, and, on the other hand, a body entrusted by the government with a public function by contract:

> ... for a body to discharge a public function, it does not need to do so under direct statutory authority. A State programme or policy, with a basis in statute or otherwise, may

[140] Ibid, para. 74 (para. 8 of the Conclusions and recommendations).

[141] Ibid, para. 29 of the Conclusions and recommendations.

[142] Ibid, paras 24–44, the key cases dealt with are: *Aston Cantlow and Wilmcote with Billesley Parochial Church Council v Wallbank* [2003] UKHL 37 (discussed below); *Marcic v Thames Water* [2002] EWCA Civ 65; *Poplar Housing and Regeneration Community Association v Donoghue* [2001] EWCA Civ 595; *Callin and ors v Leonard Cheshire Foundation* [2002] EWCA Civ 595; *R(A) v Partnerships in Care Ltd* [2002] 1 WLR 2610, [2002] EWHC 529 (Admin); *R v Hampshire Farmers' Market, ex p Beer* [2003] EWCA Civ 1056. Other cases of interest include *R (Haggerty) v St Helen's Council* [2003] EWHC 803 (Admin) (council was liable for any breach of Convention rights resulting from contractual negotiations with a private care home which resulted in the home's closure) and *Rubython v Federation Internationale de L'Automobile*, where Gray J considered that first, an application of the Act to the body would mean an unacceptable territorial application of the Act so as to impose obligations on France, and second, that the 'granting of press accreditation cannot be said to be a public authority function' *per* Gray J at p 4 of the transcript (Judgment of 6 March 2003, Queen's Bench Division, unreported). See also the suggestion that local authorities are obliged to build in Convention obligations into their contracts with private housing associations when they contract out (privatize) such services, Woolf LCJ in *Leonard Cheshire* (above) at paras 33–35; discussed by M. Carss-Frisk, 'Public Authorities: The Developing Definition', *EHRLR* (2002) 319–326, and see the critical remarks by M. Sunkin who discusses the contract idea in the light of the Joint Committee Report (above), 'Pushing Forward the Frontiers of Human Rights Protection: The Meaning of Public Authority under the Human Rights Act', *Public Law* (2004) 643–658, esp. 647–648; see further the Joint Committee Report (above) paras 110–126.   [143] See n 142 above.

[144] For an interesting analysis of the dilemmas involved, see M. Sunkin, 'Pushing Forward the Frontiers of Human Rights Protection: The Meaning of Public Authority under the Human Rights Act', *Public Law* (2004) 643–658.

delegate its powers or duties through contractual arrangements without changing the public nature of those powers or duties. Under section 6 of the Human Rights Act, there should be no distinction between a body providing housing because it itself is required to do so by statute, and a body providing housing because it has contracted with a local authority which is required by statute to provide the service. The loss of a single step in proximity to the statutory duty does not change the nature of the function, nor the nature of its capacity to interfere with Convention rights.[145]

Finally, the Report sets out its own test:

> as a matter of broad principle, a body is a functional public authority performing a public function under section 6(3)(b) of the Human Rights Act where it exercises a function that has its origin in governmental responsibilities...in such a way as to compel individuals to rely on that body for realisation of their Convention human rights.[146]

The key case to have reached the House of Lords concerned a parochial church council. It that case, the House of Lords disagreed with the Court of Appeal that the council was a public authority. The House of Lords held, first, that the council could not be considered a 'pure' or 'standard' public authority under section 6.[147] Lord Nicholls considered that the reference in section 6(1) to public authority 'is essentially a reference to a body whose nature is governmental in a broad sense of that expression'.[148] As discussed throughout this book, the nature of government is a contested concept and certainly shifts over time and from country to country. For Lord Nicholls:

> The most obvious examples are government departments, local authorities, the police and the armed forces. Behind the instinctive classification of these organisations as bodies whose nature is governmental lie factors such as the possession of special powers, democratic accountability, public funding in whole or in part, an obligation to act only in the public interest, and a statutory constitution...[149]

With regard to the parochial church council in the instant case, Lord Nicholls dealt with the Church of England, and then the council, and found that neither could be considered 'core' public authorities, and that they were 'far removed from the type of body whose acts engage the responsibility of the state under the European Convention'.[150] More specifically he stated:

> Historically the Church of England has discharged an important and influential role in the life of this country. As the established church it still has special links with central

---

[145] *The Meaning of Public Authority under the Human Rights Act, Seventh Report of Session 2003–04*, at para. 142 (para. 26 of the Conclusions and recommendations).

[146] At para. 157 (para. 31 of the Conclusions and recommendations).

[147] The Joint Committee uses the term 'pure', in the course of the argument they were referred to as 'core' public authorities. The judgment refers also to the terminology used by Clayton and Tomlinson in *The Law of Human Rights* (Oxford: Oxford University Press, 2000) at para. 5.08 which contrasts obvious public bodies with 'functional' public authorities. These latter bodies were also referred to in argument as 'hybrid' bodies. See *Aston Cantlow and Wilmcote with Billesley Parochial Church Council v Wallbank* [2003] UKHL 37, at para. 35 (*per* Lord Hope).

[148] Ibid, at para. 7.   [149] Ibid, at para. 7.   [150] Ibid, at para. 14.

government. But the Church of England remains essentially a religious organisation. This is so even though some of the emanations of the church discharge functions which may qualify as governmental. Church schools and the conduct of marriage services are two instances. The legislative powers of the General Synod of the Church of England are another. This should not be regarded as infecting the Church of England as a whole, or its emanations in general, with the character of a governmental organisation.

As to parochial church councils, their constitution and functions lend no support to the view that they should be characterised as governmental organisations or, more precisely, in the language of the statute, public authorities. Parochial church councils are established as corporate bodies under a church measure, now the Parochial Church Councils (Powers) Measure 1956. For historical reasons this unique form of legislation, having the same force as a statute, is the way the Church of England governs its affairs. But the essential role of a parochial church council is to provide a formal means, prescribed by the Church of England, whereby ex officio and elected members of the local church promote the mission of the Church and discharge financial responsibilities in respect of their own parish church, including responsibilities regarding maintenance of the fabric of the building. This smacks of a church body engaged in self-governance and promotion of its affairs.[151]

Lord Nicholls also made reference to the special care that had been taken in the Human Rights Act to protect the exercise of freedom of religion by religious organizations under section 13.[152] This section implies, on the one hand, that religious entities have duties and yet, on the other hand, that the courts should not act to deprive them of their freedoms.

Lord Nicholls was aware of the shifting sands of what constitute governmental functions and who fulfils them. He chose to argue for a flexible test to determine how to limit the second category of authorities: the 'hybrid'[153] authorities foreseen by section 6(3)(b):

> In a modern developed state governmental functions extend far beyond maintenance of law and order and defence of the realm. Further, the manner in which wide ranging governmental functions are discharged varies considerably. In the interests of efficiency and economy, and for other reasons, functions of a governmental nature are frequently discharged by non-governmental bodies. Sometimes this will be a consequence of privatisation, sometimes not. One obvious example is the running of prisons by

---

[151] Ibid, at paras 13–14.

[152] See Lord Nicholls at para. 15. Section 13 of the Act states: '(1) If a court's determination of any question arising under this Act might affect the exercise by a religious organisation (itself or its members collectively) of the Convention right to freedom of thought, conscience and religion, it must have particular regard to the importance of that right. (2) In this section "court" includes a tribunal.'

[153] See, e.g. D. Oliver, *Common Values and the Public-Private Divide* (London: Butterworths, 1999) at 237, but Oliver in her later writing cautions against the term: 'But it is not the nature of the of the *person* as "hybrid" or "functional" that matters, rather the nature of the function or activity that is in issue in the particular case. It would not be accurate to refer to a function as "hybrid", since hybrid suggests a crossbreed or mongrel. What is meant when this kind of phrase is used is that the body is not a standard public authority, but has functions, some of which are of a public and some of a private nature.' D. Oliver, 'Functions of a Public Nature under the Human Rights Act', *Public Law* (2004) 329–351, at 337.

commercial organisations. Another is the discharge of regulatory functions by organisations in the private sector, for instance, the Law Society. Section 6(3)(b) gathers this type of case into the embrace of section 6 by including within the phrase 'public authority' any person whose functions include 'functions of a public nature'. This extension of the expression 'public authority' does not apply to a person if the nature of the act in question is 'private'.[154]

The rationale for his division was based in part on an understanding that labelling a body as a 'core' public authority rather than a 'hybrid' public authority would preclude that body from ever bringing a claim as a victim before the European Court of Human Rights. The European Commission of Human Rights had prevented bodies such as local councils from making applications under the Convention; such a body was not be considered to be a 'non-governmental organization'.[155]

The test in the House of Lords, for determining whether one is dealing with a functional public authority, was said to involve taking into account the following factors: 'the extent to which in carrying out the relevant function the body is publicly funded, or is exercising statutory powers, or is taking the place of central government or local authorities, or is providing a public service'.[156] Applying this test to the Aston Parochial Church Council, Lord Nicholls explained how the test should be applied in practice to the actual case, which concerned a demand by the Council that Mr and Mrs Wallbank, as lay rectors, undertake a chancel repair to the church:

> it is not necessary to analyse each of the functions of a parochial church council and see if any of them is a public function. What matters is whether the particular act done by

[154] *Aston Cantlon and Wilmcote with Billesley Parochial Church Council v Wallbank* [2003] UKHL 37.
[155] See also Lord Hope at para. 47. See Art. 34 of the European Convention on Human Rights and P. Leach, *Taking a Case to the European Court of Human Rights* (London: Blackstone Press, 2001) at 62–76, esp. para. 5.2.12, where he cites the Commission decisions in *Ayuntamiento de M v Spain* App. 15090/89, 68 DR 209 and *Rothenthurm Commune v Switzerland* App. 13252/87, 59 DR 251. The issue was left open in *BBC v UK* App. 25978/94, 84–A DR 129. See further *Ayuntamiento de Mula v Spain* App. 55346/00, Decision of the European Court of Human Rights of 1 February 2001: 'The Court reiterates that under the settled case-law of the Convention institutions, local-government organisations are public-law bodies which perform official duties assigned to them by the Constitution and by substantive law. They are therefore quite clearly governmental organisations... In that connection, the Court reiterates that in international law the expression "governmental organisations" cannot be held to refer only to the Government or the central organs of the State. Where powers are distributed along decentralised lines, it refers to any national authority which exercises public functions. The applicant authority cannot be regarded as a person or group of individuals within the meaning of Article 34 of the Convention either. Such a construction would not be consistent with the distinction drawn in that provision between non-governmental organisations, on the one hand, and persons or groups of individuals on the other. The fact that local authorities have capacity to defend their property rights in the courts in the same way as private individuals or non-governmental organisations does not mean that they can be assimilated to private individuals or non-governmental organisations for the purposes of Article 34 of the Convention.' At pp 2 and 3 of the translation. It is suggested that the converse could also be true: the fact that an entity is treated as exercising a public function for the purposes of domestic law does not necessarily mean that it cannot claim to be a non-governmental organization for the purposes of Art. 34. The BBC represents an obvious example of an entity that might be considered both a victim in Strasbourg and perpetrator at the national level without this necessarily presenting a contradiction. [156] Ibid, at para. 12.

the plaintiff council of which complaint is made is a private act as contrasted with the discharge of a public function. The impugned act is enforcement of Mr and Mrs Wallbank's liability, as lay rectors, for the repair of the chancel of the church of St John the Baptist at Aston Cantlow. As I see it, the only respect in which there is any 'public' involvement is that parishioners have certain rights to attend church services and in respect of marriage and burial services. To that extent the state of repair of the church building may be said to affect rights of the public. But I do not think this suffices to characterise actions taken by the parochial church council for the repair of the church as 'public'. If a parochial church council enters into a contract with a builder for the repair of the chancel arch, that could hardly be described as a public act. Likewise when a parochial church council enforces, in accordance with the provisions of the Chancel Repairs Act 1932, a burdensome incident attached to the ownership of certain pieces of land: there is nothing particularly 'public' about this. This is no more a public act than is the enforcement of a restrictive covenant of which church land has the benefit.[157]

Lord Hope took a similar approach, but he felt that the act was of a private nature because the liability to repair the chancel arose from private law. He explored the issue as to whether such an obligation does nonetheless relate to a non-private act on the part of an entity exercising functions of a public nature:

It may be said that, as the church is a historic building which is open to the public, it is in the public interest that these repairs should be carried out. It is also true that the liability to repair the chancel rests on persons who need not be members of the church and that there is, as the Court of Appeal observed at p 63B, para 34, no surviving element of mutuality or mutual governance between the church and the impropriator. But none of these factors leads to the conclusion that the PCC's act in seeking to enforce the lay rector's liability on behalf of the parishioners is a public rather than a private act. The nature of the act is to be found in the nature of the obligation which the PCC is seeking to enforce. It is seeking to enforce a civil debt. The function which it is performing has nothing to do with the responsibilities which are owed to the public by the State. I would hold that section 6(5) applies, and that in relation to this act the PCC is not for the purposes of section 6(1) a public authority.[158]

Lord Scott of Foscote came to a different conclusion with regard to the question as to whether the PCC could be considered a 'person certain' performing a public function as a hybrid public authority. For him the following factors were relevant:

1. The parish church is a church of the Church of England, a church by law established.
2. It is a church to which the Anglican public are entitled to have recourse, regardless of whether they are practising members of the church, for marriage, for baptism of their children, for weddings, for funerals and burial, and perhaps for other purposes as well.
3. Members of other denominations, or even other religions, are, if parishioners, entitled to burial in the parish churchyard.

---

[157] Ibid, at para. 16. It is worth noting here that even if the Council had been found to be a public authority under s 6, Lord Nicholls would have found that the Act did not apply, as the Council was applying primary legislation which left no room for interpretation. See para. 19.

[158] Ibid, at para. 64.

4. The church is, therefore, a public building. It is not a private building from which the public can lawfully be excluded at the whim of the owner.
5. The PCC is corporate and its functions are charitable. Its members have the status of charity trustees. Charitable trusts are public trusts, not private ones.
6. A decision by a PCC to enforce a chancel repairing liability is a decision taken in the interests of the parishioners as a whole. It is not taken in pursuit of any private interests. If it were so taken, it would I think be impeachable by judicial review.[159]

He disagreed that the obligations were of a private nature, making the point that:

> ...obligations imposed by common law are not necessarily private law obligations. Whether they are so or not must depend on those to whom they are owed. The chancel repair obligations are not owed to private individuals. Private individuals cannot release them. Section 52 of the Ecclesiastical Dilapidations Measure 1923 provided a procedure whereby lay rectors liable for chancel repairs could compound their liability and thereby obtain a release from it. The procedure required there to be consultation with the PCC of the parish, the obtaining of approval from the Diocesan Dilapidations Board and payment of the requisite sum to the Diocesan Authority. The sum paid becomes trust money (see s(5)). These provisions have an unmistakable public law flavour to them. The chancel repair obligations resting on a lay rector are not, in my opinion, private law obligations.[160]

He therefore determined that the Council was a public authority for the purposes of the Human Rights Act.

Lord Rodger of Earlsferry, however, considered that the Council's role in this case could not be seen as governmental:

> In performing its duties in relation to the maintenance of the fabric of the church so that services may take place there, the PCC is doing its part to help the minister discharge his pastoral and evangelistic duties. The PCC may be acting in the public interest, in a general sense, but it is still carrying out a church rather than a governmental function. That remains the case even although, from time to time, when performing one of his pastoral duties—conducting a marriage service in the church—the minister himself may act as a public authority.[161]

Moreover, for Lord Rodgers the enforcement of common law could not bring it within the scope of a governmental function:

> ...the fact that, as part of its responsibilities in relation to the maintenance of the church fabric, the PCC may have to enforce a common law obligation against a lay rector who happens not to be a member of the Church can hardly transform the PCC into a public authority. Indeed, the very term 'lay rector' is a reminder that the common law obligation which the PCC is enforcing is the last remnant of a set of more complex rights and liabilities that were ecclesiastical in origin.[162]

---

[159] See also Lord Hope at para. 130. [160] Ibid, at para. 131. [161] Ibid, at para. 170.
[162] Ibid, at para. 171.

It is suggested that the judgment has sent a rather confusing message.[163] First, there has been a focus on those groups that would trigger direct state responsibility in Strasbourg before the European Court of Human Rights. This is unfortunate, as the European Court of Human Rights demands that governments protect against threats from all bodies, and not just offer protection from those bodies which give rise to direct responsibility.[164] The European Court rarely explains which bodies trigger direct responsibility. So the English courts have reverted to a range of bodies which by 'nature' are governmental. This is unhelpful, considering the contested nature of the natural role of government.

Second, the public authority test has been conflated with the Strasbourg Court's victim test, which draws a distinction between governmental bodies and non-governmental organizations. In order to protect the rights of entities to complain about human rights abuses under the Human Rights Act and under the Convention in Strasbourg, the judges have drawn the contours of the 'pure' public authority narrowly in order to avoid labelling bodies as governmental. The idea is that by declining to label such bodies as governmental, they will preserve such bodies' right to claim to be victims for the purposes of the Act or the Convention; i.e. that a 'hybrid' public authority may still in some circumstances qualify as a victim for the purposes of the Act and Convention.

It is unfortunate that the two notions of 'non-governmental organization' for the purposes of Article 34 ECHR—and pure public authority—are seen as forming a dichotomy. The categories are not necessarily mutually exclusive and serve completely different functions. The ambiguity surrounding whether a 'hybrid' public authority could complain of human rights violations adds to the confusion. The BBC is assumed to be a public authority for the purposes of ensuring its human rights accountability—but it is not hard to imagine situations where it may want to complain about a violation of its rights under human rights law. At the same time, one could imagine situations where its actions ought to trigger direct state responsibility in Strasbourg before the European Court of Human Rights.

Third, there are different views as to whether the enforcement of special duties under the common law by an entity takes us into the realm of a public authority acting in a public way. Lord Scott, as we saw, considered that the obligations on Mr and Mrs Wallbank to repair the church could not be considered private law obligations. For him, the common law enforcement of these obligations by the council brought the council within the definition of a public authority as a person certain exercising a public function—a hybrid public authority.

---

[163] For an excellent exegesis of the different judgments of the Lordships in this case, see P. Cane, 'Church, State and Human Rights: Are Parish Councils Public Authorities?' 120 *LQR* (2004) 41–48.

[164] See generally Ch 9, at 9.1 above. According to Wadham, Mountfield, and Edmundson (2003: 80) the approach of the English courts, whereby privatized/contracted-out services are considered outside the scope of the Human Rights Act, runs the risk of denying individuals and organizations their right to a remedy under Art. 13 of the Convention.

Fourth, there is likely to be continuing confusion based on analogies with the law of judicial review. A standard pure core public authority will not be subject to judicial review where it is carrying out certain contractual functions, such bodies will, however, be liable under the Human Rights Act.[165] Moreover, the law of judicial review has quickly evolved so that remedies are available against bodies exercising public or governmental functions and those bodies are granted certain procedural safeguards should it be determined that the proceedings fall under the judicial review procedure. The safeguards are aimed at ensuring that public bodies are not tied up with unnecessary litigation and that decisions can be made with a degree of certainty. A public/private divide has now become familiar terrain for arguments over procedure and remedies before the English courts.[166] The creation of a conceptual category of bodies performing public functions for the purposes of administrative law has had a huge impact on the debate about the scope of the category of entities performing public functions under the Human Rights Act.[167] Dawn Oliver has carefully explained how the tests have different rationales and suggested that policy arguments militate in favour of different tests under the administrative law of judicial review and the protections offered by the Human Rights Act (even though Ministers may have expected a single test).[168]

10.2.1.3 Policy Arguments Concerning the Public/Private Divide in the Human Rights Act

Dawn Oliver has been keen to restrict the temptation to offer a generous interpretation of what constitutes a public authority under the Human Rights Act; she suggests such a generous approach will have undesirable consequences beyond the human rights proceedings in issue:

> The categorisation of bodies into state and non-state pigeonholes could, if the 'state' pigeonhole became too full, result in the imposition by the body politic of regulations

---

[165] The point is well made by S. Grosz, J. Beatson, and P. Duffy, *Human Rights: The 1998 Act and the European Convention* (London: Sweet & Maxwell, 2000) at 61–67; see also Markus (2003: 83–99); Oliver (2004: 347–348).

[166] See generally D. Oliver, *Common Values and the Public-Private Divide* (London: Butterworths, 1999).

[167] See Lord Nicholls in *Aston* (n 147 above) at para. 52; *R v Hampshire Farmers' Market, ex p Beer* [2003] EWCA Civ 1056; *R(A) v Partnerships in Care Ltd* [2002] 1 WLR 2610, [2002] EWHC 529 (Admin). The argument in this last case illustrates how the courts may distinguish between private prisons (public function), or private medical facilities with patients compulsorily detained (public function) from housing associations providing a commercial service (private acts): 'The analogy between the hospital and a prison is an apt one. Even if the operation of a private prison is an activity which has become enmeshed in the activities of the public body which "subcontracted" its statutory obligations to the operators of the prison, the nature of the functions which even private prisons perform may well be enough to bring their decisions within the ambit of public law. Likewise, the need for the hospital's patients to receive care and treatment which may result in their living in the community again as a matter of public concern and interest. And those of the hospital's patients who are admitted to the hospital under section 3 of the 1983 Act (such as the Claimant) are admitted by compulsion and not by choice (a fact which Staney Burnton J. rightly considered as critical in the *Leonard Cheshire Foundation* case at [51] in distinguishing between a prison and the residential homes run by the Foundation.' At para. 25.   [168] Oliver (2004: 346–350).

and checks which could inhibit the development of institutions of civil society. In effect broad interpretations of 'public authority' and 'public function' would roll forward the frontiers of the state and roll back the frontiers of civil society, not by any means a politically neutral process.[169]

Oliver is right to point out that the determination of the public/private line is ideologically loaded, but she makes a questionable assumption that burdening 'civil society' with human rights duties is the same as expanding the power of the state. Furthermore, she assumes that, as soon as the judge decides that a body has human rights obligations, that body automatically looses its autonomy from government and its right to complain about government action which infringes its own human rights under the Convention. She points to the implications for certain bodies (such as privatized utilities, sporting associations and other 'possibly public' institutions) of a broad conception of 'public authority':

> Such bodies, as public authorities without Convention rights, would not be entitled to seek justifications for interferences by the government with the rights that are secured to private individuals and bodies under the Convention in terms of the public interests set out in the exceptions to most articles. They themselves would have no right to freedom of expression: the results of research by charities and universities, and programmes produced by the BBC, which the government found unacceptable could be suppressed without the suppression having to be justified under the exceptions in the Convention articles; the syllabuses and content of courses taught at universities could be controlled by the state without justification under the Convention articles.[170]

Raising the spectre of unstoppable government interference in university teaching may be a persuasive rhetorical device in this context—but we should pause to see if we want to follow this line of argument. I suggested above, that such an approach starts from the false assumption that there is a binary choice to be made between whether a body can be a human rights victim or a human rights abuser. I would argue that any body can be both victim and abuser.

For the moment, the BBC has not been automatically precluded from bringing complaints under the European Convention in Strasbourg. The European Commission of Human Rights did not, in fact, find it necessary to decide the status of the BBC as it found all the complaints brought by the BBC to be inadmissible; but the Commission nevertheless examined the detail of the complaints on the working assumption that the BBC does have the 'necessary status' to bring an application.[171] At the same time, complaints by a pro-life organization before

---

[169] D. Oliver, 'The Frontiers of the State: Public Authorities and Public Functions under the Human Rights Act', *Public Law* (2000) 476–493, at 477.   [170] Ibid, at 491.

[171] See, e.g. 'The Commission has considered whether the BBC is a "person, non-governmental organisation or group of individuals" within the meaning of Article 25 [now Art. 34] of the Convention. However, the Commission is not required to determine this question in the present case as, assuming that the BBC does have the necessary status to bring the application, the application is nevertheless inadmissible for the following reasons...' *British Broadcasting Corporation v UK* App. 25798/94, 18 January 1996; a similar paragraph appears in *British Broadcasting Corporation Scotland et al v UK* App. 34324/96, 23 October 1997; App. 25978/94, 84–A D & R 129.

the English courts that their political electoral broadcast was censored by the BBC
have been met with a declaration by the Court of Appeal that such a refusal by the
BBC was unlawful. The Court of Appeal examined the judgments of the
European Court of Human Rights in detail and applied the Convention's principles
to hold that the BBC had acted unlawfully.[172] Their ruling was overturned by
the House of Lords, not on the grounds that the BBC had no human rights obligations, but rather that the courts could not depart from Parliament's intention with
regard to the obligations placed on broadcasters. This meant that preference had
to be given to 'the protection of the public from being unduly distressed in their
own homes' rather than 'the requirements of freedom of political speech'.[173]

Oliver's scenario is, however, much more dramatic than suggested so far. She
describes a situation where charities, sports clubs, universities, etc. would lose
their freedom of action and could be discriminated against with impunity.

> They would not have freedom of association: so sporting bodies' membership rules and
> universities' student selection processes and criteria could be controlled by the state
> without the need to justify the control under Article 11(2). The property of such bodies
> could be expropriated, without compensation and without justification under the first
> protocol. They would have no right to respect for their privacy or correspondence.
> Having no rights, they would not be entitled not to be discriminated against on Article
> 14 grounds in the enjoyment of their rights. To treat such bodies as public authorities, in
> other words, would introduce a strong element of state corporatism into the system,
> undermining the pluralism that is supposed to be a hallmark of a liberal democracy and,
> in effect, rolling forward the frontiers of the state.[174]

This line of argumentation was picked up by Lord Nicholls in the *Aston* case, but
he restricted himself to the conclusion that a 'non-governmental organisation
within the meaning of article 34 ought not to be regarded as a "core" public
authority for the purposes of section 6'.[175] He argued for a 'generously wide scope'

---

[172] *Prolife Alliance v British Broadcasting Corporation* [2002] EWCA Civ 297. Although this was a
case of judicial review it is hard to see how the Convention would only apply under this procedure
and not in the case of a complaint under the Human Rights Act alone.

[173] *Per* Lord Nicholls at para. 16. *R v British Broadcasting Corporation, ex p Prolife Alliance* [2003]
UKHL 23. Lord Nicholls went on to refer to s 6(2): 'In the absence of a successful claim that the
offensive material restriction is not compatible with the Convention rights of ProLife Alliance, it is
not for the courts to find that broadcasters acted unlawfully when they did no more than give effect to
the statutory and other obligations binding on them. Even in such a case the effect of section 6(2) of
the Human Rights Act 1998 would have to be considered.' For the detail of s 6(2), see above; this
seems to presume that the BBC is a public authority. Lord Hoffman (at para. 58) explained how he
saw the relevance of the Convention for the BBC in a judicial review: 'The fact that no one has a right
to broadcast on television does not mean that article 10 has no application to such broadcasts. But the
nature of the right in such cases is different. Instead of being a right not to be prevented from expressing one's opinions, it becomes a right to fair consideration for being afforded the opportunity to do
so; a right not to have one's access to public media denied on discriminatory, arbitrary or unreasonable grounds.' Note Lord Walker at para. 106: 'Mr Pannick QC (for the BBC) accepts for the purposes of this appeal that the BBC is a public authority, without making any wider concession as to its
status in different contexts.'   [174] Oliver (2000: 491).

[175] *Aston* (n 147 above) at para. 47.

for the concept of public function for 'hybrid' bodies, as this would best fulfil the legislature's intention to ensure the protection of human rights.[176]

Oliver's approach may be convincing for some as regards the determination of pure/core/standard public authorities, but the risk is that this philosophy is carried over into determinations of what counts as a hybrid/functional public authority (or more accurately a 'person certain of whose functions are functions of a public nature' and where the nature of the act is *not* private (section 6(3)(b) and (5)). Oliver asks the judges to:

> . . . be wary of treating services offered either to the general public or to individuals as public functions unless they involve the exercise of coercive power or special authority, both because of difficulties in defining and limiting this form of vertical effect of the Act, and because such treatment legitimates state control of many activities by private bodies, often by individuals, thus rolling forward the frontiers of the state.[177]

The preoccupation with state control of the population can be simply met with a preoccupation with judicial protection from human rights abuses. We are simply debating whether we think laws protect or restrict freedom to act and whether we trust the judges to apply those laws. At this point much depends on one's perspective. Those running the university, sports club, or gas company may prefer a playing field unencumbered by the prospect of human rights litigation; but those excluded, dismissed, or discriminated against might not.

To be fair, Professor Oliver's approach is much more subtle. She is aware of the dangers of the operation of a public/private divide in English law and would prefer the removal of the procedural privileges that the state and its bodies enjoy under judicial review on the public side, as well as the inculcation of values such as autonomy, dignity, respect, status, and security into common law decision-making on the private side.[178] Oliver's prognosis in 1999 was that human rights issues will arise in private law disputes between 'vulnerable individuals on the one hand, and companies and other bodies in positions of power on the other'.[179] She suggests that the common law will develop in line with the Human Rights Act and the above-mentioned values, 'imposing duties of respect for individuals on those in power'.[180] Such a development of human rights obligations through the common law is considered in section 10.3.4 below.

---

[176] 'Unlike a core public authority, a "hybrid" public authority, exercising both public functions and non-public functions, is not absolutely disabled from having Convention rights. A hybrid public authority is not a public authority in respect of an act of a private nature. Here again, as with section 6(1), this feature throws some light on the approach to be adopted when interpreting section 6(3)(b). Giving a generously wide scope to the expression "public function" in section 6(3)(b) will further the statutory aim of promoting the observance of human rights values without depriving the bodies in question of the ability themselves to rely on Convention rights when necessary.' Ibid, at para. 11.

[177] Oliver (2000: 492).   [178] See generally Oliver (1999) esp. at 264.

[179] Oliver (1999: 246).

[180] Ibid. For the ways in which private law could develop these sorts of protections see also Oliver (1999: 167–200) and (2004: 329–351, at 349). See also J. Wadham and H. Mountfield, *Blackstone's Guide to the Human Rights Act 1998* (London: Blackstone Press, 1999) at 32, for the prediction that 'over time, Convention standards will infiltrate, influence and may even create new common law rights'.

10.2.2   US State Action Cases before the Supreme Court

The US Supreme Court has interpreted the Constitution as providing protection from interference with certain rights by non-state actors where there is a degree of 'state action'. Justice Scalia, delivering an opinion of the Court in 1995, stated that: 'It is fair to say that "our cases deciding when private action might be deemed that of the state have not been a model of consistency".'[181] The possible logic of the Court's approach has been pored over by commentators and has generated several studies.[182] Rather than attempt to break down the case-law into traditional categories used by commentators such as 'public function', 'state encouragement', 'government subsidies', and 'symbiotic relationship', this review of the cases will proceed according to the rights in issue.[183] Gardbaum's careful analysis of the state action cases concludes that 'the actual impact of constitutional rights on private actors is not fixed but will vary with changes in their substantive interpretation'.[184] He adds that there should no longer be a 'general constitutional consensus' that 'the reach of constitutional rights into the private sphere is definitively resolved and fixed by the state action doctrine'.[185]

10.2.2.1   Racial Discrimination by Private Entities

Although the early cases concerning racial discrimination by social clubs,[186] restaurants,[187] and parks[188] repay careful reading, the line of reasoning developed

---

[181] *Lebron v National Railroad Passenger Corp* 513 US (1995) 374, at 378, quoting *Edmonson v Leesville Concrete Co* 500 US (1991) 614, at 632, O'Connor J, dissenting.

[182] See, e.g. J. Y. Jakosa, 'Parsing Public from Private: The Failure of Differential State Action Analysis' 19 *Harv CR-CLLR* (1984) 193; H. Friendly, 'The Public-Private Penumbra: Fourteen Years Later' 130 *UPLR Review* (1982) 1289; and L. Alexander and P. Porton, *Whom does the Constitution Command?* (New York: Greenwood Press, 1988).

[183] See the helpful analysis by J. E. Nowak and R. D. Rotunda, *Constitutional Law* (St Paul, Minn: West Group, 6th edn, 2000) at 502–543.   [184] Gardbaum (2003: 459).

[185] Ibid.

[186] See *Moose Lodge No. 107 v Irvis* 407 US 163 (1972) (no state action found where a club refused to serve Blacks), the claim that the licensing by the state provided the requisite state action was rejected: 'Appellee, while conceding the right of private clubs to choose members upon a discriminatory basis, asserts that the licensing of Moose Lodge to serve liquor by the Pennsylvania Liquor Control Board amounts to such state involvement with the club's activities as to make its discriminatory practices forbidden by the Equal Protection Clause of the Fourteenth Amendment. The relief sought and obtained by appellee in the District Court was an injunction forbidding the licensing by the liquor authority of Moose Lodge until it ceased its discriminatory practices. We conclude that Moose Lodge's refusal to serve food and beverages to a guest by reason of the fact that he was a Negro does not, under the circumstances here presented, violate the Fourteenth Amendment.' At 171–172.

[187] See *Burton v Wilmington Parking Authority* 365 US 715 (1961), where a private restaurant operated under a lease from a state authority as an integral part of a public parking service, and the Supreme Court found that racial discrimination by the restaurant triggered state action and the protection of the Fourteenth Amendment.

[188] See *Evans v Newton* 382 US 296 (1966): 'The service rendered even by a private park of this character is municipal in nature. It is open to every white person, there being no selective element other than race. Golf clubs, social centers, luncheon clubs, schools such as Tuskegee was at least in origin, and other like organizations in the private sector are often racially oriented. A park, on the other hand, is more like a fire department or police department that traditionally serves the

by the Supreme Court in these cases has not been revisited by the Court in recent years. As Nowak and Rotunda point out, any form of state aid to entities engaging in racial discrimination will be prohibited for the state agency itself and so the issue of actions against private entities enjoying state subsidies may not come up.[189] Furthermore, section 1981 of the Civil Rights Act makes it illegal for schools and other private businesses, to discriminate on grounds of race; it is unlikely therefore that the issue will now arise as a constitutional issue of state action.[190]

10.2.2.2   Due Process before Private Decision-Makers

Due process cases can be seen as a separate category from racial discrimination. The Supreme Court has been unenthusiastic about extending this sort of constitutional protection into the private sphere. The Supreme Court declined to find state action even where a private school and a nursing home were essentially funded by the state.[191] Nor was state action found where the defendant was an electricity company and the petitioner had complained that she had been disconnected without due process. The Court considered that, even if there were a monopoly, there was an insufficient nexus between the company and the state, and arguments concerning 'public interest' were rejected.[192] The context of the case, and the weak protection given to due process rights in such situations, led Judge Friendly (speaking extrajudicially) to suggest that 'more state involvement will be required to produce a holding of unconstitutionality when the constitutional claim is lack of procedural due process, or even infringement of asserted First Amendment rights, than when the claim is of racial discrimination. Surely the result in *Jackson v Metropolitan Edison Co* would have been different if the company had refused to serve blacks'.[193]

community. Mass recreation through the use of parks is plainly in the public domain, *Watson v Memphis*, 373 U.S. 526; and state courts that aid private parties to perform that public function on a segregated basis implicate the State in conduct proscribed by the Fourteenth Amendment.' At 301–302 (footnote omitted).

  [189] Nowak and Rotunda (2000: 540).   [190] Ibid.

  [191] Consider *Rendell-Baker v Kohn* 457 US 83 (1982) and *Blum v Yaretski* 457 US 991 (1982) where the Supreme Court declared, respectively, that there was no 'state action' with regards to a 'private' school (99% publicly funded), and a 'private' nursing home (often funded by Medicaid).

  [192] *Jackson v Metropolitan Edison Co* 419 US 345 (1974). The Court rejected a public interest argument: 'It may well be that acts of a heavily regulated utility with at least something of a governmentally protected monopoly will more readily be found to be "state" acts than will the acts of an entity lacking these characteristics. But the inquiry must be whether there is a sufficiently close nexus between the State and the challenged action of the regulated entity so that the action of the latter may be fairly treated as that of the State itself.' At 350–351. The Court rejected an argument based on public interest: 'Doctors, optometrists, lawyers, Metropolitan, and Nebbia's upstate New York grocery selling a quart of milk are all in regulated businesses, providing arguably essential goods and services, "affected with a public interest." We do not believe that such a status converts their every action, absent more, into that of the State.' At 354.

  [193] H. Friendly, 'The Public-Private Penumbra: Fourteen Years Later' 130 *UPLR* (1982) 1289 at 1292 (footnote omitted).

10.2.2.3   *Freedom of Expression*

The Supreme Court seems to take a generous attitude to the scope of state action in cases which raise freedom of expression. The Court seems keen to bring private action within the scope of the Constitution. The case of *Marsh v Alabama* concerned a 'company town', known as Chickasaw, owned and governed by the Gulf Shipbuilding Corporation.[194] A Jehovah's Witness had been asked to stop distributing leaflets outside the post office in the 'business block'. When she refused, she was arrested by the deputy sheriff (whose salary was paid for by the company) for remaining on the premises of another after having been asked to leave. She was later convicted despite her complaints concerning the breach of her Constitutional rights. The case came before the Supreme Court, which emphasized the importance of the free circulation of ideas and its case-law upholding freedom of expression:

> As we have heretofore stated, the town of Chickasaw does not function differently from any other town. The 'business block' serves as the community shopping center and is freely accessible and open to the people in the area and those passing through. The managers appointed by the corporation cannot curtail the liberty of press and religion of these people consistently with the purposes of the Constitutional guarantees, and a state statute, as the one here involved, which enforces such action by criminally punishing those who attempt to distribute religious literature clearly violates the First and Fourteenth Amendments to the Constitution.
>
> Many people in the United States live in company-owned towns. These people, just as residents of municipalities, are free citizens of their State and country. Just as all other citizens they must make decisions which affect the welfare of community and nation. To act as good citizens they must be informed. In order to enable them to be properly informed their information must be uncensored. There is no more reason for depriving these people of the liberties guaranteed by the First and Fourteenth Amendments than there is for curtailing these freedoms with respect to any other citizen.
>
> When we balance the Constitutional rights of owners of property against those of the people to enjoy freedom of press and religion, as we must here, we remain mindful of the fact that the latter occupy a preferred position. As we have stated before, the right to exercise the liberties safeguarded by the First Amendment 'lies at the foundation of free government by free men' and we must in all cases 'weigh the circumstances and appraise . . . the reasons . . . in support of the regulation of (those) rights.' *Schneider v State*, 308 U.S. 147, 161, 60 S. Ct. 146, 151. In our view the circumstance that the property rights to the premises where the deprivation of liberty, here involved, took place, were held by others than the public, is not sufficient to justify the State's permitting a corporation to govern a community of citizens so as to restrict their fundamental liberties and the enforcement of such restraint by the application of a State statute. Insofar as the State has attempted to impose criminal punishment on appellant for undertaking to distribute religious literature in a company town, its action cannot stand.[195]

---

[194] 326 US 501 (1946).   [195] At 507–509 (footnotes omitted).

This emphasis on the balancing of competing rights and the need to look at the reasons for the limitations of any right is, perhaps, the clearest explanation of what happens in the application of human rights obligations to non-state actors. The cases are often explained in terms of nexus to the state or the symbiotic relationship between the non-state actor and the state; I suggest that we see the results of such cases in terms of the importance of the rights at issue, and the existence of alternative remedies for dealing with the interference with human rights.[196] The 'shopping centre cases' reveal how it is perhaps context, rather than any state nexus test, that is the key factor. In *Food Employees v Logan Plaza* the Supreme Court found by a majority that a private shopping mall was analogous to the private town in the *Marsh v Alabama* case discussed above:[197]

> The sole justification offered for the substantial interference with the effectiveness of petitioners' exercise of their First Amendment rights to promulgate their views through handbilling and picketing is respondents' claimed absolute right under state law to prohibit any use of their property by others without their consent. However, unlike a situation involving a person's home, no meaningful claim to protection of a right of privacy can be advanced by respondents here. Nor on the facts of the case can any significant claim to protection of the normal business operation of the property be raised. Naked title is essentially all that is at issue.
>
> The economic development of the United States in the last 20 years reinforces our opinion of the correctness of the approach taken in *Marsh*. The large-scale movement of this country's population from the cities to the suburbs has been accompanied by the advent of the suburban shopping center, typically a cluster of individual retail units on a single large privately owned tract. It has been estimated that by the end of 1966 there were between 10,000 and 11,000 shopping centers in the United States and Canada, accounting for approximately 37% of the total retail sales in those two countries.
>
> These figures illustrate the substantial consequences for workers seeking to challenge substandard working conditions, consumers protesting shoddy or overpriced merchandise, and minority groups seeking nondiscriminatory hiring policies that a contrary decision here would have. Business enterprises located in downtown areas would be subject to on-the-spot public criticism for their practices, but businesses situated in the suburbs could largely immunize themselves from similar criticism by creating a cordon sanitaire of parking lots around their stores. Neither precedent nor policy compels a result so at variance with the goal of free expression and communication that is the heart of the First Amendment.[198]

It is interesting to compare the case of *Lloyd Corp Ltd v Tanner*, where the Supreme Court, by a majority, denied priority to freedom of speech in a private shopping mall. The Courts below had followed the reasoning set out in the *Marsh* and *Logan Valley* cases just discussed. The majority opinion of Justice Powell explained the background in these terms:

> The Center had been in operation for some eight years when this litigation commenced. Throughout this period it had a policy, strictly enforced, against the distribution of

---

[196] Cf the discussion in Ch 9 above, regarding the need to protect the 'essence' of rights from being extinguished in the circumstances of cases such as *Appleby v UK*.
[197] 391 US 308 (1968).   [198] At 324–325.

handbills within the building complex and its malls. No exceptions were made with respect to handbilling, which was considered likely to annoy customers, to create litter, potentially to create disorders, and generally to be incompatible with the purpose of the Center and the atmosphere sought to be preserved.

On November 14, 1968, the respondents in this case distributed within the Center handbill invitations to a meeting of the 'Resistance Community' to protest the draft and the Vietnam war. The distribution, made in several different places on the mall walkways by five young people, was quiet and orderly, and there was no littering. There was a complaint from one customer. Security guards informed the respondents that they were trespassing and would be arrested unless they stopped distributing the handbills within the Center. The guards suggested that respondents distribute their literature on the public streets and sidewalks adjacent to but outside of the Center complex. Respondents left the premises as requested 'to avoid arrest' and continued the handbilling outside. Subsequently this suit was instituted in the District Court, seeking declaratory and injunctive relief.

The District Court, emphasizing that the Center 'is open to the general public,' found that it is 'the functional equivalent of a public business district.' 308 F. Supp., at 130. That court then held that Lloyd's 'rule prohibiting the distribution of handbills within the Mall violates . . . First Amendment rights.' 308 F. Supp., at 131.[199]

But the majority of the Court chose to distinguish this situation from the previous precedents. It was suggested that the *Logan Valley* case concerned picketing connected to a particular shop in the mall, whereas *Lloyd* concerned a general protest unconnected to the mall. Furthermore it was suggested that alternative methods for distributing the pamphlets existed in the *Lloyd* case.[200]

A further case concerning a labour dispute with a shoe company made it clear that the *Logan Valley* case had simply gone too far and was no longer authoritative. The majority opinion of the Supreme Court explained:

> . . . the fact is that the reasoning of the Court's opinion in *Lloyd* cannot be squared with the reasoning of the Court's opinion in *Logan Valley*.
>
> It matters not that some Members of the Court may continue to believe that the *Logan Valley* case was rightly decided. Our institutional duty is to follow until changed

---

[199] *Lloyd Corp v Tanner* 407 US 551 (1972) at 555–556 (footnote omitted).

[200] 'A further fact, distinguishing the present case from *Logan Valley*, is that the Union pickets in that case would have been deprived of all reasonable opportunity to convey their message to patrons of the Weis store had they been denied access to the shopping center. The situation at Lloyd Center was notably different. The central building complex was surrounded by public sidewalks, totaling 66 linear blocks. All persons who enter or leave the private areas within the complex must cross public streets and sidewalks, either on foot or in automobiles. When moving to and from the privately owned parking lots, automobiles are required by law to come to a complete stop. Handbills may be distributed conveniently to pedestrians, and also to occupants of automobiles, from these public sidewalks and streets. Indeed, respondents moved to these public areas and continued distribution of their handbills after being requested to leave the interior malls. It would be an unwarranted infringement of property rights to require them to yield to the exercise of First Amendment rights under circumstances where adequate alternative avenues of communication exist. Such an accommodation would diminish property rights without significantly enhancing the asserted right of free speech. In ordering this accommodation the courts below erred in their interpretation of this Court's decisions in *Marsh* and *Logan Valley*.' At 566–567 (footnote omitted).

the law as it now is, not as some Members of the Court might wish it to be. And in the performance of that duty we make clear now, if it was not clear before, that the rationale of *Logan Valley* did not survive the Court's decision in the *Lloyd* case.[201]

The majority considered that, if public authorities were not allowed to discriminate with regard to which speech would be allowed on public property, the Court could not allow for a distinction which allowed for labour disputes but excluded war protests:

> . . . if the respondents in the *Lloyd* case did not have a First Amendment right to enter that shopping center to distribute handbills concerning Vietnam, then the pickets in the present case did not have a First Amendment right to enter this shopping center for the purpose of advertising their strike against the Butler Shoe Co.[202]

However, the Court later reintroduced an element of flexibility by upholding a decision of the California Supreme Court that a private shopping mall could not rely on its constitutional right to property when faced with students protesting against a UN resolution concerning Zionism. The students' freedom of expression under Californian law was given priority. The Court explained: 'Our reasoning in *Lloyd*, however, does not *ex proprio vigore* limit the authority of the State to exercise its police power or its sovereign right to adopt in its own Constitution individual liberties more expansive than those conferred by the Federal Constitution.'[203] The PruneYard Shopping Center's Constitutional rights were not extinguished as:

> Here the requirement that appellants permit appellees to exercise state-protected rights of free expression and petition on shopping center property clearly does not amount to an unconstitutional infringement of appellants' property rights under the Taking Clause. There is nothing to suggest that preventing appellants from prohibiting this sort of activity will unreasonably impair the value or use of their property as a shopping center. The PruneYard is a large commercial complex that covers several city blocks, contains numerous separate business establishments, and is open to the public at large. The decision of the California Supreme Court makes it clear that the PruneYard may restrict expressive activity by adopting time, place, and manner regulations that will minimize any interference with its commercial functions. Appellees were orderly, and they limited their activity to the common areas of the shopping center. In these circumstances, the fact that they may have 'physically invaded' appellants' property cannot be viewed as determinative.[204]

The Court wants to recognize the importance of freedom of expression in the private sphere, yet clings to the idea that state action doctrine means that the Constitution can only apply where one is dealing with an entity which seems to look like a public authority. In all cases, of course, there is a degree of state action, as the law has been invoked by both sides in their dispute. But the traditional

---

[201] *Hudgens v NLRB* 424 US 507 (1976) at 518.   [202] Ibid, at 520–521.
[203] *PruneYard Shopping Center v Robins* 447 US 74 (1980) at 81.   [204] Ibid, at 83–84.

approach that constitutional rights only apply to protect one from government plays a powerful role. The Court, in retrospect, considered that it had created an exception to the rule with its decision in the *Marsh* case.[205] In contrast to the company town, the phenomenon of the massive mall has basically split the Supreme Court and the state courts as they grapple with the balance between private property rights and freedom of expression. As the Supreme Court put it in the *Lloyd* case, finding an accommodation between the rights of property owners and rights to freedom of expression is not always easy, but the 'Framers of the Constitution certainly did not think these fundamental rights of a free society are incompatible with each other'.[206] It is submitted that we are better able to see what is really going on when the courts admit that they are simply dealing with competing fundamental rights claims. Where the picture becomes more difficult to follow is when the argument is said to turn on whether the defendant (the alleged rights abuser) is said to be liable, either because the actor by its nature can be assimilated to a state actor because a traditional government function is involved, or because the state is so involved with the private actor that the private actions become coloured as state action, and therefore the non-state actor is bound to respect Constitutional rights. Another more recent case about freedom of expression illustrates the Court's doctrine on these points.

The case of *Lebron v National Railroad Passenger Corp* concerned a complaint that Amtrack had violated the First Amendment rights of Lebron who wanted to place a billboard display in Amtrack's Pennsylvania Station in New York City.[207] Lebron wanted to lease the huge illuminated display to place a photomontage criticizing the Coors family for 'its support of right-wing causes, particularly the contras in Nicaragua'.[208] The work included 'photographic images of convivial drinkers of Coors beer, juxtaposed with a Nicaraguan village scene in which peasants are menaced by a can of Coors that hurtles towards them, leaving behind a trail of fire, as if it were a missile.'[209]

Amtrak's Vice-President disapproved of the advert and referred to the policy of not allowing political advertising on this gigantic billboard (the 'Spectacular', about thirty metres long and three metres high). The first instance court ruled that the rejection by Amtrak violated the First Amendment rights of Lebron. The court found that the ties to Government made Amtrak a government actor for the purposes of Constitutional rights protection. The Court of Appeals found that Amtrak was not a government entity and that there was no state action. The Supreme Court found that, for the purposes of determining constitutional rights of individuals, government-created and controlled corporations are part of the Government itself, even though, for other purposes, Amtrak did not have governmental powers and immunities.

---

[205] See the opinion of the Court in *Hudgens v NLRB* 424 US 507 (1976) at 513.
[206] *Lloyd Corp v Tanner* 407 US 551 (1972) at 570.　　　　[207] 513 US 374 (1995).
[208] From the description of the District Court, at 513 US 374 (1995) at 377.　　　　[209] Ibid.

The Supreme Court's approach reminds us of the complexity of the public/private question and the importance of understanding the constitutional order of the state in question. Although Congress had stated, at the time Amtrak was created, that Amtrak 'will not be an agency or establishment of the United States Government', the Court was able to say that the legislature could not determine the status of Amtrak as far as Constitutional rights are concerned. In other countries too, the legislature's determination of whether or not a body has human rights obligations or not would be dispositive for the judiciary.

But this is not the only facet of the decision of interest in the present context. Note that the Court was able to digest the idea that Amtrak could be a non-state actor for the purposes of 'sovereign immunity from suit', and still be required to respect Constitutional rights because of its 'nature' under the Constitution. In the words of the Supreme Court:

> If Amtrak is, by its very nature, what the Constitution regards as the Government, congressional pronouncement that it is not such can no more relieve it of its First Amendment restrictions than a similar pronouncement could exempt the Federal Bureau of Investigation from the Fourth Amendment. The Constitution constrains governmental action 'by whatever instruments or in whatever modes that action may be taken.' *Ex parte Virginia*, 100 U.S. 339, 346–347 (1880). And under whatever congressional label.[210]

The Court can see the non-state actor as more or less governmental according to the context. This is a useful approach, as it avoids the stark choice between labelling something as public or private for all purposes. It allows one to move on to focus on the purported harm done, rather than consider subjective notions of what is the 'nature' of government or the 'nexus' with the state. When the case was finally decided, the majority of the Court of Appeals found that Amtrack was not at fault. The majority held that:

> Amtrak's decision, as a proprietor, to decline to enter the political arena, even indirectly, by displaying political advertisements is certainly reasonable. Amtrak's position as a government controlled and financed public facility, used daily by thousands of people, made it highly advisable to avoid the criticism and the embarrassments of allowing any display seeming to favor any political view. This was particularly so with respect to the Spectacular in view of its uniqueness and size.[211]

We have then, a *governmental* actor avoiding constitutional rights liability by staying out of a so-called *political* arena. The *Lebron* case illustrates the complexity of our topic. Amtrak was determined by the courts to be a non-governmental entity for the purposes of immunity, a government entity for the purposes of constitutional rights, and a public proprietor entitled to avoid the 'embarrassing' political arena for the purposes of freedom of expression. The bigger issue arises as to how one

---

[210] Ibid, at 392–393.
[211] *Lebron v National R.R. Passenger Corp* No. 937127, Court of Appeals, decided 30 October 1995, available from http://www.findlaw.com/casecode.

can expect to enforce freedom of expression in public places. Billboards and displays will either be owned by purely private entities or by government-controlled entities. If the purely private entities have no Constitutional duties to allow 'embarrassing' political expression, and the government-controlled entities can avoid their constitutional duties by adopting a 'no politics' approach, the opportunities for democratic participation and discussion are greatly reduced.

10.2.2.4   Cruel and Unusual Punishment, Privatized Prisons, and the Rejection of Functional Tests

Finally, let us turn to issues of detention in private prisons. The substantive claim here often concerns cruel and unusual punishment forbidden by the Eighth Amendment to the Constitution.[212] But to understand the approach of the Supreme Court one has to consider the procedural options open to a complainant. The Court has been prepared to admit the existence of a constitutional tort against individual federal officers (strictly speaking non-state actors, as the complaint is not against the state itself). This was to ensure that the substantive constitutional protection against cruel punishment was effective. On the other hand, analogous complaints against a private corporation running a prison and its individual private sector employees have been rejected. Such rulings cannot be understood as an indication that there is no state action, there obviously is: no private company can run a prison without a 'symbiotic relationship' with the state. It is suggested here that the apparent non-existence of a constitutional tort derives from the Supreme Court's reluctance to fashion such a constitutional tort beyond the one it invented for state officers. In *Correctional Services Corp v Malesko* the Court simply refused a remedy against the private prison by declaring that no such remedy should be created:

> Respondent now asks that we extend this limited holding [a recognition of a private constitutional tort action against federal officers] to confer a right of action for damages against private entities acting under color of federal law. He contends that the Court must recognize a federal remedy at law wherever there has been an alleged constitutional deprivation, no matter that the victim of the alleged deprivation might have alternative remedies elsewhere, and that the proposed remedy would not significantly deter the principal wrongdoer, an individual private employee. We have heretofore refused to imply new substantive liabilities under such circumstances, and we decline to do so here.[213]

So far, therefore, there is no constitutional remedy against a private prison for cruel and unusual punishment. There is, however, a separate remedy in the US Code against those who act under colour of law and violate civil rights. Title 42 of the United States Code paragraph 1983, entitled 'Civil action for deprivation of

---

[212] It reads in part: 'Excessive bail shall not be required, nor excessive fines imposed, nor cruel and unusual punishments inflicted.'   [213] *Correctional Serv. Corp v Malesko* 534 US 61 (2001) at 66.

rights', grants a civil remedy for violations of constitutional rights.[214] Prisoners in private prisons have relied on this remedy to sue the relevant corporations and their employees with regard to mistreatment. Although under this head there can be no doubt that the substantive obligations apply, a new hurdle arises. Public authorities enjoy immunity in this context. So the prisoner has to show that the prison corporation is acting in a public way ('under color of law') to bring himself within the Code's remedial provision, and yet, show that the corporation is so private that it should not enjoy the immunities provided for public entities. This is what Ronnie Lee McKnight sought to do before the Supreme Court when he sued Darryl Richardson and John Walker for the use of 'extremely tight physical restraints' in a privatized prison in Tennessee.

The US Supreme Court, by a five to four majority, rejected a functional test to determine what is public or private and, without deciding the substantive liability question, decided that private guards were to be considered differently from public guards and that they should enjoy no immunity. The reasoning is instructive for what it says about how privatization is supposed to incorporate new safeguards against human rights abuses. The approach implies a departure from the traditional rules developed for protecting individuals from abuse of power. The majority decided that 'History does *not* reveal a "firmly rooted" tradition of immunity applicable to privately employed prison guards.'[215] The majority opinion considered that private individuals operated jails in the eighteenth century in America and England and that private contractors were heavily involved in prison management in various states of the United States during the nineteenth century. The majority also considered the purpose of the immunity doctrine and decided that, in any event, such purposes could not survive the logic of the private sphere. It is possible to identify three purposes for this immunity according to the Court's opinion.

First, the necessity of providing immunity to public officials to 'serve the public good or to ensure that talented candidates were not deterred by the threat of damages suits from entering public service'.[216] Second, the immunity is to contribute to 'principled and fearless decision-making'.[217] And third, immunity is there to ensure that officials are not distracted from their governmental duties because of lawsuits. The majority quickly dismissed the suggestion that a functional test should be used to assimilate private guards to public guards: 'a purely functional approach bristles with difficulty, particularly since, in many areas, government and private industry may engage in fundamentally similar activities, ranging from

---

[214] 'Every person who, under color of any statute, ordinance, regulation, custom, or usage, of any State or Territory or the District of Columbia, subjects, or causes to be subjected, any citizen of the United States or other person within the jurisdiction thereof to the deprivation of any rights, privileges, or immunities secured by the Constitution and laws, shall be liable to the party injured in an action at law, suit in equity, or other proper proceeding for redress, except that in any action brought against a judicial officer for an act or omission taken in such officer's judicial capacity, injunctive relief shall not be granted unless a declaratory decree was violated or declaratory relief was unavailable.'

[215] *Richardson et al v McKnight* 521 US 399 (1977) at 404.   [216] Ibid, at 409.

[217] Ibid, at 408.

electricity production, to waste disposal, to even mail delivery'.[218] The majority then go on to explain why there are important differences between the public and the private in the context of excluding private operators from the immunity enjoyed by state actors. With reference to the arguments for immunity for state actors outlined above, the majority found that the first argument, i.e. that talented candidates would be deterred from applying to work in a prison where they enjoy no immunity, did not hold water in the private sphere. This is because, in the majority's view, comprehensive insurance would increase the chances of full indemnification by their private employer.

Turning to the second argument, regarding the need to avoid overly timid behaviour for fear of litigation, the majority suggested that there is no problem of unwarranted timidity in the private sphere:

> ... when a private company subject to competitive market pressures operates a prison. Competitive pressures mean not only that a firm whose guards are too aggressive will face damages that raise costs, thereby threatening its replacement, but also that a firm whose guards are too timid will face threats of replacement by other firms with records that demonstrate their ability to do both a safer and a more effective job.
>
> These ordinary marketplace pressures are present here.[219]

The judgment continues later:

> In other words, marketplace pressures provide the private firm with strong incentives to avoid overly timid, insufficiently vigorous, unduly fearful, or 'nonarduous' employee job performance. And the contract's provisions—including those that might permit employee indemnification and avoid many civil service restrictions—grant this private firm freedom to respond to those market pressures through rewards and penalties that operate directly upon its employees ... To this extent, the employees before us resemble those of other private firms and differ from government employees.[220]

This economic analysis is then supplemented with a revealing argument about the purposes of privatization today:

> Because privatization law also frees the private prison-management firm from many civil service law restraints, Tenn. Code Ann. §41-24-111 (1990), it permits the private firm, unlike a government department, to offset any increased employee liability risk with higher pay or extra benefits. In respect to this second government-immunity-related purpose then, it is difficult to find a *special* need for immunity, for the guards' employer can operate like other private firms; it need not operate like a typical government department.[221]

The four dissenting Justices preferred to determine the question on the basis of the *function* being performed and would have conferred immunity on the private guards. They rejected taking a policy approach based on the rational decision-making of

---

[218] Ibid, at 409.   [219] Ibid, at 409.   [220] Ibid, at 410.   [221] Ibid, at 411.

economic actors and suggested that the argument of the majority on policy grounds is simply wrong:

> First of all, it is fanciful to speak of the consequences of 'market' pressures in a regime where public officials are the only purchaser, and other people's money the medium of payment. Ultimately, one prison-management firm will be selected to replace another prison-management firm only if a decision is made by some *political* official not to renew the contract. See Tenn. Code Ann. §§41-24-103 to 105 (Supp. 1996). This is a government decision, not a market choice. If state officers turn out to be more strict in reviewing the cost and performance of privately managed prisons than of publicly managed ones, it will only be because they have chosen to be so. The process can come to resemble a market choice only to the extent that political actors *will* such resemblance— that is, to the extent that political actors (1) are willing to pay attention to the issue of prison services, among the many issues vying for their attention, and (2) are willing to place considerations of cost and quality of service ahead of such political considerations as personal friendship, political alliances, in-state ownership of the contractor, etc. Secondly and more importantly, however, if one assumes a political regime that *is* bent on emulating the market in its purchase of prison services, it is almost certainly the case that, short of mismanagement so severe as to provoke a prison riot, *price* (not discipline) will be the predominating factor in such a regime's selection of a contractor. A contractor's price must depend upon its costs; lawsuits increase costs [Footnote 3 in the original at this point reads: This is true even of successfully defended lawsuits, and even of lawsuits that have been insured against. The Court thinks it relevant to the factor I am currently discussing that the private prison management firm 'must buy insurance sufficient to compensate victims of civil rights torts,' *ante*, at 410. Belief in the relevance of this factor must be traceable, ultimately, to belief in the existence of a free lunch. Obviously, as civil rights claims increase, the cost of civil rights insurance increases.]; and 'fearless' maintenance of discipline increases lawsuits. The incentive to down play discipline will exist, moreover, even in those States where the politicians' zeal for market emulation and budget cutting has waned, and where prison-management contract renewal is virtually automatic: the more cautious the prison guards, the fewer the lawsuits, the higher the profits. In sum, it seems that 'market competitive' private prison managers have even greater need than civil-service prison managers for immunity as an incentive to discipline.[222]

The dissent highlights how adherence to a public/private distinction could lead to absurd results in this context: 'Today's decision says that two sets of prison guards who are indistinguishable in the ultimate source of their authority over prisoners, indistinguishable in the powers that they possess over prisoners, and indistinguishable in the duties that they owe towards prisoners, are to be treated quite differently in the matter of their financial liability.'[223]

The majority judgment has now been relied on in suits brought against private prisons with regard to the guarantees in the US Bill of Rights. A Court of Appeals has held that:

> private prison-management corporations and their employees may be sued under § 1983 by a prisoner who has suffered a constitutional injury. Clearly, confinement of

---

[222] Dissenting opinion of Justice Scalia, with whom Chief Justice Rehnquist, Justices Kennedy and Thomas joined, ibid, at 418–420.   [223] Ibid, at para. 11.

wrongdoers—though sometimes delegated to private entities—is a fundamentally governmental function. These corporations and their employees are therefore subject to limitations imposed by the Eighth Amendment.[224]

The reasoning of the Supreme Court in *Richardson v McKnight* suggests a few remarks on the effect of privatization on the determination of liability for human rights violations. First, relying on *traditional* notions of the *obvious* functions of the state can be misleading as traditions change over time; even a function as 'typical' as running prisons can be shown to have been traditionally private at one time, or may indeed become traditionally private in some countries. The public/private boundary in such situations seems contested rather than obvious.

Second, relying on the idea that the state has *delegated* certain functions may be similarly misleading. Some sectors may never have been under state control (for example the new internet services), or they may exist in competition with state functions (for example postal services).

Third, part of the *rationale* for privatization is the desire to liberate certain sectors from state regulation or 'civil service law restraints'. It seems contradictory therefore to expect that these liberated sectors will be assimilated by law to public services for the purposes of liability—even for fundamental rights claims. The rejection of 'state law' for the private sphere is not confined to North America; it can be detected in many of the countries moving away from 'state law' to a market economy in Eastern and Central Europe.[225]

Fourth, discussions over the *nature* of public and private functions thinly mask differences concerning the desired substantive outcome. Attempts at legal dividing lines will often make little sense and will draw distinctions which inevitably simply reflect majority preferences. It seems pretty pointless to attempt a meaningful distinction between functions of a private or public nature if judges within one court in one country can be so at odds on the question of the publicness of a function such as prison management.

Fifth, it is quite clear that the courts are prepared to find a non-state actor such as an employee in a private prison, *public for some purposes and private for others*. There is no such thing as a public function 'essence'. So the US Court of Appeals can rule that private prison companies and their employees are private for the

---

[224] Court of Appeals, 5th Circuit, Case 03–40493, *Billy D Rosborough v Management & Training Corp, Unidentified Shirley, Corrections Officer*, 7 November 2003, at p 5 of the transcript.

[225] Consider the comments of Andrzej Rzeplinski: 'Do we want a common space for human rights in Europe?', 30 September 1999 Warsaw meeting of the European Sections of the International Commission of Jurists. Addressing the question of the horizontal application of rights and their possible intrusion into parent/child relations he rejected the utility of a human rights approach. 'As I see it, an attempt at turning the children's relations with their parents into public law relations would be a dangerous experiment with the good experience of over 200 human generations. I am writing this from the perspective of a person who lived for several decades in a country affected by the great experiment of making people happy with omnipotent state law among other things. It will be much better for our children if the occasional cases of pathological conduct on part of the parents are dealt with under provisions of the family and possibly also the penal code.'

purposes of federal immunity, but 'public' for the purposes of falling within a bribery statute outlawing bribery of public officials; this may be defensible in terms of policy,[226] but suggests caution in expressing the view that some things are simply *obviously* public functions. Judges place entities on one side of the line in order to ensure liability—rather than for reasons which reflect some inherent quality about the entity.

Talking about privatization highlights the possible dangers for human rights protection of simple transfers of certain state activity to the private sphere. It does not mean that privatization, as such, is a violation of human rights, or that the purpose of privatization necessarily violates human rights obligations. The issue is a simple one. In privatizing, governments may decrease the level of human rights accountability for the sector concerned. Although it is possible to build in new layers of accountability as functions pass from the public to the private sphere, the point of privatization is usually to introduce flexibility rather than continue all the restrictions and liabilities which applied to state activity.[227]

10.3 INTERPRETATION OF THE LAW IN CONFORMITY WITH HUMAN RIGHTS

It was noted earlier how Lord Browne-Wilkinson considered that the European Convention on Human Rights was percolating into every aspect of those living in Britain. Steven Sedley LJ, in his Hamlyn lectures, suggested that to understand the British courts' own obligation to act compatibly with the Convention, one must ask whether the courts' obligations 'extend to developing a body of law which will protect individuals from all violations of their Convention rights from whatever source?'[228] He proposes an understanding of the way the courts will treat the Convention in the private sphere as akin to a 'cascade effect'.

The metaphors of percolation and cascade are loaded with meanings. A recent book by Duncan Watts explains that in network science the spread of diseases reaches epidemic proportions when 'percolating clusters' come into existence (he asks us to imagine the point at which an egg white becomes white when

---

[226] The Court of Appeals concluded: 'It goes without saying that the policy considerations supporting private corrections officers' *not* being entitled to qualified immunity are quite different from those concerning whether they are "public officials" for purposes of the federal bribery statute. Obviously, the Government has just as strong an interest in the integrity of private corrections officers charged with guarding federal detainees as it has in the integrity of federal corrections officers employed in federal facilities. Under such circumstances, and for purposes of the federal bribery statute, there is simply *no* basis for differing between such private and public officers.' Court of Appeals 5th Circuit, Case 99–21044, *United States of America v Thomas*, 24 January 2001, at Pt III, available from http://laws.findlaw.com/5th/9921044cr0.html.

[227] See 'Privatization' in the Introduction above.

[228] Rt Hon. Lord Justice Sedley, *Freedom, Law and Justice* (London: Sweet & Maxwell, 1999) at 23.

cooked).[229] At a critical point, these 'percolations' dramatically appear and allow the uninhibited spread of the disease. One might suggest that the sites of developing interest and expertise in the Convention could be compared to these percolating clusters, and that the absorption of the Convention has now passed a point of no return with the spread of human rights thinking into all aspects of national law. One could similarly go on to highlight the fact that 'cascades' are similarly used in network science to explain the spread of innovative ideas among decision-makers.[230] Much depends on the connections that individuals have outside their immediate sites. This might simply be taken as a starting point for the suggestion that the success of the idea that human rights obligations should be applied to non-state actors will depend, in part, on how judges see their opposite numbers developing this idea in other jurisdictions. Greater connectivity between jurisdictions (e-mail, judicial conferences, and greater attention to the case-law of international courts and tribunals) means that in some contexts judicial doctrine can now spread quite quickly across jurisdictions. One field of judicial endeavour which generates comparative judicial interest is the field of interpretation. The following discussion examines how human rights norms are affecting judicial interpretation with regard to the duties of non-state actors. This is undertaken in four headings: statutory interpretation, the court seeing itself as bound by human rights law, the development of the common law, and the recourse to human rights to underpin values in the legal system.

10.3.1   Statutory Interpretation

The topic of statutory interpretation is huge. The following discussion simply refers to situations where legislation is interpreted in cases involving private disputes, so as to shed light on the application of human rights obligations to non-state actors. We are considering here the human rights document itself, but rather normal legislation which falls to be interpreted in conformity with human rights obligations more generally. The issue has arisen in a few cases from Hong Kong and the United Kingdom.

10.3.1.1   Hong Kong

Judge Downey's judgment in *Tam Hing-yee v Wu Tai-wai* was the first decision under the Hong Kong Bill of Rights.[231] Andrew Byrnes has lauded the Judge's 'receptivity to jurisprudence from a variety of sources, including references to academic opinion'.[232] But in the end, the Judge focused, not so much on the

---

[229] D. J. Watts, *Six Degrees: The Science of a Connected Age* (New York: W. W. Norton and Co, 2003) at 183–189.   [230] Ibid, 229–255.
[231] *Tam Hing-yee v Wu Tai-wai* (1991) 1 HKPLR 1.
[232] A. Byrnes, ' "Recalcitrant Debtors" in a Town "Pollinated by Gold" ' 21 *Hong Kong Law Journal* (1991) 377–398, at 397.

approach of other jurisdictions when faced with the non-state actor issue, but on the particular provision of the Hong Kong Bill of Rights. The case turned on whether the Hong Kong Bill of Rights could be used to review legislation in a case between two private parties. Judge Downey concluded that section 3 of the Bill of Rights Ordinance conferred a power on the courts to review all legislation against the standards of the Bill of Rights even where the parties to the dispute were both private parties and no government or public authority is party to the litigation.[233] Judge Downey explained the result:

> It is, in my view, important to remember that the Ordinance only gives to the courts the power to declare that a statutory provision is repealed. It does not give the courts any power to *re-write* the legislation so as to make it conform with the Ordinance. That is a function which is rightly retained and reserved as the sole prerogative of the legislature. If a court were to declare that a particular statutory provision, wholly and indefensibly repugnant to the Bill of Rights, was only repealed in cases where the Government or some public body is the defendant, but remains in force as between private individuals, I respectfully venture to suggest that the court would be usurping a function of the legislature, and failing in its duty to take notice of, and apply, the law as laid down by the legislature.[234]

The Court of Appeal reversed this finding,[235] and the legislature then brought in an amendment to extend the scope of judicial review to legislation involving private parties, but then later chose to reverse that change—with arguably ambiguous results.[236]

The Court of Appeal felt the Judge had paid insufficient attention to section 7 of the Bill of Rights Ordinance, which states that the Ordinance binds only the Government, public authorities, and any natural or corporate person acting on their behalf.[237] The Court of Appeal accepted that the constitutional nature

---

[233] Section 3 reads: 'Effect on pre-existing legislation 1. All pre-existing legislation that admits of a construction consistent with this Ordinance shall be given such a construction. 2. All pre-existing legislation that does not admit of a construction consistent with this Ordinance is, to the extent of the inconsistency, repealed.'   [234] *Tam Hing-yee v Wu Tai-wai* (1991) 1 HKPLR 1, at 12.

[235] *Tam Hing-yee v Wu Tai-wai* (1991) 1 HKPLR 261.

[236] Following the Court of Appeal decision (see below) the Legislative Council enacted the Hong Kong Bill of Rights (Amendment) Ordinance 1997, Ordinance No. 107, to extend the scope of the Bill of Rights to allow the courts to consider legislation for conformity with the Bill of Rights in cases between private parties. The editors of the *Basic Law and Human Rights Bulletin* evaluated the subsequent legislative steps in the following way: 'That amendment was first suspended, with effect from 18 July 1997, by the Legislative Provisions (Suspension of Operation) Ordinance 1997, and then repealed on 28 February 1998 by the Hong Kong (Amendment Ordinance 1998). In view of the clear obligations under ICCPR to provide protection against violations of some rights by private parties—protection provided in part (or restored) by the Hong Kong Bill of Rights (Amendment ordinance 1997—the constitutionality of the repeal of that Ordinance must be of questionable validity in the light of article 39 of the Basic Law. Accordingly, in our view it is strongly arguable that the legislative reversal of *Tam Hing-yee* has been effective, notwithstanding the apparently unconstitutional efforts to amend it.' See A. Byrnes, J. M. M. Chan, and P. Y. Lo (eds) 5(1) *Basic Law and Human Rights Bulletin* (1999) 43. See also the criticism of the repeal by the Hong Kong Bar Association, Submission on the report of the Hong Kong Special Administrative Region to the Human Rights Committee, October 1999, at paras 29–31.   [237] See 10.2 above, for the exact wording of the Ordinance.

of the Ordinance meant it should be given a generous interpretation 'but that does not entitle a court to override the clear intention of the legislature, which we take to be, from the words "binds only the government etc" that private individuals should not be adversely affected by the ordinance'.[238] The history of the drafting of the Ordinance had been referred to by the Court at the first instance. In that context, Andrew Byrnes' discussion of how sectors of the business community had lobbied for the exclusion of 'inter-citizen' rights was specifically mentioned by Judge Downey.[239] In Byrnes' analysis: 'Business groups feared that Article 26 of the ICCPR, if enacted directly as part of Hong Kong law, might operate in combination with clause 7 of the draft Bill as a general antidiscrimination provision, rendering discrimination by private individuals unlawful.'[240] Byrnes had also highlighted the concern expressed by the Hong Kong General Chamber of Commerce at the time of the consultations on the Bill of Rights with regard to people demanding privacy rights, with regard to information shared by private institutions, and with regard to private sector fears that they could be 'subjected to nuisance litigation at the hands of "discontented employees" or "recalcitrant debtors"'.[241] There were fears that the Government could turn the Bill of Rights on private individuals and companies so that it would become a sword in the hands of government rather than a shield in the hands of the individual. Nevertheless, Byrnes argued that 'while there is a Bill of Rights which binds only the state, there will continue to be significant violations of rights by private individuals for which there is no legal remedy'.[242] The Court of Appeal addressed this protection gap and acknowledged that there was an obligation under international law to provide such protection from nonstate actors: 'We accept that the inevitable result of the interpretation which we find unavoidable is that the Ordinance does not fully comply with the intention expressed in its preamble, namely: "to provide for the incorporation into the law of Hong Kong of provisions of the International Covenant on Civil and Political Rights".'[243]

As discussed earlier, the Human Rights Committee later reminded the authorities that the Covenant creates an obligation to protect individuals from violations by private parties and noted 'with deep concern the absence of legislation providing effective protection against violations of Covenant rights by non-governmental actors'.[244] According to the Court of Appeal, there remains no room for statutory interpretation to bring domestic law into line with the relevant international obligations.

238 *Tam Hing-yee v Wu Tai-wai* (1991) 1 HKPLR, at 266.
239 *Tam Hing-yee v Wu Tai-wai* (1991) 1 HKPLR 1, at 11.
240 A. Byrnes, 'The Hong Kong Bill of Rights and Relations Between Private Individuals' in J. Chan and Y. Ghai (eds) *The Hong Kong Bill of Rights: A Comparative Approach* (Hong Kong: Butterworths Asia, 1993) 71–105, at 85.   241 Ibid, at 87.
242 Ibid, at 88.   243 *Tam Hing-yee v Wu Tai-wai* (1991) 1 HKPLR 261, at 267.
244 UN Doc. CCPR/C/79/Add.57, 9 November 1995, at para. 10, and see also the subsequent concluding observations in UN Doc. CCPR/C/79/Add.117, 12 November 1999, at para. 15.

10.3.1.2   The United Kingdom

Ian Leigh labels the national courts' use of the European Convention on Human Rights to interpret legislation in cases between two private entities 'direct statutory horizontality'.[245] Under section 3 of the Human Rights Act, a court is obliged to take into account human rights law when interpreting legislation.[246] The House of Lords was faced with this issue in a case involving a claim brought by one private party against another private party in *Ghaidan v Godin-Mendoza*. This case concerned a homosexual partner who had been denied the rights of a 'surviving spouse', and the landlord.[247] Everything turned on whether a Schedule to the Rent Act could be read in such a way as to protect the human right not to be discriminated against on grounds of sexual orientation. The relevant provisions read:

> 2(1) The surviving spouse (if any) of the original tenant, if residing in the dwelling-house immediately before the death of the original tenant, shall after the death be the statutory tenant if and so long as he or she occupies the dwelling-house as his or her residence.
>
> (2) For the purposes of this paragraph, a person who was living with the original tenant as his or her wife or husband shall be treated as the spouse of the original tenant.[248]

Lord Nicholls was explicit that the Human Rights Act had, through its inclusion of section 3, given the judges the authority to read in new words in order to avoid an application of the legislation which would violate human rights. In his words:

> ... the mere fact the language under consideration is inconsistent with a Convention-compliant meaning does not of itself make a Convention-compliant interpretation under section 3 impossible. Section 3 enables language to be interpreted restrictively or expansively. But section 3 goes further than this. It is also apt to require a court to read in words which change the meaning of the enacted legislation, so as to make it Convention-compliant.[249]

He went on to rewrite the 'unambiguous' wording so that the 'application of section 3 to paragraph 2 has the effect that paragraph 2 should be read and given effect to as though the survivor of such a homosexual couple were the surviving spouse of the original tenant'.[250] This approach was shared by three Law Lords, but Lord Millett felt that such a reading upset the democratic institutional balance between the legislature and the judiciary:

> Couples of the same sex can no more live together as husband and wife than they can live together as brother and sister. To extend the paragraph to persons who set up home

---

[245] I. Leigh, 'Horizontal Rights, the Human Rights Act and Privacy: Lessons from the Commonwealth?' (1999) 48 *ICLQ* 57–87, at 75, see also Clayton and Tomlinson (2000: 229–231).

[246] Section 3(1) reads: 'So far as it is possible to do so, primary legislation and subordinate legislation must be read and given effect in a way which is compatible with the Convention rights.'

[247] *Ghaidan v Godin-Mendoza* [2004] UKHL 30. In the Court of Appeal, Keene LJ had been clear that human rights in the European Convention were relevant to the construction of legislation even though the Court was dealing with 'litigation between two private individuals'. *Mendoza v Ghaidan* [2002] EWCA Civ 1533, at para. 37.   [248] Paras 2 and 3 of Sch 1 to the Rent Act 1977.

[249] *Ghaidan v Godin-Mendoza* [2004] UKHL 30, at para. 32.   [250] Ibid, at para. 35.

as lovers would have been a major category extension. It would have been highly controversial in 1988 and was not then required by the Convention. The practice of Contracting States was far from uniform; and Parliament was entitled to take the view that any further extension of paragraph (2) could wait for another day. One step at a time is a defensible legislative policy which the courts should respect. Housing Acts come before Parliament with some frequency; and Parliament was entitled to take the view that the question could be revisited without any great delay. It is just as important for legislatures not to proceed faster than society can accept as it is for judges; and under our constitutional arrangements the pace of change is for Parliament.[251]

Baronness Hale considered the purpose of human rights more generally and stated with regard to the dilemma before the judges: 'Democracy is founded on the principle that each individual has equal value. Treating some as automatically having less value than others not only causes pain and distress to that person but also violates his or her dignity as a human being.'[252] The next chapter examines the power of the concepts of democracy and dignity. The choice here between judicial activism or textual fidelity in terms of human rights is, to a great extent, dependent on the internal empowering legislation. For the majority of the House of Lords, the Human Rights Act 1998 expressed the will of Parliament that human rights protection should be read into legislation, even where the plain meaning could not easily support such a reading. There was a recognition by Lord Steyn that the legislature had passed over the opportunity to ask judges to interpret legislation in conformity with the Human Rights Act where this was merely 'reasonable'.[253] Again, the approach of the judiciary is informed by the model of judicial review in question. The 'reasonable' interpretation approach, associated with the New Zealand Bill of Rights Act 1990,[254] placed a greater burden on the legislature than on the judiciary to bring the law into compliance with the human rights protections in the Act.[255] On the other hand, stronger forms of Bills of Rights such

---

[251] *Ghaidan v Godin-Mendoza* [2004] UKHL 30, at para. 95.   [252] Ibid, at para. 132.

[253] See Lord Steyn at para. 44: 'Parliament specifically rejected the legislative model of requiring a reasonable interpretation.' He was referring to the New Zealand Bill of Rights Act 1990; for a discussion of the New Zealand Courts' approach to interpretation in this context, see Clayton and Tomlinson (2000: 164–167). Lord Steyn also acknowledged the influence of the *Marleasing* case where the European Court of Justice ruled that national courts have to interpret national law so as to conform with the wording and text of Directives such as Directive 68/151/EC of 9 March 1968; the Court did not demand that the national law under interpretation be specifically introduced to implement the Community law in question. *Marleasing SA v La Comercial Internacional de Alimentación SA* Case C–106/89, Judgment of 13 November 1990, [1990] ECR I–4135. See n 256 below for details.

[254] See n 253 above.

[255] Several opinions in the *Prolife* case before the House of Lords seemed to treat the issue of the balance between expression and the right not to be offended as determined by the legislature and declined to adjust the legislative framework. See *R v British Broadcasting Corporation, ex p Prolife Alliance* [2003] UKHL 23. Lord Lester has suggested that the judges 'failed to comply with the obligation imposed by s. 3 HRA to interpret the broadcasting legislation compatibly with the Conventions rights of the Pro-Life Alliance and the public'. 'The Human Rights Act 1998—Five Years On', *EHRLR* (2004) 258–271, at 268. See also E. Barendt, 'Free Speech and Abortion', *Public Law* (2003) 580.

as those found in the United States or Canada, allow the judges greater room for manoeuvre than judges applying the Human Rights Act in the United Kingdom.

The situation for the United Kingdom is, however, especially coloured by the influence of European Community law which demands that, even if unimplemented, Community Directives can not normally be invoked against non-state actors, national law has to be read, if possible, to fulfil the state's obligation to achieve the results intended by these Directives.[256] This can be seen, for example, in *Webb v EMO Air Cargo (UK) Ltd*[257] a ruling by the European Court of Justice demanding that existing national law must be read together with an EC Directive so as to preclude dismissal on grounds of pregnancy by a private employer.[258]

As for the conundrum concerning the democratic legitimacy of re-reading democratically adopted legislation in accordance with human rights principles, one solution is to differentiate legislation adopted before and after the Human Rights Act 1998. Clayton and Tomlinson, after a thoughtful analysis, have set out the following grid for understanding how the courts will approach the interpretation of legislation to ensure compatibility with the Human Rights Act:

> We suggest that, in all cases in which Convention rights are in play, the effect of section 3 is equivalent to requiring the courts to act on a presumption that the intention of the legislature was to enact a provision compatible with Convention rights. In relation to statutes passed before the Human Rights Act, section 3 can be read as, in effect, adding a statement to the effect that the statute is intended to be read in a way which is compatible with Convention rights. In the case of statutes passed after the Human Rights Act, this will be made clear by the 'statement of compatibility' with Convention rights.[259]

The key point to recall at this point is that, in cases between non-state actors such entities cannot escape the reach of the Human Rights Act where the courts are

---

[256] The approach is clearly set out in the *Marleasing* case (n 253 above) at para. 8: 'Member States' obligation arising from a directive to achieve the result envisaged by the directive and their duty under Article 5 of the Treaty to take all appropriate measures, whether general or particular, to ensure the fulfilment of that obligation, is binding on all the authorities of Member States including, for matters within their jurisdiction, the courts. It follows that, in applying national law, whether the provisions in question were adopted before or after the directive, the national court called upon to interpret it is required to do so, as far as possible, in the light of the wording and the purpose of the directive in order to achieve the result pursued by the latter and thereby comply with the third paragraph of Article 189 of the Treaty.' Art. 189 has now been replaced by Art. 249 of the Treaty Establishing the European Community, of which para. 4 reads: 'A directive shall be binding, as to the result to be achieved, upon each Member State to which it is addressed, but shall leave to the national authorities the choice of form and methods.'   [257] Case C–32/93 [1994] ECR I–3567.

[258] 'Article 2(1) [of the Sex Discrimination Act 1975] read with Article 5(1) of Directive 76/207 precludes dismissal of an employee who is recruited for an unlimited term with a view, initially, to replacing another employee during the latter's maternity leave and who cannot do so because, shortly after recruitment, she is herself found to be pregnant.' At para. 29. For the subsequent House of Lords judgment, see *Webb v EMO Air Cargo (UK) Ltd (No. 2)* [1995] 1 WLR 1454.

[259] Clayton and Tomlinson (2000: 168–169). Section 19(1) reads: 'A Minister of the Crown in charge of a Bill in either House of Parliament must, before Second Reading of the Bill—(a) make a statement to the effect that in his view the provisions of the Bill are compatible with the Convention rights ("a statement of compatibility"); or (b) make a statement to the effect that although he is unable to make a statement of compatibility the government nevertheless wishes the House to

ready to interpret relevant legislation to restrict the freedom of action of non-state actors on human rights grounds.[260] The argument that the parties do not have human rights obligations *vis-à-vis* each other, with the result that human rights need not be read into the interpretation of the legislation, has not taken hold.[261] In the *Ghaidan* case, the landlord was prevented from terminating the tenancy for the homosexual surviving partner because the relevant legislation had to be read to avoid discrimination on grounds of sexual orientation.

10.3.2   A Court Itself is Bound to Act in Conformity with Human Rights Law

As with the sections above, the extent to which a court is bound to ensure respect for human rights in claims brought against non-state actors will depend on the national legislation concerned. In South Africa, the interim Constitution originally excluded the judiciary from its list of addressees, and the Constitutional Court therefore refused to apply that Constitution directly against private actors.[262] The 1996 Constitution however, as we saw above, was adjusted to ensure horizontal effect by binding 'natural' or 'juristic person[s]' and the text additionally inserted 'the judiciary' into the relevant overarching provision.[263] According to the Constitutional Court, the fact of mentioning the judiciary does not simply mean that *all* the rights in the Bill of Rights can be enforced against non-state actors; attention has to be paid to the specific wording of section 8 (quoted in full above at 10.1.2.2).[264] Section 8(2) states that natural and juristic persons are bound by the Bill of Rights '*if, and to the extent that*' the provision is applicable. Once that test has been passed, it is for the courts to develop the common law under section 8(3). In this situation, the obligations are binding on the non-state actor and not on the judiciary. The courts will then develop, if necessary, the common law to ensure those obligations are respected.

In Canada, the language of the Charter of Rights and Freedoms[265] has been interpreted as excluding a general obligation on the courts to ensure that

proceed with the Bill.' For discussion, see Lester (2004: 261–262) and A. Lester and D. Pannick, *Human Rights Law and Practice* (London: Butterworths, 2nd edn, 2004) Ch 8.

[260] Even if the courts are not prepared to interpret legislation in this way, they may consider it appropriate to issue a declaration of incompatibility under s 4 of the 1998 Act. This can happen in cases between private parties: *Wilson v The First County Trust Ltd* [2001] EWCA Civ 633; see further *Wilson and ors v Secretary of State for Trade and Industry* [2003] UKHL 40 and the interpretation of Wadham, Mountfield, and Edmundson (2003: 70).

[261] Clayton and Tomlinson (2000: 230) set out this argument and conclude: 'It is arguable that section 6(1) *requires* a court undertaking the "act" of statutory construction to do so in accordance with section 3(1) and that, as a result, this produces "direct statutory horizontality".' See 10.3.2 below, for a discussion of this point.

[262] See *Du Plessis v De Klerk* Case CCT 8/95, 7 November 1995, discussed in 10.1.2 above. The interim Constitution had included a s 7(1) which stated: 'This Chapter shall bind all legislative and executive organs of state at all levels of government.'

[263] Section 8(1) reads: 'The Bill of Rights applies to all law, and binds the legislature, the executive, the judiciary and all organs of state.'   [264] Case CCT 53/01, 14 July 2002, esp. paras 30–33.

[265] Incorporated in the Constitution Act 1982, enacted by the Canada Act 1982 (UK), in force 17 April 1982 (except for s 15, which came into force 17 April 1985).

injunctions ordered in cases between private parties respect the Charter rights and freedoms. The Supreme Court of Canada came to this conclusion in its judgment in *Dolphin Delivery Ltd v Retail, Wholesale and Department Store Union, Local 580.*[266] The case concerned an interlocutory injunction against a trade union to prevent it picketing business premises. The Court held that the union could not rely on freedom of expression in such a private dispute and the injunction was upheld. The core factor which influenced Justice McIntyre's judgment was the text of section 32 of the Charter.[267] He held that the position and inclusion of the word 'government' led to the conclusion that it referred to the executive or administrative branch of government and not to 'government in its generic sense—meaning the whole of the governmental apparatus of the state—but to a branch of government'.[268] He continued that the Charter applies to the action of the legislative, executive, and administrative branches of government in both public and private litigation. Moreover, he added that the Charter applies whether the action depends on statute or the common law:

> To regard a court order as an element of governmental intervention necessary to invoke the *Charter* would, it seems to me, widen the scope of the *Charter* application to virtually all private litigation. All cases must end, if carried to completion, with an enforcement order and if the *Charter* precludes the making of the order, where a *Charter* right would be infringed, it would seem that all private litigation would be subject to the *Charter*.[269]

McIntyre J stated that: 'A more direct and a more precisely-defined connection between the element of government action and the claim advanced must be present before the *Charter* applies.'[270] Later he stated: 'it is difficult and probably dangerous to attempt to define with narrow precision that element of governmental intervention which will suffice to permit reliance on the *Charter* by private litigants in private litigation'.[271] What the judgment makes clear is that where one party brings a case against another relying on the common law, and no act of government is involved, the Charter is inapplicable. Later cases have softened the impact of this rule by taking the Charter into consideration in the courts' development of the common law. The point for present purposes is that the absence of an express reference to the judiciary being bound by the Charter has led to the denial of the possibility of using the Charter to mount a complaint in a purely private dispute.

Turning to New Zealand, the situation is again different and complicated by the presence of, not only the Bill of Rights Act, but also a Human Rights Act, as well as a Privacy Act.[272] The Bill of Rights Act 1990 is explicitly addressed to the

---

[266] [1986] 2 SCR 573.

[267] Section 32(1) reads: 'This Charter applies (*a*) to the Parliament and government of Canada in respect of all matters within the authority of Parliament including all matters relating to the Yukon Territory and Northwest Territories; and (*b*) to the legislature and government of each province in respect of all matters within the authority of the legislature of each province.'

[268] [1986] 2 SCR 573, at 598.   [269] Ibid, at 598–599.   [270] Ibid, at 599.

[271] Ibid, at 602.

[272] The Human Rights Act 1993 (as amended in 2001) prohibits discrimination on various grounds in the private sphere. The sphere of application is confusingly labelled 'Areas of public life'

judiciary and has been applied in developing the common law. The inclusion of the judiciary in the Act has encouraged the courts to apply the Act to the common law of defamation in litigation between private parties, although it is hard to say whether the courts now see themselves as addressees of the Bill of Rights or simply as entitled to interpret and develop the common law in line with what the Bill of Rights requires.[273]

The US Supreme Court has been seen as treating action by the courts as sufficient to trigger state action for the purposes of the Fourteenth Amendment to the Constitution. This arose in the case of *Shelley v Kraemer* and has given rise to considerable legal scholarship. This is a complicated area and we are urged to be careful about drawing conclusions from this one case. It is said that, for 'mainstream commentators', the case of *Shelley v Kraemer* 'should be confined to its facts'.[274] *Shelley v Kraemer* 'arose when a black couple bought property to which a restrictive covenant applied. A white couple who owned restricted property in the same neighbourhood sued to stop the Shelleys from taking possession of the property'.[275] The Missouri Supreme Court upheld the covenant. The case illustrates a very simple point. If a court upholds a rule under the common law which denies an individual his or her constitutional rights, the effect is the same as if the legislature had passed a law abrogating those same rights. In the words of the judgment:

> But the present cases, unlike those just discussed, do not involve action by state legislatures or city councils. Here the particular patterns of discrimination and the areas in which the restrictions are to operate, are determined, in the first instance, by the terms of agreements among private individuals. Participation of the State consists in the enforcement of the restrictions so defined. The crucial issue with which we are here confronted is whether this distinction removes these cases from the operation of the prohibitory provisions of the Fourteenth Amendment.[276]

and includes: access to public places, vehicles and facilities, education, employment, industrial and professional associations, qualifying bodies and vocational training bodies, partnerships, provision of goods and services, land, housing, and accommodation. See Pt II of the Act. A number of exceptions cover issues of competing rights such as privacy and the rights of religious organizations. On the Privacy Act and the influence of the Bill of Rights in litigation concerning privacy and freedom of expression, see R. Tobin, 'Privacy and Freedom of Expression in New Zealand' in M. Colvin (ed) *Developing Key Privacy Rights* (Oxford: Hart Publishing, 2002) 129–157.

[273] See Elias J: 'The application of the Act to the common law seems to me to follow from the language of s 3 which refers to acts of the judicial branch of the Government of New Zealand, a provision not to be found in the Canadian Charter.' *Lange v Atkinson and Australian Consolidated Press NZ Ltd* 2 NZLR [1997] 22, at 33. See also the persuasive article by Andrew Butler, 'The New Zealand Bill of Rights and private common law litigation', *New Zealand Law Journal* (August 1991) 261–266. For the subsequent judgments regarding the *Lange* case, see [1998] 3 NZLR 424 (Court of Appeal); [1999] UKPC 46 (Privy Council); [2000] NZCA 95 (Court of Appeal).

[274] Gardbaum (2003: 414).

[275] As described by J. Biskupic and E. Witt, *The Supreme Court and Individual Rights* (Washington, DC: Congressional Quarterly Inc, 3rd edn, 1996) at 261.

[276] *Shelley v Kraemer* 334 US 1 (1948) at 12–13.

Faced with this dilemma, the Supreme Court chose to see the judicial branch as part of government and therefore subject to the Constitution:[277]

> We have no doubt that there has been state action in these cases in the full and complete sense of the phrase. The undisputed facts disclose that petitioners were willing purchasers of properties upon which they desired to establish homes. The owners of the properties were willing sellers; and contracts of sale were accordingly consummated. It is clear that *but for* the active intervention of the state courts, supported by the full panoply of state power, petitioners would have been free to occupy the properties in question without restraint.[278]

This could be called a *but for* test. It illustrates when a national court may hold that a case between two purely private parties will trigger human rights protection in a situation where the national law seemingly restricts human rights protection to state actors. Courts may conceive themselves as state actors and the enforcement of the law becomes sufficient state action to trigger constitutional rights protection.

While this logic may work for the US Constitution, the Canadian courts have not followed this logic, as the courts are not seen as part of government for the purposes of the Canadian Charter. The situation in the United Kingdom is more complex. The Human Rights Act 1998 binds the courts in section 6(3)(a). The Act also binds tribunals, and from the way the Bill was introduced in Parliament, it seems that all labour law tribunals,[279] as well as the courts, should have a duty to act compatibly with the Convention in developing the common law in cases between private parties.[280] For William Wade, the result of this section (and the way it was presented in Parliament) was that 'a court cannot lawfully give

---

[277] Ibid, at 17, 'it has never been suggested that state court action is immunized from the operation of those provisions simply because the act is that of the judicial branch of the state government'.

[278] Ibid, at 17 (emphasis added).

[279] See Jack Straw (Home Secretary) House of Commons, 17 June 1998, Col. 411: ' "Tribunals" include industrial tribunals, the employment appeals tribunal, immigration adjudicators and the immigration appeals tribunal. If those bodies are not required to comply with convention rights, it is hard to think of bodies that should be. If the employment appeals tribunal were deemed not to be a public body, the cases would go straight to the court in Strasbourg.'

[280] Lord Irvine (Lord Chancellor) 'We believe that it is right as a matter of principle that organisations which are, on a reasonable view and as decided by the courts, exercising a public function should be so treated under the Bill and should have the duty, alongside other organisations having public functions, to act compatibly with the convention rights in respect of those functions. That means (among other things) that, in doing what they do, they should pay due regard to Article 8 (on privacy) as well as to Article 10 (on freedom of expression, which includes also the freedom of the press).

We also believe that it is right as a matter of principle for the courts to have the duty of acting compatibly with the convention not only in cases involving other public authorities but also in developing the common law in deciding cases between individuals. Why should they not? In preparing this Bill, we have taken the view that it is the other course, that of excluding convention considerations altogether from cases between individuals, which would have to be justified. We do not think that that would be justifiable; nor, indeed, do we think it would be practicable. As the noble and learned Lord, Lord Wilberforce, recognised, the courts already bring convention considerations to bear and I have no doubt that they will continue to do so in developing the common law and that they have the support of the noble and learned Lord in making that use of the convention. Clause 3 requires the courts to interpret legislation compatibly with the convention rights and to the fullest extent possible in all cases coming before them.' House of Lords, 24 November 1997, Col. 783.

judgment in any case in which Convention rights are in issue except in accordance with those rights [in the European Convention]'.[281] Wade's point of view has not been accepted by the majority of commentators and has been described as 'contentious' and as giving 'direct, or full horizontal effect' to human rights in the national legal order.[282] The objections focus first, on the fact that the legislation constructs a complicated test for limiting remedies to claims against 'public authorities'. It therefore seems to these commentators to defeat the clear words of this legislation if one applies the Human Rights Act to all private litigation. Second, one meets the fundamental critique that the Human Rights Act does not actually incorporate the international human rights in the Convention into the national legal order, but sets out a separate scheme for rights protection. According to Gavin Phillipson, because Parliament has not incorporated these rights for the private sphere 'it is clear that they can become in the private sphere at most legal values and principles, rather than the clear entitlements they are when exercised against public authorities'.[283] For Phillipson, it is 'self-evident' that 'a court cannot have a duty to act compatibly with rights which the parties before it do not hold'.[284]

The middle-ground adopted by some commentators has been to suggest that, although the Human Rights Act may not as such necessarily found a *cause of action* in the private sphere, it 'must be used to interpret all law before the courts'.[285] Within this broad position, there is room to dispute the extent to which the Courts remain free to develop causes of action. Murray Hunt considers

[281] Sir William Wade, 'Opinion: Human Rights and the Judiciary', *EHRLR* (1998) 520–533, at 524. See also H. W. R. Wade, 'Horizons of Horizontality' 116 *LQR* (2000) 217–224, at 224; Sir William Wade, 'Paradoxes in Human Rights Act', letter to *The Times*, 1 September 2000. Cf A. Lester and D. Pannick, 'The Impact of the Human Rights Act on Private Law: The Knight's Move' 116 *LQR* (2000) 380–385, J. Beatson and S. Grosz, 'Horizontality: a Footnote' 116 *LQR* (2000) 385–386.

[282] G. Phillipson, 'Transforming Breach of Confidence? Towards a Common Law Right of Privacy under the Human Rights' 66 *MLR* (2003) 726–758, at 729; see also Wadham, Mountfield, and Edmundson (2003: 69–71); S. Grosz, J. Beatson, and P. Duffy, *Human Rights: the 1998 Act and the European Convention* (London: Sweet & Maxwell, 2000) at 88–94; G. Phillipson, 'The Human Rights Act, "Horizontal Effect" and the Common Law: A Bang or a Whimper?' 62 *MLR* (1999) 824–849, at 827–829; G. Lightman and J. Bowers, 'Incorporation of the ECHR and its Impact on Employment Law', *EHRLR* (1995) 560–581, at 565.

[283] See Phillipson (1999: 837). See Lightman and Bowers (1995: 565).

[284] Phillipson (1999: 837). See also Lord Justice Buxton, 'The Human Rights Act and Private Law' 116 *LQR* (2000) 48–65. Buxton LJ, writing in an extrajudicial capacity, stressed (at 56) that the rights incorporated by the Act are the rights created by the Convention, for him (at 52) the '*content* cannot have changed in the course of that process of transmission. The Convention rights must therefore also be assertable only against public bodies'.

[285] Wadham, Mountfield, and Edmundson (2003: 70): 'The Convention must be used to interpret all law before the courts, but falls short of being directly horizontal as the 1998 Act does not *directly* confer any new private causes of action on individuals when their Convention rights have been violated by a private party.' The authors align themselves with Murray Hunt's (1998: 441–442) carefully argued conclusion that the Convention is 'potentially relevant in proceedings between private parties, but will fall short of being *directly* horizontally effective, because it will not confer any new private causes of action against individuals in respect of breach of Convention rights'. See further Leigh (1999: 87) and Clapham (1993: 340–342).

that this position 'requires a distinction to be drawn between the evolution of existing causes of action over time and the creation of entirely new causes of action against private parties'.[286] Such a distinction, however, may not be so easy to discern. The development of the common law may, in effect, be the creation of new remedies for violations of Convention rights by non-state actors.[287] In fact, Hunt himself seems to see this evolution as likely to involve a 'metamorphosis' of existing causes of action.[288]

More revealing, for present purposes, are the policy arguments which are thrown up to counter the suggestion that the courts, as public/government authorities, should ensure respect for human rights in private disputes. Leigh has argued that the implications of the courts being bound to apply the Convention in the private sphere would be 'profound: settled common law rules of private law would be open to reinterpretation in the light of the Human Rights Act'.[289] With regard to the right to respect for private life (enshrined in Article 8 of the ECHR), he foresees a direct application to the domestic sphere as 'destabilizing', suggesting that such 'an undesirable exercise in uncertainty risks seriously damaging the balancing of interests in the common law'.[290] Relevant common law interests absent from the Convention framework might include freedom of contract, testamentary freedom, and the right to earn a living in a chosen profession.[291] The thread which runs throughout opposition to judicial application of human rights in private law matters is the prospect of this 'uncertainty'.[292] The uncertainty is compounded by the fact that human rights *principles* are seen as indeterminate, and subject to rather open-ended glossing by the European Court of Human Rights, leaving courts with open-ended judicial discretion.[293]

For the most part, the English courts took a strict approach to this issue, admitting that they were bound as state actors to apply the Convention in private litigation, but discouraging the idea that the Convention had any relevance to non-state actors outside the existing causes of action.[294] In 2005, things took a

---

[286] Hunt (1998: 442).   [287] See the discussion by Leigh (1999: 84, footnote 118).
[288] Hunt (1998: 443).   [289] Leigh (1999: 84).   [290] Leigh (1999: 73).
[291] Leigh (1999: 73), and Phillipson (1999: 838–840).
[292] See, e.g. Leigh (1999: 73); Oliver (2004: 348); and Grosz, Beatson, and Duffy (2000: 92–93).
[293] Phillipson (1999: 842, 848).
[294] See, e.g. *Re S*: 'The House unanimously takes the view that since the 1998 Act came into force in October 2000, the earlier case law about the existence and scope of inherent jurisdiction need not be considered in this case or in similar cases. The foundation of the jurisdiction to restrain publicity in a case such as the present is now derived from convention rights under the ECHR.' [2004] UKHL 47, at para. 23. See also Baroness Hale's approach in *Campbell v MGN Ltd* [2004] UKHL 22, at para. 132: 'The 1998 Act does not create any new cause of action between private persons. But if there is a relevant cause of action applicable, the court as a public authority must act compatibly with both parties' Convention rights.' See generally paras 132–133. See also *Jammel (Yousef) v Dow Jones and Co Inc* [2005] EWCA Civ 75, at para. 55 where the Court of Appeal stayed as an abuse of the court's process a defamation claim where the damage had been minimal, their reasoning relied in part on the Human Rights Act: 'Section 6 requires the court, as a public authority, to administer the law in a manner which is compatible with Convention rights, insofar as it is possible to do so. Keeping a proper balance between the Article 10 right of freedom of expression and the protection of individual

new turn in a judgment concerning privacy claims by Michael Douglas and Catherine Zeta-Jones against *Hello!* magazine. The Court of Appeal accepted that the courts actually have a duty under human rights law to develop causes of action to give effect to both the right to privacy and the right to freedom of expression in cases involving two non-state actors.[295]

10.3.3 The Court Develops the Common Law

So far, judges have been cautious about seeming to overhaul the common law in the light of human rights principles. They have tended to treat human rights values as already prevalent in the common law. An examination of the common law then reveals that that law already balances things quite nicely. If there is to be any recalibration, one can expect that it will come in stages. Again, the metaphors are telling: commentators and judges perceive that human rights will radiate, permeate, and infiltrate the common law.

10.3.3.1 The United Kingdom

In the United Kingdom, the courts had been using the Convention to develop the common law for some time, even before the adoption of the Human Rights Act.[296] Early cases which invoked the Convention in the context of a prohibition in a will on a beneficiary becoming a Roman Catholic,[297] or a ban on 'coloured' people in a Dockers' Club,[298] came down in favour of common law freedom of 'testamentary disposition' and freedom to 'order one's private life as one chooses'. On the other hand, concern for freedom of expression protected under the Convention played a role in determining whether a profit motive may justify punitive damages in a libel action.[299] In labour law, the Convention was

---

reputation must, so it seems to us, require the court to bring to a stop as an abuse of process defamation proceedings that are not serving the legitimate purpose of protecting the claimant's reputation, which includes compensating the claimant only if that reputation has been unlawfully damaged.'

[295] *Michael Douglas, Catherine Zeta-Jones, Northern & Shell plc v Hello Ltd, Hola SA, Eduardo Sanchez Junco* [2005] EWCA Civ 595. See esp. paras 50–53: 'We conclude that, in so far as private information is concerned, we are required to adopt, as the vehicle for performing such duty as falls on the courts in relation to Convention rights, the cause of action formerly described as breach of confidence.' The judgment often uses the expressions 'right to privacy', 'infringement of privacy', and 'invasion of privacy' when dealing with the substance of the claim which was nevertheless procedurally an action for breach of confidence (brought as such in part due to the uncertainty as to whether a an action for invasion of privacy would be recognized by the courts. In the light, *inter alia*, of the *von Hannover v Germany* case (discussed in Ch 9, at 9.1.8.3 above) the Court of Appeal seems to suggest that injunctions will be available against newspapers with regard to the prospect of photographs being published which upset, and infringe on Art. 8 rights protecting privacy. See para. 253.

[296] See R. Clements, 'Bringing It All Back Home: "Rights" in English Law Before the Human Rights Act 1998' 21 *HRLJ* (2000) 134–142; M. Hunt, *Using Human Rights Law in English Courts* (Oxford: Hart Publishing, 1997).

[297] *Blathwayt v Baron Cawley* [1976] AC 397.

[298] *Dockers' Labour Club v Race Relations Board* [1974] 3 All ER 592.

[299] *Broome v Cassell & Co* [1972] AC 1027, at 1133 *per* Lord Kilbrandon, 'one must be watchful against holding the profit motive to be sufficient to justify punitive damages: to do so would be seriously to hamper what must be regarded, at least since the European Convention was ratified, as a constitutional right to free speech'.

successfully used in the Court of Appeal to bolster arguments about the right to choose one's union.³⁰⁰ The House of Lords reversed the Court of Appeal finding that freedom of association had to be mutual, so there was no common law right to choose one union over another if that union did not want someone as a member.³⁰¹

Whitehouse v Lemon concerned a private prosecution by Mary Whitehouse against *Gay News* for blasphemy. The Convention was referred to by Lord Scarman (in the majority) who was prepared to uphold the usefulness of the offence of blasphemy as well as strict liability for the publishers. Lord Scarman saw that the offence had to be interpreted in the context of the human rights guarantees in the Convention.³⁰²

More recently, in *DPP v Jones* the House of Lords was faced with an appeal by two demonstrators who had been arrested for failing to move on when asked to do so. They had been arrested for 'trespassory assembly'. They argued that this contradicted their right of access to the highway under common law. The House of Lords acknowledged that the Convention protection of freedom of assembly may be useful for determining or developing the common law. They based their ruling, however, on the common law and found that that the right of access to the highway was not automatically displaced by property rights and the exercise of the right of access did indeed extend to reasonable assembly. The interesting aspect for present purposes is the attitude taken to assembly on highways running through private property. For example, the Lord Chancellor, Lord Irvine, stated in the context of demonstrations on a highway:

> . . . there can be no basis for distinguishing highways on publicly owned land and privately owned land. The nature of the public's right of use of the highway cannot depend upon whether the owner of the sub-soil is a private landowner or a public authority. Any fear, however, that the rights of private landowners might be prejudiced by the right as defined, are unfounded. The law of trespass will continue to protect private landowners against unreasonably large, unreasonably prolonged or unreasonably obstructive assemblies upon these highways.³⁰³

---

³⁰⁰ *Cheall v APEX* [1982] 3 All ER 875.   ³⁰¹ *Cheall v APEX* [1983] 2 WLR 679.

³⁰² 'Article 9 provides that everyone has the right to freedom of religion, and the right to manifest his religion in worship, teaching, practice and observance. By necessary implication the article imposes a duty on all of us to refrain from insulting or outraging the religious feeling of others. Article 10 provides that everyone shall have the right to freedom of expression. The exercise of this freedom "carries with it duties and responsibilities" and may be subject to such restrictions as are prescribed by law and are necessary "for the prevention of disorder or crime, for the protection of health or morals, for the protection of the reputation or rights of others . . ." It would be intolerable if by allowing an author or publisher to plead the excellence of his motives and the right of free speech he could evade the penalties of the law even though his words were blasphemous in the sense of constituting an outrage upon the religious feelings of his fellow citizens. This is no way forward for a successful plural society.' *Whitehouse v Lemon* [1979] AC 617, at 665. Note, this was a 'private' prosecution which had resulted in a jury trial and conviction. The appeal to the House of Lords concerned the necessity of intention for the crime of blasphemous libel.

³⁰³ *DPP v Jones and anor* [1999] 2 All ER 257, at 265. See also Lord Hope (dissenting) at 275: 'But it has not been suggested that the right of access is different according to the public or private

Lord Hutton found that the right of the public to use the highway should include the right to hold a reasonable, peaceful public assembly on a highway which causes no obstruction to persons passing along the highway. He found that 'there is a right for members of the public to assemble together to express views on matters of public concern'.[304] Lord Hutton continued: 'I consider that the common law should now recognise that this right, which is one of the fundamental rights of citizens in a democracy, is unduly restricted unless it can be exercised in some circumstances on the public highway.'[305]

In the period following the adoption of the Human Rights Act, concern has focused on the extent to which the Convention might be used to elaborate on the law of breach of confidence to generate a common law of privacy that could be used against the media.[306] As we noted earlier, this issue was hotly debated during the passage of the Bill through Parliament. At one level, the legislative compromise of including Article 12 in the Act clearly foreshadows the expectation that the Convention will be used in common law litigation involving the media.[307] Indeed, early privacy claims brought as actions for breach of confidence have carefully considered the human rights dimension, and in effect, called for the media to consider expectations of privacy. Again, any reticence on the part of the judges probably owes more to respect for the role of the legislature than to any sense that human rights principles are inappropriate for use against non-state actors.[308] By

character of the landowner. The conclusions which I would draw from this are that the addition of the word "public" is tautologous, and that anything which we may say about the limits of the public right of access to a highway must be taken, in law, to apply to each and every highway.'

[304] Ibid, at 292.

[305] Ibid, at 292. Note also Lord Hutton's approving reference to the Canadian judgment of Lamer CJC in the Supreme Court of Canada in *Committee for the Commonwealth of Canada v Canada* (1991) 77 DLR (4th) 385, where it is said that freedom of expression cannot be limited to places where the speaker is the owner of the property.

[306] For a detailed analysis see G. Phillipson, 'Transforming Breach of Confidence? Towards a Common Law Right of Privacy under the Human Rights' 66 *MLR* (2003) 726–758; see also J. Rozenberg, *Privacy and the Press* (Oxford: Oxford University Press, 2004) for further analysis and details of the factual background to some of the cases.

[307] The section reads: '(1) This section applies if a court is considering whether to grant any relief which, if granted, might affect the exercise of the Convention right to freedom of expression. (2) If the person against whom the application for relief is made ("the respondent") is neither present nor represented, no such relief is to be granted unless the court is satisfied—(a) that the applicant has taken all practicable steps to notify the respondent; or (b) that there are compelling reasons why the respondent should not be notified. (3) No such relief is to be granted so as to restrain publication before trial unless the court is satisfied that the applicant is likely to establish that publication should not be allowed. (4) The court must have particular regard to the importance of the Convention right to freedom of expression and, where the proceedings relate to material which the respondent claims, or which appears to the court, to be journalistic, literary or artistic material (or to conduct connected with such material), to—(a) the extent to which—(i) the material has, or is about to, become available to the public; or (ii) it is, or would be, in the public interest for the material to be published; (b) any relevant privacy code. (5) In this section—"court" includes a tribunal; and "relief" includes any remedy or order (other than in criminal proceedings).'

[308] See the approach of Buxton LJ who wrote, in an extrajudicial capacity: 'To the extent that "values", as opposed to rights, can be extracted from the E.C.H.R. and thus from those parts of the E.H.C.R. that are translated into Convention Rights in English domestic law, they remain,

applying human rights principles to determine the shape of the law of confidence, the courts are already indirectly applying the Convention protection of private life to non-state actors such as the media; at the same time, respect for the principle of freedom of expression (with its limitations) is judicially imposed on non-state actors seeking to restrain or punish the media for their snooping and publications. The following two cases are discussed in order to see how this occurs in practice. The first concerns a story about Naomi Campbell leaving a Narcotics Anonymous meeting. The second concerns the publication of unauthorized wedding photos of Michael Douglas and Catherine Zeta-Jones.

Naomi Campbell's case concerned a story and picture of her entitled 'Naomi: I am a drug addict'. The picture was of her on the street after a Narcotics Anonymous session. The case against the *Daily Mirror,* for breach of confidence, reached the House of Lords. The judges were split on the outcome of the case. The majority found in favour of Naomi Campbell. All the judges were, however, clear that the values in the European Convention on Human Rights were to be applied in balancing the interests of privacy and freedom of expression. Lord Nicholls stated that the values in Articles 8 and 10 were of general application in cases between individuals even outside the context of breach of confidence.[309] Lord Hoffman drew a distinction between the enforcement of human rights obligations against the state before the European Court of Human Rights in Strasbourg, and their application against private parties in national law. He said that, while the Human Rights Act does not provide for an action to protect privacy rights against invasion by private individuals, human rights law has identified 'private information as something worth protecting as an aspect of human autonomy and dignity'.[310] He went on to explode the remnants of any remaining logic for the exclusion of non-state violators from the human rights equation:

> And this recognition has raised inescapably the question of why it should be worth protecting against the state but not against a private person. There may of course be justifications for the publication of private information by private persons which would not be available to the state—I have particularly in mind the position of the media, to which I shall return in a moment—but I can see no logical ground for saying that a person should have less protection against a private individual than he would have against

stubbornly, values whose content lives in public law. To transpose those values into private law would require an exercise in analogy: an analogy that while it might be illuminating in general terms is very difficult to justify from the provisions of the H.R.A.' R. Buxton, 'The Human Rights Act and Private Law' 116 *LQR* (2000) 48–65, at 59.

309 'The time has come to recognise that the values enshrined in articles 8 and 10 are now part of the cause of action for breach of confidence. As Lord Woolf CJ has said, the courts have been able to achieve this result by absorbing the rights protected by articles 8 and 10 into this cause of action: *A v B plc* [2003] QB 195, 202, para 4. Further, it should now be recognised that for this purpose these values are of general application. The values embodied in articles 8 and 10 are as much applicable in disputes between individuals or between an individual and a non-governmental body such as a newspaper as they are in disputes between individuals and a public authority.' *Campbell v MGN Ltd* [2004] UKHL 22, at para. 17.   310 Ibid, at para. 50.

the state for the publication of personal information for which there is no justification. Nor, it appears, have any of the other judges who have considered the matter.[311]

For Lord Hoffmann, the human rights approach 'takes a different view of the underlying value which the law protects. Instead of the cause of action being based upon the duty of good faith applicable to confidential personal information and trade secrets alike, it focuses upon the protection of human autonomy and dignity— the right to control the dissemination of information about one's private life and the right to the esteem and respect of other people'.[312] On the facts, the majority seemed to feel that the photo and story generated distress with a possible set-back for the drug therapy and that this tilted the balance in favour of protecting privacy.[313] The result and reasoning in this case had a considerable impact on the final result in the litigation concerning Michael Douglas and Catherine Zeta-Jones.

An exclusive contract had been arranged for *OK!* Magazine to publish the photographs of the wedding between Michael Douglas and Catherine Zeta-Jones. The existence of this exclusive contract was assumed to be well known to other magazines and to the wedding guests. Although the £1 million offered by *OK!* was relevant, entering into the contract was considered not to be merely for profit, but aimed at ensuring that the couple would have full control over the published photographs. The case arose because a guest surreptitiously took some photographs, smuggled them out, and sold them to a rival magazine.[314] The rival magazine, called *Hello!*, was about to publish these photos when *OK!* obtained an injunction in court. The Court of Appeal lifted the injunction and the judgment of Sedley LJ contains interesting reflections on the obligations of non-state actors in this context. In a section headed 'Common law and equity' he concluded:

> It is relevant, finally, to note that no Strasbourg jurisprudence contra-indicates, much less countermands, the establishment in national legal systems of a qualified right of privacy; and that the courts of France and Germany, to take two other signatories of the Convention, have both in recent years developed long-gestated laws for the qualified protection of privacy against both state and non-state invasion.[315]

Turning to the effect of the Human Rights Act, Sedley LJ highlighted the view that the Convention rights which protect freedom of expression (Article 10) and private life (Article 8) are applicable in cases between two private parties:

> Two initial points need to be made about s. 12 of the Act. First, by subsection (4) it puts beyond question the direct applicability of at least one article of the Convention as between one private party to litigation and another—in the jargon, its horizontal effect.

---

[311] *Campbell v MGN Ltd* [2004] UKHL 22, at para. 50.   [312] Ibid, at para. 51.
[313] See esp. para. 169 *per* Lord Carswell; para. 98 *per* Lord Hope; and para. 144 *per* Baroness Hale.
[314] For a reconstruction of events see the account by Rozenberg (2004: 39–42, 67–84).
[315] *Douglas et al v Hello! Ltd (No. 1)* [2001] QB 96, at para. 127. He goes on to reference: E. Picard, 'The right to privacy in French law' in B. S. Markesinis (ed) *Protecting Privacy: The Clifford Chance Lectures Volume Four* (Oxford: Oxford University Press, 1999) and Markesinis, *A Comparative Introduction to the German Law of Torts* (Oxford: Clarendon Press, 3rd edn, 1994) at 63–66.

Whether this is an illustration of the intended mechanism of the entire Act, or whether it is a special case (and if so, why), need not detain us here. The other point, well made by Mr Tugendhat, is that it is 'the Convention right' to freedom of expression which both triggers the section (see s. 12(1)) and to which particular regard is to be had. That Convention right, when one turns to it, is qualified in favour of the reputation and rights of others and the protection of information received in confidence. In other words, you cannot have particular regard to Article 10 without having equally particular regard at the very least to Article 8 . . .[316]

Sedley LJ saw that, in fact, a court might have to consider whether publication might threaten other relevant Convention rights, such as the right to life. In this way, the newspaper is, in effect, obliged to consider the 'full range of relevant Convention rights' in the context of its exercise of its right to freedom of expression.[317] In the end the judges weighed the competing demands for privacy and freedom of expression and favoured publication, knowing that the actual privacy claims would be dealt with at a later trial.

The judgment at the actual trial recognized that a series of cases raising breach of confidence and freedom of expression issues represented 'a fusion between the pre-existing law of confidence and rights and duties arising under the Human Rights Act.'[318] The judgment went on to determine that the photographs constituted information and were protected under the rules on confidence. There was no public interest (as understood in the Human Rights Act and the Press Code of Conduct) and, although *Hello!* was not actually denied its freedom of expression, this human right remained relevant as 'awards of damages generally can be said to affect the exercise of the Convention right to freedom of expression because a possible exposure to a substantial monetary award can deter or inhibit expression almost as completely as would an injunction.'[319] Nevertheless, the judgment came down on the side of Douglas and Zeta-Jones and the claim for breach of confidence. *Hello!* argued that the law of breach of confidence was not 'prescribed by law' as required by the European Convention on Human Rights. Lynsday J rejected this argument, saying that he considered he was not conscious of having 'extended' the law.[320] On appeal the judgment considers this issue in the light of human rights principles. The Court of Appeal concluded that, even if the restriction of freedom of expression imposed on *Hello!* could not have been said to have been 'prescribed by law' as the Convention demands, the 'proper course was for the court to attempt to bring English law into compliance with the Convention' by protecting the couple's Article 8 rights even at the expense of *Hello!*'s Article 10 rights.[321]

---

[316] Ibid, at para. 133. [317] Ibid, at para. 134.
[318] *Douglas et al v Hello! Ltd et al (No. 6)* [2003] EWHC 78, at para. 186. (The cases referred to are discussed in the Court of Appeal decision on the injunction (above), see *Venables and anor v News Group Newspapers Ltd and ors* [2001] 1 All ER 908; *A v B* [2002] 3 WLR 542; and *Campbell v MGN* [2002] EWCA Civ 1373.) [319] Ibid, at para. 203.
[320] Ibid, at para. 212.
[321] *Michael Douglas, Catherine Zeta-Jones, Northern & Shell plc v Hello Ltd, Hola SA, Eduardo Sanchez Junco* [2005] EWCA Civ 595, at para. 150.

Michael Douglas and Catherine Zeta-Jones won their argument on breach of confidence grounds and were eventually awarded £14,500 in damages (distress and inconvenience).[322] Although the Court of Appeal refused to adjust the sum of damages on appeal, they held that, in the light of the *Campbell* and *von Hannover* cases, the earlier decision to lift the injunction had been wrong. The decision to lift the injunction had failed to take into account the infringement of privacy represented by the publication of the unauthorized photographs. In the absence of a convincing public interest or freedom of the press argument, the threat of an infringement of privacy demanded protection by the courts.[323] Furthermore, the judgment noted that the modest damages awarded cannot really be seen as an adequate remedy for the infringement of privacy which took place. First, because the couple were not ready to trade their privacy with regard to unauthorized photos for any sum, and second, because such a level of damages would not serve as a deterrent to newspapers and magazines 'contemplating the publication of photographs which infringed an individual's privacy'.[324]

A final point regarding this case is worth mentioning. The Court also considered in detail claims concerning economic torts, including unlawful interference with the business of *OK!* and conspiracy to injure *OK!* by unlawful means. For our purposes the key issue is: what constitutes *unlawful* means? Here the judgment takes the human rights obligations of the magazine and considers them as part of the equation for understanding whether unlawful means had been used.[325] The Court found that unlawful means had been used; but in the end *Hello!* did not have the requisite intention to establish the relevant economic torts. *Hello!* did not have to pay damages to *OK!*.

Stepping back from the intricacies of the different causes of action in the national legal order, we can consider the overall result. The existence of international human rights obligations persuaded the Court to develop the national legal order to allow those who wish to prevent invasions of privacy by non-state actors to obtain compensation and the prospect of future protection through injunctions.

10.3.3.2   South Africa

The South African Constitutional Court has had some reservations about imposing constitutional rights thinking on the common law. Part of the explanation for this

---

[322] The case is complicated by the application of s 12 of the Human Rights Act (quoted above) and the Press Complaints Code to which it makes reference. The Code was found to have been broken through the use of a hidden camera and subterfuge by the photographer. See para. 205. The Code stated that everyone is entitled to expect respect for his or her private life (para. 3(i)); that use of long lens photography to take pictures of people in private places without their consent is unacceptable (para. 3(ii)) and it is noted that 'Private places are public or private property where there is a reasonable expectation of privacy.' On 'misrepresentation', see para. 11. Public interest is included as an exception with regard to privacy and misrepresentation.

[323] Ibid, at paras 253–254. In this context, the judgment refers only to invasion/infringement of privacy and abandons references to breach of confidence.   [324] Ibid, at para. 257.

[325] Ibid, at paras 229 and 233.

attitude resides in the delicate balance between, on the one hand, the Constitutional legal order elaborated by the Constitutional Court, and on the other hand, the national legal order developed by the other courts in South Africa. Another part of the explanation is the wording of the Constitution itself.[326] Section 8 was quoted in full above and states in part that, when courts are applying the Bill of Rights to non-state actors, if the legislation does not give effect to the right, then the courts must apply, or if necessary develop, the common law. There is here a constitutional brake on judicial activism with regard to the common law. The Constitutional Court has had little opportunity to set out much guidance in this field. In the *Holomisa* case, discussed in section 10.1.2.2 above, the Court was faced with the argument that the common law of defamation failed to protect freedom of expression, which is a constitutional entitlement for newspapers under the Constitution. The Court found that the plaintiffs need not establish the falsity of the publication to prove defamation and an assault on their dignity; and it found that the common law rule of 'reasonable' publication sufficed as a defence for the publisher in the interests of democracy. In short, it found the constitutional values of dignity and democracy were adequately protected by the common law.[327] But, even if in this case the common law was found adequate, it is clear that the Constitution has opened up the possibility of adjusting the common law to ensure that non-state actors fulfil their obligations under the Bill of Rights in the Constitution.

Max du Plessis and Jolyn Ford worry in general terms about the possible 'colonisation' of the common law by the constitutional rights instruments, not out of a desire to protect freedom of contract, or rules based on protecting reputation and confidence, but rather because they see this as disempowering for the

---

[326] Note, in addition to s 8 discussed below, s 39(2) enjoins the courts to apply the Constitution in a purposive way in all contexts: 'When interpreting any legislation, and when developing the common law or customary law, every court, tribunal or forum must promote the spirit, purport and objects of the Bill of Rights.'

[327] 'Were the Supreme Court of Appeal not to have developed the defence of reasonable publication in *Bogoshi*'s case, a proper application of constitutional principle would have indeed required the development of our common law to avoid this result. However, the defence of reasonableness developed in that case does avoid a zero-sum result and strikes a balance between the constitutional interests of plaintiffs and defendants. It permits a publisher who can establish truth in the public benefit to do so and avoid liability. But if a publisher cannot establish the truth, or finds it disproportionately expensive or difficult to do so, the publisher may show that in all the circumstances the publication was reasonable. In determining whether publication was reasonable, a court will have regard to the individual's interest in protecting his or her reputation in the context of the constitutional commitment to human dignity. It will also have regard to the individual's interest in privacy. In that regard, there can be no doubt that persons in public office have a diminished right to privacy, though of course their right to dignity persists. It will also have regard to the crucial role played by the press in fostering a transparent and open democracy. The defence of reasonable publication avoids therefore a winner-takes-all result and establishes a proper balance between freedom of expression and the value of human dignity. Moreover, the defence of reasonable publication will encourage editors and journalists to act with due care and respect for the individual interest in human dignity prior to publishing defamatory material, without precluding them from publishing such material when it is reasonable to do so.' *Khumalo v Holomisa* Case CCT 53/01, 14 July 2002, *per* O'Regan J, at para. 43.

regular common law judges faced with the abuse of private power. For them: 'Much of the total aggregate of power in society lies in the private sphere, regulated (if at all) by the private common law. In our view, the common law can be an important vehicle through which rights (or, the values which they attempt to embody) are brought home (and perhaps into the home). The common law courts can be seen as good candidates for this transformation.'[328] Their fear is that constitutional 'balancing techniques' degenerate into indeterminacy and eventually into a 'species of facile, reductive reasoning'.[329] It is perhaps too early to see if their fears are justified.

10.3.3.3   *Canada*

As we have already seen, the Canadian courts have declined to allow for a constitutional cause of action to permit claims against non-state actors with no governmental functions. On the other hand, they have elaborated a theory of how and why the common law should be developed in conformity with the Charter. In one case, Mr Hill (a Crown lawyer) had brought and won a defamation case against the Church of Scientology and their lawyer Morris Manning. He was awarded $300,000 (Canadian) by the jury.[330] The Church of Scientology and Manning sought to argue that their Charter rights had been violated. The Court rejected the argument that Hill was a government actor (even though his defamation suit was paid for by the Government). The Court also rejected the alternative argument that the common law of defamation placed too much emphasis on the need to protect reputation and was in contradiction with human rights principles concerning freedom of expression. The judgment of the Supreme Court sets out the approach of the Court:

> Historically, the common law evolved as a result of the courts making those incremental changes which were necessary in order to make the law comply with current societal values. The *Charter* represents a restatement of the fundamental values which guide and shape our democratic society and our legal system. It follows that it is appropriate for the courts to make such incremental revisions to the common law as may be necessary to have it comply with the values enunciated in the *Charter*.[331]

Cory J, delivering the judgment of the Court, explained how the Charter is to be taken into account in such circumstances. The process of considering necessary limitations under Article 1 of the Charter is not transferred to a dispute in the private sphere between non-state actors:

> When the common law is in conflict with *Charter* values, how should the competing principles be balanced? In my view, a traditional s. 1 framework for justification is not appropriate. It must be remembered that the *Charter* 'challenge' in a case involving private litigants does not allege the violation of a *Charter* right. It addresses a conflict between principles. Therefore, the balancing must be more flexible than the traditional s. 1 analysis undertaken in cases involving governmental action cases. *Charter* values,

---

[328] du Plessis and Ford (2004: 312).   [329] du Plessis and Ford (2004: 311).
[330] *Hill v Church of Scientology of Toronto* [1995] 2 SCR 1130.   [331] Ibid, at para. 92.

framed in general terms, should be weighed against the principles which underlie the common law. The *Charter* values will then provide the guidelines for any modification to the common law which the court feels is necessary.[332]

Furthermore, the burden of proving that the common law is inconsistent with the *Charter* values lies on the party making such a claim.[333] The Supreme Court went on to examine and balance the competing values underlying the protection of reputation and freedom of expression. They referred to the finding that *dignity* underlies all Charter values and that protection of reputation is essential for *democracy*.[334] These values therefore could be opposed to those that founded freedom of expression. The common law protection of reputation and the limitation that it imposes on freedom of expression in this context was held not to warrant any adjustment of the common law.[335]

10.3.4   Reliance on Human Rights to Explain the Scope of Certain Values in National Law

Outside the common law world, human/constitutional rights have been invoked to inform the interpretation of national law. In Germany a doctrinal debate erupted over the *Drittwirkung* of constitutional rights contained in the Basic Law. This is a reference to the developed German theory of the application of fundamental rights values in cases where two private parties are involved. At this point it would not be helpful to describe this theory and all its variants. Suffice to say that *Drittwirkung* is more accurately *Drittwirkung der Grundrechte*, or the third-party effect of fundamental rights. Furthermore, there exists in the doctrine a difference between *mittelbare Drittwirkung* and *unmittelbare Drittwirkung*. The former means that the values and principles surrounding constitutional fundamental rights are to be considered by the courts when they are deciding private law cases; the rights are mediated through the law. The latter means that the rights themselves can be directly applied against private bodies by the national courts. They are unmediated. This section is concerned with *mittelbare Drittwirkung*.[336]

The core of the modern doctrine is helpfully summarized by Ralf Brinktrine: the rights of the 'Basic Law are not only individual rights in the sense of defensive

---

[332] Ibid, at para. 97. Section 1 reads: 'The *Canadian Charter of Rights and Freedoms* guarantees the rights and freedoms set out in it subject only to such reasonable limits prescribed by law as can be demonstrably justified in a free and democratic society.'   [333] Ibid, at para. 98.

[334] 'Although it is not specifically mentioned in the *Charter*, the good reputation of the individual represents and reflects the innate dignity of the individual, a concept which underlies all the *Charter* rights. It follows that the protection of the good reputation of an individual is of fundamental importance to our democratic society.' Ibid, at para. 120.   [335] Ibid, at para. 141.

[336] For some of the literature, see Lewan (1968); Horan (1976); Scheuner (1971); Zanghi (1971); Brinktrine (2001); B. Markesinis and S. Enchelmaier, 'The Applicability of Human Rights as between Individuals under German Constitutional Law' in B. S. Markesinis (ed) *Protecting Privacy: The Clifford Chance Lectures Volume Four*, Oxford: Oxford University Press, 1999) 191–243; B. Markesinis, 'Privacy, Freedom of Expression, and the Horizontal Effect of the Human Rights Bill: Lessons from Germany' 115 *LQR* (1999) 47–88.

rights against the State but ... they constitute an objective order of values (*"eine objective Wertordnung"*). This objective order of values ... has a so called "radiation effect" (*"Ausstrahlungswirkung"*). This means that the system of objective values created by the Basic Law permeates the whole legal system'.[337] He goes on to explain that the German Constitutional Court has adjusted its position so that the lower courts are asked to interpret legislation that restricts basic rights in a way that balances the purpose of the legislation with the interests protected by the basic right.[338] So, in fact, the result is similar to the statutory interpretation route discussed in section 10.3.1.2 above. Let us consider how the Constitutional Court approached the issue in the *Caroline of Monaco* case (discussed in Chapter 9).

The Constitutional Court held that the Federal Court of Justice had properly interpreted the Copyright Act in accordance with the constitutional protection of freedom of the press. They held that the statutory rule concerning figures in 'contemporary society' had been correctly applied to the Princess and that freedom of expression demanded not only information but entertainment. The Court referred to 'a growing tendency in the media to do away with the distinction between information and entertainment both as regards press coverage generally and individual contributions, and to disseminate information in the form of entertainment or mix it with entertainment ("infotainment")'.[339] This entertainment fell within the scope of the application of fundamental rights and had been given the right weight in the interpretation of the legislation. The Court, however, pointed to another basic right which it felt had been given insufficient attention in deciding which photographs could be published. The Constitutional Court highlighted section 6 of the Basic Law and its focus on the protection of family life. It held that the lower courts had failed to interpret the legislation in accordance with this value.[340] The magazine subsequently undertook not to republish the particular photographs of Princess Caroline with her children.

---

[337] Brinktrine (2001: 424) footnotes omitted.

[338] For a comparative analysis of the approach taken by the German Constitutional Court see Tushnet (2003: 83–84, 94–95) who highlights the way in which the German Constitutional Court in cases such as *Lüth*, 7 BverfGe [1958] 198, ensures that the lower courts understand the relevant constitutional principle; Tushnet stresses that the Constitutional Court considered it should not review every decision by the ordinary courts. He suggests one way of understanding the different approaches of courts in South Africa, Canada, the United States, and Germany is to see the federal limits of the constitutional court and its relationship to ordinary law-making.

[339] *Caroline of Monaco v Burda Press* Judgment of 19 December 1999, translated at para. 25 of the *Von Hannover v Germany* Judgment of the European Court of Human Rights, 24 June 2004.

[340] At (cc) of the translated judgment. 'However, the constitutional requirements have not been satisfied in so far as the decisions of which the appellant complains did not take account of the fact that the right to protection of personality rights of a person in the appellant's situation is strengthened by section 6 of the Basic Law regarding that person's intimate relations with their children.' Section 6 reads: 'Article 6 [Marriage and the family; children born outside of marriage] (1) Marriage and the family shall enjoy the special protection of the state.   (2) The care and upbringing of children is the natural right of parents and a duty primarily incumbent upon them. The state shall watch over them in the performance of this duty.   (3) Children may be separated from their families against the will of their parents or guardians only pursuant to a law, and only if the parents or guardians fail in their duties or the children are otherwise in danger of serious neglect.   (4) Every mother shall be entitled

As discussed in Chapter 9, the European Court of Human Rights eventually held that the courts had failed to give proper priority to the protection of private life under Article 8 and that the publication of the other photographs could not be justified by reference to freedom of information. The explanation by the European Court of Human Rights concerning who is a public figure, and what sort of weight to give to trivial information, may influence the development of constitutional law with respect to protecting privacy from media intrusion, not only in Germany, but also throughout the states of the Council of Europe.[341]

The German theory of *Drittwirkung* has resonance outside Germany,[342] including with judges and scholars writing about the Human Rights Act in the United Kingdom. Lord Steyn, speaking extrajudicially, considered that 'the German Federal Constitutional Court has captured the right nuance by holding that the German Bill of Rights has a radiating effect throughout the legal system'.[343] Basil Markesinis has carefully considered the balancing of values undertaken by the German courts and sees an application for the UK courts in the light of the incorporation of the Convention. He suggests the question is not '*whether* we can privatise human rights but *to what extent* we should do so'.[344]

10.4 INVOKING POSITIVE OBLIGATIONS

The fourth route for judicial application of human rights obligations to non-state actors concerns the situation where a national court considers the positive human

to the protection and care of the community. (5) Children born outside of marriage shall be provided by legislation with the same opportunities for physical and mental development and for their position in society as are enjoyed by those born within marriage.'

[341] See the critique by M. A. Sanderson, 'Is *Von Hannover v Germany* a Step Backward for the Substantive Analysis of Speech and Privacy Interests?', *EHRLR* (2004) 631–644.

[342] For the suggestion that the Japanese legal order may be susceptible to *Drittwirking* thinking with regard to the application of international human rights law against private persons, see Y. Iwasawa, *International Law, Human Rights, and Japanese Law* (Oxford: Clarendon Press, 1998) at 90. Article 90 of the Japanese Civil Code states that juristic acts which are contrary to public policy or good morals are null and void. Yuji Iwasawa refers to a case that concerned a complaint against the owner of an apartment for refusing to rent the apartment to someone because he was Korean. The response of the Court was to deny the direct applicability of provisions of the Constitution 'to juridical relations between individuals'. (*X v Y (an apartment owner, a real estate agent and Osaka Prefecture)*, Osaka District Court, Judgment of 18 June 1993, HJ (1468) 122 [1993], see 37 *Japanese Annual of International Law* (1994) 152, at 153.) The Court held that the provisions have to be 'realized through a particular provision of substantive private law' and focused on the obligation of good faith finding that there had been 'no reasonable causes for the refusal' to rent the apartment. Yuji Iwasawa (1998: 201) surmises that, in its application of the good faith principle, the Court was 'likely to have been influenced by ideas of international human rights law'.

[343] He continued later: 'I am inclined to share the view of those who argue that the structure of our Act rules out direct horizontal application. If this is right, it is beyond the power of the English courts to develop a general tort of privacy. On the other hand, by its radiating effect the Act may indirectly lead to the incremental development of existing remedies which protect rights of privacy e.g. based on a duty of confidentiality.' 'Democracy Through Law' The 2002 Robin Cooke Lecture, 18 September, at 20–21. Mimeograph on file with the author.

[344] B. Markesinis, 'Privacy, Freedom of Expression, and the Horizontal Effect of the Human Rights Bill: Lessons from Germany' 115 *LQR* (1999) 47–88, at 74.

rights obligations that arise for states and non-state actors under human rights law. This may occur where state authorities are forced to take positive action to protect people from threats emanating from non-state actors. The scope of these state obligations under international law was described in Chapters 8 and 9 and will not be further elaborated here.[345] Each constitutional order has a different view as to the extent to which national courts can demand that that the *state* take positive action to protect human rights.[346] Positive obligations may also arise for *non-state actors* themselves exercising public functions and acting in fulfilment of those functions.[347] In fact, we may see that there are positive obligations for non-state actors when they have no so-called public function.

In some circumstances the national courts will have limited jurisdiction to hold the relevant actor accountable for failing to act to protect people. For example, the Human Rights Act 1998 specifically precludes the courts from holding the government accountable for failing to introduce a proposal for legislation or for failing to make primary legislation or remedial orders.[348] Under international human rights law, an international treaty body or court could find that a state has failed to introduce appropriate legal safeguards and is thus in violation of its international human rights obligations. Furthermore, at the national level, there may be another difference: cases can be brought against actors that are not states. The question arises: to what extent do these non-state actors have obligations to ensure the protection of human rights? Again, national provisions may actually prevent the application of human rights law. There will be differing criteria as to who has obligations under the national legislation. But even where the non-state actor is deemed to have human rights obligations under the national legislation, there may be restrictions on what is expected. For example, the provisions of the Human Rights Act 1998 do not apply where, as the result of primary legislation, the public authority (which could be a non-state actor) could not have acted differently or the actor is giving effect to the primary legislation.[349]

[345] Keir Starmer has suggested a useful categorization of positive obligations that flow from the interpretation of the European Convention on Human Rights that could be relevant to understanding how national courts tackle this issue. He breaks down the Strasbourg case-law into duties: to put in place a legal framework for the effective protection of Convention rights; to prevent breaches; to provide relevant information and advice regarding breaches; to respond to breaches; and to provide resources to individuals to prevent breaches. K. Starmer, 'Positive Obligations Under the Convention' in J. Jowell and J. Cooper (eds) *Understanding Human Rights Principles* (Oxford: Hart Publishing (2001) 139–159.

[346] Commentators have highlighted the very restrictive approach of the US Supreme Court in *DeShaney v Winnebago County Department of Social Services* where the Court held that the purpose of the Fourteenth Amendment was 'to protect the people from the State, not to ensure that the State protected them from each other'. 109 S Ct 998 (1989) at 1003. See Starmer (2001), Clapham (1993: 159–162), and, more generally, Tushnet (2003).

[347] See, e.g. the Canadian Supreme Court case *Eldridge v British Columbia (Attorney General)* [1997] 3 SCR 624, referred to in 10.2 above. In that case it was held that the *private* entity attracted Charter scrutiny and that the failure to provide sign language interpretation was intimately connected to the legislation which was an expression of government policy. At paras 42–51. The failure to provide these services was declared unconstitutional.   [348] See s 6(6) (supra).

[349] See s 6(2)(a) and (b) quoted in 10.2.1.1 above. It is worth noting that the parochial church council that was found by the majority of the House of Lords not to be a public authority for the purposes

Bearing in mind the existence of such limitations, it is still quite likely that the courts could conclude that an entity (public or private) has not done enough to fulfil its positive obligations to ensure the protection of human rights where the actual abuser is a purely private person. One could imagine a company running a private prison being held to account under the Human Rights Act for failing to protect the right to life where a prisoner is killed by another prisoner. Other examples have been given by Leigh with regard to situations where public authorities in charge of health, telecommunications, the press, and prosecutions could possibly be brought before the courts under the Human Rights Act for failing to protect someone from non-state actor abuses.[350] So, for example, a hospital or health authority could be a defendant in a human rights action where they failed to prevent journalists from taking distressing photographs of a patient against his will.[351]

The positive obligations may, however, be invoked in a yet more indirect way; by focusing on the courts as such.[352] A newspaper may be found to have a duty to refrain from publishing the name of a convicted criminal, where there is a danger to the life of that person. In one case, two boys aged 10 had killed a two-year-old boy, they were convicted and imprisoned; they were to be released at age 18. The two boys brought a case for an injunction to prevent newspapers from publishing details about their new identities. Dame Elizabeth Butler-Sloss issued an injunction 'against the world' and, while suggesting that there was no direct duty stemming from the Human Rights Act as newspapers were not public authorities under section 6, she held that the Court was such a public authority and that it had to ensure that the Convention was respected:[353] 'The duty on the court, in my view, is to act compatibly with convention rights in adjudicating upon existing common law causes of action, and that includes a positive as well as a negative obligation.'[354]

The special point here is that the right to privacy was not sufficient to restrict the newspaper's freedom of expression. The judge based her decision on the threats to life and the possibility of inhuman and degrading treatment under Articles 2 and 3 of the European Convention. She recalled that these Articles are

of the Human Rights Act (discussed in 10.2.1.2 above), would have had the defence that it was acting in order to give effect to a provision of primary legislation had the courts found that it was in fact a public authority. *Aston Cantlow and Wilmcote with Billesley Parochial Church Council v Wallbank* [2003] UKHL 37, *per* Lord Nichols, at para. 19.

350 Leigh (1999: 78–80).

351 See Leigh's example at (1999: 80) referring to the litigation in *Kaye v Robertson* [1991] FSR 62.

352 For a discussion see Leigh (1999: 80–82).

353 *Venables and anor v News Group Newspapers Ltd and ors* [2001] 1 All ER 908, at 917 (para. 24) 'It is clear that, although operating in the public domain and fulfilling a public service, the defendant newspapers cannot sensibly be said to come within the definition of public authority in s 6(1) of the 1998 Act. Consequently, convention rights are not directly enforceable against the defendants; see ss 7(1) and 8 of the 1998 Act. That is not, however, the end of the matter, since the court is a public authority, see s 6(3), and must itself act in a way compatible with the convention, see s 6(1), and have regard to European jurisprudence, see s 2.' The judgment goes on to consider a number of European cases, including *Osman v UK* (discussed in Ch 9 above), which develop the notion of positive obligations under the Convention.   354 Ibid, at 918 (para. 27).

not confined to violence by state actors but cover the duty to protect individuals from private violence. She continued: 'I recognise also that the threats to the life and physical safety of the claimants do not come from those against whom the injunctions are sought. But the media are uniquely placed to provide the information that would lead to the risk that others would take the law into their own hands and commit crimes against the claimants.'[355]

10.5   LIMITS TO HUMAN RIGHTS IN THE PRIVATE SPHERE

If one accepts that non-state actors have human rights obligations, it becomes necessary to answer some tricky questions concerning the limits to this extension of human rights into the private sphere. First, some human rights obligations may indeed have greater scope when the obligations fall on the state rather than on non-state actors. This is reflected in expressions found in certain constitutions that proclaim that the human rights provisions will be applied 'as appropriate' against non-state actors. Second, at the philosophical level, there may be a difference between rights against the state and rights against private individuals or other non-state actors; the reason is simple. When one claims a right to information from the state, the state can only rely on limitations such as national security or public order. When one invokes the same right against a private entity, that entity often has human rights too. So, if one claims the right to inform the public about what a politician or pop star looks like naked, one is met with a counter-claim of the human right to privacy. When one claims rights to distribute information about the state, the state cannot claim a human right to privacy. The state has no human rights.

But this slick distinction should not be overstated. The state will also have the obligation to protect the rights of others. Therefore it is quite likely that the state will respond to a human rights claim with a counter-claim that its actions are indeed based on the need to protect the same values and human rights in particular. Let us now consider possible limitations to the application of human rights obligations and see how we can develop ideas for understanding the limits to the enforcement of human rights obligations on non-state actors through the courts.

10.5.1   Subsidiarity and Complementarity as Tools for Limiting the Human Rights Obligations of Non-State Actors

There is considerable concern that a conception of human rights obligations applicable against private actors will diminish or distract from the primary set of

---

[355] *Venables and anor v News Group Newspapers Ltd and ors* [2001] 1 All ER 908, at 931–932 (para. 76). Compare the approach taken by the House of Lords with regard to asylum seekers fearing violence from non-state actors, dealt with in Ch 8 at 8.6 above.

human rights obligations which are said to rest with the state. I have sought to show that these fears do not justify impunity for violations of human rights committed by non-state actors. The problem remains: how to regulate the relationship between the primary obligations for states and the secondary set of obligations for non-state actors.

This issue has been seen by some in terms of subsidiarity or complementarity. Theo van Boven has suggested 'if a wrong can be attributed only to non-state actors, then they should be held responsible as far as reparations are concerned. However, whenever the wrongs can be attributed to the state by acts, or by legislation, or by state practice, then certainly the state is primarily responsible. This is still the traditional approach: that [the] state is responsible for human rights'.[356] His concern came in the context of a suggestion by another commentator that a principle of subsidiarity should apply in the context of reparations for human rights violations so that 'reparation should be provided in the first place by the individuals who committed the violation, while the state should intervene only when reparation cannot be obtained from them'.[357] As Doug Cassels stated in the same context, such a subsidiarity principle would place an unreasonable burden on human rights litigators: as 'it suggests that one might need to exhaust the remedies against individual perpetrators before reparations could be sought from states'.[358] However, it may make sense to rework the principle so that there is no hierarchy but a simple complementarity whereby the state has an international obligation to ensure its legal system protects the victims of human rights abuses through, in Sadaro's words, 'the international civil responsibility' of 'individuals and other non-state entities'.

One way to consider the issue of human rights in the private sphere is by reference back to the state's international obligation to ensure respect for human rights from threats posed by non-state actors. A complementarity principle here would mean that the domestic court is simultaneously applying human rights law against a private actor and ensuring that the state is complying with its international obligations. The national court is doing both things at the same time. Complementarity expresses this function beautifully.

10.5.2 The Availability of Non-Human Rights Remedies and the Question of Cost

An issue which is rarely mentioned in the debate over the horizontality of human rights protection is that the examples which dog the debate concerning racial

---

[356] Report of *Expert Seminar on Reparation for Victims of Gross and Systematic Human Rights Violations in the Context of Political Transitions Expert seminar on reparation for victims of gross and systematic human rights violations in the context of political transitions* (hereinafter 'Expert Seminar (2002)') Leuven, 10 March 2002 (Antwerpen: Universiteit Antwerpen, 2002) at 61.

[357] P. Sardaro, 'The right to reparation for gross and systematic violations from the perspective of general international law' in *Expert Seminar* (2002) 15–24, at 19.

[358] *Expert Seminar* (2002: 60).

discrimination in employment, restaurants, and clubs have been overtaken by protective non-discrimination legislation. For example, in the context of the twenty-five states of the European Union, various directives cover sex discrimination in the workplace, as well as private discrimination, on grounds of race, religion, age, disability, and sexual orientation. Other states usually have national law which protects against discrimination in the private sphere, and where this is lacking the state may be failing to fulfil its human rights obligations. But often such human rights abuses by non-state actors will be actionable through the simple application of the criminal or civil law. The costs involved in mounting a human rights (or constitutional) challenge, either to the existing law, or against the actions of a non-state actor, will usually act as a dissuasive force and encourage the use of normal remedies. The idea that constitutional human rights will become diluted, diminished, or trivialized through their application against non-state actors is not borne out when one examines those jurisdictions where this is possible. In most cases, lawyers will bring a case under the appropriate law without recourse to human rights provisions. The South African Constitutional Court has not been swamped with cases alleging violations of human rights by non-state actors. Most systems will sever redundant human rights claims where the law already provides a remedy. In fact, in the United Kingdom, the Human Rights Act specifically refers to the relevance of other remedies in the context of any award of damages for a violation of human rights.[359]

Most human rights complaints at the national level will be resolved taking into account a combination of these factors: the appropriateness of applying the right against the non-state actor in question; the availability of alternative remedies; an appreciation of whether the constitutional text allows for a cause of action; the finality of the judgment for the development of the law by the legislature; and lastly, if one is being honest, the *intuition* of the judges concerning the values at stake. (This is discussed further in the next section.) These factors will vary from jurisdiction to jurisdiction. What will remain central for any theory for balancing rights will be, not so much the nuances in the constitutional text, but rather the judicial weight given to the values which underpin the protection of human rights.

Mark Tushnet has recently offered the insight that the application of constitutional rights to the private sector can proceed on two paths determined by one's vision of the social democratic state. First, there is the assumption that the state should control the 'effective social power exercised by market actors through their control of valuable social resources such as property and opportunities for employment'.[360] Second, he suggests that social welfare rights could be achieved in a market context by getting private institutions to 'absorb some of the social welfare obligations created by the constitution'.[361] It is suspicion of both of these projects that provokes the strong reaction to proposals to extend human rights to non-state actors. With regard to the first view, the idea of an extension of human

---

[359] See s 8(3).   [360] (2003: 91).   [361] Ibid, at 92.

rights obligations to private law by a Supreme Court in charge of national law breeds concern that the national/federal state is encroaching on local autonomy and into the private sector itself. The protective mantle of constitutional rights are seen as meddlesome and illegitimate. As to the second view, there is the familiar concern that by encouraging human rights obligations for non-state actors under constitutional law one is absolving the state of its human rights responsibilities and shifting the burden onto the private sector.

Both concerns are well-founded. My position is that the debate too quickly degenerates into two binary questions: should private sector obligations be generated by the legislature or by judges? And, should these human rights obligations fall on the state or on the private sector? This chapter has attempted to show that the answer to each question can be 'both', if you so desire. Most of the time, private human rights abuses will be in breach of existing national law, but it makes sense to ask judges to extend constitutional/human rights protection where this national law is lacking. Most of the time, private entities will not be asked to fulfil the human rights obligations of the state, but where private entities seriously threaten the values underlying the protection of human rights (democracy and dignity) then it makes sense to extend human rights obligations to them.

10.5.3 An *Instinctive* Understanding of the Limits of Non-State Actor Obligations through Emphasis on the Rights of the Non-State Actor

It is difficult to articulate a set of hierarchical values which facilitate the resolution of dilemmas at the limits of the application of human rights in the private sphere. Those opposed to such an extension often resort to the example of judicial interference in personal choices about whom to ask to dinner, or to whom one should be allowed to refuse to rent a flat. Rather than finding theoretical explanations of why a landlord might not be allowed to limit access to his rented accommodation— but a flat-sharer might be allowed to choose a flatmate, it is possible to refer the reader to a variety of attempts to draw the boundary between the reasonable and the unreasonable application of human rights to the private sphere.

Three constitutional lawyers have recently looked at this conundrum. They have sought, in their defence of the application of national constitutional rights to the private sphere, to show that there are limits which take into consideration respect for privacy, intimacy, freedom of contract, and private property.[362]

The first approach comes in the context of a review of the state action doctrine in the United States, but the logic has been influential elsewhere. It starts from the idea (examined above) that all reliance on law brings an actor within the constraints of the Constitution. However, in the thesis presented by Stephen Gardbaum, the application to non-state actors is tempered by 'procedural limitations' so that

---

[362] Although freedom of contract and the right to trade are not international human rights, as we saw in Ch 9 above, the European Court of Human Rights has placed considerable emphasis on the rights of a commercial owner of a shopping mall to the right to property under the European Convention.

where the law allows for no cause of action on any grounds, then the plaintiff cannot rely on constitutional rights against a private party.[363] Gardbaum presents the limits of the application of US constitutional rights to the private sphere in the following way:

> ... complete immunity from constitutional scrutiny applies only to actions by private actors (a) that do not invoke, or otherwise rely on, any law, or (b) for which the victim has no relevant cause of action. As far as the latter is concerned, there may occasionally be situations where, although a private actor relies on a law, say to discriminate on grounds of race, there is no relevant, existing nonconstitutional cause of action that the victim can employ as plaintiff to challenge the law. So where *A*, a private club that denies membership to African Americans, relies on the rules of property law to physically eject *B*, an African American, from its premises, *B* may sue for the tort of assault and allege that the law relied on by *A* is unconstitutional. But where *C* relies on the rules of property law to give change only to white beggars and not to black, there may be no common law tort or statutory cause of action that would enable a black beggar to challenge the constitutionality of the rules of property law relied on.[364]

For Mark Tushnet, also starting from the debate concerning the US Constitution, the classic problem can be resolved through admitting that the private party accused of violating human rights has himself/herself/itself human rights. One then simply openly weighs the conflicting rights. Tushnet has suggested that, in response to the standard American hypothetical that suggests that it can not be correct to allow that 'a white racist could be held liable for failing to invite a black neighbor to a holiday party in the racist's living room', one should simply note that 'in this situation another constitutional norm—here, a right to intimate association—must be balanced against the anti-discrimination norm'.[365]

Lastly the conundrum has been dealt with by Ahron Barak, President of the Israeli Supreme Court, who writing extra-judicially, canvassed the arguments for and against horizontal effect in any context. According to Barak the 'primary argument against the application of constitutional human rights in private law is that recognition of these rights in relations between private individuals will deeply harm human rights themselves, primarily the individual's autonomy of will'.[366] For Barak, the general solution lies in a judicial balancing exercise and for him the solution to the common hypothetical is simply *intuitive*:

> My intuition tells me that the restaurant owner has an obligation to give service, that is, to make a contract, without discriminating on the basis of gender, race or religion. By contrast, the same intuition tells me that the private party renting out a room in his apartment is entitled to choose a lodger as he sees fit. This intuition is based primarily on the proper balance between the freedom to make a contract of the restaurant owner and the apartment owner and the right of the persons seeking the service (food or dwelling) not to be discriminated against. I accept that the restaurant owner and apartment owner

[363] Gardbaum (2003: 421).   [364] Ibid, at 422.   [365] Tushnet (2003: 93).
[366] Barak (2001: 35).

have the constitutional freedom to decide with whom to have to contract. Similarly, I accept that the person wishing to dine in the restaurant or rent the room is entitled not to be discriminated against (whether by the State or by private parties) and that if he is refused on the basis of gender, religion or race, this constitutes discrimination.

In balancing these rights when they conflict, the right of the person not to be discriminated against prevails in the restaurant example and the freedom to enter or not to enter into a contract prevails in the case of the apartment owner. The rationale at the base of this balance is rooted in the concept that the freedom to make a contract is stronger when it relates to a person's privacy, while it is weaker when directed against the public at large. Similarly, the right not to be discriminated against is strongest when service is offered to the general public and a person is segregated from that public on the basis of race, gender or religion. The right not be discriminated against diminishes in strength where the service, by its very nature, is not 'open' to all and is provided on a personal basis.[367]

Barak's solution is that the right not to be discriminated against is always weighed against the non-state actor's freedom to contract, but that the balance comes down in favour of the restaurant client due to the fact that the service is offered to all, whereas the lodger comes up against another human right, the right to privacy which, in contrast to the restaurant context, arises outside a situation where services have to be offered to all.

These hypotheticals go some way to explaining the limits of human rights in the private sphere, but they fail to really capture the grey zone. Recourse to the notion of an intimate sphere, or the right to develop intimate relations, can quickly become turned into a protected zone which excludes the protection of the law for those subjected to domestic violence and other abuses.

In the end, the hypothetical examples posit easy extremes. One can agree that the courts cannot interfere with personal choices about charitable giving (even if the preferences are based on religion or some other prohibited ground) and we can agree that restaurants cannot exclude people on the ground of the colour of their skin. But what about employer's policies that result in dismissal for pregnancy? Or an employer's toleration of racist abuse? Should the victims be entitled to complain in court on the basis of a violation of their human rights? My suggestion is that rather than seeking to erect a boundary based on whether facilities are 'open to the public' (which simply begs the question again of what is a 'public' and 'private' affair) we should admit that every human rights complaint is potentially admissible against a non-state actor. Whether it should succeed will depend on the values at stake and whether the essence of those values is about to be extinguished in a way which has serious consequences. My suggestion is that the key values at stake in such disputes are dignity and democracy. These concepts are examined in greater detail in the next chapter.

---

[367] Barak (2001: 39).

11

Dignity and Democracy

It is time to address the emerging paradoxes at the heart of this investigation. If we are serious about protecting the democratic principle that everyone should be able to communicate their ideas to others in the polity, we have to accept some inroads on personal freedoms concerning property, commerce, and privacy. Democracy may demand a wide-ranging circulation of ideas, even at the expense of absolute respect for private property and private relations. But democracy also demands that rules are made in ways whereby there is accountability to those who are governed by those rules. This latter democratic principle partly explains the reticence of judges at the national level to extend constitutional protections to the private sphere so as to create causes of action against non-state actors. In the absence of a clear democratic will to extend these obligations in this way, judges are cautious and can call on this principle of democracy to justify their caution.

So we may have a first democratic principle, requiring that judges apply human rights law to override traditional rules concerning the protection of property, commerce, and reputation. And, paradoxically, various actors appeal to a second democratic principle, to demand that judges refrain from applying human rights law in the absence of a clear legislative mandate.

A further paradox emerges when one considers the broader aims of human rights. Human rights law is imbued with values, including democracy, but a key justificatory argument for respecting human rights is the importance of protecting human dignity. Human dignity, as a *raison d'être* for human rights, is reflected, not only in international instruments, but also in various constitutional orders. A Justice of the South African Constitutional Court has articulated the complementary nature of the two concepts in the context of human rights claims: 'Freedom of expression is integral to a democratic society for many reasons. It is constitutive of the dignity and autonomy of human beings. Moreover, without it, the ability of citizens to make responsible political decisions and to participate effectively in public life would be stifled.'[1] The same judge goes on in this context to situate dignity as the paramount goal. 'However, although freedom of expression is fundamental to our democratic society, it is not a paramount value. It must be construed in the context of the other values enshrined in

---

[1] *Khumalo et al v Holomisa* Case CCT 53/01, 14 July 2002, O' Reagan J, at para. 21.

our Constitution. In particular, the values of human dignity, freedom and equality.'[2] Similar foundational thinking concerning human dignity is prevalent outside this particular constitutional context.[3]

Once one accepts the proposition that human rights are ultimately concerned with the protection of human dignity and that assaults on that dignity have to be prevented, remedied, and punished, there is little room left for arguments about the state or non-state character of the assailant. On the other hand, when one makes a dignity-based claim against a non-state actor, that actor may also rely on the importance of respect for dignity and base a counter-claim on the same foundational value. But, again, one should not make too much of this distinction; claims against the state are often met with the response that the state has to protect the rights of others and that the state is simply protecting dignity rather than disrespecting it.

Similarly, the argument that judicial extension of human rights into the private sphere is somehow anti-democratic can be countered by thinking more generally about the role of the judge. Human rights rules with regard to state actors have been developed over the years and deliver a degree of predictability and accessibility, but that development has often been through judicial activism and in spite of the democratic will. The cautious approach of the courts to the extension of human rights obligations to private actors and judicial deference to the legislature means that cases involving allegations of human rights violations by non-state actors are rather unlikely to spawn a slew of legislative codes regulating private abuses of human rights. Judicial abdication should not therefore be seen as appropriate deference in the face of a passive legislature (in particular when one admits that human rights should protect minority interests and not only those who can mobilize for legislative change).[4]

If one's fear is *gouvernement des juges*, the legitimacy of the judicial function in the interpretation of human rights must apply equally to the public and the private sphere. However, those who oppose the horizontal extension of human rights into the sphere of private law suggest that this would lead to judges choosing

---

[2] *Khumalo et al v Holomisa*, at para. 25.

[3] Recall the approach of the Canadian Supreme Court in *Hill v Church of Scientology of Toronto* [1995] 2 SCR 1130, where it was said (at para. 20) that the 'innate dignity of the individual [was] a concept which underlies all the *Charter* rights'.

[4] Cf Sprigman and Osborne: 'Compare the situation where the alleged rights infringer is not the legislature but a private actor, acting pursuant not to legal power created by the legislature but under the common law. The offender here is not an entity, like the legislature, beyond the practical reach of the ordinary law. She is fully subject to the power of the legislature to enact corrective legislation, whether that power be used to ban discrimination against gays and lesbians by private corporations, restrain exploitation of workers in mines, ban corporal punishment in private schools, or for any other purpose that the legislature determines will give effect to constitutional rights. In that situation, it best serves the fundamental structure of the Constitution, and the principle of majority rule embedded in that structure, that the victim, along with other citizens who feel offended by the offending private conduct, should mobilise politically in an effort to obtain legislative redress, rather than relief from a politically non-responsible judge.' C. Sprigman and M. Osborne, 'Du Plessis is *not* Dead: South Africa's 1996 Constitution and the Application of the Bill of Rights to Private Disputes' 15 *SAJHR* (1999) 25–51, at 49.

between competing constitutional rights, an exercise which may be contrasted with the application of a single right.[5] As mentioned above, I suggest that, even in the application of a single human/constitutional right, the judge will still, in effect, be balancing competing rights.

11.1 DIGNITY

We saw in the previous chapter that, when faced with a direct clash of human rights claims between two private bodies we may need to ask, not which rights have been given priority by the legislator, but rather, what is the underlying aim of the human right in question? One of the major justifications for the protection of human rights is the need to protect and enhance human dignity. This concept has spawned a vast literature in the field of human rights and we can only scratch the surface here.[6]

11.1.1 Philosophical Foundations of Dignity

In considering the meaning given to the notion of dignity one may recall Kant's reflections on the inner worth of human beings and our duties towards other human beings which flow from this dignity:

> But a human being regarded as a *person*, that is, as the subject of a morally practical reason, is exalted above any price; for as a person (*homo noumenon*) he is not to be valued merely as a means to the ends of others or even to his own ends, but as an end in himself, that is, he possesses a *dignity* (an absolute inner worth) by which he exacts *respect* for himself from all other rational beings in the world. He can measure himself with every other being of this kind and value himself on a footing of equality with them.[7]

This may not necessarily be how everyone conceives their dignity, and their reasons for demanding respect, but it does represent an early exploration and influential articulation of why some people consider dignity worth respecting and protecting. The normative aspect of this claim to be accorded respect by everyone (and not just the government) is asserted by Kant later in the same chapter:

> Every human being has a legitimate claim to respect from his fellow human beings and is *in turn* bound to respect every other. Humanity itself is dignity; for a human

---

⁵ Ibid, at 43.

⁶ See, e.g. D. Kretzmer and E. Klein (eds) *The Concept of Human Dignity in Human Rights Discourse* (The Hague: Kluwer, 2002); R. Brownsword, 'Freedom of Contract, Human Rights and Human Dignity' in D. Friedmann and D. Barak-Erez (eds) *Human Rights in Private Law* (Oxford: Hart Publishing, 2001) 181–199; O. Schachter, 'Human Dignity as a Normative Concept' 77 *AJIL* (1983) 848–854; M. S. McDougal, H. D. Lasswell, and L. C. Chen, *Human Rights and World Public Order* (Newhaven, Conn: Yale University Press, 1980).

⁷ I. Kant, *The Metaphysics of Morals* (1797) M. Gregor (trans) (Cambridge: Cambridge University Press, 1996) at 186.

being cannot be used merely as a means by any human being (either by others or even by himself) but must always be used at the same time as an end. It is just in this that his dignity (personality) consists, by which he raises himself above all other beings in the world that are not human beings and yet can be used, and so over all *things*. But just as he cannot give himself away at any price (this would conflict with his duty of self esteem), so neither can he act contrary to the equally necessary self-esteem of others, as human beings, that is he is under obligations to acknowledge, in a practical way, the dignity of humanity in every other human being. Hence there rests on him a duty regarding the respect that must be shown to every other human being.[8]

Kant had earlier expressed a practical imperative in the following way: 'Act in such a way that you treat humanity, whether in your own person or in the person of another, always at the same time as an end and never simply as a means.'[9] Such Kantian logic is behind the notion of dignity, seen as particularly influential in the secular human rights movement.[10] In fact, Lou Henkin goes so far as to state that:

> The human rights idea and ideology begin with an *ur* value or principle (derived perhaps from Immanuel Kant), the principle of *human dignity*. Human rights discourse has rooted itself entirely in human dignity and finds its complete justification in that idea. The content of human rights is defined by what is required by human dignity—nothing less, perhaps nothing more.[11]

Human rights philosophers, anxious to avoid an over-reliance on religion or law, have taken as a starting point the consciousness of those subject to humiliation, and 'generate' human rights in the following way:

> Human dignity inheres in all human being qua human beings. Human rights constitute one expression of it. Human dignity is a quality which is always present in but also more than and above its various expressions. This human dignity has to do with dignity which inheres in oneself as a human being and possesses a dimension as interiority as it relates to one's self-perception. The external recognition of this dignity by another constitutes the basis of human rights. Respecting them devolves on the other party as its duty. In this way, human dignity, human rights, and human duty become intertwined in a web of relationships. Take two human beings, A and B. Both possess human dignity within themselves in their awareness that they are human beings. B's recognition of this human dignity of A gives rise to A's human rights, which it is B's duty to respect. Similarly, it is A's duty to respect B's human rights, which flow from B's human dignity.[12]

---

[8] *The Metaphysics of Morals*, at 209.

[9] *Grounding for the Metaphysics of Morals* (1785) J. W. Ellington (trans) (Indianapolis: Hacket Publishing, 1981) at 36.

[10] P. Quinn, 'Christian Ethics and Human Rights' in J. Runzo, N. M. Martin, and A. Sharma (eds) *Human Rights and Responsibilities* (Oxford: Oneworld Publications, 2003) 233–245, at 234.

[11] L. Henkin, 'Religion, Religions and Human Rights' 26 *Journal of Religious Ethics* (1998) 229, at 231.

[12] A. Sharma, 'The Religious Perspective Dignity as a Foundation for Human Rights Discourse' in Runzo, Martin, and Sharma (2003) 67–76, at 71.

Human dignity is linked to human rights from the opening of the Universal Declaration through to the International Covenant and the regional treaties;[13] indeed many human rights instruments and treaties not only recall the importance of protecting human dignity, but actually specifically provide for its concrete protection as such.[14]

---

[13] For an examination of the background to inclusion of dignity in the Universal Declaration of Human Rights, see K. Dicke, 'The Founding Function of Human Dignity in the Universal Declaration of Human Rights' in Kretzmer and Klein (2002: 111–120).

[14] See the second preambular paragraph of the UN Charter: 'We the peoples of the United Nations determined . . . to reaffirm faith in fundamental human rights, in the dignity and worth of the human person.' The Universal Declaration of Human Rights opens with: 'Whereas recognition of the inherent dignity and of the equal and inalienable rights of all members of the human family is the foundation of freedom, justice and peace in the world', and then proclaims in its first Article: 'All human beings are born equal in dignity and rights', and later includes Art. 22 (everyone entitled to the rights indispensable for his dignity and the free development of his personality) and Art. 23 (the right of everyone who works to 'just remuneration ensuring for himself and his family an existence worthy of human dignity'). The second preambular paragraphs of both the Covenant on Civil and Political Rights and the Covenant on Economic, Social and Cultural Rights recognize 'that these rights derive from the inherent dignity of the human person'. The Proclamation of Tehran (The First World Conference on Human Rights, 1968) states in para. 5: 'The primary aim of the United Nations in the sphere of human rights is the achievement by each individual of the maximum freedom and dignity', and later urges 'all peoples and governments to . . . redouble their efforts to provide for all human beings a life consonant with freedom and dignity and conducive to physical, mental, social and spiritual welfare'. Mention should also be made of regional or non-universal instruments such as the American Declaration on the Rights and Duties of Man (1948) which begins: 'All men are born free and equal in dignity and rights, and, being endowed by nature with reason and conscience, they should conduct themselves as brothers one to another. The fulfilment of duty by each individual is a prerequisite to the rights of all. Rights and duties are interrelated in every social and political activity of man. While rights exalt individual liberty, duties express the dignity of that liberty.' The American Convention on Human Rights (1969) includes multiple references to dignity as an element to be protected with regard to deprivation of liberty, forced labour, and the protection of privacy: Arts 5(2), 6(2), and 11(1). The Helsinki Final Act (1975) declares that states 'will promote and encourage the effective exercise of civil, political, economic, social, cultural and other rights and freedoms all of which derive from the inherent dignity of the human person and are essential for his free and full development' (Principle VII, para. 2). The African Charter on Human and Peoples' Rights refers to the struggle of the African people for dignity in the eighth preambular paragraph, and guarantees every individual the right to respect for the dignity inherent in a human being (Art. 5). The Protocol to the African Charter on Human and Peoples' Rights on the Rights of Women in Africa (2003) includes a freestanding article entitled 'Right to Dignity: Article 3', which states that 'Every woman shall have the right to dignity inherent in a human being' and obliges states 'to adopt and implement appropriate measures to ensure the protection of every woman's right to respect for her dignity'. Art. 1(a) of the Cairo Declaration on Human Rights in Islam (1990), adopted by the member states of the Islamic Conference, reads: 'All human beings form one family whose members are united by submission to God and descent from Adam. All men are equal in terms of basic human dignity and basic obligations and responsibilities, without any discrimination on grounds of race, colour, language, sex, religious belief, political affiliation, social status or other consideration. True faith is the guarantee for enhancing such dignity along the path to human perfection.' The Arab Charter on Human Rights (1994) began: '*Given* the Arab nation's belief in human dignity since God honoured it by making the Arab World the cradle of religions and the birthplace of civilizations which confirmed its right to a life of dignity based on freedom, justice and peace.' The revised 2004 version begins: 'Proceeding from the faith of the Arab nation in the dignity of the human person whom God has exalted since the Creation and that the Arab nation is the cradle of religions and the homeland of civilizations with lofty human values that affirm the human right to a life of dignity based on freedom, justice and equality.' The Council of Europe treaties

Moreover, as Klaus Dicke has pointed out,[15] the UN General Assembly actually determined in 1986 that new human rights instruments should 'derive from the inherent dignity and worth of the human person'.[16] The appeal of dignity can be further witnessed in other related spheres. The United States National Security Council's report to the President in 1950 stated that the 'Fundamental Purpose of the United States' was laid down in the preamble to the Constitution and its 'essence' is 'to assure the integrity and vitality of our free society, which is founded on the dignity and worth of the individual'.[17] The foundational concept of dignity has furthermore been relied on by judges applying human rights instruments, such as the European Convention on Human Rights, which make no mention of the word.[18] Interestingly, respect for human dignity has even been seen as a foundation for the Caux Round Table Principles for Business.[19]

11.1.2   Protection of Dignity as an End in Itself

More than 170 governments meeting in Vienna at the Second World Conference on Human Rights in 1993 chose human dignity as the value that generated human rights, and stressed the need for human beings to be central to any consideration of the protection of human rights. The Declaration and Programme of

focused on democracy in the early years, but recent treaties have highlighted the importance of protecting human dignity. The Convention for the Protection of Human Rights and Dignity of the Human Being with Regard to the Application of Biology and Medicine (1997) not only includes the protection of dignity in the title but also includes strong assertions in the preamble, where it is stated that the contracting parties are: 'Convinced of the need to respect the human being both as an individual and as a member of the human species and recognizing the importance of ensuring dignity of the human being' and 'Conscious that the misuse of biology and medicine may lead to acts endangering human dignity'. See also the Additional Protocol concerning Biomedical Research (2005), Art. 1: 'Parties to this Protocol shall protect the dignity and identity of all human beings and guarantee everyone, without discrimination, respect for their integrity and other rights and fundamental freedoms with regard to any research involving interventions on human beings in the field of biomedicine.' See also the protocols on Transplantation of Organs and Tissues of Human Origin (2002), (Art. 1) and on the Prohibition of Cloning Human Beings (1998) (preamble).

[15] Dicke (2002: 119).

[16] The full paragraph reads: '4. Invites Member States and United Nations bodies to bear in mind the following guidelines in developing international instruments in the field of human rights; such instruments should, inter alia: (a) Be consistent with the existing body of international human rights law; (b) Be of fundamental character and derive from the inherent dignity and worth of the human person; (c) Be sufficiently precise to give rise to identifiable and practicable rights and obligations.' GA Res. 41/120, 4 December 1986. See also P. Alston, 'Conjuring Up New Human Rights: A Proposal for Quality Control' 78 *AJIL* (1984) 607–621.

[17] 'NSC 68: United States Objectives and Programs for National Security', 7 April 1950, at Pt II.

[18] J. A. Frowein, 'Human Dignity in International Law' in Kretzmer and Klein (2002) 121–132. Note also the judgment of the House of Lords (applying the European Convention on Human Rights) in *R v Secretary of State for Education and Employment et al ex p Williamson et al* [2005] UKHL 15, at paras 23, 28, 57, 59, 64, 67, 76, 77, 81, 83, and 84. The case is discussed below.

[19] J. Farrar, *Corporate Governance in Australia and New Zealand* (Oxford: Oxford University Press, 2001) at 415.

Action reveals in the preamble the foundational quality accorded to human dignity. The World Conference *recognized* and *affirmed*:

> ... that all human rights derive from the dignity and worth inherent in the human person, and that the human person is the central subject of human rights and fundamental freedoms, and consequently should be the principal beneficiary and should participate actively in the realization of these rights and freedoms.

The Declaration and Programme of Action goes on to use the concept of dignity nine more times in contexts such as biomedical advances, gender-based violence, indigenous people, poverty and social exclusion, and torture.[20] Since the Vienna Conference, the protection of human dignity has been written into a number of new Constitutions (including the Constitution for Europe),[21] and the French *Conseil Constitutionnel* in 1994 held that the protection of human dignity was a principle with constitutional force.[22]

---

[20] Pt I, para. 11: 'Everyone has the right to enjoy the benefits of scientific progress and its applications. The World Conference on Human Rights notes that certain advances, notably in the biomedical and life sciences as well as in information technology, may have potentially adverse consequences for the integrity, dignity and human rights of the individual, and calls for international cooperation to ensure that human rights and dignity are fully respected in this area of universal concern.' Para. 18: 'Gender-based violence and all forms of sexual harassment and exploitation, including those resulting from cultural prejudice and international trafficking, are incompatible with the dignity and worth of the human person, and must be eliminated. This can be achieved by legal measures and through national action and international cooperation in such fields as economic and social development, education, safe maternity and health care, and social support.' Para. 20: 'The World Conference on Human Rights recognizes the inherent dignity and the unique contribution of indigenous people to the development and plurality of society and strongly reaffirms the commitment of the international community to their economic, social and cultural well-being and their enjoyment of the fruits of sustainable development.' Para. 25: 'The World Conference on Human Rights affirms that extreme poverty and social exclusion constitute a violation of human dignity and that urgent steps are necessary to achieve better knowledge of extreme poverty and its causes, including those related to the problem of development, in order to promote the human rights of the poorest, and to put an end to extreme poverty and social exclusion and to promote the enjoyment of the fruits of social progress.' Pt I, para. 55: 'The World Conference on Human Rights emphasizes that one of the most atrocious violations against human dignity is the act of torture, the result of which destroys the dignity and impairs the capability of victims to continue their lives and their activities.'

[21] The Charter of Fundamental Rights of the European Union, adopted in Nice in 2000, not only centred human rights on human dignity, but also fixed human dignity as the first foundation of the European Union itself. 'Conscious of its spiritual and moral heritage, the Union is founded on the indivisible, universal values of human dignity, freedom equality and solidarity;' Compare Art. I-2 of the Constitution for Europe: 'The Union is founded on the values of respect for human dignity, freedom, democracy, equality, the rule of law and respect for human rights, including the rights of persons belonging to minorities. These values are common to the Member States in a society in which pluralism, non-discrimination, tolerance, justice, solidarity and equality between women and men prevail.' Art. 1 of the Charter is entitled 'human dignity' and simply states: 'Human dignity is inviolable. It must be respected and protected.' See also the identical Title I Dignity, Art. II-62 of the Treaty establishing a Constitution for Europe, EU Doc. CIG 87/2/04, Rev. 2, 29 October 2004.

[22] For an explanation by Jaques Robert, Member of the French *Conseil Constitutionnel*, see 'The Principle of Human Dignity' in *The principle of respect for human dignity* (1999) European Commission for Democracy through Law, Proceedings of the UniDem Seminar, Montpellier 2–6 July 1998 (Strasbourg: Council of Europe) Collection Science and Technique of Democracy, No. 26, pp 43–56.

This decision of the *Conseil Constitutionnel* was taken in the context of draft legislation on the human body and its products, medically assisted procreation, and prenatal diagnosis. The advance of medical research in these areas has led, not only to new legal protections for dignity, but also to an understanding that 'threats to human dignity come not only from the power of the state, but can come also from science; hence the need, at the dawn of new body-manipulating technologies, to reaffirm and consecrate human dignity as a constitutional principle to be obeyed by all authorities'.[23] The UNESCO Universal Declaration on the Human Genome and Human Rights starts with a chapter on human dignity and the human genome,[24] and later uses the importance of dignity to prohibit cloning.[25] There seems to be near universal approval of the need to protect human dignity in the face of scientific advances concerning our genetic make-up. Dignity in this context seems synonymous with individual uniqueness and worth. In response to the prospect of being able to select births and manipulate the genes of babies in the future, ethicists and law-makers have coalesced around the principle of respect for human dignity and addressed their recommendations, not only to states, but also to 'private science policy makers'.[26]

Roger Brownsword has highlighted that the concept of human dignity appears in modern debates 'in two very different roles, in one case acting in support of individual autonomy (human dignity as empowerment) and, in the other case, acting as a constraint on autonomy (human dignity as constraint)'.[27] Although he sees both as anchored in Kant, he has explained how the two concepts may be in competition:

> According to the first conception, it is because humans have a distinctive value (their intrinsic dignity) that they have rights qua humans. Commonly, it is the capacity for autonomous action that is equated with human dignity and this, in turn, generates a regime of human rights organised around the protection of individual autonomy. In this way, respect for human dignity empowers individuals by protecting their choices against the unwilled interferences of others . . . By contrast, the second conception presents human dignity as a value that stands over and above individual choice and consent . . . Individual and joint autonomy is thus constrained—actions no matter how free, that compromise human dignity (whether the dignity of the acting individual or dignity as recognised by the community at large) are simply off limits.[28]

[23] Dominique Rousseau, 'Concluding Report' in *The principle of respect for human dignity* (n 22 above) 102–106, at 104.

[24] Art. 1 reads: 'The human genome underlies the fundamental unity of all members of the human family, as well as the recognition of their inherent dignity and diversity. In a symbolic sense, it is the heritage of humanity.' Art. 2 states: 'a) Everyone has a right to respect for their dignity and for their rights regardless of their genetic characteristics. b) That dignity makes it imperative not to reduce individuals to their genetic characteristics and to respect their uniqueness and diversity.' The declaration was adopted by the UNESCO General Conference on 11 November 1999.

[25] Art. 11: 'Practices which are contrary to human dignity, such as reproductive cloning of human beings, shall not be permitted. States and competent international organizations are invited to co-operate in identifying such practices and in taking, at national or international level, the measures necessary to ensure that the principles set out in this Declaration are respected.' See also Arts 6, 10, and 12, which all refer to human dignity.   [26] Art. 13.

[27] (2001: 191).   [28] (2001: 183–184).

Although these different conceptions of dignity may reflect a philosophical predilection for empowerment or constraint,[29] one need not conclude that the concept of human dignity inevitably pulls in opposite directions for each human rights problem. In the context of human rights and biomedicine, the Convention on Human Rights and Biomedicine fits the protective (constraining) approach by prohibiting commerce in body parts. Arguments based on empowerment, autonomy, or self-determination, founded on a particular conception of human dignity, will be met with the alternative conception that the human rights rule is designed to constrain sales rather than empower purchasers and vendors.

Another arena where one encounters international norms concerning the protection of dignity is that of working conditions. The European Union has adopted a series of directives concerned with sex discrimination,[30] racial discrimination,[31] and discrimination based on religion or belief, disability, age, or sexual orientation.[32] These Directives include violations of dignity in the definition of discrimination and state that such violations amount to harassment. This development takes us beyond a discrimination regime that looks at comparisons between different groups, and focuses on the effect on the victim of having a hostile working environment. According to Article 2(3) of the Directive on equal treatment in employment:

> Harassment shall be deemed to be a form of discrimination within the meaning of paragraph 1, when unwanted conduct related to any of the grounds referred to in Article 1 takes place with the purpose or effect of *violating the dignity* of a person and of creating an intimidating, hostile, degrading, humiliating or offensive environment.[33]

The significance of the Directives in the present context is enhanced by the fact they are explicitly extended to the private sphere. For example, the equal treatment Directive applies: 'to all persons, as regards both the public and private sectors, including public bodies'.[34]

Perhaps the zenith of the prohibition on attacks on dignity is the international criminalization of 'outrages upon personal dignity, in particular humiliating and degrading treatment' in international and internal armed conflict contained in the context of the Rome Statute of the International Criminal Court 1998.[35] These provisions are based on Common Article 3 of the four Geneva Conventions of 1949 and Protocol II of 1977, Article 4(2)(e) (internal armed conflict), and Article 75(2)(b) of Protocol I of 1977 (international armed conflict). They were first explicitly criminalized in the Statute for the International Tribunal for Crimes committed in Rwanda, which criminalized in Article 4(e) 'Outrages upon personal dignity, in particular humiliating and degrading treatment, rape, enforced

---

[29] Brownsword (2001: 184).
[30] Directive 2002/73/EC, [2002] OJ L269/15, 5 October 2002.
[31] Directive 2000/43/EC, [2002] OJ L180/22, 19 July 2000.
[32] Directive 2000/78/EC, [2002] OJ L303/16, 2 December 2000.
[33] Ibid, Art. 2(3) (emphasis added).   [34] Ibid, Art. 3(1).
[35] Art. 8(2)(b)(xxi) and (c)(ii).

prostitution and any form of indecent assault.'[36] Interestingly, this criminalization originated from violence in an internal conflict rather than an inter-state conflict. The various cases which have included charges of 'outrages upon personal dignity' have included first, a Bosnian Croat prison warden in *de facto* control of a prison detaining Bosnian Muslims in the context of the armed conflict against the Bosnian government forces; and second, a non-state businessman, the civilian director of a tea factory in Rwanda.

In the *Aleksovski* case, which concerned the treatment of Bosnian Muslims in Kaonik prison, the International Criminal Tribunal for the former Yugoslavia went out of its way to stress the foundational aspect of respect for human dignity:

> It is unquestionable that the prohibition of acts constituting outrages upon personal dignity safeguards an important value. Indeed, it is difficult to conceive of a more important value than that of respect for the human personality. It can be said that the entire edifice of international human rights law, and of the evolution of international humanitarian law, rests on this founding principle.[37]

The case reveals another aspect to the quest for respect for human dignity that is vital to an understanding of the value of this concept for developing human rights theory. The Tribunal explains in a long passage that it is the subjective feelings of the victim that determine whether the rule has been violated. In one paragraph, there is a shift from a set of rules focused on the perpetrator to a victim-orientated approach:

> An outrage upon personal dignity is an act which is animated by contempt for the human dignity of another person. The corollary is that the act must cause serious humiliation or degradation to the victim. It is not necessary for the act to directly harm the physical or mental well-being of the victim. It is enough that the act causes real and lasting suffering to the individual arising from the humiliation or ridicule. The degree of suffering which the victim endures will obviously depend on his/her temperament. Sensitive individuals tend to be more prone to perceive their treatment by others to be humiliating and, in addition, they tend to suffer from the effects thereof more grievously. On the other hand, the perpetrator would be hard-pressed to cause serious distress to individuals with nonchalant dispositions because such persons are not as preoccupied with their treatment by others and, even should they find that treatment to be humiliating, they tend to be able to cope better by shrugging it off. Thus, the same act by a perpetrator may cause intense suffering to the former, but inconsequential discomfort to the latter. This difference in result is occasioned by the subjective element. In the prosecution of an accused for a criminal offence, the subjective element must be tempered by objective factors; otherwise, unfairness to the accused would result because his/her culpability would depend not on the gravity of the act but wholly on the sensitivity of the victim. Consequently, an objective component to the *actus reus* is

---

[36] For a discussion of the case-law and the scope of these crimes, see K. Kittichaisaree, *International Criminal Law* (Oxford: Oxford University Press, 2001) at 196.

[37] *Prosecutor v Aleksovski* Case IT–95–14/1–T, 25 June 1999, at para. 54.

apposite: the humiliation to the victim must be so intense that the reasonable person would be outraged.[38]

The Tribunal found that, in the actual circumstances where the detainees were extremely vulnerable, the violence constituted an outrage upon personal dignity and the accused was held responsible under Article 3 of the Statute for this 'violation of the laws or customs of war'.

The second example concerns Alfred Musema-Uwimana. Musema was the Director of the Gisovu Tea Factory. He was indicted with various counts, including charges relating to outrages upon personal dignity. The International Criminal Tribunal for Rwanda took the opportunity to elaborate on the different types of outrages upon personal dignity listed in Article 4(e) of the Statute. The Tribunal distinguished humiliating and degrading treatment from torture by stating that, not only would the motives of the perpetrator differ but in relation to the former *there is no requirement that the acts be committed under state authority*.[39]

Focusing on the war crime of outrages upon personal dignity reveals three developments: first, an acceptance that the protection of human dignity requires consideration of the violations from the victim's perspective; second, a connection to a state or a military force is not required for this particular international crime; and third, human dignity has a powerful appeal as a foundational value for the whole of human rights and international humanitarian law.

Finally, in the influential *Furundžija* judgment, the Yugoslavia Tribunal returned to the concept of dignity in order to conclude that forced oral penetration must be considered rape:

> The essence of the whole corpus of international humanitarian law as well as human rights law lies in the protection of the human dignity of every person, whatever his or

---

[38] At para. 56, and see the Appeals Chamber Judgment in Case IT–95–14/1–A, at paras 36–37. With regard to the *mens rea* of the offence of outrages upon personal dignity, see para. 27 of the Appeals Chamber Judgment, which suggests that, contrary to what was indicated by the Trial Chamber, the prosecution does not have to prove an intent to humiliate or ridicule. Note also the discussion in para. 26 concerning the prohibition of outrages upon personal dignity as a category of inhuman treatment punishable under Art. 2(b) as a grave breach of the Geneva Conventions. This relates to Arts 50/51/130/147, respectively, of the four Geneva Conventions of 1949. Although the conflict in this case was seen as internationalized due to the role of Croatia, Aleksovski was actually only convicted with regard to outrages on personal dignity as a violation of the laws and customs of war and not with regard to the grave breaches counts. The Appeals Chamber revised the sentence from 2½ years' imprisonment to 7 years.

[39] *Prosecutor v Musema* Case ICTR–96–13–T, 13 January 2000, at para. 285: '*Humiliating and degrading treatment*: Subjecting victims to treatment designed to subvert their self-regard. Like outrages upon personal dignity, these offenses may be regarded as a lesser forms of torture; moreover ones in which the motives required for torture would not be required, nor would it be required that the acts be committed under state authority.' Note the discussion in Ch 10, at 10.1.1 above, of the later Appeals Chamber ruling that torture, in fact, requires no such state authority: *Prosecutor v Kunarac, Kovać and Vukovič* Case IT–96–23 and IT–96–23/1–A, Judgment of the ICTY (Appeals Chamber), 12 June 2002, para. 148.

her gender. The general principle of respect for human dignity is the basic underpinning and indeed the very *raison d'être* of international humanitarian law and human rights law; indeed in modern times it has become of such paramount importance as to permeate the whole body of international law.[40]

It is often assumed that the principle of respect for human dignity is confined to incidents of inhuman or degrading treatment. But, as suggested in *Furundžija*, respect for human dignity is an imperative which applies beyond the simple injunction to treat people under one's control in a humane way.

11.1.3   The Dignity Paradox

Twenty years ago, Oscar Schachter highlighted the fact that the dignity of the human person as a basic ideal is 'so generally recognized as to require no independent support. It has acquired a resonance that leads it to be invoked widely as a legal and moral ground for protest against degrading and abusive treatment. No other ideal seems so clearly accepted as a universal social goal'.[41]

Starting from the Kantian imperative that individuals are not to be treated merely as instruments or objects of the will of others, he posits three implications: first, that a high priority be accorded to individual choices with regard to issues of beliefs, way of life, attitudes, and the conduct of public affairs. This means that there can be no imposition of beliefs and attitudes, nor can there be any extension of governmental authority into personal and familial areas of human life. For Schachter, there is 'The question of the proper boundaries between the public and the private, and between the sphere governed by the "general will" and that left to the individual remains to be answered in particular cases. But the idea that such boundaries need to be drawn and that an appropriate priority should be accorded to individual choices is not without significance. It clearly runs counter to many existing political ideologies and practices.'[42]

At first sight there appears to be a paradox. The centrality of the value of human dignity has been resorted to in order to reconstruct a theory of human rights that is unencumbered by a public/private divide; and yet the protection of dignity demands a defined private sphere in which individuals must be free to make choices without interference from government. But recognition of the human need to make choices free from interference does not necessarily lead to a no-go area, where the individual is unprotected from attacks on his or her dignity. It is true that the importance of protecting a private sphere has been used in the past to justify non-interference by the police in cases of domestic violence, the legality of rape within marriage, and to uphold the legality of racially exclusive clubs and

---

[40] *Prosecutor v Furundžia* Case IT–95–17/1–T, 10 December 1998, at para. 183.
[41] Schachter (1983: 849).   [42] Ibid, at 850.

associations.[43] However, I would suggest that the value of dignity demands both protection of the right to make choices about all aspects of life, *and* protection from attacks on dignity in both public and private spheres of life. The confusion arises because it is assumed that only state/public attacks on human dignity should be protected. By shifting to a victim's perspective it becomes obvious that dignity should be protected from public and private attacks. Schachter makes the point that: 'Affronts to dignity may come from nonofficial sources.'[44] In sum, I am suggesting that moving away from a conception of human rights regulating the social contract between the citizen and the state, and towards a conception, founded on the need to protect human dignity, permits an understanding of human rights protection as requiring legal protection from all threats to human dignity (whether they are considered state or non-state actors).

Yet this general conclusion may be unworkable in practice. There is said to be a difference between judges weighing individual freedom against state interference and the inevitable balancing that will occur when judges weigh competing human rights of private entities. Gavin Anderson is surely correct in his assertion that a simple appeal to dignity is not sufficient to guide courts in an intelligible way when deciding the rights and wrongs of claims against private individuals or non-state actors.[45]

It may be possible to suggest a more specific meaning for the term dignity in the context of human rights protection. We have already seen that in Schachter's analysis a first aspect of dignity requires that individuals be given space to make choices with regard to different aspects of their lives. A second aspect is the fact that, while an individual should not be subjected to collective responsibility for the acts of groups, human dignity 'embraces a recognition that the individual self is part of larger collectivities and that they, too, must be considered in the meaning of the inherent dignity of the human person'.[46] This means that the groups as well as individuals have to be protected through human rights law. The third aspect requires consideration of the material needs of human beings. Schachter concludes: 'Economic and social arrangements cannot therefore be excluded from a consideration of the demands of dignity. At the least, it requires recognition of a minimal concept of distributive justice that would require satisfaction of the essential needs of everyone.'[47]

I would suggest that concern for dignity has at least four aspects:

(1) the prohibition of all types of inhuman treatment, humiliation, or degradation by one person over another;

---

[43] See the cases discussed in A. Clapham, *Human Rights in the Private Sphere* (Oxford: Clarendon Press, 1993) at 304–308.   [44] Schachter (1983: 852).

[45] G. W. Anderson, 'Rights and the Art of Boundary Maintenance' 60 *MLR* (1997) 120–132, at 131. (Book review article on *Human Rights in the Private Sphere* (1993)).

[46] Schachter (1982: 851).   [47] Ibid.

(2) the assurance of the possibility for individual choice and the conditions for 'each individual's self-fulfilment',[48] autonomy,[49] or self-realization;[50]

(3) the recognition that the protection of group identity and culture may be essential for the protection of personal dignity;

(4) the creation of the necessary conditions for each individual to have their essential needs satisfied.

The first aspect covers direct abuses and may even rise to the level of an international crime. The last three aspects might involve less direct physical violence but could concern a non-state actor denying the opportunity for self-fulfilment: denying the right to associate, to make love, to take part in social life, to express one's intellectual, artistic, or cultural ideas, to enjoy a decent standard of living and health care. This composite entitlement is reflected in Article 22 of the Universal Declaration of Human Rights: 'Everyone, as a member of society, has the right to social security and is entitled to realization, through national effort and international co-operation and in accordance with the organization and resources of each State, of the economic, social and cultural rights indispensable for his dignity and the free development of his personality.'

If the overriding aim is to protect the victim's dignity, then that victim has to be protected from everyone, states and non-state actors. It matters not whether the actor has public functions, is financed by the state, or is simply a private individual. Inhuman and degrading treatment can be just as damaging whether meted out by a private security guard or an officer in the police force. The concept of dignity should be understood in its widest sense. It concerns not only the absence of indignities, but also ensuring access to basic amenities that allow for the full development of the human personality.

As discussed in Chapters 4 and 6 above, it is sometimes suggested that non-state actors only have obligations to *respect* human rights. In other words, that they have only negative obligations. I would go further. Non-state actors must also have obligations to protect human rights and to allow for the full-realization of the human potential. Those employers who deny pregnant women working in garment factories reasonable hours or the right to pre-natal care are denying them their human right to enjoy the highest attainable standard of physical and mental

---

[48] See *Lingens v Austria* Judgment of the European Court of Human Rights, 8 July 1986, at para. 41.

[49] See J. Raz, *The Morality of Freedom* (Oxford: Clarendon Press, 1986); J. Maritain, *The Rights of Man and Natural Law* D. C. Anson (trans) (New York: Charles Scribner's Sons, 1943) at 9: 'It [the common good of society] involves, as its chief value, the highest possible attainment (that is the highest compatible with the good of the whole) of persons to their lives as persons, and to their freedom of expression or autonomy—on to the gift of goodness which in their turn flow from it'. And (at 44) 'the most fundamental aspiration of the person is the aspiration towards the *liberty of expansion and autonomy*'.

[50] J. Galtung defines violence as 'anything avoidable that impedes human self-realization' and interprets 'human self-realization' as satisfaction of human needs. See *Transarmament and the Cold War: Peace Research and the Peace Movement* (Copenhagen: Christian Ejlers, 1988) at 271.

health.[51] This right is enshrined in Article 12 of the International Covenant on Economic, Social and Cultural Rights. In addition, such women are being prevented from enjoying their rights under Articles 22 and 25 of the Universal Declarations of Human Rights.

Can this assertion be grounded in the same philosophical roots that inspired the philosophy of human rights? What are the limits of our duty to ensure the protection of the dignity of others, do we merely have a negative duty not to attack the dignity of others, or do we have positive duties that go beyond a simple non-interference principle? Does the practical imperative not to treat other people as ends extend to positive duties to enhance their dignity? Here Kant may have provided the answer in his early *Grounding for the Metaphysics of Morals*:

> . . . concerning meritorious duty to others, the natural end that all men have is their own happiness. Now humanity might indeed subsist if nobody contributed anything to the happiness of others, provided he did not intentionally impair their happiness. But this, after all, would harmonize only negatively and not positively with humanity as an end itself, if everyone does not also strive, as much as he can, to further the ends of others. For the ends of any subject who is an end in himself must as far as possible be my ends also, if that conception of an end in itself is to have its full effect in me.[52]

The Kantian reasoning provides us with some justification as to why human rights should be respected and why we all have duties to respect the rights of others. While this reasoning may be adopted by some moral philosophers, and may even be reflected in international texts, more work still remains to be done to relate the sense of obligation to the moral universe of different cultures and peoples. Some of the most controversial rifts arise in the context of attempts to diffuse the tension between duties to God and duties under such a dignity-based morality. Abou El Fadl, in a chapter entitled 'The Human Rights Commitment in Modern Islam' draws attention to the dangers of simplistic readings which assert that 'Islam presented a genuine and authentic expression of international human rights'.[53] He offers his own reasoning in the following format:

> God created human beings as individuals, and their liability in the Hereafter is individually determined as well. To commit oneself to safeguarding and protecting the well-being of the individual is to take God's creation seriously. Each individual embodies a virtual universe of divine miracles—in body, soul, and mind. Why should a Muslim commit himself/herself to the rights and well-being of a fellow human being? The answer is because God has already made such a commitment when God invested so much of the

---

[51] N. Klein, *No Logo* (London: Flamingo, 2001) at 222; Human Rights Watch, *No Guarantees: Sex Discrimination in Mexico's Maquiladora Sector* (1996), Human Rights Watch, *Mexico—A Job or Your Rights: Continued Sex Discrimination in Mexico's Maquiladora Sector* (1998b).

[52] *Grounding for the Metaphysics of Morals* (1785) J. W. Ellington (trans) (Indianapolis: Hacket Publishing, 1981) at 37.

[53] K. Abou El Fadl, 'The Human Rights Commitment in Modern Islam' in J. Runzo, N. M. Martin, and A. Sharma (eds) *Human Rights and Responsibilities* (Oxford: Oneworld Publications, 2003) 301–364, at 307.

God-self in each and every person. This is why the Qur'an asserts that whoever kills a fellow human being unjustly, it is as if he/she has murdered all of humanity—it is as if the killer has murdered the divine sanctity and defiled the very meaning of divinity . . .

The real issue is that as Muslims we have been charged with safeguarding the well-being and dignity of human beings, and we have also been charged with achieving justice.[54]

The invocation of humanity and dignity remind us that there may be multiple foundations for human rights beyond the Enlightenment and the European constitutional model. Modern universal human rights law cannot, and should not, derive the actual rights from eighteenth-century philosophical Europeans; it must be based on a participatory process, whereby different peoples and cultures continue to determine what these obligations are.[55] The processes by which this happens in international law are well known, and the development of human rights law through the United Nations is part of this process. But for some writers, such as An-Na'im, 'human rights need to be "owned" by different peoples around the world, instead of being perceived as simply another facet of Western hegemony'.[56]

To achieve change from within religious and other communities, there needs to be protection for dissident voices and arguments. The foundation for protection of such pluralistic participation is often understood under the term democracy.

11.2 DEMOCRACY

Looking at the ways democracy is referred to helps to reveal why human rights mechanisms enjoy the support they do. Democracy has started to achieve a new sort of resonance in international relations. Not only is it used as a quality which is considered essential for ensuring the accountability of transnational corporations,[57] the legitimacy of international organizations, such as the United Nations and the European Union, democracy also promotes dignity, by highlighting that individuals not only need to be treated with respect, but also ought to be able to participate in decision-making in an environment that allows for a full and frank discussion of ideas and demands. This environment is not limited to national

---

[54] *Human Rights and Responsibilities*, at 338–389.

[55] J. Tully, 'The Kantian Idea of Europe: Critical and Cosmopolitan Perspectives' in A. Padgen (ed) *The Idea of Europe: From Antiquity to the European Union* (Cambridge: Cambridge University Press, 2002) 331–358.

[56] A. A. An-Na'im, 'The Synergy and Interdependence of Human Rights, Religion, and Secularism' in Runzo, Martin, and Sharma (2003) 27–49, at 40.

[57] See Judith Richter 'If democratic—that is people centred and participatory—policy-making is brought to the centre of considerations, then democratic control over transnational corporations becomes more feasible to consider and explore, and the political debate can become refocused from one of corporate responsibility towards one of corporate public accountability.' *Holding Corporations Accountable: Corporate Conduct, International Codes, and Citizen Action* (London: Zed Books, 2001) at 210.

borders, as appeals for democratization are extended to the international system as well. According to Boutros Boutros-Ghali, 'just like democratization within States, democratization at the international level is based on and aims to promote the dignity and worth of the individual being and the fundamental equality of all person and all peoples.'[58]

Susan Marks, in her book-length treatment of competing conceptions of 'democracy' in international legal argument, distinguishes the evocative conception of 'low intensity democracy' from the democratic principle of 'rule by the people on a footing of equality'.[59] Instead of focusing on minimalist democracy, whereby periodic elections determine who is to govern, she highlights a wider vision variously labelled: popular democracy, participatory democracy, strong democracy, discursive democracy, deliberative democracy, and communicative democracy. Marks highlights a number of points arising from this distinction:

> In the first place, democracy cannot be conceived purely as an 'institutional arrangement', organizational form or checklist of procedures. Rather, it must be understood as an ongoing process of enhancing the possibilities for self-rule and the prospects for political equality, against a background of changing historical circumstances. Nor, secondly, can democracy be grasped simply as a 'method of government.' While modern democracy is incompatible with forms of political organization developed for small city-states, the institutions of representative government can and must coexist with expanded opportunities for involvement by ordinary citizens in public affairs. The Rousseauian notion of democracy as a form of society retains pertinence, if not for the reasons of self-realization that he had in mind, then at least on the prudential ground that active citizenship is necessary to ensure that those who rule do so in the interests of all and not just in their own interests. Thirdly, political legitimacy cannot be approached as a matter of episodic procedure. The fact that parliaments are subject to periodic popular recall is not, of itself, sufficient to justify public power. Democracy demands that state authority be required to justify itself to the citizenry on a continuing basis. To enable this, a democratic polity must include a vigorous 'public sphere', that is to say, an arena distinct from the institutions of the state in which citizens can come together to define collective goals, shape public policies and evaluate governmental activity. Fourthly, political equality must be seen to require more than the constitutional guarantee of civil rights. Universal suffrage has not put an end to inequalities in the capacity of citizens to exercise and influence state power, because that capacity is affected by disparities in society. Subordinate socio-economic status tends to reinforce, and be reinforced by, political marginalization. Efforts to ensure political and civil rights must therefore go hand in hand with moves to secure respect for social, economic, and cultural rights. Finally the homogeneity of the democratic 'people' cannot be assumed. Since the social disparities which affect participation in public processes are systematically correlated (*inter alia*) to divisions of gender, ethnicity, and other group affiliation, political equality

---

[58] *An Agenda for Democratization* (New York: United Nations, 1996) UN Doc. DPI/1867, at para. 66.
[59] S. Marks, *The Riddle of All Constitutions: International Law, Democracy, and a Critique of Ideology* (Oxford: Oxford University Press, 2000) at 58.

must not be understood in terms of (a particular) identity. Rather, it must be approached in terms of the need to ensure that differences among citizens do not operate as disadvantages. Democracy must be conceived as requiring that all citizens have the chance to participate in decision-making which affects them all.[60]

The value of relying on participatory democracy as a way of understanding the human rights obligations of non-state actors is that it demonstrates that democracy needs a public space or public sphere in which to develop. The protection of this public sphere has nothing to do with protecting existing state institutions. This public space fills the gap between what happens in the official organs of the state and the intimate thoughts of the individual. As soon as we, as individuals, seek to influence how decisions are taken which affect us, we find ourselves in this public space, which needs to be kept as participatory and open as possible, if we are to enjoy progress towards greater democracy.

11.2.1   The Democracy Paradox

Sprigman and Osborne, writing in the context of the South African Constitution, posit a hypothetical case of a black South African man who applies to join a political party that advocates white supremacy and is limited to whites. They suggest that both parties to the eventual dispute before the courts will invoke fundamental rights. On the one hand, the black applicant will invoke equality, while on the other hand, the white party chief will invoke freedom of association. They suggest that the text of the Constitution offers no hint as to how to rank these rights: 'On the contrary, the enterprise of ranking rights requires a political choice, and political choice in a democracy is the terrain of legislatures, not courts.'[61] For them, one's choices become not only limited, but risk being limited on the say-so of the judges: 'If the equality right applies directly to private relationships, my irrational and capricious decision to leave property to one relative and not another, to bar my door to Jehovah's Witnesses, or . . . to refuse to invite women to my bridge club, is rendered potentially justiciable.'[62]

These examples could be countered with the arguments developed in Chapter 1 with regard to the 'trivialization argument', but they are not really the core of

---

[60]   *The Riddle of All Constitutions: International Law, Democracy, and a Critique of Ideology*, at 59–60.

[61]   C. Sprigman and M. Osborne, 'Du Plessis is *not* Dead: South Africa's 1996 Constitution and the Application of the Bill of Rights to Private Disputes' 15 *SAJHR* (1999) 25–51, at 43. Cf Halton Cheadle and Dennis Davis, who accept the starting point that the inclusion of the provisions on direct horizontal effect in the new Constitution appears 'to hand to an unelected elite the power to develop rules to govern the conduct of citizens—a power that in any conception of democracy is the preserve of the democratically elected legislature. It is then a provision, that on the face of it, at odds with the deepest commitments of our Constitution.' H. Cheadle and D. Davis, 'The Application of the 1996 Constitution in the Private Sphere '13 *SAJHR* (1997) 44–66, at 56. They go on to argue, however, that the sections in the Constitution (8(2) and (3)) allowing for horizontal effect 'do not disable the proper functioning of a democracy but are constitutive of it'.

[62]   Ibid, at 46.

Sprigman and Osborne's attack on the extension of human rights to the private sphere. The key issue is again democratic legitimacy. Sprigman and Osborne's objection is based on their 'conviction that the kind of *ad hoc* value choices involving the balancing of autonomy against equality that lie at the heart of private discrimination, are appropriately allocated in the first instance to the legislature'.[63] Once the issue has been determined by the legislature, they would have no quarrel with the courts reviewing the Act of Parliament to see whether the legislature struck the right balance. This critique has some merit, but it is still hard to see why the weighing of values becomes more acceptable when the case involves legislation or the acts of public officials. In the end, as we shall see below in the context of corporal punishment, in reviewing official acts the judges may still be faced with both sides claiming the need to protect fundamental rights, and these claims may indeed each be founded on the importance of the value of human dignity. Such dignity claims seem as difficult to rank in the public sphere as in the private sphere.

Gavin Anderson has argued that adjudicating rights disputes involves inevitable 'boundary maintenance' between the public and private spheres, and that when this is carried out by the courts, such adjudication is really only a concealed exercise in protecting existing property rights:

> If we take first the question of the legitimate bounds of the courts' role in testing legislation against human rights norms, we could ask why it is that, when courts are enforcing private values against public bodies they have been regarded as engaged in legitimate activity. This essentially rests on the idea that courts are engaged in matters of law and not high politics; for example, that human rights represent neutral principles through the application of which courts can allow individuals to pursue their own conception of the good life free from unnecessary interference. This neutrality is, of course, a myth: the process of protecting existing distributions of property entitlements which courts are engaged in when they enforce private rights rests on assumptions that existing distributions of wealth and power form a natural starting point for human rights discourse which are as controversial as when a legislature might decide to pursue redistributive policies. To the extent that the power of review can be justified, it relies on these assumptions remaining hidden, and the fact that this has been successfully achieved for so long is testimony to the triumph of the rhetoric of rights. Can this fiction be sustained when courts may be called on to apply public values in the private sphere?[64]

Anderson considers that the 'enforcement of private values is what comes "naturally" to courts adjudicating human rights claims'.[65] And he sees a significant legitimacy problem:

> The difficulty is, however, that in order for the courts to achieve any meaningful intervention to limit private power, they need to abandon the familiar legal language of

[63] Ibid, at 46.

[64] Anderson (1997: 129–130); see also L. M. Seidman, 'Public Principle and Private Choice: The Uneasy Case for a Boundary Maintenance Theory of Constitutional Law' 96 *YLJ* (1987) 1006–1059.   [65] Ibid, at 131.

property rights and concepts of formal equality . . . the rub is that as soon as the courts discard the legal language of private rights, the law/politics distinction starts to disintegrate . . . Lifting the veil from the law/politics distinction destroys the (perceived) legitimacy courts have under the classical liberal account; we now have no compelling reason to privilege the courts' view of these issues.[66]

This is a sophisticated critique. But one could venture two responses. First, it is true that the rhetoric of rights has been used to entrench property entitlements and the existing distribution of wealth. But modern international human rights law cannot be so easily assimilated to property/wealth entitlements under national law. When the Duke of Westminster sought to use the European Convention on Human Rights to challenge the transfer of ownership (freeholds) of residential property in London to his tenants, the European Court of Human Rights found that international human rights law allowed the legislature to privilege the moral entitlements of long-term tenants over the Duke's private law possessions. The human right to the enjoyment of possessions under the European Convention was limited by the legitimate deprivation of these possessions by the government 'in the public interest'.[67] The Court held that 'Parliament's belief in the existence of a social injustice was not such as could be characterized as manifestly unreasonable.'[68] The Strasbourg Court held that the national legislature was to enjoy a wide margin of appreciation in interpreting social and economic policies. Even the level of compensation required by the Convention is flexible where the government is pursuing social justice; human rights law does not require compensation at full market value.[69] The question of whether a human rights approach would simply entrench existing inequalities and injustices was also at the heart of the discussion of the new South African Constitution. The solution in the South African Constitution includes a generous provision for legitimate interference with private property rights in the public interest.[70] The conservative effect of the judicial protection of property rights in the past should not automatically lead us to reject the progressive possibilities of using human rights law in the future.

But there is a second sting in Anderson's critique. How does one justify an extension of the power of the judges from the scrutiny of governmental action for conformity with human rights standards into the boundless sphere of private relations? If we reject the sacrosanct nature of private property rights and put our faith in

---

[66] Anderson, *YLJ*, at 130.　　　　[67] See Art. 1 of Protocol 1 to the ECHR.

[68] *James and ors* Judgment of 21 February 1986, at para. 49.

[69] 'Article 1 does not, however, guarantee a right to full compensation in all circumstances. Legitimate objectives of "public interest", such as pursued in measures of economic reform or measures designed to achieve greater social justice, may call for less than reimbursement of the full market value. Furthermore, the Court's power of review is limited to ascertaining whether the choice of compensation terms falls outside the State's wide margin of appreciation in this domain.' Ibid, at para. 54.

[70] See s 25(3), which states that the amount of compensation to be paid for any expropriated property is to be determined with regard to all the relevant circumstances, including 'the history of the acquisition and use of the property' Section 25(4)(a) states: 'For the purposes of this section . . . the public interest includes the nation's commitment to land reforms to bring about equitable access to all South Africa's natural resources.'

values such as human dignity, are we leaving law and asking judges to be our moral guides? The answer calls for a radical admission that judges are already guided by values and morality. By asking them to apply the same morality in the private sphere that they apply to state actors we are only asking for non-discrimination with regard to the victims and perpetrators. If we accept that the protection of dignity is worth fighting for, then why not apply it in all spheres? This is certainly the modern approach to human rights law, and again is reflected in new settlements such as the South African Constitution, which states in section 12(1): 'Everyone has the right to freedom and security of the person, which includes the right—
. . . (c) to be free from all forms of violence from either public or private sources.'[71]

If we accept that judges form part of the machinery to protect human dignity, it seems unrealistic to suggest that the democratic legitimacy of the legislature should foreclose appeal to legal protection through the courts. Of course at the theoretical level it is hard to make a case for giving judges the power to annul provisions contained in legislation—but this is not necessarily what the application of human rights law through the courts requires.[72] As we saw in Chapter 10 above, judicial application of human rights law is more likely to be an interpretative exercise than a usurpation of legislative prerogative.

* * *

This examination of contemporary applications of the values of dignity and democracy points to their evolving nature and new considerations which demand that human beings can enjoy dignity and democracy even where the threats to these values come from non-state actors. I have suggested that careful consideration of the value of dignity as a foundation of human rights requires us to prevent and punish assaults on dignity whether they are perpetrated by state or by non-state actors. If human rights law is founded on the importance of the protection of human dignity, then human rights law must cover this wider approach. I have also suggested that in human rights law, taking democracy seriously demands the fullest protection for freedom of expression, association, assembly, and participation in all levels of decision-making which might affect us. In order to ensure this conception of democracy, human rights law has to ensure that a public space is protected from unnecessary restrictions imposed by state and non-state actors. Of course, the metaphor of space should be understood to include cyberspace.[73]

---

[71] See also s 1: 'The Republic of South Africa is one, sovereign, democratic state founded on the following values: (a) Human dignity, the achievement of equality and the advancement of human rights and freedoms', see also ss 7(1) and 10: 'Everyone has inherent dignity and the right to have their dignity respected and protected.' And s 8(2) which states that the Bill of Rights binds natural and juristic persons. This is discussed in detail in Ch 10, at 10.1.2 above.

[72] The exact arrangements with regard to the UK were dealt with in Ch 10 above. For a general discussion regarding the legitimacy of judicial review, see L. Favoreu and J. A. Jolowicz (eds) *Contrôle juridictionnel des lois* (Paris: Economica, 1986), See also L. Tribe 'The Futile Search for Legitimacy' in *Constitutional Choices* (Cambridge, Mass: Harvard University Press, 1985) Ch 1, esp. at 6–7.

[73] See C. R. Sunstein, *Designing Democracy: What Constitutions Do* (Oxford: Oxford University Press, 2001) at 21, who deals with the 'preconditions for maintaining a republic. We have seen that

Several cases discussed in Chapter 10 contained a recurring clash, between an individual's right to privacy to be protected as part of the obligation to respect personal dignity, and the private media's appeal to the importance of freedom of expression in a democratic society. These cases suggest that a careful assessment of the facts will illustrate which value is most under threat. Where privacy concerns publicity about a medical condition and freedom of expression concerns newspaper sales, the balance came down on the side of the protection of human dignity.

In other constitutional contexts the clash may be presented, not so much as dignity versus democracy, but rather as autonomy versus participation. Personal autonomy may be presented as a right to choose the trade union of one's choice and to have one's ideas respected within the union.[74] Participation may even be presented as the overriding value suggesting a right to be admitted to an association and determine its policies.[75] According to Andrew Butler, in the context of labour relations, the extension of human rights into the private sphere has meant that the Irish courts have ruled that 'a trade union cannot seek to deny a person's right to disassociate, nor can it conduct its internal affairs in a manner which violates the dictates of fair procedures. The presence of a governmental action threshold test would have prevented the courts from considering these cases, and would have allowed private power to be used in a way abusive of the rights of other citizens.'[76] The concern is, however, that courts might not always recognize that an association should be free to define its membership and arrange its own rules for decision-making and representation. At that point, even though the associations may be set up to protect personal autonomy and participation, these same values are used to undermine those associations.

In sum, the values of dignity and democracy, or autonomy and participation, can be called on to defend and limit most human rights. Once we admit that we are weighting appeals to the same value from both sides we can fashion a jurisprudence that is more transparent about the choices being made.

---

the essential factor is a well-functioning system of free expression . . . To be sure, such a system depends on restraints on official censorship of controversial ideas and opinions. But it also depends on more than that. It also depends on some kind of public domain, in which a wide range of speakers have access to a diverse public—and also to particular institutions and practices, against which they wish to launch objections. Above all, a republic, or at least a heterogeneous one, depends on arenas in which citizens with varying experiences and prospects, and different views about what is good and right, are able to meet with one another, and to consult.' His concern is with the prospect of so many technological possibilities for discussion and opinion that people may be tempted to filter out what they do not want to confront. 'But to the extent that new technologies increase people's ability to wall themselves off from topics and opinions they would prefer to avoid, they also create serious dangers.' At 202.

[74] See A. S. Butler, 'Constitutional Rights in Private Litigation: A Critique and Comparative Analysis' 22 *Anglo-American Law Review* (1993) 1–41, at 28–30, discussing *Rodgers v ITGWU* [1978] ILRM 51.

[75] See, in particular, the discussion by Butler (1993: 31–32) discussing the Irish cases *Tierney v Amalgamated Society of Woodworkers* [1959] IR 254 and *Murphy v Stewart* [1973] IR 97.

[76] Ibid, at 31.

11.3   AN EXAMPLE: FREEDOM OF RELIGION AND CORPORAL PUNISHMENT IN PRIVATE SCHOOLS

To illustrate this point let us consider a case from the South African Constitutional Court. In *Christian Education South Africa v Minister of Education*, a law prohibiting corporal punishment in schools was challenged as violating the rights of parents of children in private schools.[77] The parents had consented to the use of corporal punishment in these schools and claimed that the law violated their rights to privacy; their freedom of religion, belief, and opinion; their right to establish independent educational institutions; their right to use their language and participate in the cultural life of their choice; and their right to enjoy their culture and practice their religion. The Minister contended that corporal punishment infringed constitutional rights, in that the parents' claim was inconsistent with the following constitutional rights: the right to equality; the right to have one's inherent dignity respected and protected; freedom and security of the person; and the rights of the child to be protected from maltreatment, neglect, abuse, or degradation.

For Sachs J, the balancing exercise took the following form: 'the proportionality exercise has to relate to whether the failure to accommodate the appellant's religious belief and practice by means of the exemption for which the appellant asked, can be accepted as reasonable and justifiable in an open and democratic society based on human dignity, freedom and equality'.[78] Sachs J offered insights into the judicial method, pointing out that, in the area of religious freedom, 'balancing becomes doubly difficult'.[79] This is 'first because of the problems of weighing considerations of faith against those of reason, and secondly because of the problems of separating out what aspects of an activity are religious and protected by the Bill of Rights and what are secular and open to regulation in the ordinary way'. He eschewed a simple labelling of practices as religious or secular as they are often 'simultaneously both'.[80] And he avoided recourse to a division between public and private because, again, both notions are in play. He found that the Constitution contemplated the importance of the right to freedom of religion in an 'open and democratic society', and he also found that the right to act according to one's beliefs 'is one of the key ingredients of any persons' dignity'.[81] In fact, he continued: 'Religious belief has the capacity to awake concepts of self-worth and human dignity which form the cornerstone of human rights.'[82]

So we have appeals to both democracy and dignity as the fundamental foundational values underpinning the right in question, the right to religion. The ban on corporal punishment did not deprive parents of their 'general right and capacity to bring up their children according to their Christian beliefs'.[83] The issue was

---

[77] Case CCT4/00, Judgment of 18 August 2000, [2000] (4) SA 757 (CC); [2000] (10) BCLR 1051(CC).   [78] Ibid, at para. 32.
[79] Ibid, at para. 34.   [80] Ibid, at para. 35.   [81] Ibid, at para. 36.
[82] Ibid, at para. 36.   [83] Ibid. at para. 38.

whether the ban on corporal punishment was an unjustifiable limitation on that right. What values were said to underlie the counter-argument of the state with regard to its rule banning corporal punishment in religious independent schools (one could call them non-state actors)? The Minister contended that 'the core value of human dignity in our Bill of Rights did not countenance the use of physical force to achieve scholarly correction'.[84] This was of course met with the argument that 'for believers, including the children involved, the *indignity* and degradation lay not in the punishment, but in the defiance of the scriptures represented by leaving the misdeeds unpunished; subjectively, for those who shared the religious outlook of the community, no *indignity* at all was involved'.[85]

For one side the rule is essential to protect human dignity—for the other side the rule itself led to indignity. Similarly, as we saw above, democracy can be invoked to support both sides of the argument. Democracy demands protection for minority beliefs, and democracy demands that in principle the will of the legislature is applied to all and is not subverted by the judges. Recourse to democracy theory, or some foundational theory based on dignity, was in the end not determinative for the judge. Context counted. Three contextual points deserve mention at this point.

First, the judgments from the South African and Namibian courts had already come down against the use of corporal punishment in general, based on international human rights law focused on the protection of human dignity. Second, the 1996 Constitution specifically set out that 'Everyone has the right to freedom and security of the person, which includes the right . . . to be free from all forms of violence from either public or private sources'.[86] This right reinforces the obligations on states to ensure respect for human rights in the private sphere and finds a mirror in international human rights law.[87] Third, South Africa's past was crucial to understanding Parliament's wish:

> . . . to make a radical break with an authoritarian past. As part of its pedagogical mission, the Department sought to introduce new principles of learning in terms of which problems were solved through reason rather than force . . . The ban was part of a comprehensive process of eliminating state-sanctioned use of physical force as a method of punishment. The outlawing of physical punishment in the school accordingly represented more than a pragmatic attempt to deal with disciplinary problems in a new way. It had a principled and symbolic function, manifestly intended to promote respect for the dignity and physical and emotional integrity of all children.[88]

Against this background, the Constitutional Court determined that the scales came down in favour of the generality of the law, rather than the claimed religious exception. In the end, the parents were not really being asked to choose between 'obeying the law of the land or following their conscience'.[89]

---

[84] Case CCT 4/00 Judgment of 18 August 2000, at para. 43.   [85] Ibid, at para. 43 (emphasis added).

[86] Section 12(c).   [87] See Ch 8 above.   [88] Ibid, at para. 50.   [89] Ibid, at para. 51.

In the wake of this case, the House of Lords found themselves faced with a similar claim under the Human Rights Act 1998. The case was brought by head teachers, teachers, and parents of children at four independent schools and was based on the claim that there had been a violation of the right to freedom of religion as protected under Article 9 of the European Convention on Human Rights.[90] For these teachers and parents, 'part of the duty of education in the Christian context is that teachers should be able to stand in the place of parents and administer physical punishment to children who are guilty of indiscipline'.[91] The aim of such discipline is 'to help form godly character'.[92]

The opinion of Lord Nicholls circumscribed the right in question with the implicit precondition of protection of human dignity:

> . . . a belief must satisfy some modest, objective minimum requirements. These threshold requirements are implicit in article 9 of the European Convention and comparable guarantees in other human rights instruments. The belief must be consistent with basic standards of human dignity or integrity. Manifestation of a religious belief, for instance, which involved subjecting others to torture or inhuman punishment would not qualify for protection.[93]

Having found that 'smacking' did not necessarily take the belief outside the protection offered by Article 9, he went on to find that the prohibition on corporal punishment was a matter of social policy, where Parliament was entitled to lead public opinion, and that the restrictions were prescribed by law and necessary in a democratic society for the protection of the rights of others. Baronness Hale focused on the international human rights obligations more generally, including Article 28(2) of the Convention on the Rights of the Child, which demands that states 'take all appropriate measures to ensure that school discipline is administered in a manner consistent with the child's human dignity'. She also highlighted the positive obligations of the state under Articles 3 and 8 of the European Convention, but concluded that these obligations did not necessarily cover the punishment at issue. The Convention on the Rights of the Child set out a broader sphere of protection.[94]

These two cases illustrate the centrality of human dignity to the judicial approach to weighing human rights. Dignity was at issue for both parents and children. The governments were charged with protecting dignity, but the question for the courts in both cases boiled down to whether the legislature got the balance right. To return to Brownsword's categories, we can see that the common conception of *dignity as empowerment for autonomy*, has been overtaken by the second conception of *dignity as constraint*. It is suggested that, in both jurisdictions, the relevant judges felt comfortable favouring dignity as constraint, as the constraints in each case had been fully debated by the democratically elected legislature.

---

[90] *R v Secretary of State for Education and Employment et al, ex p Williamson et al* [2005] UKHL 15.
[91] Ibid, at para 9.   [92] Ibid, at para. 9.
[93] Ibid, at para. 23. See also Lord Walker, at para. 64.
[94] Ibid, at para. 86.

Although both cases were brought against the state rather than against a
non-state actor, the issue was essentially the human rights of children versus the
human rights of parents. Thinking about the different conceptions of dignity in
play may bring us closer to understanding how to apply human rights obligations
to non-state actors. What has emerged throughout this study is that, whatever
conception of dignity is invoked, the judicial enforcement of human rights is
never very far away from questions concerning the democratic legitimacy of such
a process.

11.4   SUMMARY REGARDING DIGNITY AND DEMOCRACY

I have suggested that recourse to the concepts of dignity and democracy in the
context of human rights claims against non-state actors should take into consideration various paradoxes. Positing dignity as the supreme value may simply invite
both sides to frame their case in terms of indignities suffered. How then to protect
one's dignity at the expense of another's dignity? We witnessed an approach which
acknowledged that, although dignity may be relevant to claims relating to
parental religious convictions over corporal punishment, to limit the right was not
necessarily to extinguish it. On the other hand, arguments over the dignity of the
child fell to be understood as legitimate constraints on others' actions. I suggested
that judicial conviction in the *dignity as constraint* approach was marked where the
constraints had been democratically adopted after proper deliberation.[95]

With regard to democracy, we saw that some of those most antagonistic to the
judicial enforcement of human rights obligations against non-state actors were
concerned with the anti-majoritarian aspects of such a development through the
delegation of crucial decisions to unelected judges. The paradox is that a democracy respecting human rights requires the fullest possible circulation of ideas, yet
respecting human rights also demands a degree of protection of privacy and private property to the exclusion of those wanting to contribute to democratic
debate. With the privatization of public space seemingly comes increased protection of rights for some, and diminished opportunities to exercise their rights for
others.

As with dignity, we can see democracy as simultaneously empowering and as a
legitimate form of constraint. In some circumstances, the protection of democracy will demand constraints on individuals' human rights in order to ensure that
the fullest possible deliberation takes place. Those in power may often be least
interested in ensuring that such a debate takes place and may baulk at the idea of
legislating such constraints. Therefore we have to trust the judges to juggle
commitments to dignity and democracy in the context of individual complaints.

---

[95] On the concept of deliberative democracy, see Sunstein (2001).

Where the legislature has failed to address the best way to properly protect either dignity or democracy from assaults by private actors, human rights law may demand judicial intervention. Judges will usually be careful not to cause a constitutional crisis by usurping the legislature. Judges can, as we have seen, usually find interpretative devices to ensure that the enjoyment of human rights is protected from the actions of non-state actors. The democratic challenge posed by the judicial application of human rights law to the private sphere may be more apparent than real.

12

Complexity, Complicity, and Complementarity

Rather than write a set of conclusions, it seems appropriate to regroup some of the suggestions developed in this book around three recurring concepts: complexity, complicity, and complementarity.[1]

12.1 COMPLEXITY

In sum, the development of the human rights obligations of non-state actors is complex due to at least three factors: first is the rather unspecified and evolving nature of the obligations as they are adapted from the traditional realm of state obligations to obligations for non-state actors. Second, although international law binds states and non-state actors, the obligations vary in scope according to the context. Third, the complexity of modern life means that we have to try to disentangle complex networks and the influence and support that different actors lend each other before we can respond to enforce human rights obligations. Let us look at each of these factors in turn.

First, the notion of individuals having concrete duties under international law as opposed to national law was clearly enunciated, really for the first time, in the Nuremberg judgment delivered by the International Military Tribunal (IMT). Until the Nuremberg trials, war crimes trials had been held at the national level under national military law. The international laws of war, such as the Hague Convention of 1907, prohibited certain methods of waging war. But, in the words of the judgment: 'yet the Hague Convention nowhere designates such practices as criminal, nor is any sentence prescribed, nor any mention made of a court to try and punish offenders'.[2]

---

[1] This chapter builds on previous attempts to organize some thoughts around these concepts, see, e.g. A. Clapham, 'Issues of complexity, complicity and complementarity: from the Nuremberg trials to the dawn of the new International Criminal Court' in P. Sands (ed) *From Nuremberg to The Hague: The Future of International Criminal Justice* (Cambridge: Cambridge University Press, 2003) 30–67.

[2] *Trial of German Major War Criminals (Goering et al)*, International Military Tribunal (Nuremberg) Judgment and Sentence 30 September and 1 October 1946, (London: HMSO) Cmd. 6964, at 40.

Despite the lack of clear duties for individuals or other non-state actors, the Tribunal determined that:

> The law of war is to be found not only in treaties, but in the customs and practices of states which gradually obtained universal recognition, and from general principles of justice applied by jurists, and practised by military courts. This law is not static, but by continual adaptation follows the needs of a changing world. Indeed, in many cases treaties do no more than express and define for more accurate reference the principles of law already existing.[3]

This marked the beginning of a new way of thinking about international law as going beyond obligations on states and attaching duties to individuals involving criminal responsibility. As we have seen, human rights law then developed the prohibitions on genocide, crimes against humanity, disappearances, and torture, to generate crimes outside the context of armed conflict. The result is *complex*, for a lawyer, because the law develops from being addressed to one set of duty-holders to another, both of which have simultaneous duties under the international law in question. Moreover, the same act can give rise to multiple responsibilities. We have, first, the responsibility of the state under international law for the violation of its international obligations under a treaty or customary law obligation, and then second, we simultaneously have, *inter alia*, the responsibility of the individual. But to really understand the scope of the obligations in question, we have to consider the context. Some non-state actors will have greater responsibilities, depending on their role and power.[4]

In the context of international crimes committed in Rwanda it was enough to have been the mayor of a village and to have encouraged rapes by one's presence,[5] or the director of the tea plantation and allow trucks to be used to hunt down and exterminate civilians. In this last situation, the International Criminal Tribunal for Rwanda found Mr Musema criminally responsible under international law for genocide and crimes against humanity. He was given a life sentence. Aggravating circumstances which were raised at the sentencing stage included the fact that he took no steps to prevent the participation of the tea factory employees or the use of its vehicles in the attacks.[6]

As we saw throughout the study, human rights obligations come in many different packages. At the simplest level, they arise as treaty obligations for states. But we encountered customary international obligations which arise for states, and inter-governmental organizations as well as other non-state actors. International criminal law was found to bind private individuals. National law clearly applied human rights obligations to non-state actors and we encountered non-traditional

---

[3] *Trial of German Major War Criminals (Goering et al)*, at 40.

[4] Just as some states will be expected to do more under human rights treaties depending on their available resources and what can be reasonably expected in the circumstances.

[5] *Akayesu* Case ICTR–96–4–T, Judgment of 2 September 1998.

[6] *Alfred Musema* Case ICTR–96–13–T, Judgment of 27 January 2000.

methods for holding non-state actors accountable through 'deeds of commitment', agreements subject to arbitration, and the establishment of mechanisms to monitor compliance by corporations with the OECD Guidelines.

Even when we focus on an inter-governmental organization, corporation, or *de facto* government as the bearer of human rights obligations, we are faced with the myriad of connections that obscure the relationship between the non-state actor and the actual human rights victim. The sub-contracting of services, the support and bribes offered to rebel forces, and the harbouring of terrorists all pose complicated questions of attribution and responsibility. This complexity has generated demands to 'lift the lid' and 'pierce the veil' to highlight the responsibilities of those who assist others to commit human rights violations. Part of the response to this complicated situation has been to develop legal responsibility through charges of complicity— and it is worth recalling that the etymology of complicity can be traced to the Latin word *complicare*, and, as noted in the *Oxford English Dictionary*, the second listed meaning for complicity is: 'state of being complex'.

12.2   COMPLICITY

The concept of complicity is familiar in both national and international criminal law.[7] We saw in Chapter 6 above that the concept has been developed in the context of corporate responsibility to cover, not only situations where the corporation knowingly assists in an illegal act, but also where it benefits from the abuses committed by others. Corporate complicity has become the kernel of attempts to hold corporations accountable for human rights abuses. The concept of complicity allows human rights groups to invoke the familiar international human rights law framework for states, and then go on to show how corporate activity, which contributes to such state behaviour, amounts to complicity in a state's violations of international law. Complicity is the concept which helps lawyers and human rights organizations to fuse the state/non-state actor divide and apply international human rights law to non-state actor corporations. We might also note here that complicity has been relied on by commentators to link the Taliban with Al Qaeda in order to justify military action in Afghanistan.[8] Moreover, focusing on the accomplices has been central to international prosecutions concerning Rwanda and the former Yugoslavia.[9] Finally, with regard to

[7] See, e.g. E. van Sliedregt, *The Criminal Responsibility of Individuals for Violations of International Humanitarian Law* (The Hague: TMC Asser Press, 2003) at 41–114, esp. 87–94.

[8] R. Wolfrum and C. E. Philipp, 'The Status of the Taliban: Their Obligations and Rights under International Law' 6 *Max Planck Yearbook of United Nations Law* (2002) 559–601, esp. at 595–601. See further Ch 7, at 7.4. above

[9] C. Eboe-Osuji, ' "Complicity in Genocide" versus "Aiding and Abetting Genocide" ' 3 *Journal of International Criminal Justice* (2005) 56–81; see also W. Schabas, 'Enforcing international humanitarian law: Catching the accomplices' 83 *Review of the International Committee of the Red Cross* (2001) 439–459.

suicide-bombing, it is self-evident that catching the accomplices may be one of the only tools in the legal toolbox. But the notion of complicity takes on a life of its own beyond legal argumentation.

The point is that when different actors label certain activity 'complicity', they deliberately evoke conceptions of criminality and blameworthiness even if, strictly speaking, the activity would not give rise to criminal liability in a court of law.

The concept of complicity is at the heart of contemporary questions of morality and ethics. As political and economic life becomes more diffuse with decisions being taken at various degrees of proximity to us, we may wonder how complicit we are in wrongdoing through our action or inaction. In a book entitled *Complicity*, Christopher Kutz introduces his subject in the following way: [10]

> Try as we might to live well, we find ourselves connected to harms and wrongs, albeit by relations that fall outside the paradigm of individual, intentional wrongdoing. Here are some examples: buying a table made of tropical wood that comes from a defoliated rainforest, or owning stock in a company that does business in a country that jails political dissenters; being a citizen of a nation that bombs another country's factories in a reckless attack on terrorists, or inhabiting a region seized long ago from its aboriginal occupants; helping to design an automobile the manufacturer knowingly sells with a dangerously defective fuel system, or administering a national health care bureaucracy that carelessly allows the distribution of HIV-contaminated blood.

For Kutz, these examples fall in a moral grey zone: 'Although in each of these cases we stand outside the shadow of evil, we still do not find the full light of the good.'[11] His modern look at the legal and moral dimensions of complicity forces us to consider our expanding notions of community, as our actions often have effects far beyond our immediate surroundings, and affect people to whom we may now have an increasing sense of responsibility. In Kutz's words: 'The hidden promise of complicity is the conception of community upon which it draws'.[12]

Of course, complicity in war crimes or genocide has been given a specific legal meaning in particular trials,[13] and we examined how this might be applied to corporations under the Alien Tort Claims Act in Chapter 6. But thinking about complicity more generally does force all of us to consider how our actions affect the lives of others around the world. The increasing reliance on complicity as a central concept in human rights complaints reflects, in my view, an increased sense of solidarity with the victims of human rights abuses in other countries. It reflects a sense that the complainer recognizes that there are now increased responsibilities which stretch across borders and that the bearers of those responsibilities are not simply a rarefied group of temporary leaders. The responsibility extends to all of us.

---

[10] C. Kutz, *Complicity: Ethics and Law for a Collective Age* (Cambridge: Cambridge University Press, 2000) at 1.   [11] Ibid, at 1.
[12] Ibid, at 259.   [13] Eboe-Osuji (2005).

12.3   COMPLEMENTARITY

When Niels Bohr, the Danish theoretical physicist, announced the complementarity principle in the 1920s, he was explaining that, in order to have complete knowledge of a phenomenon at the atomic level, one needs a description of both the wave and the particle properties of phenomena such as light and electrons. As suggested in Chapter 1, scientists were confused by the fact that they viewed the phenomenon under examination either as waves or as particles depending on the experimental equipment used. The complementarity concept reminds us that the observation of an event depends on both the observer and the viewing apparatus. We coined this the 'jurisdictional filter' in Chapter 1.

Complementarity allows us also to see things differently in three contexts. First, an entity can be regarded as public and private at the same time. An entity such as the BBC may be non-governmental for the purposes of bringing a complaint before the European Court of Human Rights, and yet be performing a public function so that it can be a defendant in a claim brought against it under the Human Rights Act 1998. An entity such as Amtrak in the United States can be a governmental entity for the purposes of determining the rights of citizens under the Bill of Rights in the US Constitution, but still not be an agency of the US Government for the purposes of sovereign immunity from suit and with regard to inherent governmental powers.

Second, complementarity allows us to see the multiplicity of actors involved in a human rights infringement. The act may give rise to responsibility for a state, an individual, and an organization. The jurisdictional filter of an international or national court may blinker us from seeing the multiple overlapping layers of responsibility. A single act of genocide could give rise to individual criminal responsibility under customary international law. The act may also be attributable to an organization. In addition, where the act is attributable to a state, there may be state responsibility under both customary international law and the Genocide Convention of 1948. State responsibility may arise because the behaviour of a state official is attributable to the state in question, or it could be that the state is accused of failing through omission to fulfil its positive obligations to protect someone within its jurisdiction, or to prosecute the alleged perpetrator. In short, international law provides that a single event can generate multiple violations. Detecting state responsibility or individual criminal responsibility does not foreclose the possibility that there have also been violations of international law by other entities. It is even conceivable the acts generate simultaneous criminal and civil violations of international law.[14]

---

[14] See Arts 57 and 58 of the ILC Articles on state responsibility annexed to GA Res. A/Res/56/83, adopted 12 December 2001. Art. 57: 'These articles are without prejudice to any question of the responsibility under international law of an international organization, or of any State for the conduct of an international organization'. Art.58: 'These articles are without prejudice to any question of

Third, the act could give rise to multiple breaches of national law, international human rights law, international humanitarian law, and international criminal law. Additionally, the actions could give rise to simultaneous breaches of a non-binding instrument such as the OECD Guidelines for Multinational Enterprises. The fact that one is in breach of a 'voluntary' set of Guidelines does not mean that one cannot also be simultaneously in breach of national law or even international criminal law. The trade unions' approach to the Guidelines is at pains to stress that the Guidelines are 'not an alternative to effective regulation of companies, worker capital strategies or the negotiation of collective agreements, but they can be an important *complement*.' [15] While all of these breaches may be happening simultaneously, we only appreciate them according to the filter we are using to examine the human rights situation. As suggested earlier, the national court may be simultaneously applying human rights law against a private actor and ensuring that the state is complying with its international obligations. Which one you notice depends on how you look at it.

12.4   FINAL COMMENTS

In the twentieth century, innovative physicists adapted their vocabulary to explain new ways of thinking about the sub-atomic world, as the traditional Newtonian understanding of the laws of physics gave way to a more complete understanding of the atomic world. At their heart was the recognition that 'classical physics is just that idealization in which we can speak about parts of the world without any reference to ourselves'.[16] Complementarity was used in part by physicists like Niels Bohr to explain the importance of how observation changes what we measure. It introduces us ourselves as essential factors in the search for knowledge and understanding. 'In this way quantum theory reminds us, as Bohr has put it, of the old wisdom that when searching for harmony in life one must never forget that in the drama of existence we are ourselves both players and spectators.'[17]

---

the individual responsibility under international law of any person acting on behalf of a State.' The ILC Commentary explains that Art. 58 was drafted so as not to preclude any development with regard to international civil liability for individuals. 'So far this principle has operated in the field of criminal responsibility, but it is not excluded that developments may occur in the field of individual civil responsibility. As a saving clause article 58 is not intended to exclude that possibility; hence the use of the general term "individual responsibility".' Commentary to Art. 58 at para. 2, UN Doc. A/56/10, *Report of the ILC 53rd Session*, adopted 10 August 2001, at p 364.

[15] J. Evans, General Secretary of the Trade Union Advisory Committee to the OECD (TUAC) 'OECD Guidelines—one tool for corporate social accountability' (2003), available at http://www.responsiblepractice.com/english/standards/tuac.

[16] W. Heisenberg, *Physics and Philosophy* (London: Penguin Classics, 2000) at 22–23 (first published 1962).   [17] Ibid, at 25.

Bibliography

Abi-Saab, G. (1971), 'The International Law of Multinational Corporations: A Critique of American Legal Doctrines' in *Annales d'études internationales* 97.

—— (1979), 'Wars of National Liberation in the Geneva Conventions and Protocols' 165 *RCADI* 353.

—— (1984), 'Progressive Development of the Principles and Norms of International Law Relating to the New International Economic Order' (Report of the Secretary-General: UN Doc. A/39/504/Add.1).

—— (1995), 'Diplomatie multilatérale et développement du droit international: le rôle des résolutions de l'Assemblée générale' in V.-Y. Ghebali and D. Kappeler (eds) *Multiple Aspects of International Relations: études à la mémoire du professeur Jean Siotis* (Brussels: Bruylant) 83.

—— (1996), *Cours Général de Droit International Public* 207 *RCADI* (The Hague: Martinus Nijhoff).

—— (2001), 'The concept of "war crimes"' in S. Yee and W. Tieya (eds) *International Law in the Post-Cold War World: Essays in memory of Li Haopei* (London: Routledge) 99.

Abou El Fadl, K. (2003), 'The Human Rights Commitment in Modern Islam' in J. Runzo, N. M. Martin, and A. Sharma (eds) *Human Rights and Responsibilities* (Oxford: Oneworld Publications) 301.

Ackerman, B. A. (1985), 'Beyond *Carolene Products*' 98 *HLR* 713.

Addo, M. K. and N. Grief (1998), 'Does Article 3 of the European Convention on Human Rights Enshrine Absolute Rights?' 9 *EJIL* 510.

Alexander, L. and P. Porton (1988), *Whom does the Constitution Command?* (New York: Greenwood Press).

Alfredsson, G. and A. Eide (eds) (1999), *The Universal Declaration of Human Rights* (The Hague: Martinus Nijhoff).

Alkema, E. A. (1988), 'The Third-Party Applicability or "Drittwirkung" of the European Convention on Human Rights' in F. Matscher and H. Petzold (eds) *Protecting Human Rights: The European Dimension (Studies in Honour of Gérard J. Wiarda)* (Cologne: Carl Heymanns Verlag) 33.

Alldridge, P. (ed) (1999), *Personal Autonomy, the Private Sphere and Criminal Law: A Comparative Study* (Oxford: Hart Publishing).

Alston, P. (1979), 'The United Nations' Specialized Agencies and Implementation of the International Covenant on Economic, Social, and Cultural Rights' 18 *Col JTL* 79.

—— (1982), 'International Trade as an Instrument of Positive Human Rights Policy' 4 *HRQ* 155.

—— (1993), 'Labor Rights Provisions in US Trade Law: Aggressive Unilateralism?' 14 *HRQ*.

—— (1997), 'The Myopia of the Handmaidens: International Lawyers and Globalization' 3 *EJIL* 435.

—— (ed) (1999), *The EU and Human Rights* (Oxford: Oxford University Press).

—— (1999), 'Transplanting Foreign Norms: Human Rights and Other International Legal Norms in Japan' 10 *EJIL* 625.

Alston, P. (2001), 'Downsizing the State in Human Rights Discourse' in N. Dorden and P. Gifford (eds) *Democracy and the Rule of Law* (Washington, DC: Congressional Quarterly Press) 357.

—— (2004), ' "Core Labour Standards" and the Transformation of the International Labour Rights Regime' 15 *EJIL* 457.

—— (2004), *A Human Rights Perspective on the Millennium Development Goals: Paper prepared as a contribution to the work of the Millennium Project Task Force on Poverty and Economic Development* (on file with the author).

Ambos, K. (1999), 'Article 25' in O. Triffterer (ed) *Commentary on the Rome Statute of the International Criminal Court* (Baden-Baden: Nomos) 475.

Amerasinghe, C. F. (1967), *State Responsibility for Injuries to Aliens* (Oxford: Clarendon Press).

—— (1995), 'International Personality Revisited' 47 *AJPIL* 123.

—— (1996), *Principles of the Institutional Law of International Organizations* (Cambridge: Cambridge University Press).

Amnesty International *Human Rights and Peacekeeping* (AI Index IOR 40/001/1994).

—— (1998), *Human Rights Principles for Companies* (AI Index ACT 70/001/98).

—— (2000) *'Collateral Damage' or Unlawful Killings? Violations of the Laws of War by NATO during Operation Allied Force* (AI Index EUR 70/025/2000).

—— (2000), *Respect, protect, fulfil—Women's human rights: State responsibility for abuses by 'non-state actors'* (AI Index IOR 50/001/00).

—— (2000), *Sudan: The Human Price of Oil* (AI Index AFR 54/001/00 ERR).

—— (2002), *Guatemala the lethal legacy of impunity* (AI Index AMR 34/009/2002).

—— (2003), *Iraq: On Whose Behalf? Human Rights and the Economic Reconstruction Process in Iraq* (AI Index MDE 14/128/2003).

—— (2004), *It's in our hands: Stop violence against women* (AI Index ACT 77/001/2004).

—— (2004), *Kosovo (Serbia and Montenegro): 'So does that mean I have rights?' Protecting the human rights of women and girls trafficked for forced prostitution in Kosovo* (AI Index EUR 70/010/2004).

—— (2004), *Making Rights a Reality: The Duty of States to Address Violence Against Women* (AI Index ACT 77/049/2004).

—— (2004), *The UN Human Rights Norms for Business: Towards Legal Accountability* (AI Index IOR 42/001/2004).

Amnesty International (UK) and The Prince of Wales Business Leaders Forum (2000), *Human rights: is it any of your business?* (London: AIUK).

Amnesty International (Business Group), 'Human Rights Guidelines for Pension Fund Trustees', http://www.amnesty.org.

Amnesty International (UK) (2000), *Global trade, labour and human rights* (London: AIUK).

—— and C. Avery (2000), *Business and Human Rights in a Time of Change* (London: AIUK).

An-Na'im, A. A. (ed) (1992), *Human Rights in Cross-Cultural Perspectives: A Quest for Consensus* (Philadelphia, Pa: University of Pennsylvania Press).

—— (2003), 'The Synergy and Interdependence of Human Rights, Religion, and Secularism' in J. Runzo, N. M. Martin, and A. Sharma (eds) *Human Rights and Responsibilities* (Oxford: Oneworld Publications) 27.

Anderson, G. W. (1997), 'Rights and the Art of Boundary Maintenance' 60 *MLR* 120.

Androf, J. and M. McIntosh (2001), *Perspectives on Corporate Citizenship* (Sheffield: Greenleaf Publishing).

Antunes, J. E. (1994), *Liability of Corporate Groups: Autonomy and Control in Parent-Subsidiary Relationships in US, German and EU Law—An International and Comparative Perspective* (Deventer: Kluwer).

Arajärvi, P. (1999), 'Article 26' in G. Alfredsson and A. Eide (eds) *The Universal Declaration of Human Rights* (The Hague: Martinus Nijhoff) 551.

Arend, A. C. (1999), *Legal Rules and International Society* (New York: Oxford University Press).

Ascoly, N. and I. Zeldenrust (2002), 'Working with codes: perspectives from the Clean Clothes Campaign' in R. Jenkins, R. Pearson, and G. Seyfang (eds) *Corporate Responsibility & Labour Rights: Codes of Conduct in the Global Economy* (London: Earthscan) 172.

Aziz, N. (1999), 'The Human Rights Debate in an Era of Globalization' in P. Van Ness (ed) *Debating Human Rights* (London: Routledge) 32.

Bantekas, I., S. Nash, and M. Mackarel (2001), *International Criminal Law* (London: Cavendish).

Banton, M. (1996), *International Action against Racial Discrimination* (Oxford: Oxford University Press).

Barak, A. (2001), 'Constitutional Human Rights and Private Law' in D. Friedmann and D. Barak-Erez (eds) *Human Rights in Private Law* (Oxford: Hart Publishing) 13.

Bassiouni, M. C. (ed) (1999), *International Criminal Law* (Ardsley: Transnational, 2nd edn).

Batruch, C. (2004), 'Oil and conflict: Lundin Petroleum's experience in Sudan' in A. J. K. Bailes and I. Frommelt (eds) *Business and Security: Public-Private Sector Relationships in a New Security Environment* (Oxford: Oxford University Press) 148.

Bazyler, M. J. (2000), 'Nuremberg in America: Litigating the Holocaust in United States Courts' 34 *URLR* 1.

—— (2003), *Holocaust Justice: The Battle for Restitution in America's Courts* (New York: New York University Press).

Beatson, J. and Y. Cripps (eds) (2000), *Freedom of Expression and Freedom of Information: Essays in Honour of Sir David Williams* (Oxford: Oxford University Press).

Bekker, P. H. F. (1994), *The Legal Position of Intergovernmental Organizations: A Functional Necessity Analysis of Their Legal Status and Immunities* (Dordrecht: Martinus Nijhoff).

Bennoune, K. (1997), ' "A Practice which Debases Everyone Involved": Corporal Punishment under International Law' in Association for the Prevention of Torture *20 ans consacrés à la réalisation d'une idée* (Geneva: APT) 203.

Benvenisti, E. and G. Nolte (eds) (2004), *The Welfare State, Globalization and International Law* (Berlin: Springer verlag).

Betten, L. and N. Grief (1998), *EU Law and Human Rights* (London: Longman).

Beyani, C. and D. Lilly (2001), *Regulating private military companies: options for the UK Government* (London: International Alert).

Bianchi, A. (1994), 'Denying State Immunity to Violators of Human Rights' 46 *AJPIL* 195.

—— (1997), 'Globalization of Human Rights: The Role of Non-State Actors' in G. Teubner (ed) *Global Law Without a State* (Aldershot: Dartmouth) 179.

Birkenshaw, P. (1988), *Freedom of Information: The Law, the Practice and the Ideal* (London: Weidenfeld and Nicholson).

Biskupic, J. and E. Witt (1996), *The Supreme Court and Individual Rights* (Washington, DC: Congressional Quarterly, Inc, 3rd edn).

Blake, N. and R. Husain (2003), *Immigration, Asylum and Human Rights*, (Oxford: Oxford University Press).

Blank, K. L. (2002), *The Role of International Financial Institutions in International Humanitarian Law: Report from the International Humanitarian Law Working Group* (Washington, DC: United States Institute of Peace).

Blanpain, R. (1979), *The OECD Guidelines for Multinationals and Labour Relations 1967–1979: experience and review* (Deventer: Kluwer).

Blowfield, M. (2002), 'ETI: a multi-stakeholder approach' in R. Jenkins, R. Pearson, and G. Seyfang (eds) *Corporate Responsibility & Labour Rights: Codes of Conduct in the Global Economy* (London: Earthscan) 184.

Boisson de Chazournes, L. (1999), 'Public Participation in Decision-Making: The World Bank Inspection Panel' in E. Brown Weiss, A. Rigo Sureda, and L. Boisson de Chazournes (eds) *The World Bank, International Financial Institutions and the Development of International Law* (Washington, DC: American Society of International Law, Studies in Transnational Legal Policy, No. 31) 84.

—— (2000), 'Policy Guidance and Compliance: The World Bank Operational Standards' in D. Shelton (ed) *Commitment and Compliance: The Role of Non-Binding Norms in the International legal System* (Oxford: Oxford University Press) 281.

—— (2001), 'Le Panel d'Inspection de la Banque modiale: à propos de la complexification de l'espace public international', *Revue Générale de Droit International Public* 145.

—— and M. M. Mbengue (2002), 'Le rôle des organes de réglement des différends de l'OMC dans le développement du droit: á propos des OGM' in J. Bourrinet and S. Maljean-Dubois (eds) *Le commerce international des organisms génétiquement modifiés* (Paris: la documentation Française) 177.

—— and P. Sands (eds) (1999), *International Law, The International Court of Justice and Nuclear Weapons* (Cambridge: Cambridge University Press).

Bone, A. (2004), 'Conflict diamonds: the De Beer Group and the Kimberly Process' in A. J. K. Bailes and I. Frommelt (eds) *Business and Security: Public-Private Sector Relationships in a New Security Environment* (Solna/Oxford: SIPRI/Oxford University Press) 129.

Bottigliero, I. (2004), *Redress for Victims of Crimes Under International Law* (Leiden: Martinus Nijoff).

Bottomley, S. and D. Kinley (eds) (2002),*Commercial Law and Human Rights* (Dartmouth: Ashgate).

Bourloyannis-Vrailas, M.-C. (1995), 'The Convention on the Safety on United Nations and Associated Personnel' 44 *ICLQ* 560.

Boustany, K. (1998), 'Brocklebank: A Questionable Decision of the Court Martial Appeal Court of Canada' 1 *Yearbook of International Humanitarian Law* 371.

Boyle, K. and A. Baldaccini (2001), 'A Critical Evaluation of International Human Rights Approaches to Racism' in S. Fredman (ed) *Discrimination and Human Rights, The Case of Racism* (Oxford: Oxford University Press) 135.

Brackman, A. C. (1989), *The Other Nuremberg: The Untold Story of the Tokyo War Crimes Trials* (London: Collins).

Bradley, K. St C. (1999), 'Reflections on the Human Rights Role of the European Parliament' in P. Alston (ed) *The EU and Human Rights* (Oxford: Oxford University Press) 839.

Brandtner, B. and A. Rosas (1998), 'Human Rights and the External Relations of the European Community: An Analysis of Doctrine and Practice' 9 *EJIL* 469.

—— (1999), 'Trade Preferences and Human Rights' in P. Alston (ed) *The EU and Human Rights* (Oxford: Oxford University Press) 699.

Brett, R. (1998), 'Non-governmental human rights organizations and international humanitarian law', *IRRC* 531.

Brierly, J. L. (1928), 'The Theory of Implied State Complicity in International Claims' 9 *British Year Book of International Law* 42.

Brinktrine, R. (2001), 'The Horizontal Effect of Human Rights in German Constitutional Law: The British debate on horizontality and the possible role model of the German doctrine of "*mittelbare Drittwirkung der Grundrechte*" ' *EHRLR* 421.

Brown Weiss, E. (ed) (1997), *International Compliance with Nonbinding Accords* (Washington, DC: American Society of International Law).

—— A. Rigo Sureda, and L. Boisson de Chazournes (eds) (1999), *The World Bank, International Financial Institutions and the Development of International Law* (Washington, DC: American Society of International Law, Studies in Transnational Legal Policy, No. 31).

Brownlie, I. (1958), 'International Law and the Activities of Armed Bands' 7 *ICLQ* 712.

—— (1980), 'Legal Effects of Codes of Conduct for MNEs: Commentary' in N. Horn (ed) *Legal Problems of Codes of Conduct for Multinational Enterprises* (Deventer: Kluwer) 39.

—— (1993), 'The Decisions of Political Organs of the United Nations and the Rule of Law' in R. St J. Macdonald (ed) *Essays in Honour of Wang Tieya* (Dordrecht: Martinus Nijhoff) 91.

—— (2003), *Principles of Public International Law* (Oxford: Oxford University Press, 6th edn).

Brownsword, R. (2001), 'Freedom of Contract, Human Rights and Human Dignity' in D. Friedmann and D. Barak-Erez (eds) *Human Rights in Private Law* (Oxford: Hart Publishing) 181.

Bruderlein, C. (2000), 'The role of non-state actors in building human security: the case of armed groups in intra-state wars' (Geneva: Centre for Humanitarian Dialogue) http://www.ihlresearch.org/ihl/.

Bruno, K. K. J. (2000), 'Tangled Up in Blue: Corporate Partnerships at the United Nations' (Transnational Resource & Action Center) http://www.corpwatch.org.

Brysk, A. (2000), *Human Rights and Private Wrongs: Constructing Global Civil Society* (New York and London: Routledge).

Buergenthal, T. (1998), 'The Normative and Institutional Evolution of International Human Rights' 19 *HRQ* 703.

—— (1999), 'The World Bank and Human Rights' in E. Brown Weiss, A. Rigo Sureda, and L. Boisson de Chazournes (eds) *The World Bank, International Financial Institutions and the Development of International Law* (Washington, DC: American Society of International Law, Studies in Transnational Legal Policy, No. 31) 95.

Burgers, J. H. and H. Danelius (1988), *The United Nations Convention Against Torture* (The Hague: Martinus Nijhoff).

Burley, A.-M. (1989), 'The Alien Tort Statute and the Judiciary Act of 1789: A Badge of Honor' 83 *AJIL* 461.

Butler, A. S. (August 1991), 'The New Zealand Bill of Rights and private common law litigation', *New Zealand Law Journal* 261.

—— (1993), 'Constitutional Rights in Private Litigation: A Critique and Comparative Analysis' 22 *Anglo-American Law Review* 1.

Buxton, R. (2000), 'The Human Rights Act and Private Law' 116 *LQR* 48.

Byrnes, A. (1991), ' "Recalcitrant Debtors" in a Town "Pollinated by Gold" ' 21 *Hong Kong Law Journal* 377.

—— (1992), 'Equality and Non-Discrimination' in R. Wacks (ed) *Human Rights in Hong Kong* (Hong Kong: Oxford University Press) 225.

—— (1993), 'The Hong Kong Bill of Rights and Relations Between Private Individuals' in J. Chan and Y. Ghai (eds) *The Hong Kong Bill of Rights: A Comparative Approach* (Hong Kong: Butterworths Asia) 71.

CAFOD (2004), *Clean up your Computer: Working conditions in the electronics sector*, http://www.cafod.org.uk/policy_and_analysis/policy_papers/clean_up_your_computer_report.

Cahier, P. (1992), *Changements et Continuité du Droit International* 195 *RCADI* (Dordrecht: Martinus Nijhoff).

Campbell, G. (2002), *Blood Diamonds: Tracing the Deadly Path of the World's Most Precious Stones*, (Boulder, Col: Westview).

Campbell, T., K. D. Ewing, and A. Tomkins (2001), *Sceptical Essays on Human Rights* (Oxford: Oxford University Press).

Cane, P. (2004), 'Church, State and Human Rights: Are Parish Councils Public Authorities?' 120 *LQR* 41.

Cannizzaro, E. (ed) (2002), *The European Union as an Actor in International Relations* (The Hague: Kluwer Law International).

Carlier, J.-Y. (1999), 'The Geneva refugee definition and the "theory of the three scales" ' in F. Nicholson and P. Twomey (eds) *Refugee Rights and Realities: Evolving International Concepts and Regimes* (Cambridge: Cambridge University Press) 37.

Carrillo-Suárez (1999), 'Hors de logique: contemporary issues in international humanitarian law as applied to internal armed conflict' 15 *American University International Law Review* 1.

Carruthers, S. (2004), 'Beware of Lawyers Bearing Gifts: A Critical Evaluation of the Proposals on Fundamental Rights in the EU Constitutional Treaty', *EHRLR* 424.

Carss-Frisk, M. (2002), 'Public Authorities: The Developing Definition', *EHRLR* 319.

Cass, B. (1992), 'The Limits of the Public/Private Dichotomy: A Comment on Coady and Coady' in P. Alston, S. Parker, and J. Seymour (eds) *Children, Rights and the Law* (Oxford: Oxford University Press) 140.

Cassese, A. (1980), 'Mercenaries: Lawful Combatants or War Criminals?', *Zeitschrift für ausländisches öffentliches Recht und Völkerrecht* 1.

—— (1981), 'The Status of Rebels under the 1977 Geneva Protocol on Non-International Armed Conflicts' 30 *ICLQ* 416.

—— (1984), 'Wars of National Liberation' in C. Swinarski (ed) *Studies and Essays in International Humanitarian Law and Red Cross Principles: Essays in Honour of Jean Pictet* (The Hague: Martinus Nijhoff) 314.

—— (1986), *International Law in a Divided World* (Oxford: Oxford University Press).

—— (1990), *Human Rights in a Changing World* (Cambridge: Polity Press).

—— (1995), *Self-determination of Peoples: A Legal Reappraisal* (Cambridge: Cambridge University Press).

—— (1996), 'The International Court of Justice and the right of peoples to self-determination' in V. Lowe and M. Fitzmaurice (eds) *Fifty Years of the International Court of Justice: Essays in Honour of Sir Robert Jennings* (Cambridge: Grotius/Cambridge University Press) 351.

—— (1999), 'The Statute of the International Criminal Court: Some Preliminary Reflections' 10 *EJIL* 141.

—— (2000), 'The Martens Clause: Half a Loaf or Simply Pie in the Sky?' 11 *EJIL* 193.

—— (2003), *International Criminal Law* (Oxford: Oxford University Press).

—— (2003), 'Terrorism as an International Crime' in A. Bianchi (ed) *Enforcing International Law Norms Against Terrorism* (Oxford: Hart Publishing) 213.

—— (2005), *International Law* (Oxford: Oxford University Press, 2nd edn).

—— P. Gaeta, and J. R. W. D. Jones (2002), *The Rome Statute of the International Criminal Court: A Commentary* (Oxford: Oxford University Press).

Cate, F. H. (1997), *Privacy in the Information Age* (Washington, DC: Brookings Insitution Press).

Caux Round Table (2000), 'Principles for Business', http://www.cauxroundtable.org.

Cerney, P. (1999), 'Globalization, governance and complexity' in A. Prakash and J. Hart (eds) *Globalization and Governance* (London: Routledge) 188.

Chan, J. (1999), *The Annotated Ordinances of Hong Kong: Hong Kong Bill of Rights Ordinance (Chapter 383)* (Hong Kong: Butterworths Asia).

Chandhoke, N. (2002), 'The Limits of Global Society' in M. Glasius, M. Kaldor, and H. Anheirer (eds) *Global Civil Society 2002* (Oxford: Oxford University Press) 35.

Charlesworth, H. (1995), 'Worlds Apart: Public/Private Distinctions in International Law' in M. Thornton (ed) *Public and Private: Feminist Legal Debates* (Oxford: Oxford University Press) 243.

Charnovitz, S. (1997), 'Trade, Employment and Labour Standards: The OECD Study and Recent Developments in the Trade and Labor Standards Debate' 11 *Temple International and Comparative Law Journal* 131.

—— (1998), 'The Moral Exception in Trade Policy' 38 *Virg JIL* 689.

—— (2002), *Trade Law and Global Governance* (London: Cameron May).

Cheadle, H. and D. Davis (1997), 'The Application of the 1996 Constitution in the Private Sphere' 13 *SAJHR* 44.

Chetail, V. (2003), 'The contribution of the International Court of Justice to international humanitarian law' 85, (850) *IRRC* 235.

Chinkin, C. (1998), 'International law and human rights' in T. Evans (ed) *Human Rights Fifty Years On: A reappraisal* (Manchester: Manchester University Press) 105.

—— (1999), 'A Critique of the Public/Private Dimension' 10 *EJIL* 387.

Cholewinski, R. (1997), *Migrant Workers in International Human Rights Law: Their Protection in Countries of Employment* (Oxford: Clarendon Press).

Christian Aid (2001), *The scorched earth: oil and war in Sudan*, http://www.christian-aid.org.uk/indepth/0103suda/sudanoil.htm.

—— (2004), *Behind the mask: The real face of corporate social responsibility*, http://www.christian-aid.org.uk/indepth/0401csr/csr_behindthemask.pdf.

Churchill, R. R. and U. Khaliq (2004), 'The Collective Complaints System of the European Social Charter: An Effective Mechanism for Ensuring Compliance with Economic and Social Rights' 15 *EJIL* 417.

Clapham, A. (1993), *Human Rights in the Private Sphere* (Oxford: Clarendon Press).

Clapham, A. (2000), 'The Question of Jurisdiction Under International Criminal Law Over Legal Persons: Lessons from the Rome Conference on an International Criminal Court' in M. Kamminga and S. Zia-Zarifi (eds) *Liability of Multinational Corporations Under International Law* (The Hague: Kluwer) 139.

—— (2001), 'Revisiting *Human Rights in the Private Sphere*: Using the European Convention on Human Rights to Protect the Right of Access to the Civil Courts' in C. Scott (ed) *Torture as Tort: Comparative Perspectives on the Development of Transnational Human Rights Litigation* (Oxford: Hart Publishing) 513.

—— (2001), 'Sanctions and Economic, Social and Cultural Rights' in V. Gowlland-Debbas (ed) *United Nations Sanctions and International Law* (The Hague: Kluwer) 131.

Clayton, R. and H. Tomlinson (2000), *The Law of Human Rights (Volume 1)* (Oxford: Oxford University Press).

Clements, L. J. (1994), *European Human Rights: Taking a case under the Convention* (London: Sweet & Maxwell).

Clements, R. (2000), 'Bringing It All Back Home: "Rights" in English Law Before the Human Rights Act 1998' 21 *HRLJ* 134.

Coffee, J. C. (1981), ' "No Soul to Damn: No Body to Kick": An Unscandalized Inquiry into the Problem of Corporate Punishment' 79 *Mich LR* 386

Cohn, H. H. (1983), 'On the Meaning of Human Dignity', *Israel Yearbook of Human Rights* 228.

Compa, L. A. and S. F. Diamond (eds) (1996), *Human Rights, Labour, and International Trade* (Philadelphia, Pa: University of Philadelphia Press).

Condorelli, L., A.-M. La Rosa, and S. Scherrer (eds) (1996), *Les Nations unies et le droit international humanitaire: Actes du colloque international 19, 20, 21 octobre 1995*, (Paris: Pedone).

Cooper, J. (2000), 'Horizontality: The Application of Human Rights Standards in private Disputes' in P. Havers and R. English (eds) *An Introduction to Human Rights and the Common Law* (Oxford: Hart Publishing) 53.

Cottier, T., J. Pauwelyn, and E. Bürgi (eds) (2005) *Human Rights and International Trade* (Oxford: Oxford University Press).

Craven, M. (1995), *The International Covenant on Economic, Social and Cultural Rights: a Perspective on its Development* (Oxford: Oxford University Press).

Crawford, J. (2002a), *The International Law Commission's Articles on State Responsibility: Introduction, Text and Commentaries* (Cambridge: Cambridge University Press).

—— (2002b), Declaration in *The Presbyterian Church of Sudan et al v Talisman Energy Inc, Republic of the Sudan* Civil Action 01 CV 9882 (AGS), US District Court for the Southern District of New York (May 2002).

—— and P. Alston (eds) (2000), *The Future of UN Human Rights Treaty Monitoring* (Cambridge: Cambridge University Press).

—— and S. Olleson (2003), 'The Nature and Forms of International Responsibility' in M. Evans (ed) *International Law*, (Oxford: Oxford University Press) 445.

Cutler, C. A. (2001), 'Critical Reflections on the Westphalian assumptions of international law and organization: a crisis of legitimacy' 27 *Review of International Studies* 133.

Daes, E.-I. A. (1983), 'The Individual's Duties to the Community and the Limitations on Human Rights and Freedoms under Article 29 of the Universal Declaration of Human Rights' (UN Doc. E/CN.4/Sub.2/432/Rev.2).

—— (1992), *Status of the Individual and Contemporary International Law: Promotion, Protection and Restoration of Human Rights at National, Regional and International Levels* (New York: UN Study Series).

Danish Human Rights and Business Project, the Confederation of Danish Industries, the Danish Centre for Human Rights, and the Industrialization Fund for Developing Countries (2000), 'Defining the Scope of Business Responsibility for Human Rights Abroad', http://www.humanrights.dk.

Darrow, M. (2003a), *Between Light and Shade: The World Bank, the International Monetary Fund, and International Human Rights Law* (Oxford: Hart Publishing).

—— (2003b), 'Human Rights Accountability of the World Bank and IMF: Possibilities and Limits of Legal Analysis' 12(1) *Social and Legal Studies* 133.

David, E. (1978), *Mercenaires et volontaires internationaux en droit des gens* (Brussels: Editions de L'Université de Bruxelles).

—— (1999), 'Conclusions', *Revue belge de droit international* 115.

De Búrca, G. (2004), 'Beyond the Charter: How Enlargement has enlarged the Human Rights Policy of the EU' 27 *Ford ILJ* 679.

De Doelder, H. and K. Tiedemann (eds) (1996), *La Criminalisation du Comportement Collectif* (The Hague: Kluwer).

De Feyter, K. (2001), 'Corporate Governance and Human Rights', Institut international des droits de l'homme, *Commerce mondial et protection des droits de l'homme: les droits de l'homme à l'épreuve de la globalisation des échanges economiques* (Brussels: Bruylant) 71.

De Schutter, O. (2005), 'The Accountability of Multinationals for Human Rights Violations in European Law' in P. Alston (ed) *Non-State Actors and Human Rights* (Oxford: Oxford University Press).

De Waal, J., I. Currie, and G. Erasmus (2001), *The Bill of Rights Handbook* (Lansdowne, Ont: Juta, 4th edn).

De Witte, B. (1999), 'The Past and Future Role of the European Court of Justice in the Protection of Human Rights' in P. Alston (ed) *The EU and Human Rights* (Oxford: Oxford University Press) 859.

Decew, J. W. (1997), *In Pursuit of Privacy: Law, Ethics, and the Rise of Technology* (Ithaca, NY: Cornell University Press).

Detter, I. (2000), *The Law of War* (Cambridge: Cambridge University Press, 2nd edn).

Dicke, K. (2002), 'The Founding Function of Human Dignity in the Universal Declaration of Human Rights' in D. Kretzmer and E. Klein (eds) *The Concept of Human Dignity in Human Rights Discourse* (The Hague: Kluwer) 111.

Dickson B. (1999), 'The Horizontal Application of Human Rights Law' in A. Hegarty and S. Leonard (eds) *Human Rights: An Agenda for the 21st Century* (London: Cavendish) 59.

Diller, J. M. and D. A. Levy (1997), 'Notes and Comments: Child Labor, Trade and Investments: Toward the Harmonization of International Law' 91 *AJIL* 663.

Dine, J. (2005), *Companies, International Trade and Human Rights* (Cambridge: Cambridge University Press).

Dinstein, Y. (2004), *The Conduct of Hostilities under the Law of International Armed Conflict* (Cambridge: Cambridge University Press).

—— and M. Tabory (eds) (1996), *War Crimes in International Law* (The Hague: Martinus Nijhoff).

Douglas-Scott, S. (2004), 'The Charter of Fundamental Rights as a Constitutional Document', *EHRLR* 37.

Drake, S. (2005), 'Twenty years after *Von Colson*: the impact of "indirect effect" on the protection of the individual's Community rights' 30 *European Law Review* 329.

Drucker, P. F. (1997), 'The Global Economy and the Nation-State' 76 *Foreign Affairs* 159.

Drzemczewski, A. (1979), 'The European Human Rights Convention and Relations between Private Parties' 26 *NILR* 163.

——(1983), *European Human Rights Convention in Domestic Law* (Oxford: Clarendon Press).

Drzewicki, K. (1999), 'Internationalization and Juridization of Human Rights' in R. Hanski and M. Suski (eds) *An Introduction to the International Protection of Human Rights* (Turku: Institute for Human Rights, 2nd edn) 25.

Du Plessis, M. and J. Ford (2004), 'Developing the Common Law Progressively—Horizontality, the Human Rights Act and the South African Experience', *EHRLR* 286.

Dunne, T. and N. J. Wheeler (eds) (1999), *Human Rights in Global Politics* (Cambridge: Cambridge University Press).

Dupuy, P.-M. (2002), *L'unité de l'ordre juridique international: Cours général de droit international public (2000)* 297 *RCADI* (Leiden: Martinus Nijhoff).

Eboe-Osuji, C. (2005), ' "Complicity in Genocide" versus "Aiding and Abetting Genocide" ' 3 *Journal of International Criminal Justice* 56.

Eide, A., C. Krause, and A. Rosas (eds) (2001), *Economic, Social and Cultural Rights: A Textbook* (Dordrecht: Martinus Nijhoff, 2nd edn).

——T. Meron, and A. Rosas (1995), 'Combating Lawlessness in Gray Zone Conflicts Through Minimum Humanitarian Standards' 89 *AJIL* 215.

Eissen, M.-A. (1962), 'The European Convention on Human Rights and the Duties of the Individual' 32 *Nordisk Tidsskrift for International Ret* 229.

Etzioni, A. (1990), *The Limits of Privacy* (New York: Basic Books).

Evans, J. (2003), 'OECD Guidelines—one tool for corporate social accountability', http://www.responsiblepractice.com/english/standards/tuac/.

Evans, M. D. and R. Murray (eds) (2002), *The African Charter on Human and Peoples' Rights; The System in Practice, 1986–2000* (Cambridge: Cambridge University Press).

Evrigenis, D. (1982), 'Recent Case-Law of the European Court of Human Rights on Articles 8 and 10 of the European Convention on Human Rights' 3 *HRLJ* 121.

Ewing, A. P. (2004), 'Understanding the Global Compact Human Rights Principles', UN Global Compact Office & OHCHR, *Embedding Human Rights in Business Practice* (New York: UN Global Compact Office) 29.

Ewing, K. D. (2004), 'The Futility of the Human Rights Act', *Public Law* 829.

Fagan, A. (2001), 'Determining the Stakes: Binding and Non-Binding Bills of Rights' in D. Friedmann and D. Barak-Erez (eds) *Human Rights in Private Law* (Oxford: Hart Publishing) 73.

Falk, R. A. (2000), *Human Rights Horizons: The Pursuit of Justice in a Globalizing World* (London: Routledge).

Farrar, J. (2001), *Corporate Governance in Australia and New Zealand* (Oxford: Oxford University Press).

Fatouros, A. A. (1983), 'Transnational Enterprise in the Law of State Responsibility' in R. B. Lillich (ed) *International Law of State Responsibility for Injuries to Aliens* (Charlottesville, Virg: University Press of Virginia) 361.

—— (1997), 'National Legal Persons on International Law' in R. Bernhardt (ed) *Encyclopedia of Public International Law*, vol. 1 (Amsterdam: Elsevier) 495.

Favoreu, L. and J. A. Jolowicz, (eds) (1986), *Contrôle juridictionnel des lois* (Paris: Economica).

Feeney, P. (2002), 'The Relevance of the OECD Guidelines for Multinational Enterprises to the Mining Sector and the Promotion of Sustainable Development' 10 *The Centre for Energy, Petroleum and Mineral Law and Policy Journal*, http://www.dundee.ac.uk/cepmlp/journal/html/vol10/article10–6.html.

Feller, E., V. Türk, and F. Nicholson, (eds) (2003), *Refugee Protection in International Law: UNHCR's Global Consultations on International Protection* (Cambridge: Cambridge University Press).

Fleck, D. (2003), 'Humanitarian Protection Against Non-State Actors' in J. A. Frowein, K. Scharioth, I. Winkelmann, and R. Wolfrum (eds) *Verhandeln für den Frieden—Negotiating for Peace: Liber Amicorum Tono Eitel* (Berlin: Springer Verlag) 69.

Foqué, R. (1998), 'Global Governance and the Rule of Law: Human Rights and General Principles of Good Global Governance' in K. Wellens (ed) *International Law: Theory and Practice* (The Hague: Martinus Nijhoff) 25.

Forcese, C. (1999), 'Deterring "Militarized Commerce": The Prospect of Liability for "Privatized" Human Rights Abuses' 31 *Ottawa Law Review* 171.

Forde, M. (1985), 'Non-Governmental Interferences with Human Rights' 56 *British Year Book of International Law* 253.

Foster, M. (ed) (2001), *Engaging non-state actors in a landmine ban: a pioneering conference*, Conference held in Geneva, 24–25 March 2000 (Quezon City, Philippines: Conference Organizers).

Fox, H. (2003), 'International Law and Restraints on the Exercise of Jurisdiction by National Courts of States' in M. Evans (ed) *International Law* (Oxford: Oxford University Press) 357.

Francioni, F. (1996), 'International "soft law": a contemporary assessment' in V. Lowe and M. Fitzmaurice (eds) *Fifty Years of the International Court of Justice: Essays in Honour of Sir Robert Jennings* (Cambridge: Grotius) 167.

Fredman, S. (ed) (2001), *Discrimination and Human Rights: The Case of Racism* (Oxford: Oxford University Press).

—— (2001), 'Scepticism under Scrutiny: Labour Law and Human Rights' in T. Campbell, K. D. Ewing, and A. Tomkins (eds) *Sceptical Essays on Human Rights* (Oxford: Oxford University Press) 197.

Friedmann, D. and D. Barak-Erez (eds) (2001), *Human Rights in Private Law* (Oxford: Hart Publishing).

Friedmann, W. (1964), *The Changing Structure of International Law* (London: Stevens and Sons).

Friendly, H. (1982), 'The Public-Private Penumbra: Fourteen Years Later' 130 *UPLR* 1289.

Frowein, J. A. (1986), 'Fundamental Human Rights as a Vehicle of Legal Integration in Europe' in M. Cappelletti, M. Seccombe, and J. H. H. Weiler (eds) *Integration through Law: Europe and the American Federal Experience*, vol. i, book 3 (Berlin: Walter de Gruyter) 300.

—— (1992), 'De Facto Régime' in R. Bernhardt (ed) *Encyclopedia of Public International Law*, vol. 1 (Amsterdam: Elsevier) 966.

—— (2002), 'Human Dignity in International Law' in D. Kretzmer and E. Klein (eds) *The Concept of Human Dignity in Human Rights Discourse* (The Hague: Kluwer) 121.

Fudge, J. (1987), 'The Public/Private Distinction: The Possibilities of and the Limits to the Use of Charter Litigation to Further Feminist Struggles', *Osgoode Hall Law Journal* 485.

—— (2001), 'The Canadian Charter of Rights: Recognition, Redistribution, and the Imperialism of the Courts' in T. Campbell, K. D. Ewing, and A. Tomkins (eds) *Sceptical Essays on Human Rights* (Oxford: Oxford University Press) 335.

Fédération Internationale des Ligues des Droits de l'Homme (1999), *The World Trade Organisation and Human Rights: Position paper* (No. 285/2).

Gaeta, P. (1996), 'The Dayton Agreements and International Law' 7 *EJIL* 147.

Garcia-Rubio, M. (2001), *On the Application of Customary Rules of State Responsibility by the WTO Dispute Settlement Organs* (Geneva: Graduate Institute of International Studies, Studies and Working Papers).

Gardbaum, S. (2003), 'The "Horizontal Effect" of Constitutional Rights' 102 *Mich LR* 387.

Gearty, C. (2001), 'Tort Law and the Human Rights Act' in T. Campbell, K. D. Ewing, and A. Tomkins (eds) *Sceptical Essays on Human Rights* (Oxford: Oxford University Press) 243.

Geneva Call (2002), *Seeking Rebel Accountability: Report of the Geneva Call Mission to the MILF in the Philippines, 3–8 April 2002* (Geneva: Geneva Call).

Ghai, Y. (1997), 'Rights, Duties and Responsibilities' 7(4) *Human Rights Solidarity—(Asia Human Rights Commission Newsletter)* 9.

Gianviti, F. (30 May 2001), 'Economic, Social and Cultural Rights and the International Monetary Fund', paper presented to meeting organized by the UN Committee on Economic Social and Cultural Rights, on file with the author.

Giddens, A. (1999), *Runaway World* (London: Profile Books).

Gillies, D. (1993), 'Human Rights, Governance, and Democracy: The World Bank's Problem Frontiers' 11 *NQHR* 3.

Glasius, M. (2002), 'Expertise in the Cause of Justice: Global Civil Society Influence on the Statute for an International Criminal Court' in M. Glasius, M. Kaldor, and H. Anheirer (eds) *Global Civil Society 2002* (Oxford: Oxford University Press) 137.

Gold, J. (1996), *Interpretation: The IMF and International Law* (Dordrecht: Kluwer).

Goldsmith, A. (1996), 'Seeds of Exploitation: Free Trade Zones in the Global Economy' in J. Mander and E. Goldsmith (eds) *The Case against the Global Economy: and for a turn toward the local* (San Francisco: Sierra Club Books) 267.

Goldsmith, Lord (2004), 'The Charter of Rights—A Brake Not an Accelerator', *EHRLR* 473.

Gomien, D., D. Harris, and L. Zwaak (1996), *Law and Practice of the European Convention on Human Rights and the European Social Charter* (Strasbourg: Council of Europe).

Goodman, F. I. (1982), 'Professor Brest on State Action and Liberal Theory and a Postscript to Professor Stone' 130 *UPLR* 1331.

Goodwin-Gill, G. (1996), *The Refugee in International Law* (Oxford: Oxford University Press, 2nd edn).

Gowlland-Debbas, V. (1999), 'The Right to Life and Genocide: The Court and an International Public Policy' in L. Boisson de Chazournes and P. Sands (eds) *International Law, The International Court of Justice and Nuclear Weapons* (Cambridge: Cambridge University Press) 315.

Graefrath, B. (1996), 'Complicity in the Law of International Responsibility', *Revue belge de droit international* 370.

Greenwood, C. (1998), 'International Humanitarian Law and United Nations Military Operations' 1 *Yearbook of International Humanitarian Law* 3.

—— 'International Humanitarian Law (Laws of War)' in F. Kalshoven (ed) *The Centennial of the First International Peace Conference* (The Hague: Kluwer) 161.

—— (2002a), 'International law and the "war against terrorism"' *International Affairs* 301.

—— (2002b), Declaration in *The Presbyterian Church of Sudan et al v Talisman Energy Inc, Republic of the Sudan* Civil Action 01 CV 9882 (AGS), US District Court for the Southern District of New York (7 May 2002, filed 13 May 2002).

—— (2003), 'The Law of War (International Humanitarian Law)' in M. Evans (ed) *International Law* (Oxford: Oxford University Press) 789.

Grenier, M. (2003), 'Communicating Human Rights: a summary of recent trends in European annual reports' 2 (1) *New Academy Review* 76.

Grossman, R. L. and F. Adams (1996), 'Exercising Power Over Corporations Through State Charters' in J. Mander and E. E. Goldsmith (eds) *The Case Against the Global Economy: and for a turn toward the local* (San Francisco, Cal: Sierra Club Books) 374.

Grosz, S., J. Beatson, and P. Duffy (2000), *Human Rights: the 1998 Act and the European Convention* (London: Sweet & Maxwell).

Guillaume, G. (2001), 'La Cour internationale de Justice et les droits de l'homme', in Asia-Europe Foundation, *The Fourth Informal ASEM Seminar on Human Rights* (Singapore: ASEF) 21.

Gutman, R. and D. Rieff (eds) (1999), *Crimes of War: What the Public Should Know* (New York: W. W. Norton and Co).

Hannum, H. (1995/6), 'The Status of the Universal Declaration of Human Rights in National and International Law' 25 *Georgia Journal of International and Comparative Law* 287.

Hanski, R. and M. Suski (eds) (1999), *An Introduction to the International Protection of Human Rights: A Textbook* (Turku: Åbo Akademi University, Institute for Human Rights, 2nd edn).

Hansmann, H. and R. Kraakman (2004), 'What is Corporate Law?' in R. Kraakman, P. Davies, H. Hansmann, G. Hertig, K. Hopt, H. Kanda, and E. Rock (eds) *The Anatomy of Corporate Law: A Comparative and Functional Approach* (Oxford: Oxford University Press) 1.

Harding, C. (2001), 'Statist assumptions, normative individualism and new forms of personality: evolving a philosophy of international law for the twenty-first century' 1 *Non-State Actors and International Law* 107.

Harker, J. (2000), *Human Security in Sudan: the Report of a Canadian Assessment Mission* (prepared for the Canadian Department of Foreign Affairs and International Trade).

Harris, D., M. O'Boyle, and C. Warbrick (1995), *Law of the European Convention on Human Rights* (London: Butterworths).

Hathaway, J. C. (1991), *The Law of Refugee Status* (Ontario: Butterworths).

—— (ed) (1997), *Reconceiving International Refugee Law* (Dordrecht: Martinus Nijhoff).

Hemingway, S. (2002), 'Excess Baggage? The Responsibility of Companies and Individuals for Human Rights Violations Within the Tourism Industry', *Human Rights Law Review Student Supplement 2001–2002* 49.

Henckaerts, J.-M. and L. Doswald-Beck (2005), *Customary International Humanitarian Law—Volume 1: Rules* (Cambridge: Cambridge University Press).

Henkin, L. (1993), 'The Mythology of Sovereignty' in R. St J. MacDonald (ed) *Essays in Honour of Wang Tieya* (Dordrecht/Boston/London: Martinus Nijhoff) 351.

—— (1999), 'The Universal Declaration at 50 and the Challenge of Global Markets' 25 *Brooklyn JIL* 17.

Henzelin, M. (2000), *Le principe de l'universalité en droit pénal international: droit et obligation pour le Etats de poursuivre et juger selon le principe de l'universalité* (Brussels: Bruylant).

Heyns, C. (2002), 'Civil and Political Rights in the African Charter' in M. D. Evans and R. Murray (eds) *The African Charter on Human and Peoples' Rights: The System in Practice, 1986–2000*, (Cambridge: Cambridge University Press) 137.

Higgins, R. (1978), 'Conceptual thinking about the individual in international law' 4 *BJIS* 1.

—— (1994), *Problems and Process: International Law and How We Use It* (Oxford: Clarendon Press).

—— (1998), 'The International Court of Justice and Human Rights' in K. Wellens (ed) *International Law: Theory and Practice* (The Hague: Martinus Nijhoff) 691.

Hillemanns, C. (October 2003), 'UN Norms on the Responsibilities of Transnational Corporations and Other Business Enterprises with regard to Human Rights', *German Law Journal*, http://www.germanlawjournal.com /pdf/Vol04No10/PDF_Vol_04_No_ 10_1065-1080_European_Hillemanns.pdf.

Hofmann, R. (ed) (1999), *Non-State Actors as New Subjects of International Law: International Law—From the Traditional State Order Towards the Law of the Global Community* (Berlin: Duncker & Humblot).

Holmes, J. T. (1999), 'The Principle of Complementarity' in R. S. Lee (ed) *The International Criminal Court, The Making of the Rome Statute* (The Hague, London, Boston: Kluwer) 41.

Holmqvist, C. (2005), 'Private Security Companies: The Case for Regulation' (Stockholm: SIPRI Policy Paper No. 9).

Horan, M. J. (1976), 'Contemporary Constitutionalism and Legal Relationships between Individuals' 25 *ICLQ* 848.

Horn, N. (ed) (1980), *Legal Problems of Codes of Conduct for Multinational Enterprises* (Deventer: Kluwer).

Howse, R. (2002), 'Human Rights in the WTO: Whose Rights, What Humanity? Comment on Petersmann' 13 *EJIL* 651.

—— and M. Mutua (2000), *Protecting Human Rights in a Global Economy: Challenges for the World Trade Organization* (Montreal: International Centre for Human Rights and Democracy).

Human Rights Research and Education Centre, 'The International Code of Ethics for Canadian Business', http://www.uottawa.ca.

Human Rights Watch (1991), *Criminal Injustice Violence against Women in Brazil.*

—— (1996), *No Guarantees: Sex Discrimination in Mexico's Maquiladora Sector.*

—— (1998a), *Colombia: Human Rights Concerns Raised by the Security Arrangements of Transnational Oil Companies.*

—— (1998b), *Mexico—A Job or Your Rights: Continued Sex Discrimination in Mexico's Maquiladora Sector.*

—— (1999a), 'Oil Companies Complicit in Nigerian Abuses', *Nigeria—Human Rights Watch World Report 1999.*

—— (1999c), *The Enron Corporation: Corporate Complicity in Human Rights Violations*.

—— (2000), 'United Nations Global Compact', *Corporations and Human Rights*.

—— (2002a), *From the Household to the Factory: Sex Discrimination in the Guatemalan Labor Force*.

—— (2002b), *Tainted Harvest: Child Labor and Obstacles to Organizing on Ecuador's Banana Plantations*.

—— (2004), *Sudan, Oil, and Human Rights*.

—— (2005), *The Curse of Gold*.

—— (2005), *No Exit: Human Rights Abuses Inside the MKO Camps*.

Hunt, M. (1997), *Using Human Rights Law in English Courts* (Oxford: Hart Publishing).

—— (1998), 'The Effect on the Law of Obligations' in B. S. Markesinis (ed) *The Impact of the Human Rights Bill on English Law: The Clifford Chance Lectures, Volume 3* (Oxford: Oxford University Press) 159.

—— (1998), 'The Horizontal Effect of the Human Rights Act', *Public Law* 423.

—— (2001), 'The "Horizontal Effect" of the Human Rights Act: Moving beyond the Public-Private Distinction' in J. Jowell and J. Cooper (eds) *Understanding Human Rights Principles* (Oxford: Hart Publishing) 161.

Hunt, P. (1998), 'State Obligations, Indicators, Benchmarks, and the Right to Education' 4 *Human Rights Law and Practice* 109.

Hunter, J. (2000), 'The Multilateral Agreement on Investment and the Review of the OECD Guidelines for Multinational Enterprises' in M. Kamminga and S. Zia-Zarifi (eds) *Liability of Multinational Corporations Under International Law* (The Hague: Kluwer) 197.

Ignatieff, M. (1998), *The Warrior's Honor: Ethnic War and the Modern Conscience* (New York: Metropolitan Books).

—— (2003), *Empire Lite: Nation-building in Bosnia, Kosovo and Afghanistan* (London: Vintage).

Ijalaye, D. A. (1978), *The Extension of Corporate Personality in International Law* (New York: Oceana).

Ingadottir, T. (2001), *The International Criminal Court, The Trust Fund for Victims (Article 79 of the Rome statute) A Discussion Paper* (Project on International Court and Tribunals).

—— (ed) (2003), *The International Criminal Court: Recommendations on Policy and Practice—Financing, Victims, Judges, and Immunities* (New York: Transnational).

Institute of International Law (2003), *L'application du droit international humanitaire et des droits fondamentaux de l'homme dans les conflits armés auxquels prennent part des entités non étatiques: résolution de Berlin du 25 août 1999—The application of international humanitarian law and fundamental human rights in armed conflicts in which non-state entities are parties: Berlin resolution of 25 August 1999 (commentaire de Robert Kolb) Collection "résolutions" n° 1* (Paris: Pedone).

International Chamber of Commerce and International Organisation of Employers (2004), *The Sub-Commission's Draft Norms*.

International Council on Human Rights Policy (2000), *Ends and Means: human rights approaches to armed groups* (Versoix: ICHRP).

—— (2002), *Beyond Voluntarism: Human rights and the developing international legal obligations of companies* (Versoix: ICHRP).

—— (2003), *Deserving Trust: Issues of Accountability for Human Rights NGOs (Draft Report)* (Versoix: ICHRP).

International Institute of Human Rights (1969), *René Cassin Amicorum discipulorumque liber (4 vols)* (Paris: Pedone).

International Law Association (2000), *Final Report on the Exercise of Universal Jurisdiction in respect of Gross Human Rights Offences*, London Conference.

International Organisation of Employers (2000), 'The IOE and the Global Compact', http://www.un.org/partners/business/partners/gcevent/associations/ioe.htm.

International Peace Academy and FAFO AIS (2004), *Business and International Crimes: Assessing the Liability of Business Entities for Grave Violations of International Law* (Oslo: Fafo-report 467).

Iwasawa, Y. (1998), *International Law, Human Rights, and Japanese Law* (Oxford: Clarendon Press).

Jacobs, F. G. and R. C. A. White (1996), *The European Convention on Human Rights* (Oxford: Clarendon Press, 2nd edn).

Jägers, N. (1999), 'The Legal Status of the Multinational Corporation under International Law', in M. K. Addo (ed) *Human Rights Standards and the Responsability of Transantional Corporations* (The Hague: Kluwer) 259.

—— (2002), *Corporate Human Rights Obligations: in Search of Accountability* (Antwerp: Intersentia).

Jakosa, J. Y. (1984), 'Parsing Public from Private: The Failure of Differential State Action Analysis' 19 *Harv CR-CLLR* 193.

Jawara, F. and A. Kwa (2004), *Behind the Scenes at the WTO: the real world of international trade negotiations* (London: Zed Books).

Jayawickrama, N. (2002), *The Judicial Application of Human Rights Law: National Regional and International Jurisprudence* (Cambridge: Cambridge University Press).

Jenkins, R. (2002), 'The political economy of codes of conduct' in R. Jenkins, R. Pearson, and G. Seyfang (eds) *Corporate Responsibility & Labour Rights: Codes of Conduct in the Global Economy* (London: Earthscan) 13.

—— R. Pearson, and G. Seyfang (eds) (2002), *Corporate Responsibility & Labour Rights: Codes of Conduct in the Global Economy* (London: Earthscan).

Jennings, R. and A. Watts (eds) (1996), *Oppenheim's International Law*, vol. i (London: Longman, 9th edn).

Jochnick, C. (1999), 'Confronting the Impunity of Non-State Actors: New Fields for the Promotion of Human Rights' 21 *HRQ* 56.

Jones, C. (1999), *Global Justice: Defending Cosmopolitanism* (Oxford: Oxford University Press).

Joseph, S. (2004), *Corporations and Transnational Human Rights Litigation* (Oxford: Hart Publishing).

Joseph, S., J. Schultz, and M. Castan (eds) (2004), *The International Covenant on Civil and Political Rights: Cases, Materials, and Commentary* (Oxford: Oxford University Press, 2nd edn).

Jungk, M. (1999), 'A Practical Guide to Addressing Human Rights Concerns for Companies Operating Abroad' in M. Addo (ed) *Human Rights Standards and the Responsibility of Transnational Corporations* (The Hague: Kluwer) 171.

Justice, D. W. (2002), 'The international trade union movement and the new codes of coduct' in R. Jenkins, R. Pearson, and G. Seyfang (eds) *Corporate Responsibility & Labour Rights: Codes of Conduct in the Global Economy* (London: Earthscan) 90.

Kaldor, M., H. Anheirer, and M. Glasius (eds) (2003), *Global Civil Society 2003* (Oxford: Oxford University Press).

Kalshoven, F. and E. Zegveld, (2001), *Constraints on the Waging of War* (Geneva: ICRC, 3rd edn).

Kamminga, M. T. (1999), 'Holding Multinational Corporations Accountable for Human Rights Abuses: A Challenge for the EC' in P. Alston (ed) *The EU and Human Rights* (Oxford: Oxford University Press) 553.

—— and S. Zia-Zarifi (eds) (2000), *Liability of Multinational Corporations Under International Law* (The Hague: Kluwer).

Kapur, D. and R. Webb (2000), *Governance-Related Conditionalities of the International Financial Institutions* (New York and Geneva: United Nations, UNCTAD, Centre for International Development Harvard University).

Keefe, P. R. (12 August 2004), 'Iraq: America's Private Armies', *New York Review of Books* 48.

Kell, G. and J. G. Ruggie (1999), 'Global markets and Social legitimacy: The case of the "Global Compact"' (paper presented at an international conference: Governing the Public Domain beyond the era of the Washington Consensus? Redrawing the Line Between the State and the Market, York University, Toronto, 4–6 November 1999.)', http://www.unglobalcompact.org/gc/unweb.nsf/content/gkjr.htm.

Kennedy, D. (1982), 'The Status of the Decline of the Public/Private Distinction' 130 *UPLR* 1349.

Kinley, D. and S. Joseph (2002), 'Multinational corporations and human rights: questions about their relationship' 27 *ALJ* 7.

—— and J. Tadaki (2004), 'From Talk to Walk: the Emergence of Human Rights Responsibilities for Corporations at International Law' 44 *Virg JIL* 931.

Kittichaisaree, K. (2001), *International Criminal Law* (Oxford: Oxford University Press).

Klabbers, J. (1998), 'Presumptive Personality: The European Union in International Law' in M. Koskenniemi (ed) *International Law Aspects of the European Union* (The Hague: Kluwer) 231.

—— (2002), *An Introduction to International Institutional Law* (Cambridge: Cambridge University Press).

Klare, K. E. (1982), 'The Public/Private Distinction in Labor Law' 130 *UPLR* 1358.

Klein, N. (2001), *No Logo* (London: Flamingo).

—— (2002), *Fences and Windows: Dispatches from the Front Lines of the Globalization Debate* (London: Flamingo).

Klein, P. (1998), *La responsabilité des organisations internationals: dans les ordres juridiques internes et en droit des gens* (Brussels: Bruylant).

Klein, P. (1999), 'Les institutions financières internationales et les droits de la personne', *Revue belge de droit international* 97.

Klug, F. (2000), *Values for a Godless Age: The Story of the United Kingdom's New Bill of Rights* (Harmondsworth: Penguin).

Kneebone, S. (2005), 'Women Within The Refugee Construct: "Exclusionary Inclusion" In Policy And Practice—The Australian Experience' 17 *IJRL* 7.

Kooijmans, P. H. (1998), 'The Security Council and Non-State Entities as Parties to Conflicts', in K. Wellens (ed) *International Law: Theory and Practice* (The Hague: Martinus Nijhoff) 333.

Koskenmäki, R. (2004), 'Legal Implications Resulting from State Failure in Light of the Case of Somalia' 73 *NJIL* 1.

Koskenniemi, M. (2003), 'What is International Law For?' in M. Evans (ed) *International Law* (Oxford: Oxford University Press) 89.

Kothari, M. (1999), 'Globalisation, Social Action and Human Rights' in M. Mehra (ed) *Human Rights and Economic Globalisation: Directions for the WTO* (Uppsala: Global Publications Foundation, International NGO Committee on Human Rights in Trade and Investment, International Coalition for Development Action) 37.

Kraakman, R., P. Davies, H. Hansmann, G. Hertig, K. J. Hopt, H. Kanda, and E. B. Rock (2004), *The Anatomy of Corporate law: A Comparative and Functional Approach* (Oxford: Oxford University Press).

Krebber, S. (2004), 'The Search for Core Labour Standards in Liberalized Trade' in E. Benvenisti and G. Nolte (eds) *The Welfare State, Globalization and International Law* (Berlin: Springer Verlag) 175.

Kretzmer, D. and F. K. Hazan (eds) (2000), *Freedom of Speech and Incitement Against Democracy* (The Hague: Kluwer).

—— and E. Klein (eds) (2002), *The Concept of Human Dignity in Human Rights Discourse* (The Hague: Kluwer).

Krüger, H. C. and C. A. Nøgaard (1993), 'The Right of Application', in R. St J. Macdonald, F. Matscher, and H. Petzold (eds) *The European System for the Protection of Human Rights* (Dordrecht: Martinus Nijhoff) 657.

Kutz, C. (2000) *Complicity: ethics and law for a collective age* (Cambridge: Cambridge University Press).

Kwakwa, E. (2000), 'Article 1 F(c) Acts Contrary to the Purposes and Principles of the United Nations' 12 *IJRL* 79.

Kälin, W. (2000), *Guiding Principles on Internal Displacement: Annotations* (Washington, DC: American Society of International Law, Studies in Transnational Legal Policy, No. 32).

Lattimer, M. and P. Sands (eds) (2003), *Justice for Crimes Against Humanity* (Oxford: Hart Publishing).

Lauterpacht, E. (1998), 'International Law and Private Foreign Investment', http://ww.law.indiana.edu/glsj/vol4/no2/laupgp.html.

—— and D. Bethlehem (2001), 'The Scope and Content of the Principle of Non-refoulement: Opinion' (Geneva: UNHCR).

Lauterpacht, H. (1950), *International Law and Human Rights* (London: Stevens & Sons).

—— (1970), E. Lauterpacht (ed) *Collected Papers*, vol. 1 (Cambridge: Cambridge University Press).

Lawand, K. (2003), 'Reviewing the Legal Regime', Looking Back, Looking Forward—International Campaign to Ban Landmines Workshop on Engaging Non-State Actors in a Landmine Ban, Conference, 13 September 2003, Bangkok.

Lawson, R. (1998), 'Out of Control. State Responsibility and Human Rights: Will the ILC's Definition of the "Act of State" meet the Challenges of the 21st Century?' in M. Castermans, F. van Hoof, and J. Smith (eds) *The Role of the Nation-State in the 21st Century* (The Hague: Kluwer) 91.

Lawyers Committee for Human Rights (1993), *The World Bank: Governance and Human Rights*.

Leach, P. (2001), *Taking a Case to the European Court of Human Rights* (London: Blackstone Press).

Leary, V. A. (1996), 'Human Rights at the ILO: Reflections on Making the ILO More "User Friendly" ', in A. A. Cançado (ed) *The Modern World of Human Rights, Essays in Honor of Thomas Buergenthal* (San José: Inter-American Institute of Human Rights) 375.

—— (1996), 'The Paradox of Workers' Rights as Human Rights' in L. A. Compa and S. F. Diamond (eds) *Human Rights, Labour, and International Trade* (Philadelphia, Pa: University of Philadelphia Press) 22.

—— (1996), 'Workers' Rights and International Trade: the Social Clause (GATT, ILO, NAFTA, U.S. Laws)' in J. N. Bhagwati and R. E. Hudec (eds) *Fair Trade and Harmonization: Volume 2 Legal Analysis* (Cambridge, Mass: MIT Press) 177.

—— (1997a), 'Nonbinding Accords in the Field of Labor' in E. Brown Weiss (ed) *International Compliance with Nonbinding Accords* (Washington, DC: American Society of International Law) 247.

—— (1997b), 'The WTO and the Social Clause: Post Singapore' 1 *EJIL* 118.

Leckie, S. (1998), 'Another Step Towards Indivisibility: Identifying the Key Features of Violation of Economic, Social and Cultural Rights' 20 *HRQ* 81.

Leigh, I. (1999), 'Horizontal Rights, the Human Rights Act and Privacy: Lessons from the Commonwealth?' 48 *ICLQ* 57.

Leivo, T. (1995), 'Against Whom May the Direct Effect of EC Directives be Relied Upon?' VI *The Finnish Yearbook of International Law* 565.

Lenaerts, K. and E. de Smijter (2000), 'The European Union as an Actor under International Law' 19 *Yearbook of European Law* 95.

Lester, A. (2004), 'The Human Rights Act 1998—Five Years On', *EHRLR* 258.

—— (2005), 'The utility of the Human Rights Act: a reply to Keith Ewing', *Public Law* 249.

—— and D. Pannick (2004), *Human Rights Law and Practice* (London: Butterworths, 2nd edn).

Leuprecht, P. (1999), 'The World Trade Organisation—Another Playground of Pan-Economic Ideology?' in M. Mehra (ed) *Human Rights and Economic Globalisation: Directions for the WTO* (Uppsala: Global Publications Foundation, International NGO Committee on Human Rights in Trade and Investment, International Coalition for Development Action) 15.

Lewan, K. M. (1968), 'The Significance of Constitutional Rights for Private Law: Theory and Practice in West Germany' 17 *ICLQ* 571.

Lightman, G. and J. Bowers (1995), 'Incorporation of the ECHR and its Impact on Employment Law', *EHRLR* 560.

Lillich, R. B. (1980), 'Duties of States Regarding the Civil Rights of Aliens' 161 *RCADI* (Alphen aan den Rijn: Sijthoff and Noordhoff) 329.

Litvin, D. (November 2003–December 2003), 'Human Rights are Your Business', *Foreign Policy* (electronic version).

Lopez-Hutado, C. (2002), 'Social Labeling and WTO Law' 5 *JIEL* 719.

—— (2005), 'The WTO Legal System and International Human Rights', PhD thesis, Graduate Institute of International Studies.

Lorber, P. (2004), 'Labour Law' in S. Peers and A. Ward (eds) *The European Union Charter of Fundamental Rights* (Oxford: Hart Publishing) 211.

Lupi, N. (1998), 'Report by the Enquiry Commission on the Behaviour of Italian Peace-keeping Troops in Somalia' 1 *Yearbook of International Humanitarian Law* 375.

MacKinnon, C. (1993), 'Crimes of War Crimes of Peace', in S. Shute and S. Hurley (eds) *On Human Rights: the Amnesty Lectures* (New York: Basic Books) 83.

Malanczuk, P. (1997), *Akehurst's Modern Introduction to International Law* (London: Routledge, 7th edn).

—— (2000), 'Multinational Enterprises and Treaty-making—A Contribution to the Discussion on Non-State Actors and the "Subjects of International Law"' in V. Gowlland-Debbas (ed) *Multilateral Treaty-Making: The Current Status of Challenges to and Reforms Needed in the International Legislative Process* (The Hague: Martinus Nijhoff) 45.

Mandel, M. (1989), *The Charter of Rights and the Legalization of Politics in Canada* (Toronto: Wall & Thompson).

Marceau, G. (2002), 'WTO Dispute Settlement and Human Rights' 13 *EJIL* 753.

Markesinis, B. (1999), 'Privacy, Freedom of Expression, and the Horizontal Effect of the Human Rights Bill: Lessons from Germany' 115 *LQR* 47.

—— and J.-B. Auby, C. Waltjen, and S. Deakin (eds) (1999), *The Tortious Liability of Statutory Bodies* (Oxford: Hart Publishing).

—— and S. Enchelmaier (1999), 'The Applicability of Human Rights as between Individuals under German Constitutional Law' in B. S. Markesinis (ed) *Protecting Privacy: The Clifford Chance Lectures Volume Four* (Oxford: Oxford University Press) 191.

Marks, S. (2000), *The Riddle of All Constitutions: International Law, Democracy, and a Critique of Ideology* (Oxford: Oxford University Press).

—— and A. Clapham (2005), *International Human Rights Lexicon* (Oxford: Oxford University Press).

Markus, K. (2003), 'What is Public Power: The Courts' Approach to the Public Authority Definition Under the Human Rights Act' in J. Jowell and J. Cooper (eds) *Delivering Rights: How the Human Rights Act is Working* (Oxford: Hart Publishing) 77.

Maslen, S. (2004), *Commentaries on Arms Control Treaties, Volume I, The Convention on the Prohibition of the Use, Stockpiling, Production, and Transfer of Anti-Personnel Mines and on their Destruction* (Oxford: Oxford University Press).

Matas, D. (1997), 'Armed Opposition Groups' 24 *Manitoba Law Journal* 621.

—— (2001), 'The law: tool to engage non-state actors in a landmine ban' in M. Foster (ed) *Engaging non-state actors in a landmine ban: a pioneering conference*, Conference held in Geneva, 24–25 March 2000 (Quezon City, Philippines: Conference Organizers) 130.

Matscher, F. and H. Petzold (eds) (1988), *Protecting Human Rights: The European Dimension (Studies in Honour of Gérard J. Wiarda)* (Cologne: Carl Heymanns Verlag).

Matua, M. (2002), *Human Rights: A Political and Cultural Critique* (Philadelphia, Pa: University of Pennsylvania Press).

Mayes, T. (2002), *Restraint or Revelation: free speech and privacy in a confessional age* (London: Spiked).

McBeth, A. (2005), 'Holding the Purse Strings: The Continuing Evolution of Human Rights Law and the Potential Liability of the Finance Industry for Human Rights Abuses' 23 *NQHR* 7.

McCorquodale, R. and R. La Forgia (2001), 'Taking off the Blindfolds: Torture by Non-State Actors' 1 *Human Rights Law Review* 189.

McCoubrey, H. (1998), *International Humanitarian Law* (Aldershot: Ashgate, 2nd edn).

McCrudden, C. and A. Davies (2000), 'A Perspective on Trade and Labor Rights' 3 *JIEL* 43.

McIntosh, M., D. Leipziger, K. Jones, and G. Coleman (1998), *Corporate Citizenship: Successful strategies for responsible companies* (Great Britain: Financial Times Pitman Publishing).

McIntosh, M., R. Thomas, D. Leipziger, and G. Coleman (2003), *Living Corporate Citizenship: Strategic routes to socially responsible business* (London: Prentice Hall).

McKenzie, E. (1994), *Privatopia* (Newhaven, Conn: Yale University Press).

Meeran, R. (1999), 'The Unveiling of Transnational Corporations', in M. K. Addo (ed) *Human Rights Standards and the Responsibility of Transnational Corporations* (The Hague: Kluwer) 161.

Mégrét, F. and F. Hoffmann (2003), 'The UN as Human Rights Violator? Some Reflections on the United Nations Changing Human Rights Responsibilities' 25 *HRQ* 314.

Mehra, M. (ed) (1999), *Human Rights and Economic Globalisation: Directions for the WTO* (Uppsala: Global Publications Foundation, International NGO Committee on Human Rights in Trade and Investment, International Coalition for Development Action) 15.

Meng, W. (2004), 'International Labour Standards and International Trade Law' in E. Benvenisti and G. Nolte (eds) *The Welfare State, Globalization and International Law* (Berlin: Springer Verlag) 371.

Meron, T. (1983), 'On the Inadequate Reach of Humanitarian and Human Rights Law and the Need for a New Instrument' 77 *AJIL* 589.

——(1985), 'The Meaning and Reach of the International Convention on the Elimination of All Forms of Racial Discrimination' 79 *AJIL* 283.

——(1987), *Human Rights in Internal Strife: Their International Protection* (Cambridge: Grotius).

——(1989), *Human Rights and Humanitarian Norms as Customary Law*, (Oxford: Clarendon Press).

——(2004), *International Law in the Age of Human Rights—General Course on Public International Law* 301 *RCADI* (Leiden: Martinus Nijhoff).

Michael, J. (1994), *Privacy and Human Rights: An International and Comparative Study, with Special Reference to Developments in Informational Technology* (Paris/Aldershot: UNESCO/Dartmouth).

Moir, L. (2002), *The Law of Internal Armed Conflict* (Cambridge: Cambridge University Press).

Monbiot, G. (2003), *The Age of Consent: A Manifesto for a New World Order* (London: Flamingo).

Monshipouri, M., C. E. Welsh, and E. T. Kennedy (2003), 'Multinational Corporations and the Ethics of Global Responsibility: Problems and Possibilities' 25 *HRQ* 965.

Moore, M. (2003), *A World Without Walls: Freedom, Development, Free Trade and Global Governance* (Cambridge: Cambridge University Press).

Morsink, J. (1999), *The Universal Declaration of Human Rights: Origins, Drafting, and Intent* (Philadelphia, Pa: University of Pennsylvania Press).

Mowbray, A. (2004), *The Development of Positive Obligations under the European Convention on Human Rights by the European Court of Human Rights* (Oxford: Hart Publishing).

Muchlinski, P. T. (1999), *Multinational Enterprises and the Law* (Oxford: Blackwell).

——(2001a), 'Human rights and multinationals: is there a problem?' 77 *International Affairs* 31.

——(2001b), 'Corporations in International Litigation: Problems of Jurisdiction and the United Kingdom Asbestos Cases' 50 *ICLQ* 1.

——(2003), 'Human Rights, Social Responsibility and the Regulation of International Business: The Development of International Standards by Intergovernmental Organization' 3 *Non-State Actors and International Law* 123.

Mundlak, G. (2001), 'Human Rights and the Employment Relationship: A Look Through the Prism of Juridification' in D. Friedmann and D. Barak Erez (eds) *Human Rights in Private Law* (Oxford: Hart Publishing) 297.

Murray, C. (1983), 'The Status of the ANC and SWAPO in International Humanitarian Law' 100 *South African Law Journal* 402.

—— (1984), 'The 1977 Geneva Protocols and Conflict in Southern Africa' 33 *ICLQ* 462.

Murray, J. (2002), 'Labour rights/corporate responsibilities: the role of ILO labour standards' in R. Jenkins, R. Pearson, and G. Seyfang (eds) *Corporate Responsibility & Labour Rights: Codes of Conduct in the Global Economy* (London: Earthscan) 31.

Murray, R. (2000), *The African Commission on Human and Peoples' Rights and International Law* (Oxford: Hart Publishing).

Musah, A.-F. and J. 'Kayode Fayemi (eds) (2000), *Mercenaries: An African Security Dilemma* (London: Pluto Press).

Möller, J. T. (2001), 'The Independent Inspection Panel of the World Bank—Comparison with other Inspection Complaints Procedures' in G. Alfredsson and R. Ring (eds) *The Inspection Panel of the World Bank* (The Hague: Kluwer) 219.

Nair, R. (1998), 'Confronting the Violence Committee by Armed Opposition Groups' 1 *Yale HRDLJ* 1.

Naqvi, Y. (2003) 'Amnesty for war crimes: Defining the limits of international recognition' 85 (851) *IRRC* 581.

Nelson, J. (2000), *The Business of Peace: The private sector as a partner in conflict prevention and resolution* (London: Council on Economic Priorities; The Prince of Wales Business Leaders Forum).

Nelson, W. N. (1981), 'Human Rights and Human Obligations' in J. R. Pennock and J. W. Chapman (eds) *Human Rights: Nomos XXIII* (New York: New York University Press) 281.

Noortmann, M. (2001), 'Non-State Actors in International Law' in B. Arts, M. Noortmann, and B. Reinalda (eds) *Non-State Actors in International Relations* (Aldershot: Ashgate) 59.

Novartis Foundation for Sustainable Development, The Prince of Wales International Business Leaders Forum (2004), *Human Rights and the Private Sector: International Symposium Report* (Basel/London: Novartis Foundation/PWIBLF).

Nowak, J. E. and R. D. Rotunda (2000), *Constitutional Law* (St Paul, Minn: West Group, 6th edn).

Nowrot, K. (1999), 'Legal Consequences of Globalization: The Status of Non-Governmental Organizations Under International Law' 6 *Global Legal Studies Journal* 579.

Nozick, R. (1974), *Anarchy, State and Utopia* (Oxford: Basil Blackwell).

Obokata, T. (2005), 'Smuggling of Human Beings from a Human Rights Perspective: Obligations of Non-State and State Actors under International Human Rights Law' 17 *IJRL* 394.

O'Connell, D. P. (1970), *International Law*, vol. 1 (London: Stevens and Sons, 2nd edn).

OECD (2000a), *OECD Guidelines for Multinational Enterprises: Review 2000*, DAFFE/IME/WPG(2000)9.

—— (2000b), *OECD Guidelines for Multinational Enterprises: Frequently asked questions*, http://www.oecd.org/daf/investment/guidelines/faq.htm.

—— (2001), *The OECD Guidelines for Multinational Enterprises: Text, Guidelines, Commentary*, DAFFE/IME/WPG(2000)15 Final.

OHCHR (2000), *Business and Human Rights: A Progress Report*, http://www.unhchr.ch/business.htm.

—— (2000), *Business and Human Rights: An Update*, http://www.unhchr.ch/businesupdate.htm.

—— (2004), 'OHCHR Briefing Paper on The Global Compact and Human Rights: Understanding Sphere of Influence and Complicity', UN Global Compact Office & OHCHR, *Embedding Human Rights in Business Practice* (New York: UN Global Compact Office) 14.

Oliver, D. (1999), *Common Values and the Public-Private Divide* (London: Butterworths).

—— (2000), 'The Frontiers of the State: Public Authorities and Public Functions under the Human Rights Act', *Public Law* 476.

—— (2001), 'Comment: Chancel Repairs and the Human Rights Act', *Public Law* 651.

—— (2004), 'Functions of a Public Nature under the Human Rights Act', *Public Law* 329.

Oppenheim, L. (1920), R. F. Roxburgh (ed) *International Law: A Treatise* (London: Longmans, 3rd edn).

—— (1952), H. Lauterpacht (ed) *International Law: a Treatise (Disputes, War and Neutrality)*, vol. II (London: Longman, 7th edn).

O'Rourke, D. (2002), 'Monitoring the monitors: a critique of corporate third-party labour monitoring' in R. Jenkins, R. Pearson, and G. Seyfang (eds) *Corporate Responsibility & Labour Rights: Codes of Conduct in the Global Economy* (London: Earthscan) 196.

Orrego Vicuna, F. (2004), *International Dispute Settlement in an Evolving Global Society: Constitutionalization, Accessibility, Privatization* (Cambridge: Cambridge University Press).

Ouguerouz, F. (2003), *The African Charter on Human and Peoples' Rights: A Comprehensive Agenda for Human Dignity and Sustainable Democracy in Africa* (The Hague: Martinus Nijhoff).

Ovey, C. and R. C. A. White (2002), *Jacobs & White, The European Convention on Human Rights* (Oxford: Oxford University Press, 3rd edn).

Palawankar, U. (1993), 'Applicability of international humanitarian law to United Nations peace-keeping forces', *IRRC* 227.

—— (1994), *Symposium on Humanitarian Action and Peace-Keeping Operations: Report* (Geneva: ICRC).

Paringaux, R.-P. (December 2000), 'De la complicité avec les dictatures au "capitalisme éthique": "Business" pétrole et droits humains', *Le Monde Diplomatique* 4.

Pasqualucci, J. M. (2003), *The Practice and Procedure of the Inter-American Court of Human Rights* (Cambridge: Cambridge University Press).

Paust, J. J. (1983), 'Remarks' 77 *Proceedings of the American Society of International Law* 186.

—— (1992), 'The Other Side of Right: Private Duties Under Human Rights Law' 5 *Harv HRJ* 51.

—— (2002), 'Human Rights Responsibilities of Private Corporations' 35 *Van JTL* 801.

—— M. C. Bassiouni, S. A. Williams, M. Scharf, J. Gurulé, and B. Zagaris, (1996), *International Criminal Law; Cases and Materials* (Durham, NC: Carolina Academic Press).

Pauwelyn, J. (2003), *Conflict of Norms in Public International Law: How WTO Law Relates to other Rules of International Law* (Cambridge: Cambridge University Press).

Peers, S. and A. Ward (eds) (2004), *The European Union Charter of Fundamental Rights* (Oxford: Hart Publishing).

Pejic, J. (2000), 'Article 1F(a): The Notion of International Crimes' 12 *IJRL* 11.

Penna, L. R. (1984), 'Customary International Law and Protocol I: An Analysis of Some Provisions' in C. Swinarski (ed) *Studies and Essays in International Humanitarian Law and Red Cross Principles: Essays in Honour of Jean Pictet* (The Hague: Martinus Nijhoff) 201.

Petersmann, E.-U. (2000), 'The WTO Constitution and Human Rights' 3 *JIEL* 19.

—— (2002), *The GATT/WTO Dispute Settlement System: International Law, International Organizations and Dispute Settlement* (London: Kluwer).

—— (2002), 'Taking Human Dignity, Poverty and Empowerment of Individuals More Seriously: Rejoinder to Alston' 13 *EJIL* 845.

—— (2002), 'Time for a United Nations "Global Compact" for Integrating Human Rights into the Law of Worldwide Organizations: Lessons from European Integration' 13 *EJIL* 621.

Phillipson, G. (1999), 'The Human Rights Act, "Horizontal Effect" and the Common Law: A Bang or a Whimper?' 62 *MLR* 824.

—— (2003), 'Transforming Breach of Confidence? Towards a Common Law Right of Privacy under the Human Rights Act' 66(5) *MLR* 726.

Ping-Fat, S. (2003), 'Universities and Public Authorities' 167 *Justice of the Peace* 91.

Pisillo Mazzeschi, R. (1989), *'Due diligence' e resonsibilità internazionale degli stati* (Milan: Giuffrè).

Pityana, N. B. (2002), 'The Challenge of Culture for Human Rights in Africa: the African Charter in a Comparative Context' in M. D. Evans and R. Murray (eds) *The African Charter on Human and Peoples' Rights; The System in Practice, 1986–2000* (Cambridge: Cambridge University Press) 219.

Plender, R. and N. Mole (1999), 'Beyond the Geneva Convention: constructing a *de facto* right of asylum from international human rights instruments' in F. Nicholson and P. Twomey (eds) *Refugee Rights and Realities: Evolving International Concepts and Regimes* (Cambridge: Cambridge University Press) 81.

Prechal, S. (1995), *Directives in European Community Law: A Study of Directives and Their Enforcement in National Courts* (Oxford: Clarendon Press).

Prove, P. (1999), 'Human Rights at the World Trade Organization?' in M. Mehra (ed) *Human Rights and Economic Globalisation: Directions for the WTO* (Uppsala: Global Publications Foundatation, International NGO Committee on Human Rights in Trade and Investment, International Coalition for Development Action) 23.

Quinn, P. (2003), 'Christian Ethics and Human Rights' in J. Runzo, N. M. Martin, and A. Sharma (eds) *Human Rights and Responsibilities* (Oxford: Oneworld Publications) 233.

Qureshi, A. H. (1999), *International Economic Law*, (London: Sweet & Maxwell).

Rakhoff, T. D. (2001), 'Enforcement of Employment Contracts and the Anti-Slavery Norm' in D. Friedmann and D. Barak-Erez (eds) *Human Rights in Private Law* (Oxford: Hart Publishing) 283.

Ramasastry, A. (1998), 'Secrets and Lies? Swiss Banks and International Human Rights' 31 *Van JTL* 325.

—— (2002), 'Corporate Complicity: From Nuremberg to Rangoon An Examination of Forced Labor Cases and Their Impact on the Liability of Multinational Corporations' 20 *Berkeley JIL* 91.

Ratner, S. R. (2001), 'Corporations and Human Rights: A Theory of Legal Responsibility' 111 *YLJ* 443.

—— (2004), 'Overcoming Temptations to Violate Human Dignity in Times of Crisis: On the Possibilities for meaningful Self-Restraint' 5 *Theoretical Inquiries in Law* 81, http://www.bepress.com/til/default/vol5/iss1/art3/.

Rautenbach, I. (2000), 'The bill of rights applies to private law and binds private persons', *Journal of South African Law (TSAR)* 296.

Raymond, J. (1980), 'A Contribution to the Interpretation of Article 13 of the European Convention on Human Rights' 5 *Human Rights Review* 161.

—— (1988), 'L'Article 1 du Protocole additionnel et les rapports entre particuliers' in F. Matscher and H. Petzold (eds) *Protecting Human Rights: The European Dimension (Studies in Honour of Gérard J. Wiarda)* (Cologne: Carl Heymanns Verlag) 531.

Raz, J. (1986), *The Morality of Freedom* (Oxford: Clarendon Press).

Reich, A. (2004), 'Core Labour Standards and the WTO: Beware of Unilateralism!—A Response to Werner Meng' in E. Benvenisti and G. Nolte (eds) *The Welfare State, Globalization and International Law* (Berlin: Springer Verlag) 395.

Reichberg, G. M. (2002), 'The hard questions of international business: some guidelines from the ethics of war' in H. von Weltzein Hoivik (ed) *Moral Leadership in Action: Building and Sustaining Moral Competence in European Organizations* (Cheltenham: Edward Elgar) 304.

Reid, K. (1998), *A Practitioner's Guide to the European Convention on Human Rights* (London: Sweet & Maxwell).

Reidel, E. H. (2000a), 'Recognition of Beligerency' in R. Bernhardt (ed) *Encyclopedia of Public International Law*, vol. IV (Amsterdam: Elsevier) 47.

—— (2000b), 'Recognition of Insurgency' in R. Bernhardt (ed) *Encyclopedia of Public International Law*, vol. IV (Amsterdam: Elsevier) 54.

Reinisch, A. (2000), *International Organisations before National Courts* (Cambridge: Cambridge University Press).

Reisman, W. M. and D. L. Stevick (1998), 'The Applicability of International Law Standards to United Nations Economic Sanctions Programmes' 9 *EJIL* 86.

Richter, J. (2001), *Holding Corporations Accountable: Corporate Conduct, International Codes, and Citizen Action* (London: Zed Books).

Riedel, E. and M. Will (1999), 'Human Rights Clauses in External Agreements of the EC' in P. Alston (ed) *The EU and Human Rights* (Oxford: Oxford University Press) 723.

Rieff, D. (2002), *A Bed for the Night: Humanitarianism in Crisis* (London: Vintage).

Rigaux, F. (1991), 'Transnational Corporations' in M. Bedjaoui (ed) *International Law: Achievements and Prospects* (Dordrecht: Martinus Nijhoff) 121.

Rigo Sureda, A. (2002), 'Process Integrity and Institutional Independence in International Organizations: the Inspection Panel and the Sanctions Committee of the World Bank' in L. Boisson de Chazournes, C. Romano, and R. Mackenzie (eds) *International Organizations and International Dispute Settlement: Trends and Prospects* (New York: Transnational Publishers) 165.

Rishmawi, M. (1998), 'Situation of human rights in Somalia', UN Doc. E/CN.4/1998/96.

—— (1999), 'Situation of human rights in Somalia', UN Doc. E/CN.4/1999/103.

Robinson, M. (1998), 'The business case for human rights' in Financial Times Management, *Visions of ethical business* (London: Financial Times Professional) 14–17.

Rodley, N. (1993), 'Can Armed Opposition Groups Violate Human Rights?' in K. E. Mahoney and P. Mahoney (eds) *Human Rights in the Twenty-first Century* (Dordrecht: Martinus Nijhoff) 297.

Rorty, R. (1993), 'Human Rights, Rationality, and Sentimentality' in S. Shute and S. Hurley (eds) *On Human Rights: The Oxford Amnesty Lectures* (Oxford: Oxford University Press) 111.

Roucounas, E. (2005), 'Non-State Actors: Areas of International Responsibility in Need of Further Exploration' in M. Ragazzi (ed) *International Responsibility Today: Essays in Memory of Oscar Schachter* (Leiden: Brill) 391.

Rowbottom, J. (2005), 'Property and Participation: A Right of Access for Expressive Activities', *EHRLR* 186.

Rozenberg, J. (2004), *Privacy and the Press* (Oxford: Oxford University Press).

Runzo, J., N. M. Martin, and A. Sharma (eds) (2003), *Human Rights and Responsibilities in the World Religions* (Oxford: Oneworld Publications).

Ryniker, A. (1999), 'Quelques commentaires à propos de la Circulaire du Secrétaire général des Nations Unies du 6 août 1999', *Revue internationale de la Croix-Rouge* 795.

Saland, P. (1999), 'International Criminal Law Principles' in R. S. Lee (ed) *The International Criminal Court, The Making of the Rome Statute* (The Hague: Kluwer) 189.

Salzman, J. (2000), 'Labour Rights, Globalization and Institutions: The Role and Influence of the Organization for Economic Cooperation and Development' 21 *Mich JIL* 769.

Sanderson, M. A. (2004), 'Is *Von Hannover v Germany* a Step Backward for the Substantive Analysis of Speech and Privacy Interests?', *EHRLR* 631.

Sandoz, Y., C. Swinarski, and B. Zimmermann (eds) (1987), *Commentary on the Additional Protocols of 8 June 1977 to the Geneva Conventions of 12 August 1949* (Geneva/Dordrecht: ICRC/Nijhoff).

Sands, P. (1998), 'Treaty, Custom and the Cross-fertilization of International Law' 1 *Yale HRDLJ* 3.

—— (2000a), 'Arbitrating environmental disputes', Unpublished draft remarks on the occasion of the annual ICSID-ICC-AAA Colloquium, 10 November 2000, Washington, DC, on file with the author.

—— (2000b), 'Vers une transformation du droit international? Institutionnaliser le doute' in P.-M. Dupuy and C. Leben (eds) *Cours et travaux* (Paris, Université Panthéon-Assas (Paris II)/Institut des hautes études internationales de Paris: Pedone) 180.

—— and P. Klein (2001), *Bowett's Law of International Institutions*, (London: Sweet & Maxwell).

Santos, S. M., (2002), 'Geneva Call's Deed of Commitment for Armed Groups: An Annotation' in *Seeking Rebel Accountability: Report of the Geneva Call Mission to the MILF in the Philippines, 3–8 April 2002* (Geneva: Geneva Call) 82.

—— (2003), 'A Critical Reflection on The Geneva Call Instrument and Approach in Engaging Armed Groups on Humanitarian Norms: A Southern Perspective', *Curbing Human Rights Violations by Non-State Armed Groups, Conference 13–15 November 2003, The Armed Groups Project, Centre for International Relations, Liu Institute—University of British Columbia.*

Sardaro, P. (2002), 'The right to reparation for gross and systematic violations from the perspective of general international law', *Expert Seminar on Reparation for Victims of Gross and Systematic Human Rights Violations in the Context of Political Transitions* (Antwerp: University of Antwerp) 15.

Sassòli, M. (2000), 'Possible Legal Mechanisms to Improve Compliance by Armed Groups with International Humanitarian Law and International Human Rights Law', Conference Paper, University of Quebec in Montreal, available through www.ihlresearch.org/ihl/.

—— (2002), 'Droit international pénal et droit pénal interne: le case des territoires se trouvent sous administration internationale' in M. Henzelin and R. Roth (eds) *Le droit pénal à l'épreuve de l'internationalisation* (Paris/Geneva/Brussels: LGDG/Georg/Bruylant) 119.

—— and A. A. Bouvier (1999), *How Does Law Protect in War?* (Geneva: ICRC).

Schabas, W. A. (2000), *Genocide in International Law: The Crime of Crimes* (Cambridge: Cambridge University Press).

—— (2001), 'Enforcing international humanitarian law: Catching the accomplices' 83 *IRRC* 439.

Schachter, O. (1983), 'Human Dignity as a Normative Concept' 77 *AJIL* 848.

Scheuner, U. (1971), 'Fundamental Rights and the Protection of the Individual against Social Groups and Powers in the Constitutional System of the Federal Republic of Germany' in International Institute of Human Rights, *René Cassin Amicorum discipulorumque liber (4 vols)*, vol. iii (Paris: Pedone) 253.

Schmid, A. P. (1997), 'Non-State Actors: Organized Crime, Human Rights NGOs and the United Nations' in SIM Studie- en Informatiecentrum Mensenrechten (Netherlands Institute of Human Rights) *The Legitimacy of the United Nations: Towards an Enhanced Legal Status of Non-State Actors, SIM Special No. 19*, 125.

Schreier, F. and M. Caparini (2005), 'Privatising Security: Law, Practice and Governance of Private Military and Security Companies' (Geneva: Geneva Centre for the Democratic Control of Armed Forces, Occasional Paper No. 6).

Schwartz, B. (1977), *The Great Rights of Mankind: A History of the American Bill of Rights* (New York: Oxford University Press).

Schwebel, S. M. (1996), 'The Treatment of Human Rights and of Aliens in the International Court of Justice' in V. Lowe and M. Fitzmaurice (eds) *Fifty Years of the International Court of Justice: Essays in Honour of Sir Robert Jennings* (Cambridge: Grotius) 327.

Schwelb, E. (1966), 'The International Convention on the Elimination of All Forms of Racial Discrimination' 15 *ICLQ* 996.

Scott, C. (2001), 'Multinational Enterprises and Emergent Jurisprudence on Violations of Economic, Social and Cultural Rights' in A. Eide, C. Krause, and A. Rosas (eds) *Economic, Social and Cultural Rights: A Textbook* (Dordrecht: Martinus Nijhoff, 2nd edn) 563.

—— (ed) (2001), *Torture as Tort: Comparative Perspectives on the Development of Transnational Human Rights Litigation* (Oxford: Hart Publishing).

—— (2001), 'Translating Torture into Transnational Tort: Conceptual Divides in the Debate on Corporate Accountability for Human Rights Harms' in C. Scott (ed) *Torture as Tort: Comparative Perspectives on the Development of Transnational Human Rights Litigation* (Oxford: Hart Publishing) 45.

Scott, S. V. (1998), 'International Lawyers: Handmaidens, Chefs, or Birth Attendants: A Response to Philip Alston' 9 *EJIL* 750.

Sedley, S. (1999), *Freedom, Law and Justice* (London: Sweet & Maxwell).

Seidl-Hohenveldern, I. (1987), *Corporations in and under International Law* (Cambridge: Grotius).

—— (1992), 'International Economic Law' (Dordrecht: Martinus Nijhoff, 2nd edn).

Seidman, L. M. (1987), 'Public Principle and Private Choice: The Uneasy Case for a Boundary Maintenance Theory of Constitutional Law' 96 *YLJ* 1006.

Shamir, R. (2004), 'Between Self-Regulation and the Alien Tort Claims Act: On the Contested Concept of Corporate Social Responsibility' 38 *Law & Society Review* 635.

Sharma, A. (2003), 'The Religious Perspective: Dignity as a Foundation for Human Rights Discourse' in J. Runzo, N. M. Martin, and A. Sharma (eds) *Human Rights and Responsibilities* (Oxford: Oneworld Publications) 67.

Shaw, M. (2003), *International Law* (Cambridge: Cambridge University Press, 5th edn).

Shell (1998), *Business and Human Rights: A Management Primer*.

—— (1999), *Shell Report: People, planet and profits: An act of commitment*.

Shelton, D. (1990), 'Private Violence, Public Wrongs, and the Responsibility of States' 13 *Ford ILJ* 1.

—— (1999), *Remedies in International Human Rights Law* (Oxford: Oxford University Press).

Shihata, I. F. I. (1988), 'The World Bank and Human Rights: An Analysis of the Legal Issues and the Record of Achievements' 17 *Denver Journal of International Law and Policy* 39.

—— (1991), *The World Bank in a Changing World: Selected Essays* (Dordrecht: Martinus Nijhoff).

—— (1992), 'Human Rights, Development, and International Financial Institutions' 8 *American University Journal of International Law and Policy* 27.

—— (ed) (1995), *The World Bank in a Changing World: Selected Essays and Lectures*, vol. II (The Hague: Martinus Nijhoff).

—— (1995), 'Human Rights, Development, and International Financial Institutions' in I. F. I. Shihata (ed) *The World Bank in a Changing World: Selected Essays and Lectures*, vol. II (The Hague: Martinus Nijhoff) 553.

—— (1997a), 'The World Bank and Human Rights', mimeographed note dated November 1997 on file with the author.

—— (1997b), 'The World Bank and Human Rights', *Österreichische außenpolitische Dokumentation, Special Issue* 'The universal protection of human rights: Translating international commitments into national action' 40th International Seminar for Diplomats, Helbrunn Castle, Salzburg, Austria, 28 July–1 August 1997, 191.

—— (1997c), 'Democracy and Development' 46 *ICLQ* 635.

Shiner, R. A. (2003), *Freedom of Commercial Expression* (Oxford: Oxford University Press).

Shraga, D. (1996), 'The United Nations as an actor bound by international humanitarian law', in L. Condorelli, A.-M. La Rosa, and S. Scherrer (eds) *Les Nations unies et le droit international humanitaire: Actes du colloque international 19, 20, 21 octobre 1995* (Paris: Pedone) 317.

—— (2000), 'UN Peacekeeping Operations: Applicability of International Humanitarian Law and Responsibility for Operations-Related Damage' 94 *AJIL* 406.

—— and R. Zacklin (1994), 'The Applicability of International Humanitarian Law to United Nations Peace-keeping Operations: Conceptual, Legal and Practical Issues' in U. Palawankar (ed) *Symposium on Humanitarian Action and Peace-Keeping Operations* (Geneva: ICRC) 39.

Simma, B. (1995), 'International Human Rights and General International Law: A Comparative Analysis', *AEL*, vol. IV Book 2 (The Hague: Martinus Nijhoff) 153.

Simmonds, R. (1968), *Legal Problems Arising from the United Nations Military Operations in the Congo* (The Hague: Martinus Nijhoff).

Singer, P. W. (2004), *Corporate Warriors: The Rise of the Privatized Military*, (Ithaca, NY: Cornell University Press).

—— (2004), 'The Private Military Industry and Iraq: What Have We Learned and Where to Next?' (Geneva: Geneva Centre for the Democratic Control of Armed Forces).

—— (2004), 'War, Profits, and the Vacuum of Law: Privatized Military Firms and International Law', vol. 42 *Col JTL* 521.

Singh, R. (1999), 'Privacy and the Media: The Impact of the Human Rights Bill' in B. S. Markesinis (ed) *Protecting Privacy: The Clifford Chance Lectures Volume Four* (Oxford: Oxford University Press) 169.

Skogly, S. I. (1999), 'The Position of the World Bank and the International Monetary Fund in the Human Rights Field' in R. Hanski and M. Suski (eds) *An Introduction to the International Protection of Human Rights* (Turku: Institute for Human Rights, Åbo Akademi, 2nd edn) 231.

—— (2001), *The Human Rights Obligations of the World Bank and the International Monetary Fund* (London: Cavendish).

Slaughter, A.-M. (1997), 'The Real New World Order' 76 *Foreign Affairs* 183.

Smillie, I. (2003), *Motherhood, Apple Pie and False Teeth* (Ottawa: Partnership Africa Canada, Occasional Paper No. 10, The Diamonds and Human Security Project).

Smyth, M. (2000), *Business and the Human Rights Act* (Bristol: Jordans).

Société Française Pour le Droit International (2005), *Colloque du Mans: Le sujet en droit international* (Paris: Pedone).

Sornarajah, M. (2004), *The International Law on Foreign Investment* (Cambridge: Cambridge University Press, 2nd edn).

Sphere Project (2000), *Humanitarian Charter and Minimum Standards in Disaster Response* (Oxford: Oxfam Publishing).

Spicer, T. (1999), *An Unorthodox Soldier: Peace and War and the Sandline Affair* (Edinburgh: Mainstream Publishing).

Spielmann, D. (1998), 'Obligations positives et effet horizontal des dispositions de la Convention' in F. Sudre (ed) *L'interpretation de la Convention européenne des droits de l'homme* (Brussels: Nemesis) 133.

Sprigman, C. and M. Osborne (1999), 'Du Plessis is *not* Dead: South Africa's 1996 Constitution and the Application of the Bill of Rights to Private Disputes' 15 *SAJHR* 25.

Starmer, K. (2001), 'Positive Obligations Under the Convention' in J. Jowell and J. Cooper (eds) *Understanding Human Rights Principles* (Oxford: Hart Publishing) 139.

Stephens, B. (2004), 'Upsetting Checks and Balances: The Bush Administration's Efforts to Limit Human Rights Litigation' 17 *Harv HRJ* 170.

—— and M. Ratner (1996), *International Human Rights Litigation in U.S. Courts* (Irvington-on-Hudson, NY: Transnational).

Stessens, G. (1994), 'Corporate Criminal Liability: A Comparative Perspective' 43 *ICLQ* 493.

Sudre, F. (2000), 'Les "obligations positives" dans la jurisprudence européennes des droits de l'homme' in P. Mahoney, F. Matscher, H. Petzold, and L. Wildhaber (eds) *Protecting Human Rights: The European Perspective—Studies in memory of Rolv Ryssdal* (Cologne: Carl Heymanns) 1359.

Sullivan, D. (1993), 'The Public/Private Distinction in International Human Rights Law' in J. Peters and A. Wolper (eds) *Women's Rights: Human Rights* (New York: Routledge) 126.

Sullivan, R. and D. Hogan (2002), 'The Business Case for Human Rights—The Amnesty International Perspective' in S. Bottomley and D. Kinley (eds) *Commercial Law and Human Rights* (Dartmouth: Ashgate) 69.

—— R. Lake, and J. Kirsty Thomas (2003), 'Why Should Investors Care about Human Rights?' 2(1) *New Academy Review* 37.

Sunkin, M. (2004), 'Pushing Forward the Frontiers of Human Rights Protection: The Meaning of Public Authority under the Human Rights Act', *Public Law* 643.

Sunstein, C. (2001), *Republic.com* (Princeton, NJ: Princeton University Press).

—— (2001), *Designing Democracy: What Constitutions Do* (Oxford: Oxford University Press).

Swinarski, C. (ed) (1984), *Studies and Essays in International Humanitarian Law and Red Cross Principles: Essays in Honour of Jean Pictet* (The Hague: Martinus Nijhoff).

Szasz, P. (1995), 'General Law Making Processes' in O. Schachter and C. C. Joyner (eds) *United Nations Legal Order*, vol. 1 (Cambridge: Cambridge University Press) 35.

Teubner, G. (1997), "Global Bukowina": Legal Pluralism in the World Society', in G. Teubner (ed) *Global Law Without a State* (Aldershot: Dartmouth) 3.

Thadani, P. Z. (2000), 'Regulating Corporate Human Rights Abuses: Is *UNOCAL* The Answer?' 42 *William and Mary Law Review* 619.

Thomas, C. (1998), 'International Financial Institutions and social and economic rights: an exploration' in T. Evans (ed) *Human Rights Fifty Years On: A reappraisal* (Manchester: Manchester University Press) 161.

Thornton, M. (ed) (1995), *Public and Private: Feminist Legal Debates* (Melbourne: Oxford University Press).

Thuan, C. (1984), 'Sociétés transnationales et droits de l'homme' in C. Thuan (ed) *Multinationales et droits de l'homme* (Paris: PUF) 43.

Thürer, D. (1999), 'The Emergence of Non-Governmental Organizations and Transnational Enterprises in International Law and the Changing Role of the State' in R. Hofmann (ed) *Non-State Actors as New Subjects of International Law: International Law—From the Traditional State Order Towards the Law of the Global Community* (Berlin: Duncker & Humblot) 37.

Tobin, R. (2002), 'Privacy and Freedom of Expression in New Zealand' in M. Colvin (ed) *Developing Key Privacy Rights* (Oxford: Hart Publishing) 129.

Tomuschat, C. (1999), 'Individual Reparation Claims in Instances of Grave Human Rights Violations: The Position under General International Law' in A. Randelzhofer and C. Tomuschat (eds) *State Responsibility and the Individual: Reparation in Instances of Grave Violations of Human Rights* (The Hague: Martinus Nijhoff) 1.

—— (2001), *International Law: Ensuring the Survival of Mankind on the Eve of a New Century: General Course on Public International Law* 281 *RCADI* (The Hague: Martinus Nijhoff).

—— (2002), 'The International Responsibility of the European Union' in E. Cannizzaro (ed) *The European Union as an Actor in International Relations* (The Hague: Kluwer) 177.

—— (2003), *Human Rights: Between Idealism and Realism* (Oxford: Oxford University Press).

—— (2004), 'The Applicability of Human Rights Law to Insurgent Movements' in H. Fischer, U. Froissart, W. Heintschel von Heinegg, and C. Raap (eds) *Krisensicherung und Humanitärer Schutz—Crisis Management and Humanitarian Protection: Festschrift für Dieter Fleck* (Berlin: Berliner Wissenschafts-Verlag) 573.

Tribe, L. (1985), *Constitutional Choices* (Cambridge, Mass: Harvard University Press).

Tully, S. (2001), 'The 2000 Review of the OECD Guidelines for Multinational Enterprises' 50 *ICLQ* 394.

Tushnet, M. (2003), 'The issue of state action/horizontal effect in comparative constitutional law' 1 *International Journal of Constitutional Law* 79.

—— (2001), 'Scepticism about Judicial Review: A Perspective from the United States' in T. Campbell, K. D. Ewing, and A. Tomkins (eds) *Sceptical Essays on Human Rights* (Oxford: Oxford University Press) 359.

Türk, V. (2002), 'Non-State Agents of Persecution' in V. Chetail and V. Gowlland-Debbas (eds) *Switzerland and the International Protection of Refugees* (The Hague: Kluwer) 95.

UNCTAD, (1997a), *World Investment Report: Transnational Corporations, Market Structure and Competition Policy.*

—— (1997b), *Transnational Corporations, Market Structure and Competition Policy*, UNCTAD/ITE/IIT/5 (Overview).

United Nations (1995), *United Nations Civilian Police Handbook* (Turin: International Training Centre of the ILO).

—— (June 2000), *The United Nations System and The Business Community: Guidance for the Resident Coordinator System (Working Draft).*

Utting, P. (2000), 'Business Responsibility for Sustainable Development', *Geneva 2000, The Next Step in Social Development* (Geneva: United Nations Research Institute for Social Development).

—— (2002), 'Regulating Business via Multistakeholder Initiatives: A Preliminary Assessment' in Non-Governmental Liaison Service (NGLS) *Voluntary Approaches to Corporate Responsibility: Readings and a Resource Guide* (Geneva: NGLS/UNRISD) 61.

van Boven, T. (1998), 'A Universal Declaration of Human Responsibilities?' in B. Van der Heijden and B. Tahzib-Lie (eds) *Reflections on the Universal Declaration on Human Rights* (The Hague: Martinus Nijhoff) 73.

—— (2000), 'Non-State Actors; Introductory Comments [1997]' in F. Coomans, C. Flinterman, F. Grünfeld, I. Westendorp, and J. Willems (eds) *Human Rights from Exclusion to Inclusion; Principles and Practice: An Anthology from the Work of Theo van Boven*, (The Hague: Kluwer) 363.

—— (2001), 'Discrimination and Human Rights Law: Combating Racism' in S. Fredman (ed) *Discrimination and Human Rights: The Case of Racism* (Oxford: Oxford University Press) 111.

van den Bogaert, S. (2002), 'Horizontality: The Court Attacks?' in C. Barnard and J. Scott (eds) *The Law of the Single European Market* (Oxford: Hart Publishing) 123.

van der Walt, J. (2001), 'Progressive Indirect Horizontal Application of the Bill of Rights: Towards a Co-operative Relation Between Common-Law and Constitutional Jurisprudence' 17 *SAJHR* 341.

van der Wolf, W.-J. (2002), *The Future and Futurity of the Public-Private Distinction in the View of the Horizontal-Application of Fundamental Rights* (Nijmegen: Wolf Legal Productions).

van Dijk, P. (1988), 'The Interpretation of "Civil Rights and Obligations" by the European Court of Human Rights: One More Step to Take' in F. P. H. Matscher and H. Petzold (eds) *Protecting Human Rights: The European Dimension (Studies in Honour of Gérard J. Wiarda)* (Cologne: Carl Heymanns) 134.

—— and G. J. H. van Hoof (1990), *Theory and Practice of the European Convention on Human Rights* (The Hague: Kluwer, 2nd edn).

—— (1998), *Theory and Practice of the European Convention on Human Rights* (The Hague: Kluwer, 3rd edn).

Van Genugten, W. J. M. (2000), 'The Status of Transnational Corporations in International Public Law: with special reference to the case of Shell' in A. Eide, H. O. Bergesen, and P. R. Goyer (eds) *Human Rights and the Oil Industry* (Antwerp: Intersentia) 71.

Van Sliedregt, E. (2003), *The Criminal Responsibility of Individuals for Violations of International Humanitarian Law* (The Hague: TMC Asser Press).

Verhoosel, G. (2003), 'The Use of Investor-State Arbitration under Bilateral Investment Treaties to Seek Relief for Breaches of WTO Law' 6 *JIEL* 493.

Vieira De Mello, S. (2003), 'Human Rights: what role for business?' 2(1) *New Academy Review* 19.

Vigny, J.-D. and C. Thompson (2002), 'Fundamental Standards of Humanity: What Future?' 20 *NQHR* 185.

Wade, H. R. W. (1998), 'Opinion: Human Rights and the Judiciary', *EHRLR* 520.

—— (2000), 'Horizons of Horizontality' 116 *LQR* 217.

Wadham, J. and H. Mountfield (1999), *Blackstone's Guide to the Human Rights Act 1998* (London: Blackstone Press).

—— and A. Edmundson (2003), *Blackstone's Guide to the Human Rights Act 1998* (Oxford: Oxford University Press, 3rd edn).

Waldron, J. (ed), (1984), *Theories of Rights* (Oxford: Oxford University Press).

Ward, H. (2001), *Governing Multinationals: the Role of Foreign Direct Liability* (London: Royal Institute of International Affairs, Briefing Paper New Series No. 18).

Watts, D. J. (2003), *Six Degrees: The Science of a Connected Age* (New York: W.W. Norton and Co).

Wedgwood, R. (1999), 'Legal Personality and the Role of Non-Governmental Organizations and Non-State Political Entities in the United Nations System' in R. Hofmann (ed) *Non-State Actors as New Subjects of International Law: International Law—From the Traditional State Order Towards the Law of the Global Community*, (Berlin: Duncker & Humblot) 21.

Weenink, A. (2001), 'The Relevance of Being Important or the Importance of Being Relevant? State and Non-State Actors in International Relations Theory' in B. Arts, M. Noortmann, and B. Reinalda (eds) *Non-State Actors in International Relations* (Aldershot: Ashgate) 59.

Weiler, J. H. H. (1999), *The Constitution of Europe: "Do the new clothes have an emperor?" and other essays on European integration* (Cambridge: Cambridge University Press).

Weissbrodt, D. (1998), 'Non-State Entities and Human Rights within the Context of the the Nation-State in the 21st Century' in M. Castermans-Holleman, F. van Hoof, and J. Smith (eds) *The Role of the Nation-State in the 21st Century* (Dordrecht: Kluwer) 175.

—— and M. Kruger (2003), 'Norms on the Responsibilities of Transnational Corporations and Other Business Enterprises with Regard to Human Rights' 97 *AJIL* 901.

Wells, C. (2001), *Corporations and Criminal Responsibility* (Oxford: Oxford University Press, 2nd edn).

Wendland, L. (2002), *A Handbook on State Obligations under the UN Convention against Torture* (Geneva: Association for the Prevention of Torture).

Wetherill, S. (2004), 'The Internal Market' in S. Peers and A. Ward (eds) *The European Union Charter of Fundamental Rights* (Oxford: Hart Publishing) 183.

Wilde, R. (1998), '*Quis Custodiet Ipsos Custodes?*: Why and How UNHCR Governance of Development Refugee Camps Should be Subject to International Human Rights Law' 1 *Yale HRDLJ* 107.

—— (2001), 'The Complex Role of the Legal Adviser when International Organizations Administer Territory', *Proceedings of the 95th Annual Meeting of the American Society of International Law* 251.

—— (2001), 'From Danzig to East Timor and Beyond: The Role of International Territorial Administration' 95 *AJIL* 583.

—— (2004), 'The Accountability of International Organizations and the Concepts of Functional Duality' in W. P. Heere (ed) *From Government to Governance: The Growing Impact of Non-State Actors on the International and European Legal System* (The Hague: TMC Asser Press) 164.

Willetts, P. (ed) (1998), 'Political globalization and the impact of NGOs upon transnational companies' in J. Mitchell (ed) *Companies in a World of Conflict* (London: Royal Institute of International Affairs) 195.

Williams, A. (2004), *EU Human Rights Policies: A Study in Irony* (Oxford: Oxford University Press).

Wilshaw, R. (2002), 'Code Monitoring in the informal Fair Trade sector: the experience of Oxfam GB' in R. Jenkins, R. Pearson, and G. Seyfang (eds) *Corporate Responsibility & Labour Rights: Codes of Conduct in the Global Economy* (London: Earthscan) 209.

Wilshire, D. (2003), 'Non-State Actors and the Definition of a Refugee in the United Kingdom: Protection, Accountability or Culpability?' 15 *IJRL* 68.

Wilson, H. A. (1988), *International Law and the Use of Force by National Liberation Movements* (Oxford: Oxford University Press).

Wirth, D. A. (2000), 'Compliance with Non-Binding Norms of Trade and Finance' in D. Shelton (ed) *Commitment and Compliance: The Role of Non-Binding Norms in the International legal System* (Oxford: Oxford University Press) 330.

Wolfrum, R. and C. E. Philipp (2002), 'The Status of the Taliban: Their Obligations and Rights under International Law' 6 *Max Planck Yearbook of United Nations Law* 559.

Woods, N. (2001), 'Making the IMF and World Bank more accountable', 77 *International Affairs* 83.

Woolman, S. (1998), 'Application (Revison Service 3)' in M. Chalskalson, J. Kentridge, J. Klaaren, G. Marcus, D. Spitz, and S. Woolman (eds) *Constitutional Law of South Africa* (Kenwyn: Juta) para. 10.1–68.

World Bank (1998a), *Development and Human Rights: The Role of the World Bank* (Washington, DC: World Bank).

—— (January 1998b), *Fraud and Corruption under Bank-Financed Contracts: Procedures for Dealing with Allegations against Bidders, Suppliers, Contractors, or Consultants* (Washington, DC: World Bank).

Wright, J. (2001), *Tort Law & Human Rights* (Oxford: Hart Publishing).

Yates, G. T. (1983), 'State Responsibility for Nonwealth Injuries to Aliens in the Postwar Era' in R. B. Lillich (ed) *International Law of State Responsibility for Injuries to Aliens*, (Charlottesville, Virg: University Press of Virginia) 213.

Young, R. M. and M. Molina (1998), 'IHL and Peace Operations: Sharing Canada's lessons learned from Somalia' 1 *Yearbook of International Humanitarian Law* 362.

Zacklin, R. (1996), 'General Report' in L. Condorelli, A.-M. La Rosa, and S. Scherrer (eds) *Les Nations unies et le droit international humanitaire: Actes du colloque international 19, 20, 21 octobre 1995*, (Paris: Pedone) 39.

Zadek, S. (2001), *The Civil Corporation: The New Economy of Corporate Citizenship* (London/Sterling, Virg: Earthscan).

Zander, M. (1985), *A Bill of Rights?* (London: Sweet & Maxwell, 3rd edn).

Zappalà, S. (2003), *Human Rights in International Criminal Proceedings* (Oxford: Oxford University Press).

Zegveld, L. (2002), *Accountability of Armed Opposition Groups in International Law* (Cambridge: Cambridge University Press).

Zia-Zarifi, S. (1999), 'Suing Multinational Corporations in the U.S. for Violating International Law' *UCLA JILFA* 81.

Ziegler, J. (1999), *The Swiss, the Gold, and the Dead: How Swiss Bankers Helped Finance the Nazi War Machine* (London: Penguin).

Index